New Zealand's North Island (Te Ika-a-Māui)

Bay of Islands & Northland
p105

Auckland
p44

Waikato & Coromandel Peninsula
p147

Rotorua & the Bay of Plenty
p257

The East Coast
p298

Taupo & the Central Plateau
p230

Taranaki & Whanganui
p197

Wellington Region
p330

THIS EDITION WRITTEN AND RESEARCHED BY

Brett Atkinson,

Sarah Bennett, Charles Rawlings-Way, Lee

Jan 2015

Contents

PLAN YOUR TRIP

Welcome to the North Island 4

New Zealand – North Island Map 6

The North Island's Top 15 8

Need to Know 18

If You Like 20

Month by Month 23

Itineraries 27

Active North Island 29

Regions at a Glance 40

WELLINGTON P332

TONGARIRO NATIONAL PARK P246

ON THE ROAD

AUCKLAND 44
Auckland 46
Hauraki Gulf Islands . . . 81
Waiheke Island 82
Great Barrier Island 90
West Auckland 94
Titirangi 94
Waitakere Ranges 95
Karekare 95
Piha 96
Kumeu & Around 97
Muriwai Beach 98
Helensville 98
North Auckland 99
Long Bay Regional Park 99
Shakespear Regional Park 99
Orewa 99
Waiwera 100
Puhoi 100
Mahurangi & Scandrett Regional Parks 101
Warkworth 101
Matakana & Around 102
Leigh 103
Goat Island Marine Reserve 104
Pakiri 104

BAY OF ISLANDS & NORTHLAND 105
Whangarei District 108
Mangawhai 108
Waipu & Bream Bay 109
Whangarei 110
Whangarei Heads 115
Tutukaka Coast & the Poor Knights Islands 115
Russell Road 117

Bay of Islands 118
Russell 122
Paihia & Waitangi 125
Urupukapuka Island 129
Kerikeri 129
The Far North 132
Matauri & Tauranga Bays 132
Whangaroa Harbour 133
Doubtless Bay 134
Karikari Peninsula 135
Cape Reinga & Ninety Mile Beach 136
Kaitaia 138
Ahipara 138
Hokianga 140
Kauri Coast 143

WAIKATO & COROMANDEL PENINSULA 147
Waikato 149
Rangiriri 150
Ngaruawahia & Around . . 151
Hamilton 151
Raglan 157
Te Awamutu 161
Rangiaowhia 162
Wharepapa South 163
Cambridge 163
Matamata 164
Te Aroha 165
The King Country 166
Kawhia 167
Otorohanga 168
Waitomo Caves 169
Te Kuiti 173
Taumarunui 175
Owhango 176
Coromandel 176
Miranda 178
Thames 178
Coromandel Town 181

Contents

Far North Coromandel . . 184
Whitianga. 186
Coroglen &
Whenuakite 189
Hahei 189
Hot Water Beach 190
Tairua 191
Puketui Valley 192
Opoutere 192
Whangamata. 192
Waihi & Around. 193
Karangahake Gorge 195
Paeroa 196

TARANAKI & WHANGANUI 197

New Plymouth 200
Mt Taranaki
(Egmont National
Park) 207
Surf Highway 45 211
Whanganui. 213
Whanganui National
Park 219
Palmerston North 224
Manawatu Gorge
& Around 228

TAUPO & THE CENTRAL PLATEAU 230

Taupo 232
Turangi & Around 243
The Central Plateau . . . 246
Tongariro National
Park 246
Whakapapa Village. 250
National Park Village 251
Ohakune. 253
Waiouru 256
Taihape & Around. 256

ROTORUA & THE BAY OF PLENTY . . . 257

Rotorua 259
Bay of Plenty. 276
Tauranga 276
Mt Maunganui. 282
Papamoa 287
Matakana Island. 287
Katikati. 287
Te Puke. 288
Whakatane 289
Whakaari
(White Island). 293
Ohope. 294
Opotiki 295

THE EAST COAST . . 298

East Cape. 299
Pacific Coast Highway. . .299
Gisborne 305
Te Urewera National
Park 312
Hawke's Bay 314
Napier. 315
Hastings, Havelock
North & Around 323
Cape Kidnappers 327
Central Hawke's Bay 328
Kaweka &
Ruahine Ranges 329

WELLINGTON REGION 330

Wellington 332
Kapiti Coast. 353
Paekakariki 354
Waikanae & Around 355
The Wairarapa. 356
Martinborough 357
Cape Palliser. 358
Greytown 359
Masterton & Around 360

UNDERSTAND

The North Island
Today 364
History 366
Environment 376
Maori Culture 383
The Kiwi Psyche 391
Arts & Music 396

SURVIVAL GUIDE

Directory A–Z 402
Transport 415
Language. 423
Index. 429
Map Legend. 438

SPECIAL FEATURES

Active North Island . . 29
Environment 376
Maori Culture 383
The Kiwi Psyche 391

Welcome to the North Island

Packing in cosmopolitan cities, authentic experiences of indigenous Maori culture, and the country's bubbling volcanic heart, the North Island is an exceedingly versatile destination.

Volcanic Thrills

Welcome to one of the planet's youngest countries, at least in geological terms. Ascend the volcanic cones surrounding Auckland for super city views, before heading south to Rotorua for hot mud spa treatments and helicopter journeys to the jagged volcanic summit of Mt Tarawera. Head due south to Lake Taupo, the legacy of one of the planet's biggest-ever volcanic eruptions, and now gateway to Tongariro National Park. Ski or snowboard on Mt Ruapehu's still-active slopes, or negotiate a steady path past Mt Ngauruhoe's brooding volcanic cone on the Tongariro Alpine Crossing.

Outdoor Experiences

New Zealand's South Island usually gets the kudos, but the oft-overlooked North Island also features a sublime combination of forests, mountains and beaches. Tackle one of the North Island's 'Great Walks' – the Whanganui Journey even offers a river journey by canoe or kayak – or spend a few hours wandering through the accessible wilderness of the Coromandel Peninsula. Day trips from vibrant Auckland can include kayaking to dormant volcanoes or canyoning and abseiling down forested waterfalls.

Food, Wine & Beer

Kiwi food was once a bland echo of a British Sunday dinner, but these days NZ chefs dip into New World culinary oceans for inspiration, especially Pacific flavours.

Try some Maori faves: *paua* (abalone), *kina* (sea urchin) and *kumara* (sweet potato). Thirsty? NZ's cool-climate wineries have been collecting award trophies for decades now, and the vineyard restaurants of the Hawke's Bay region are seriously good. The North Island's booming craft-beer scene also deserves serious scrutiny – keep an eye out for brews from Hallertau, Liberty and Crouchers. And with a firmly entrenched coffee culture, you can always find a decent double-shot.

Maori Culture

The all-conquering All Blacks rugby team, with its awesome Maori players, is just one example of how Maori culture impresses itself on contemporary Kiwi life: across the North Island you can hear Maori language, watch Maori TV, see *marae* (meeting houses), join in a *hangi* (Maori feast), or catch a cultural performance with traditional Maori song, usually a blood-curdling *haka* (war dance). Venture to the North Island's East Cape for the most authentic Maori experiences.

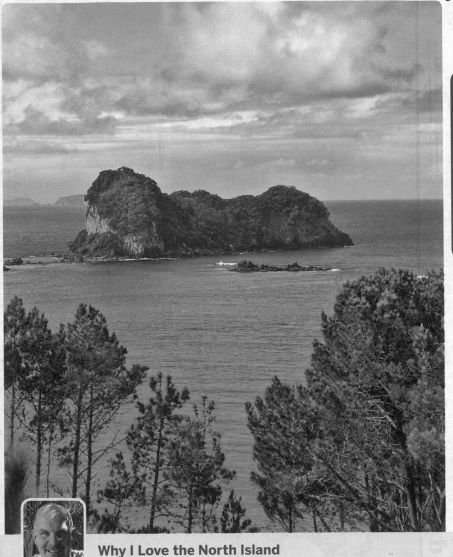

Why I Love the North Island

By Brett Atkinson, Author

Born in the shadow of Mt Ngongotaha in Rotorua, and now resident in Auckland, I've been exploring the North Island with family and friends for most of my life. Favourite places include the bush and beaches of the Coromandel Peninsula, the wine and food scenes of Hawke's Bay, and the rough and tumble volcanic landscapes of Tongariro National Park. For craft beer, culture and coffee, the national capital of Wellington is always appealing, and Auckland's growing ethnic diversity and cosmopolitan vibe makes it New Zealand's most exciting and international city.

For more about our authors, see page 440

Above: Mahurangi Island, near Hahei (p189)

New Zealand – North Island

ELEVATION

2000m
1500m
1250m
1000m
750m
500m
250m
0

100 km
60 miles

Bay of Islands
Scattered islands amid aquamarine waters (p118)

Hauraki Gulf
Wining & dining on Waiheke Island (p81)

Coromandel
Brilliant beaches & forest-clad escapes (p176)

East Cape
Authentic immersion in Maori culture (p299)

Auckland
Island-hopping & great urban eating (p44)

SOUTH PACIFIC OCEAN

TASMAN SEA

To Tokelau

To Kermadec Islands

Cape Reinga
Waitiki Landing
North Cape
Great Exhibition Bay
Karikari Peninsula
Kaitaia
Kerikeri
Kaikohe
Opononi
Hokianga Harbour
Bay of Islands
Russell
Cape Brett
Dargaville
Whangarei
Poor Knights Islands
Hen & Chicken Islands
Wellsford
Warkworth
Kaipara Harbour
Northern River
Helensville
Auckland
Manukau Harbour
Hauraki Gulf
Great Barrier Island
Cape Colville
Coromandel Peninsula
Coromandel Town
Whitianga
Hahei
Ramarama
Thames
Huntly
Te Aroha
Lake Waikato
Mayor Island
Whakaari (White Island)
Cape Runaway

Waitomo Caves
Accessible & adventurous
underground thrills (p169)

Rotorua
Maori culture &
volcanic activity (p259)

Whanganui National Park
Riverside history, heritage
& adventure (p219)

Wellington
Craft beer, coffee
& culture (p332)

Hawke's Bay
Gourmet exploring amid
historic vineyards (p314)

Napier
Colourful & stylish
art deco townscape (p315)

Tongariro National Park
World-beating
one-day alpine walk (p246)

SOUTH PACIFIC OCEAN

To Chatham
Islands

40°S

38°S

178°E

176°E

172°E

40°S

38°S

Hicks Bay
East Cape
Ruatoria
Te Kaha
Tokomaru
Bay
Tolaga Bay
Gisborne
Poverty
Bay
Mahia
Peninsula

Opotiki
Ohope
Whakatane
Matahata
Lake
Rotorua
Rotorua
Murupara
Lake
Waikaremoana
Wairoa
Hawke
Bay
Napier
Cape
Kidnappers
Hastings

Tauranga
Bay of
Plenty

Raglan
Hamilton
Cambridge
Otorohanga
Kawhia
Waitomo Caves
Te Kuiti
Waikato River

Taupo
Lake
Taupo
Turangi
Mt Ngauruhoe
Mt Tongariro
Tongariro
National Park
Ohakune
Waiouru
Taihape

Owhango
National Park
Mt Ruapehu
Taumarunui

Waipawa
Waipukurau

Dannevirke
Woodville
Manawatu
Gorge
Palmerston North

Cape
Turnagain

Whanganui
National Park
Whanganui

North
Taranaki
Bight

New Plymouth
Mt Taranaki
(Mt Egmont)
Stratford
Opunake
Hawera

South
Taranaki
Bight

Levin

Paraparaumu
Kapiti
Island
Paekakariki

Upper
Hutt
Masterton
Greytown
Martinborough
Lake
Wairarapa

Cape Palliser

Lower Hutt
WELLINGTON
Cook Strait

Marlborough
Sounds

Picton

Tasman
Bay
Golden
Bay
Nelson
Collingwood

Karamea

Mokau River
Rangitikei River
Whanganui River
Manawatu River

The North Island's
Top 15

Hauraki Gulf

1 A yachtie's paradise, the island-studded Hauraki Gulf (p81) is Auckland's aquatic playground, sheltering its harbour and east coast bays and providing ample excuse for the City of Sails' pleasure fleet to breeze into action. Despite the busy maritime traffic, the gulf has its own resident pods of whales and dolphins. Rangitoto Island is an icon of the city – its near-perfect volcanic cone provides the backdrop for many a tourist snapshot. With beautiful beaches, acclaimed wineries and upmarket eateries, Waiheke is Auckland's most popular island escape. Waiheke Island (p82)

Urban Auckland

2 Held in the embrace of two harbours and built on the remnants of long extinct volcanoes, Auckland (p46) isn't your average metropolis. It's regularly rated one of the world's most liveable cities and with some recent regeneration projects from the waterfront to the city's art gallery, its star is in the ascendant. Auckland is also blessed with good beaches, flanked by wine regions, and it has a large enough population to support a thriving dining, drinking and live-music scene. Cultural festivals are celebrated with gusto in this ethnically diverse city, which has the world's largest Pacific Islander population.

1

Waitomo Caves

3 Waitomo (p169) is a must-see – an astonishing maze of subterranean caves, canyons and rivers perforating the northern King Country limestone. Black-water rafting is the big lure here (similar to white-water rafting, but through a dark cave), plus glowworm grottoes, underground abseiling and more stalactites and stalagmites than you'll ever see in one place again. Above ground, Waitomo township is a quaint collaboration of businesses: a craft brewery, a cafe, a holiday park and some decent B&Bs. But don't linger in the sunlight – it's party time downstairs.

Geothermal Rotorua

4 The first thing you'll notice about Rotorua (p259) is the smell of sulphur, meaning this geothermal hot spot is a tad whiffy. But volcanic activity is what everyone comes to see, with gushing geysers, bubbling mud, steaming cracks in the ground, and boiling pools of mineral-rich water. Rotorua is definitely unique, a fact exploited by some commercially savvy local businesses. But you don't have to spend a fortune, and there are plenty of affordable (and free) volcanic encounters to be had in parks, Maori villages or just along the roadside.

Bay of Islands

5 Turquoise waters lapping in pretty bays, dolphins frolicking at the bows of boats, pods of orcas gliding gracefully by: chances are these are the kind of images that drew you to New Zealand in the first place, and these are exactly the kind of experiences that the Bay of Islands (p118) delivers so well. Whether you're a hardened sea dog or a confirmed landlubber, there are myriad options to tempt you out on the water to explore the 150-odd islands that dot this beautiful bay.

Rugby

6 Rugby union is New Zealand's national game and governing sporting preoccupation. If your timing's good you might catch the revered national team (and reigning world champions), the All Blacks, in action. The 'ABs' are resident gods – mention Richie McCaw or Dan Carter in any conversation and you'll win friends for life. Watch some kids chasing a ball around a suburban field on a Saturday morning, or yell along with the locals in a small-town pub as the big men collide on the big screen.

East Cape

7 Get right off the beaten track around NZ's easternmost region (p299), a twisting and turning coastal procession of isolated bays and coves, many punctuated during summer with the crimson blooms of the pohutukawa tree. Nowhere else in NZ is everyday Maori culture and society quite so evident, with quiet villages and *marae* (Maori meeting places) tucked into sleepy bays. Several East Cape tour operations are run by members of the local Ngati Porou *iwi* (tribe), providing the opportunity for authentic and heartfelt interaction with travellers.
East Cape Lighthouse (p303)

Wellington

8 Voted the 'coolest little capital in the world' by Lonely Planet's *Best in Travel* a few years back, windy Wellington (p332) lives up to the mantle by keeping things fresh and dynamic. Long famed for a vibrant arts and music scene, fuelled by excellent espresso and more restaurants per head than New York, Wellington has a host of craft-beer bars that have now elbowed in on the action. Edgy yet sociable, colourful yet often dressed in black, Wellington is big on the unexpected and unconventional. Erratic weather only adds to the excitement.

Maori Culture

9 New Zealand's indigenous Maori culture is both accessible and engaging: join in a *haka* (war dance); chow down at a traditional *hangi* (Maori feast cooked in the ground), carve a pendant from bone or *pounamu* (jade), learn some Maori language, or check out an authentic cultural performance with song, dance, legends, arts and crafts. Big-city and regional museums around the North Island are crammed with Maori artefacts and historical items, but this is a living culture: vibrant, potent and contemporary.

TIM GRAHAM / GETTY IMAGES ©

Auckland's Pacific Island Culture

10 Welcome to 'The Big Taro', where around 180,000 residents of Polynesian descent make Auckland the capital of the South Pacific. The influence of Pacific Islanders from Samoa, the Cook Islands, Tonga, Niue, Fiji, Tokelau and Tuvalu is evident throughout Auckland. On the sports field, the city's professional teams showcase the best of Polynesian power, especially the NZ Warriors rugby league team. Immerse yourself in Pacific Island culture at the weekly Otara market, or time your visit for March's annual Pasifika Festival. Performers at the Pasifika Festival (p61)

Coromandel Peninsula

11 A stunning peninsula combining sweeping beaches, quirky coastal landscapes, and rugged bush-clad mountains, the Coromandel region (p176) is a perfect and relaxing escape from the energy and verve of Auckland. The area's hippie and alternative lifestyle roots linger, with organic farms, New Age retreats and well-marked – and sometimes challenging – trails crisscrossing the peninsula's inland spine. Other options for active adventure include sea kayaking around Cathedral Cove, followed by a DIY natural spa pool at nearby Hot Water Beach. Cathedral Cove (p189)

Napier Art Deco

12 Volcanically active NZ is known as the 'Shaky Isles', and seven decades before the Christchurch earthquakes of 2010 and 2011, the country was impacted by a significant seismic event. When a magnitude 7.8 earthquake struck the North Island's east coast in 1931, many brick buildings in the cities of Napier and Hastings collapsed. Reconstruction harnessed the art deco and Spanish mission architectural fashions of the day, and now Napier (p315) is a showcase of art deco design. Visit during February's Art Deco Weekend for the complete 1930s experience.

11

12

15

Hawke's Bay Wine Country

13 Wine has been crafted in the Hawke's Bay region (p314) since 1851, with many more-recent vineyards now joining iconic local wineries such as Mission Estate and Church Road. The emphasis is on excellent Bordeaux-style reds and chardonnay, and many wineries also incorporate good vineyard restaurants. Farmers markets and a tasty menu of other gourmet and artisan producers make it easy for foodie travellers to craft a DIY exploration of the region, and smart lodge and B&B accommodation often celebrate stunning rural and coastal locations.

Tongariro Alpine Crossing

14 At the centre of the North Island, Tongariro National Park presents an alien landscape of alpine desert punctuated by three smoking and smouldering volcanoes. The Tongariro Alpine Crossing (p248) offers the perfect taste of what the park has to offer, skirting the bases of two of the mountains and providing views of craters, brightly coloured lakes, and the vast Central Plateau stretching out beyond. It's for these reasons that it's often rated as one of the world's best single-day wilderness walks.

Whanganui National Park

15 After frantic jetboating or river rafting in other parts of the North Island, slow right down with a canoe or kayak trip down the history-rich Whanganui River in the gloriously isolated Whanganui National Park (p219). Snaking 329km from its source on Mt Tongariro to the Tasman Sea, it's the country's longest navigable river, and tracks through brooding native bush scattered with the remains of historical villages and trading stops. If you're more keen on a driving holiday, the spidery Whanganui River Road is equally spectacular. Bridge to Nowhere (p220), Whanganui River

Need to Know

For more information, see Survival Guide (p401)

Currency
New Zealand dollar ($)

Language
English, Maori and New Zealand Sign Language

Visas
Citizens of Australia, the UK and 56 other countries don't need visas for NZ (length of stay allowances vary). Other countries' citizens require visas. See www.immigration.govt.nz.

Money
ATMs are widely available, especially in larger cities and towns. Credit cards accepted in most hotels and restaurants.

Mobile Phones
Australian and European phones will work on NZ's networks, but not most American or Japanese phones. Use global roaming or a local SIM card and pre-paid account.

Time
New Zealand time is GMT/UTC plus 12 hours (two hours ahead of Australian Eastern Standard Time).

When to Go

Paihia
GO Feb–Apr

Auckland
GO Feb–Apr

Rotorua
GO Oct–Dec

Taupo
GO Jul–Oct (skiing)
or Feb–Apr

Wellington
GO Dec–Feb

High Season
(Dec–Feb)

➡ Summer with busy beaches, outdoor explorations, festivals and sporting events.

➡ Pay more for big-city accommodation.

➡ It's school holiday time with local families hitting popular beaches.

Shoulder
(Mar–Apr)

➡ Fine weather, short queues, kids in school and warm(ish) ocean.

➡ Evenings supping Kiwi wines and beers.

➡ Spring (Sep–Nov) is also shoulder season: local businesses aren't stressed by summer crowds yet.

Low Season
(May–Aug)

➡ Head for the slopes of Mt Ruapehu for brilliant southern hemisphere skiing.

➡ No crowds, good accommodation deals and a seat in any restaurant.

➡ Watch the All Blacks rugby team in welcoming local pubs.

Useful Websites

100% Pure New Zealand
(www.newzealand.com) Official tourism site.

Department of Conservation
(www.doc.govt.nz) DOC parks and camping info.

Destination New Zealand
(www.destination-nz.com) Resourceful tourism site.

Lonely Planet (www.lonely-planet.com/new-zealand) Destination information, hotel bookings, traveller forum and more.

Te Ara (www.teara.govt.nz) Online encyclopedia of NZ.

Important Numbers

Regular NZ phone numbers have a two-digit area code followed by a seven-digit number. When dialling within a region, the area code is still required. Drop the initial 0 if dialling from abroad.

NZ country code	☏64
International access code from NZ	☏00
Emergency (ambulance, fire, police)	☏111
Directory assistance	☏018
International directory	☏0172

Exchange Rates

Australia	A$1	NZ$1.10
Canada	C$1	NZ$1.09
China	Y10	NZ$1.90
Euro zone	€1	NZ$1.62
Japan	¥100	NZ$1.16
Singapore	S$1	NZ$0.94
UK	UK£1	NZ$1.98
US	US$1	NZ$1.19

For current exchange rates see www.xe.com.

Daily Costs

Budget:
Less than $130

➡ Dorm beds or campsites: $25–35 per night

➡ Big-city food markets for self-catering bargains

➡ Explore NZ with a money-saving bus pass

Midrange:
$130–250

➡ Double room in a midrange hotel/motel: $100–200

➡ Midrange restaurant, a movie or a live band, and a few beers at a pub

➡ Hire a car and explore further

Top End:
Over $250

➡ Double room in top-end hotel: from $200

➡ Three-course meal in a classy restaurant: $80

➡ Take a guided tour, go shopping or hit some ritzy bars

Opening Hours

Opening hours vary seasonally (eg the Bay of Islands is quiet during winter), but use the following as a general guide:

Banks 9.30am–4.30pm Monday to Friday; some 9am–noon Saturday

Cafes 7am–4pm

Pubs & Bars noon–late

Restaurants noon–2.30pm and 6.30–9pm

Shops 9am–5.30pm Monday to Friday; 9am to noon or 5pm Saturday

Supermarkets 8am–7pm, often 9pm or later in cities

Arriving in the North Island

Auckland International Airport (p78)

Bus – 24-hour Airbus Express at least every 10 to 30 minutes

Shuttle Bus – Pre-booked, 24-hour door-to-door services

Taxi – Around $70; 45 minutes to the city

Wellington Airport (p351)

Bus – Airport Flyer every 15 minutes 6.30am to 9.30pm

Shuttle Bus – Pre-booked, 24-hour door-to-door services

Taxi – Around $30; 20 minutes to the city

Getting Around

The North Island is surprisingly large and spread out and many roads are two-lane country byways: getting from A to B requires some thought.

Car Travel at your own tempo, explore remote areas and visit regions with no public transport. Hire cars in major towns. Driving is on the left; the steering wheel is on the right.

Bus Reliable, frequent services around the country (usually cheaper than flying).

Plane Fast-track your holiday with affordable, frequent, fast internal flights.

Train One scenic route from Auckland to Wellington transiting through Tongariro National Park.

For much more on **getting around**, see p415

If You Like...

Cities

Auckland Sydney for beginners? We prefer 'Seattle minus the rain', infused with vibrant South Pacific culture. (p46)

Wellington All the lures you'd expect in a capital city, packed into what is really just a very big town. A treat for walkers. (p332)

Hamilton New Zealand's fourth-biggest town doesn't raise much of a blip on the tourist radar, but the bar scene, restaurants, museum and Waikato River all deserve a second look. (p151)

New Plymouth First appearances can definitely be deceiving. Beyond New Plymouth's laid-back provincial charm is a winning selection of cosmopolitan museums and galleries, great cafes and restaurants. (p200)

Beaches

Karekare Classic black sand beach west of Auckland with wild surf (Eddie Vedder nearly drowned here), so be careful. (p95)

Hahei Iconic Kiwi beach on the Coromandel, with mandatory side trips to Cathedral Cove and Hot Water Beach. (p189)

Wainui Beach On the North Island's East Coast, with surfing, sandcastles, sunshine... the quintessential Kiwi beach for all travelling beach bums. BYO Jack Johnson tunes. (p308)

Manu Bay NZ's most famous surf break (seen *Endless Summer?*) peels ashore south of Raglan. There's not much sand, but the left-hand point break is what you're here for. (p160)

History

Waitangi Treaty Grounds In the Bay of Islands, where the contentious Treaty of Waitangi was first signed by Maori chiefs and the British Crown. (p126)

Te Papa Wellington's vibrant treasure-trove museum, where history, both Maori and Pakeha, speaks, sparkles, shakes. (p338)

Whanganui River Road Drive alongside the slow-curling Whanganui River past Maori towns and groves of deciduous trees, remnants of failed Pakeha farms. (p219)

Russell New Zealand's first capital used to be a rambunctious and rowdy haven for boozing sailors, but now it's a pretty harbourside village with historic sites aplenty. (p122)

Maori Culture

Auckland The country's biggest city is renowned for having the planet's biggest Pacific Island population, but a handful of excellent Maori tour operators also showcase Auckland's indigenous culture and history. (p58)

Rotorua Catch a cultural performance at one of several venues: experience a *haka* (war dance) and a *hangi* (Maori feast), with traditional song, dance, folklore and storytelling. (p271)

Footprints Waipoua Explore the staggeringly beautiful Waipoua Kauri Forest on Northland's West Coast with a Maori guide. (p142)

Taiami Tours Heritage Journeys Help paddle a *waka* (Maori canoe) along the sleepy Waitangi River to Haruru Falls. Tours include being welcomed onto a *marae* (meeting place) by the passionate Mihaka family. (p121)

Museums

Auckland Museum A classical Greek-temple design housing a superb collection of Maori and Pacific Islander artefacts, with wonderful guided tours. (p52)

Voyager – New Zealand Maritime Museum From the earliest Maori migrations to the yachting heroics of the America's Cup, seafaring and sailing has been important to the city of Auckland. (p49)

Te Papa The country's biggest and best museum is in Wellington – brilliant by any measure and a much-loved national showcase of the history, culture and geography of NZ. (p338)

Puke Ariki New Plymouth's snazzy waterfront museum is dappled with Maori, colonial and wildlife exhibits...and a great cafe! (p200)

Rotorua Museum Learn about Rotorua's volcanic and spa town history before exploring the art and culture of the local Te Arawa Maori people at this excellent museum. (p261)

Tramping

Cape Reinga Coastal Walkway A 53km Northland long-haul, which can be easily bitten off as a series of short, scenic strolls. (p136)

Mt Taranaki short walks You can loop around the mountain or bag the summit, but a couple of hours spent strolling on its photogenic flanks is equally rewarding. (p207)

Hillary Trail Invest an active four days tackling this very spectacular coastal trail named after 'Sir Ed'. There are good campsites along the way and regular access to Auckland's West Coast surf beaches. (p95)

Tongariro Alpine Crossing Strike out on what is reputedly NZ's best one-day walk, featuring spectacular alpine and volcanic scenery. Spend a few extra days and incorporate interesting summit diversions up Mts Ngauruhoe and Tongariro. (p248)

Top: Te Papa Museum (p338), Wellington
Bottom: Cathedral Cove (p189), Coromandel Peninsula

Pubs, Bars & Beer

Wellington craft-beer scene
Malthouse and Hashigo Zake are just two of around 20 craft-beer bars in the capital (something to do with thirsty politicians?). (p348)

Hamilton Hamilton's Hood and Victoria Sts offer up great pubs and bars and it's just a short hop to Good George in Frankton. (p155)

Auckland The country's biggest city is developing as a hoppy hub. Head to Galbraith's Alehouse, Hallertau or Brothers Beer for Auckland microbrewed goodness. (p74)

Rotorua The crafty team at Rotorua's Croucher Brewing Co create some of the country's best brews. Check them out at their Brew bars in Rotorua (p270) or Tauranga (p281).

Foodie Experiences

Eating in Auckland New restaurants, ethnic culinary enclaves and a growing food-truck scene all make Auckland New Zealand's eating capital. (p66)

Bay of Plenty kiwifruit Pick up a dozen fuzzy, ripe and delicious kiwifruit from roadside stalls for as little as $1-a-dozen. (p288)

Wellington Everyone accepts the nation's capital is a hotspot for craft beer and coffee, but classy fine dining, casual cafes, and authentic ethnic eateries also line Wellington's streets. (p345)

Hawke's Bay Combine dining in the vineyard restaurants of Hawke's Bay with exploring farmers markets and roadside stalls in this fertile and productive region. (p326)

Wine Regions

Martinborough A small-but-sweet wine region a day-trip from Wellington: easy cycling and easy-drinking pinot noir. (p357)

Waiheke Island Auckland's favourite weekend playground has a hot, dry microclimate: perfect for Bordeaux-style reds and rosés. (p82)

Hawke's Bay One of NZ's oldest established wine areas is still one of the country's best. Combine history and wine tasting at the Mission Estate winery. (p326)

Matakana From NZ's oldest wine areas to one of its newest. Around an area north of Auckland, Matakana combines an expanding boutique vineyard scene, brilliant beaches, and a great weekly farmers market. (p102)

Markets

Otara Market Multicultural and edgy, Auckland's Saturday morning Otara Market brims with buskers, arts and crafts, fashions and food. The city's Polynesian community is prominent. (p78)

River Traders Market
Whanganui's riverside market is a Saturday-morning fixture: up to 100 stalls, with a particularly good farmers market (p218)

Harbourside Market Wellington's obligatory fruit and veg pit stop, complemented by fancy artisan produce in the adjacent City Market. (p345)

La Cigale The profound French influence of this weekend Auckland farmers market is joined by a tasty array of other stalls to reflect the increasingly cosmopolitan population of Auckland. Three nights a week the space is converted to house a quirkily informal bistro. (p73)

Extreme Activities

SkyWalk & SkyJump, Auckland Sky Tower New Zealand's adrenaline-pumping extreme scene permeates even downtown Auckland. (p57)

Waitomo black-water rafting Don a wetsuit, a life vest and a helmet with a torch attached, and rampage along an underground river. (p171)

Zorbing Go on – you've always wanted to bounce down a Rotorua hillside ensconced in a giant inflatable globe. And no, it's not true there's a secret office in Wellington dreaming up new extreme sports. (p263)

Skydiving Old school thrills maybe, in the land of weird and wonderful activities, but skydiving above Taupo is one of the world's best spots to leap from a perfectly safe aircraft. (p237)

Festivals

Pasifika Festival Every March, Auckland's Western Springs is transformed into a slice of the tropical South Pacific. Dine on Polynesian food, learn the finer points of Pacific dance, and experience authentic island culture without booking a flight to Fiji or Samoa. (p61)

WOMAD Is New Plymouth's Bowl of Brooklands one of NZ's best outdoor concert venues? When the world music fiesta of WOMAD comes to town in March, there's simply no debate. (p204)

Pohutukawa Named after the scarlet-bloomed tree that punctuates the North Island coastline during summer, the Pohutukawa Festival brightens the entire Coromandel Peninsula with art, music, food and wine every November. (p149)

Month by Month

TOP EVENTS

National Jazz Festival, April

New Zealand International Sevens, February

WOMAD, March

World of Wearable Art Award Show, September

Pasifika Festival, March

January

New Zealand peels its eyes open after New Year's Eve, gathers its wits and gets set for another year. Great weather, cricket season in full swing and happy holidays for the locals.

✹ Festival of Lights

New Plymouth's Pukekura Park is regularly dubbed a 'jewel', but the gardens really sparkle during this festival (www.festivalof lights.co.nz). It's a magical scene: pathways glow and trees are impressively lit with thousands of lights. Live music, dance and kids' performances too.

February

The sun is shining, the nights are long, and the sav blanc and pale ale are chillin' in the fridge: this is prime party time across NZ. Book your festival tickets (and beds) in advance!

✹ Waitangi Day

On 6 February 1840, the Treaty of Waitangi was signed between Maori chiefs and the British Crown. The day remains a public holiday across NZ, and in Waitangi itself (the Bay of Islands) there are guided tours, concerts, market stalls and family entertainment.

✹ New Zealand International Arts Festival

This month-long spectacular (www.festival.co.nz) happens in Wellington in February to March every even-numbered year, and is sure to spark your imagination. NZ's cultural capital exudes artistic enthusiasm with theatre, dance, music and visual arts, and there are international acts aplenty.

✹ Fringe NZ

More music, theatre, comedy, dance and visual arts in Wellington, but not the mainstream stuff from the New Zealand International Arts Festival. This festival (www.fringe.co.nz) highlights the more unusual, emerging, controversial, low-budget and/or downright weird acts.

✹ Splore

Explore Splore (www.splore.net), a cutting-edge outdoor summer fest in Tapapakanga Regional Park, southeast of Auckland. Contemporary live music, performance and visual arts, safe swimming, pohutukawa trees, and the company of very laid-back locals. Come here to chill out.

☆ New Zealand International Sevens

February sees the world's top seven-a-side rugby teams in Wellington (www.sevens.co.nz): everyone from heavyweights such as Australia and South Africa, to minnows like the Cook Islands and Kenya. A great excuse for a party, and fancy dress is also encouraged.

March

March brings a hint of autumn, with harvest time in the vineyards and orchards and long, dusky evenings with plenty of festivals plumping out the calendar. Locals unwind post-tourist season.

✺ Te Matatini National Kapa Haka Festival

This engrossing Maori *haka* (war dance) competition (www.tematatini. co.nz) happens in early March in odd-numbered years. Venues vary: 2015 will be Christchurch and in 2017 it will be in Hawke's Bay. And it's not just the *haka*: expect traditional song, dance, storytelling and other performing arts.

☆ WOMAD

Local and international music, arts and dance performances fill New Plymouth's Brooklands Bowl to overflowing (www. womad.co.nz). An evolution of the world-music festival dreamed up by Peter Gabriel, who launched the inaugural UK concert in 1990. Perfect for families (usually not too loud).

✺ Auckland International Cultural Festival

Auckland's increasingly diverse mix of cultures is showcased at this excellent one-day festival (www. facebook.com/Culturalfestival) in late March. Look forward to lots of ethnic food, music and dance performances, and a fascinating glimpse into the city's cosmopolitan future.

✺ Pasifika Festival

With around 140,000 Maori and notable communities of Tongans, Samoans, Cook Islanders, Niueans, Fijians and other South Pacific Islanders, Auckland has the largest Polynesian community in the world. These vibrant island cultures come together at this annual fiesta (www.aucklandnz. com/pasifika) in Western Springs Park.

April

April is when canny travellers hit NZ: the ocean is still swimmable and the weather still mild, with nary a tourist or queue in sight. Easter means pricey accommodation everywhere.

✺ National Jazz Festival

Every Easter Tauranga hosts the longest-running jazz fest (www.jazz. org.nz) in the southern hemisphere. The line-up is invariably impressive (Kurt Elling, Keb Mo), and there's plenty of fine NZ food and wine to accompany the finger-snappin' sonics.

May

The nostalgia of autumn runs deep: party nights are long gone and another chilly Kiwi winter beckons. Thank goodness for the Comedy Festival! Farmers markets overflow with good value and organic eating.

✺ New Zealand International Comedy Festival

Three-week laugh-fest (www.comedyfestival. co.nz) in May with venues across Auckland, Wellington and various regional centres: Whangarei to Invercargill with all the mid-sized cities in between. International gag-merchants (such as Arj Barker and Danny Bhoy) line up next to home-grown talent.

June

It's the beginning of the ski season, so time to head to Mt Ruapehu. For everyone else, head north: the Bay of Plenty is always sunny, and is it just us, or is Northland underrated?

✺ Matariki

Maori New Year is heralded by the rise of Matariki (aka Pleiades star cluster) in May and the sighting of the new moon in June. Remembrance, education, music, film, community days and tree planting take place, mainly around Auckland and Northland.

July

Wellington's good citizens clutch collars, shiver and hang out in bookshops and cafes. The All Blacks kick off the international rugby season, so find a pub and get cheering. Yes, even you Aussies.

✦✦ NZ International Film Festival

After separate film festivals (www.nzff.co.nz) in both Auckland and Wellington, a selection of flicks hits the road for screenings in regional North Island towns from July to November. Movie buffs in Masterton and Palmerston North get very excited – understandably so.

☆ Russell Birdman

Birdman rallies are just so '80s... But they sure are funny! This one in Russell (www.russellbirdman.co.nz) features the usual cast of costumed contenders propelling themselves off a jetty in pursuit of weightlessness. Bonus points if your name is Russell.

August

Land a good deal on accommodation pretty much anywhere except around Mt Ruapehu's ski scene. Winter is almost spent, but there's still not much happening outside. Music, great pubs and art are your saviours.

✦✦ Taranaki International Arts Festival

Beneath the slopes of Mt Taranaki, August used to be a time of quiet repose. Not any more: this whiz-bang arts festival (www.taft.co.nz/artsfest) in New Plymouth now shakes the winter from the city with music, theatre, dance, visual arts and parades.

Top: Women peforming a *kapa haka* during Waitangi Day celebrations

Bottom: Members of a Tongan group at the Pasifika Festival

✯✯ Jazz & Blues Festival

You might think that the Bay of Islands is all about sunning yourself on a yacht while dolphins splash saltwater on your stomach. In the depths of winter, this jazzy little festival (www.jazz-blues.co.nz) will give you something else to do.

September

Spring has sprung! The amazing and surprising World of WearableArt Award Show is always a hit. And will someone please beat Canterbury in the annual ITM rugby cup final?

✯✯ World of WearableArt Award Show

A bizarre (in the best possible way) two-week long Wellington event (www.worldofwearableart.com) featuring amazing hand-crafted garments. Entries from the show are displayed at the World of WearableArt & Classic Cars Museum across Cook Strait in Nelson after the event.

October

This post-rugby and pre-cricket season leaves sports fans twiddling their thumbs. Maybe it's time to head east to Gisborne? October is shoulder season, with reasonable accommodation rates, minimal crowds and no competition for the good campsites.

✯✯ Feast Gisborne

Around Labour Day Weekend – in the back half of the month – Gisborne's proud winemakers pair with local foodies and artisan producers to showcase the region's tasty goodies. There's lots of great music too (www.feastgisborne.co.nz).

November

Across Northland, the Coromandel Peninsula, Bay of Plenty and the East Coast, NZ's iconic pohutukawa trees erupt with brilliant crimson blooms. The weather is picking up, and a few tourists are starting to arrive.

✯✯ Pohutukawa Festival

Coromandel comes alive with markets, picnics, live music, kiteflying, snorkelling and poetry (www.pohutukawafestival.co.nz). It's all very clean-living and above-board – not everything has to be about drinking, dancing and

decadence. And just look at those pohutukawa trees!

✯ Lake Taupo Cycle Challenge

Feeling fit? Try cycling 160km around Lake Taupo and then talk to us. Held on the last Saturday in November, the event (www.cyclechallenge.com) is open to individuals and teams, and has been judged one of the world's six best recreational rides.

December

Summer! The crack of leather on willow resounds across the nation's cricket pitches and office workers surge towards the finish line. Everyone gears up for Christmas: avoid shopping centres like the plague.

☆ Rhythm & Vines

Wine, music and song in sunny east coast Gisborne on New Year's Eve (www.rhythmandvines.co.nz). Top DJs, hip-hop acts, bands and singer-songwriters compete for your attentions. Or maybe you'd rather just drink some chardonnay and kiss someone on the beach?

Itineraries

 2 WEEKS **Northern Highlights**

Discover the harbours, beaches and Pacific culture of **Auckland**, before heading north to the **Bay of Islands**. At **Waitangi**, explore colonial history and New Zealand's indigenous Maori culture, before hitting the water to swim with dolphins.

Return to Auckland and detour east to the rugged **Coromandel Peninsula** for bushwalking and sea kayaking. Stay overnight in the sleepy beach community of **Hahei**. Then follow looping SH25 around the peninsula to the historic mining town of **Waihi**, before continuing to **Tauranga**, gateway to beachy **Mt Maunganui**.

Head south to **Rotorua** for the classic combo of bubbling thermal activity and vibrant Maori culture. Splash out on a helicopter ride for stunning views of **Mt Tarawera** and the surrounding lakes. Continue south to **Lake Taupo** for jetboating thrills or the more relaxed appeal of trout fishing. If you're feeling brave, bungy jump from 47m above the Waikato River.

Follow the coves of the lake's picturesque eastern shore to **Tongariro National Park**, where there's good winter skiing, and the Tongariro Alpine Crossing, judged one of the world's best one-day walks.

Cape Reinga
Doubtless Bay
Ninety Mile Beach
Mangonui
Ahipara
BAY OF ISLANDS
SOUTH PACIFIC OCEAN
Hokianga
Poor Knights Islands
Tutukaka
Coromandel Peninsula
TASMAN SEA
West Coast Beaches
Hahei
Auckland
Hot Water Beach
Whakaari (White Island)
East Cape
Waitomo Caves
Te Kuiti
Rotorua
Kaituna River
Whakatane
Lake Taupo
Gisborne
Tongariro National Park

Beaches, Volcanoes & Maori Culture
Action Stations

Beaches, Volcanoes & Maori Culture

From energetic and cosmopolitan **Auckland**, head north to sleepy **Tutukaka** for diving around **Poor Knights Islands**. Kayaking, paddle boarding and snorkelling are also available. Further north combine sailing and dolphin swimming trips at **Doubtless Bay** with possibly the world's best fish and chips at **Mangonui**. Continue to windswept **Cape Reinga**, the end of the road for NZ's SH1.

Venture south, skirting the windswept expanses of **Ninety Mile Beach**, before hitting **Ahipara** and traversing massive sand dunes on sand yachts or quad bikes. Continue to **Hokianga** for a taste of colonial history, before heading south through Auckland to **Whakatane**. Take a boat or helicopter out to **Whakaari** (White Island), NZ's most active volcano.

Meander on the SH35 around the **East Cape**, a procession of hidden coves and bays. Here locally owned tourism operators showcase NZ's indigenous Maori culture. Maybe go horse riding on the beach or try a *hangi* (Maori feast). Continue to **Gisborne** for excellent wines and craft beers. NZ's iconic combination of active adventure and stunning scenery is definitely not restricted to the South Island.

Action Stations

Kick off in **Auckland** with the vertiginous combination of SkyWalk and SkyJump. Slow down with a twilight sea-kayaking trip across the harbour, before heading to the **West Coast Beaches** for canyoning down bush-clad waterfalls.

Take the long way round to the **Coromandel Peninsula** for the legendary beach town of **Hahei** and more kayaking around stunning Cathedral Cove. Finish the day – if the tides are in your favour – by digging a natural spa pool at nearby **Hot Water Beach**.

Back on the road, head to **Rotorua**, where action options include zorbing, jetboating, mountain biking and a downhill luge. White-water rafting and river sledging on the nearby Grade V **Kaituna River** are exciting, especially the 7m drop over the Okere Falls.

Continue south to **Lake Taupo** for skydiving with mountain views and bungy jumping above the Waikato River, before completing the superb Tongariro Alpine Crossing, a stunning one-day tramp in **Tongariro National Park**. Saving the best for last, head back north to **Te Kuiti** and experience black-water rafting at **Waitomo Caves**.

Plan Your Trip
Active North Island

Featuring volcanic lakes, arcing beaches and bush-clad rivers, the North Island's scenery can be experienced through an exciting menu of active adventure. Tramp along coastal pathways, undertake thrilling sports like zorbing and bungy jumping, or create personal memories of surfing, skiing and mountain biking at the bottom of the planet.

Trekking in the North Island

Trekking (aka bushwalking, hiking, or tramping as Kiwis call it) is the perfect vehicle for a close encounter with the North Island's natural beauty. There are thousands of kilometres of tracks here – some well marked (including three of New Zealand's celebrated 'Great Walks'), some barely a line on a map – plus an excellent network of huts enabling trampers to avoid lugging tents and (in some cases) cooking gear. Before plodding off into the forest, get up-to-date information from the appropriate authority – usually the Department of Conservation (DOC) or regional i-SITE visitor information centres.

Planning Your Tramp

When to Go

Mid-December–late January Tramping high season is during the school summer holidays, starting a couple of weeks before Christmas – avoid it if you can.

January–March The summer weather lingers into March: wait until February if you can, when tracks are less crowded.

Top Adventures

Top Short Tramps
Tongariro Alpine Crossing, Tongariro National Park; Kohi Point Walkway, Whakatane; Mangawhai Cliff Top Walkway, Northland; Pinnacles, Coromandel Peninsula

Top Anti-Gravity Activities
There are many locations to go bungy jumping, but in Auckland you can make the leap of faith from the Sky Tower; the downhill thrill of zorbing takes place in Rotorua; the sweep and swoosh of the Swoop and Shweeb is also in Rotorua

Top White-Water Rafting Trips
Tongariro River, Taupo; Kaituna River, Rotorua

Top Mountain-Biking Tracks
Ohakune Old Coach Road, Central Plateau; Redwoods Whakarewarewa Forest, Rotorua; 42 Traverse, Central Plateau

Top Surf Spots
Manu Bay, Raglan; Waikanae Beach, Gisborne; Mount Beach, Mt Maunganui

June–August Winter is not the time to be out in the wild, especially at altitude – some paths close in winter because of snow and there are correspondingly lower levels of facilities and services.

What to Bring

Primary considerations: your feet and your shoulders. Make sure your footwear is as tough as old boots and that your pack isn't too heavy. If you're camping or staying in huts without stoves, bring a camping stove. Also bring insect repellent to keep sandflies away, and don't forget your scroggin – a mixture of dried fruit and nuts (and sometimes chocolate) for munching en route.

Books

DOC publishes detailed books on the flora and fauna, geology and history of NZ's national parks, plus leaflets (50c to $2) detailing hundreds of NZ walking tracks.

Lonely Planet's *Tramping in New Zealand* describes around 50 walks of various lengths and degrees of difficulty. Mark Pickering and Rodney Smith's *101 Great Tramps* has suggestions for two- to six-day tramps around the country. The companion guide, *202 Great Walks: the Best Day Walks in New Zealand,* by Mark Pickering, is handy for shorter, family-friendly

excursions. New trampers should check out *Don't Forget Your Scroggin* by Sarah Bennett and Lee Slater – all about being safe and happy on the track. The *Birdseye Tramping Guides* from Craig Potton Publishing have fab topographical maps, and there are countless books covering tramps and short urban walks around NZ – scan the bookshops.

Maps

The topographical maps produced by Land Information New Zealand (LINZ) are a safe bet. Bookshops don't often have a good selection of these, but LINZ has map sales offices in major cities and towns, and DOC offices often sell LINZ maps for local tracks. Outdoor stores also stock them. The LINZ map series includes park maps (national, state and forest), dedicated walking-track maps, and detailed 'Topo50' maps (you may need two or three of these per track).

Online Resources

www.trampingtracks.co.nz Descriptions, maps and photos of long and short tramps all over NZ.

www.tramper.co.nz Articles, photos, forums and excellent track and hut information.

www.trampingnz.com Region-by-region track info with readable trip reports.

www.peakbagging.org.nz Find a summit and get up on top of it.

www.topomap.co.nz Online topographic maps of the whole country.

Track Classification

Tracks in NZ are classified according to various features, including level of difficulty. We loosely refer to the level of difficulty as easy, medium, hard or difficult. The widely used track classification system is as follows:

Short Walk Well formed; allows for wheelchair access or constructed to 'shoe' standard (ie walking boots not required). Suitable for people of all ages and fitness levels.

Walking Track Easy and well-formed longer walks; constructed to 'shoe' standard. Suitable for people of most ages and fitness levels.

Easy Tramping Track or **Great Walk** Well formed; major water crossings have bridges and track junctions have signs. Light walking boots required.

TRACK SAFETY

Thousands of people tramp across NZ without incident, but every year a few folks meet their maker in the mountains. Some trails are only for the experienced, fit and well-equipped – don't attempt these if you don't fit the bill. Ensure you are healthy and feel comfortable walking for sustained periods.

NZ's climatic changeability subjects high-altitude walks to snow and ice, even in summer: always check weather and track conditions before setting off, and be ready for conditions to change rapidly. Consult a DOC visitor centre and leave your intentions with a responsible person before starting longer walks.

Also see www.mountainsafety.org.nz and www.metservice.co.nz for weather updates.

RESPONSIBLE TRAMPING

If you went straight from the cradle into a pair of hiking boots, some of these tramping tips will seem ridiculously obvious; others you mightn't have considered. Online, the 'leave no trace' website (www.lnt.org) is a great resource for low-impact hiking, and the DOC site (www.camping.org.nz) has plenty more responsible camping tips. When in doubt, ask DOC or i-SITE staff.

The ridiculously obvious:

➡ Time your tramp to avoid peak season: fewer people equals less stress on the environment and fewer snorers in the huts.

➡ Carry out *all* your rubbish. Burying rubbish disturbs soil and vegetation, encourages erosion, and animals will probably dig it up anyway.

➡ Don't use detergents, shampoo or toothpaste in or near watercourses (even if they're biodegradable).

➡ Use lightweight kerosene, alcohol or Shellite (white gas) stoves for cooking; avoid disposable butane gas canisters.

➡ Where there's a toilet, use it. Where there isn't one, dig a hole and bury your by-product (at least 15cm deep, 100m from any watercourse).

➡ If a track passes through a muddy patch, just plough straight on through – skirting around the outside increases the size of the bog.

You mightn't have considered:

➡ Wash your dishes 50m from watercourses; use a scourer, sand or snow instead of detergent.

➡ If you *really* need to scrub your bod, use biodegradable soap and a bucket, at least 50m from any watercourse. Spread the waste water around widely to help the soil filter it.

➡ If open fires are allowed, use only dead, fallen wood in existing fireplaces. Leave any extra wood for the next happy camper.

➡ Keep food-storage bags out of reach of scavengers by tying them to rafters or trees.

➡ Feeding wildlife can lead to unbalanced populations, diseases and animals becoming dependent on handouts. Keep your dried apricots to yourself.

Tramping Track Requires skill and experience; constructed to 'boot' standard. Suitable for people of average physical fitness. Water crossings may not have bridges.

Route Requires a high degree of skill, experience and navigation skills. Well-equipped trampers only.

Great Walks

Three of NZ's nine official 'Great Walks' are on the North Island, and one is actually a highly regarded river trip. Natural beauty abounds, but prepare yourself for crowds, especially during summer.

All three of the North Island's Great Walks are described in Lonely Planet's *Tramping in New Zealand,* and are detailed in pamphlets provided by DOC visitor centres.

To tramp these tracks you'll need to buy **Great Walk Tickets** before setting out. These track-specific tickets cover you for hut accommodation (from $22 to $54 per adult per night, depending on the track and season) and/or camping ($6 to $18 per adult per night). You can camp only at designated camping grounds. In the off-peak season (May to September), you can use **Backcountry Hut Passes** ($92 per adult, valid for six months) or pay-as-you-go **Backcountry Hut Tickets** (huts $5 to $15, camping $5) instead of Great Walk tickets on North Island Great Walks except for the Lake Waikaremoana Track.

Prices for kids aged 11 to 17 are half those listed here; kids 10 and under stay for free. We hear whispers of hut tickets being phased out over coming years:

Great Walks

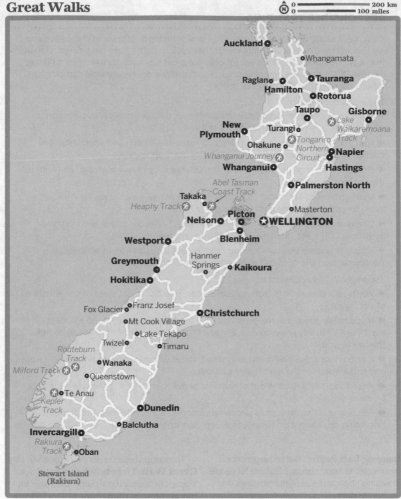

Backcounty Hut Passes are the way of the future.

There's a booking system in place for Great Walk huts and campsites. Trampers must book their chosen accommodation and specify dates when they purchase Great Walk Tickets. Bookings are required year-round for the Lake Waikaremoana Track. For the Tongariro Northern Circuit and the Whanganui Journey, bookings are required for the peak season only (October to April).

Bookings and ticket purchases can be made online (www.doc.govt.nz), by email

(greatwalksbooking@doc.govt.nz), or via DOC offices close to the tracks. Bookings open mid-July each year.

Other North Island Tracks

Of course, there are a lot more walks in the North Island than just the great ones! Try these selections on for size:

Cape Reinga Coastal Walkway A 50km, three-day, easy beach tramp (camping only) in Northland. A 132km six- to eight-day route is also possible.

Mt Holdsworth–Jumbo Circuit A medium-to-hard, three-day tramp in Holdsworth Forest Park, scaling alpine Mt Holdsworth.

Pouakai Circuit A 25km, two- to three-day loop in the lowland rainforest, cliffs and subalpine forest at the foot of Mt Taranaki in Egmont National Park.

Tongariro Alpine Crossing A brilliant 18km, one-day, medium tramp through Tongariro National Park.

Backcountry Huts & Conservation Campsites

Huts

DOC maintains more than 950 backcountry huts in NZ's national and forest parks. Hut categories comprise:

Basic huts Just a shed!

Standard huts No cooking equipment and sometimes no heating, but mattresses, water supply and toilets.

Serviced huts Mattress-equipped bunks or sleeping platforms, water supply, heating, toilets and sometimes cooking facilities.

Details about the hut services can be found on the DOC website. Backcountry hut fees per adult, per night range from free to $52, with tickets bought in advance at DOC visitor centres (some huts can also be booked online: visit www.doc.govt.nz). Children under 10 can use huts for free; 11- to 17-year-olds are charged half price. If you do a lot of tramping DOC sells a six-month Backcountry Hut Pass applicable to most huts except Great Walk huts in peak season (October to April, during which

time you'll need Great Walk tickets). In the low season (May to September), backcountry hut tickets and passes can also be used to procure a bunk or campsite on some Great Walks.

Depending on the hut category, a night's stay may use one or two tickets. Date your tickets and put them in the boxes provided at huts. Accommodation is on a first-come, first-served basis.

Campsites

DOC also manages 250 'Conservation Campsites' (usually vehicle accessible) with categories as follows:

Basic campsites Basic toilets and water; free and unbookable.

Standard campsites Toilets and water supply, and perhaps barbecues and picnic tables; $5 to $16; unbookable.

Serviced campsites Full facilities: flush toilets, tap water, showers and picnic tables. They may also have barbecues, a kitchen and laundry; $7 to $19; bookable via DOC visitor centres.

Children aged five to 17 pay half-price for Conservation Campsites; kids four and under stay free.

Guided Walks

If you're new to tramping or just want a more comfortable experience than the DIY alternative, several companies can escort you through the wilds, usually staying in comfortable huts (showers!), with meals cooked and equipment carried for you.

Places on the North Island where you can sign up for a guided walk include

THE NORTH ISLAND'S THREE 'GREAT WALKS'

Walk	Distance	Duration	Difficulty	Description
Lake Waikaremoana Track	46km	3–4 days	Easy to medium	Lake views, bush-clad slopes and swimming in Te Urewera National Park
Tongariro Northern Circuit	41km	3–4 days	Medium to hard	Through the active volcanic landscape of Tongariro National Park; see also Tongariro Alpine Crossing
Whanganui Journey	145km	5 days	Easy	Canoe or kayak down the Whanganui River in Whanganui National Park

TE ARAROA

Epic! **Te Araroa** (www.teararoa.org. nz) is a 3000km tramping trail from Cape Reinga in NZ's north to Bluff in the south (or the other way around). The route links existing tracks with new sections. Built over a decade, mostly by volunteers, it's one of the longest hikes in the world: check the website for maps and track notes, plus blogs and videos from hardy types who have completed the end-to-end epic.

Mt Taranaki, Lake Waikaremoana and Tongariro National Park. Prices for a four-night guided walk start at around $1800, and rise towards $2200 for deluxe guided experiences.

Getting There & Away

Getting to and from trailheads can be problematic, except for popular trails serviced by public and dedicated trampers' transport. Having a vehicle only helps with getting to one end of the track (you still have to collect your car afterwards). If the track starts or ends down a dead-end road, hitching will be difficult.

Of course, tracks accessible by public transport are also the most crowded. An alternative is to arrange private transport, either with a friend or by chartering a vehicle to drop you at one end, then pick you up at the other. If you intend to leave a vehicle at a trailhead, don't leave anything valuable inside – theft from cars in isolated areas is a significant problem.

Skiing & Snowboarding on the North Island

Global warming is triggering a worldwide melt, but NZ remains an essential southern hemisphere destination for snow bunnies, with downhill skiing, cross-country (Nordic) skiing and snowboarding all passionately pursued. Heliskiing, where choppers lift skiers to the top of long, isolated stretches of virgin snow, also has its fans. The North Island ski season is generally

June to October, though it can vary depending on annual weather conditions.

Planning Your Snow Session

Where to Go

On the North Island, the volcanic landscape of Mt Ruapehu in Tongariro National Park showcases the Whakapapa and Turoa resorts, while club areas such as Tongariro's Tukino and Taranaki's Manganui are publicly accessible and usually less crowded and cheaper than the commercial fields.

Practicalities

NZ's commercial ski areas aren't generally set up as 'resorts' with chalets, lodges or hotels. Rather, accommodation and après-ski carousing are often in surrounding towns, connected with the slopes via daily shuttles. Many club areas have lodges you can stay at, subject to availability.

Visitor information centres in NZ and international Tourism New Zealand offices have info on the various ski areas and can make bookings and organise packages. Lift passes cost anywhere from $60 to $100 per adult per day (half-price for kids). Lesson and lift packages are available in most areas. Ski/snowboard equipment rental starts at around $50 per day (cheaper for multiday hire).

Online Resources

www.brownbearski.co.nz Brilliant reference detailing all of NZ's ski areas.

www.mtruapehu.com The go-to website for information on Whakapapa and Turoa.

www.snow.co.nz Reports, cams and ski info across the country.

www.nzsnowboard.com Snowboarding information.

North Island Ski Areas

Tongariro National Park

Whakapapa & Turoa (p249) On either side of Mt Ruapehu, these well-run twin resorts comprise NZ's largest ski area. Whakapapa has 30 intermediate groomed runs, plus snowboarding, cross-country, downhill, a terrain park and the highest lift access in NZ. Drive from Whakapapa Village (6km; free parking), or shuttle-bus in from

National Park Village, Taupo, Turangi or Whakapapa Village. Smaller Turoa has a beginners' lift, plus snowboarding, downhill and cross-country skiing. There's free parking or shuttle-bus transport from Ohakune 17km away, which has the North Island's liveliest post-ski scene.

Tukino (p250) Club-operated Tukino is on Mt Ruapehu's east, 46km from Turangi. It's quite remote, 14km down a gravel road from the sealed Desert Rd (SH1), and you need a 4WD vehicle to get in. Uncrowded, with mostly beginner and intermediate runs.

Taranaki

Manganui (p208) Offers volcano-slope, club-run skiing on the eastern slopes of spectacular Mt Taranaki in the Egmont National Park, 22km from Stratford (and a 20-minute walk from the car park). Ski off the summit when conditions permit: it's a sweaty two-hour climb to the crater, but the exhilarating 1300m descent compensates.

Extreme North Island

The North Island's astounding natural assets encourage even the laziest lounge lizards to drag themselves outside and get active. 'Extreme' sports are abundant and supremely well organised here. Mountaineering is part of the national psyche; skydiving, mountain biking, jetboating and rock climbing are well established; and pants-wetting, illogical activities like bungy jumping have become everyday pursuits. While adrenaline-pumping activities obviously have some element of risk, the perception of danger is part of the thrill. (Just make sure you have travel insurance anyway.)

Bungy Jumping

Bungy jumping was made famous by Kiwi AJ Hackett's 1986 plunge from the Eiffel Tower, after which he teamed up with champion NZ skier Henry van Asch to turn the endeavour into a profitable enterprise. The South Island resort town of Queenstown is the spiritual home of bungy, but Taupo, Taihape, Auckland and Rotorua on the North Island all offer the opportunity to leap bravely into the void on a giant rubber band.

Caving

Caving (aka spelunking) opportunities abound in NZ's honeycombed karst (limestone) regions. In the North Island, you'll find local clubs and organised tours around Auckland, Waitomo and Whangarei.

Useful resources:

➡ **Wellington Caving Group** (www.caving. org.nz)

➡ **Auckland Speleo Group** (www.asg. org.nz)

➡ **New Zealand Speleological Society** (www.caves.org.nz)

Horse Trekking

Unlike some other parts of the world where beginners get led by the nose around a paddock, horse trekking in NZ lets you really get out into the countryside – on a farm, forest or beach. Rides range from one-hour jaunts (from around $50) to week-long, fully catered treks.

On the North Island Taupo, the Coromandel Peninsula, Waitomo, Pakiri, Ninety Mile Beach, Rotorua, the Bay of Plenty and East Cape are top places for an equine encounter.

For info and operator listings:

➡ **100% Pure New Zealand** (www. newzealand.com)

➡ **True NZ Horse Trekking** (www.truenz. co.nz/horsetrekking)

➡ **Auckland SPCA Horse Welfare Auxiliary Inc** (www.horsetalk.co.nz)

Jetboating

Hold onto your breakfast: passenger-drenching 360-degree spins ahoy!

On the North Island the Whanganui, Motu, Rangitaiki and Waikato Rivers are excellent for jetboating, and there are sprint jets at the Agrodome in Rotorua. Jetboating around the Bay of Islands in Northland is also de rigueur.

Parasailing & Kiteboarding

Parasailing (dangling from a modified parachute that glides over the water, whilst being pulled along by a speed-boat/jetski) is perhaps the easiest way for humans to achieve assisted flight. After a half-day of instruction you should be able to do

CYCLE TOURING

OK, so cruising around the country on a bicycle isn't necessarily 'extreme', but it is super-popular in NZ, especially during summer. Most towns offer bike hire at either backpacker hostels or specialist bike shops, with bike repair shops in bigger towns.

The $50-million **Nga Haerenga, The New Zealand Cycle Trail** (www.nzcycletrail.com/) is a national network of bike trails from Kaitaia to Bluff, featuring 22 'Great Rides', a similar concept to tramping's 'Great Walks'. Some sections are still in the developmental stages, but some stages are open: see the website for updates.

Online resources:

→ **Independent Cycle Tours** (www.cyclehire.co.nz)

→ **Paradise Press** (www.paradise-press.co.nz) Produces *Pedallers' Paradise* booklets by Nigel Rushton.

limited solo flights. Tandem flights in the North Island happen at Te Mata Peak in Hawke's Bay.

Kiteboarding (aka kitesurfing), where a mini parachute drags you across the ocean on a mini surfboard, can be attempted at Paihia, Tauranga, Mt Maunganui, Raglan and Wellington. You can tee up lessons at most of these places, too. Karikari Peninsula near Cape Reinga on NZ's northern tip is a kiteboarding mecca.

Mountain Biking

The North Island is laced with quality mountain-biking opportunities. Mountain bikes can be hired in Taupo and Rotorua, and both cities have bicycle repair shops.

Companies will take you up to the summit of Mt Ruapehu, so you can hurtle down without the grunt-work of getting to the top first. Rotorua's Redwoods Whakarewarewa Forest offers famously good mountain biking, as does the 42 Traverse near the township of National Park (close to Tongariro National Park). Other North Island options include Woodhill Forest, Waihi, Te Aroha, Te Mata Peak and Makara Peak in Wellington.

Some traditional tramping tracks are open to mountain bikes, but DOC has restricted access in many cases due to track damage and the inconvenience to walkers, especially at busy times. Never cycle on walking tracks in national parks unless it's permissible (check with DOC), or you risk heavy fines and the unfathomable ire of hikers.

→ **Classic New Zealand Mountain Bike Rides** (www.kennett.co.nz) Details short and long rides all over NZ.

→ **New Zealand Mountain Biker** (www.nzmtbr.co.nz) A magazine which comes out every two months.

Rock Climbing

Time to chalk up your fingers and don some natty little rubber shoes. On the North Island, popular rock-climbing areas include Auckland's Mt Eden Quarry; Whanganui Bay, Kinloch, Kawakawa Bay and Motuoapa near Lake Taupo; Mangatepopo Valley and Whakapapa Gorge on the Central Plateau; Humphries Castle and Warwick Castle on Mt Taranaki; and Piarere and Wharepapa South in the Waikato.

Climb New Zealand (www.climb.co.nz) has the low-down on the gnarliest overhangs around NZ, plus access and instruction info.

Scuba Diving

NZ is prime scuba territory, with warm waters up north, brilliant sea-life and plenty of interesting sites.

Around the North Island, get wet at the Bay of Islands Maritime and Historic Park, the Hauraki Gulf Maritime Park, the Bay of Plenty, Great Barrier Island, Goat Island Marine Reserve, the Alderman Islands, Te Tapuwae o Rongokako Marine Reserve near Gisborne, and Sugar Loaf Islands Marine Park near New Plymouth. The Poor Knights Islands near Whangarei are reputed to have the best diving in NZ (with the diveable wreck of the Greenpeace flagship *Rainbow Warrior* nearby).

Expect to pay anywhere from $180 for a short introductory, pool-based scuba course; and around $600 for a four-day,

Above: Rock climbing, Whanganui Bay, Lake Taupo

Right: Surfing lesson at Raglan (p157)

MATTHEW MICAH WRIGHT / GETTY IMAGES ©

SURFING IN NEW ZEALAND

As a surfer I feel particularly guilty in letting the reader in on a local secret – NZ has a sensational mix of quality waves perfect for beginners and experienced surfers. As long as you're willing to travel off the beaten track, you can score some great, uncrowded waves. The islands of NZ are hit with swells from all points of the compass throughout the year. So, with a little weather knowledge and a little effort, numerous options present themselves. Point breaks, reefs, rocky shelves and hollow sandy beach breaks can all be found – take your pick!

Surfing has become increasingly popular in NZ and today there are surf schools up and running at most premier surf beaches. It's worth doing a bit of research before you arrive: **Surfing New Zealand** (www.surfingnz.co.nz) recommends a number of surf schools on its website. If you're on a surf holiday in NZ, consider purchasing a copy of the *New Zealand Surfing Guide* by Mike Bhana.

Surf.co.nz (www.surf.co.nz) provides information on many great surf spots, but most NZ beaches hold good rideable breaks. Here are some of the ones I particularly enjoy on the North Island:

Waikato Raglan, NZ's most famous surf break and usually the first stop for overseas surfies

Coromandel Whangamata

Bay of Plenty Mt Maunganui, now with a 250m artificial reef that creates huge waves, and Matakana Island

Taranaki Fitzroy Beach, Stent Rd and Greenmeadows Point all lie along the 'Surf Highway'

East Coast Hicks Bay, Gisborne city beaches and Mahia Peninsula

Wellington Region Beaches such as Lyall Bay, Castlepoint and Tora

NZ water temperatures and climate vary greatly from north to south. For comfort while surfing, wear a wetsuit. In summer on the North Island you can get away with a spring suit and boardies, while in winter you'll need to use a 2–3mm steamer.

Josh Kronfeld, surfer and former All Black

PADI-approved, ocean dive course. One-off organised boat- and land-based dives start at around $170.

Resources include:

➡ **New Zealand Underwater Association** (www.nzu.org.nz)

➡ **Dive New Zealand** (www.divenewzealand.com)

Skydiving

Feeling confident? For most first-time skydivers, a tandem skydive will help you make the leap, even if common sense starts to get the better of you. Tandem jumps involve training with a qualified instructor, then experiencing up to 45 seconds of free fall before your chute opens. The thrill is worth every dollar (around $250/300/350 for an 8000/10,000/12,000ft jump, extra for a DVD/photograph). The **New Zealand Parachute Federation** (www.nzpf.org) is the governing body.

Sea Kayaking

Sea kayaking is a fantastic way to see the coast and get close to wildlife you'd otherwise never see.

Highly rated sea kayaking areas around the North Island include the Hauraki Gulf (particularly off Waiheke and Great Barrier Islands), the Bay of Islands and Coromandel Peninsula. Other North Island kayaking locations include Auckland's Waitemata Harbour, Hahei, Raglan and East Cape. Useful resources:

➡ **Kiwi Association of Sea Kayakers** (KASK; www.kask.org.nz)

➡ **Sea Kayak Operators Association of New Zealand** (www.skoanz.org.nz)

White-Water Rafting, Kayaking & Canoeing

There are almost as many white-water rafting and kayaking possibilities as there are rivers in NZ, with no shortage of companies to get you into the rapids. Rivers are graded from I to VI, with VI meaning 'unraftable'. On the rougher stretches there's usually a minimum age limit of 12 or 13 years.

Popular North Island rafting rivers include the Rangitaiki, Wairoa, Motu, Mokau, Mohaka, Waitomo, Tongariro and Rangitikei. There is also the Kaituna Cascades near Rotorua, with its 7m drop at Okere Falls.

Canoeing is so popular on the North Island's Whanganui River that it's been designated one of NZ's 'Great Walks'. You can also dip your paddle into Lake Taupo and Lake Rotorua. Some backpacker hostels close to canoe-friendly waters have Canadian canoes and kayaks for hire (or for free), and loads of commercial operators run guided trips.

Resources include:

➡ **New Zealand Rafting Association** (NZRA; www.nz-rafting.co.nz)

➡ **Whitewater NZ** (www.rivers.org.nz)

➡ **New Zealand Kayak** (www.canoeandkayak.co.nz)

Regions at a Glance

Experience Auckland's confident and cosmopolitan Pacific buzz before heading north for the Bay of Islands' combination of colonial history, Maori heritage and sweeping beaches amid isolated coves. The Coromandel Peninsula features yet more bush-clad beaches, and New Zealand's indigenous Maori culture bubbles away proudly in volcanic Rotorua and around the remote East Cape, quite probably the North Island's most quintessentially laid-back region. Further inland, the country's violent volcanic past produced the wonders of Lake Taupo and Tongariro National Park, now a haven for skiers, trampers, and anglers looking to lure a plump rainbow trout. Wine and foodie treats abound in Hawke's Bay and Gisborne, while Wellington is arty and caffeine-fuelled proof that capital cities definitely don't have to be boring.

Auckland

Coastline
Eating & Drinking
Volcanoes

Beaches

From the calm, child-friendly bays facing the Hauraki Gulf, to the black sand, surf beaches of the west coast, Auckland's water-lovers really are spoilt for choice.

Restaurants, Bars & Cafes

Auckland has some of the nation's best fine dining and ethnic restaurants, a lively cafe and bar scene, and wine regions on three of its flanks. Coffee and craft beer are also booming here.

A Unique Landscape

Auckland is, quite literally, a global hot spot, with more than 50 separate volcanoes forming a unique topography. Take a hike up one of the landscape's dormant cones for a high, wide and handsome city panorama.

p44

Bay of Islands & Northland

Coastline
Wilderness
History

Beaches & Bays

Bay after beautiful bay line Northland's east coast, making it a favourite with families, surfers and anglers. To the west, long windswept beaches stretch for miles, in places forming towering sand dunes.

Ancient Forests

Kauri forests once blanketed the entire north, and in the pockets where these giants remain, particularly in the Waipoua Forest, they're an imposing sight.

Kerikeri & Waitangi

New Zealand was settled top down by both Maori and Europeans, with missionaries erecting the country's oldest surviving buildings in Kerikeri. In nearby Waitangi, the treaty that founded the modern nation was first signed.

p105

Waikato & Coromandel Peninsula

Coastline
Towns
Caves

Beaches & Surf

Around Raglan you'll find safe swimming and world-class surf at legendary Manu Bay. Beaches on the Coromandel are extremely popular in summer, but splendid isolation can still be found.

Smalltown Vibe

Smaller towns in the Waikato like Te Aroha, Cambridge, Matamata and Raglan have great pubs, cafes, restaurants and friendly locals. The Coromandel's goldrush roots are in Thames and Coromandel Town.

Waitomo Caves

Don't miss Waitomo Caves, NZ's most staggering cave site. Rafting along underground rivers (black-water rafting) is popular, or you can just float through amazing grottoes of glow-worms.

p147

Taranaki & Whanganui

National Parks
Underrated Cities
Beaches

National Parks

Whanganui National Park offers canoeing and kayaking on the Whanganui River. Near New Plymouth, Mt Taranaki is a picture-perfect peak with fabulous tramping.

Underrated Cities

New Plymouth, Whanganui and Palmerston North are mid-sized cities often overlooked by travellers. You'll find fantastic restaurants and bars, great coffee, wonderful museums and friendly folk.

Beaches

South of New Plymouth are black sand beaches and gnarly breaks. Whanganui offers remote beaches, while south of Palmerston North, Horowhenua District has acres of empty sand.

p197

Taupo & the Central Plateau

Wilderness Scenery
Outdoor Activities

Lake & Rivers

New Zealand's mightiest river is borne from New Zealand's greatest lake: aquatic pursuits in picturesque settings abound (kayaking, sailing, fishing). The water is famously chilly, but hot springs bubble up on the lakeside and riverbank.

Epic Landscapes

The three steaming, smoking, occasionally erupting volcanoes at the heart of the North Island are an imposing sight, with the focus on skiing in winter and tramping at other times.

Extreme Taupo

Skydiving, bungy jumping, white-water rafting, jetboating, mountain biking, wakeboarding, parasailing, skiing – you want thrills? You got 'em.

p230

Rotorua & the Bay of Plenty

Geothermal Activity
Maori Culture
Activities

Volcanic Hubbub

The Rotorua landscape is littered with geysers, thermal vents, hot mineral springs and boiling mud pools. NZ's most active volcano, Whakaari (White Island), is 48km off the coast of Whakatane.

Maori Cultural Experiences

Engage with Maori culture in Rotorua: a slew of companies offer cultural experiences for travellers, most involving traditional dance and musical performance, a *haka* (war dance) and a *hangi* (Maori feast).

Outdoor Sports

Try paragliding, surfing, skydiving, zorbing, jetboating, blokarting, white-water rafting, mountain biking, kayaking... or just swim at the beach.

p257

The East Coast

·······································

Coastline
Wine
Architecture

·······································

Coastal Scenery

Follow in the wake of early Maori and James Cook along this stretch of coastline, home to the East Cape Lighthouse and Cape Kidnappers' gaggling gannets.

Gisborne & Hawke's Bay Wine Regions

Sip your way through Gisborne's bright chardonnays, then head to Hawke's Bay for seriously good Bordeaux-style reds and excellent winery dining at some of New Zealand's historic vineyards.

Art-Deco Napier

Napier's art-deco town centre is a magnet for architecture lovers. Time your visit for the annual art-deco weekend, an extravaganza of music, wine, cars and costumes.

p298

Wellington Region

·······································

Arts
Eating & Drinking
Nightlife

·······································

Museums & Galleries

Crowbarred into the city centre are a significant collection of quality display spaces, including the highly interactive Te Papa museum and internationally flavoured City Gallery.

Cafe & Beer Culture

With more than a dozen roasters and scores of hip cafes, Wellington remains the coffee capital of New Zealand. The city also hosts a hip and happening craft-beer scene and great dining.

Bar Hopping

Between the boho bars around Cuba St and Courtenay Pl's glitzy drinking dens, you should find enough to keep you entertained until sun-up.

p330

On the Road

**Bay of
Islands &
Northland**
p105

Auckland
p44

**Waikato &
Coromandel
Peninsula**
p147

**Rotorua & the
Bay of Plenty**
p257

**The East
Coast**
p298

**Taupo & the
Central Plateau**
p230

**Taranaki &
Whanganui**
p197

**Wellington
Region**
p330

Auckland

📓 09 / POP 1.42 MILLION

Includes ➡

Sights 46
Activities..................... 56
Tours.......................... 58
Festivals & Events 60
Sleeping...................... 63
Eating 66
Drinking & Nightlife 74
Entertainment............. 76
Shopping 77
Hauraki Gulf Islands.....81
West Auckland............. 94
North Auckland 99

Best Places to Eat

➡ Depot (p67)

➡ Ima (p68)

➡ Blue Breeze Inn (p71)

➡ Little Bird (p69)

➡ St Heliers Bay Bistro (p73)

Best Places to Stay

➡ Hotel de Brett (p63)

➡ Auckland Takapuna Oaks (p66)

➡ Verandahs (p64)

➡ 23 Hepburn (p64)

Why Go?

Paris may be the city of love, but Auckland is the city of many lovers, according to its Maori name, Tamaki Makaurau. Those lovers so desired this place that they fought over it for centuries.

It's hard to imagine a more geographically blessed city. Its two harbours frame a narrow isthmus punctuated by volcanic cones and surrounded by fertile farmland. From any of its numerous vantage points you'll be surprised how close the Tasman Sea and Pacific Ocean come to kissing and forming a new island.

Whether it's the ruggedly beautiful west-coast surf beaches, or the glistening Hauraki Gulf with its myriad islands, the water's never far away. And within an hour's drive from the city's high-rise heart, there are dense tracts of rainforest, thermal springs, wineries and wildlife reserves. No wonder Auckland is regularly rated one of the world's top cities for quality of life and liveability.

When to Go

➡ Auckland has a mild climate, with the occasional chilly frost in winter and high humidity in summer.

➡ Summer months have an average of eight days of rain, but the weather is famously fickle, with 'four seasons in one day' possible at any time of the year.

➡ If you're after a big-city buzz, don't come between Christmas and New Year, when Aucklanders desert the city for the beach en masse; the sights remain open but many cafes and restaurants close, some not surfacing again until well into January.

Auckland Highlights

1 Going with the flows, exploring Auckland's fascinating **volcanic field** (p57)

2 Getting back to nature on the island sanctuaries of the beautiful **Hauraki Gulf** (p81)

3 Being awed by the Maori *taonga* (treasures) of the **Auckland Museum** (p52)

4 Going west to the mystical and treacherous black sands of **Karekare** (p95) and **Piha** (p96)

5 Swimming with the fishes at **Goat Island Marine Reserve** (p104)

6 Schlepping around world-class wineries and beaches on **Waiheke Island** (p82)

7 Buzzing around the cafes, restaurants and bars of **Ponsonby** (p69)

8 Soaking up the Polynesian vibe at the **Pasifika Festival** (p61), held in March at Western Springs Park

AUCKLAND

History

Maori occupation in the Auckland area dates back around 800 years. Initial settlements were concentrated on the Hauraki Gulf islands, but gradually the fertile isthmus beckoned and land was cleared for growing food.

Over hundreds of years Tamaki's many different tribes wrestled for control of the area, building *pa* (fortified villages) on the numerous volcanic cones. The Ngati Whatua *iwi* (tribe) from the Kaipara Harbour took the upper hand in 1741, occupying the major *pa* sites. During the Musket Wars of the 1820s they were decimated by the northern tribe Ngapuhi, leaving the land all but abandoned.

At the time the Treaty of Waitangi was signed in 1840, Governor Hobson had his base in the Bay of Islands. When Ngati Whatua chief Te Kawau offered 3000 acres of land for sale on the northern edge of the Waitemata Harbour, Hobson decided to create a new capital, naming it after one of his patrons, George Eden (Earl of Auckland).

Beginning with just a few tents on a beach, the settlement grew quickly, and soon the port was busy exporting the region's produce, including kauri timber. However, it lost its capital status to centrally located Wellington after just 25 years.

Since the beginning of the 20th century Auckland has been NZ's fastest-growing city and its main industrial centre. Political deals may be done in Wellington, but Auckland is the big smoke in the land of the long white cloud.

In 2010 the municipalities and urban districts that made up the Auckland Region were merged into one 'super city', and in 2011 the newly minted metropolis was given a buff and shine to prepare it for hosting the Rugby World Cup. The waterfront was redeveloped, the art gallery and zoo were given a makeover, and a swag of new restaurants and bars popped up – leaving a more vibrant city in the cup's wake.

⊙ Sights

Auckland is a city of volcanoes, with the ridges of lava flows forming its main thoroughfares and its many cones providing islands of green within the sea of suburbs. As well as being by far the largest, it's also the most multicultural of New Zealand's cities. A sizeable Asian community rubs shoulders with the biggest Polynesian population of any city in the world.

The traditional Kiwi aspiration for a freestanding house on a quarter-acre section has resulted in a vast, sprawling city. The CBD was long ago abandoned to commerce, and inner-city apartment living has only recently caught on. While geography has been kind, city planning has been less so. Unbridled and ill-conceived development has left the centre of the city with plenty of architectural embarrassments. To get under Auckland's skin, you're best to head to the streets of Victorian and Edwardian villas in its hip inner-city suburbs.

⊙ City Centre

★ **Auckland Art Gallery** GALLERY
(Map p50; www.aucklandartgallery.com; cnr Kitchener & Wellesley Sts; admission varies for special exhibitions; ⊙10am-5pm) **FREE** Following a significant 2011 refurbishment, Auckland's premier art repository now has a stunning glass-and-wood atrium grafted onto its 1887 French-chateau frame. Along with important works by Pieter Bruegel the Younger, Guido Reni, Picasso, Cézanne, Gauguin and Matisse, it also showcases the best of NZ art. Highlights include the intimate 19th-

ESSENTIAL AUCKLAND

Eat Amid the diverse and cosmopolitan scene of Ponsonby Central

Drink West Auckland craft beers at Hallertau in Riverhead

Read *Under the Mountain* (1979) – Maurice Gee's teenage tale of slimy things lurking under Auckland's volcanoes

Listen to *Pure Heroine* (2013) – savvy lyrics and beats from Devonport's very own Lorde

Watch *Matariki* (2010) – five interwoven multicultural stories set in South Auckland

Festival Pasifika

Online www.aucklandnz.com; www.lonelyplanet.com/new-zealand/auckland

Area code ☑ 09

AUCKLAND IN...

Two Days

Start by acquainting yourself with the inner city. Take our **walking tour** (p59) from Karangahape Rd (K Rd) to the Wynyard Quarter, stopping along the way to have at least a quick whiz around the NZ section of the **Auckland Art Gallery**. Catch a ferry to **Devonport**, head up North Head and cool down at **Cheltenham Beach** (weather and tide permitting), before ferrying back to the city for dinner.

On day two, head up **One Tree Hill**, wander around **Cornwall Park** and then visit the **Auckland Museum** and **Domain**. Take a trip along **Tamaki Drive**, stopping at **Bastion** or **Achilles Point** to enjoy the harbour views. Spend the evening dining and bar hopping in **Ponsonby**.

Four Days

On the third day, get out on the **Hauraki Gulf**. Catch the ferry to **Waiheke Island** and divide your time between the beaches and the wineries.

For your final day, head west. Grab breakfast in **Titirangi** before exploring the **Waitakere Ranges Regional Park**, **Karekare** and **Piha**. Freshen up for a night on the town on **K Rd** or **Britomart**.

---

century portraits of tattooed Maori subjects by Charles Goldie, and the starkly dramatic text-scrawled canvasses of Colin McCahon. Free tours depart from the main entrance daily at 11.30am and 1.30pm.

Albert Park   PARK

(Map p50) On the city's eastern flank, Albert Park is a Victorian formal garden bordering **Auckland University**'s campus, and incorporates a row of stately Victorian merchant houses (Princes St) and **Old Government House** (Map p50; Waterloo Quadrant). The latter was the colony's seat of power from 1856 until 1865, when Wellington became the capital. The stately **University Clock Tower** (1926) has influences from art nouveau (the incorporation of NZ flora and fauna into the decoration), and the Chicago School.

At the centre of the campus is a wall of the Albert Barracks (1847), a fortification that enclosed 9 hectares, including Albert Park, during the New Zealand Wars.

Sky Tower   LANDMARK

(Map p50; www.skycityauckland.co.nz; cnr Federal & Victoria Sts; adult/child $28/11; ⊗8.30am-10.30pm) ⌀ The impossible-to-miss Sky Tower looks like a giant hypodermic giving a fix to the heavens. Spectacular lighting renders it space-age at night and the colours change for special events. At 328m it is the southern hemisphere's tallest structure. A lift takes you up to the observation decks in 40 stomach-lurching seconds; look down

through the glass floor panels if you're after an extra kick. Visit at sunset and have a drink in the Sky Lounge Cafe & Bar.

The Sky Tower is also home to the Sky-Walk (p57) and SkyJump (p57).

Civic Theatre   ARCHITECTURE

(Map p50; www.civictheatre.co.nz; cnr Queen & Wellesley Sts) The 'mighty Civic' (1929) is one of seven 'atmospheric theatres' remaining in the world and a fine survivor from cinema's Golden Age. The auditorium has lavish Moorish decoration, and the starlit southern-hemisphere sky in the ceiling (complete with cloud projections) gives the illusion of being under a night sky. It's mainly used for touring musicals, international concerts and film-festival screenings.

Even if nothing is scheduled, try and sneak a peek at the foyer, an Indian indulgence with elephants and monkeys hanging from every conceivable fixture. Buddhas were planned to decorate the street frontage but were considered too risqué at the time – they chose neoclassical naked boys instead!

St Patrick's Cathedral   CHURCH

(Map p50; www.stpatricks.org.nz; 43 Wyndham St; ⊗7am-7pm) Auckland's Catholic cathedral (1907) is one of the city's loveliest buildings. Polished wood and Belgian stained glass lend warmth to the interior of the majestic Gothic Revival church. There's a historical display in the old confessional on the left-hand side.

Auckland

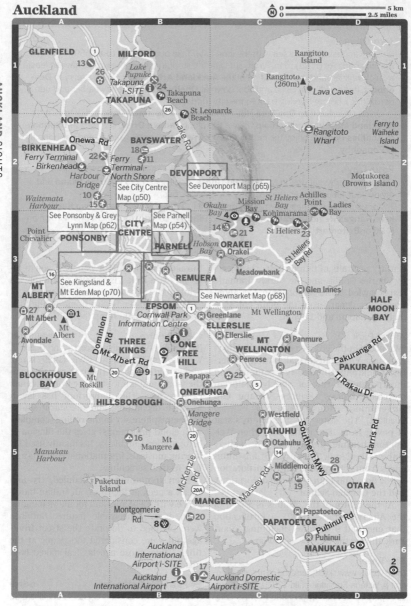

0 ——— 5 km
0 ——— 2.5 miles

N

Britomart, Viaduct Harbour & Wynyard Quarter

Stretching for only a small grid of blocks above the train station, Britomart is a compact enclave of historic buildings and new developments that has been transformed into one of the city's best eating, drinking and shopping precincts. Most of Auckland's top fashion designers have recently decamped to the Britomart area from further uptown in High St.

Auckland

⊙ Sights
1 Alberton A4
2 Auckland Botanic Gardens................. D6
3 Bastion Point......................................C3
4 Kelly Tarlton's Sealife
   Aquarium C3
5 One Tree Hill.....................................B4
6 Rainbow's End....................................D6
7 Stardome Observatory.........................B4
8 Villa Maria Estate................................B6
9 Wallace Arts Centre..............................B4

⊕ Activities, Courses & Tours
10 Auckland Bridge Climb &
   Bungy A2
11 CharterLink..B2
12 Coast to Coast Walkway.....................B4
13 Dive Centre..A1
14 Fergs Kayaks.......................................C3
15 Gulfwind A2
   Penny Whiting Sailing School ....(see 15)

⊜ Sleeping
16 Ambury Regional Park B5
17 Auckland Airport Campervan
   Park...B6
18 Auckland Takapuna Oaks....................B2
19 Grange Lodge......................................C5
20 Jet Park B6
21 Nautical Nook......................................C3

⊗ Eating
22 Engine Room A2
23 St Heliers Bay Bistro C3
   Takapuna Beach Cafe ....(see 24)
24 The Commons.......................................B1

⊜ Entertainment
25 Mt Smart Stadium...............................C4
26 North Shore Events Centre.................A1

⊜ Shopping
27 Avondale Sunday Market A4
28 Otara Market D5

Once a busy commercial port, the Viaduct Harbour was given a major makeover for the 1999/2000 and 2003 America's Cup yachting events. It's now a fancy dining and boozing precinct, and guaranteed to have at least a slight buzz any night of the week. Historical plaques, public sculpture and the chance to gawk at millionaires' yachts make it a diverting place for a stroll.

Connected to the Viaduct by a raiseable bridge, Wynyard Quarter opened in advance of another sporting tournament, 2011's Rugby World Cup. With its public plazas, waterfront cafes, events centre, fish market and children's playground, it has quickly become Auckland's favourite new place to promenade. At the adjacent Silo Park (p63) area, free outdoor Friday night movies and weekend markets have become summertime institutions, and new restaurants have further boosted the precinct's culinary buzz.

**Voyager – New Zealand
Maritime Museum** MUSEUM
(Map p50; ☑09-373 0800; www.maritimemuseum.co.nz; 149-159 Quay St; admission adult/child $17/8.50, with harbour cruise $29/14.50; ⊙9am-5pm, free guided tours at 10.30am & 1pm) This museum traces NZ's seafaring history, from Maori voyaging canoes to the America's Cup. Recreations include a tilting 19th-century steerage-class cabin and a 1950s beach store and bach (holiday home). *Blue Water Black Magic* is a tribute to Sir Peter Blake, the Whitbread-Round-the-World and America's Cup–winning yachtsman who was murdered in 2001 on an environmental monitoring trip in the Amazon. There are also optional one-hour harbour cruises on the *Ted Ashby,* a ketch-rigged sailing scow.

Auckland Fish Market MARKET
(Map p50; www.aucklandfishmarket.co.nz; 22-32 Jellicoe St; ⊙6am-7pm) Early-morning auctions combine with fish shops, cafes and restaurants, and a seafood-cooking school.

⊙ Mt Eden

Mt Eden VOLCANO
(Maungawhau; Map p70; ⊙road access 7am-11pm) From the top of Auckland's highest volcanic cone (196m) the entire isthmus and both harbours are laid bare. The symmetrical crater (50m deep) is known as Te Ipu Kai a Mataaho (the Food Bowl of Mataaho, the god of things hidden in the ground) and is highly *tapu* (sacred). Do not enter it, but feel free to explore the remainder of the mountain. The remains of *pa* terraces and food storage pits are clearly visible.

Drive to the top or join the fitness freaks jogging or trudging up. Tour buses are banned from the summit, but shuttles will transport infirm passengers to the top from the car park on the lower slopes.

Eden Garden GARDENS
(Map p68; www.edengarden.co.nz; 24 Omana Ave; adult/child $8/6; ⊙9am-4pm) On Mt Eden's eastern slopes, and noted for its camellias, rhododendrons and azaleas.

City Centre

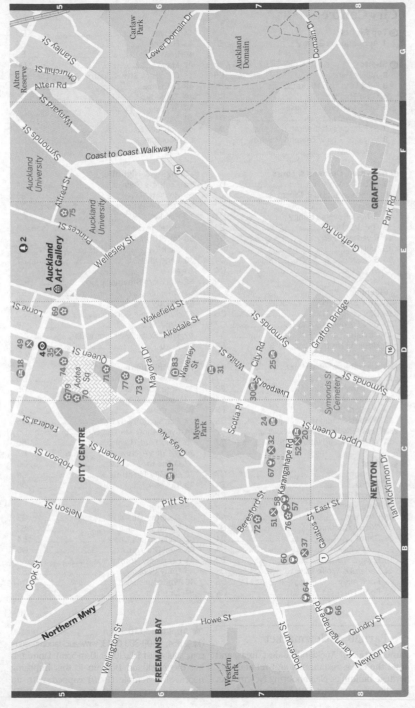

GRAFTON

Park Rd

Grafton Rd

Coast to Coast Walkway

Auckland Domain

Lower Domain Dr

Carlaw Park

Domain Dr

Stanley St

Churchill St

Alten Rd

Alten Reserve

Wynyard St

Symonds St

Auckland University

Alfred St

Princes St

Auckland University

Wellesley St

1 Auckland Art Gallery 🏛

2

Lorne St

69 🏛

Wakefield St

Airedale St

Symonds St

Grafton Bridge

Symonds St Cemetery

Symonds St

16

49 ✕
35 ◉
4 ◉
74 🏛
18 🏬
79 🏛
Aotea Sq
70 Sq
77 🏛
73 🏛

Queen St

Mayoral Dr

83 🏬
Waverley St
31 🍴
White St

City Rd

25 🏛

Liverpool St

30 🍴

24 🏛

Upper Queen St

NEWTON

Ian McKinnon Dr

16

Federal St

CITY CENTRE

Hobson St

Vincent St

Greys Ave

Myers Park

Scotia Pl

Nelson St

Pitt St

19 🍴

32 ✕
67 ✕
52 ✕
57

Karangahape Rd

51 ✕ 58 ✕
76 ✕
72

Beresford St

Galatos St East St

37 ✕
60

1

64

66

Karangahape Rd

Gundry St

Newton Rd

Hopetoun St

Howe St

Western Park

Wellington St

Cook St

Northern Mwy

FREEMANS BAY

City Centre

◎ **Top Sights**
1 Auckland Art Gallery E5

◎ **Sights**
2 Albert Park E5
3 Auckland Fish Market B1
4 Civic Theatre D5
5 Old Government House F4
6 Sky Tower D4
7 St Patrick's Cathedral D3
8 Voyager – New Zealand Maritime
   Museum D2

◉ **Activities, Courses & Tours**
9 360 Discovery D2
10 Auckland Jet Boat Tours C1
11 Fullers E2
12 G-MAX Reverse Bungy D4
13 GreatSights E2
14 Riverhead Ferry D2
15 Sail NZ D2
16 SkyJump C4
17 SkyWalk C4

◎ **Sleeping**
18 Attic Backpackers D5
19 City Lodge C6
20 City Travellers C7
21 CityLife D4
22 Hotel de Brett E3
23 Jucy Hotel F3
24 Kiwi International Hotel C7
25 Langham D7
26 Nomads Auckland E3
27 Quadrant F4
28 Waldorf Celestion F3
29 Waldorf Stadium G3
30 YHA Auckland City D7
31 YHA Auckland International D7

◎ **Eating**
32 Alleluya C7
33 Baduzzi B1
34 Box of Bird E3
35 Burgerfuel D5
36 Clooney A4
37 Coco's Cantina B7
38 Depot D4
39 Dida's Freemans Bay B4
40 Ebisu F2
41 Federal & Wolfe D3
42 Food Alley D3
43 Food Truck Garage C4

44 Grove D3
45 Hansan E4
46 Ima E3
47 Masu D4
   O'Connell Street Bistro .... (see 22)
48 Ortolana E2
49 Remedy D5
50 Revive D3
51 Satya B7
52 Scullery C7
53 Soul Bar D2
   Zap 4 .... (see 34)

◎ **Drinking & Nightlife**
54 Brothers Beer B4
55 Cassette Nine E3
56 Ding Dong Lounge D3
57 Family B7
   Hotel de Brett .... (see 22)
58 Ink & Coherent B7
59 Jack Tar B1
60 Legend B7
61 Mo's D3
62 Northern Steamship Co. E2
63 Orleans E3
64 Thirsty Dog B7
65 Tyler Street Garage F2
66 Urge A8
67 Wine Cellar & Whammy Bar C7
68 Xuxu E2

◎ **Entertainment**
69 Academy Cinemas D5
70 Aotea Centre D5
71 Auckland Town Hall D5
72 Centurian B7
73 Classic Comedy Club D6
74 Event Cinemas D5
75 Maidment Theatre E5
76 NZ Film Archives D6
77 Q Theatre D6
78 SkyCity Theatre C4
79 Ticketek D5

◎ **Shopping**
80 Countdown G3
81 Karen Walker E2
82 Pauanesia E4
83 Real Groovy D6
84 Strangely Normal E4
85 Unity Books E3
86 Whitcoulls D4
87 Zambesi F2

◎ Parnell & Newmarket

Parnell is one of Auckland's oldest areas, and amid the cafes, restaurants and retailers are heritage buildings. Neighbouring Newmarket is a shopping precinct with boutiques.

★ **Auckland Museum**   MUSEUM
(Map p54; ☎ 09-309 0443; www.aucklandmuseum.com; adult/child $25/10; ⊙ 10am-5pm) Dominating the Auckland Domain is this imposing neoclassical temple (1929) capped with an impressive copper-and-glass dome (2007).

The displays of Pacific Island and Maori artefacts on the ground floor are essential viewing. Highlights include a 25m war canoe and an extant carved meeting house (remove your shoes before entering). There's also a fascinating display on Auckland's volcanic field, including an eruption simulation, and the upper floors showcase military displays, fulfilling the building's dual role as a war memorial.

Hour-long museum highlights tours (included with admission) depart at 10.45am, 12.45pm and 2.15pm. Admission options incorporating Maori culture and performances are also available.

Auckland's main Anzac commemorations take place at dawn on 25th of April at the cenotaph in the museum's forecourt.

Auckland Domain PARK
(Map p54) Covering about 80 hectares, this green swathe contains sports fields, interesting sculpture, formal gardens, wild corners and the **Wintergarden** (Map p54; www.wintergardenpavilion.co.nz; ⊙9am-5.30pm Mon-Sat, 9am-7.30pm Sun Nov-Mar, 9am-4.30pm Apr-Oct) FREE, with its fernery, tropical house, cool house, cute cat statue, coffee kiosk and neighbouring cafe. The mound in the centre of the park is all that remains of Pukekaroa, one of Auckland's volcanoes. At its humble peak, a totara surrounded by a palisade honours the first Maori king.

Holy Trinity Cathedral CHURCH
(Map p54; www.holy-trinity.org.nz; Parnell Rd; ⊙10am-3pm) Auckland's Anglican cathedral is a hodgepodge of architectural styles, especially compared to **St Mary's** (1886) next door, a wooden Gothic Revival church with a burnished interior and interesting stained-glass windows. Holy Trinity's windows are also notable, especially the rose window by English artist Carl Edwards, which is particularly striking above the simple kauri altar.

Parnell Rose Gardens GARDENS
(Map p54; 85-87 Gladstone Rd; ⊙7am-7pm) These formal gardens are blooming excellent from November to March. A stroll through the park leads to peaceful **Judges Bay** and tiny **St Stephen's Chapel** (Map p54; Judge St), built for the signing of the constitution of NZ's Anglican Church (1857).

Highwic HISTORIC BUILDING
(Map p68; www.historic.org.nz; 40 Gillies Ave; adult/child $9/free; ⊙10.30am-4.30pm Wed-Sun) A marvellous Carpenter Gothic house (1862), sitting amid lush, landscaped grounds.

Kinder House HISTORIC BUILDING
(Map p54; www.kinder.org.nz; 2 Ayr St; entry by donation; ⊙noon-3pm Wed-Sun; 🐾) Built of volcanic stone, this 1857 home displays the watercolours and memorabilia of Reverend Dr John Kinder (1819–1903), headmaster of the Church of England Grammar School.

Ewelme Cottage HISTORIC BUILDING
(Map p54; www.historic.org.nz; 14 Ayr St; adult/child $8.50/free; ⊙10.30am-4.30pm Sun) Built in 1864 for a clergyman, this storybook cottage is in exceptionally good condition.

⊙ Tamaki Drive

This scenic, pohutukawa-lined road heads east from the city, hugging the waterfront. In summer it's a jogging/cycling/rollerblading blur.

A succession of child-friendly, peaceful swimming beaches starts at Okahu Bay. Around the headland is Mission Bay, a popular beach with an iconic art-deco fountain, historic mission house, restaurants and bars. Safe swimming beaches Kohimarama and St Heliers follow. Further east along Cliff Rd, the Achilles Point lookout offers panoramic views. At its base is Ladies Bay, popular with nudists.

Buses 745 to 769 from Britomart follow this route.

Kelly Tarlton's Sealife Aquarium AQUARIUM
(Map p48; ☑09-531 5065; www.kellytarltons.co.nz; 23 Tamaki Dr; adult/child $36/20; ⊙9.30am-5pm) 🐟 Sharks and stingrays swim over and around you in transparent tunnels that were once stormwater tanks. You can also enter the tanks in a shark cage with snorkel ($95), or dive into the tanks ($165). Other attractions include the Penguin Discovery tour (daily 10am, $199 per person) where just four visitors per day can get up close with Antarctic penguins. For all experiences, book online for a 10% to 20% discount and to check times.

A free shark-shaped shuttle bus departs from 172 Quay St (opposite the ferry terminal) on the half-hour from 9.30am to 3.30pm.

Bastion Point PARK
(Map p48; Hapimana St) Politics, harbour views and lush lawns combine on this pretty headland with a chequered history. An elaborate cliff-top garden mausoleum honours Michael Joseph Savage (1872–1940), the country's first Labour prime minister, whose socialist reforms left him adored by the populace. Follow the lawn to one of the many WWII gun embankments that line the harbour.

Parnell

Waitemata Harbour

Tamaki Dr

Judges Bay

Dove-Myer Robinson Park

Quay St

The Strand

Alten Reserve

Parnell Rise

York St

Earle St

Farnham St

Garfield St

Cleveland Rd

Judges Bay Rd

Judge St

Windsor St

Ruskin Rd

Avon St

Gladstone Rd

Cheshire St

Scarborough Tce

Alberon Reserve

Coast to Coast Walkway

PARNELL

St Georges Bay Rd

Parnell Rd

St Stephens Ave

Takutai St

Domain Dr

Brighton Rd

Hobson Bay

Football Rd

1 **Auckland Museum**

St Mary's Church

Cathedral Pl

Laurie Ave

Devonport

With well-preserved Victorian and Edwardian buildings and loads of cafes, Devonport is a short ferry trip from the city. There are also two volcanic cones to climb and easy access to the first of the North Shore's beaches.

For a self-guided tour of historic buildings, pick up the *Old Devonport Walk* pamphlet from the i-SITE. Bikes can be hired from the ferry terminal.

Ferries to Devonport (adult/child return $11/5.80, 12 minutes) depart from the Auckland Ferry Building every 30 minutes (hour-ly after 8pm) from 6.15am to 11.15pm (until 1am Friday and Saturday), and from 7.15am to 10pm on Sundays and public holidays. Some Waiheke Island and Rangitoto ferries also stop here.

Mt Victoria & North Head VOLCANO
Mt Victoria (Takarunga; Map p65; Victoria Rd) and **North Head** (Maungauika; Map p65; Takarunga Rd; ⊙ 6am-10pm) were Maori *pa* and they remain fortresses of sorts, with the navy maintaining a presence. Both have gun embankments and North Head is riddled with tunnels, dug at the end of the 19th cen-

Parnell

◎ **Top Sights**
  1 Auckland Museum...............................B5

◎ **Sights**
  2 Auckland Domain..............................A5
  3 Ewelme Cottage................................C5
  4 Holy Trinity Cathedral.........................C5
  5 Kinder House....................................C5
  6 Parnell Rose Gardens.........................C3
  7 St Stephen's Chapel..........................D2
  8 Wintergarden..................................A5

⊕ **Activities, Courses & Tours**
  9 Parnell Baths.....................................D2

⊜ **Sleeping**
  10 City Garden Lodge C4
  11 Lantana Lodge.................................C3
  12 Parnell Inn.......................................B4
  13 Quality Hotel Parnell.........................C4
  14 Quest Carlaw Park............................A3

⊗ **Eating**
  15 Burgerfuel.......................................B4
  16 La Cigale C3

◉ **Entertainment**
  17 ASB Tennis Centre............................A3
     Ticketmaster...........................(see 18)
  18 Vector Arena....................................A2

tury in response to the Russian threat, and extended during WWI and WWII. The gates are locked at night, but that's never stopped teenagers from jumping the fence for scary subterranean explorations.

Between the two, Cambria Reserve stands on the remains of a third volcanic cone that was largely quarried away.

Navy Museum   MUSEUM
(Map p65; www.navymuseum.mil.nz; Torpedo Bay; ◷10am-5pm) FREE The navy has been in Devonport since the earliest days of the colony. Its history is on display at this well-presented and often moving museum, focusing on the stories of the sailors themselves.

◉ Western Springs

Auckland Zoo   ZOO
(Map p70; www.aucklandzoo.co.nz; Motions Rd; adult/child $25/10; ◷9.30am-5pm, last entry 4.15pm) ⏺ At this modern, spacious zoo, the big foreigners tend to steal the attention from the timid natives, but if you can wrestle the kids away from the tigers and orang-utans, there's a well-presented NZ section. Called *Te Wao Nui,* it's divided into six ecological zones: Coast (seals, penguins), Islands (mainly lizards, including NZ's pint-sized dinosaur, the tuatara), Wetlands (ducks, herons, eels), Night (kiwi, naturally, along with frogs, native owls and weta), Forest (birds) and High Country (cheekier birds and lizards).

Frequent buses (adult/child $3.40/2) run from the Britomart Transport Centre to bus stop 8124 on Great North Rd, from where it is a 700m walk to the zoo's entrance. See www.at.govt.nz.

Western Springs   PARK
(Map p70; Great North Rd) Parents bring their children to this picturesque park for the popular adventure playground. It's a picnic spot and a good place to get acquainted with playful pukeko (swamp hens), easygoing ducks and pushy, bread-fattened geese. Formed by a confluence of lava flows, more than 4 million litres bubble up into the central lake daily. From the city, catch any bus heading west via Great North Rd (adult/child $3.40/2). By car, take the Western Springs exit from the North Western Motorway. Until 1902 this was Auckland's main water supply.

MOTAT   MUSEUM
(Museum of Transport & Technology; Map p70; www.motat.org.nz; 805 Great North Rd; adult/child $16/8; ◷10am-5pm) This technology boffin's paradise is spread over two sites and 19 hectares. In **MOTAT Great North Rd** look out for former Prime Minister Helen Clark's Honda 50 motorbike and the pioneer village. **MOTAT Meola Rd** features the Aviation Display Hall with rare military and commercial planes. The two sites are linked by a vintage tram (free with admission, $2 otherwise), which passes the park and zoo. It's a fun kids' ride whether you visit MOTAT or not.

◉ Other Suburbs

One Tree Hill   PARK
(Maungakiekie; Map p48; www.cornwallpark.co.nz) This volcanic cone was the isthmus' key *pa* and the greatest fortress in the country, and from the top (182m) there are 360-degree views. At the summit is the grave of John Logan Campbell, who gifted the land to the city in 1901 and requested that a memorial be built to the Maori people on the summit. Nearby is

the stump of the last 'one tree'. Allow time to explore surrounding Cornwall Park with its mature trees and Acacia Cottage (1841).

The information centre has fascinating interactive displays illustrating what the *pa* would have looked like when 5000 people lived here. Near the excellent children's playground, the **Stardome Observatory** (Map p48; ☑ 09-624 1246; www.stardome.org.nz; 670 Manukau Rd; admission to exhibits free, shows adult/child $10/8; ☺ 10am-3pm Mon, 9.30am-4.30pm & 6.30-9.30pm Wed-Fri) **FREE** offers regular stargazing and planetarium shows that aren't dependent on Auckland's fickle weather (usually 8pm Wednesday to Sunday; phone ahead or check the website).

To get to One Tree Hill from the city take a train to Greenlane and walk 1km along Green Lane West. By car, take the Greenlane exit of the Southern Motorway and turn right into Green Lane West.

Wallace Arts Centre   GALLERY
(Map p48; www.tsbbankwallaceartscentre.org.nz; Pah Homestead, 72 Hillsborough Rd, Hillsborough; ☺ 10am-3pm Tue-Fri, 10am-5pm Sat & Sun) **FREE** Housed in a gorgeous 1879 mansion with views to One Tree Hill and the Manakau Harbour, the Wallace Arts Centre is endowed with contemporary New Zealand art from an extensive private collection, which is changed every four to six weeks. Have lunch on the verandah and wander amongst the magnificent trees in the surrounding

---

ONE TREE TO RULE THEM ALL

Looking at One Tree Hill, your first thought will probably be 'Where's the bloody tree?' Good question. Up until 2000 a Monterey pine stood at the top of the hill. This was a replacement for a sacred totara that was chopped down by British settlers in 1852. Maori activists first attacked the foreign usurper in 1994, finishing the job in 2000. It's unlikely that another tree will be planted until local land claims have moved closer to resolution, but you can bet your boots that when it does happen, the tree will be a native.

Auckland's most beloved landmark achieved international recognition in 1987 when U2 released the song 'One Tree Hill' on their acclaimed *The Joshua Tree* album. It was only released as a single in NZ, where it went to number one.

---

park. The art is also very accessible, ranging from a life-size skeletal rugby ruck to a vibrant Ziggy Stardust painted on glass.

Bus 299 (Lynfield) departs every 15 minutes from Wellesley St in the city (near the Civic Theatre) and heads to Hillsborough Rd ($4.50, about 40 minutes).

Auckland Botanic Gardens   GARDENS
(Map p48; www.aucklandbotanicgardens.co.nz; 102 Hill Rd, Manurewa; ☺ 8am-6pm mid-Mar–mid-Oct, 8am-8pm mid-Oct–mid-Mar) **FREE** This 64-hectare park has over 10,000 plants (including threatened species), dozens of gardens and an infestation of wedding parties. By car, take the Southern Motorway, exit at Manurewa and follow the signs. Otherwise take the train to Manurewa ($6.80, 40 minutes) and then walk along Hill Rd (1.5km).

Alberton   HISTORIC BUILDING
(Map p48; www.historic.org.nz; 100 Mt Albert Rd; adult/child $9/free; ☺ 10.30am-4.30pm Wed-Sun) A classic colonial mansion (1863), Alberton featured as a backdrop for some scenes in *The Piano*. It's a 1km walk from Mt Albert train station.

Rainbow's End   AMUSEMENT PARK
(Map p48; www.rainbowsend.co.nz; 2 Clist Cres; Superpass unlimited rides adult/child $52/42; ☺ 10am-5pm) 🚲 It's a bit dull by international standards but Rainbow's End has enough rides (including a corkscrew rollercoaster) to keep the kids happy all day.

🏃 Activities

Nothing gets you closer to the heart and soul of Auckland than sailing on the Hauraki Gulf. If you can't afford a yacht cruise, catch a ferry instead.

Visitors centres and public libraries stock the city council's *Auckland City's Walkways* pamphlet, which has a good selection of urban walks, including information on the Coast to Coast Walkway (p58).

Trading on the country's action-packed reputation, Auckland has sprouted its own set of thrill-inducing activities. Look around for backpacker reductions or special offers before booking anything.

Sailing

Sail NZ   SAILING
(Map p50; ☑ 0800 397 567; www.explorenz.co.nz; Viaduct Harbour) 🚲 Shoot the breeze on a genuine America's Cup yacht (adult/child $160/115) or head out on a 'Whale & Dolphin Safari' (adult/child $160/105); dolphins

> **DON'T MISS**
>
> ## AUCKLAND VOLCANIC FIELD
>
> Some cities think they're tough just by living in the shadow of a volcano. Auckland's built on 50 of them and, no, they're not all extinct. The last one to erupt was Rangitoto about 600 years ago and no one can predict when the next eruption will occur. Auckland's quite literally a hot spot – with a reservoir of magma 100km below, waiting to bubble to the surface. But relax: this has only happened 19 times in the last 20,000 years.
>
> Some of Auckland's volcanoes are cones, some are filled with water and some have been completely quarried away. Moves are afoot to register the field as a World Heritage Site and protect what remains. Most of the surviving cones show evidence of terracing from when they formed a formidable series of Maori *pa*. The most interesting to explore are Mt Eden (p49), One Tree Hill (p55) and Rangitoto, but Mt Wellington (Maungarei), Mt Albert (Owairaka), Mt Roskill (Puketapapa), Lake Pupuke, Mt Mangere and Mt Hobson (Remuwera) are all worth a visit.

are spotted 90% of the time and whales 75%. The *Pride of Auckland* fleet of glamorous large yachts offers 90-minute Harbour Sailing Cruises (adult/child $75/55), 2½-hour Dinner Cruises ($120/85) and full-day Sailing Adventures (adult/child $165/125).

CharterLink   SAILING
(Map p48; ☑ 09-445 7114; www.charterlink.co.nz; Bayswater Marina; per day $395-1126) Well-maintained older yachts, luxury yachts and catamarans.

Gulfwind   SAILING
(Map p48; ☑ 09-521 1564; www.gulfwind.co.nz; Westhaven Marina) Charters (half-/full day $445/895) and small-group sailing courses (two days $595).

Penny Whiting Sailing School   SAILING
(Map p48; ☑ 09-376 1322; www.pennywhiting.com; Westhaven Marina; course $750) Runs 15-hour learners' courses either as five afternoon lessons or over two weekends.

Extreme Sports

SkyWalk   EXTREME SPORTS
(Map p50; ☑ 0800 759 925; www.skywalk.co.nz; Sky Tower, cnr Federal & Victoria Sts; adult/child $145/115; ⊙10am-4.30pm) SkyWalk involves circling the 192m-high, 1.2m-wide outside halo of the Sky Tower without rails or a balcony. Don't worry, they're not completely crazy – there is a safety harness.

SkyJump   EXTREME SPORTS
(Map p50; ☑ 0800 759 586; www.skyjump.co.nz; Sky Tower, cnr Federal & Victoria Sts; adult/child $225/175; ⊙10am-5pm) This thrilling 11-second, 85km/h base wire leap from the observation deck of the Sky Tower is more like a parachute jump than a bungy. Combine it with the SkyWalk in the Look & Leap package ($290).

Auckland Bridge Climb & Bungy   BUNGY
(Map p48; ☑ 09-360 7748; www.bungy.co.nz; Curran St, Herne Bay; climb adult/child $120/80, bungy $150/120) Climb up or jump off the Auckland Harbour Bridge.

NZ Skydive   SKYDIVING
(☑ 09-373 5778; www.nzskydive.co.nz; 12,000ft $330) Tandem skydives from Mercer airfield, 55km south of Auckland. A free shuttle for overseas visitors is available from Auckland.

G-MAX Reverse Bungy   BUNGY
(Map p50; ☑ 09-377 1328; cnr Albert & Victoria Sts; ride $40; ⊙9am-10pm Sun-Thu, 10am-2am Fri & Sat) Imagine a giant slingshot with yourself as the projectile as you're reverse-bungyed 60m into the air.

Diving

Dive Centre   DIVING
(Map p48; ☑ 09-444 7698; www.divecentre.co.nz; 97 Wairau Rd, Takapuna; PADI Open Water $599) PADI courses and diving charters.

Kayaking

Fergs Kayaks   KAYAKING
(Map p48; ☑ 09-529 2230; www.fergskayaks.co.nz; 12 Tamaki Dr, Okahu Bay; ⊙9am-6pm) Hires kayaks and paddleboards (per hour/day from $20/50), bikes (per hour/day $20/120) and inline skates (per hour/day $15/30). Day and night guided kayak trips are available to Devonport (8km, three hours, $95) or Rangitoto Island (13km, six hours, $120).

Auckland Sea Kayaks   KAYAKING
(☑ 0800 999 089; www.aucklandseakayaks.co.nz) Guided trips (including lunch) to Rangitoto ($175, 10 hours) and Motukorea (Browns Island; $135, six hours). Multiday excursions also available.

DON'T MISS

NORTH SHORE BEACHES
....

Fine swimming beaches stretch from North Head to Long Bay. The gulf islands shelter them from strong surf, making them safe for supervised children. Aim for high tide unless you fancy a lengthy walk to waist-deep water. **Cheltenham Beach** is a short walk from Devonport. **Takapuna Beach**, closest to the Harbour Bridge, is Auckland's answer to Bondi and the most built up. Nearby **St Leonards Beach**, popular with gay men, requires clambering over rocks at high tide.

Other Water Activities
Auckland Jet Boat Tours JETBOATING
(Map p50; ☑ 050 825 5382; www.aucklandjetboattours.co.nz; floating pavilion, 220 Quay St; adult/child incl museum $85/45) Take a 35-minute blast around the harbour.

New Zealand Surf'n'Snow Tours SURFING
(☑ 09-828 0426; www.newzealandsurftours.com; 5-/12-day tour $799/1699) Day-long surfing courses including transport, gear and two two-hour lessons ($120). Day tours usually head to Piha (year-round; with/without own gear $50/99), while five- and 12-day tours include accommodation in Ahipara (October to May only).

Parnell Baths SWIMMING
(Map p54; www.parnellbaths.co.nz; Judges Bay Rd, Parnell; adult/child $6.30/free; ☉6am-8pm Mon-Fri, 8am-8pm Sat & Sun) Outdoor saltwater pools with an awesome 1950s mural.

Olympic Pools & Fitness Centre SWIMMING
(Map p68; www.theolympic.co.nz; 77 Broadway, Newmarket; adult/child $8/5; ☉5.30am-9.30pm Mon-Fri, 7am-8pm Sat & Sun) Pools, gym, sauna, steam room and crèche.

Ballooning
Balloon Expeditions BALLOONING
(☑09-416 8590; www.balloonexpeditions.co.nz; flight $340) Hour-long flights in a hot-air balloon at sunrise, including breakfast and bubbles.

Tramping
Coast to Coast Walkway WALKING
(Map p48; www.aucklandcity.govt.nz) Right across the country from the Tasman to the Pacific (actually, only 16km), this walk

encompasses One Tree Hill, Mt Eden, the Domain and the University, keeping mainly to reserves rather than city streets. Do it in either direction: starting from the Viaduct Basin and heading south, it's marked by yellow markers and milestones; heading north from Onehunga there are blue markers. Our recommendation? Catch the train to Onehunga and finish up at the Viaduct's bars.

From Onehunga Station, take Onehunga Mall up to Princes St, turn left and pick up the track at the inauspicious park by the motorway.

ᑕ Tours
Cultural Tours
Potiki Adventures CULTURAL TOUR
(☑ 021 422 773; www.potikiadventures.co.nz; adult/child from $150/80) Tours to Waiheke Island and explorations of Auckland from a Maori cultural perspective.

Tamaki Hikoi CULTURAL TOUR
(☑0800 282 552; www.tamakihikoi.co.nz; 1-/3hr $40/95) Guides from the Ngati Whatua *iwi* (tribe) lead various Maori cultural tours, often including walking and a cultural performance.

TIME Unlimited CULTURAL TOUR
(☑09-446 6677; www.newzealandtours.travel) ✒ Cultural, walking and sightseeing tours from a Maori perspective.

Food & Wine
NZ Winepro WINE TASTING
(☑09-575 1958; www.nzwinepro.co.nz; tours $85-275) Explores Auckland's wine regions, combining tastings with sightseeing.

Wine Trail Tours WINE TASTING
(☑09-630 1540; www.winetrailtours.co.nz) Small-group tours around West Auckland wineries and the Waitakere Ranges (half-/full day $115/245); further afield to Matakana ($255), or a combo of the two ($255).

Fine Wine Tours WINE TASTING
(☑0800 023 111; www.insidertouring.co.nz) Tours of Kumeu, Matakana and Waiheke wineries, including four-hour Kumeu tour ($199), with cheese ($229) and a six-hour tour including Muriwai Beach ($245).

The Big Foody Food Tour GUIDED TOUR
(☑021 481 177, 0800 366 386 877; www.thebigfoody.com; per person $65-165) Small-group city tours including market visits, visits to artisan producers, and lots of tastings.

City Walk
City Centre Ramble

START ST KEVIN'S ARCADE,
KARANGAHAPE RD
FINISH WYNYARD QUARTER
LENGTH 4.5KM; AROUND THREE HOURS

Start among the secondhand boutiques of
① St Kevin's Arcade and take the stairs
down to Myers Park. Look out for the repro-
duction of **② Michelangelo's Moses** at the
bottom of the stairs. Continue through the
park, taking the stairs on the right just before
the overpass to head up to street level.

Heading down Queen St, you'll pass the
③ Auckland Town Hall and **④ Aotea Sq**,
the civic heart of the city. On the next corner
is the wonderful **⑤ Civic Theatre** (p47).
Turn right on Wellesley St and then left
onto Lorne St. Immediately to your right is
⑥ Khartoum Pl, with tiling that celebrates
NZ women as the first in the world to win the
vote.. Head up the stairs to the **⑦ Auckland
Art Gallery** (p46).

Behind the gallery is **⑧ Albert Park** (p47).
Cross through it and turn left into Princes St,
where a row of **⑨ Victorian merchant's
houses** faces the **⑩ University Clock Tower**.
Cut around behind the clock tower to **⑪ Old
Government House** and then follow the di-
agonal path back to Princes St. The attractive
building on the corner of Princes St and Bowen
Ave was once the city's main **⑫ synagogue**.

Head down Bowen Ave and cut through
the park past the **⑬ Chancery precinct** to
⑭ High St with its good cafes and shopping.
Take a left onto **⑮ Vulcan Lane**, lined with
historic pubs. Turn right onto Queen St and
follow it down to the **⑯ Britomart Train Station**, housed in the former central post office.
You're now standing on reclaimed land – the
original shoreline was at Fort St. Detour to
the nearby **⑰ Britomart precinct** for good
bars, restaurants, and fashion boutiques.

From the Britomart Train Station, turn left
on Quay St and head to **⑱ Viaduct Harbour**, bustling with bars and cafes, and then
continue over the bridge to the rejuvenated
⑲ Wynyard Quarter.

Walking

Waitakere Tours   TRAMPING

(☎0800 492 482; www.waitakeretours.co.nz; per day $150) Lifelong Westies (West Aucklanders) offer guided tours of the west-coast beaches, and guided walks in the Waitakeres.

Bush & Beach   TRAMPING, WINE TASTING

(☎09-837 4130; www.bushandbeach.co.nz) 🏃 Guided walks in the Waitakere Ranges and along west-coast beaches (half-/full day $140/225, including transfers); three-hour city minibus tours ($75); and food, wine and art tours in either Matakana or Kumeu (half-/full day $219/310).

Auckland Ghost Tours   WALKING TOUR

(☎09-630 5721; www.aucklandghosttours.com; adult/child $50/25) Stories of Auckland's scary side on a two-hour walking tour of the central city.

Hiking NZ   TRAMPING

(☎0800 697 232; www.hikingnewzealand.com) Runs 'hiking safaris' leaving from Auckland, including Far North ($1280, six days), and Volcanoes & Rainforest ($2480, 10 days).

Bus Tours

Explorer Bus   BUS TOUR

(☎0800 439 756; www.explorerbus.co.nz; adult/child $40/20) 🏃 This hop-on, hop-off service departs from the Ferry Building every hour from 10am to 3pm (more frequently in summer), heading to 14 tourist sites around the central city.

Gray Line   BUS TOUR

(☎0800 698 687; www.graylinetours.co.nz; adult/child $59/29.50; ⊙departs 9.30am) 🏃 Three-hour bus tour of Auckland's highlights.

GreatSights   BUS TOUR

(Map p50; ☎0800 744 487; www.greatsights.co.nz; adult/child $59/29; ⊙departs 9.45am) 🏃 The city highlights on a three-hour bus tour.

AUCKLAND FOR CHILDREN

All of the east coast beaches (St Heliers, Kohimarama, Mission Bay, Okahu Bay, Cheltenham, Narrow Neck, Takapuna, Milford, Long Bay) are safe for supervised kids, while sights such as Rainbow's End, Kelly Tarlton's, Auckland Museum and Auckland Zoo are all firm favourites. Parnell Baths has a children's pool, but on wintry days, head to the thermal pools at Parakai or Waiwera.

Toru Tours   SIGHTSEEING

(☎027 457 0011; www.torutours.com; $69) The three-hour Express Tour will depart with just one booking – ideal for solo travellers.

Cruises

Riverhead Ferry   CRUISE

(Map p50; ☎09-376 0819; www.riverheadferry.co.nz; Pier 3, Ferry Building; tour $35) Harbour and gulf cruises including a 90-minute jaunt up the inner harbour to Riverhead, returning after two hours' pub time.

Fullers   CRUISE

(Map p50; ☎09-367 9111; www.fullers.co.nz; Ferry Building, 99 Quay St; adult/child $40/20; ⊙10.30am & 1.30pm) Daily 1½-hour harbour cruises including Rangitoto and a free return ticket to Devonport.

Other Tours

Auckland Seaplanes   SCENIC FLIGHTS

(☎09-390 1121; www.aucklandseaplanes.com; from $150 per person) Flights in a cool 1960s floatplane that explore Auckland's harbour and islands.

Red Carpet Tours   FILM LOCATIONS

(☎09-410 6561; www.redcarpet-tours.com) Day trips to Hobbiton/Matamata ($255), or all around Middle Earth across 14 days ($6650).

🎭 Festivals & Events

Also see www.aucklandnz.com.

Auckland Anniversary Day Regatta SPORTS (www.regatta.org.nz) The 'City of Sails' lives up to its name; Monday of last weekend in January.

Laneway Festival   MUSIC (www.lanewayfestival.com.au) International indie bands in a one-day festival on Anniversary Day.

Music In Parks   MUSIC (www.musicinparks.co.nz) Free gigs from January until March.

Movies In Parks   FILM (www.moviesinparks.co.nz) Free movies in February and March.

Lantern Festival   CULTURAL (www.asianz.org.nz) Three days of Asian food and culture in Albert Park to welcome the Lunar New Year (usually held in early February).

Auckland Pride Festival   GAY & LESBIAN (www.aucklandpridefestival.org.nz) Two-week festival of music, arts, sport and culture in

February celebrating the LGBT community. Highlights include the Auckland Pride Parade and the **Big Gay Out** (www.biggayout.co.nz).

Devonport Food & Wine Festival FOOD & WINE
(www.devonportwinefestival.co.nz; admission $30) Across two days in mid-February.

Splore MUSIC
(www.splore.net; Tapapakanga Regional Park) Three days of camping and music (generally of the dancy and soulful variety), held by the beach in mid-February. Headliners include big-name international acts.

Auckland Cup Week SPORTS
(www.ellerslie.co.nz; Ellerslie Racecourse) The year's biggest horse race; early March.

Auckland Arts Festival ARTS
(www.aucklandfestival.co.nz) Held over three weeks in March in odd-numbered years, this is Auckland's biggest celebration of the arts.

Pasifika Festival CULTURAL
(www.aucklandnz.com/pasifika) Western Springs Park hosts this giant Polynesian party with cultural performances, food and craft stalls; held early to mid-March.

Polyfest CULTURAL
(www.asbpolyfest.co.nz; Sports Bowl, Manukau) Massive Auckland secondary schools' Maori and Pacific Islands cultural festival held in mid-March.

Auckland International Cultural Festival CULTURAL
(www.facebook.com/Culturalfestival; May Rd, War Memorial Park, Mt Roskill) One-day festival with ethnic food stalls and cultural displays and performances; late March.

Royal Easter Show AGRICULTURAL
(www.royaleastershow.co.nz; ASB Showgrounds, 217 Green Lane West) It's supposedly agricultural but most people attend for the funfair rides.

NZ International Comedy Festival COMEDY
(www.comedyfestival.co.nz) Three-week laugh-fest with local and international comedians; late April to early May.

Out Takes FILM, GAY & LESBIAN
(www.outtakes.org.nz; Rialto Cinemas) Gay and lesbian film festival; late May to early June.

NZ International Film Festival FILM
(www.nzff.co.nz) Art-house films from mid-July.

MAORI NEW ZEALAND: AUCKLAND

Evidence of Maori occupation is literally carved into Auckland's volcanic cones. The dominant *iwi* of the isthmus was Ngati Whatua, but these days there are Maori from almost all of NZ's *iwi* living here.

For an initial taste of Maori culture, start at Auckland Museum (p52), where there's a wonderful Maori collection and a culture show. For a more personalised experience, take a tour with TIME Unlimited (p58), Potiki Adventures (p58) or Ngati Whatua's Tamaki Hikoi (p58), or visit the *marae* and recreated village at Te Hana (p101).

AUCKLAND FESTIVALS & EVENTS

Auckland Art Fair ARTS
(www.artfair.co.nz; The Cloud, Queens Wharf, Quay St) Lots of art for sale in August in odd-numbered years.

NZ Fashion Week FASHION
(www.nzfashionweek.com) In early September.

Auckland International Boat Show SPORTS
(www.auckland-boatshow.com) Boat show held in September.

Heritage Festival CULTURAL
(www.aucklandcouncil.govt.nz) Two weeks of (mainly free) tours of Auckland's neighbourhoods and historic buildings; mid-September.

Diwali Festival of Lights CULTURAL
(www.asianz.org.nz) Music, dance and food from Auckland's Indian community; mid-October.

Grey Lynn Park Festival CULTURAL
(www.greylynnparkfestival.org) Free festival of arts and crafts, food stalls, and live music in one of Auckland's more interesting inner suburbs; third Saturday in November.

Santa Parade PARADE
(www.santaparade.co.nz) Along Queen St before partying in Aotea Sq; last Sunday of November.

Christmas in the Park FAMILY
(www.christmasinthepark.co.nz) Mid-December Christmas concert and party in Auckland Domain.

AUCKLAND

Ponsonby & Grey Lynn

Ponsonby & Grey Lynn

Sleeping
1	23 Hepburn	D3
2	Abaco on Jervois	B1
3	Brown Kiwi	B1
4	Great Ponsonby Arthotel	B2
5	Ponsonby Backpackers	C3
6	Verandahs	D4

Eating
7	Bird on a Wire	C2
8	Blue Breeze Inn	C3
9	Burgerfuel	C4
10	Cocoro	C3
11	Dizengoff	C2
12	Fred's	C3
13	Il Buco	C3
14	Landreth & Co	C2
15	Little Bird	C2
	Mekong Baby	(see 11)
16	MooChowChow	D4

17	Ponsonby Central	C3
18	Ponsonby Road Bistro	C3
19	Ponsonby Village International Food Court	D4
20	Prego	C3
21	Queenie's	D2
22	Satya	D4

Drinking & Nightlife
23	Dida's Wine Lounge & Tapas Bar	B1
24	Golden Dawn	C4
25	Poof	C3

Shopping
26	Karen Walker	C4
27	New World	D2
28	Texan Art Schools	C3
29	Women's Bookshop	C3
	Zambesi	(see 18)

Silo Park Markets FILM
(www.silopark.co.nz; Wynyard Quarter) Classic movies screened outdoors on a Friday night, and markets with food trucks, DJs and craft stalls on Friday nights and Saturday afternoons; December to Easter.

🛏 Sleeping

🏨 City Centre

Auckland has plenty of luxury hotels, with several international chains taking up inner-city real estate. At the other extreme, any backpackers who leave with a bad impression of Auckland have invariably stayed in crummy, noisy digs in the city centre. Not all of the cheap city accommodation is bad, but you'll find much better hostels in inner suburbs like Ponsonby, Parnell, Freemans Bay and Mt Eden, and central Auckland is still easily reached by bus.

Attic Backpackers HOSTEL $
(Map p50; ☑09-973 5887; www.atticbackpackers.co.nz; 31 Wellesley St W; dm $26-33, s/tw/d $50/78/78; @🛜) Centrally located Attic Backpackers features contemporary and colourful decor, spotless and modern facilities, and a cool rooftop area for meeting other travellers.

Kiwi International Hotel HOTEL $
(Map p50; ☑09-379 6487; www.kiwihotel.co.nz; 411 Queen St; r $59-109, apt $169; P🛜) Rooms – most with en suite bathrooms – definitely are compact, but they're clean and well kept, and the location bordering Queen St and Karangahape Rd is very convenient.

Jucy Hotel HOTEL $
(Map p50; ☑09-379 6633; www.jucyhotel.com; 62 Emily Pl; hostel s/d $54/79, hotel r $109; P@🛜) This zippy budget hotel is from the Jucy car-rental company. Rooms in the main section have en suites, and there's a hostel wing with bunks and shared bathrooms.

YHA Auckland International HOSTEL $
(Map p50; ☑0800 278 299, 09-302 8200; www.yha.co.nz; 5 Turner St; dm $32, r $90-105; P🛜) Clean and brightly painted, this 170-bed YHA has a friendly vibe, good security, a games room and lots of lockers.

YHA Auckland City HOSTEL $
(Map p50; ☑0800 278 299, 09-309 2802; www.yha.co.nz; 18 Liverpool St; dm/s/d $27/60/85; 🛜) 🖉 Struggle up one of the city's steepest streets

to this big, impersonal tower block near the K Rd party strip. The rooms are clean and well kept, some with views and terraces.

Nomads Auckland HOSTEL $
(Map p50; ☑09-300 9999; www.nomadsauckland.com; 16 Fort St; dm $25-37, r $96-116; @🛜) This bustling backpackers has a cafe, bar, travel agency, female-only floor and a roof deck with sauna and spa. The private rooms have TVs but not all have windows.

Waldorf Celestion APARTMENT $$
(Map p50; ☑09-280 2200; www.celestion-waldorf.co.nz; 19-23 Anzac Ave; apt $170-277) 🖉 A rash of Waldorfs have opened in recent years, all presenting similar symptoms: affordable, modern apartments in city-fringe locations. We prefer this one for its stylish red, black and grey colour palette.

CityLife HOTEL $$
(Map p50; ☑09-379 9222; www.heritagehotels.co.nz/citylife-auckland; Durham St; apt $179-339; P@🛜🏊) 🖉 A worthy tower-block hotel offering numerous apartments over dozens of floors, ranging from studios to three-bedroom suites. Facilities include a heated lap pool, gym, valet parking and a babysitting service.

Waldorf Stadium APARTMENT $$
(Map p50; ☑09-337 5300; www.stadium-apartments-hotel.co.nz; 40 Beach Rd; apt $150-330) 🖉 This large newish block has spacious (if generic) family-friendly apartments with double-glazing to keep out the road noise.

City Lodge HOTEL $$
(Map p50; ☑09-379 6183; www.citylodge.co.nz; 150 Vincent St; s $79, d $103-119; @🛜) 🖉 YMCA-run and purpose-built tower for the budget market. The tiny rooms and stamp-sized bathrooms make for clean and secure accommodation. There's an industrial-style kitchen and comfy lounge.

★**Hotel de Brett** BOUTIQUE HOTEL $$$
(Map p50; ☑09-925 9000; www.hoteldebrett.com; 2 High St; r $300-600; @🛜) This hip, refurbished historic hotel has been zhooshed up with stripy carpets and clever designer touches in every nook of the extremely comfortable rooms. Prices include breakfast, free broadband and a pre-dinner drink.

Quadrant HOTEL $$$
(Map p50; ☑09-984 6000; www.thequadrant.com; 10 Waterloo Quadrant; apt $250-380; 🛜) 🖉 Slick, central and full of all the whiz-bang gadgets,

this apartment-style complex is an excellent option. The only catch is that the units are tiny and the bathrooms beyond small.

🛏 Freemans Bay

Verandahs
HOSTEL $

(Map p62; ☑ 09-360 4180; www.verandahs.co.nz; 6 Hopetoun St; dm $28-32, s $56, d $74-94, tr $96; P@🛜) Ponsonby Rd, K Rd and the city are an easy walk from this grand hostel, housed in two neighbouring villas overlooking the mature trees of Western Park. Definitely one of Auckland's best backpackers.

23 Hepburn
B&B $$$

(Map p62; ☑ 09-376 0622; www.23hepburn.co.nz; 23 Hepburn St; r $210-250; P🛜) The three boutique rooms are a symphony in muted whites and creams. Continental breakfast is left in your fridge the previous evening to enjoy at your leisure.

🛏 Ponsonby & Grey Lynn

Ponsonby Backpackers
HOSTEL $

(Map p62; ☑ 09-360 1311; www.ponsonby-backpackers.co.nz; 2 Franklin Rd; dm $26-28, s/d $45/62; P@🛜) This elegant two-storied turreted villa has a friendly vibe, sunny rooms, and a nice garden area. Central Auckland is a pleasant 20-minute walk away, and the buzz of Ponsonby Rd is right on your doorstep.

Brown Kiwi
HOSTEL $

(Map p62; ☑ 09-378 0191; www.brownkiwi.co.nz; 7 Prosford St; dm $28-31, s/d $52/72; @🛜) This low-key hostel is tucked away in a busy-by-day commercial strip, a stone's throw from Ponsonby's good shopping and grazing opportunities. The garden courtyard is made for mooching.

Abaco on Jervois
MOTEL $$

(Map p62; ☑ 09-360 6850; www.abaco.co.nz; 57 Jervois Rd; r $135-155, ste $194-215; P) A contemporary, neutral-toned motel including stainless-steel kitchenettes (with dish drawers and ovens) and fluffy white towels for use in the spa. The darker rooms downstairs are priced accordingly.

Great Ponsonby Arthotel
B&B $$$

(Map p62; ☑ 09-376 5989; www.greatpons.co.nz; 30 Ponsonby Tce; r $265-400; P@) 🖉 In a quiet cul-de-sac near Ponsonby Rd, this deceptively spacious Victorian villa has gregarious hosts, impressive sustainability practices

and great breakfasts. Studio apartments open onto an attractive rear courtyard.

🛏 Newton

City Travellers
HOSTEL $

(Map p50; ☑ 09-377 6027; www.kroadcitytravellers.co.nz; 146 Karangahape Rd; dm $29-33, s/tw/d $61/76/76; @🛜) Smaller hostel well located on bustling and bohemian Karangahape Rd.

Langham
HOTEL $$$

(Map p50; ☑ 09-379 5132; www.auckland.langhamhotels.co.nz; 83 Symonds St; r $220-390, ste $510-2430; P@🛜🏊) 🖉 The Langham's service is typically faultless, the beds are heavenly, and its day spa is one of Auckland's best.

🛏 Mt Eden

Bamber House
HOSTEL $

(Map p70; ☑ 09-623 4267; www.bamberhouse.co.nz; 22 View Rd; dm $26-28, s $57, d $72-90; P@🛜) 🖉 The original house here is a mansion of sorts, with some nicely maintained period trimmings and large grounds. The new prefab cabins have less character but come with en suites.

Pentlands
HOSTEL $

(Map p70; ☑ 09-638 7031; www.pentlands.co.nz; 22 Pentland Ave; dm $25-28, s/d $46/68; P@🛜) Set down a peaceful tree-lined cul-de-sac, this powder-blue villa has stylish rooms, a sunny deck with a barbecue, and quiet tables on the lawn.

Oaklands Lodge
HOSTEL $

(Map p70; ☑ 09-638 6545; www.oaklands.co.nz; 5a Oaklands Rd; dm $25-27, s $43-50, d $62-68; P@🛜) In a leafy cul-de-sac, this bright, well-kept hostel is close to Mt Eden village and city buses.

Bavaria
GUESTHOUSE $$

(Map p70; ☑ 09-638 9641; www.bavariabandbhotel.co.nz; 83 Valley Rd; s $95-130, d $150-180; P@🛜) This spacious villa offers large, airy rooms and a buffet breakfast. The communal TV lounge, dining room and deck all encourage mixing and mingling.

Eden Park B&B
B&B $$$

(Map p70; ☑ 09-630 5721; www.bedandbreakfastnz.com; 20 Bellwood Ave; s $135-150, d $235-250; 🛜) 🖉 The hallowed turf of Auckland's legendary Eden Park rugby ground is only a block away and, while the rooms aren't overly large, they mirror the Edwardian elegance of this fine wooden villa.

Devonport

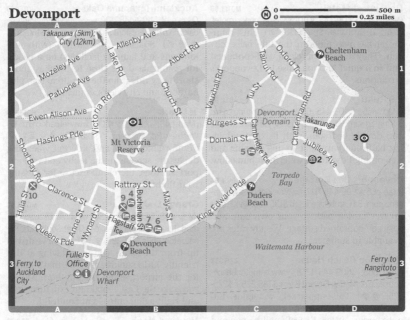

Parnell & Newmarket

City Garden Lodge HOSTEL **$**
(Map p54; ☑09-302 0880; www.citygardenlodge.
co.nz; 25 St Georges Bay Rd; dm $28-30, s/d
$56/72; P@☎) Occupying a character-
filled, two-storey house, this well-run
backpackers has a lovely garden and high-
ceilinged rooms.

Lantana Lodge HOSTEL **$**
(Map p54; ☑09-373 4546; www.lantanalodge.
co.nz; 60 St Georges Bay Rd; dm $27-31, s $58,
d $70-74; P☎) There are only eight rooms
available in this cosy villa on a quiet street.
It's not flash, but it's clean enough to be
homely.

Quest Carlaw Park APARTMENT **$$**
(Map p54; ☑09-304 0521; www.questcarlawpark.
co.nz; 15 Nicholls Lane; apt $170-335; P@☎)
🖉 It's in an odd spot but this set of smart,
modern apartments is handy for Parnell, the
city and the Domain, and if you've got a car
you're practically on the motorway.

Parnell Inn MOTEL **$$**
(Map p54; ☑09-358 0642; www.parnellinn.co.nz;
320 Parnell Rd; r $105-130; P@☎) You'll get a
chipper welcome from the friendly folks at
this good-looking, revamped motel. Rooms

Devonport

Sights
1	Mt Victoria	B2
2	Navy Museum	D2
3	North Head	D2

Sleeping
4	Devonport Motel	B2
5	Devonport Sea Cottage	C2
6	Hampton Beach House	B3
7	Parituhu	B3
8	Peace & Plenty Inn	B3

Eating
9	Bette's Bar & Eatery	B2
10	Calliope Road Cafe	A2

3 and 4 have great harbour views and some
rooms have kitchenettes.

Quality Hotel Parnell HOTEL **$$**
(Map p54; ☑09-303 3789; www.theparnell.co.nz;
20 Gladstone Rd; r $150-310; P☎) More than
100 motel rooms and units are available in
this recently renovated complex. The newer
north wing has great harbour views.

Devonport

Devonport has beautiful Edwardian B&Bs
within a relaxing ferry ride of the city.

Devonport Motel
MOTEL $$

(Map p65; ☑09-445 1010; www.devonportmotel.co.nz; 11 Buchanan St; r $150; ☏) This mini-motel has two units in the tidy back garden. They're modern, clean, self-contained and in a quiet location close to Devonport's attractions.

Parituhu
B&B $$

(Map p65; ☑09-445 6559; www.parituhu.co.nz; 3 King Edward Pde; r $125-155; ☏) There's only one double bedroom (with its own adjoining bathroom) available in this relaxing and welcoming Edwardian waterfront bungalow.

Devonport Sea Cottage
COTTAGE $$

(Map p65; ☑09-445 7117; www.devonportseacottagenz.com; 3a Cambridge Tce; d $130-150; ☏) Head up the garden path to your own cute and cosy self-contained cottage. Weekly rates are available in summer.

Hampton Beach House
B&B $$$

(Map p65; ☑09-445 1358; www.hamptonbeachhouse.co.nz; 4 King Edward Pde; s $185-225, r $225-325; @☏) This upmarket, waterside Edwardian B&B has tasteful rooms that open onto a rear garden. Expect quality linen and gourmet breakfasts.

Peace & Plenty Inn
B&B $$$

(Map p65; ☑09-445 2925; www.peaceandplenty.co.nz; 6 Flagstaff Tce; s $195-265, d $265-465; P☏) ✆ Stocked with antiques, this perfectly located, five-star Victorian house has romantic and luxurious en suite rooms with TVs, flowers, free sherry/port and local chocolates.

Other Areas

Auckland Airport

Campervan Park
CARAVAN PARK $

(Map p48; ☑09-256 8527; www.aucklandairport.co.nz; Jimmy Ward Crescent, Mangere; sites from $29; ☏) Caravan park with powered spaces, toilets and showers, all within 1km of the terminals. It's a great option for those wanting to rest up after arriving on a long flight.

Ambury Regional Park
CAMPSITE $

(Map p48; ☑09-366 2000; www.arc.govt.nz; Ambury Rd, Mangere; sites per adult/child $6/3) A slice of country in suburbia, this regional park is also a working farm. Facilities are limited (a vault toilet, warm showers and not much shade) but it's handy to the airport, right on the water and dirt cheap.

Auckland Takapuna Oaks
HOTEL $$

(Map p48; ☑09-445 7100; www.aucklandtakapunaoaks.co.nz; 1 Beresford St, Bayswater; apt $160-300; P@☏) Spacious apartments (with full kitchens and laundry facilities) on a peaceful peninsula that's close to beaches and a short ferry ride from the city. Breakfast, plus harbour and city views, is included.

Jet Park
HOTEL $$

(Map p48; ☑09-275 4100; www.jetpark.co.nz; 63 Westney Rd, Mangere; r $120-150; @☏⛟) ✆ Comfortable rooms and a decent vibe; with departure screens in the lobby and free airport shuttles, there's no excuse for missing your flight.

Grange Lodge
MOTEL $$

(Map p48; ☑09-277 8280; www.manukauaccommodation.co.nz; cnr Grange & Great South Rds, Papatoetoe; units $125-190; ☏) ✆ If you've driven up from the south, consider staying at this friendly little suburban motel that's handy for the airport. From the Southern Motorway, take the East Tamaki Rd exit, turn right and right again onto Great South Rd.

Nautical Nook
B&B $$

(Map p48; ☑09-521 2544; www.nauticalnook.com; 23b Watene Cres, Orakei; s/d $108/162; ☏) If you're a sailing buff you'll find a kindred spirit in Keith, who runs this cosy homestay with his wife Trish. The lounge and terrace have views over the harbour, and the beach is close.

✕ Eating

Because of its size and ethnic diversity, Auckland tops the country when it comes to dining options and quality. Lively eateries have sprung up to cater to the many Asian students, and offer inexpensive Japanese, Chinese and Korean staples. If you're on a budget, you'll fall in love with the city's food halls.

Aucklanders demand good coffee, so you never have to walk too far to find a decent cafe, especially in suburbs like Ponsonby, Mt Eden and Kingsland. Some double as wine bars or have gourmet aspirations, while others are content to fill their counters with fresh, reasonably priced snacks.

The hippest new foodie enclaves are Britomart (the blocks above the train station) and Federal St (under the Sky Tower), and recent openings have also resurrected and reinforced the culinary reputation of Ponsonby. The Wynyard Quarter west of Viaduct Harbour and the new City Works Depot on Wellesley St are also up-and-coming areas.

You'll find large supermarkets in most neighbourhoods: there's a particularly handy **Countdown** (Map p50; 76 Quay St; ☉24hr) at the bottom of town and a **New World** (Map p62; 2 College Hill, Freemans Bay; ☉7am-midnight) by Victoria Park. Self-caterers should consider the Otara Market (p78) and Avondale Sunday Market (p78) for cheap, fresh vegetables and La Cigale (p73) for fancier fare and local artisan produce.

City Centre

Food Truck Garage
CAFE $

(Map p50; www.foodtruckgarage.co.nz; 90 Wellesley St, City Works Depot; mains $10-14; ☉11am-10pm, limited menu 3-5pm; 🖉) 🍃 In the funky new City Works Depot, the Food Truck Garage serves up healthy versions of fast food classics like burgers, tacos and wraps. Across the menu there's definitely no trade-off of taste for wellbeing.

Food Alley
FOOD HALL $

(Map p50; 9 Albert St; mains $7-13; ☉10.30am-10pm) There's Chinese, Indonesian, Indian, Thai, Vietnamese, Turkish, Malaysian, Korean and Japanese all on offer at this no-frills food hall.

Hansan
VIETNAMESE $

(Map p50; www.hansan.co.nz; 22-24 Kitchener St; mains $10-16; ☉11am-10pm) Great value Vietnamese food, just a short walk from Queen St. There's another **branch** (Map p68; 55 Nuffield St; ☉11am-10pm) in Newmarket.

Remedy
CAFE $

(Map p50; 1 Wellesley St; snacks & mains $8-16; ☉6.30am-6pm Mon-Fri, 9am-3pm Sat) Quirky inner-city spot with excellent coffee, and the old-school thrills of a book exchange.

Revive
VEGETARIAN $

(Map p50; www.revive.co.nz; 24 Wyndham St; mains $11-13; ☉11am-8pm Mon-Thu, 11am-3pm Fri; 🖉) Vegetarian heaven with an enticing salad bar and economical daily meal deals.

Zap 4
THAI $

(Map p50; www.zap.getcellgroup.cpm; 10 Commerce St; mains $12-17; ☉11am-9pm) All your Thai favourites with a side order of bustling ambience.

★ Depot
MODERN NZ $$

(Map p50; www.eatatdepot.co.nz; 86 Federal St; dishes $17-32; ☉7am-late) TV chef Al Brown's first Auckland eatery offers first-rate Kiwi comfort food in informal surrounds

AUCKLAND'S MULTICULTURAL MENU

Around 30% of New Zealanders live in Auckland, and the country's biggest city is also the most ethnically diverse. With immigration – especially from Asia – has come a more cosmopolitan restaurant scene, and savvy Auckland foodies (and a few of the city's top chefs) keenly explore central fringe neighbourhoods for authentic tastes of the city's multicultural present and future.

Head to Dominion Rd in Balmoral – catch bus 258 ($3.40) from stop 7058 near the intersection of Queen St and Wellesley St – and get off at stop 8418 to be in the centre of Auckland's best Chinese food. Our favourites are **Barilla Dumplings** (571 Dominion Rd, Balmoral; snacks & mains $8-20; ☉11.30am-midnight) and **Shaolin Kung Fu Noodle** (636 Dominion Rd, Balmoral; ☉11.30am-11.30pm Fri-Wed, 5-11.30pm Thu), and **Spicy Joint** (533 Dominion Rd; mains $10-20; ☉noon-late Wed-Mon, 5pm-late Tue) does excellent Sichuan food.

A few blocks west – catch bus 233 ($3.40) from stop 7022 in Victoria St East to stop 8316 on Sandringham Rd – for the best of the city's Indian and Sri Lankan restaurants. **Jai Jalaram Khaman** (570 Sandringham Rd, Sandringham; snacks & mains $7-15; ☉11.30am-10pm; 🖉) does excellent vegetarian Gujarati food, and, a few doors away, **7 Siri's** (580 Sandringham Rd, Sandringham; mains $10-15; ☉11.30am-10pm Wed-Sun, 5-10pm Tue; 🖉) Sri Lankan highlight is the 'lump rice', a prosaically named but very tasty array of curries and sambal.

At the city's bustling **night markets** (www.aucklandnightmarket.co.nz) – held at a variety of suburban locations from Thursday to Saturday – around 80 ethnic food stalls offer cuisine from Argentina and Samoa, to Hungary and Turkey. Most convenient for travellers is the Onehunga market on a Thursday night. Catch a train ($4.50) from Britomart to Onehunga and walk around 650m to the Dress-Smart Outlet Shopping Centre.

If you're in town in late-March, the Auckland International Cultural Festival (p61) offers a very tasty peek into the city's ethnically diverse future, and, online, **Cheap Eats** (www.cheapeats.co.nz) scours Auckland for the city's best ethnic food for under $20.

Newmarket

N 0 _____ 500 m
0 _____ 0.25 miles

Newmarket

◎ Sights
1	Eden Garden	A2
2	Highwic	B2

⊕ Activities, Courses & Tours
3	Olympic Pools & Fitness Centre	B1

⊗ Eating
4	Basque Kitchen Bar	B1
5	Hansan	B2
6	Teed St Larder	B1

⊕ Entertainment
7	Rialto	B1

🏠 Shopping
8	Karen Walker	B2
9	Texan Art Schools Newmarket	B2
10	Zambesi Newmarket	B1

(communal tables, butcher tiles and a constant buzz). Dishes are designed to be shared, and a pair of clever shuckers serve up the city's freshest clams and oysters.

Ima   MIDDLE EASTERN **$$**
(Map p50; ☑ 09-300 7252; www.imacuisine.co.nz; 57 Fort St; breakfast $11-20, lunch $16-24, dinner shared dishes $18-30; ⊙7am-2.30pm Mon-Fri, 5.30-10.30pm Tue-Sat) Named after the Hebrew word for mother, the menu blends Israeli, Palestinian, Yemeni and Lebanese dishes. Try the *shakshuka* (baked eggs in a spicy tomato sauce) for breakfast or lunch, or rustle up a group for Ima's excellent shared dinners.

Federal & Wolfe   CAFE **$$**
(Map p50; 10 Federal St; mains $12-21; ⊙7am-3pm Mon-Sat; 🛜) 🌱 Packing crates and mismatched chairs lend an air of recycled chic to this corner cafe. Look forward to first-rate coffee and delicious food, much of it organic and free range.

Grove   MODERN NZ **$$$**
(Map p50; ☑ 09-368 4129; www.thegroverestaurant.co.nz; St Patrick's Sq, Wyndham St; mains $45, tasting menu with/without wine pairing $240/145; ⊙noon-3pm Thu-Fri, 6pm-late Mon-Sat) Romantic fine dining at its best: the room is cosy and moodily lit, the menu encourages sensual experimentation and the service is effortless. If you can't find anything to break the ice from the extensive wine list, give it up mate – it's never going to happen.

O'Connell Street Bistro   FRENCH **$$$**
(Map p50; ☑ 09-377 1884; www.oconnellstbistro. com; 3 O'Connell St; two-course lunch $60, din-

ner $28-45; ⊘ lunch Mon-Fri, dinner Mon-Sat) O'Connell St is a grown-up treat, with elegant decor and wonderful food and wine, satisfying lunchtime powerbrokers and dinnertime daters alike. If you're dining before 7.30pm, a fixed-price menu is available (two/three courses $37/43).

Masu
JAPANESE $$$

(Map p50; www.skycityauckland.co.nz; 90 Federal St, SKYCITY Grand Hotel; mains $30-45, tasting menu $88; ⊘ noon-3pm & 5.30pm-late) Superb Japanese food – especially from the sushi bar and the robata grill – and the added attraction of refreshing cocktails made from *shochu* (Japanese liquor).

Britomart, Viaduct Harbour & Wynyard Quarter

Baduzzi
ITALIAN $$

(Map p50; ✒ 09-309 9339; www.baduzzi.co.nz; cnr Jellicoe St & Fish Lane; small plates $10-20, mains $22-32; ⊘ 11.30am-late) This smart and sassy eatery does sophisticated spins on meatballs – try the crayfish (lobster) ones – and other robust but elegant Italian dishes. Cosy up in the intimate booths, grab a seat at the bar, or soak up some Auckland sunshine outside.

Ortolana
MEDITERRANEAN $$

(Map p50; www.britomart.org/ortolana; 31 Tyler St; small plates & mains $15-32; ⊘ 7am-11pm) Mediterranean and regional Italian flavours feature at this stylish restaurant with a spacious al fresco area. Much of the produce comes from the owners' small farm in rural West Auckland. There's a no-bookings policy, so try and dine between the busy lunch and dinner services.

Ebisu
JAPANESE $$$

(Map p50; www.ebisu.co.nz; 116-118 Quay St; large plates $30-36; ⊘ noon-late Mon-Fri, 5pm-late Sat & Sun) Ebisu specialises in *izakaya,* a style of drinking and eating that eschews Japanese formality, yet doesn't involve food being flung around the room or chugging along on a conveyor belt. This large bar gets it exactly right, serving exquisite plates designed to be shared.

Soul Bar
MODERN NZ $$$

(Map p50; ✒ 09-356 7249; www.soulbar.co.nz; Viaduct Harbour; mains $22-42; ⊘ 11am-late) Eating seafood by the water is a must in Auckland; this modernist gastrodome boasts an unbeatable see-and-be-seen location.

Freemans Bay

Queenie's
CAFE $$

(Map p62; ✒ 09-378 8977; www.queenies.co.nz; 24a Spring St; breakfast & lunch $11-25, dinner $28-29; ⊘ 8am-10pm Wed-Sat, 8am-3pm Sun-Tue) Kiwiana reigns supreme at this eccentric corner cafe with one wall devoted to a 1950s paint-by-numbers Maori maiden mural. The food is a step up from standard cafe fare, with an adventurous menu justifying the prices. Bistro-style dinners kick in from Wednesday to Saturday.

Clooney
MODERN NZ $$$

(Map p50; ✒ 09-358 1702; www.clooney.co.nz; 33 Sale St; mains $40-46, seven-course tasting menu with/without wine pairings $235/140; ⊘ 6pm-late Tue-Sun, noon-3pm Fri) Like the Hollywood actor of the same name, Clooney is suave, stylish and extremely sophisticated, suited up in basic black. While the taste combinations are complex, the results are faultless – which, coupled with impeccable service, puts Clooney firmly in the pricey-but-worth-it category.

Ponsonby & Grey Lynn

Auckland's busiest restaurant-cafe-bar strip is so damn cool it has its own website (www.iloveponsonby.co.nz).

★ Little Bird
CAFE $

(Map p62; www.littlebirdorganics.co.nz; 1a Summer St; mains $9-16; ⊘ 7am-4pm; ✍) ☙ Welcome to an 'unbakery', where virtually everything on the menu is prepared uncooked, but still very tasty and healthy. Tuck into dishes studded with açaí berries, quinoa and organic fruit, and there are even bagels, pad thai and tacos. Also great are the juices, smoothies and cakes.

Il Buco
PIZZA $

(Map p62; www.ilbuco.co.nz; 113 Ponsonby Rd; pizza per slice $6; ⊘ 8am-9pm Mon-Fri, to 8pm Sat & Sun; ✍) Delicious pizza by the slice – including vegetarian options – and tasty Italian nibbles like stuffed mushrooms and potato croquettes. Arrive before lunchtime for the best selection.

Dizengoff
CAFE $

(Map p62; 256 Ponsonby Rd; mains $7-19; ⊘ 6.30am-5pm) This stylish shoebox crams in a mixed crowd of corporate and fashion types, gay guys, Ponsonby denizens and travellers. Mouth-watering scrambled eggs, tempting counter food, heart-starting coffee, plus a great stack of reading material.

AUCKLAND

Kingsland & Mt Eden

GRAFTON

500 m
0.25 miles

France St

NEWTON

20

Symonds St

Khyber Pass Rd

Nugent Rd

Bastion Rd

Normanby Rd

12

24 18

EDEN
TERRACE

Mt Eden Rd

Enfield St

Edwin St

Mt Eden

Clive Rd

P

3

Oaklands Rd

15 8
Stokes Rd

MT EDEN

Bellevue Rd

Esplanade Rd

Sherbourne St

5

Penthand Ave

Woodford Rd

6

Valley Rd

Prospect Tce

Spicy Joint (660m);
Shaolin Kung Fu Noodle (780m);
Barilla Dumplings (830m)

Horoeka Ave

Wynyard St

View Rd

Bellevue Rd

Ian McKinnon Dr

Newton Rd

19

11

Dominion Rd

Valley Rd

6

ARCH
HILL

16

Bond St

Central Rd

New North Rd

Onslow Rd

Walters Rd

Bellwood Ave

7

14

King Edward Pde

GREY
LYNN

Crummer Rd

Great North Rd

North Western Mwy

Kingsland Ave

13 16

KINGSLAND

10

21 22

25

Kingsland

Eden
Park

23

Reimers Ave

SANDRINGHAM

Sandringham Rd

School Rd

17

Surrey Cres

WESTERN
SPRINGS

Western Springs Rd

Morningside Dr

New North Rd

MORNINGSIDE

Morningside

Sainsbury Rd

Jai Jalaram Khaman (1.2km);
7 Stri (1.3km)

Bullock Track

2

Old Mill Rd

4

1

Great North Rd

St. Lukes Rd

Linwood Ave

MT
ALBERT

Asquith Ave

Baldwin
Ave

Kingsland & Mt Eden

⊙ Sights
1 Auckland Zoo	A1
2 MOTAT	B2
3 Mt Eden	G4
4 Western Springs	A2

🛏 Sleeping
5 Bamber House	F3
6 Bavaria	F3
7 Eden Park B&B	E4
8 Oaklands Lodge	G4
9 Pentlands	F4

🍴 Eating
10 Atomic Roastery	D3
11 Burgerfuel	E3
12 French Cafe	G1
13 Fridge	D3
14 Merediths	E4
15 Molten	G4
16 Petra Shawarma	D3
17 Sake Bar 601	C3

🍷 Drinking & Nightlife
18 Galbraith's Alehouse	G1
19 Ginger Minx	E3
20 Kings Arms Tavern	F1
Liquid Molten	(see 15)
21 Neighbourhood	D3
22 Portland Public House	D3

⊙ Entertainment
23 Eden Park	D3
24 Power Station	G1

🛍 Shopping
25 Royal Jewellery Studio	D3

Fred's   CAFE $
(Map p62; 181 Ponsonby Rd; snacks & mains $7-16) This funky little spot features home-style baking, good coffee, and interesting fare like coconut porridge, *menemen* (Turkish baked eggs), and breakfast bruschetta. Scour the stacks of cool magazines inside or chill in the compact garden.

Bird on a Wire   SANDWICHES, CAFE $
(Map p62; www.birdonawire.co.nz; 234 Ponsonby Rd; sandwiches & burgers $8-14, salads $11-21; ⊙11am-9.30pm) Tasty sandwiches and healthy burgers, seasonal salads, and rotisserie chickens to take away. Select your baste of choice – like Jamaican jerk or salsa verde – and you're sorted. There's another smaller **Box of Bird** (Map p50; 12 Commerce St; ⊙10am-7pm Mon-Fri) branch in the central city.

Ponsonby Village
International Food Court   FOOD HALL $
(Map p62; www.ponsonbyfoodcourt.co.nz; 106 Ponsonby Rd; mains $8-20; ⊙10am-10pm; 🍴) Italian, Japanese, Malaysian, Chinese, Turkish, Thai, Lao and Indian flavours all on offer, and excellent Vietnamese and Indonesian.

Burgerfuel   BURGERS $
(Map p62; www.burgerfuel.com; 114 Ponsonby Rd; burgers $6-13; 🍴) 🌿 Gourmet burgers. Also has branches in the **city** (Map p50; 291 Queen St; ⊙10am-11pm), **Parnell** (Map p54; 187 Parnell Rd; ⊙11am-10pm) and **Mt Eden** (Map p70; 214 Dominion Rd; ⊙11am-10pm).

★ Blue Breeze Inn   CHINESE $$
(Map p62; 🕿09-360 0303; www.thebluebreezeinn. co.nz; 146 Ponsonby Rd, Ponsonby Central; small plates $10-18, larger plates $26-38; ⊙5pm-late) Regional Chinese flavours combine with a funky retro Pacific ambience. The waitstaff are sassy, the rum cocktails are deliciously strong, and menu standouts include steamed buns with Peking pork belly and pickled cucumber, and cumin-spiced lamb.

Ponsonby Central   CAFES, RESTAURANTS $$
(Map p62; www.ponsonbycentral.co.nz; 136-138 Ponsonby Rd; mains $15-35; ⊙11.30am-10.30pm Sun-Wed, 11.30am-midnight Thu-Sat) From Auckland's best pizza to Argentinean, Thai and Japanese, loads of flavour-filled restaurants and cafes fill this upmarket laneway collection of eateries and gourmet food shops.

MooChowChow   THAI $$
(Map p62; 🕿09-360 6262; www.moochowchow. co.nz; 23 Ponsonby Rd; dishes $16-30; ⊙noon-3pm Tue-Fri, 5.30pm-late Mon-Sat) It's Thai, Nahm Jim, but not as we know it. Bangkok's street food has been channelled into this supremely Ponsonby mooching spot without missing a piquant note. Killer Asian-inspired cocktails, too. Be ready to share a table with other diners.

Mekong Baby   ASIAN $$
(Map p62; www.mekongbaby.com; 262 Ponsonby Rd; mains $24-32; ⊙noon-late Tue-Sun) Stylish and buzzing restaurant and bar offering excellent Southeast Asian flavours, mainly from Vietnam, Cambodia and Laos. Try the goat curry.

Satya   INDIAN $$
(Map p62; 🕿09-361 3612; www.satya.co.nz; 17 Great North Rd; mains $11-26; ⊙11.30am-2.30pm Mon-Sat, 5.30-10pm daily; 🍴) Hugely popular, this humble-looking and humbly priced eatery

has the best *dahi puri* (chickpea, potato and yoghurt on a pappadam) in town. Also on **K Rd** (Map p50; ☑09-377 0007; 271 Karanahape Rd; ⊙11.30am-2.30pm Mon-Sat, 5.30-10pm daily).

Ponsonby Road Bistro INTERNATIONAL $$

(Map p62; ☑09-360 1611; www.ponsonbyroadbistro.co.nz; 165 Ponsonby Rd; mains $25-36; ⊙noon-3pm Mon-Fri, 5.30pm-late Mon-Sat) Portions are large at this modern, upmarket restaurant with an Italian/French sensibility and first-rate service. Imported cheese and wine are a highlight, and the crispy-based pizzas make a delicious shared snack.

Prego ITALIAN $$

(Map p62; ☑09-376 3095; www.prego.co.nz; 226 Ponsonby Rd; mains $23-40; ⊙noon-midnight) This friendly and stylish Italian restaurant covers all the bases, with a fireplace in winter and a courtyard in summer.

Landreth & Co CAFE $$

(Map p62; www.landrethandco.co.nz; 272 Ponsonby Rd; mains $11-25; ⊙6.30am-4pm; 🐾) A popular brunch spot with a sunny rear courtyard and free wi-fi. It's fully licensed, just in case you feel the urge for a beer with your truffled eggs.

Cocoro JAPANESE $$$

(Map p62; ☑09-360 0927; www.cocoro.co.nz; 56a Brown St; dishes $7-28, degustation $85; ⊙noon-2pm & 5.30-10pm Tue-Sat) Japanese elegance infuses everything about this excellent restaurant, from the soft lighting and chic decor, to the delicate flavours of the artistically arranged food. Dishes are designed to be shared.

✕ Newton

K Rd is known for its late-night clubs, but cafes and plenty of inexpensive ethnic restaurants are mixed in with the vintage clothing stores, secondhand boutiques, tattooists and adult shops.

Alleluya CAFE $

(Map p50; St Kevin's Arcade, Karangahape Rd; mains $10-19; ⊙9am-5.30pm Mon-Sat, to 3pm Sun; 🐾) To the bohemian denizens of K Rd, Alleluya means good coffee, moreish cakes and lots of vegetarian options. It's situated at the end of the city's hippest arcade, with windows offering a wonderful snapshot of the city skyline.

Scullery CAFE $$

(Map p50; 166 Karangahape Rd; mains $12-20; ⊙7am-6.30pm Sun-Wed, to 9pm Thu-Sat; 🐾) 🍃 Healthy breakfast options include mush-

room ragu with halloumi cheese, and the Korean-tinged beef tacos are great for lunch. From Thursday to Saturday dinner is served with a small selection of local wine and craft beer, and a zingy quartet of cocktails.

Coco's Cantina ITALIAN $$

(Map p50; www.cocoscantina.co.nz; 376 Karangahape Rd; mains $25-32; ⊙5pm-late Tue-Sat) Rub shoulders with Auckland's hipsters and foodsters at this bustling cantina where the wait for a table is part of the experience. Propping up the bar is hardly a hardship: the ambience and drinks list see to that. The rustic menu is narrowly focused, seasonal and invariably delicious.

French Cafe FRENCH $$$

(Map p70; ☑09-377 1911; www.thefrenchcafe.co.nz; 210 Symonds St; mains $46, tasting menu with/without wine pairings $220/140; ⊙noon-3pm Fri, 6pm-late Tue-Sat) The legendary French Cafe has been rated as one of Auckland's top restaurants for more than 20 years now and it still continues to excel. The cuisine is nominally French-influenced, but chef Simon Wright sneaks in lots of tasty Asian and Pacific Rim touches.

✕ Kingsland

Petra Shawarma MIDDLE EASTERN $

(Map p70; 482 New North Rd; mains $10-15; ⊙11am-late) Owned by a friendly Jordanian family, Petra serves up lighter, healthier kebabs, and the dips and salads are also worth the short train ride to Kingsland.

Atomic Roastery CAFE $

(Map p70; www.atomiccoffee.co.nz; 420c New North Rd; snacks $9-10; ⊙8am-3pm Mon-Sat, 9am-2pm Sun) Java hounds should follow their noses to this, one of the country's best-known coffee roasters. Tasty accompaniments include pies served in mini-frypans, bagels, salads and cakes.

Fridge CAFE $$

(Map p70; 7.30am-4pm; 507 New North Rd; mains $9-22; ⊙breakfast & lunch) Gourmet pies, healthy salads and wraps, and drool-inducing cakes.

Sake Bar 601 JAPANESE $$

(Map p70; ☑09-849 7268; www.601newnorthroad.co.nz; 601 New North Rd; mains $20-35; ⊙11.30am-1.30pm & 6-9.30pm Tue-Sat) Order a frosty Sapporo beer and watch the friendly Japanese surf-crazy owners prepare some of the best sushi and sashimi in town. Other standouts are the tempura prawns and terikayi chicken. The compact restaurant is very popular, so book ahead.

Mt Eden

Merediths
MODERN NZ $$$

(Map p70; ☑ 09-623 3140; www.merediths.co.nz; 365 Dominion Rd; 6-9 course degustation $90-140; ☺ noon-3pm Fri, 6pm-late Tue-Sat) Dining at Merediths is the culinary equivalent of blackwater rafting - tastes surprise you at every turn, you never know what's coming next and you're left with a sense of breathless exhilaration.

Molten
MODERN NZ $$$

(Map p70; ☑ 09-638 7236; www.molten.co.nz; 422 Mt Eden Rd; mains $29-37; ☺ noon-3pm Wed-Fri, 6pm-late Mon-Sat) Under the volcano's shadow, Molten oozes neighbourhood charm and erupts with flavour. The consistently excellent menu takes advantage of seasonal produce to create innovative meals.

Parnell & Newmarket

Teed St Larder
CAFE $

(Map p68; www.teedstreetlarder.co.nz; 7 Teed St; ☺ 8am-4pm) Polished concrete floors, beer crate tables and colourful oversized lampshades set the scene at Newmarket's best cafe. There are plenty of enticing cooked items on the menu but it's hard to go past the delicious sandwiches and tarts.

Basque Kitchen Bar
TAPAS $

(Map p68; ☑ 09-523 1057; www.basquekitchenbar.co.nz; 61 Davies Cres; tapas $7-15; ☺ 4.30pm-late Mon-Thu & Sat, noon-late Fri) This dark little bar serves delectable tapas accompanied by Spanish wine, beers and sherry. The braised octopus and the chorizo and prawns are both excellent; leave room for dessert of *churros* (Spanish doughnuts).

La Cigale
FRENCH $$

(Map p54; ☑ 09-366 9361; www.lacigale.co.nz; 69 St Georges Bay Rd; cafe mains $8-18, bistro mains $34; ☺ cafe 9am-4pm Mon-Fri, bistro dinner Wed-Fri from 6pm, market 9am-1.30pm Sat & Sun) Catering to Francophile foodies, this warehouse stocks French imports and has a patisserie-laden cafe. During the weekend farmers markets, this *cigale* (cicada) really chirps, with stalls laden with local artisan produce. From Wednesday to Friday the space is converted into a quirky evening bistro. Booking ahead is recommended.

Devonport

Calliope Road Cafe
CAFE $

(Map p65; 33 Calliope Rd; mains $9-18; ☺ 8am-3pm Wed-Mon) Devonport's best cafe is a little back from the main tourist strip, and serves a tasty mix of cafe classics and Southeast Asian dishes to locals in the know.

Bette's Bar & Eatery
CAFE, BAR $

(Map p65; www.facebook.com/bettesdevonport; 8 Victoria St; tapas $15-18; ☺ 11am-late) Decent wine, cocktails and beer, and good tapas and bar snacks make for a top spot to chill out after exploring Devonport.

Other Areas

★ St Heliers Bay Bistro
MODERN NZ $$

(Map p48; www.stheliersbaybistro.co.nz; 387 Tamaki Dr; mains $14-26; ☺ 7am-11pm) Catch the bus along pretty Tamaki Dr to this classy eatery with harbour views. No bookings are taken, but the switched-on crew soon find space for diners. Look forward to dishes infused with mainly Mediterranean and Middle Eastern flavours.

Takapuna Beach Cafe
CAFE $$

(Map p48; www.takapunabeachcafe.co.nz; 22 The Promenade; mains $15-27; ☺ 7am-late; ☑) Sophisticated cafe fare, combined with excellent views of Takapuna Beach, sees this cafe constantly buzz If you can't snaffle a table, grab an award-winning ice cream - our favourite is the salted caramel - and take a lazy stroll along the beach.

Engine Room
MODERN NZ $$$

(Map p48; ☑ 09-480 9502; www.engineroom.net.nz; 115 Queen St, Northcote; mains $34-36; ☺ 6pm-late Tue-Sat, noon-2.30pm Fri) One of Auckland's best restaurants, this informal eatery serves up lighter-than-air goats cheese soufflés, inventive mains and oh-my-God chocolate truffles. It's worth booking ahead and catching the ferry to Northcote wharf; the restaurant is a further 1km walk away.

The Commons
MODERN NZ $$$

(Map p48; ☑ 09-929 2791; www.thecommons.co.nz; 21 Hurstmere Rd, Takapuna; bar snacks $9-16, mains $36; ☺ 11.30am-late) Part of a culinary makeover of a former department store - other adjacent eateries include good Mexican and Italian flavours - The Commons is a spacious and sophisticated combination of elegant restaurant and buzzy bar.

Drinking & Nightlife

Auckland's nightlife is quiet during the week – for some vital signs, head to Ponsonby Rd, Britomart or the Viaduct. K Rd wakes up late on Friday and Saturday; don't even bother staggering this way before 11pm.

 City Centre

Brothers Beer
BEER HALL

(Map p50; www.brothersbeer.co.nz; 90 Wellesley St, City Works Depot; ⊙noon-10pm Wed-Sat, noon-8pm Tue & Sun, closed Mon) Our favourite Auckland bar combines industrial decor with 18 taps crammed with Brothers' own brews and guest beers from NZ and further afield. Hundreds more bottled beers await chilling in the fridges, and bar food includes top-notch pizza. Check the website for occasional tap takeovers.

Mo's
BAR

(Map p50; www.mosbar.co.nz; cnr Wolfe & Federal Sts; ⊙4pm-3am Mon-Fri, 6pm-3am Sat) There's something about this tiny corner bar that makes you want to invent problems just so the barperson can solve them with soothing words and an expertly poured martini.

Hotel de Brett
BAR

(Map p50; www.hoteldebrett.com; 2 High St; ⊙noon-late) Grab a beer in the corner bar, a cocktail in the chic art-deco house bar, or nab a spot by the fire in the atrium, which is an interesting covered space fashioned from the alleyway between the old buildings.

Cassette Nine
CLUB

(Map p50; www.cassettenine.com; 9 Vulcan Lane; ⊙noon-late Tue-Sat) Hipsters gravitate to this eccentric bar/club for music ranging from live indie to international DJ sets.

Ding Dong Lounge
CLUB

(Map p50; www.facebook.com/dingdongloungenz; 26 Wyndham St; admission varies; ⊙8pm-4am Wed-Sat) Rock, indie and alternative sounds from live bands and DJs.

Britomart, Viaduct Harbour & Wynyard Quarter

Tyler Street Garage
BAR

(Map p50; www.tylerstreetgarage.co.nz; 120 Quay St; ⊙11.30am-late) Just in case you were in any doubt that this was actually a garage, they've left the parking lines painted on the concrete floor. A compact roof terrace looks over the wharves.

Jack Tar
PUB

(Map p50; www.jacktar.co.nz; 34-37 Jellicoe St, North Wharf; ⊙10am-late Mon-Thu, 8am-late Fri-Sun) A top spot for a late-afternoon/early-

---

GAY & LESBIAN AUCKLAND

The Queen City (as it's known for completely coincidental reasons) has by far the country's biggest gay population, with the bright lights attracting gays and lesbians from all over the country. However, the even brighter lights of Sydney eventually steal many of the 30- to 40-somethings, leaving a gap in the demographic. There are a handful of gay venues, but they only really kick off on the weekends.

For the latest, see the fortnightly newspaper *Express* (available from gay venues) or www.gaynz.com. The year's big events are the Auckland Pride Festival (p60) and the Out Takes (p61) film festival.

Venues change with alarming regularity, but these ones were the stayers at the time of research:

Family (Map p50; www.familybar.co.nz; 270 Karangahape Rd, Newton) Trashy, brash and young, this bar can be a lot of fun, with dancing into the wee hours.

Urge (Map p50; www.urgebar.co.nz; 490 Karangahape Rd, Newton; ⊙9pm-late Thu-Sat, 3-7pm Sun) Older and hairier, this black-painted pocket-sized venue has DJs on Friday and Saturday nights.

Poof (Map p62; www.facebook.com/PoofonPonsonby; 212 Ponsonby Rd, Ponsonby; ⊙5pm-late Tue-Sat) Cocktail bar with a colourful pop-culture vibe.

Legend (Map p50; www.facebook.com/legend.co.nz; 373 Karangahape Rd, 1st fl; ⊙10pm-4am Thu-Sun) Friendly, clubby vibe, drag shows and excellent views of the city.

Centurian (Map p50; www.centuriansauna.co.nz; 18 Beresford St, Newton; admission before/after 3pm $23/28; ⊙11am-2am Sun-Thu, 11am-6am Fri & Sat) Gay men's sauna.

evening beer or wine amid the relaxed vibe of the waterfront Wynyard Quarter. Try the prawn and sweet chilli pizza or the salt-and-pepper-squid salad.

Xuxu
COCKTAIL BAR

(Map p50; cnr Galway & Commerce Sts; ⊙3pm-late Mon-Sat) A winning combination of Asian-tinged cocktails and bar snacks inspired by Vietnamese street food. DJs kick in around weekends.

Orleans
BAR, LIVE MUSIC

(Map p50; www.orleans.co.nz; 48 Customs St; ⊙11.30am-midnight Sun-Thu, to 4am Fri & Sat) This South Pacific gumbo spin on a southern US jazz bar has wicked cocktails, and live jazz and blues every night. Bar snacks include po'boy sandwiches.

Northern Steamship Co.
PUB

(Map p50; www.northernsteamship.co.nz; 122 Quay St; ⊙11am-late) Standard lamps hang upside down from the ceiling while the mural behind the bar dreams of NZ summer holidays in this good-looking large pub near the train station.

Ponsonby & Grey Lynn

Along Ponsonby Rd, the line between cafe, restaurant, bar and club gets blurred. A lot of eateries also have live music or become clubs later on.

Golden Dawn
BAR

(Map p62; www.goldendawn.co.nz; 134b Ponsonby Rd, cnr Ponsonby Rd & Richmond Rd; ⊙4pm-late Tue-Thu, from 3pm Fri-Sun) Occupying an old shopfront and an inviting stables yard, this hip late-night drinking den regularly hosts happenings including DJs and live bands. There's also excellent food on offer ($12 to $16), including pulled-pork rolls, and prawn buns with Japanese mayo and chilli. Entrance is via the unmarked door just around the corner on Richmond Rd.

Freida Margolis
BAR

(www.facebook.com/FreidaMargolis; 440 Richmond Rd, West Lynn; ⊙4pm-late) Formerly a butchers – look out for the West Lynn Organic Meats sign – this corner location is now a great little neighbourhood bar with a backstreets-of-Bogotá ambience. Loyal locals sit outside with their well-behaved dogs, supping on sangria, wine and craft beer, snacking on sliders and platters, and enjoying eclectic sounds from the owner's big vinyl collection.

AUCKLAND TOP 10 PLAYLIST

Download these Auckland songs to your MP3 player:

➡ 'Grey Lynn Park' – The Veils (2011)

➡ 'Auckland CBD Part Two' – Lawrence Arabia (2009)

➡ 'Forever Thursday' – Tim Finn (2008)

➡ 'Riverhead' – Goldenhorse (2004)

➡ 'A Brief Reflection' – Nesian Mystik (2002)

➡ 'Hopetoun Bridge' – Dave Dobbyn (2000)

➡ 'New Tattoo' – Hello Sailor (1994)

➡ 'Dominion Road' – The Mutton Birds (1992)

➡ 'Andy' – The Front Lawn (1989)

➡ 'One Tree Hill' – U2 (1987)

Dida's Wine Lounge & Tapas Bar
WINE BAR

(Map p62; www.glengarrywines.co.nz; 54 Jervois Rd; ⊙11.30am-midnight) Great food and an even better wine list attract a grown-up crowd. There's an associated wine store, providore and cafe next door, and another, more food-focused branch in Freemans Bay (Map p50; cnr Sale & Wellesley Sts; tapas $7-12; ⊙8am-6pm Sun & Mon, 7am-8pm Tue-Sat).

Newton

Wine Cellar & Whammy Bar
BAR, LIVE MUSIC

(Map p50; www.facebook.com/thewhammybar; St Kevin's Arcade, Karangahape Rd; ⊙5pm-midnight Mon-Thu, 5.30pm-2am Fri & Sat) Secreted downstairs in an arcade, this bar is dark, grungy and very cool, with regular live music in the neighbouring Whammy Bar from Thursday to Saturday.

Galbraith's Alehouse
BREWERY, PUB

(Map p70; www.alehouse.co.nz; 2 Mt Eden Rd; ⊙noon-11pm) Brewing real ales and lagers on site, this cosy English-style pub offers bliss on tap. There are always more craft beers on the guest taps, and the food's also very good.

Kings Arms Tavern
LIVE MUSIC, PUB

(Map p70; www.kingsarms.co.nz; 59 France St; ⊙varies by event) Auckland's leading small venue for local and up-and-coming international bands.

Ink & Coherent
CLUB

(Map p50; www.inkcoherent.co.nz; 262 & 268 Karangahape Rd) Neighbouring venues for serious dance aficionados, sometimes hosting big-name DJs.

Thirsty Dog
LIVE MUSIC, PUB

(Map p50; www.thirstydog.co.nz; 469 Karangahape Rd) Pub with comedy, folk, reggae and poetry slams.

Mt Eden

Liquid Molten
WINE BAR, TAPAS

(Map p70; www.molten.co.nz; 42 Mt Eden Rd; ☺4pm-late Mon-Sat) Grab a spot in the cosy leather banquettes or venture out the back to the al fresco garden. Either way enjoy a grown up but relaxed ambience, a great wine and beer list, and innovative bar food.

Ginger Minx
BAR

(Map p70; www.facebook.com/GingerMinxNZ; 117 Valley Rd; ☺4pm-3am Wed-Sun) Quirky decor, retro furniture, and a serious attitude to cocktails feature at this hipsterish neighbourhood bar.

Kingsland

Neighbourhood
BAR

(Map p70; www.neighbourhood.co.nz; 498 New North Rd; ☺11am-late; ☎) With picture windows overlooking Eden Park and a front terrace that's pick-up central after dark, this upmarket pub is the place to be either side of rugby fixtures. DJs play on weekends.

Portland Public House
BAR, LIVE MUSIC

(Map p70; 463 New North Rd; ☺noon-late Tue-Sun) With mismatched furniture, cartoon-themed art, and lots of hidden nooks and crannies, the Portland Public House is like spending a few lazy hours at a good mate's place. It's also an excellent location for live music.

☆ Entertainment

For listings, check the *NZ Herald's Time Out* magazine on Thursday and again in its Saturday edition. Visit www.kroad.co.nz for Karangahape Rd bars and clubs.

Tickets for most major events can be bought from the following:

Ticketek
TICKETING AGENCY

(Map p50; ☏0800 842 538; www.ticketek.co.nz) Outlets include Real Groovy (p77) and Sky-City Theatre (Map p50; ☏09-363 6000; www.skycity.co.nz; cnr Victoria & Federal Sts).

Ticketmaster
TICKETING AGENCY

(Map p54; ☏09-970 9700; www.ticketmaster.co.nz) Outlets at Real Groovy (p77), Vector Arena (p76), Aotea Centre (p77).

Live Music

Power Station
LIVE MUSIC

(Map p70; www.powerstation.net.nz; 33 Mt Eden Rd; admission varies) Midrange venue popular with up-and-coming overseas acts and established Kiwi bands.

Vector Arena
STADIUM

(Map p54; ☏09-358 1250; www.vectorarena.co.nz; Mahuhu Cres; admission varies; ☺9am-2pm) Auckland's top indoor venue for major touring acts.

Cinema

Most cinemas offer cheaper rates on weekdays before 5pm; Tuesday is usually bargain day.

Rialto
CINEMA

(Map p68; ☏09-369 2417; www.rialto.co.nz; 167 Broadway, Newmarket; adult/child $16.50/10) Mainly art-house and international films, plus better mainstream fare and regular specialist film festivals.

Academy Cinemas
CINEMA

(Map p50; ☏09-373 2761; www.academycinemas.co.nz; 44 Lorne St, City; adult/child $15.50/10) Foreign and art-house films in the basement of the Central Library.

Event Cinemas
CINEMA

(Map p50; ☏09-369 2400; www.eventcinemas.co.nz; Level 3, 297 Queen St, City; adult/child $17/12) Blockbusters, bowling alley and food court.

NZ Film Archives
CINEMA

(Map p50; ☏09-379 0688; www.filmarchive.org.nz; 300 Karangahape Rd, Newton; ☺11am-5pm Mon-Fri) Around 2000 Kiwi feature films, documentaries and TV shows, which you can watch for free on a computer monitor.

Theatre, Classical Music & Comedy

Auckland's main arts and entertainment complex is grouped around Aotea Sq. Branded The Edge (☏09-357 3355; www.theedge.co.nz), it comprises the Town Hall, Civic Theatre (p47) and Aotea Centre.

Auckland Town Hall
CLASSICAL MUSIC

(Map p50; 305 Queen St) This elegant Edwardian venue (1911) hosts the NZ Symphony Orchestra (www.nzso.co.nz) and Auckland Philharmonia (www.apo.co.nz). Also used by international rock bands.

Aotea Centre
THEATRE
(Map p50; 50 Mayoral Dr; ⊕9am-5.30pm Mon-Fri, Sat & Sun 10am-4pm) Theatre, dance, ballet and opera. **NZ Opera** (www.nzopera.com) regularly performs here.

Q Theatre
THEATRE
(Map p50; ☑09-309 9771; www.qtheatre.co.nz; 305 Queen St) Theatre by various companies and intimate live music. **Silo Theatre** (www.silotheatre.co.nz) often performs here.

Classic Comedy Club
COMEDY
(Map p50; ☑09-373 4321; www.comedy.co.nz; 321 Queen St; tickets $5-27) Performances on Mondays and from Wednesday to Saturday.

Maidment Theatre
THEATRE
(Map p50; ☑09-308 2383; www.maidment.auckland.ac.nz; 8 Alfred St) The University's theatre often stages **Auckland Theatre Company** (www.atc.co.nz) productions.

Sport

Eden Park
RUGBY, CRICKET
(Map p70; www.edenpark.co.nz; Reimers Ave, Kingsland) This stadium for top rugby (winter) and cricket (summer) tests by the **All Blacks** (www.allblacks.com) and the **Black Caps** (www.blackcaps.co.nz), respectively. Also home ground for **Auckland Rugby** (www.aucklandrugby.co.nz), the **Blues** (www.theblues.co.nz) Super Rugby team, and **Auckland Cricket** (www.aucklandcricket.co.nz). Catch the train from Britomart to Kingsland and follow the crowds.

Mt Smart Stadium
RUGBY, FOOTBALL
(Map p48; www.mtsmartstadium.co.nz; Maurice Rd, Penrose) Home ground for the **Warriors** (www.warriors.co.nz) rugby league team, **Auckland Football Federation** (www.aucklandfootball.org.nz) and **Athletics Auckland** (www.athleticsauckland.co.nz). Also *really* big concerts.

North Shore Events Centre
BASKETBALL
(Map p48; ☑09-443 8199; www.nseventscentre.co.nz; Argus Pl, Wairau Valley) Along with Vector Arena, this is one of the two home courts of the **NZ Breakers** (www.nzbreakers.co.nz) basketball team and an occasional concert venue.

ASB Tennis Centre
TENNIS
(Map p54; www.aucklandtennis.co.nz; 1 Tennis Lane, Parnell) In January the women's **ASB Classic** (www.asbclassic.co.nz) is held here, followed by the men's **Heineken Open** (www.heinekenopen.co.nz).

🔒 Shopping

Followers of fashion should head to the Britomart Precinct, Newmarket's Teed and Nuffield Sts, and Ponsonby Rd. For vintage clothing and secondhand boutiques try K Rd or Ponsonby Rd.

🔒 City Centre

Real Groovy
MUSIC
(Map p50; www.realgroovy.co.nz; 438 Queen St; ⊕9am-7pm Sat-Wed, 9am-9pm Thu & Fri) Masses of new, secondhand and rare releases in vinyl and CD format, as well as concert tickets, giant posters, DVDs, books, magazines and clothes.

Pauanesia
GIFTS
(Map p50; www.pauanesia.co.nz; 35 High St; ⊕9.30am-6.30pm Mon-Fri, 10am-4.30pm Sat & Sun) Homewares and gifts with a Polynesian and Kiwiana influence.

Unity Books
BOOKS
(Map p50; www.unitybooks.co.nz; 19 High St; ⊕8.30am-7pm Mon-Thu, 8.30am-8pm Fri, 9am-6pm Sat, 11am-6pm Sun) Independent bookshop.

Strangely Normal
CLOTHING
(Map p50; www.strangelynormal.com; 19 O'Connell St; ⊕10am-5pm Mon-Sat, 11am-4pm Sun) Quality, NZ-made, men's tailored shirts straight out of *Blue Hawaii* sit alongside hipster hats, sharp shoes and cufflinks.

Karen Walker
CLOTHING
(Map p50; www.karenwalker.com; 18 Te Ara Tahuhu, The Pavilions, Britomart Precinct; ⊕10am-6pm) Join Madonna and Kirsten Dunst in wearing Walker's cool (but pricey) threads. Also

---

AUCKLAND, THE BIG TARO

There are nearly 180,000 Pacific Islanders (PI) living in Auckland, making it the world's principal Polynesian city. Samoans are by far the largest group, followed by Cook Islanders, Tongans, Niiueans, Fijians, Tokelauans and Tuvaluans. The biggest PI communities can be found in South Auckland and pockets of West and Central Auckland.

Like the Maori renaissance of recent decades, Pasifika has become a hot commodity for Auckland hipsters. You'll find PI motifs everywhere: in art, architecture, fashion, homewares, movies and especially in music.

in **Ponsonby** (Map p62; 128a Ponsonby Rd) and **Newmarket** (Map p68; 6 Balm St).

Zambesi CLOTHING
(Map p50; www.zambesi.co.nz; 56 Tyler St; ⊘10am-6pm) Iconic NZ label much sought after by local and international celebs. Also in **Ponsonby** (Map p62; 169 Ponsonby Rd) and **Newmarket** (Map p68; 38 Osborne St).

Whitcoulls BOOKS
(Map p50; www.whitcoulls.co.nz; 210 Queen St; ⊘8am-6pm) Main branch of the biggest local chain.

🔒 Ponsonby & Grey Lynn

Women's Bookshop BOOKS
(Map p62; www.womensbookshop.co.nz; 105 Ponsonby Rd; ⊘10am-6pm) Excellent independent bookshop.

Texan Art Schools ART & CRAFTS
(Map p62; www.texanartschools.co.nz; 95 Ponsonby Rd; ⊘9.30am-5.30pm) A collective of 200 local artists sell their wares here. Also in **Newmarket** (Map p68; 366 Broadway).

🔒 Kingsland

Royal Jewellery Studio JEWELLERY
(Map p70; www.royaljewellerystudio.com; 486 New North Rd; ⊘10am-5pm) Work by local artisans, including beautiful Maori designs and authentic *pounamu* (greenstone) jewellery.

🔒 Other Areas

Otara Market MARKET
(Map p48; Newbury St; ⊘6am-noon Sat) Held in the car park between the Manukau Polytech and the Otara town centre, this market has a palpable Polynesian atmosphere and is good for South Pacific food, music and fashions. Take bus 497 from Britomart ($6.80, 50 minutes).

Avondale Sunday Market MARKET
(Map p48; www.avondalesundaymarkets.co.nz; Avondale Racecourse, Ash St; ⊘6am-noon Sun) Strong Asian and Polynesian atmosphere and good for fresh produce. Take the train from Britomart station to Avondale.

ℹ Information

INTERNET ACCESS
Auckland Council offers free wi-fi in parts of the city centre, Newton, Ponsonby, Kingsland, Mt Eden and Parnell. All public libraries offer free

wi-fi, and internet cafes catering to gaming junkies are scattered about the inner city.

MEDIA
Metro Glossy monthly magazine covering Auckland issues in depth.

New Zealand Herald (www.nzherald.co.nz) The country's biggest daily newspaper.

The Denizen (www.thedenizen.co.nz) The newest cafes, bars and restaurants in town.

MEDICAL SERVICES
Auckland City Hospital (☑09-367 0000; www.adhb.govt.nz; Park Rd, Grafton; ⊘24hr) The city's main hospital has a dedicated accident and emergency (A&E) service.

Auckland Metro Doctors & Travelcare (☑09-373 4621; www.aucklandmetrodoctors.co.nz; 17 Emily Pl; ⊘9am-5.30pm Mon-Fri, 10am-2pm Sat) Health care for travellers, including vaccinations and travel consultations.

Starship Children's Hospital (☑09-367 0000; www.adhb.govt.nz; Park Rd, Grafton; ⊘24hr) Has its own A&E department.

TOURIST INFORMATION
For more information about i-SITE centres, see www.aucklandnz.com.

Auckland Domestic Airport i-SITE (Map p48; ☑09-256 8480; ⊘7am-9pm) In the Air New Zealand terminal.

Auckland International Airport i-SITE (Map p48; ☑09-275 6467; ⊘24hr) On your left as you exit the customs hall.

Cornwall Park Information Centre (Map p48; ☑09-630 8485; www.cornwallpark.co.nz; Huia Lodge; ⊘10am-4pm)

Devonport i-SITE (Map p65; ☑09-446 0677; www.northshorenz.com; Devonport Wharf; ⊘8.30am-5pm; 🕾)

DOC Auckland Information Centre (Department of Conservation; Map p50; ☑09-379 6476; www.doc.govt.nz; 137 Quay St, Princes Wharf; ⊘9am-5pm Mon-Sat)

Karanga Plaza Kiosk (Map p50; www.waterfrontauckland.co.nz; Wynyard Quarter; ⊘10am-5.30pm)

Princes Wharf i-SITE (Map p50; ☑09-307 0612; 137 Quay St; ⊘9am-5.30pm)

SkyCity i-SITE (Map p50; ☑09-363 7182; SkyCity Atrium, cnr Victoria & Federal Sts; ⊘8am-8pm)

Takapuna i-SITE (Map p48; ☑09-486 8670; 34-36 Hurstmere Rd; ⊘8.30am-5pm Mon-Fri, 10am-3pm Sat & Sun)

ℹ Getting There & Away

AIR
Auckland is the main international gateway to NZ, and a hub for domestic flights. **Auckland International Airport** (AKL; Map p48; ☑09-275

0789; www.aucklandairport.co.nz; Ray Emery Dr, Mangere) is 21km south of the city centre. It has separate international and domestic terminals, each with a tourist information centre. A free shuttle service operates every 15 minutes (5am to 10.30pm) between the terminals and there's also a signposted footpath (about a 10-minute walk). Both terminals have left-luggage facilities, ATMs and car-rental desks, although you may get better rates from companies in town.

For flights to Great Barrier Island, see p93.

Air New Zealand (☑09-357 3000; www.airnewzealand.co.nz) Flies to Kaitaia, Kerikeri, Whangarei, Hamilton, Tauranga, Whakatane, Gisborne, Rotorua, Taupo, New Plymouth, Napier, Whanganui, Palmerston North, Masterton, Wellington, Nelson, Blenheim, Christchurch, Queenstown and Dunedin.

Jetstar (☑0800 800 995; www.jetstar.com) To Wellington, Christchurch, Queenstown and Dunedin.

Sunair (☑0800 786 847; www.sunair.co.nz) To Whitianga (one way $160).

BUS

Coaches depart from 172 Quay St, opposite the Ferry Building, except for InterCity services, which depart from **SkyCity Coach Terminal** (Map p50; ☑09-913 6220; 102 Hobson St). Many southbound services also stop at the airport.

Go Kiwi (☑07-866 0336; www.go-kiwi.co.nz) Daily Auckland City–International Airport–Thames–Tairua–Whitianga shuttles.

InterCity (www.intercity.co.nz)

Naked Bus (☑0900 62533; www.nakedbus. com) Naked Buses travel along SH1 as far north as Kerikeri (four hours) and as far south as Wellington (12 hours), as well as heading to Tauranga (3½ hours) and Napier (12 hours). The cost of calling their helpline is $1.99 per minute.

CAR, CARAVAN & CAMPERVAN
Hire

Auckland has many hire agencies around Beach Rd and Stanley St close to the city centre.

A2B (☑0800 545 000; www.a2b-car-rental. co.nz; 167 Beach Rd; ⊙8am-5pm) Cheap older cars with no visible hire-car branding.

Apex Car Rentals (☑09-307 1063; www.apex-rentals.co.nz; 156 Beach Rd; ⊙8am-5pm)

Budget (☑09-976 2270; www.budget.co.nz; 163 Beach Rd; ⊙7am-6pm Mon-Fri, 8am-5pm Sat & Sun)

Escape (☑0800 216 171; www.escaperentals. co.nz; 39 Beach Rd; ⊙8am-5pm) Eccentrically painted campervans.

Kea, Maui & Britz (☑09-255 3910; www.maui. co.nz; 36 Richard Pearse Dr, Mangere; ⊙8am-6pm)

Gateway 2 NZ (☑050 822 5587; www.gateway2nz.co.nz; 50 Ascot Rd, Mangere; ⊙8am-6pm)

Gateway Motor Home Hire (☑09-296 1652; www.motorhomehire.co.nz; 33 Spartan Rd, Takanini)

Go Rentals (☑09-257 5142; www.gorentals. co.nz; George Bolt Memoral Drive, Bay 2-10, Cargo Central; ⊙6am-10pm)

Hertz (☑09-367 6350; www.hertz.co.nz; 154 Victoria St; ⊙7.30am-5.30pm)

Jucy (☑0800 399 736; www.jucy.co.nz; 2-16 The Strand; ⊙8am-5pm)

Kea Campers (☑09-448 8800; www.keacampers.com; 36 Richard Pearse Drive, Mangere; ⊙8am-4.30pm)

NZ Frontiers (☑09-299 6705; www.newzealandfrontiers.com)

Omega (☑09-377 5573; www.omegarentals. com; 75 Beach Rd; ⊙8am-5pm)

Quality Rentals (☑0800 680 123; www.qualityrental.co.nz; 8 Andrew Baxter Dr, Mangere; ⊙8am-4pm)

Thrifty (☑09-309 0111; www.thrifty.co.nz; 150 Khyber Pass Rd; ⊙8am-5pm)

Wilderness Motorhomes (☑09-255 5300; www.wilderness.co.nz; 21 Rennie Drive, Mangere; ⊙8am-5pm)

Purchase

Mechanical inspection services are on hand at secondhand car fairs, where sellers pay to display their cars.

Auckland Car Fair (☑09-529 2233; www. carfair.co.nz; Ellerslie Racecourse, Green Lane

PLANE DELAYED?
TIME FOR A TIPPLE!

Clearly the roar of jets doesn't bother grapes, as NZ's most awarded winery is just 4km from the airport. The park-like grounds of **Villa Maria Estate** (Map p48; www.villamaria.co.nz; 118 Montgomerie Rd; platters $40-50, lunch $28-35; ⊙9am-6pm Mon-Fri, 9am-4pm Sat & Sun) are a green oasis in the encircling industrial zone. A series of concerts is held here every January and February featuring big international artists popular with the 40- to 50-something wine-swilling demographic.

Short tours ($5) take place at 11am and 3pm. There's a charge for tastings ($5), but lingering over wine and cheese on the terrace sure beats hanging around the departure lounge.

East; display fee $35; ⊙ 9am-noon Sun) Auckland's largest car fair.

City Car Fair (☑ 09-837 7817; www.aucklandcitycarfair.co.nz; 155 Fanshawe St; display fee $25; ⊙ 8am-1pm Sat)

MOTORCYCLE

NZ Motorcycle Rentals (☑ 09-486 2472; www.nzbike.com; 72 Barrys Point Rd, Takapuna; per day $145-360) Guided tours of NZ also available.

TRAIN

Northern Explorer (☑ 0800 872 467; www.kiwirailscenic.co.nz) trains leave from **Britomart station** (Queen St) at 7.50am on Monday, Thursday and Saturday and arriving in Wellington at 6.25pm. Stops include Hamilton (2½ hours), Otorohanga, (three hours), Tongariro National Park (5½ hours), Ohakune (6½ hours), Palmerston North (9½ hours) and Paraparaumu (11 hours). Standard fares to Wellington range from $119 to $186, but some discounted seats are available at $99 (first in, first served).

ⓘ Getting Around

TO & FROM THE AIRPORT

A taxi between the airport and the city usually costs between $65 and $85, more if you strike traffic snarls.

Airbus Express (☑ 09-366 6400; www.airbus.co.nz; one way/return adult $16/28, child $6/12) Runs between the terminals and the city, every 10–15 minutes from 7am to 7pm and at least hourly through the night. Stops include Mt Eden Rd or Dominion Rd (on request), Symonds St, Queen St and the Ferry Building. Reservations are not required; buy a ticket from the driver or online. The trip usually takes less than an hour (longer during peak times).

Super Shuttle (☑ 0800 748 885; www.supershuttle.co.nz) This convenient door-to-door shuttle charges $29 for one person heading between the airport and a city hotel; the price increases for outlying suburbs. Save money by sharing a shuttle.

BICYCLE

Auckland Transport (☑ 09-366 6400; www.at.govt.nz) publishes free cycle maps, available from public buildings such as stations, libraries and i-SITEs. Bikes can be taken on ferries and trains for free (dependent on available space), but only folding bikes are allowed on buses.

Adventure Cycles (☑ 09-940 2453; www.adventure-auckland.co.nz/adventurecycles; 9 Premier Ave, Western Springs; per day $30-40, per week $120-160, per month $260-350; ⊙ 7.30am-7pm Thu-Mon) Hires road, mountain and touring bikes, runs a buy-back scheme, and does repairs.

CAR & MOTORCYCLE

Auckland's motorways jam badly at peak times, particularly the Northern and Southern Motorways. It's best to avoid them between 7am and 9am, and from 4pm to 7pm. Things also get tight around 3pm during term time, which is the end of the school day.

Expect to pay for parking in central Auckland from 8am to 6pm from Monday to Saturday. Most parking meters are pay-and-display; display tickets inside your windscreen. You usually don't have to pay between 6pm and 8am or on Sunday, but check the meters and parking signs carefully.

Prices can be steep at parking buildings. Better value are the council-run open-air parks near the old train station at 126 Beach Rd ($8 per day) and on Ngaoho Pl, off The Strand ($6 per day).

PUBLIC TRANSPORT

Auckland's public transport system is run by a hodgepodge of different operators, but there is now an integrated AT HOP smartcard (www.athop.co.nz), which provides discounts of around 10% on most buses, trains and ferries. AT HOP cards cost $10 (nonrefundable), so are really only worthwhile if you're planning on an extended stay in Auckland.

The **Auckland Transport** (☑ 09-366 6400; www.at.govt.nz) information service covers buses, trains and ferries and has an excellent trip-planning feature. A Discovery Pass provides a day's transport on most trains and buses and on North Shore ferries ($16); buy it on the bus or train or at Fullers offices.

Bus

Bus routes spread their tentacles throughout the city and you can purchase a ticket from the driver. Many services terminate around Britomart station. Some bus stops have electronic displays giving an estimate of waiting times, but be warned, they are often inaccurate.

Single-ride fares in the inner city are $1 for an adult and $0.60 for a child. If you're travelling further afield there are fare stages from $1.90/1.10 (adult/child) to $10.30/6.10.

The most useful services are the environmentally friendly Link Buses that loop in both directions around three routes (taking in many of the major sights) from 7am to 11pm:

City Link (adult/child $0.50/0.30, free for AT HOP cardholders, every seven to 10 minutes) Britomart, Queen St, Karangahape Rd, with some buses connecting to Wynyard Quarter.

Inner Link ($1.90, every 10 to 15 minutes) Queen St, SkyCity, Victoria Park, Ponsonby Rd, Karangahape Rd, Museum, Newmarket, Parnell and Britomart.

Outer Link (maximum $3.40, every 15 minutes) Art Gallery, Ponsonby, Herne Bay, Westmere, MOTAT 2, Pt Chevalier, Mt Albert, St Lukes Mall, Mt Eden, Newmarket, Museum, Parnell, University.

Ferry

Auckland's Edwardian baroque **Ferry Building** (Map p50; Quay St) sits at the end of Queen St.

360 Discovery (Map p50; ✆ 0800 360 3472; www.360discovery.co.nz; Pier 4, 139 Quay St; cruise adult/child $27/17, three-day pass $35/21; ⊙10am, noon & 2.30pm) Ferries to Coromandel, Gulf Harbour, Motuihe, Rotoroa and Tiritiri Matangi.

Fullers (Map p50; ✆ 09-367 9111; www.fullers. co.nz; Ferry Building, 99 Quay St) Ferries to Bayswater, Birkenhead, Devonport, Great Barrier Island, Half Moon Bay, Northcote, Motutapu, Rangitoto and Waiheke leave directly behind the Ferry Building

Sealink (✆ 09-300 5900; www.sealink.co.nz) Ferries to Great Barrier Island leave from Wynyard Wharf, along with some car ferries to Waiheke, but most of the ferries to Waiheke leave from Half Moon Bay in East Auckland.

Train

Auckland's train services are limited and infrequent but the trains are generally clean, cheap and on time – although any hiccup on the lines can bring down the entire network. For timetables and trip planning see www.at.govt.nz.

Impressive Britomart station (p80) has food retailers, foreign-exchange facilities and a ticket office. Downstairs are left-luggage lockers.

There are just four train routes: west to Waitakere, south to Onehunga, and two run south to Pukekohe. Services are at least hourly from around 6am to 8pm (later on the weekends). Buy a ticket from machines or ticket offices at train stations. All trains have wheelchair ramps.

TAXI

Auckland's many taxis usually operate from ranks, but they also cruise popular areas. **Auckland Co-op Taxis** (✆ 09-300 3000; www.3003000.co.nz) is one of the biggest companies; has a surcharge for transport to and from the airport and ships, and for phone orders.

HAURAKI GULF ISLANDS

The Hauraki Gulf, stretching between Auckland and the Coromandel Peninsula, is dotted with *motu* (islands) and gives the Bay of Islands stiff competition in the beauty stakes. Some islands are only minutes from the city and make excellent day trips. Winesoaked Waiheke and volcanic Rangitoto really shouldn't be missed. Great Barrier requires more effort (and cash) to get to, but provides an idyllic escape from modern life.

There are 47 islands in the Hauraki Gulf Maritime Park, administered by DOC. Some are good-sized islands, others are no more than rocks jutting out of the sea. They're loosely put into two categories: recreation and conservation. The recreation islands can easily be visited and their harbours are dotted with yachts in summer. The conservation islands, however, have restricted access. Permits are required to visit some, while others are closed refuges for the preservation of rare plants and animals, especially birds.

The gulf is a busy highway for marine mammals. Sei, minke and Bryde's whales are regularly seen in its outer reaches, along with orcas and bottlenose dolphins. You might even spy a passing humpback.

Rangitoto & Motutapu Islands

POP 75

Sloping elegantly from the waters of the gulf, 259m **Rangitoto** (www.rangitoto.org), the largest and youngest of Auckland's volcanic cones, provides a picturesque backdrop to all of the city's activities. As recently as 600 years ago it erupted from the sea and was probably active for several years before settling down. Maori living on **Motutapu** (Sacred Island; www.motutapu.org.nz), to which Rangitoto is now joined by a causeway, certainly witnessed the eruptions, as footprints have been found embedded in ash, and oral history details several generations living here before the eruption.

Rangitoto makes for a great day trip. Its harsh scoria slopes hold a surprising amount of flora (including the world's largest pohutukawa forest) and there are excellent walks, but you'll need sturdy shoes and plenty of water. Although it looks steep, up close it's shaped more like an egg sizzling in a pan. The walk to the summit only takes an hour and is rewarded with sublime views. At the top a loop walk goes around the crater's rim. A walk to lava caves branches off the summit walk and takes 30 minutes return. There's an information board with walk maps at the wharf.

Motutapu, in contrast to Rangitoto, is mainly covered in grassland, which is grazed by sheep and cattle. Archaeologically, this is a very significant island, with the traces of centuries of continuous human habitation etched into its landscape.

At Home Bay on Motutapu there's a **DOC campsite** (www.doc.govt.nz; adult/child $6/3) with only basic facilities (running water and a flush toilet). Bring cooking equipment, as open fires are forbidden, and book on-line. It's a three-hour walk from **Rangitoto wharf** (Map p48); Fullers run a weekend-only service to Home Bay in the summer months.

In 2011 both islands were officially declared predator-free after an extensive eradication programme. Endangered birds such as takahe and tieke (saddleback) have been released and others such as kakariki and bellbirds have returned of their own volition.

❶ Getting There & Around

Fullers (☎09-367 9111; www.fullers.co.nz; Ferry Building, 99 Quay St; adult/child return Auckland or Devonport $29/14.50) Has ferry services to Rangitoto from Auckland's Ferry Building (20 minutes, three daily on weekdays, four on weekends) and Devonport (two daily). It also offers the Volcanic Explorer (adult/child incl ferry $60/30; ⊙departs 9.15am & 12.15pm), a guided tour around the island in a canopied 'road train'.

Motuihe Island

Between Rangitoto and Waiheke Islands, 176-hectare Motuihe has a lovely white-sand beach and a fascinating history. There are three *pa* sites, last occupied by the Ngati Paoa tribe. The island was sold in 1840 (for a heifer, blankets, frocks, garden tools, pots and pans) and from 1872 to 1941 served as a quarantine station. During WWI the dashing swashbuckler Count von Luckner launched a daring escape from the island (where he was interned with other German and Austrian nationals), making it 1000km to the Kermadec Islands before being recaptured.

Motuihe has been rendered pest-free and is now subject to a vigorous reforestation project by enthusiastic volunteers. As a result, endangered birds have returned, including the loquacious tieke.

Apart from the trust's headquarters, the only accommodation on the island is a basic **DOC campsite** (www.doc.govt.nz; adult/child $6/3); only toilets and water are provided, and booking ahead online is essential. There are no permanent residents or shops, except for a lunchtime kiosk during January.

❶ Getting There & Away

360 Discovery (☎0800 360 3472; www.360discovery.co.nz; adult/child return $28/17.50) A ferry taking one hour departs from Auckland daily at 8.45am, returning at 3.30pm.

Waiheke Island

POP 8300

Waiheke is 93 sq km of island bliss just a 35-minute ferry ride from the CBD. Once they could hardly give land away here; nowadays multimillionaires rub shoulders with the old-time hippies and bohemian artists who gave the island its green repute. Auckland office workers fantasise about swapping the daily motorway crawl for a watery commute and a warm, dry microclimate.

On Waiheke's city side, emerald waters lap at rocky bays, while its ocean flank has some of the region's best sandy beaches. While beaches are the big drawcard, wine is a close second. There are 19 boutique wineries to visit, many with swanky restaurants and breathtaking city views. The island also boasts galleries and craft stores.

Waiheke has been inhabited since at least the 14th century, most recently by Ngati Paoa, and there are more than 40 *pa* sites scattered around the island. Europeans arrived with the missionary Samuel Marsden in the early 1800s and the island was soon stripped of its kauri forest.

There are petrol stations in Oneroa, Ostend and Onetangi, ATMs in Oneroa and Ostend, and a supermarket in Ostend.

◉ Sights & Activities

Beaches

Waiheke's two best beaches are **Onetangi**, a long stretch of white sand at the centre of the island, and **Palm Beach**, a pretty little horseshoe bay between Oneroa and Onetangi. Both have nudist sections; head west just past some rocks in both cases. **Oneroa** and neighbouring **Little Oneroa** are also excellent, but you'll be sharing the waters with moored yachts in summer. Reached by an unsealed road through farmland, **Man O' War Bay** is a compact beach that's excellent for swimming.

Wineries

Goldie Vineyard   WINERY
(www.goldiewines.co.nz; 18 Causeway Rd; tastings $10, refundable with purchase; ⊙tasting room noon-4pm daily, cafe noon-4pm Sat & Sun & daily late Dec–mid-Jan) Founded as Goldwater

Estate in 1978, this is Waiheke's pioneering vineyard. The tasting room sells well-stocked baskets for a picnic amongst the vines ($60 for two people).

Passage Rock   WINERY
(☑ 09-372 7257; www.passagerockwines.co.nz; 438 Orapiu Rd; ⊗ noon-4pm Sat & Sun Aug-Dec, daily Jan, Wed-Sun Feb-Apr) Excellent pizza among the vines.

Man O' War Vineyards   WINERY
(www.manowarvineyards.co.nz; Man O' War Bay; ⊗ 11am-6pm summer, to 4.30pm winter) Settle in with a tapas platter and a glass of Man O' War's Valhalla chardonnay at our favourite Waiheke winery. If the weather is good, go for a swim in beautiful Man O' War Bay.

Stonyridge   WINERY
(☑ 09-372 8822; www.stonyridge.com; 80 Onetangi Rd; tastings per wine $3-15; ⊗ 11.30am-5pm) 🍽 Famous organic reds, an atmospheric cafe, tours ($10, 35 minutes, 11.30am Saturday and Sunday) and the occasional dance party.

Wild On Waiheke   WINERY, BREWERY
(☑ 09-372 3434; www.wildonwaiheke.co.nz; 82 Onetangi Rd; tastings per beer or wine $2; ⊗ 11am-4pm Thu-Sun, daily in summer) This winery and microbrewery offers tastings, archery, laser clay shooting, pétanque, a sandpit and a giant chess board.

Art & Culture
The *Waiheke Art Map* brochure, free from the i-SITE, lists galleries and craft stores.

Artworks Complex   ARTS CENTRE
(2 Korora Rd; 📶) The Artworks complex houses a **community theatre** (☑ 09-372 2941; www.artworkstheatre.org.nz), an **art-house cin**ema (☑ 09-372 4240; www.waihekecinema.net; adult/child $14/7), an attention-grabbing **art gallery** (☑ 09-372 9907; www.waihekeartgallery. org.nz; ⊗ 10am-4pm) FREE and **Whittaker's Musical Museum** (☑ 09-372 5573; www.musical-museum.org; ⊗ 1-4pm, live shows 1.30pm Sat) FREE, a collection of antique concert instruments. This is also the place for free internet access, either on a terminal at the **library** (⊗ 9am-5.30pm Mon-Fri, 10am-4pm Sat; 📶) or on their wi-fi network.

Stony Batter Historic Reserve HISTORIC SITE
(www.fortstonybatter.org; Stony Batter Rd; adult/child $8/5; ⊗ 9am-5pm) At the eastern end of the island, Stony Batter has WWII tunnels and gun emplacements that were built in 1941 to defend Auckland's harbour. The 20-minute walk from the carpark leads through private farmland and derives its name from the boulder-strewn fields. Bring a torch and cash.

Waiheke Museum
& Historic Village   MUSEUM
(www.waihekemuseum.org.nz; 165 Onetangi Rd; admission by donation; ⊗ noon-4pm Wed, Sat & Sun) Displays Islander artefacts in six restored buildings.

Dead Dog Bay   GARDENS
(www.deaddogbay.co.nz; Margaret Reeve Lane; adult/child $10/free; ⊗ 10am-5pm) Wander steep pathways through rainforest, wetlands and gardens scattered with sculpture.

Connells Bay   GARDENS
(☑ 09-372 8957; www.connellsbay.co.nz; Cowes Bay Rd; adult/child $30/15; ⊗ by appointment, late Oct-late Mar) A pricey but excellent private sculpture park featuring a stellar roster of NZ artists. Admission is by way of a two-hour guided tour; book ahead.

LOCAL KNOWLEDGE

WAIHEKE ISLAND

Thirty years ago, Waiheke Island was home to an eclectic mix of outlaws who could not (or chose not to) live in 'normal' society: hippies and hermits, alternative healers and writers, potters and pot growers, and everything in between. Sometime in the late '80s, Waiheke was 'discovered', and it's quite a different place now. But even with all the changes – fine dining, vineyards and luxury holiday homes – Waiheke Island's identity and spirit are still undeniable. The beautiful weather remains the same, as do the phenomenal vistas, the lush bush and native birds, the chooks in your neighbours' backyards, the feeling that everything deserves to move a little slower (we call it 'Waiheke time'), the smell of honeysuckle, the crystal waters, the best fish and chips ever, the house I was born in and, probably, still a few pot growers. Waiheke was, and remains, like nowhere else on the planet.

Zoë Bell, Stuntwoman & Actor

Waiheke Island

5 km
2.5 miles

Inset (Enlargement):

Hekerua Bay
Queens Dr
SURFDALE
Oneroa Bay
Little Oneroa Beach
Ocean View Rd
Tawa St
Kiwi St
Oneroa Beach
ONEROA
BLACKPOOL
Burrell Rd
The Esplanade
Haruhi Bay
Blackpool Beach
Tahatai Rd
16
18
24
19
23
20
1

Main map:

Thumb Point
Hooks Bay
Stony Batter (220m)
Opopo Bay
Man O' War Bay
Cowes Bay Rd
Cowes Bay
Waiheke Channel
Omaru Bay
Orapiu Wharf
Orapiu Rd
Te Haahi-Goodwin Reserve
Maunganui (231m)
Te Muttuku Bay
McLeods Bay
Awaawaroa Rd
Awaawaroa Bay
Man O' War Bay Rd
Onetangi Reserve
Waiheke Rd
HAURAKI GULF
Onetangi Bay
Onetangi Beach
ONETANGI
Ostend Rd
Carsons Rd
Whakanewha Regional Park
OMIHA
Rocky Bay
Gordons Rd
Te Whau Dr
Palm Beach
PALM BEACH
Causeway Rd
OSTEND
Car Ferry Wharf
Te Whau Point
Kennedy Point
See Enlargement
ONEROA
Fossil Bay
Matiatia Wharf
Matiatia Bay
Atawhai Whenua Reserve
Auckland (18km)
Tamaki Strait
Awaawaroa Bay

7
5
2
6
27
30
10
29
17
22
9
8
21
3
26
14
4
28
25
15
11
12
13

Waiheke Island

◎ Sights
Art Gallery..(see 1)
1 Artworks Complex.................................F3
2 Connells Bay..E4
3 Dead Dog Bay.......................................B3
4 Goldie Vineyard.....................................B3
5 Man O' War Vineyards...........................E2
6 Passage Rock..E3
7 Stony Batter Historic Reserve...............E2
8 Stonyridge..C3
9 Waiheke Museum & Historic
　Village...C3
Whittaker's Musical Museum........ (see 1)
Wild On Waiheke............................(see 8)

◉ Activities, Courses & Tours
10 EcoZip Adventures................................C3
11 Fullers...A2
12 Ross Adventures...................................A2

◉ Sleeping
13 Cable Bay Views...................................A2
14 Enclosure Bay.......................................B2
15 Fossil Bay Lodge...................................A2
16 Hekerua Lodge......................................G3
17 Kina..C2

18 Punga Lodge..G3
19 Tawa Lodge..G3
20 The Oyster Inn......................................F3
21 Whakanewha Regional Park
　Campsite...C4

◉ Eating
Cable Bay.......................................(see 13)
22 Casita Miro...C2
23 Delight..F3
24 Dragonfired..G3
25 Mudbrick..A3
26 Ostend Market......................................B3
27 Poderi Crisci...D3
Solar Eating House........................(see 23)
28 Te Whau...B3
The Oyster Inn ....(see 20)
Wai Kitchen....................................(see 20)

◉ Drinking & Nightlife
29 4th Avenue Eatery & Bar.......................C2
30 Charlie Farley's.....................................C2

◉ Entertainment
Art-House Cinema ....(see 1)
Community Theatre.........................(see 1)

Walks

Ask at the i-SITE about the island's beautiful coastal walks (ranging from one to three hours) and the 3km Cross Island Walkway (from Onetangi to Rocky Bay). Other tracks traverse **Whakanewha Regional Park**, a haven for rare coastal birds and geckos, and the Royal Forest & Bird Protection Society's three reserves: **Onetangi** (Waiheke Rd), **Te Haahi-Goodwin** (Orapiu Rd) and **Atawhai Whenua** (Ocean View Rd).

Other Activities

Hike Bike Ako　　WALKING, CYCLING
(☑ 021 465 373; www.hikebikeako.co.nz; hiking adult/child $99/79, biking & combination $139) Explore the island on a guided walking (three hours) or biking (five hours) tour, or a combination (five hours) of both. Tours all include pick up from the ferry, lunch at a cafe or vineyard, and Maori legends, history and culture. There's a minimum age of seven for walking and 16 for biking.

Ross Adventures　　KAYAKING
(☑ 09-372 5550; www.kayakwaiheke.co.nz; Matiatia Beach; half-/full-day trips $85/145, per hr hire from $25) It's the fervently held opinion of Ross that Waiheke offers kayaking every bit as good as the legendary Abel Tasman National Park. He should know – he's been offering guided

kayak trips for over 20 years. Experienced sea kayakers can comfortably circumnavigate the island in four days, exploring hidden coves and sand spits inaccessible by land.

EcoZip Adventures　　ZIPLINE
(☑ 0800 246 947; www.ecozipadventures.co.nz; Trig Hill Rd; adult/child $99/69) With vineyard, native bush and ocean views, three separate 200m stretches make for an exciting ride, and there's a gentle 1.5km walk back up through the bush after the thrills. Costs include free transfers from Matiatia Wharf or Oneroa if you don't have your own transport.

Tours

Ananda Tours　　FOOD & WINE
(☑ 09-372 7530; www.ananda.co.nz) Gourmet wine and food tours ($120), and a wine connoisseurs' tour ($230). Small-group, informal tours can be customised, including visits to artists' studios.

Fullers　　. FOOD & WINE
(☑ 09-367 9111; www.fullers.co.nz) Runs a 'Wine on Waiheke' tour (adult $119, 4½ hours, departs Auckland 1pm) visiting three of the island's top wineries, and includes a platter of nibbles; 'Taste of Waiheke' (adult $129, 5½ hours, departs Auckland 11am) includes three wineries plus an olive grove and light

lunch. There's also a 1½-hour Explorer Tour (adult/child $52/26, departs Auckland 10am, 11am and noon). All prices include the ferry and an all-day local bus pass.

Sunshine Tours FOOD & WINE
(☑ 09-372 6127; www.waihekeislandadventures.com) Scenic tours ($45) and vineyard tours ($45).

Waiheke Executive Transport WINE, CULTURAL
(☑ 0800 372 200; www.waiheketransport.co.nz) Options include island highlights tours ($26) and wine tours ($110 to $115).

✦ Festivals & Events

Sculpture on the Gulf ARTS
(www.sculptureonthegulf.co.nz) A 2.5km cliff-top sculpture walk, held for three weeks from late January in odd-numbered years.

**Waiheke Island of
Wine Vintage Festival** WINE, FOOD, MUSIC
(www.waihekevintagefestival.co.nz; ⊘ late Mar-early Apr) Held for the first time in 2014, featuring a week of jazz and classical concerts in the vines, plus art exhibitions, a farmers market, and food and wine matching. Seventeen different vineyards are involved, and shuttle buses travel between the different locations.

**Waiheke Island International
Jazz Festival** MUSIC
(www.waihekejazzfestival.co.nz; prices vary by event) Local and international acts across the island from Friday to Sunday during Easter.

⛏ Sleeping

Waiheke is so popular in the summer holidays that many locals rent out their houses and bugger off elsewhere. You'll need to book ahead and even then there are very few bargains. Prices drop considerably in winter, especially midweek. For midrange accommodation, a good option is to book a holiday home through www.bookabach.co.nz or www.holidayhouses.co.nz, but you'll need transport to get around.

Fossil Bay Lodge CABIN $
(☑ 09-372 8371; www.fossilbay.webs.com; 58 Korora Rd; s $49, d $80-125, tents $80-105; ☜) Three cute cabins open onto a courtyard facing the main building, which houses the toilets, a communal kitchen and living area, and a compact upstairs apartment. Recently added are two cosy bell tents for 'glamping' accommodation, and apart from the occasional squawking duck – or toddler from the adjacent Steiner kindergarten – it's a peaceful place.

Hekerua Lodge HOSTEL $
(☑ 09-372 8990; www.hekerualodge.co.nz; 11 Hekerua Rd; sites from $18, dm $30-36, s $55, d $90-120; @☜☒) This secluded hostel is surrounded by native bush and has a barbecue, stone-tiled pool, sunny deck, casual lounge area and its own walking track. It's far from luxurious, but it has a laid-back and social feel, no doubt assisted by the cool, neutral decor and the serene images of Buddha scattered about.

Kina HOSTEL $
(☑ 09-372 8971; www.kinabackpackers.co.nz; 421 Seaview Rd; dm $28-34, s/tw $55/72, d $72-90; @☜) This old-style, well-positioned hostel has a large garden and lawn overlooking Onetangi Beach. Relatively compact dorms and private rooms are shared between an older building and a newer wing, and it's run efficiently by a Kiwi couple with young children and a friendly Border Collie.

**Whakanewha Regional
Park Campsite** CAMPSITE $
(☑ 09-366 2000; www.arc.govt.nz; Gordons Rd; sites per adult/child $13/6) A pretty but basic campsite with toilets, gas barbecues and drinking water. Self-contained campervans can stay in the adjacent Poukaraka Flats campground.

Tawa Lodge GUESTHOUSE $$
(☑ 09-372 9434; www.pungalodge.co.nz; 15 Tawa St; r $120, apt $175-240; ☜) Between the self-contained cottage at the front and the apartment at the rear are three reasonably priced loft rooms sharing a small kitchen and bathroom. Look forward to excellent ocean views from the shared deck.

Punga Lodge B&B $$
(☑ 09-372 6675; www.pungalodge.co.nz; 223 Ocean View Rd; r $145-150, units $140-200; @☜) Both the colourful en suite rooms in the house and the self-contained garden units have access to decks looking onto a lush tropical garden. There's a spa, and prices include homemade breakfast, afternoon tea and wharf transfers.

The Oyster Inn BOUTIQUE HOTEL $$$
(☑ 09-372 2222; www.theoysterinn.co.nz; 124 Ocean View Rd; r $285-335) With a breezy and cool ambience inspired by classic American Cape Cod style, The Oyster Inn has just three luxury rooms in the heart of Oneroa. Guests are picked up from the ferry at Matiatia wharf in a retro VW combi van, and this attention to luxurious detail is further enhanced with chic decor, stellar bathroom products and personalised service.

Enclosure Bay
B&B $$$

(☎09-372 8882; www.enclosurebay.co.nz; 9 Great Barrier Rd; r $375, ste $450-499) If you're going to shell out for a luxury B&B you're going to want something a little special, and that's certainly what's offered here. Each of the three guest rooms have sumptuous views and balconies, and the owners subscribe to the nothing's-too-much-trouble school of Kiwi hospitality.

Cable Bay Views
APARTMENTS $$$

(☎09-372 2901; www.cablebayviews.co.nz; 103 Church Bay Rd; d $250; ☜) These three modern, self-contained studio apartments have stellar vineyard views and are handily close to a couple of Waiheke's best vineyard restaurants. Check the website for good midweek and off-peak discounts.

✖ Eating

Waiheke has some excellent eateries and, if you're lucky, the views will be enough to distract from the hole being bored into your hip pocket.

Dragonfired
PIZZERIA $

(Little Oneroa Beach; mains $8-16; ☺10.30am-8.30pm; ⚑) Specialising in 'artisan wood-fired food', this caravan by the beach serves the three Ps: pizza, polenta plates and pocket bread. It's easily Waiheke's best place for cheap eats.

Ostend Market
MARKET $

(www.ostendmarketwaiheke.co.nz; War Memorial Hall, Belgium St; ☺7.30am-1pm Sat) Fresh local produce, and local craft and secondhand knick-knacks.

Wai Kitchen
CAFE $$

(www.waikitchen.co.nz; 1/149 Ocean View Rd, Oneroa; mains $17-23; ☺9am-4pm, extended summer) Why? Well firstly there's the lively menu that abounds with Mediterranean and Asian flavours. Then there's the charming service and the breezy ambience of this glassed-in wedge, facing the *wai* (water).

Casita Miro
SPANISH $$

(☎09-372 7854; www.mirovineyard.co.nz; 3 Brown St, Onetangi; dishes $19-40; ☺noon-3pm daily, 6-10pm Thu-Sat Jan-Feb, reduced hours in winter) A wrought iron and glass pavilion backed with a Gaudi-esque mosaic garden is the stage for a very entertaining troupe of servers who will guide you through the menu of delectable *ración tapas* – dishes bigger than regular tapas, designed to be shared.

The Oyster Inn
SEAFOOD, MODERN NZ $$

(☎09-372 2222; www.theoysterinn.co.nz; 124 Ocean View Rd; mains $23-36; ☺11am-late) The Oyster Inn is a popular destination for Auckland's smart set. It has an excellent seafood-skewed bistro menu, oysters and champagne, and a buzzy but relaxed vibe that's part bar and part restaurant. Brunch from 11am on the verandah is a great way to ease into another Waiheke day.

Delight
CAFE, TURKISH $$

(☎09-372 9035; www.delightcafe.co.nz; 29 Waikare Rd, Oneroa; mains $14-23, mezze $10-19; ☺8am-3pm) If you're bored with eggs Benedict, try one of the piquant breakfast tagines at this stylish cafe/mezze bar. Paninis, wraps and salads are served along with more traditional mezze, and the views are just as delicious.

Solar Eating House
CAFE, BAR $$

(139 Oceanview Rd; mains $15-24; ☺8am-9.30pm) ⚑ With a spacious outdoor area and ocean views, Solar is our relaxed choice for the first coffee – or beer or glass of wine – of the day. Lots of local organic and sustainable produce underpins the menu.

Poderi Crisci
ITALIAN $$

(☎09-372 2148; www.podericrisci.co.nz; 205 Awaawaroa Rd; mains $24-33; ☺noon-3pm Thu-Mon, extended hrs in summer) Poderi Crisci has quickly gained a sterling reputation for its food, particularly its legendary four-hour long lunches on Sundays ($65 per person). Italian varietals and olives have been planted alongside the existing vines. Definitely worth the drive into the restaurant's isolated valley.

Te Whau
WINERY $$$

(☎09-372 7191; www.tewhau.com; 218 Te Whau Dr; mains $37-42; ☺11am-5pm Wed-Mon, 6.30pm-late Sat Nov-Easter, reduced hrs in winter) ⚑ Perched on the end of Te Whau peninsula, this winery restaurant has exceptional views, food and service, and one of the finest wine lists you'll see in the country. Try its own impressive Bordeaux blends, merlot, chardonnay and rosé for $3 per taste (11am to 5pm).

Cable Bay
WINERY $$$

(☎09-372 5889; www.cablebayvineyards.co.nz; 12 Nick Johnstone Dr; two/three courses $72/90; ☺noon-3pm & 6pm-late daily) ⚑ Impressive ubermodern architecture, sculpture and beautiful views set the scene for this acclaimed restaurant. The food is sublime, but if the budget won't stretch to a meal, stop in for a wine tasting (from $8), or snacks from the small-plates menu ($10 to $15) on the terrace from 11am.

Mudbrick WINERY $$$
(☑09-372 9050; www.mudbrick.co.nz; 126 Church Bay Rd; mains $42-49, tasting menu with/without wine $190/110; ⊙11.30am-3.30pm & 6pm-10.30pm) Auckland and the gulf are at their glistening best when viewed from Mudbrick's picturesque verandah. The winery also offers tours and tastings (from $10, 10am to 5pm).

🍷 Drinking & Nightlife

You'll find bars in Oneroa and pubs in Surfdale and Ostend.

Charlie Farley's BAR
(www.charliefarleys.co.nz; 21 The Strand, Onetangi; ⊙8.30am-late) It's easy to see why the locals love this place when you're supping on a Waiheke wine or beer under the pohutukawa on the beach-gazing deck.

4th Avenue Eatery & Bar PUB, CAFE
(www.fourthavenue.co.nz; 1 Fourth Ave, Onetangi) Part bar and part bistro, all served up with cool and classy decor and Onetangi Beach views from the sunny deck. There's a good selection of tap beers and decent shared plates and platters ($20 to $49).

ℹ️ Information

Waiheke Island i-SITE (☑09-372 1234; www.waihekenz.com; 118 Ocean View Rd; ⊙9am-5pm) As well as the very helpful main office, there's a (usually unstaffed) counter in the ferry terminal at Matiatia Wharf.

ℹ️ Getting There & Away

360 Discovery (☑0800 360 3472; www.360discovery.co.nz) You can pick up the 360 Discovery tourist ferry at Orapiu on its journey between Auckland and Coromandel Town. However, note that Orapiu is quite remote and not served by buses.

Fullers (☑09-367 9111; www.fullers.co.nz; return adult/child $36/18; ⊙5.20am-11.45pm Mon-Fri, 6.25am-11.45pm Sat, 7am-9.30pm Sun) Frequent passenger ferries from Auckland's Ferry Building to Matiatia Wharf (on the hour from 9am to 5pm), some via Devonport.

Sealink (☑09-300 5900; www.sealink.co.nz; adult/child/car/motorcycle return $36.50/20/152/58; ⊙4.30am-6.30pm Mon-Thu, 4.30am-8pm Fri, 6am-6.30pm Sat & Sun) Runs car ferries to Kennedy Point, mainly from Half Moon Bay (east Auckland) but some leave from Wynyard Wharf in the city. The ferry runs at least every two hours and takes 45 minutes (booking essential).

ℹ️ Getting Around

BIKE

Various bicycle routes are outlined in the *Bike Waiheke!* brochure, available from the wharf and the i-SITE; be prepared for a few hills.

Waiheke Bike Hire (☑09-372 7937; www.waihekebikehire.co.nz; Matiatia Wharf) Hires mountain bikes (half-/full day $25/35) from their base near the wharf and at the Oneroa i-SITE.

Waiheke E Bikes (☑027 467 883, 022 050 2233; www.waihekeebikes.co.nz; per day $50) Parts of Waiheke are quite hilly, so ease the load with these hybrid machines combining pedalling with electric motors. If you order two bikes, they'll pick you up and return you to the ferry for free.

BUS

The island has regular bus services, starting from **Matiatia Wharf** and heading through Oneroa (adult/child $1.60/0.80, five minutes) on their way to all the main settlements, as far west as Onetangi (adult/child $4.40/2.40, 30 minutes); see **Auckland Transport** (☑09-366 6400; www.at.govt.nz) for timetables. A day pass (adult/child $9/5.50) is available from the Fullers counter at Matiatia Wharf.

Waiheke Vineyard Hopper (☑09-367 9111; www.waihekevineyardhopper.co.nz; per person $20; ⊙Dec 26-early Feb) Handy option with dedicated shuttles travelling around eight different Waiheke vineyards every 40 minutes during summer. A $54 pass also includes ferry tickets and local Waiheke buses.

CAR, MOTORBIKE & SCOOTER

Fun Rentals (☑09-372 8001; www.funrentals.co.nz; 14a Belgium St, Ostend; per day car/scooter/4WD from $59/49/59)

Rent Me Waiheke (☑09-372 3339; www.rentmewaiheke.co.nz; 14 Ocean View Rd, Matiatia; per day cars/scooters $59/49)

Waiheke Auto Rentals (☑09-372 8998; www.waihekerentals.co.nz; Matiatia Wharf; per day car/scooter from $69/79)

Waiheke Rental Cars (☑09-372 8635; www.waihekerentalcars.co.nz; Matiatia Wharf; per day car/4WD from $59/79)

TAXI

Island Taxis (☑0800 372 4111; www.island-taxis.co.nz)

Waiheke Express Taxis (☑0800 700 789; www.waihekeexpresstaxis.co.nz)

Waiheke Independent Taxis (☑0800 300 372)

Rotoroa Island

From 1911 to 2005 the only people to have access to this blissful little island on the far side of Waiheke were the alcoholics and drug addicts who came (or were sentenced) here to dry out, and the Salvation Army staff who cared for them. In 2011, after 100 years, 82-hectare **Rotoroa** (☑ 0800 76 86 76; www.rotoroa.org.nz; access fee $5) opened to the public, giving visitors access to three sandy swimming beaches and the social history and art displays in the restored buildings of the former treatment centre. There are also three well-appointed, wildly retro holiday homes for rent ($375 to $650), and excellent hostel accommodation in dorms (per person $35) in the former Superintendent's House.

ℹ️ Getting There & Away

360 Discovery (☑ 0800 360 3472; www.360discovery.co.nz; adult/child from Auckland $49/29, from Orapiu $21/13) From Auckland the ferry takes 75 minutes, stopping at Orapiu on Waiheke Island en route. There are four boats per week from Labour Day in October to Easter (daily in January) and two boats per week over the cooler months.

Tiritiri Matangi Island

This magical, 220-hectare, predator-free **island** (www.tiritirimatangi.org.nz) is home to the tuatara (a prehistoric lizard) and lots of endangered native birds, including the very rare and colourful takahe. Other birds that can be seen here include the bellbird, stitchbird, saddleback, whitehead, kakariki, kokako, little spotted kiwi, brown teal, NZ robin, fernbird and penguins; 78 different species have been sighted in total. The saddleback was once close to extinction, with just 150 left, but now there are more than 600 on Tiritiri alone. To experience the dawn chorus in full flight, stay overnight at the **DOC bunkhouse** (☑ 09-425 7812; www.doc.govt.nz; adult/child $30/20); book well ahead and ensure there's room on the ferry.

The island was sold to the Crown in 1841, deforested, and farmed until the 1970s. Since 1984 hundreds of volunteers have planted 250,000 native trees and the forest cover has regenerated. An 1864 lighthouse stands on the eastern end of the island.

ℹ️ Getting There & Away

360 Discovery (☑ 0800 360 3472; www.360discovery.co.nz; return Auckland/Gulf Harbour $69/37; ⊗ Wed-Sun) Book a guided walk ($5) with your ferry ticket; the guides know where all the really cool birds hang out.

Motuora Island

Halfway between Tiritiri Matangi and Kawau, Motuora has 80 predator-free hectares and is used as a kiwi 'crèche'. There's a wharf on the west coast of the island, but you'll need your own boat to get here. The **DOC campsite** (☑ 027-492 8586; www.doc.govt.nz; adult/child $6/3) requires bookings and provides toilets, cold showers and water. There's also a cottage that sleeps five ($52); bring your own linen and food.

Kawau Island

POP 300

Kawau Island lies 50km north of Auckland off the Mahurangi Peninsula. There are few proper roads through the island, the residents relying mainly on boats. The main attraction is **Mansion House** (adult/child $4/2; ⊗ noon-2pm), an impressive wooden manor extended from an 1845 structure by Governor George Grey, who purchased the island in 1862. It houses a fine collection of Victoriana, including some of Grey's effects, and is surrounded by the original exotic gardens. A set of short walks (10 minutes to two hours) are signposted from Mansion House, leading to beaches, the old copper mine, and a lookout; download DOC's *Kawau Island Historic Reserve* map (www.doc.govt.nz).

🛏️ Sleeping & Eating

Kawau Lodge　　　　　　　B&B $$$
(☑ 09-422 8831; www.kawaulodge.co.nz; North Cove; s $160, d $210-245) 🏄 This ecoconscious boutique hotel has its own jetty, wraparound decks and views. Meals ($10 to $75) can be arranged, as can excursions.

Mansion House Cafe Restaurant　　CAFE $$
(☑ 09-422 8903; lunch $12-18, dinner $18-28; ⊗ hours vary) If you haven't packed a picnic, this idyllically situated eatery serves all-day breakfasts, sandwiches and hearty evening meals.

❶ Getting There & Away

Kawau Water Taxis (📞0800 111 616; www.kawaucruises.co.nz) Daily ferries from Sandspit to Kawau (adult/child return $55/31) and a water-taxi service (minimum charge $142.50). The Super Cruise (adult/child $68/30, barbecue lunch $27/15) departs Sandspit at 10.30am and circles the island, delivering the post to 75 different wharves.

Great Barrier Island

POP 860

Named Aotea (meaning cloud) by the Maori, and Great Barrier (due to its position at the edge of the Hauraki Gulf) by Captain James Cook, this rugged and exceptionally beautiful place falls in behind South, North and Stewart as NZ's fourth-largest island (285 sq km). It closely resembles the Coromandel Peninsula to which it was once joined, and like the Coromandel it was once a mining, logging and whaling centre. Those industries have long gone and today two-thirds of the island is publicly owned and managed by DOC.

Great Barrier has unspoilt beaches, hot springs, old kauri dams, a forest sanctuary and a network of tramping tracks. Because there are no possums on the island, the native bush is lush.

Although only 88km from Auckland, Great Barrier seems a world – and a good many years – away. The island has no supermarket, no electricity supply (only private solar, wind and diesel generators) and no main drainage (only septic tanks). Many roads are unsealed and petrol costs are high. Mobile-phone reception is very limited and there are no banks, ATMs or street lights.

From around mid-December to mid-January is the peak season, so make sure you book transport, accommodation and activities well in advance.

Tryphena is the main settlement, 4km from the ferry wharf at Shoal Bay. Strung out along several kilometres of coastal road, it consists of a few dozen houses and a handful of shops and accommodation places. From the wharf it's 3km to Mulberry Grove, and then another 1km over the headland to Pa Beach and the Stonewall Store (p93).

The airport is at **Claris**, 12km north of Tryphena, a small settlement with a general store, bottle shop, laundrette, garage, pharmacy and cafe.

Whangaparapara is an old timber town and the site of the island's 19th-century whaling activities. **Port Fitzroy** is the other main harbour on the west coast, a one-hour drive from Tryphena. These four main settlements have fuel available.

✘ Activities

Water Sports

The beaches on the west coast are safe, but care needs to be taken on the surf-pounded eastern beaches. **Medlands Beach**, with its wide sweep of white sand, is one of the most beautiful and accessible beaches on the island. Remote **Whangapoua**, in the northeast, requires more effort to get to, while **Kaitoke**, **Awana Bay** and **Harataonga** on the east coast are also worth a visit.

Okiwi Bar has an excellent right-hand break, while Awana has both left- and right-hand breaks. Pohutukawa trees shelter the pretty bays around Tryphena.

Diving is excellent, with shipwrecks, pinnacles, lots of fish and more than 33m visibility at some times of the year.

Hooked on Barrier DIVING, FISHING
(📞09-429 0740; www.hookedonbarrier.co.nz; 89 Hector Sanderson Rd; half-/full-day charter $700/1200) Hires out diving, snorkelling, fishing, surfing and kayaking gear, and runs fishing, diving and sightseeing charters.

Mountain Biking

With rugged scenery and relatively little traffic on the roads, mountain biking is a popular activity. There's a designated 25km ride beginning on Blind Bay Rd, Okupu, winding beneath the Ahumata cliffs before crossing Whangaparapara Rd and beginning the 15km Forest Rd ride through beautiful forest to Port Fitzroy. Cycling on other DOC walking tracks is prohibited.

Tramping

The island's very popular walking tracks are outlined in DOC's free *Great Barrier Island (Aotea Island)* booklet. Before setting out, make sure you're properly equipped with water and food, and be prepared for both sunny and wet weather.

The most popular easy walk is the 45-minute **Kaitoke Hot Springs Track**, starting from Whangaparapara Rd and leading to natural hot springs in a bush stream. Check the temperature before getting in and don't put your head under the water.

Windy Canyon, which is only a 15-minute walk from Aotea Rd, has spectacular rock outcrops and affords great views of the island. From Windy Canyon, an excellent trail continues for another two to three hours through scrubby forest to Hirakimata (Mt Hobson, 621m), the highest point on the island, with views across the Hauraki Gulf and Coromandel. Near the top of the mountain are lush forests and a few mature kauri trees that survived the logging days. From Hirakimata it is 40 minutes south to Mt Heale Hut or two hours west through forest and past a kauri driving dam to Kaiaraara Hut, where it's another 45 minutes on to Port Fitzroy.

A more challenging tramp is the hilly **Tramline Track** (five hours), which starts on Aotea Rd and follows old logging tramlines to Whangaparapara Harbour. The initial stages of this track are not maintained and in some parts the clay becomes slippery after rain.

Of a similar length, but flatter and easier walking, is the 11km **Harataonga Coastal Walk** (five hours) which heads from Harataonga Bay to Whangapoua.

Many other trails traverse the forest, taking between 30 minutes and five hours. The **Aotea Track** combines bits of other paths into a three-day walk, overnighting in each of the huts.

See p94 for details of shuttle buses to and from the trailheads.

🛏 Sleeping

Unless you're camping, Great Barrier isn't a cheap place to stay. At pretty much every price point you'll pay more than you would for a similar place elsewhere. In the off-seaon, however, rates drop considerably. **Island Accommodation** (✆09-429 0995; www.islandaccommodation.co.nz) offers a booking service, which is handy for finding self-contained houses for longer stays. Check accommodation and island information websites for packages including flights and car rental. Note that accommodation rates soar for around two weeks following Christmas and the island also gets very busy during this time.

Medlands Beach Backpackers　HOSTEL $
(✆09-429 0320; www.medlandsbeach.com; 9 Mason Rd; dm $35, d/units from $70/120) Chill out in the garden of this house on the hill, overlooking beautiful Medlands Beach. The backpackers' area is simple, with a little double cabin for romantic budgeteers at a slight remove from the rest. The self-contained houses sleep up to six.

Crossroads Lodge　HOSTEL $
(✆09-429 0889; www.xroadslodge.com; 1 Blind Bay Rd; dm/s/d $30/50/75; @🛜) This low-key backpackers is 2km from the airfield and close to forest walks and hot springs. Mountain bikes can be hired, and golf clubs can be borrowed to play on the nearby nine-hole golf course.

Kaiaraara & Mt Heale Huts　HUT $
(www.doc.govt.nz; dm per adult/child $15/7.50) These DOC huts in the Great Barrier Forest have bunk beds, cold running water, chemical toilets and a kitchen/dining area. Bring your own sleeping bag and cooking/eating equipment and book online. Mt Heale Hut sleeps 20 people and has a gas cooker, but Kaiaraara Hut (which sleeps 24) doesn't. Both must be booked in advance.

DOC Campsites　CAMPSITE $
(✆09-379 6476; www.doc.govt.nz; site per adult/child $10/5) There are campsites at Harataonga Bay, Medlands Beach, Akapoua Bay, Whangapoua, The Green (Whangaparapara) and Awana Bay. All have basic facilities, including water, cold showers (except for at The Green), toilets and a food-preparation shelter. You need to bring your own gas cooking stove as open fires are prohibited. Book in advance online.

Aotea Lodge　APARTMENT $$
(✆09-429 0628; www.aotealodge.com; 41 Medland Rd; units $100-150; 🛜) A well-tended, sunny garden surrounds these reasonably priced units, perched on the hill just above Tryphena. They range from a two-bedroom house to an unusual mezzanine unit loaded with bunks, and each has its own cooking facilities.

Shoal Bay Lodge　APARTMENT $$
(✆09-429 0890; www.shoalbaylodge.co.nz; 145 Shoal Bay Rd; apt $160-290) Hidden among the trees these comfy self-contained apartments offer sea views, bird song and solar power. Best is the three-bedroom lodge with its sunset-guzzling deck.

Tipi & Bob's Waterfront Lodge　MOTEL $$$
(✆09-429 0550; www.waterfrontlodge.co.nz; 38 Puriri Bay Rd; units $195-250) West of Tryphena, these smart motel-style units have some wonderful sea views and very helpful owners. The complex includes a restaurant and bar, and there's also a compact double room available for $135.

Great Barrier Island

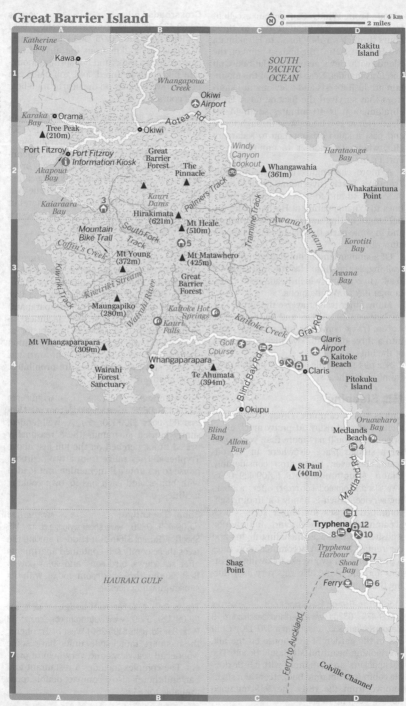

N

0 ——————————— 4 km
0 ——————————— 2 miles

Katherine Bay

Kawa ⊙

Whangapoua Creek

Okiwi Airport ✈

SOUTH PACIFIC OCEAN

Rakitu Island

Karaka Bay

Orama ⊙

Tree Peak
▲ (210m)

Okiwi ⊙

Aotea Rd

Port Fitzroy ⊙

Port Fitzroy
ⓘ Information Kiosk

Akapoua Bay

Great
Barrier
Forest

The
Pinnacle ▲

Windy Canyon Lookout 🚻

Whangawahia ▲ (361m)

Harataonga Bay

Whakatautuna
Point

Kaiaraara Bay

3

Kauri Dams

Hirakimata ▲
(621m)

Mt Heale ▲
(510m)

Palmers Track

Tramline Track

Awana Stream

Korotiti Bay

Coffin's Creek

Mountain
Bike Trail

South Fork Track

5 🏕

Mt Young ▲
(372m)

Mt Matawhero ▲
(425m)

Awana Bay

Kiwiriki Track

Kiwiriki Stream

Great
Barrier
Forest

Maungapiko ▲
(280m)

Wairahi River

Kaitoke Hot Springs ♨

Kauri
Falls

Kaitoke Creek

Gray Rd

Mt Whangaparapara ▲
(309m)

Golf
Course ⛳

2 🏨

Claris
Airport ✈

Kaitoke
Beach

9 ✕ 11 🔒

Claris

Whangaparapara ⊙

Te Ahumata ▲
(394m)

Blind Bay Rd

Pitokuku
Island

Wairahi
Forest
Sanctuary

Okupu ⊙

Blind Bay

Allom Bay

Oruawharo Bay

Medlands
Beach 🏨 4

St Paul ▲
(401m)

Medland Rd

5

HAURAKI GULF

1 🏨

Tryphena

8 🏨 12
🔒 ✕ 10

Shag
Point

Tryphena Harbour

7 🏨

Shoal Bay

Ferry ⚓

🏨 6

Ferry to Auckland

Colville Channel

Great Barrier Island

⊕ **Activities, Courses & Tours**
Hooked on Barrier .... (see 11)

🛏 **Sleeping**
1 Aotea Lodge D6
2 Crossroads Lodge C4
3 Kaiaraara Hut A2
4 Medlands Beach Backpackers............D5
5 Mt Heale Hut..B3
6 Shoal Bay Lodge D6
7 Sunset Waterfront Lodge D6
8 Tipi & Bob's Waterfront Lodge D6

✖ **Eating**
9 Claris Texas C4
Currach Irish Pub...................... (see 10)
Tipi & Bob's.................................... (see 8)
10 Wild Rose D6

🛍 **Shopping**
11 Aotea Community Art Gallery............. C4
12 Stonewall Store...................................... D6

Sunset Waterfront Lodge　　　MOTEL $$$
(☑09-429 0051; www.sunsetlodge.co.nz; Mulberry Grove; apt $195-245) Gaze across the lawn to the sea from the attractive studio units, or fight over who's going to get the pointy room in the two-bedroom A-frame villas. There's a small shop and cafe next door.

✖ Eating & Drinking

In summer, most places are open daily but for the rest of the year the hours can be sporadic. A monthly guide to opening hours is on www.thebarrier.co.nz, but it pays to call ahead for an evening meal.

Self-caterers will find small stores in Tryphena, Claris, Whangaparapara and Port Fitzroy. The **Stonewall Store** (82 Blackwell Dr; ⊕8.30am-6pm) in Tryphena has a good selection of wine, beer and locally grown produce, and also operates a small al fresco market from 10am on Saturday mornings.

Wild Rose　　　CAFE $
(☑09-429 0905; Blackwell Dr; mains $11-21; ⊕10am-3pm Wed-Sun; ☑) ✒ Wild Rose does the best impersonation of an Auckland cafe on the island, albeit with the addition of local crowd-pleasers such as toasted sandwiches and legendary burgers. It uses freerange, organic and sustainable local produce whenever possible.

Claris Texas　　　CAFE $
(129 Hector Sanderson Rd; mains $7-18; ⊕8am-4pm; 📶) While it doesn't live up to the promise of its quirky name, this is the best gap-filler in the centre of the island, serving cooked breakfasts, nachos, salads and pies.

Currach Irish Pub　　　PUB $$
(☑09-429 0211; www.currachirishpub.co.nz; Blackwell Dr; mains $19-30; ⊕from 4pm) This lively, child-friendly pub has a changing menu of seafood, steak and burgers, and is the island's main social centre. Rub shoulders with local musos on jam nights.

Tipi & Bob's　　　RESTAURANT $$$
(☑09-429 0550; www.waterfrontlodge.co.nz; 38 Puriri Bay Rd; breakfast $16-20, dinner $34-40; ⊕8.30-10am & 5.30-10pm) Serving simple but satisfying meals in large portions, this popular haunt has an inviting deck overlooking the harbour. There's a cheaper pub menu in the bar.

🛍 Shopping

Aotea Community Art Gallery　ARTS & CRAFTS
(80 Hector Sanderson Rd; ⊕10.30am-3.30pm) This eclectic showcase for the island's artsy fraternity sells everything from paintings and sculpture to handmade soap and local honey.

ⓘ Information

There's an information kiosk at the GBI Rent-A-Car office (p94) in Claris. Claris Texas cafe has internet access.

Great Barrier Island i-SITE (www. greatbarriernz.com; Claris Airport; ⊕11am-noon Mon, Wed & Fri, 8am-2.30pm Sat, extended in summer) Brochures including their own *Great Barrier Island* pamphlet with useful information and a handy map.

Port Fitzroy Information Kiosk (☑09-429 0848; www.thebarrier.co.nz; ⊕9.30am-3pm Mon-Sat) Privately run kiosk that publishes the *Great Barrier Island Visitor Information Guide*.

ⓘ Getting There & Away

AIR

FlyMySky (☑09-256 7025, 0800 222 123; www.flymysky.co.nz) Flies at least three times a day to Claris from Auckland. Cheaper flights are available if you travel to the island on a Sunday or leave on a Friday ($89), and there's a special return fare for flying one way and ferrying the other (adult/child $187/138).

Great Barrier Airlines (☑ 09-275 9120, 0800 900 600; www.greatbarrierairlines.co.nz) Departs from Auckland Domestic Airport (at least twice daily) and North Shore Aerodrome (at least daily) for the 30-minute flight to Claris. In summer it also flies from Whangarei.

Sunair (☑ 0800 786 847; www.sunair. co.nz; one way $150-190) Flies to Claris from Whitianga and Tauranga daily.

BOAT

Fullers (☑ 09-367 9111; www.fullers.co.nz; Ferry Building, 99 Quay St) Runs the fastest services (2½ hours) from Auckland's Ferry Building to Shoal Bay and Port Fitzroy from mid-December to the end of January, as well as around Labour Weekend in late October and on the Easter long weekend. Passengers only.

SeaLink (☑ 09-300 5900, 0800 732 546; www.sealink.co.nz) Runs car ferries from three to five days a week from Wynyard Wharf in Auckland to Tryphena's Shoal Bay (six hours).

ⓘ Getting Around

Most roads are narrow and windy but even small hire cars can handle the unsealed sections. Many of the accommodation places will pick you up from the airport or wharf if notified in advance.

Aotea Car Rentals (☑ 0800 426 832; www. aoteacarrentals.co.nz; Mulberry Grove) Rents cars (from $60), 4WDs (from $80) and vans (from $99). Rental clients can use Great Barrier Travel trampers shuttles for free.

GBI Rent-A-Car (☑ 09-429 0062; www.great-barrierisland.co.nz; 67 Hector Sanderson Rd) Has a somewhat battered fleet of cars starting at $40 and 4WDs from $70. They also operate shuttle services from Claris to Tryphena ($20), Medlands ($15), Whangaparapara ($20) and Port Fitzroy ($30, minimum four passengers), as well as trampers shuttles. There's a $5 flagfall for solo passengers; call ahead to book.

Great Barrier Travel (☑ 09-429 0474, 0800 426 832; www.greatbarriertravel.co.nz) Runs shuttles between Tryphena and Claris (timed to meet all the planes and boats), a daily shuttle from Claris to Port Fitzroy, and transfers to and from the walking tracks. Call ahead to confirm times and to book.

WEST AUCKLAND

West Auckland epitomises rugged: wild black-sand beaches, bush-shrouded ranges, and mullet-haired, black-T-shirt-wearing 'Westies'. The latter is just one of several stereotypes of the area's denizens. Others include the back-to-nature hippie, the eccentric bohemian artist and the dope-smoking surfer dude, all attracted to a simple life at the edge of the bush.

Add to the mix Croatian immigrants, earning the fertile fields at the base of the Waitakere Ranges the nickname 'Dallie Valley' after the Dalmatian coast where many hailed from. These pioneering families planted grapes and made wine, founding one of NZ's major industries.

Titirangi

POP 3200

This little village marks the end of Auckland's suburban sprawl and is a good place to spot all of the stereotypes mentioned above over a coffee, wine or cold beer. Once home to NZ's greatest modern painter, Colin McCahon, there remains an artsy feel to the place. Titirangi means 'Fringe of Heaven' – an apt name for the gateway to the Waitakere Ranges. This is the last stop for petrol and ATMs on your way west.

◎ Sights

McCahon House   MUSEUM
(www.mccahonhouse.org.nz; 67 Otitori Bay Rd; admission $5; ⊙10am-3pm Wed, Sat & Sun) It's a mark of the esteem in which Colin McCahon is held that the house he lived and painted in during the 1950s has been opened to the public as a mini-museum. The swish pad next door is home to the artist lucky enough to win the McCahon Arts Residency. Look for the signposts pointing down Park Rd, just before you reach Titirangi village.

Lopdell House Gallery   GALLERY
(www.lopdell.org.nz; 418 Titirangi Rd; ⊙10am-4.30pm) FREE An excellent modern art gallery housed in the former Hotel Titirangi (1930), on the edge of the village. A significant restoration from 2012–2014 has further restored the building's heritage glory.

🛏 Sleeping & Eating

Fringe of Heaven   B&B $$$
(☑ 09-817 8682; www.fringeofheaven.com; 4 Otitori Bay Rd; r $230) Surrounded by native bush, this Frank Lloyd Wright–inspired house offers glorious views over Manukau Harbour, an outdoor bath, glowworms in the garden and a songbird choir – all within 20 minutes of the city centre.

Hardware Cafe
CAFE $$

(www.hardwarecafe.org.nz; 404 Titirangi Rd; brunch $10-18, dinner $18-28; ⊙6am-4.30pm Sun-Tue, 6am-late Wed-Sat) This popular licensed cafe serves delicious, reasonably priced cooked breakfasts and lunches along with tempting counter food. More substantial evening meals start from $18.

Waitakere Ranges

This 160-sq-km wilderness was covered in kauri until the mid-19th century, when logging claimed most of the giant trees. A few stands of ancient kauri and other mature natives survive amid the dense bush of the regenerating rainforest, which is now protected inside the Waitakere Ranges Regional Park. Bordered to the west by wildly beautiful beaches on the Tasman Sea, the park's rugged terrain makes an excellent day trip from Auckland.

⊙ Sights & Activities

Arataki
VISITORS CENTRE

(☑09-817 0077; www.arc.govt.nz; Scenic Dr; ⊙9am-5pm) ⚓ As well as providing information on the 250km of trails within the park, this impressive centre also features Maori carvings and spectacular views. The carvings at the entrance depict the ancestors of the Kawerau *iwi*. You can also book here for several basic campsites (adult/child $6/4) within the park. A 1.6km nature trail opposite the centre leads visitors past labelled native species, including mature kauri.

Hillary Trail & Other Tracks
TRAMPING

(www.arc.govt.nz/hillarytrail) Arataki Vistor Centre is the starting point for this challenging 70km trail honouring Everest-conqueror Sir Edmund Hillary. It can be tackled in stages or in its four-day entirety, staying at campsites along the way. Walkers head to the coast at Huia, then continue past Whatipu, Karekare, Piha and Anawhata. From here continue up the coast to Te Henga and Muriwai, or head through bush to the Cascades Kauri to end at Swanson train station.

Other noted walks in the park include the Kitekite Track (1.8km, 30 minutes one way), the Fairy Falls Track (5.6km, 2½-hour loop) and the Auckland City Walk (1.5km, one-hour loop).

Rain Forest Express
RAILWAY

(☑09-302 8028; www.watercare.co.nz; 280 Scenic Dr; 2½hr trip adult/child $25/12) Departs from

Jacobsons' Depot and follows an old logging track through several tunnels deep into the bush. You'll need to book well ahead; check the website for the schedule. Less regular are the 3½-hour twilight trips (adult/child $28/14), offering glimpses of glowworms and cave weta.

Waitakere Tramline Society
RAILWAY

(☑09-818 4946; www.waitakeretramline.org.nz; adult/child $15/5) Runs four scenic trips every Sunday that pass through a glowworm tunnel en route to the Waitakere Falls and Dam. Trips start from the end of Christian Rd, which runs south of Swanson station. Closed temporarily at the time of writing; check the website for the latest.

AWOL Canyoning Adventures
CANYONING

(☑09-834 0501; www.awoladventures.co.nz; ⊙half-/full day $160/195) Offers plenty of slippery, slidey, wet fun in Piha Canyon and the Blue Canyon, including glowworm-illuminated night trips ($185); transfers from Auckland are included.

Karekare

Few stretches of sand have more personality than Karekare. Those prone to metaphysical musings inevitably settle on descriptions such as 'spiritual' and 'brooding'. Perhaps

---

LOCAL KNOWLEDGE

HILLARY TRAIL

My family grew up loving Auckland's wild west coast, where the Tasman Sea pounds the black-sand beaches and black-back gulls ride the westerlies. Our family has walked and explored and lived out here for nearly a century and this is also where we came to grieve after my mother and sister were killed in 1975, where the invigorating salty air and the marvellous wild vistas to the Tasman Sea worked like a balm for our broken hearts. My father would come here to dream up and then prepare for new expeditional challenges. It seemed the right sort of environment for someone like him: not a passive coastline, but active and exciting, with huge cliffs, crashing waves, thick bush and a tantalising far-away horizon.

Peter Hillary,
Mountaineer & Explorer

history has left its imprint: in 1825 it was the site of a ruthless massacre of the local Kawerau *iwi* by Ngapuhi invaders. Wild and gorgeously undeveloped, this famous beach has been the setting for onscreen moments both high- and lowbrow, from Oscar-winner *The Piano*, to *Xena, Warrior Princess*.

From the car park the quickest route to the black-sand beach involves wading through a stream. Karekare rates as one of the most dangerous beaches in the country, with strong surf and ever-present rips, so don't even think about swimming unless the beach is being patrolled by lifeguards (usually only in summer). In 1995 Pearl Jam singer Eddie Vedder nearly drowned here while visiting Neil Finn's Karekare pad.

Follow the road over the bridge and up along Lone Kauri Rd for 100m, where a short track leads to the pretty **Karekare Falls**. This leafy picnic spot is the start of several walking tracks.

Karekare has no shops of any description and no public transport. To get here take Scenic Dr and Piha Rd until you reach the well-signposted turn-off to Karekare Rd.

Piha

If you notice an Auckland surfer dude with a faraway look, chances are they're daydreaming about Piha... or just stoned. This beautifully rugged, iron-sand beach has long been a favourite for refugees from the city's stresses – whether for day trips, weekend teenage parties or family holidays.

Although Piha is popular, it's also incredibly dangerous, with wild surf and strong undercurrents; so much so that it's spawned its own popular reality TV show, *Piha Rescue*. If you don't want to inadvertently star in it, always swim between the flags, where lifeguards can provide help if you get into trouble.

Piha may be bigger and more populated than Karekare, but there's no supermarket, liquor shop, bank or petrol station, although there is a small general store that doubles as a cafe, takeaway shop and post office.

◉ Sights & Activities

The view of the coast as you drive down Piha Rd is spectacular. Perched on its haunches near the centre of the beach is **Lion Rock** (101m), whose 'mane' glows golden in the evening light. It's actually the eroded core of an ancient volcano and a Maori *pa* site. A path at the south end of the beach takes you to some great lookouts. At low tide you can walk south along the beach and watch the surf shooting through a ravine in another large rock known as the **Camel**. A little further along, the waves crash through the **Gap** and form a safe swimming hole. A small colony of blue penguins nests at the beach's north end.

For surfboard hire, refer to the Piha Store and Piha Surf Shop listings.

🛏 Sleeping & Eating

Piha Beachstay – Jandal Palace   HOSTEL $
(☑ 09-812 8381; www.pihabeachstay.co.nz; 38 Glenesk Rd; dm $33, r $80-120; @ 🛜) Attractive and ecofriendly, this wood-and-glass lodge has extremely smart facilities. It's 1km from the beach but there's a little stream at the bottom of the property and bushwalks nearby. In winter an open fire warms the large communal lounge.

Piha Domain Motor Camp   CAMPSITE $
(☑ 09-812 8815; www.pihabeach.co.nz; 21 Seaview Rd; sites from $15, s/d cabin $50/60; 🛜) Smackbang on the beach, this well-kept campsite is great for those seeking an old-fashioned, cheap-as-chips, no-frills, family holiday. To keep unruly teens at bay, under 20s must be accompanied by parents. The cabins are tiny.

Piha Surf Accommodation   CABIN $
(☑ 09-812 8723; www.pihasurf.co.nz; 122 Seaview Rd; caravans & cabins $60-90) Each basic but charmingly tatty caravan has its own linen, TV, fridge, cooker and long-drop toilet, and they share a very simple shower. The private cabins have the same rudimentary bathroom arrangement but are a more comfortable option.

Black Sands Lodge   APARTMENT $$
(☑ 021 969 924; www.pihabeach.co.nz/Black-Sands-Lodge.htm; Beach Valley Rd; cabin $130, apt $180-220; 🛜) These two modern conjoined apartments with private decks match their prime location with attractive touches such as stereos and DVD players. The cabin is kitted out in a 1950s Kiwiana bach style and shares a bathroom with the main house. Bikes and wi-fi are free for guests, and in-room massage and lavish dinners can be arranged on request.

Piha Store   BAKERY $
(Seaview Rd; snacks $2-10; ◉ 7.30am-5.30pm) Call in for pies and other baked goods, groceries and ice creams. The attached Lion Rock Surf Shop rents surfboards (two

hours/half-day/day $20/30/40) and body boards ($10/20/30).

Piha Cafe
CAFE $$

(20 Seaview Rd; mains $14-23; ⊘ 8.30am-4pm Mon-Thu, 8.30am-7pm Fri-Sun) 🍴 Big-city standards mesh seamlessly with sand-between-toes informality at this attractive ecofriendly cafe. Cooked breakfasts and crispy pizzas provide sustenance for a hard day's surfing. After the waves, head back for a cold beverage on the deck.

🛍 Shopping

West Coast Gallery
ARTS & CRAFTS

(www.westcoastgallery.co.nz; Seaview Rd; ⊘ 10am-5pm Wed-Sun) The work of more than 180 local artists is sold from this small not-for-profit gallery next to the Piha fire station.

Piha Surf Shop
OUTDOOR EQUIPMENT

(www.pihasurf.co.nz; 122 Seaview Rd; ⊘ 8am-5pm) A family-run venture, with well-known surfboard designer Mike Jolly selling his wares and wife Pam selling a small range of crafts. Surfboards (per three hours/day $25/35), wet suits ($8/15) and body boards ($15/25) can be hired, and private surfing lessons can be arranged.

ℹ Getting There & Away

There's no public transport to Piha, but **NZ Surf'n'Snow Tours** (☏ 09-828 0426; www. newzealandsurftours.com; one way $25, return trip incl surfing gear $99) provides shuttles when the surf's up. **Go Hitch** (☏ 0800 467 442; www.gohitch.co.nz; per person $40; ⊘ departs 8.30am & 10.30am Sat & Sun) also operates a Piha shuttle from downtown Auckland and Ponsonby on weekends.

Te Henga (Bethells Beach)

Breathtaking Bethells Beach is reached by taking Te Henga Rd at the northern end of Scenic Dr. It's another raw, black-sand beach with surf, windswept dunes and walks, such as the popular one over giant sand dunes to Lake Wainamu (starting near the bridge on the approach to the beach).

Kumeu & Around

West Auckland's main wine-producing area still has some vineyards owned by the original Croatian families who kick-started NZ's wine industry. The fancy eateries that have mushroomed in recent years have done lit-

tle to dint the relaxed farmland feel to the region, but everything to encourage an afternoon's indulgence on the way back from the beach or the hot pools. Most cellars offer free tastings.

🍴 Eating & Drinking

Tasting Shed
TAPAS $$

(☏ 09-412 6454; www.thetastingshed.co.nz; 609 SH16; dishes $5-24; ⊘ 4-10pm Wed & Thu, noon-11pm Fri-Sun) Complementing its rural aspect with rustic chic decor, this slick eatery conjures up delicious dishes designed to be shared. It's not strictly tapas, as the menu strays from Spain, and appropriates flavours from Asia, the Middle East, Croatia, Serbia, Italy and France.

Hallertau
BREWERY

(☏ 09-412 5555; www.hallertau.co.nz; 1171 Coatesville-Riverhead Hwy, Riverhead; shared plates $11-15, mains $24-31; ⊘ 11am-midnight) Hallertau offers tasting paddles ($14) of its craft beers served on a vine-covered terrace edging the restaurant. Regular guest beers, good food, and occasional weekend DJs and live music make it very popular with Auckland's hopheads.

Soljans Estate
WINERY

(www.soljans.co.nz; 366 SH16; mains $19-33; ⊘ tastings 9am-5.30pm, cafe 9.30am-3pm) One of the pioneering Croat-Kiwi family vineyards, Soljans has a wonderful cafe offering brunch, Dalmatian-style squid and Vintner's platters crammed with Mediterranean treats.

Riverhead
PUB

(www.theriverhead.co.nz; cnr Queen & York Sts, Riverhead; mains $20-31; ⊘ 11am-late Mon-Fri, 10am-late Sat & Sun) A blissful terrace, shaded by oak trees and overlooking the river, makes this 1857 hotel a memorable drink stop, even if the menu doesn't quite live up to its gastropub ambitions. Make a day of it, with a boat cruise (p60) from the city to the pub's own jetty.

Kumeu River
WINERY

(www.kumeuriver.co.nz; 550 SH16; ⊘ 9am-5pm Mon-Fri, 11am-5pm Sat) Owned by the Brajkovich family, this winery produces one of NZ's best chardonnays, among other varietals.

Coopers Creek
WINERY

(www.cooperscreek.co.nz; 601 SH16, Huapai; ⊘ 10.30am-5.30pm) Buy a bottle, spread out a picnic in the attractive gardens and, from January to Easter, enjoy Sunday afternoon jazz sessions.

ⓘ Getting There & Away

From central Auckland, Kumeu is 25km up the Northwestern Motorway (SH16). Helensville-bound buses head here from Lower Albert St (adult/child $7.90/4.50, 50 minutes), but you'll really need a car or bike to get around.

Muriwai Beach

Yet another rugged black-sand surf beach, stretching 60km, Muriwai Beach's main claim to fame is the **Takapu Refuge gannet colony**, spread over the southern headland and outlying rock stacks. Viewing platforms get you close enough to watch (and smell) these fascinating seabirds. Every August hundreds of adult birds return to this spot to hook up with their regular partners and get busy – expect lots of outrageously cute neck-rubbing, bill-touching and general snuggling. The net result is a single chick per season; December and January are the best times to see the little fellas testing their wings before embarking on an impressive odyssey.

Nearby, a couple of short tracks will take you through beautiful native bush to a lookout that offers views along the length of the beach. Wild surf and treacherous rips mean that swimming is safe only when the beach is patrolled (swim between the flags). Apart from surfing, Muriwai Beach is a popular spot for hang gliding, parapunting, kiteboarding and horse riding. There are also

---

THE GREAT GANNET OE

After honing their flying skills, young gannets get the ultimate chance to test them – a 2000km journey to Australia. They usually hang out there for several years before returning home, never to attempt the journey again. Once back in the homeland they spend a few years waiting for a piece of waterfront property to become available in the colony, before settling down with a regular partner to nest – returning to the same patch of dirt every year. In other words, they're your typical New Zealander on their OE (Overseas Experience). Why are they called Kiwis again?

---

tennis courts, a golf course and a cafe that doubles as a takeaway chippie.

Helensville

POP 2600

A smattering of heritage buildings, antique shops and cafes makes village-like Helensville a good whistle-stop for those taking SH16 north.

🏃 Activities

Parakai Springs   THERMAL POOLS
(www.parakaisprings.co.nz; 150 Parkhurst Rd; adult/child $20/10; ⊙10am-9pm) Aucklanders bring their bored children to Parakai, 2km northwest of Helensville, on wet wintry days as a cheaper alternative to Waiwera. It has large thermally heated swimming pools, private spas ($8 per hour) and a couple of hydroslides.

**Woodhill Mountain
Bike Park**   MOUNTAIN BIKING
(☑027 278 0949; www.bikepark.co.nz; Restall Rd, Woodhill; adult/child $7/2, bike hire per hr $30; ⊙9am-5pm Thu-Tue, 10am-10pm Wed) Maintains many challenging tracks (including jumps and beams) within Woodhill Forest, 14km south of Helensville.

Tree Adventures   OUTDOORS
(☑0800 827 926; www.treeadventures.co.nz; Restall Rd, Woodhill; courses $16-40; ⊙9.30am-5.30pm) A set of high-ropes courses within Woodhill Forest, consisting of swinging logs, nets, balance beams, Tarzan swings and a flying fox.

4 Track Adventures   QUAD BIKES
(☑09-420 8104; www.4trackadventures. co.nz; Restall Rd, Woodhill; 1½/2½/3½hr tours $155/255/295) Rattle through Woodhill Forest (and along Muriwai Beach on the longer tours) on a quad bike. Pick up from Auckland is available at $50 per person.

ⓘ Information

Helensville Library (Commercial Rd; 🛜)
Visitor Information Centre (☑09-420 8060; www.helensville.co.nz; 87 Commercial Rd; ⊙10am-4pm Mon-Sat) Pick up free brochures detailing the *Helensville Heritage Trail* and *Helensville Riverside Walkway*.

ⓘ Getting There & Away

Bus 60 heads from Lower Albert St in Auckland (near Britomart) to Helensville ($10.30, 1½ hours).

NORTH AUCKLAND

The Auckland supercity sprawls 90km north of the CBD to just past the point where SH16 and SH1 converge at Wellsford. Beaches, regional parks, tramping trails, quaint villages, wine, kayaking and snorkelling are the main drawcards.

Long Bay Regional Park

The northernmost of Auckland's east coast bays, Long Bay is a popular family picnic and swimming spot, attracting over a million visitors a year. A three-hour-return coastal walk heads north from the sandy beach to the Okura River, taking in secluded Grannys Bay and Pohutukawa Bay (which attracts nude bathers).

Regular buses head to Long Bay from Albert St in the city (adult/child $6.80/4, one hour). If you're driving, leave the Northern Motorway at the Oteha Valley Rd exit, head towards Browns Bay and follow the signs.

Shakespear Regional Park

Shooting out eastward just before Orewa, the Whangaparaoa Peninsula is a heavily developed spit of land with a sizable South African expat community. At its tip is this gorgeous 376-hectare regional park, its native wildlife protected by a 1.7km pest-proof fence.

Sheep, cows, peacocks and pukeko ramble over the grassy headland, while pohutukawa-lined Te Haruhi Bay provides great views of the gulf islands and the city. Walking tracks take between 40 minutes and two hours, exploring native forest, WWII gun embankments, Maori sites and lookouts. If you can't bear to leave, there's an idyllic beachfront campsite (☏09-301 0101; www.arc.govt.nz; adult/child $13/6) with flush toilets and cold showers.

It's possible to get here via a torturous two-hour bus trip from Albert St. The one-way fare is $10.30, so it's best to buy a $16 Discovery day pass. An alternative is to take the 360 Discovery (☏0800 360 3472; www.360discovery.co.nz; adult/child $14/8.30) ferry service to Gulf Harbour, a Noddytown development of matching townhouses, a marina, country club and golf course. Enquire at the ferry office about picking up a bus or taxi from here. Alternatively, walk or cycle the remaining 3km to the park. The ferry is a good option for cyclists wanting to

skip the boring road trip out of Auckland; carry-on bikes are free.

Orewa

POP 7400

Locals have fears that Orewa is turning into NZ's equivalent of Queensland's Gold Coast, but until they start exporting retirees and replacing them with bikini-clad parking wardens that's unlikely to happen. It is, however, very built-up and high-rise apartment towers have begun to sprout.

◎ Sights & Activities

Orewa Beach   BEACH
Orewa's 3km-long stretch of sand is its main drawcard. Being in the gulf, it's sheltered from the surf but it's still patrolled by lifeguards in the peak season.

Alice Eaves Scenic Reserve   FOREST
(Old North Rd) Ten hectares of native bush with labelled trees, a *pa* site, a lookout and easy short walks.

Millennium Walkway   WALKING
Starting from South Bridge this 8km route loops through various parks before returning along the beach; follow the blue route markers.

Snowplanet   SNOW SPORTS
(www.snowplanet.co.nz; 91 Small Rd, Silverdale; day pass adult/child $66/47; ◎10am-10pm Sat-Thu, 10am-midnight Fri) Snowplanet offers indoor skiing, tobogganing and snowboarding throughout the year. It's just off SH1, 8km south of Orewa.

⌬ Sleeping

Orewa Beach Top 10   HOLIDAY PARK $
(☏09-426 5832; www.orewaholidaypark.co.nz; 265 Hibiscus Coast Hwy; sites $40, units $60-115; @) ✦ Taking up a large chunk of the beach's south end, this well-kept park has excellent facilities but road noise can be a problem.

Orewa Motor Lodge   MOTEL $$
(☏09-426 4027; www.orewamotorlodge.co.nz; 290 Hibicus Coast Hwy; units $170-190; ☏) One of the motels lining Orewa's main road, this complex has scrupulously clean wooden units prettied up with hanging flower baskets. There's also a spa pool.

Waves   APARTMENT $$$
(☏09-427 0888; www.waves.co.nz; cnr Hibiscus Coast Hwy & Kohu St; units $175-299; ☏) Like a

ℹ WHICH HIGHWAY?

From Auckland, the multilane Northern Motorway (SH1) bypasses Orewa and Waiwera on a **tolled section** (☑0800 40 20 20; www.tollroad.govt.nz; per car & motorbike $2.20). It will save you about 10 minutes, provided you pay online or by phone (in advance or within five days of your journey) rather than stopping to queue at the toll booths.

Between Christmas and New Year SH1 can be terribly gridlocked heading north between the toll road and Wellsford; SH16 through Kumeu and Helensville is a sensible alternative. The same is true if heading south in the first few days of the New Year.

motel only much flasher, this complex offers spacious, self-contained apartments, and the downstairs units have gardens and spa baths. It's only a few metres from the beach.

 Eating

Asahi　　　　　　　　　　　　JAPANESE $
(6 Bakehouse Lane; mains $11-20; �9am-3pm Mon, 9am-9pm Tue-Sat) Excellent for a sushi fix, with good bento boxes ($21.50).

Casablanca　　　　　　　TURKISH, CAFE $$
(www.casablancacafenz.co.nz; 336 Hibiscus Coast Hwy; mains $13-30; � 10am-late Mon-Fri, 9am-late Sat & Sun) Turkish, North African and Mediterranean flavours feature at this buzzy cafe. Try the hearty baked Moorish eggs and you'll be set for the next chapter of your Kiwi road trip.

ℹ Information

Orewa Information Centre (☑09-426 5338; www.orewabeach.co.nz; 40-46 Orewa Sq; �९am-3.30pm Mon-Fri, 10am-noon Sat) Part of the local Citizens Advice Bureau.

ℹ Getting There & Away

Direct buses run between Orewa and Albert St in the city (adult/child $10.30/6.10, 1¼ hours), as well as Shakespear Regional Park (adult/child $1.90/1.10, 50 minutes) and Waiwera (adult/child $1.90/1.10, 10 minutes).

Waiwera

This pleasant river-mouth village has a great beach, but it's the *wai wera* (hot waters) that people come here for. Warm mineral water bubbles up from 1500m below the surface to fill the 19 pools of the **Waiwera Thermal Resort** (☑09-427 8800; www.waiwera.co.nz; 21 Main Rd; adult/child $26/15; �9am-9pm). There's a movie pool, 10 big slides, barbecues, private tubs ($40) and a health spa. Luxury modern houses have also been built nearby (doubles $180); enquire about indulgence packages.

Squeezed between the Waiwera and Puhoi Rivers, the exquisite 134-hectare **Wenderholm Regional Park** (☑09-366 2000; www.arc.govt.nz; sites per adult/child $13/6, houses $120-145) has a diverse ecology, abundant bird life, beaches and walks (30 minutes to 2½ hours). **Couldrey House** (www.historicouldreyhouse.co.nz; adult/child $5/free; �1-4pm Sat & Sun, daily Jan), the original homestead dating from the 1860s, is now a museum. The campsite provides only tap water and long-drop toilets, and the council also rents two comfortable self-contained houses.

Bus 895 from Auckland's Albert St heads to Waiwera (adult/child $10.30/6.10, one hour) via Orewa.

Puhoi

POP 450

Forget dingy cafes and earnest poets – this quaint village is a slice of the real Bohemia. In 1863 around 200 German-speaking immigrants from the present-day Czech Republic settled in what was then dense bush.

◉ Sights & Activities

Church of Sts Peter & Paul　　　　CHURCH
(www.holyname.org.nz; Puhoi Rd) The village's pretty Catholic church dates from 1881 and has an interesting tabernacle painting (a copy of one in Bohemia), stained glass and statues.

Bohemian Museum　　　　　　　MUSEUM
(www.puhoihistoricalsociety.org.nz; Puhoi Rd; adult/child $3/free; �(1-4pm Sat & Sun, daily Christmas-Easter) Tells the story of the hardship and perseverance of the original Bohemian pioneers.

Puhoi River Canoe Hire　　　　CANOEING
(☑09-422 0891; www.puhoirivercanoes.co.nz; 84 Puhoi Rd) ✿ Hires kayaks and Canadian canoes, either by the hour (kayak/canoe $25/50) or for an excellent 8km downstream journey from the village to Wenderholm Regional Park (single/double kayak $50/100, including return transport). Bookings are essential.

✕ Eating & Drinking

Puhoi Valley   CAFE $$
(www.puhoivalley.co.nz; 275 Ahuroa Rd; mains $13-22; ⊙10am-4pm) Renowned across NZ, Puhoi Valley cheese features heavily on the menu of this upmarket cheese shop and cafe, set blissfully alongside a lake, fountain and children's playground. In the summer there's music on the lawn, perfect with a gourmet ice cream.

Puhoi Hotel   PUB
(www.puhoipub.co.nz; cnr Saleyards & Puhoi Rds; ⊙10am-10pm) There's character and then some in this 1879 pub, with walls completely covered in old photos, animal heads and vintage household goods.

Puhoi Cottage   TEAHOUSE
(www.puhoicottage.co.nz; 50 Ahuroa Rd; ⊙10am-4pm Fri-Sun) Drop in for a Devonshire cream tea ($11).

❶ Getting There & Away

Puhoi is 1km west of SH1. The turn-off is 2km past the Johnstone Hills tunnel.

Mahurangi & Scandrett Regional Parks

Straddling the head of Mahurangi Harbour, **Mahurangi Regional Park** (✆09-366 2000; www.arc.govt.nz; sites from $6, baches $120-145) has three distinct fingers: Mahurangi West, accessed from a turn-off 3km north of Puhoi; Scott Point on the eastern side, with road access 16km southeast of Warkworth; and isolated Mahurangi East, which can only be reached by boat. This boater's paradise incorporates areas of coastal forest, *pa* sites and a historic homestead and cemetery. Its

sheltered beaches offer prime sandy spots for a dip or picnic and there are loop walks ranging from 1½ to 2½ hours. Accommodation is available in four basic campsites and four baches sleeping six to eight. Campervans can also park for $6 per person.

On the way to Mahurangi West you'll pass **Zealandia Sculpture Garden** (✆09-422 0099; www.zealandiasculpturegarden.co.nz; 138 Mahurangi West Rd; admission $10; ⊙by appointment Nov-Mar), where the work of Terry Stringer is showcased within impressive architecture and grounds.

On the ocean side of the Mahurangi Peninsula, **Scandrett Regional Park** (✆09-366 2000; www.arc.govt.nz; bach $145) has a sandy beach, walking tracks, patches of regenerating forest, another historic homestead, more *pa* sites and great views towards Kawau Island. Three baches (sleeping six to eight) are available for rent and there's room for campervans ($6 per person).

Warkworth

POP 3300
River-hugging Warkworth makes a pleasant pit stop, its dinky main street retaining a village atmosphere.

◉ Sights

Dome Forest   FOREST
(SH1) Two kilometres north of Warkworth, a track leads through this regenerating forest to the Dome summit (336m). On a fine day you can see the Sky Tower from a lookout near the top. The summit walk takes about 1½ hours return, or you can continue for a gruelling seven-hour one-way tramp through the Totara Peak Scenic Reserve, exiting on Govan Wilson Rd.

WORTH A TRIP

TE HANA TE AO MARAMA

You'll see the terraces of a lot of historic *pa* (fortified village) sites etched into hillsides all around NZ, but if you want to get an idea of how these fortified villages actually looked, take a guided tour of the re-created *pa* at **Te Hana Te Ao Marama** (www.tehana.co.nz; 307-308 SH1, Te Hana). Tours leave on the hour from 10am to 3pm daily (adult/child $25/13). The daytime tours can be combined with a *powhiri* (formal welcome) on to the very real *marae* next door, with some packages including a meal and a cultural concert.

For the most atmospheric experience, take one of the Friday night *Starlight Tours* (adult/child $100/50, bus from Auckland $25 extra), where you'll be on the receiving end of a *powhiri*, have a meal within the *marae* complex and then proceed into the dramatically lit village for a guided tour and concert.

Sheepworld FARM
(www.sheepworldfarm.co.nz; SH1; adult/child $15/8, incl show $28/10; ⊙9am-5pm) This agricultural attraction offers farm experiences for little city slickers (pony rides, lamb feeding) and the ubiquitous sheep and dog show, including a shearing demonstration (showtimes 11am and 2pm).

Warkworth & District Museum MUSEUM
(www.wwmuseum.orcon.net.nz; Tudor Collins Dr; adult/child $8/2; ⊙9am-3pm) Pioneer-era detritus is displayed at this small local museum. Of more interest is the surrounding **Parry Kauri Park**, which harbours a couple of giant kauri trees, including the 800-year-old McKinney kauri (girth 7.6m).

✖ Eating & Drinking

Chocolate Brown CAFE, SWEETS $$
(www.chocolatebrown.co.nz; 6 Mill Lane; mains $10-20; ⊙8.30am-4pm) Decked out with quirky NZ-themed art – mostly for sale – this cafe turns out excellent coffee, robust eggy breakfasts and delicious homestyle baking. Definitely leave room for a few cacao-infused goodies from the chocolate shop next door; there are also plenty of gift packs for the folks back home.

Ransom Wines WINERY
(www.ransomwines.co.nz; Valerie Close; tasting with purchase free, otherwise donation to Tawharanui Open Sanctuary $5; ⊙10am-5pm Tue-Sun) Well signposted from SH1, about 3km south of Warkworth, Ransom produces great food wines and showcases them with good-value tasting platters (per person $20), crammed with smoked meats and local cheeses. A tasting flight of five wines is $12.

Tahi Bar CRAFT BEER
(www.tahibar.com; 1 Neville St; ⊙noon-late Wed-Sun) Tucked down a quiet laneway, Tahi features eight ever-changing taps of New Zealand craft beer. It's an exceptionally friendly spot with decent platters and pub grub and a rustic and sunny deck.

🔒 Shopping

Honey Centre FOOD
(www.honeycentre.co.nz; cnr SH1 & Perry Rd; ⊙8.30am-5pm) About 5km south of Warkworth, the Honey Centre makes a diverting pit stop, with its cafe, free honey tasting and glass-fronted hives. The shop sells all sorts of bee-related products, from candles to mead.

ℹ Information

Warkworth i-SITE (☎09-425 9081; www.warkworthnz.com; 1 Baxter St; ⊙8.30am-5pm Mon-Fri, 9am-3pm Sat & Sun)

ℹ Getting There & Away

InterCity (☎09-583 5780; www.intercity.co.nz) and **Naked Bus** (www.nakedbus.com) services both pass through town, en route between Auckland and the Bay of Islands.

Matakana & Around

Around 15 years ago, Matakana was a nondescript rural village with a handful of heritage buildings and an old-fashioned country pub. Now the locals watch bemused as Auckland's chattering classes idle away the hours in stylish wine bars and cafes. The striking **Matakana Cinemas** (☎09-422 9833; www.matakanacinemas.co.nz; 2 Matakana Valley Rd) complex has a domed roof reminiscent of an Ottoman bathhouse, and an excellent **farmers market** (www.matakanavillage.co.nz; ⊙8am-1pm Sat) is held in its shadow.

The reason for this growth is the area's boutique wineries, which are developing a name for pinot gris, merlot, syrah and a host of obscure varietals. Local vineyards are detailed in the free *Matakana Coast Wine Country* (www.matakanacoast.com) and *Matakana Wine Trail* (www.matakanawine.com) brochures. Both are available from the Matakana Information Centre in the foyer of the cinema.

◉ Sights & Activities

★ **Tawharanui Regional Park** BEACH
(☎09-366 2000; www.arc.govt.nz; Takatu Rd) A partly unsealed road leads to this 588-hectare reserve at the end of a peninsula. This special place is an open sanctuary for native birds, protected by a pest-proof fence, while the northern coast is a marine park (bring a snorkel). There are plenty of walking tracks (1½ to four hours) but the main attraction is **Anchor Bay**, one of the region's finest white-sand beaches. Camping is allowed at two basic sites near the beach (adult/child $13/6) and there's a six-person bach for hire ($145).

Blue Adventures WATER SPORTS
(☎022 630 5705; www.blueadventures.co.nz; lessons per hour $60-75) Based in Matakana, but offering kitesurfing, paddle boarding and

wakeboarding lessons, and tours from Auckland to Mangawhai. Also jetboat tours (per person $75 to $300) along the Matakana coast.

Matakana Cycle Hire BICYCLE RENTAL
(☑09-423 0076; www.matakanabicyclerental.co.nz; 951 Matakana Rd; half-/full-day hire $30/40, tours from $60) Bike hire to explore local vineyards and beaches.

Omaha Beach BEACH
The nearest swimming beach to Matakana, Omaha has a long stretch of white sand, good surf and ritzy holiday homes.

Brick Bay Sculpture Trail PARK
(www.brickbaysculpture.co.nz; Arabella Lane, Snells Beach; adult/child $12/8; ⊙10am-5pm) After taking an hour-long artistic ramble through the beautiful grounds of Brick Bay Wines, recuperate with a wine tasting at the architecturally impressive cafe.

Morris & James ARTS & CRAFTS
(www.morrisandjames.co.nz; 48 Tongue Farm Rd; ⊙9am-5pm) FREE Watch the potters at work during the free daily tour (11.30am) or just call in to check out the colourful finished products and the courtyard cafe.

🛏 Sleeping

Sandspit Holiday Park HOLIDAY PARK $
(☑09-425 8610; www.sandspitholidaypark.co.nz; 1334 Sandspit Rd; sites from $17, units $70-120; @🛜) A camping ground masquerading as a pioneer village, this place incorporates historic buildings and faux shopfronts into its facilities. It's right by the water at Sandspit.

Matakana Country Lodge B&B $$$
(☑09-422 3553; www.matakanacountry.co.nz; 149 Anderson Rd; r $275-375; 🛜🐾) It's only five minutes from Matakana by way of an unsealed road and a long driveway, but this lodge offers tranquillity in bucketloads and expansive views over the countryside. The three guest rooms have the run of the entire villa, including the kitchen, pool and spa.

🍴 Eating & Drinking

Charlie's Gelato Garden ICE CREAM $
(www.charliesgelato.co.nz; 17 Sharp Rd; ice cream $4-6, pizza from $5; ⊙9am-5pm, reduced hours in winter) Superb sorbet and gelato made from fresh fruit and interesting ingredients – try the liquorice or ginger beer flavours – and excellent wood-fired pizzas during summer from Friday to Sunday.

**Mahurangi River
Winery & Restaurant** WINERY $$$
(☑09-425 0306; www.mahurangiriver.co.nz; 162 Hamilton Rd; mains $24-36, platters $25-45; ⊙11am-4pm Thu-Mon Feb-Dec, 11am-4pm daily Jan) Expansive vineyard views partner with a relaxed ambience and savvy food at this rural spot off Sandspit Rd.

The Matakana PUB $$
(www.matakana.co.nz; 11 Matakana Valley Rd; mains $17-25; ⊙noon-late) Following a trendy makeover, Matakana's heritage pub now features quirky decor, Matakana wines and craft beers, and decent bistro food including local Mahurangi oysters. Occasional DJs and live acts enliven the cool outdoor space.

Plume WINERY $$
(☑09-422 7915; www.plumerestaurant.co.nz; 49a Sharp Rd; mains $29-40; ⊙11am-3pm Wed-Sun, 6pm-late Fri & Sat) Plume has rural views from its terrace and an adventurous menu that jumps from China to Spain by way of Thailand and India.

Vintry WINE BAR
(☑09-423 0251; www.thevintry.co.nz; 2 Matakana Valley Rd; tastings from $5; ⊙10am-10pm) In the Matakana Cinemas complex, this wine bar serves as a one-stop cellar door for all the local producers.

ℹ Information

Matakana Information Centre (☑09-422 7433; www.matakanainfo.org.nz; 2 Matakana Valley Rd; ⊙10am-1pm) In the foyer of the cinema complex.

ℹ Getting There & Away

Matakana village is a 10km drive northeast of Warkworth along Matakana Rd; there's no public transport. Ferries for Kawau Island leave from Sandspit, 8km east of Warkworth along Sandspit Rd.

Leigh
POP 390

Appealing little Leigh (www.leighbythesea.co.nz) has a picturesque harbour dotted with fishing boats, and a decent swimming beach at Matheson Bay. Long-standing Goat Island Dive & Snorkel (☑0800 348 369; www.goatislanddive.co.nz; 142a Pakiri Rd; mask, snorkel & fin hire $22, dive trips incl equipment $110-250, PADI Open Water $499) offers PADI courses and boat dive trips in the Hauraki Gulf throughout the year.

Apart from its proximity to Goat Island, the town's other claim to fame is the legendary **Leigh Sawmill** (☑09-422 6019; www.sawmillcafe.co.nz; 142 Pakiri Rd; mains $14-35; ⊙10am-late daily Jan–mid-Feb, 10am-3pm Mon-Wed & 10am-late Thu-Sun mid-Feb–Mar, 10am-late Thu-Sun Apr-Nov), a spunky little pub and beer garden that's a regular stop on the summer rock circuit, sometimes attracting surprisingly big names. If you imbibe too much at the on-site **microbrewery** (⊙1.30-5pm Fri & Sat), there's accommodation inside the old sawmill shed, including basic backpacker rooms (from $25) and massive doubles with en suites (from $125). Alternatively, you can rent the Cosy Sawmill Family Cottage (from $300, sleeps 10).

Goat Island Marine Reserve

Only 3km from Leigh, this 547-hectare aquatic area was established in 1975 as the country's first marine reserve. In less than 40 years the sea has reverted to a giant aquarium, giving an impression of what the NZ coast must have been like before humans arrived. You only need step knee deep into the water to see snapper (the big fish with blue dots and fins), blue maomao and stripy parore swimming around. There are dive areas all round Goat Island, which sits just offshore, or you can snorkel or dive directly from the beach.

Excellent interpretive panels explain the area's Maori significance (it was the landing place of one of the ancestral canoes) and provide pictures of the species you're likely to encounter. Colourful sponges, forests of seaweed, boarfish, crayfish and stingrays are common sights, and if you're very lucky you may see orcas and bottle-nosed dolphins. Visibility is claimed to be at least 10m, 75% of the time.

A **glass-bottomed boat** (☑09-422 6334; www.glassbottomboat.co.nz; adult/child $28/15) provides an opportunity to see the underwater life while staying dry. Trips last 45 minutes and run from the beach all year round, weather permitting; ring to check conditions and to book.

Staffed by marine experts and graduate students from the University of Auckland, the recently opened **Goat Island Marine Discovery Centre** (☑09-923 3645; www.goatislandmarine.co.nz; Goat Island Rd, Leigh; adult/child/family $10/5/20; ⊙10am-4pm daily mid-Dec–March) is packed with interesting exhibitions on the ecosystem of the marine reserve, and is definitely worth visiting before venturing into Goat Island's waters. The interactive displays and the tide pool full of marine creatures is great for children. Phone ahead for opening hours outside of mid-December to March.

You can usually rent kayaks and snorkelling gear right from the beach. Snorkelling gear (from $9) and wetsuits (from $12) can also be hired at **Seafriends** (☑09-422 6212; www.seafriends.org.nz; 7 Goat Island Rd; ⊙9am-7pm), further up the road, which also has saltwater aquariums and a cafe.

Pakiri

Blissful Pakiri Beach, 12km past Goat Island (4km of the road is unsealed), is an unspoilt expanse of white sand and rolling surf – a large chunk of which is protected as a regional park.

Right by the water, **Pakiri Beach Holiday Park** (☑09-422 6199; www.pakiriholidaypark.co.nz; 261 Pakiri River Rd; sites from $50, units $80-400) has a shop and tidy units of varying degrees of luxury in a secure setting under the shade of pohutukawa.

Just 6km on from Pakiri is **Pakiri Horse Riding** (☑09-422 6275; www.horseride-nz.co.nz; Rahuikiri Rd), which has more than 80 horses available for superb bush-and-beach rides, ranging from one hour ($65) to multiday 'safaris'. Accommodation is provided in basic but spectacularly situated beachside **cabins** (dm/cabin $35/155) or in a comfortable four-bedroom **house** ($500), secluded among the dunes.

Bay of Islands & Northland

🗐 09

Includes ➡

Mangawhai 108

Waipu & Bream Bay .. 109

Whangarei 110

Tutukaka Coast & the
Poor Knights Islands.. 115

Russell Road 117

Bay of Islands 118

Russell 122

Paihia & Waitangi 125

Kerikeri 129

Cape Reinga &
Ninety Mile Beach 136

Hokianga 140

Kauri Coast 143

Best Places to Eat

➡ à Deco (p114)

➡ Havana Cabana (p117)

➡ Bennetts (p109)

➡ Food at Wharepuke (p132)

Best Places to Stay

➡ Endless Summer Lodge (p139)

➡ Relax a Lodge (p130)

➡ Tree House (p140)

➡ Kahoe Farms Hostel (p134)

Why Go?

For many New Zealanders, the phrase 'up north' conjures up sepia-toned images of family fun in the sun, pohutukawa in bloom and dolphins frolicking in pretty bays. From school playgrounds to work cafeterias, owning a bach (holiday house) 'up north' is a passport to popularity.

Beaches are the main drawcard and they're here in profusion. Visitors from more crowded countries are flummoxed to wander onto beaches without a scrap of development or another human being in sight. The west coast shelters the most spectacular remnants of the ancient kauri forests that once blanketed the top of the country; the remaining giant trees are an awe-inspiring sight and one of the nation's treasures.

It's not just natural attractions that are on offer: history hangs heavily here. The site of the earliest settlements of both Maori and Europeans, Northland is unquestionably the birthplace of the nation.

When to Go

➡ Northland's beaches go crazy at New Year and remain busy throughout the January school holidays, with the long, lazy days of summer usually continuing into February and March.

➡ The 'winterless north' boasts a subtropical climate, most noticeable from Kerikeri upwards, which averages seven rainy days per month in summer but 16 in winter.

➡ In winter the average highs hover around 16°C and the average lows around 7°C.

➡ Temperatures are often a degree or two warmer than Auckland, especially on the east coast.

Bay of Islands & Northland Highlights

1 Splashing about, body surfing, sunbathing and strolling at **Matauri Bay** (p132)

2 Watching oceans collide while souls depart at **Cape Reinga** (p136)

3 Paying homage to the ancient kauri giants of the **Waipoua Forest** (p143)

4 Diving at one of the world's top spots, the **Poor Knights Islands** (p115)

5 Frolicking with dolphins and claiming your own island paradise among the many in the **Bay of Islands** (p118)

6 Surfing the sand dunes at **Ninety Mile Beach** (p136) or Hokianga's **North Head** (p140)

7 Delving into history and culture at the **Waitangi Treaty Grounds** (p126)

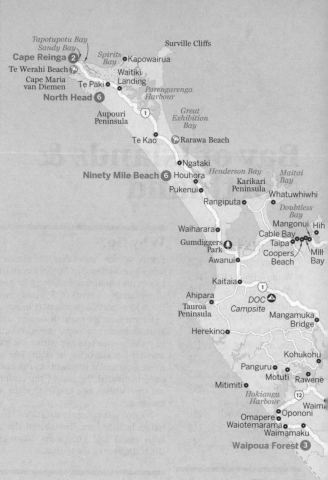

Tapotupotu Bay
Sandy Bay
Cape Reinga 2
Te Werahi Beach
Cape Maria
van Diemen
North Head 6
Spirits
Bay
Kapowairua
Waitiki
Landing
Te Paki
Surville Cliffs
Parengarenga
Harbour
Aupouri
Peninsula
Great
Exhibition
Bay
Te Kao
Rarawa Beach
Ngataki
Ninety Mile Beach 6 Houhora
Pukenui
Henderson Bay
Karikari
Peninsula
Maitai
Bay
Whatuwhiwhi
Rangiputa
Doubtless
Bay
Waiharara
Gumdiggers
Park
Awanui
Mangonui Hih
Cable Bay
Taipa
Coopers
Beach
Mill
Bay
Kaitaia
Ahipara
Tauroa
Peninsula
DOC
Campsite
Mangamuka
Bridge
Herekino
Kohukohu
Panguru
Mitimiti
Motuti
Rawene
Hokianga
Harbour
Omapere
Waiotemarama
Opononi
Waima
Waimamaku
Waipoua Forest 3

TASMAN
SEA

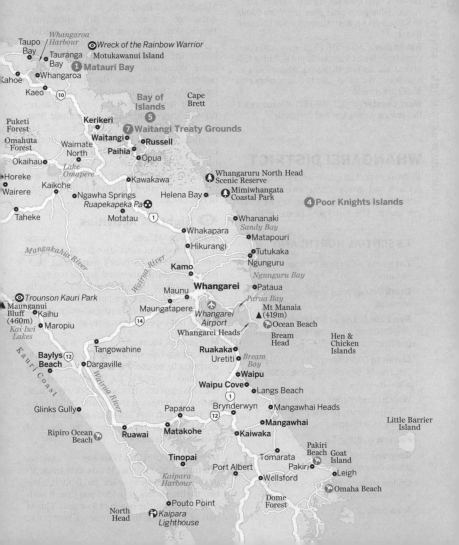

SOUTH PACIFIC OCEAN

0 — 50 km
0 — 25 miles

Whangaroa Harbour

Taupo Bay
Tauranga Bay
Whangaroa
Kahoe
Kaeo

1 Matauri Bay

● Wreck of the Rainbow Warrior
○ Motukawanui Island

10

Puketi Forest
Omahuta Forest
Okaihau
Horeke
Wairere
Taheke

Kerikeri
7 Waitangi Treaty Grounds
Waitangi
Waimate North
Lake Omapere
Paihia
● **Russell**
Opua

Bay of Islands
5

Cape Brett

Kaikohe
Kawakawa
Ngawha Springs
Ruapekapeka Pa
Motatau

1

⬧ Whangaruru North Head Scenic Reserve
⬧ Mimiwhangata Coastal Park
Helena Bay

4 Poor Knights Islands

Mangakahia River
Whakapara
Hikurangi
Sandy Bay
Whananaki
Matapouri
Tutukaka
Ngunguru

Kamo

Waitma River

Ngunguru Bay

Maunu
Whangarei
Pataua

Trounson Kauri Park
▲ Maunganui Bluff (460m)
Maropiu
Kai Iwi Lakes

Maungatapere
Whangarei Airport
Whangarei Heads

Parua Bay
Mt Manaia ▲ (419m)
○ Ocean Beach

Bream Head

Hen & Chicken Islands

14

Tangowahine
Baylys Beach 12
Dargaville

Ruakaka
Uretiti
Bream Bay

Waitma River

Glinks Gully

Waipu
Waipu Cove
Langs Beach
Mangawhai Heads

Paparoa
Brynderwyn
Mangawhai

Little Barrier Island

Ripiro Ocean Beach
Ruawai
Matakohe
Kaiwaka

12

Pakiri Beach
Goat Island

Tinopai
Tomarata
Pakiri
Leigh

Port Albert
Wellsford
○ Omaha Beach

Kaipara Harbour

North Head
● Pouto Point
Kaipara Lighthouse

Dome Forest

ℹ Getting There & Around

AIR

Air New Zealand (☑0800 737 000; www.air-newzealand.co.nz) Daily flights from Auckland to Whangarei, Kerikeri and Kaitaia, and from Wellington to Whangarei.

Great Barrier Airlines (☑0800 900 600, 09-275 9120; www.greatbarrierairlines.co.nz) Friday and Sunday flights from November to March that link Whangarei to Great Barrier Island.

BUS

InterCity (☑09-583 5780; www.intercity.co.nz) InterCity and associated Northliner services head from Auckland to Kerikeri via Waipu, Whangarei and Paihia; and from Paihia to Kaitaia via Kerikeri, Mangonui and Coopers Beach.

Naked Bus (☑09-006 2533; www.nakedbus.com) Daily buses from Auckland to Paihia (3¾ hours), via Warkworth, Waipu, Whangarei and Kawakawa. Note that calls to this number cost $1.99 per minute.

West Coaster (☑021 380 187) Weekday shuttles linking Whangarei and Dargaville.

WHANGAREI DISTRICT

To truly experience this area you'll need to get wet, and scores of beaches offer opportunities for swimming, surfing or just splashing about. The hot spots heave with Kiwi

---

ESSENTIAL NORTHLAND

Eat Kumara, Dargaville's knobbly claim to fame

Drink Orange juice, Kerikeri's signature squeeze

Read *The House of Strife* (1993), Maurice Shadbolt's riveting novel set during the Northland War

Listen to *Cape Reinga Way* (2011) by The Nukes, ukeleles heading to the afterlife

Watch *Land of the Long White Cloud* (2009) – fishing philosophers on Ninety Mile Beach

Festival Waitangi Day

Go green Sing to the trees with Footprints Waipoua

Online www.northlandnz.com; www.kauricoast.com

Area code ☑09

---

holidaymakers at peak times, but even then it's possible to find isolated stretches of sand where your footprints are the only ones.

North of Whangarei, the Tutukaka Coast is one of the planet's top three coastlines, according to *National Geographic Traveler* magazine, and the late Jacques Cousteau rated the neighbouring Poor Knights Islands as one of the world's best dive sites.

Online, see www.whangareinz.com.

Mangawhai

POP 2400

Mangawhai Village sits at the base of a horseshoe harbour, but it's Mangawhai Heads, 5km further on, that's really special.

Various Maori tribes inhabited the area before the 1660s, when Ngati Whatua became dominant. In 1807, Ngati Whatua defeated Ngapuhi from the north in a major battle, letting the survivors escape. One of them was Hongi Hika, who in 1825 returned, armed with muskets obtained from Europeans. The ensuing bloodbath all but annihilated Ngati Whatua and the district became *tapu* (sacred, taboo). British squatters moved in and were rewarded with land titles by the government in the 1850s. Ceremonies were only performed to lift the *tapu* in the 1990s.

◎ Sights & Activities

Mangawhai Heads BEACH
A narrow spit of sand stretches for kilometres to form the harbour's south head, sheltering a seabird sanctuary. Across the water sits the holiday town with a surf beach at its northern tip. Lifesavers patrol on weekends in summer and daily during school holidays, but it's not especially dangerous.

Mangawhai Museum MUSEUM
(www.mangawhai-museum.org.nz; Molesworth Dr; admission by donation; ⊙10.30am-1pm Thu-Sun) Scheduled to open by the time you read this, the Mangawhai Historical Society's new museum occupies a spectacular building on the main road that links Mangawhai Village to Mangawhai Heads; check out the roof shaped like a stingray.

Mangawhai Cliff Top Walkway TRAMPING
Starting at Mangawhai Heads, this track affords extensive views of sea and land. It takes two to three hours, provided you time it with a return down the beach at low tide. This is part of Te Araroa, the national walking track.

🛏 Sleeping

Coastal Cow Backpackers   HOSTEL $
(☑ 09-431 5246; www.mangawhaibackpackers.com; 299 Molesworth Dr, Mangawhai Heads; dm $28, s $55-88, d & tw $66-95) This homely hostel has simple rooms decorated with a quirky bovine theme. There's also a self-contained unit ($95).

Milestone Cottages   APARTMENTS $$
(☑ 09-431 4018; www.milestonecottages.co.nz; 27 Moir Pt Rd, Mangawhai Heads; apt $125-170; ☀) A Pasifika paradise, with lush tropical gardens and self-contained apartments. A walking track leads to a compact beach that's great for swimming and kayaking.

Mangawhai Lodge   B&B $$$
(☑ 09-431 5311; www.seaviewlodge.co.nz; 4 Heather St, Mangawhai Heads; s/d $185/190, unit $175-220; @🛜) 🗗 Smartly furnished rooms have access to a picture-perfect wraparound verandah at this boutique B&B, which also features great views.

🍴 Eating & Drinking

Mangawhai Market   MARKET $
(Moir St; ⊙9am-1pm Sat) Held in the library hall in Mangawhai Village, this is a good place to stock up on organic produce (including wine and olive oil) and peruse local craft. Another market is held on Sunday mornings in the Mangawhai Heads Domain from mid-October to Easter.

Bennetts   CAFE $$
(☑ 09-431 5072; www.bennettsofmangawhai.com; 52 Moir St, Mangawhai Village; mains $13-23; ⊙shop 9.30am-4.30pm, cafe 9am-4pm Mon-Fri, from 8.30am Sat & Sun) Rural Europe comes to Mangawhai at this atmospheric *chocolaterie*, *gelateria* and cafe, where you can sit by the fountain while dining on French and Italian flavours and sipping a glass of wine.

Sail Rock Cafe   CAFE $$
(12a Wood St, Mangawhai Heads; mains $13-32; ⊙9.30am-late, closed Wed outside of summer) The standout here is the salt-and-pepper squid, plus there are Kiwi craft brews on tap and dairy-free and gluten-free menu options. Good pizzas ($13 to $25) are also available for take away.

Frog & Kiwi   CAFE $$
(www.facebook.com/FrogAndKiwiRestaurant; The Hub, 6 Molesworth Dr, Mangawhai Village; breakfast & lunch $9-21, dinner $32-38; ⊙9am-2.30am & 6-10pm) This French-Kiwi cafe and bistro does great counter food, good-value $12 lunch specials – also available to take away – and more refined French classics at night.

Mangawhai Tavern   PUB, LIVE MUSIC
(www.mangawhaitavern.co.nz; Moir St; ⊙11am-late) One of the country's oldest pubs – built in 1865 – the tavern's harbourside location is a top spot for an afternoon beer. There's live music most Saturday nights and Sunday afternoons, and across the Christmas-New Year period some of NZ's top bands rock the garden bar.

ℹ Information

Visitor Information Centre (☑ 09-431 5090; www.mangawhai.co.nz) Staffed sporadically (mainly on weekends and in summer), but there are information boards outside.

Waipu & Bream Bay

POP 1854

The original 934 British settlers came to Waipu from Scotland via Nova Scotia (Canada) between 1853 and 1860. These dour Scots had the good sense to eschew frigid Otago, where so many of their kindred settled, for sunnier northern climes. The story comes to life through holograms, a short film and interactive displays at the **Waipu Museum** (www.waipumuseum.co.nz; 36 The Centre; adult/child $8/3; ⊙10am-4pm).

Only 10% of current residents are direct descendants of the original Scots, but there's a big get-together on 1 January every year, when the **Highland Games** (www.waipugames.co.nz; adult/child $15/5), established in 1871, take place in Caledonian Park. Just south of Waipu township, there's good swimming at **Waipu Cove** and **Langs Beach**.

There are also excellent walks in the area, including the **Waipu Coastal Trail**, which heads south from Waipu Cove – around to Langs Beach, passing the **Pancake Rocks** on the way. The 2km **Waipu Caves Walking Track** starts at Ormiston Rd and passes through farmland and a scenic reserve en route to a large cave containing glowworms and limestone formations; bring a torch, a compass and sturdy footwear to delve the depths.

Bream Bay has miles of blissfully deserted beach, blighted only slightly by a giant oil refinery at the north end. At **Uretiti**, a stretch of beach south of a **DOC campsite** (www.doc.govt.nz; SH1; sites per adult/child $10/5) is unofficially considered 'clothing optional'. Over

New Year the crowd is evenly split between Kiwi families, serious European nudists and gay guys.

🛏 Sleeping

Waipu Wanderers Backpackers HOSTEL $
(☎ 09-432 0532; www.waipu-hostel.co.nz; 25 St Marys Rd; dm/s/d $30/45/66; 🛜) There are only three rooms at this friendly backpackers in Waipu township. Look forward to free fruit in season.

Ruakaka Reserve Motor Camp HOLIDAY PARK $
(☎ 09-432 7590; www.motorcamp.co.nz; 21 Ruakaka Beach Rd; sites from $30, cabins $50-90; 🛜) Priced and positioned somewhere between a DOC campsite and a holiday park, this ginormous motor camp offers simple facilities on a grassy area fronting the beach and rivermouth at Ruakaka.

Stonehouse GUESTHOUSE $$
(☎ 09-432 0432; www.stonehousewaipu.co.nz; 641 Cove Rd; apt $80-160; 🛜) Nestled between the road to Waipu Cove and a saltwater lagoon, this Cornish-style house built of stone slabs offers three brightly decorated, self-contained units. They range from the budget-orientated 'cutesy' (with a double sofa bed and six bunks), to more comfortable rooms which can be rented individually or as a three-room apartment.

🍴 Eating

Cafe Deli CAFE $
(29 The Centre; mains $10-22; ⊗ 9am-4pm) Enticing salads, pasta, muffins and organic, fairtrade coffee are served at this attractive little cafe on Waipu's main drag.

Pizza Barn ITALIAN $$
(2 Cove Rd; mains $19-30; ⊗ 11.30am-late Wed-Sun Apr-Nov, daily Dec-Mar) Popular platters, light fare and great pizzas ($12 to 26) go well with cold beer when this cool place morphs into a bar.

Two Fish Cafe CAFE $$
(www.twofishcafe.co.nz; 910 Cove Rd; mains $18-30; ⊗ 9am-8pm Thu-Sun Apr-Jun & Aug-Dec, 9am-late daily Jan-Mar, closed Jul) Grab a spot on the deck of this heritage cottage near Waipu Cove and devour excellent home baking, good pizzas and quite possibly Northland's best gourmet fish burger.

ℹ Information

Tourist brochures and internet access are available at the museum.

ℹ Getting There & Away

Waipu Cove can be reached by a particularly scenic route that heads from Mangawhai Heads through Langs Beach. Otherwise turn off SH1 38km south of Whangarei.

InterCity and Naked Bus both operate bus services.

Whangarei

POP 52,900

Northland's only city is surrounded by natural beauty, and its compact town centre offers plenty of rainy-day diversions. There's a thriving artistic community, some good walks, and interesting cafes and bars.

⊙ Sights

◎ Town Basin

This attractive riverside marina is home to vintage car and clock museums, cafes, shops, public art and an information centre. It's a great place for a stroll, with a marked **Art**

MAORI NZ: NORTHLAND

Known to Maori as Te Tai Tokerau, this region has a long and proud Maori history and today has one of the country's highest percentages of Maori people. Along with East Cape, it's a place where you might hear Maori being spoken. In mythology the region is known as the tail of the fish of Maui.

Maori sites of particular significance include Cape Reinga, the Waitangi Treaty Grounds, Ruapekapeka Pa Historic Reserve and, in the Waipoua Forest, Tane Mahuta.

Maori cultural experiences are offered by many local operators, including Footprints Waipoua, Sandtrails Hokianga, Motuti Marae, Ahikaa Adventures, Sand Safaris, Terenga Paraoa, Native Nature Tours, Taiamai Tours, Rewa's Village and Culture North. Many businesses catering to travellers are owned or run by Maori individuals or *hapu* (subtribal) groups. **Tai Tokerau Tourism** (www.taitokerau.co.nz) lists many of them on its website.

Walk and **Heritage Trail**. An **artisans market** is held on Saturdays from October to April under the shade of the pedestrian bridge.

★**Whangarei Art Museum** GALLERY
(www.whangareiartmuseum.co.nz; The Hub, Town Basin; admission by donation; ⊘10am-4pm) Accessed through the Hub information centre (p115), Whangarei's public gallery has an interesting permanent collection, the star of which is a 1904 Maori portrait by Goldie. Also planned is a new **Hundertwasser Art Centre**, based on architectural plans by the late Austrian artist, Friedensreich Hundertwasser. See www.hundertwasser.co.nz for details of the campaign to raise support and funding of the project. A model of the proposed building is in the information centre.

★**Clapham's Clocks** MUSEUM
(www.claphamsclocks.com; Town Basin; adult/child $8/4; ⊘9am-5pm) This very interesting collection of 1400 ticking, gonging and cuckooing timepieces constitutes the National Clock Museum.

◉ City Centre

Old Library Arts Centre GALLERY
(www.oldlibrary.org.nz; 7 Rust Ave; ⊘10am-4pm Tue-Thu) **FREE** The work of local artists is exhibited in this wonderful art-deco building. Check the website for occasional concerts. Set between the old and new libraries is **Pou**, an intriguing sculpture consisting of 10 large poles carved with Maori, Polynesian, Celtic, Croatian and Korean motifs. Grab an interpretive pamphlet from the library.

Botanica & Cafler Park GARDENS
(First Ave & Water St; ⊘10am-4pm) **FREE** Native ferns, tropical plants and cacti are displayed in this little council-run fernery, set on the edge of cute Cafler Park. The park encloses the Waiarohia Stream and includes a rose garden and a scented garden.

◉ Surrounds

Abbey Caves CAVE
(Abbey Caves Rd) **FREE** Abbey Caves is an undeveloped network of three caverns full of glowworms and limestone formations, 6km east of town. Grab a torch, strong shoes, a mate for safety, and prepare to get wet. The surrounding reserve is a forest of crazily shaped rock extrusions. If you're staying at neighbouring Little Earth Lodge, you can borrow helmets and hire head torches.

Kiwi North MUSEUM, WILDLIFE
(www.kiwinorth.co.nz; 500 SH14, Maunu; adult/child $15/5; ⊘10am-4pm) Five kilometres west of Whangarei, this complex includes 19th-century buildings and a museum displaying Maori and colonial artefacts. A gecko and kiwi house offers a rare chance to see the country's feathery fave in a darkened nocturnal house.

Native Bird Recovery Centre WILDLIFE CENTRE
(www.nbr.org.nz; 500 SH14, Maunu; ⊘10am-4.30pm Tue-Thu, 1-4.30pm Mon & Fri) **FREE** This avian hospital nurses sick and injured birds back to health. Say hi to the talking tuis.

Whangarei Falls WATERFALL
(Otuihau; Ngunguru Rd) Short walks around these 26m-high falls provide views of the water cascading over the edge of an old basalt lava flow. The falls can be reached on the Tikipunga bus ($3, no service on Sundays), leaving from Rose St in the city.

AH Reed Memorial Kauri Park FOREST
(Whareora Rd) A grove of immense 500-year-old kauri trees has been preserved in this lush tract of native bush, where a cleverly designed boardwalk leads you effortlessly up into the canopy. To get here, head north on Bank St and turn right into Whareora Rd.

Quarry Gardens GARDENS
(www.whangareiquarrygardens.org.nz; Russell Rd; admission by donation; ⊘8am-5pm) Green-fingered volunteers have transformed this old quarry into a blissful park with a lake, waterfalls, pungent floral aromas, wild bits, orderly bits and lots of positive energy. To get here, take Rust Ave, turn right into Western Hills Dr and then left into Russell Rd.

Quarry Arts Centre ARTS CENTRE
(www.quarryarts.org; 21 Selwyn Ave; ⊘9.30am-4.30pm) **FREE** An eccentric village of artists' studios and co-operative galleries where you can often pick up well-priced art and craft.

Kingdom of Zion ZOO
(☑09-435 0110; www.kingdomofzion.co.nz; Gray Rd, Kamo; adult/child/family from $60/25/150; ⊘9am-5pm) An essential destination if you're a fan of big cats, with more than 30 lions, tigers, cheetahs and leopards. A variety of tours is available – most popular is the Feed Tour (adult/child $80/30) – and there are also behind-the-scenes opportunities to meet the cats. Kingdom of Zion is around

Whangarei

(Map of Whangarei with the following labels)

Quarry Gardens (1.6km);
Whangarei Views (2.2km)

à Deco
(1.4km)

Coronation
Scenic
Reserve

6 ◉ Selwyn Ave

Waiarohia
Stream

Mansfield Tce

Grey St

Vinery La

Norfolk St

Dent St

Laurie
Hall
Park

Rathbone St

Rust Ave

13
18 Butter
Factory La

James St

Western Hills Dr

Cafler
Park

4
5

Bank St

15
21
10

Third Ave

Second Ave

16 22

Water St

14
Vine St

11

Central Ave

First Ave

3 ◉

InterCity
Rose St

Walton St

Clyde St

8
9

Northland
Coach &
Travel Centre

Albert St

Maunu Rd

Kirikiri Stream

Porowini Ave

Tarewa Rd

Railway Rd

Whangarei
i-SITE (1km)

9km northwest of Whangarei. A return shuttle bus ($25) leaves from the Town Basin daily at 1.15pm.

🏃 Activities

The free *Whangarei Walks* brochure, available from the i-SITE (p115), has maps and detailed descriptions of some excellent local tracks. The **Hatea River Walk** follows the river from the Town Basin to the falls (three hours return). Longer tracks head through **Parihaka Reserve**, which is just east of the Hatea River and encompasses the remnants of a volcanic cone (241m) and a major *pa* (fortified village) site. The city is spread out for inspection from the lookout at the top, which is accessible by car. Other tracks head through **Coronation Scenic Reserve**, an expanse of bush immediately west of the centre that includes two *pa* sites and abandoned quarries.

Skydive Ballistic Blondes   SKYDIVING
(📞0800 695 867; www.skydiveballisticblondes.co.nz; 12,000ft tandem $320) Not only is this the oddest-named skydiving outfit in the country, it's also the only one licensed to land on the beach (Ocean Beach or Paihia).

Pacific Coast Kayaks   KAYAKING
(📞09-436 1947; www.nzseakayaking.co.nz; hire 4/8hr $60/80, tours $40-130) Hires kayaks and offers guided paddles to various Whangarei region locations.

👉 Tours

Pupurangi Hire & Tour   CULTURAL TOUR
(📞09-438 8117; www.hirentour.co.nz; Jetty 1, Riverside Dr; ⊙9.30am-5.30pm Oct-Apr, weekends only May-Sep) Various hour-long tours of Whangarei, all with a Maori flavour, including *waka* (canoe) trips on the river ($35). Also hires kayaks (per hour $17), *waka* ($25), aquacycles ($17) and bikes ($15).

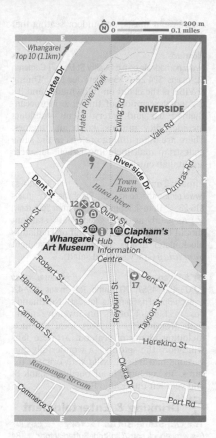

Whangarei

◎ Top Sights
| 1 | Clapham's Clocks | F3 |
| 2 | Whangarei Art Museum | E3 |

◎ Sights
3	Botanica & Cafler Park	C3
4	Old Library Arts Centre	C2
5	Pou	C2
6	Quarry Arts Centre	B1

⊕ Activities, Courses & Tours
| 7 | Pupurangi Hire & Tour | E2 |

⌷ Sleeping
| 8 | BK's Pohutukawa Lodge | A3 |
| 9 | Lodge Bordeaux | A3 |

⊗ Eating
10	Fresh	D3
11	La Familia	D3
12	Mokaba	E2
13	Nectar	D2
14	Nomad	D3
15	Pimarn Thai	D3
16	Whangarei Growers' Market	C3

⊙ Drinking & Nightlife
| 17 | Brauhaus Frings | F3 |
| 18 | The Old Stone Butter Factory | D2 |

⊞ Shopping
19	Bach	E2
20	Burning Issues	E2
21	Kathmandu	D3
22	Tuatara	C3

Terenga Paraoa　　　　CULTURAL TOUR
(☑ 09-430 3083; departs Town Basin; adult/child morning $55/30, afternoon $32/20; ◷ 9.30am & 1pm) Guided Maori cultural tours taking in Whangarei Harbour, Mt Manaia (115), the Kauri Park and, in the mornings, Parihaka *pa*.

⌷ Sleeping

Little Earth Lodge　　　　HOSTEL $
(☑ 09-430 6562; www.littleearthlodge.co.nz; 85 Abbey Caves Rd; dm/s/d/tr $31/68/72/93; @ ☎) Set on a farm 6km from town and right next to Abbey Caves, Little Earth makes most other hostels look downright shabby. Forget dorm rooms crammed with nasty, spongy bunks: settle down in a proper cosy bed with nice linen and a maximum of two room-mates. Resident critters include miniature horses Tom and Jerry, and the lovable pooch Muttley.

**Whangarei Falls
Holiday Park & Backpackers**　　HOSTEL $
(☑ 09-437 0609; www.whangareifalls.co.nz; 12 Ngunguru Rd, Glenbervie; dm $26-28, s $42-52, d & tw $56-66; ☎ ▣) Located 5km from Whangarei CBD but a short walk from Whangarei Falls, with good-value cabins and dorms, some with small kitchenettes. There's also room for tents and campervans.

Whangarei Top 10　　　HOLIDAY PARK $
(☑ 09-437 6856; www.whangareitop10.co.nz; 24 Mair St; sites from $21, units $75-130; ☎) ⍝ This centrally located riverside holiday park has friendly owners, a better-than-average set of units, and supershiny stainless-steel surfaces. Mair St is off Hatea Dr, north of the city centre.

Whangarei Views　　　　B&B $$
(☑ 09-437 6238; www.whangareiviews.co.nz; 5 Kensington Heights Rise; s/d/apt $109/139/149; @ ☎) Modern and peaceful, with a self-contained

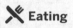

two-bedroom flat downstairs and a B&B room in the main part of the house. To get here, follow the directions to Quarry Gardens (p111). Kensington Heights Rise is off Russell Rd, and yes, the views are excellent.

BK's Pohutukawa Lodge
MOTEL $$

(☑09-430 8634; www.pohutukawalodge.co.nz; 362 Western Hills Dr; units $125-150; @ 🛜) Just west of town, this nicely furnished motel has 14 units with well-kept facilities and ample parking.

Lodge Bordeaux
MOTEL $$$

(☑09-438 0404; www.lodgebordeaux.co.nz; 361 Western Hills Dr; apt $195-230; @ 🛜) Lodge Bordeaux has tasteful units with stellar kitchens and bathrooms (most with spa baths), private balconies and access to excellent wine. To get here, take Rust Ave and turn left into Western Hills Dr.

✖ Eating

Nectar
CAFE $

(www.nectarcafe.co.nz; 88 Bank St; mains $12-20; ⊙7am-3pm Mon-Fri, 8am-2pm Sat) 🖉 Nectar offers the winning combination of friendly staff, fairtrade coffee, and generous servings from a menu full of Northland produce. Check out the urban views from the back windows, and settle in for a lazy brunch of Israeli baked eggs with organic quinoa.

Fresh
CAFE $

(12 James St; mains $10-22; ⊙7.30am-4pm Sat-Wed, 7.30am-7pm Thu & Fri) Fresh as a daisy, and with supersized-flower photography on the walls, this chic cafe serves up great coffee and interesting breakfasts. It's open later for after-work drinks on Thursday and Friday.

La Familia
CAFE $

(www.lafamila.co.nz; 84 Cameron St; mains $10-15, pizzas $12-19; ⊙7am-4pm Tue-Sat, 9am-2.30pm Sun) Versatility rules at this cosy corner location. Good pastries, counter food and coffee segue to robust Italian-themed mains and pizzas for lunch. At the time of writing, the owners were also planning on opening for dinner on Friday and Saturday nights.

Whangarei Growers' Market
MARKET

(Water St; ⊙6.30-11am Sat) Stock up on local produce at this farmers market.

Mokaba
CAFE $$

(www.mokabacafe.co.nz; Town Basin; mains $9-21; ⊙8am-5pm) The best of the Town Basin's cafes has outdoor tables overlooking the for-est of yacht masts, and indoor seating that segues into a gallery.

Nomad
MOROCCAN $$

(www.nomadcafe.co.nz; Quality St Mall, 71 Cameron St; mains $24-28; ⊙5pm-late Tue-Sat) 'Dining & Vibe' is the claim on the window, and it's a good description of this chic Moroccan-themed bar and eatery. Menu standouts include spicy prawns, kofta and tagines. There are other dining options in the same pedestrian mall including Israeli, Japanese and Italian cuisine.

Pimarn Thai
THAI $$

(www.pimarnthai.co.nz; 12 Rathbone St; mains $16-23; ⊙11am-2.30pm Mon-Sat, from 5pm daily; 🖉) As gaudy as every good Thai restaurant should be, Pimarn features all of Thailand's blockbuster dishes, including an excellent *yum talay* (spicy seafood salad).

★ à Deco
MODERN NZ $$$

(☑09-459 4957; 70 Kamo Rd; mains $37-42; ⊙noon-3pm Fri, 6pm-late Tue-Sat) Northland's best restaurant offers an inventive menu that prominently features local produce, including plenty of seafood. Art-deco fans will adore the setting – a wonderfully curvaceous marine-style villa with original fixtures. To get here, head north on Bank St and veer left into Kamo Rd.

🍷 Drinking & Entertainment

The Old Stone Butter Factory
CAFE, BAR

(www.facebook.com/OldStoneButterFactory; 84 Bank St; ⊙10am-late Mon-Sun) Occupying a converted bank building, this tapas and cocktail bar hosts live musicians on Fridays. As the hours dissolve, DJs kick in. It's also a popular spot for touring Kiwi bands and musos, and has interesting beers and wine. The sunny courtyard is also a good spot for a coffee.

Brauhaus Frings
BREWERY

(www.frings.co.nz; 104 Dent St; ⊙10am-10pm) This popular microbrewery has good beers, a terrace, wood-fired pizzas, and live music on Wednesday (jam night) and every second Sunday from 4pm. It's usually closed by 10pm on weekdays, but can push on to 3am on weekends.

🔒 Shopping

See also Quarry Arts Centre (p111).

Tuatara ART & CRAFTS
(www.tuataradesignstore.co.nz; 29 Bank St; ⊙9.30am-5pm Mon-Fri, 8am-2pm Sat) Maori and Pasifika design, art and craft.

Bach ART & CRAFTS
(www.thebach.org.nz; Town Basin; ⊙9.30am-4.30pm) Co-op store representing over 100 Northland artisans.

Burning Issues ART & CRAFTS
(www.burningissuesgallery.co.nz; Town Basin; ⊙10am-5pm) Glassware, ceramics and jewellery.

Kathmandu OUTDOOR EQUIPMENT
(www.kathmandu.co.nz; 22 James St; ⊙9am-5.30pm Mon-Fri, 9am-4pm Sat, 10am-3pm Sun) Outdoor gear and travel clothing.

ℹ Information

DOC Office (☎09-470 3300; www.doc.govt.nz; 2 South End Ave, Raumanga; ⊙8.30am-4pm Mon-Fri) Located on South End Ave; turn right off SH1 around 2km south of central Whangarei.

Hub Information Centre (☎09-430 1188; Town Basin; ⊙8.30am-5pm Mon-Fri, 9am-4pm Sat & Sun; ⊛) More central branch of the i-SITE, in the foyer of the Art Museum.

Whangarei i-SITE (☎09-438 1079; www.whangareinz.com; 92 Otaika Rd/SH1; ⊙8.30am-5pm Mon-Fri, 9am-4pm Sat & Sun; ⊛) Information, cafe, toilets and internet access.

ℹ Getting There & Around

AIR
Whangarei Airport (WRE; ☎09-436 0047; www.whangareiairport.co.nz; Handforth St) Whangarei Airport is at Onerahi, 6km southeast of the centre. Air New Zealand and Great Barrier Airlines flights both service Whangarei. Taxis into town cost around $30. A city bus stops 400m away on Church St ($3, 18 buses on weekdays, seven on Saturdays).

BUS
Bus services to Whangarei are run by InterCity, whose buses stop outside the **Northland Coach & Travel Centre** (☎09-438 3206; 3 Bank St; ⊙8am-5pm Mon-Fri, 8.30am-2.30pm Sat & Sun), and Naked Buses, whose buses stop at the Hub (p115), in the Town Basin. West Coaster shuttles also service Whangarei.

TAXI
A1 Cabs (☎0800 438 3377)

Whangarei Heads

Whangarei Heads Rd winds 35km along the northern reaches of the harbour to the Heads' entrance, passing mangroves and picturesque pohutukawa-lined bays. Holiday homes, B&Bs and galleries are dotted around the water-hugging small settlements. There are great views from the top of **Mt Manaia** (419m), a sheer rock outcrop above McLeod Bay, but prepare for a lung- and leg-busting 1½-hour climb.

Bream Head caps off the craggy finger of land. A five-hour one-way walking track from **Urquharts Bay** to **Ocean Beach** passes through the **Bream Head Scenic Reserve** and lovely **Smugglers Bay** and **Peach Cove**.

Magnificent Ocean Beach stretches for miles on the other side of the headland. There's decent surfing to be had and lifeguards patrol the beach in summer. A detour from **Parua Bay** takes you to glorious **Pataua**, a small settlement that lies on a shallow inlet linked to a surf beach by a footbridge.

🛏 Sleeping & Eating

Kauri Villas B&B $$
(☎09-436 1797; www.kaurivillas.com; 73 Owhiwa Rd, Parua Bay; d $130-175; ⊛) Perched on a hill with views back over the harbour to Whangarei, this pretty blue-trimmed villa has an old-world feel, due in part to some very chintzy wallpaper. The decor's more restrained in the self-contained lodge and annex rooms.

Parua Bay Tavern PUB $$
(www.paruabaytavern.co.nz; 1034 Whangarei Heads Rd; meals $15-31; ⊙11.30am-late) A magical spot on a summer's day, this friendly pub is set on a thumb-shaped peninsula, with a sole pohutukawa blazing red against the green water. Grab a seat on the deck, a cold beverage and a decent pub meal.

Tutukaka Coast & the Poor Knights Islands

If Goat Island Marine Reserve whetted your appetite, diving at the Poor Knights is the feast followed by a wafer-thin mint that might cause your stomach to explode. Apart from the natural underwater scenery, two decommissioned navy ships have been sunk nearby for divers to explore.

Following the road northeast of Whangarei for 26km, you'll first come to the sweet village of **Ngunguru** near the mouth of a broad river. **Tutukaka** is 1km further on, its marina bustling with yachts, dive crews and game-fishing boats.

From Tutukaka the road heads slightly inland, popping out 10km later at the golden sands of **Matapouri**. A blissful 20-minute coastal walk leads from here to **Whale Bay**, fringed with giant pohutukawa trees.

Continuing north from Matapouri, the wide expanse of **Sandy Bay**, one of Northland's premier surf beaches, comes into view. Long-boarding competitions are held here in summer. The road then loops back to join SH1 at Hikurangi. A branch leading off from this road doubles back north to the coast at **Whananaki**, where there are more glorious beaches and the **Otamure Bay DOC campsite** (☑ 09-433 8402; www.doc.govt. nz; sites per adult/child $10/5).

🏃 Activities

Dive trips leave from Tutukaka and cater for both first-timers and experts. There are some excellent walks along the coast. Pick up a copy of the *Tutukaka Coast Tracks & Walks* brochure from the Whangarei i-SITE (p115).

Dive! Tutukaka   DIVING
(☑ 0800 288 882; www.diving.co.nz; Marina Rd; 2 dives incl gear $249) 🏊 Dive courses and excursions, including a five-day PADI open-water course ($799). For nondivers, the Perfect Day Ocean Cruise ($149) includes lunch and snacks, snorkelling in the marine reserve, kayaking through caves and arches,

paddle boarding, and sightings of dolphins (usually) and whales (occasionally). Cruises run from November to April, departing at 11am and returning at 4.15pm. In off months, snorkellers can tag along on the dive boats. Dive! Tutukaka has twice-daily shuttles from Whangarei for its customers ($20).

Yukon Dive   DIVING
(☑ 09-434 4506; www.yukon.co.nz; 2 dives incl full gear $245) An owner-operator offering dive trips for a maximum of 12 people at a time.

Tutukaka Surf Experience   SURFING
(☑ 09-434 4135; www.tutukakasurf.co.nz; Marina Rd; 2hr lesson $75) Runs surf lessons at 9.30am most days in summer and on the weekends otherwise, operating from whichever beach has the best beginner breaks that day. Also hires surfboards (per day $45) and stand-up paddle boards (per day $20).

🛏 Sleeping

Lupton Lodge   B&B $$
(☑ 09-437 2989; www.luptonlodge.co.nz; 555 Ngunguru Rd; s $125-155, d $170-245; @ 🛜 🌊) The rooms are spacious, luxurious and full of character in this historic homestead (1896), peacefully positioned in farmland halfway between Whangarei and Ngunguru. Wander the orchard, splash around the pool or shoot some snooker in the guest lounge.

Pacific Rendezvous   MOTEL $$
(☑ 09-434 3847; www.pacificrendezvous.co.nz; Motel Rd; apt $199-250) Perfectly situated for spectacular views on the south head of Tutukaka harbour, this is a great choice for families and small groups. Most of the units are 1960s duplexes with multiple bedrooms, but they're all individually owned and decorated.

MARINE RICHES AT THE POOR KNIGHTS

Established in 1981, the Poor Knights marine reserve is rated as one of the world's top-10 diving spots. The islands are bathed in a subtropical current from the Coral Sea, so varieties of tropical and subtropical fish not seen in other NZ waters can be observed here. The waters are clear, with no sediment or pollution problems. The 40m to 60m underwater cliffs drop steeply to the sandy bottom and are a labyrinth of archways, caves, tunnels and fissures that attract a wide variety of sponges and colourful underwater vegetation. Schooling fish, eels and rays are common (including manta rays in season).

The two main volcanic islands, Tawhiti Rahi and Aorangi, were home to the Ngai Wai tribe, but since a raiding-party massacre of 1825 the islands have been *tapu* (forbidden). Even today the public is barred from the islands, in order to protect their pristine environment. Not only do tuatara and Butler's shearwater breed here, but there are unique species of flora, such as the Poor Knights lily.

✖ Eating & Drinking

★ **Havana Cabana**   SOUTH AMERICAN $
(www.havanacabana.co.nz; 23 McAuslin Rd, Sandy
Bay; snacks & meals $5-16; ☺ 11am-8pm daily Box-
ing Day to early Feb, Sat & Sun only early Feb-Easter)
Nestled away near the beach at Sandy Bay,
around 20 minutes' drive north of Tutukaka,
this colourful caravan turns out excellent
Cuban and South American food. Tuck into
empanadas, tacos, great roast pork Cuban
sandwiches, or Caribbean jerk pulled pork,
all washed down with Cuban coffee or frozen pina coladas.

Schnappa Rock   CAFE, BAR $$
(www.schnapparock.co.nz; cnr Marina Rd & Mar-
lin Pl; breakfast/lunch $10-27, dinner $26-35, bar
snacks $8-19; ☺ 8am-late, closed Sun night Jun-
Oct) ✎ Filled with expectant divers in the
morning and those capping off their Perfect
Days in the evening, this cafe-restaurant-bar
is often buzzing. Top NZ bands sometimes
play on summer weekends.

Marina Pizzeria   PIZZERIA $$
(www.marinapizzeria.co.nz; Tutukaka Marina;
pizzas $15-30; ☺ 4pm-late Fri, 10am-late Sat &
Sun) Everything is homemade at this excellent takeaway and restaurant – the bread,
the pasta, the pizza and the ice cream.
Hearty breakfasts are served from 10am on
weekends.

Russell Road

The quickest route to Russell takes SH1 to
Opua and then crosses by ferry. The old Russell Rd is a snaking scenic route that adds
about half an hour to the trip.

The turn-off is easy to miss, located 6km
north of Hikurangi at Whakapara (look
for the sign to Oakura). Stop after 13km
at the **Gallery & Cafe** (www.galleryhelena-
bay.co.nz; 1392 Old Russell Rd, Helena Bay; mains
$14-18; ☺ 10am-5pm) high above Helena Bay
for fairtrade coffee, scrummy cake, amazing views and interesting Kiwiana art and
craft.

At **Helena Bay** an unsealed detour leads
8km to **Mimiwhangata Coastal Park**,
which features sand dunes, pohutukawa
trees, jutting headlands and picturesque
beaches. DOC-managed accommodation
includes a simple but comfortable cottage,
and a beach house ($613 per week), both
of which sleep seven to eight people. Basic

camping (per adult/child $10/5) is available
at secluded Waikahoa Bay.

Back on Russell Rd, you'll find the **Farm**
(☎ 09-433 6894; www.thefarm.co.nz; 3632 Russell Rd; sites from $13, dm/s/d $20/30/80), a
rough-and-ready backpackers that rambles
through various buildings, including an
old woolshed fitted out with a mirror ball.
The rooms are basic, and the Farm is popular with trail bikers during the summer
holidays; off season it's a chilled-out rustic
escape. On offer are horse treks (1½ hours,
$50) or motorbike rides (one hour $60)
through the 1000-acre working farm.

At an intersection shortly after the Farm,
Russell Rd branches off to the left for an
unsealed, winding section traversing the
Ngaiotonga Scenic Reserve. Unless you're
planning to explore the forest (there are two
short walks: the 20-minute **Kauri Grove
Nature Walk** and the 10-minute **Twin Bole
Kauri Walk**), you're better off veering right
onto the sealed Rawhiti Rd.

After 2.6km, a side road leads to the
**Whangaruru North Head Scenic Re-
serve**, which has beaches, walking tracks
and fine scenery. A loop route from DOC's
Puriri Bay Campsite (☎ 09-433 6160; www.
doc.govt.nz; sites per adult/child $10/5) leads
up to a ridge, offering a remarkable coastal
panorama.

If you want to head directly to Russell,
continue along Rawhiti Rd for another 7km
before veering left onto Manawaora Rd,
which skirts a succession of tiny idyllic bays
before reconnecting with Russell Rd.

Otherwise take a detour to isolated
Rawhiti, a small Ngapuhi settlement where
life still revolves around the *marae* (meeting house). Rawhiti is the starting point
for the tramp to Cape Brett, a tiring eight-
hour, 16.3km walk to the top of the peninsula, where overnight stays are possible in
DOC's **Cape Brett Hut** (dm $15). The hut
must be booked in advance. An access fee
is charged for crossing private land (adult/
child $30/15), which you can pay at the
Paihia i-SITE (p129). Another option is to
take a water taxi to Cape Brett lighthouse
from Russell or Paihia and walk back.

A shorter one-hour walk leads through
Maori land and the **Whangamumu Scenic
Reserve** to **Whangamumu Harbour**. There
are more than 40 ancient Maori sites on the
peninsula and the remains of an unusual
whaling station.

BAY OF ISLANDS

The Bay of Islands ranks as one of NZ's top tourist drawcards, and the turquoise waters of the bay are punctuated by around 150 undeveloped islands. In particular, Paihia has excellent budget accommodation, and boat trips and water sports are very popular.

The Bay of Islands is also a place of enormous historical significance. Maori knew it as Pewhairangi and settled here early in their migrations. As the site of NZ's first permanent British settlement (at Russell), it is the birthplace of European colonisation in the country. It was in this region that the Treaty of Waitangi was drawn up and first signed in 1840; the treaty remains the linchpin of race relations in NZ today.

 Activities

The Bay of Islands offers some fine subtropical diving, made even better by the sinking of the 113m navy frigate HMNZS *Canterbury* in Deep Water Cove near Cape Brett. Local operators also head to the wreck of the *Rainbow Warrior* off the Cavalli Islands, about an hour north of Paihia by boat. Both offer a colourful feast of pink anemones, yellow sponges and abundant fish life.

There are opportunities for kayaking or sailing around the bay, either on a guided tour or by renting and going it alone. Cruises and dolphin swimming are also available.

Dive North   DIVING
(☑09-402 5369; www.divenorth.co.nz; reef & wreck $225) Based in Kerikeri but offering free pick-ups from Paihia.

Paihia Dive   DIVING
(☑09-402 7551; www.divenz.com; Williams Rd, Paihia; reef & wreck $229) Combined reef and wreck trips to either the *Canterbury* or the *Rainbow Warrior*.

Dive Ops   DIVING
(☑0800 387 892, 09-402 5454; www.diveops.co.nz; 2 dives incl equipment $230-280) Family-run diving operators, based out of Paihia.

Island Kayaks & Bay Beach Hire   KAYAKING, BOATING
(☑09-402 6078; www.baybeachhire.co.nz; Marsden Rd, Paihia; half-day kayaking tour $69; ⊙9am-5.30pm) Hires kayaks (from $15 per hour), sailing catamarans ($50 first hour, $40 per additional), motor boats ($85 first hour, $25 per additional), mountain bikes ($35 per day), boogie boards ($25 per day), fishing rods ($10 per day), wet suits and snorkelling gear (both $20 per day).

Coastal Kayakers   KAYAKING
(☑0800 334 661; www.coastalkayakers.co.nz; Te Karuwha Pde, Paihia) Runs guided tours (half-/full day $85/115, minimum two people) and multiday adventures. Kayaks (per hour/half-/full day $15/40/50) can also be rented for independent exploration.

Flying Kiwi Parasail   PARASAILING
(☑0800 359 691; www.parasail-nz.co.nz; solo $99, tandem each $89, child $69) Departs from both Paihia and Russell wharves for NZ's highest parasail (1200ft).

Tango Jet Ski & Island Boat Tours   BOAT TOUR, JETSKIING
(☑0800 253 8752; www.tangojetskitours.co.nz; boat tours/jetski hire from $65/100) Zip around the bay in a speedy inflatable boat or skipper your own jetski. Jetskis can take two people.

Great Escape Yacht Charters   SAILING
(☑09-402 7143; www.greatescape.co.nz) Offers introductory sailing lessons (two-day course $445) and longer options.

POU HERENGA TAI TWIN COAST CYCLE TRAIL

Planned to be completed by late 2014, this cycle route stretches from the Bay of Islands clear across the country to the Hokianga Harbour. OK, so that's only 84km, but as far as we're concerned that still gives you boasting rights when you get home. The complete route will travel from Opua via Kawakawa, Ngawha Springs, Kaikohe and finish up in Horeke.

At the time of research, around half of the total distance had been completed, and most popular was a 20km section from Kaikohe to Okaihau, starting west of Kaikohe and passing through an abandoned rail tunnel before skirting Lake Omapere. For maps, tips and updates on the progress of the trail, see www.nzcycletrail.com. Visit www.toptrail.co.nz for details of bike hire and shuttle transport, including from Paihia if you're staying in the Bay of Islands.

Bay of Islands

Northland Paddleboarding   PADDLE BOARDING
(☑ 027 777 1035; www.northlandpaddleboarding.
co.nz; beginner lessons per hr $50) Lessons and
guided cruises.

Horse Trek'n   HORSE RIDING
(☑ 027 233 3490; www.horsetrekn.co.nz; 2hr ride
$120) Through the Waitangi Forest.

☞ Tours

Where do you start? First by praying for
good weather, as torrential rain or choppy
seas could exclude some options. The Paihia
i-SITE (p129) and accommodation operators
can book tours.

Boat

Options include sailing boats, jetboats and
large launches. Boats leave from either
Paihia or Russell, calling into the other town
as their first stop.

One of the bay's most striking islands
is **Piercy Island (Motukokako)** off Cape
Brett, at the bay's eastern edge. This steep-
walled rock fortress features a vast natural
arch – the famous **Hole in the Rock**. Provided the conditions are right, most boat
tours will pass right through the heart of the
island. En route it's likely you'll encounter
bottlenose and common dolphins, and you
may see orcas, other whales and penguins.

The best way to explore the bay is under
sail. Either help crew the boat (no experience required), or just spend the afternoon
island-hopping, sunbathing, swimming,
snorkelling, kayaking and fishing.

Explore NZ   CRUISE, SAILING
(☑ 09-402 8234; www.explorenz.co.nz; cnr
Marsden & Williams Rds, Paihia) ☞ The four-
hour Swim with the Dolphins Cruise (adult/
child $89/45, additional $15 to swim) departs at 8am and 12.30pm. The four-hour
Discover the Bay Cruise (adult/child $99/49)
departs at 9am and 1.30pm, heading to the
Hole in the Rock and stopping at Urupukapuka Island. There are also combo options
available including a bus trip along Ninety
Mile Beach.

Another option (December to March
only) is a day sail on *Lion NZ* (adult/child
$110/70), the 80ft maxi yacht used by the
late Sir Peter Blake in racing around the
world and from Sydney to Hobart.

Fullers Great Sights   CRUISES
(☑ 0800 653 339; www.dolphincruises.co.nz; Paihia
Wharf) ☞ The four-hour Dolphin Cruise
(adult/child $95/50) departs daily at 9am
and 1.30pm, actively seeking out dolphins en
route to the Hole in the Rock, and stopping
at Urupukapuka Island on the way back. You

ⓘ SWIMMING WITH DOLPHINS

Cruises offering the opportunity to interact with wild dolphins operate all year round. They have a high success rate and you're generally offered a free trip if dolphins aren't sighted. Dolphin swims are subject to weather and sea conditions, with restrictions if calves are present.

It's totally up to the dolphins as to whether they choose to swim with you or not. You'll need to be a strong swimmer to keep abreast with them – even when they're humouring you by cruising along at half-speed.

Only three operators are licensed for dolphin swimming: Explore NZ (p119), Fullers (p119) and the yacht Carino (p120). All pay a portion of the cost towards marine research, via DOC.

won't visit the Hole in the Rock on the four-hour Dolphin Eco Experience (adult/child $109/55, departs 8am and 12.30pm); the focus is finding dolphins to swim with.

The full-day Cream Trip (adult/child $119/60) follows the mail route around the bay and includes dolphin swimming. A glamorous option for an overnight cruise from September to April is on the launch *Ipipiri*, with accommodation in en-suite state rooms from $299 per person. Meals and kayaking, snorkelling and island walks are included.

R Tucker Thompson   SAILING
(✆09-402 8430; www.tucker.co.nz) ⚓ Run by a charitable trust with an education focus, the *Tucker* is a majestic tall ship offering day sails (adult/child $145/73, including a barbecue lunch) and late-afternoon cruises (adult/child $59/30).

Rock   CRUISE
(✆0800 762 527; www.rocktheboat.co.nz; dm/s/d from $158/346/376) ⚓ A former vehicle ferry that's now a floating hostel, the *Rock* has dorms, private rooms and a bar. The cruise departs at 5pm and includes a barbecue and seafood dinner with live music, then time spent island-hopping, fishing, kayaking, snorkelling and swimming the following day. Day cruises only are $98 per person.

Carino   SAILING, DOLPHIN SWIMMING
(✆09-402 8040; www.sailingdolphins.co.nz; adult/child $114/69) ⚓ This 50ft catamaran is the only yacht licensed for swimming with dolphins. A barbecue lunch is available for $6.

Ecocruz   SAILING
(✆0800 432 627; www.ecocruz.co.nz; dm/d $650/1500) ⚓ Three-day/two-night sailing cruise aboard the 72ft ocean-going yacht *Manawanui*. Prices include accommodation, food, fishing, kayaking and snorkelling.

She's a Lady   SAILING
(✆0800 724 584; www.bay-of-islands.com; day sail $97) On day sails go snorkelling or paddle a see-through-bottom kayak. Charter boats for longer trips and a sailing school.

Phantom   SAILING
(✆0800 224 421; www.yachtphantom.com; adult/child $110/60) A fast 50ft racing sloop, known for its wonderful food. BYO beer and wine allowed.

Gungha II   SAILING
(✆0800 478 900; www.bayofislandssailing.co.nz; day sail $95) A 65ft ocean yacht with a friendly crew; lunch included.

Mack Attack   JETBOATING
(✆0800 622 528; www.mackattack.co.nz; 9 Williams Rd, Paihia; adult/child $95/40) An exhilarating, high-speed 1½-hour jetboat trip to the Hole in the Rock.

Bus

It's cheaper and quicker to take trips to Cape Reinga from Ahipara, Kaitaia or Doubtless Bay, but if you're short on time, several long day trips (10 to 12 hours) leave from the Bay of Islands. They all drive one way along Ninety Mile Beach, stopping for sandboarding on the dunes.

Fullers (p119) runs regular bus tours and backpacker-oriented versions, both stopping at Puketi Forest. The standard, child-friendly version (adult/child $135/68) includes an optional lunch at Pukenui. It also runs **Awesome NZ** (✆0800 653 339; www.awesomenz.com; tours $119) tours, with louder music, more time sandboarding, and stops to chuck a frisbee around at Tapotupotu Bay and devour fish and chips at Mangonui.

Dune Rider by Explore NZ (p119; adult/child $149/110) also samples Mangonui's feted fish and chips and includes a stop at Gumdiggers Park.

Transport options to the Hokianga and Waipoua Forest are limited, so a day trip makes sense if you don't have your own car or if you're time starved. Discover Hokianga by Fullers (p119; adult/child $112/65) takes in Tane Mahuta and Wairere Boulders in an eight-hour tour with local Maori guides.

Cultural

Native Nature Tours   CULTURAL TOUR, TRAMPING
(☏0800 668 873; www.nativenaturetours.co.nz; 581 Tipene Rd, Motatau; day treks $145-235, overnight $375) A local Maori couple formally welcome you to their *marae* and lead treks on their ancestral lands, including visits to sacred sites and an introduction to Maori food and medicine. Other options include tree planting, and overnight stays include a traditional *hangi* (earth-cooked meal) and glowworm-spotting.

**Taiamai Tours
Heritage Journeys**   CULTURAL TOURS, CANOEING
(☏09-405 9990; www.taiamaitours.co.nz; 2½hr tour $135; ☉10am & 1pm Oct-Apr) ⌀ Paddle a traditional 50ft carved *waka* (canoe) from the Waitangi bridge to the Haruru Falls. The Ngapuhi hosts wear traditional garb, and perform the proper *karakia* (incantations) and share stories.

Other Tours

Salt Air   SCENIC FLIGHTS
(☏09-402 8338; www.saltair.co.nz; Marsden Rd, Paihia) Scenic flights include a five-hour light-aircraft and 4WD tour to Cape Reinga and Ninety Mile Beach ($425), and helicopter flights out to the Hole in the Rock ($230).

A new tour even lands on the famed island (from $379).

Total Tours   FOOD & WINE
(☏0800 264 868; www.totaltours.co.nz) Explore around Kerikeri on a half-day Food, Wine and Craft tour ($65) or half-day wine tour ($75).

✹ Festivals & Events

Tall Ship Race   SPORTS
Held in Russell on the first Saturday after New Year's Day.

Waitangi Day   CULTURE
Various ceremonial events at Waitangi on 6 February.

Country Rock Festival   MUSIC
(www.country-rock.co.nz; festival pass $50) Second weekend in May.

Russell Birdman   LUNACY
(www.russellbirdman.co.nz) Lunatics with various flying contraptions jump off wharf into frigid (July) waters.

Jazz & Blues Festival   MUSIC
(www.jazz-blues.co.nz; festival pass $50) Second weekend in August.

Weekend Coastal Classic   SPORTS
(www.coastalclassic.co.nz) NZ's largest yacht race, from Auckland to the Bay of Islands, held on Labour Weekend in October.

**Bay of Islands Food
& Wine Festival**   FOOD, WINE
(www.paihianz.co.nz/it_festival; adult/child $45/15; ☉11am-6pm) Food, wine and local music in Paihia on the last Saturday of October.

WORTH A TRIP

HOLD ON UNTIL KAWAKAWA

Kawakawa is just an ordinary Kiwi town, located on SH1 south of Paihia, but the public toilets (60 Gillies St) are anything but. They were designed by Austrian-born artist and eco-architect Friedensreich Hundertwasser, who lived near Kawakawa in an isolated house without electricity from 1973 until his death in 2000. The most photographed toilets in NZ are typical Hundertwasser – lots of organic wavy lines decorated with ceramic mosaics and brightly coloured bottles, and with grass and plants on the roof. Other examples of his work can be seen in Vienna and Osaka.

Kawakawa also has a railway line running down the main street. Take a 45-minute spin pulled by **Gabriel the Steam Engine** (☏021 171 2697; www.bayofislandsvintagerailway.org.nz; adult/child $20/5; ☉10.45am, noon, 1.15pm, 2.30pm Fri-Sun, daily school holidays).

South of town, a signpost from SH1 points to **Kawiti Glowworm Caves** (☏09-404 0583; www.kawiticaves.co.nz/; 49 Waiomio Rd; adult/child $15/7.50; ☉8.30am-4.30pm). Explore the insect-illuminated caverns with a 30-minute subterranean tour. Guided tours only.

Minibus tours from Paihia to Kawakawa and the caves are offered by Russell Mini Tours (p123).

Russell

POP 720

Although it was once known as 'the hellhole of the Pacific', those coming to Russell for debauchery will be sadly disappointed: they've missed the orgies on the beach by 170 years. Instead they'll find a historic town with gift shops and B&Bs, and, in summer, you can rent kayaks and dinghies along the Strand.

Before it was known as a hellhole, or even as Russell, it was Kororareka (Sweet Penguin), a fortified Ngapuhi village. In the early 19th century the tribe permitted it to become Aotearoa's first European settlement. It quickly became a magnet for rough elements such as fleeing convicts, whalers and drunken sailors. By the 1830s dozens of whaling ships at a time were anchored in the harbour. Charles Darwin described it in 1835 as full of 'the refuse of society'.

In 1830 the settlement was the scene of the so-called Girls' War, when two pairs of Maori women were vying for the attention of a whaling captain called Brind. A chance meeting between the rivals on the beach led to verbal abuse and fighting. This minor conflict quickly escalated as family members rallied around to avenge the insult and harm done to their respective relatives. Hundreds were killed and injured over a two-week pe-riod before missionaries managed to broker a peace agreement.

After the signing of the Treaty of Waitangi in 1840, Okiato (where the car ferry now leaves from) was the residence of the governor and the temporary capital. The capital was officially moved to Auckland in 1841 and Okiato, which was by then known as Russell, was eventually abandoned. The name Russell ultimately replaced Kororareka.

◉ Sights

Pompallier Mission　　　HISTORIC BUILDING
(www.pompallier.co.nz; The Strand; tours adult/child $10/free; ◷10am-4pm) Built in 1842 to house the Catholic mission's printing press, this rammed-earth building is the mission's last remaining building in the western Pacific. A staggering 40,000 books were printed here in Maori. In the 1870s it was converted into a private home, but it is now restored to its original state, complete with tannery and printing workshop.

Christ Church　　　CHURCH
(Church St) English naturalist Charles Darwin made a donation towards the cost of

Russell

◉ 0 ─── 200 m
Ⓝ 0 ─── 0.1 miles

Russell

◎ Sights
1 Christ Church	A2
2 Haratu	A2
3 Pompallier Mission	A3
4 Russell Museum	A2

◎ Activities, Courses & Tours
| 5 Russell Mini Tours | A2 |

◎ Sleeping
6 Arcadia Lodge	B3
7 Commodore's Lodge	A2
8 Duke of Marlborough	A2
9 Hananui Lodge & Apartments	A2
10 Pukeko Cottage	B3
11 Russell Motel	B3
12 Russell Top 10	B1

◎ Eating
Duke of Marlborough	(see 8)
13 Gables	A2
14 Hone's	A2
15 Newport Chocolates	A2
The Wharf	(see 5)
16 Tuk Tuk	A2

◎ Drinking & Nightlife
| 17 Pub 'round the Corner | A2 |

◎ Shopping
| 18 Just Imagine | A1 |

HONE HEKE & THE NORTHLAND WAR

Just five years after he had been the first signatory to the Treaty of Waitangi, Ngapuhi chief Hone Heke was so disaffected that he planned to chop down Kororareka's flagstaff, a symbol of British authority, for the fourth time. Governor FitzRoy was determined not to let that happen and garrisoned the town with soldiers and marines.

On 11 March 1845 the Ngapuhi staged a diversionary siege of the town. It was a great tactical success, with Chief Kawiti attacking from the south and another party attacking from Long Beach. While the troops rushed off to protect the township, Hone Heke felled the Union Jack on Maiki (Flagstaff Hill) for the fourth and final time. The British were forced to evacuate to ships lying at anchor. The captain of the HMS *Hazard* was wounded severely in the battle and his replacement ordered the ships' cannons to be fired on the town; most of the buildings were razed. The first of the New Zealand Wars had begun.

In the months that followed, British troops (united with Hokianga-based Ngapuhi) fought Heke and Kawiti in several battles. During this time the modern *pa* (fortified village) was born, effectively the world's first sophisticated system of trench warfare. It's worth stopping at **Ruapekapeka Pa Historic Reserve** (Ruapekapeka Rd), off SH1 south of Kawakawa, to see how impressive these fortifications were. Here you can wander the site of the last battle of the Northland War, brought to life through detailed information boards. Eventually Heke, Kawiti and George Grey (the new governor) made their peace, with no side the clear winner.

building the country's oldest church (1836). The graveyard's biggest memorial commemorates Tamati Waka Nene, a powerful Ngapuhi chief from the Hokianga who sided against Hone Heke in the Northland War. The church's exterior has musket and cannonball holes dating from the 1845 battle.

Maiki HILL
(Flagstaff Rd) Overlooking Russell, this is the hill where Hone Heke chopped down the flagpole four times. You can drive up but the view justifies a climb. Take the track west from the boat ramp along the beach at low tide, or head up Wellington St.

Tapeka Point LOOKOUT, BEACH
North of Russell, on the other side of Maiki hill, Tapeka Rd heads down to a sandy beach in the shadow of a craggy headland. A *pa* once stood at the top of the hill. Follow the pathway for views stretching to the far northern reaches of the Bay of Islands.

Long Beach BEACH
(Long Beach Rd) About 1.5km behind Russell (an easy walk or cycle) is this placid, child-friendly beach. Turn left (facing the sea) to visit Donkey Bay, a small cove that is an unofficial nudist beach.

Russell Museum MUSEUM
(www.russellmuseum.org.nz; 2 York St; adult/child $7.50/2; ☉10am-4pm) This small, modern museum has a well-presented Maori section, a large 1:5-scale model of Captain Cook's *Endeavour*, and a 10-minute video on the town's history.

Haratu CULTURAL BUILDING
(www.kororarekanz.com; cnr The Strand & Pitt St; walking tours adult/child $20/10; ☉gallery 11am-3pm, walking tours 11am & 2pm) Run by the local *marae* society, Haratu has Maori art and craft, mostly available for purchase. There are also audiovisual displays and information boards. One-hour guided walks featuring Maori stories are available in summer and by arrangement other times. It's volunteer-run, so opening times can vary.

Tours

Russell Mini Tours MINIBUS
(☎0800 646 486; www.russellminitours.com; cnr The Strand & Cass St; adult/child $29/15; ☉tours 10am, 11am, 1pm, 2pm, 3pm & 4pm) Minibus tour around historic Russell with commentary. Tours departing Paihia (adult/child $40/20) visiting Kawakawa and the Kawiti Glowworm Caves are also available.

Sleeping

Russell has a few decent midrange options. There are several small budget lodges, but you'll need to book ahead at busy times. If budget is not a consideration, Russell does luxury B&Bs very well.

Wainui
HOSTEL $

(☑09-403 8278; www.pelnet.org/wainui; 92d Te Wahapu Rd; dm/r $28/66; ☎) Hard to find but worth the effort, this modern bush retreat with direct beach access has only two rooms that share a pleasant communal space. It's 5km from Russell on the way to the car ferry. Take Te Wahapu Rd and then turn right into Waiaruhe Way.

Ferry Landing Backpackers
HOSTEL $

(☑09-403 7985; www.ferrylandingrussell.co.nz; 395 Aucks Rd, Okiato Pt; dm/s/d $30/50/60; @☎) More like a homestay than a hostel, with only two rooms on offer within the owners' house. It sits on the hill directly above the ferry landing in Okiato – you'll need a car to get here.

Russell-Orongo Bay Holiday Park
HOLIDAY PARK $

(☑09-403 7704; www.russellaccommodation.co.nz; 5960 Russell Rd; unpowered/powered site $40/44, teepee $80-90, cabins & units $80-165; @☎☒) ✍ Surrounded by 14 acres studded with native forest and birdlife, this relaxed holiday park is around 3km from Russell after departing the ferry from Opua to Okiato. The wide range of accommodation includes a quirky teepee and comfortable self-contained units.

Russell Top 10
HOLIDAY PARK $

(☑09-403 7826; www.russelltop10.co.nz; 1 James St; sites/cabins/units from $41/80/140; @☎) ✍ This leafy park has a small store, good facilities, wonderful hydrangeas, tidy cabins and nice units. Showers are clean, but metered.

Pukeko Cottage
HOSTEL $

(☑09-403 8498; www.pukekocottagebackpackers.co.nz; 14 Brind Rd; per person $30; ☎) More like staying at a mate's place than a hostel, this homely house has just two bedrooms for rent and a caravan in the back garden. It's certainly not dirty, but the cleanliness is bloke-standard. Barry, the artist owner, is always up for a chat.

Lesley's B&B Homestay
B&B $$

(☑09-403 7099; www.lesleys.co.nz; 1 Pomare Rd; s $110-150, d $140-180; ☎) Rooms are bright and colourful at this welcoming B&B owned by a well-travelled local artist. Breakfasts are legendary – the owner Lesley is also a trained chef – and the guests can fire up the barbecue. Gardens and palms surround the property, and the attractions and cafes of Russell are a 10-minute walk away.

Russell Motel
MOTEL $$

(☑09-403 7854; www.motelrussell.co.nz; 16 Matauwhi Rd; units $130-165; ☎☒) Sitting amid well-tended gardens, this old-fashioned motel offers a good range of units and a kidney-shaped pool that the kids will love. The studios are a little dark but you really can't quibble for this price in central Russell.

Duke of Marlborough
HISTORIC HOTEL $$

(☑09-403 7829; www.theduke.co.nz; 35 The Strand; r $165-360; ☎) Holding NZ's oldest pub licence, the Duke boasts about 'serving rascals and reprobates since 1827', although the building has burnt down twice since then. The upstairs accommodation ranges from small, bright rooms in a 1930s extension to snazzy, spacious doubles facing the water.

Arcadia Lodge
B&B $$$

(☑09-403 7756; www.arcadialodge.co.nz; 10 Florance Ave; d $200-270; ☎) ✍ The characterful rooms of this 1890 hillside house are decked out with interesting antiques and fine linen, while the breakfast is probably the best you'll eat in town – organic, delicious and complemented with spectacular views from the deck.

Commodore's Lodge
MOTEL $$$

(☑09-403 7899; www.commodoreslodgemotel.co.nz; 28 The Strand; units $200-310; ☎☒) Being the envy of every passer-by makes up for the lack of privacy in the front apartments that face the waterfront promenade. Spacious, nicely presented units are the order of the day here, along with a small pool and free kayaks, dinghies and bikes.

Orongo Bay Homestead
LODGE $$$

(☑09-403 7527; www.thehomestead.co.nz; Aucks Rd; r $585; ☎) ✍ This wooden homestead (c 1860) was NZ's first American consulate, located a discreet 4km from Russell's rabble. Accommodation is by way of three stylishly plush rooms in the converted barn facing a chocolate-box lake. Breakfast is memorable and dinners are by arrangement.

Hananui Lodge & Apartments
MOTEL $$$

(☑09-403 7875; www.hananui.co.nz; 4 York St; units $185-320; ☎) Choose between sparkling motel-style units in the trim waterside lodge or apartments in the newer block across the road. Pick of the bunch are the upstairs waterfront units with views straight over the beach.

✕ Eating & Drinking

For a country so hooked on cafe culture and a town so touristy, it's disappointing that Russell doesn't have more on offer.

Newport Chocolates CAFE, SWEETS $
(www.newportchocolates.co.nz; 3 Cass St; chocolates around $3; ☉10am-5pm) Delicious artisan chocolates – handmade on site – with flavours including raspberry, lime and chilli, and, our favourite, caramel and sea salt. Also a top spot for rich hot chocolate and refreshing frappes.

Gables MODERN NZ $$
(✆09-403 7670; www.thegablesrestaurant.co.nz; 19 The Strand; lunch $19-25, dinner $25-32; ☉noon-3pm Fri-Mon, from 6pm Thu-Mon) Serving an imaginative take on Kiwi classics (lamb, beef and lots of seafood), the Gables occupies an 1847 building on the waterfront, built using whale vertebrae for foundations. Ask for a table by the windows for watery views and look forward to local produce including oysters, cheese and Kerikeri citrus fruits.

Duke of Marlborough PUB $$
(www.theduke.co.nz; 35 The Strand; lunch $12-32, dinner $24-37; ☉11am-late) There's no better spot in Russell to while away a few hours, glass in hand, than the Duke's sunny deck. Thankfully the upmarket pub grub matches the views, plus there's an excellent wine list and a great selection of NZ craft beers.

Tuk Tuk THAI $$
(www.tuktukrestaurant.co.nz; 19 York St; mains $18-24; ☉10.30am-11pm; ✐) Thai fabrics adorn the tables and Thai favourites fill the menu. In clement weather grab a table out front and watch Russell's little world go by.

The Wharf CAFE $$
(www.thewharfrussell.co.nz; 29 The Strand; breakfast $12-18, dinner $25-35; ☉11am-3pm & 5pm-late Wed-Sun) Cosy, nautical-themed nook with a focus on well-prepared seafood, meaty stonegrill dishes and lighter tapas-style plates. Good-value breakfasts will set you up for the day's exploring.

Hone's PIZZERIA, BAR $$
(York St; pizza $19-27; ☉noon-late summer only) Head out to the pebbled courtyard behind the Gables restaurant for wood-fired pizza, cold beer and a good vibe.

Pub 'round the Corner PUB
(19 York St; ☉noon-late) A cool, cosy tavern with pool tables and a local's vibe.

🛍 Shopping

Just Imagine... ARTS & CRAFTS
(www.justimagine.co.nz; 25 York St; ☉10am-5pm) Glassware, paintings and gifts.

ℹ Information

Russell Booking & Information Centre (✆09-403 8020; www.russellinfo.co.nz; Russell Pier; ☉8am-5pm, later in summer)

ℹ Getting There & Away

The quickest way to reach Russell by car is via the car ferry (car/motorcycle/passenger $11/5.50/1), which runs every 10 minutes from Opua (5km from Paihia) to Okiato (8km from Russell), between 6.40am and 10pm. Buy your tickets on board. If you're travelling from the south, a scenic alternative is Russell Rd.

On foot, the easiest way to reach Russell is on a passenger ferry from Paihia (adult/child one way $7/3, return $12/6). They run from 7am to 7pm (until 10pm October to May), generally every 20 minutes but hourly in the evenings. Buy your tickets on board or at the i-SITE (p129) in Paihia.

Paihia & Waitangi

POP 1800

The birthplace of NZ (as opposed to Aotearoa), Waitangi inhabits a special, somewhat complex place in the national psyche – aptly demonstrated by the mixture of celebration, commemoration, protest and apathy that accompanies the nation's birthday (Waitangi Day, 6 February).

It was here that the long-neglected and much-contested Treaty of Waitangi was first signed between Maori chiefs and the British Crown, establishing British sovereignty or something a bit like it, depending on whether you're reading the English or Maori version of the document. If you're interested in coming to grips with NZ's history and race relations, this is the place to start.

Joined to Waitangi by a bridge, Paihia would be a fairly nondescript coastal town if it wasn't the main entry point to the Bay of Islands. If you're not on a tight budget, catch a ferry to Russell, which is far nicer.

Paihia

Paihia

Sights
1 Opua Forest	A3
2 St Paul's Church	C2

Activities, Courses & Tours
3 Explore NZ	C2
4 Fullers Great Sights	C2
5 Island Kayaks & Bay Beach Hire	C2
6 Mack Attack	C2
7 Paihia Dive	C2
8 Salt Air	C2

Sleeping
9 Admiral's View Lodge	C3
10 Allegra House	B2
11 Cap'n Bob's Beachhouse	A1
12 Peppertree Lodge	C3
13 Pickled Parrot	C3
14 Seabeds	A1
15 Tarlton's Lodge	D3

Eating
16 35 Degrees South	C2
17 Alfresco's	C2
18 Countdown	A1
19 El Cafe	C2
Paihia Farmers Market	(see 3)

Drinking & Nightlife
20 Bay of Islands Swordfish Club	C2
21 Pipi Patch Bar	C3
22 Sauce	C2

There are some good walks in the area, including an easy 5km track that follows the coast from Opua to Paihia.

Sights & Activities

★ **Waitangi Treaty Grounds** HISTORIC SITE
(☏09-402 7437; www.waitangi.net.nz; 1 Tau Henare Dr; adult/child $25/free; ◷9am-5pm Mar-Dec, to 7pm Jan-Feb) 🌿 Occupying a headland draped in lawns and bush, this is NZ's most significant historic site. Here, on 6 February 1840, the first 43 Maori chiefs, after much

discussion, signed the Treaty of Waitangi with the British Crown; eventually, over 500 chiefs would sign it.

The Treaty House was built in 1832 as the four-room home of British resident James Busby. It's now preserved as a memorial and museum containing displays, including a copy of the treaty. Just across the lawn, the magnificently detailed *whare runanga* (meeting house) was completed in 1940 to mark the centenary of the treaty. The fine carvings represent the major Maori tribes.

Near the cove is the 35m *waka taua* (war canoe), also built for the centenary. A photographic exhibit details how it was fashioned from gigantic kauri logs.

The importance of the treaty is well understood by a NZ audience, but visitors might find it surprising that there's not more information displayed here about the role it has played in the nation's history: the long litany of breaches by the Crown, the wars and land confiscations that followed, and the protest movement that led to the current process of redress for historic injustices.

International visitors will get more out of what is already quite a pricey admission fee if they pay extra for a guided tour ($10) or cultural performance ($15). The 30-minute performance (11am and 1pm) demonstrates traditional Maori song and dance, including the *haka* (war dance). The Ultimate Combo (adult/child $40/free) is a combined ticket including tour and performance. Other options include a Maori Cultural Workshop (adult/child $60/35), and a *hangi* and concert (adult/child $105/50, Wednesday and Saturday December to March) at the Treaty Ground's Whare Waka (p128) cafe.

Entry is free to NZ citizens upon presentation of a passport or drivers licence.

Haruru Falls
WATERFALL
(Haruru Falls Rd) A walking track (1½ hours one way, 5km) leads from the Treaty Grounds along the Waitangi River to these attractive horseshoe falls. Part of the path follows a boardwalk through the mangroves. Otherwise you can drive here, turning right off Puketona Rd onto Haruru Falls Rd.

St Paul's Church
CHURCH
(Marsden Rd) The characterful St Paul's was constructed of Kawakawa stone in 1925, and stands on the site of NZ's first church, a simple *raupo* (bulrush) hut erected in 1823. Look for the native birds in the stained glass above the altar – the kotare (kingfisher) represents Jesus (the king plus 'fisher of men'), while the tui (parson bird) and kereru (wood pigeon) portray the personalities of the Williams brothers (one scholarly, one forceful), who set up the mission station here.

Opua Forest
FOREST
Just behind Paihia, this regenerating forest has walking trails ranging from 10 minutes to five hours. A few large trees have escaped axe and fire, including some big kauri. Walk up from School Rd for about 30 minutes to good lookouts. Information on Opua Forest walks is available from the i-SITE. Drive into the forest by taking Oromahoe Rd west from Opua.

🛏 Sleeping

If your budget is more flexible, Russell has more atmosphere, but Paihia is more convenient and has motels, apartments and B&Bs on the waterfront and around the surrounding hills. Paihia has an excellent range of hostels, and Kings Rd is the main 'backpackers' row'.

Seabeds
HOSTEL $
(☑ 09-402 5567; www.seabeds.co.nz; 46 Davis Cres; dm/s/d/apt $28/68/85/95; @ 🛜) Offering comfortable, friendly, stylish budget digs in a converted motel, Seabeds is one of Paihia's best hostels. Little design touches give it a stylish ambience, and it's in a quieter location than most of Paihia's more social hostels along Kings Rd.

Peppertree Lodge
HOSTEL $
(☑ 09-402 6122; www.peppertree.co.nz; 15 Kings Rd; dm $25-28, r $72-110; @ 🛜) Simple, clean rooms with high ceilings and good linen, plus bikes, racquets, kayaks and two barbecues for guests' use, making this a sociable choice.

Pickled Parrot
HOSTEL $
(☑ 09-402 6222; www.pickledparrot.co.nz; Greys Lane; sites per person $19, dm $26, r $66-84; @ 🛜) Surrounded by tropical plants, this friendly, well-maintained backpackers' stalwart has cute cabins, free bikes and a good vibe.

Cap'n Bob's Beachhouse
HOSTEL $
(☑ 09-402 8668; www.capnbobs.co.nz; 44 Davis Cres; dm/s/tw/d $25/49/64/86; @ 🛜) This small backpackers is a homely place, with sea views from the verandah, and more than a touch of easygoing charm.

Beachside Holiday Park
HOLIDAY PARK $
(☑ 09-402 7678; www.beachsideholiday.co.nz; 1290 SH11; sites/units from $18/65; @ 🛜) 🏊 Wake up at the water's edge at this sheltered camping ground, south of the township. The angular lemon cabins have 1970s charm, and there are kayaks for hire.

Bay of Islands Holiday Park
HOLIDAY PARK $
(☑ 09-402 7646; www.bayofislandsholidaypark. co.nz; 678 Puketona Rd; site/unit from $38/70; @ 🛜 🏊) Under tall trees by a set of shallow rapids on the Waitangi River, 7km down Puketona Rd, this wonderful holiday park has excellent units and shady campsites.

Tarlton's Lodge
B&B **$$**

(📞 09-402 6711; www.tarltonslodge.co.nz; 11 Sullivans Rd; r $175-220; 🛜🌊) Striking architecture combines with modern decor in this hilltop B&B with expansive bay views. All three suites have their own outdoor spa, perfect for a romantic stay. Look forward to excellent breakfasts.

Baystay B&B
B&B **$$**

(📞 09-402 7511; www.baystay.co.nz; 93a Yorke Rd, Haruru Falls; r $140-175; @🛜) Enjoy valley views from the spa pool of this slick, gay-friendly establishment. Yorke Rd is off Puketona Rd, just before the falls. Minimum stay of two nights; no children under 12.

Cook's Lookout
MOTEL **$$**

(📞 09-402 7409; www.cookslookout.co.nz; Causeway Rd; r $145-175, apt $255; 🛜🌊) Cook's Lookout is an old-fashioned motel with friendly owners, breathtaking views and a solar-heated swimming pool. Take Puketona Rd towards Haruru Falls, turn right into Yorke Rd and then take the second right.

Admiral's View Lodge
MOTEL **$$**

(📞 09-402 6236; www.admiralsviewlodge.co.nz; 2 MacMurray Rd; apt $120-195; @) This hillside lodge offers natty units with balconies just begging for a relaxed sunset gin and tonic. Some have spa baths and bay views.

Allegra House
B&B **$$$**

(📞 09-402 7932; www.allegra.co.nz; 39 Bayview Rd; r $220-245, apt $275; @🛜) Offering quite astonishing views of the bay from an eyrie high above the township, Allegra has three handsome B&B rooms and a spacious self-contained apartment.

✖ Eating

El Cafe
CAFE, SOUTH AMERICAN **$**

(2 Kings Rd; snacks $5-10; ⊙8am-5pm) Excellent Chilean-owned cafe with the best coffee in town and good breakfast burritos, tacos, empanadas and Latin American sweet treats. The smoothies are also great on on a warm Bay of Islands day. Say *hola* to owner Javier for us.

Shippey's
FISH & CHIPS **$**

(www.shippeys.com; Waitangi Bridge; mains $7-16; ⊙11am-late) Tuck into fresh fish and chips served as the good Lord intended them – in newspaper with a cold beverage in hand – onboard a permanently moored 19th-century tall ship. The views over the inlet and bay are magical, particularly at sunset.

Paihia Farmers Market
MARKET **$**

(www.bayofislandsfarmersmarket.org.nz; Village Green; ⊙2-5.30pm Thu) Stock up on local fruit, vegetables, pickles, preserves, honey, fish, smallgoods, eggs, cheese, bread, wine and oil, straight from the producer.

Countdown
SUPERMARKET **$**

(6 Puketona Rd; ⊙7am-9pm) The main place to stock up on provisions.

Whare Waka
CAFE **$$**

(Waitangi Treaty Grounds; mains $15-24; ⊙9am-5pm) Located beside a pond studded with ducks, backed by bush and overlooking the Treaty Grounds, the Whare Waka cafe is a top spot for good cafe fare during the day, and to return to for a *hangi* dinner on Wednesday and Saturday evenings from December to March.

Alfresco's
PUB **$$**

(📞 09-402 6797; www.alfrescosrestaurantpaihia. com; 6 Marsden Rd; breakfast & lunch $12-20, dinner $18-33; ⊙8am-late) Locals flock to this casual restaurant-cafe-bar for great food – including lots of local seafood – and reasonable prices. Settle in for live music from 3pm to 6pm every Sunday afternoon. There's Happy Hour bar prices from 3pm to 6pm every day too.

35 Degrees South
MODERN NZ, SEAFOOD **$$**

(www.35south.co.nz; 69 Marsden Rd; shared plates $10-15, mains $25-30) Service was a bit disorganised when we visited, but you can't beat the over-the-water location in central Paihia. The menu is at its best with local oysters and fish and the shared small plates. Try the tempura fish tortillas, and maybe share a dessert of Dutch raisin doughnuts.

Drinking

God bless backpackers: they certainly keep the bars buzzing. There are plenty of places along Kings Rd and in the town centre to explore, so don't feel hemmed in by our list.

Pipi Patch Bar
BAR

(18 Kings Rd; ⊙5pm-late) The party hostel has the party bar: a popular spot with large video screens and a decent terrace. You'll be shuffled inside at midnight to keep the neighbours happy – although most of them are backpackers who'll be here anyway.

Sauce
BEER

(Marsden Rd; pizza $12-22; ⊙11am-late Tue-Sun) Design-your-own pizzas plus the added attraction of excellent craft beer on tap from Hamilton's Good George Brewery.

Bay of Islands Swordfish Club BAR
(Swordy; www.swordfish.co.nz; upstairs, 96 Marsden Rd; ☺4pm-late) Great views, cold beer and tall tales abound at this brightly lit club-bar where creatures from the deep protrude from every available surface. Decent burgers, steaks and seafood ($12 to $28) are also served.

ℹ Information

Bay of Islands i-SITE (☎09-402 7345; www. northlandnz.com; Marsden Rd; ☺8am-5pm Mar–mid-Dec, to 7pm mid-Dec–Feb) Information and bookings.

ℹ Getting There & Around

All buses serving Paihia, such as InterCity and Naked Bus, stop at the Maritime Building by the wharf.

Ferries depart regularly for Russell.

For bikes, visit Bay Beach Hire (p118).

Urupukapuka Island

The largest of the bay's islands, Urupukapuka is a tranquil place criss-crossed with walking trails and surrounded by aquamarine waters. Native birds are plentiful thanks to a conservation initiative that has rendered this and all of the neighbouring islands predator free; check that there aren't any rats, mice or ants stowing away on your boat or in your gear before leaving the mainland.

Most of the regular boat tours moor at Otehei Bay for a little island time; if you want to stay over, you can usually arrange to split the trip up and return at a later date. There are **DOC campsites** (www.doc.govt.nz; sites per adult/child $10/5) at Cable, Sunset and Urupukapuka Bays, which have water supplies, cold showers (except Sunset Bay) and composting toilets; bring food, a stove and fuel.

The **Waterfront Bar & Cafe** (www.oteheibay.co.nz; Otehei Bay; mains $15-25; ☺11am-8pm) serves light meals and snacks to boat-tour passengers, and at the height of summer also offers evening meals. Kayaks can be rented on the island from **Bay of Islands Kayaking** (☎021 272 3353; www.bayofislands-kayaking.co.nz; hire from $10, island transfer & guided paddle $160).

Kerikeri

POP 6500

Kerikeri means 'dig dig', which is apt, as lots of digging goes on around the area's fertile farmland. Famous for its oranges, Kerikeri also produces kiwifruit, vegetables and wine. If you're looking for some backbreaking, poorly paid work that the locals aren't keen to do, your working holiday starts here.

A snapshot of early Maori and Pakeha (European New Zealander) interaction is offered by a cluster of historic sites centred on the picturesque river basin. In 1819 the powerful Ngapuhi chief Hongi Hika allowed Rev Samuel Marsden to start a mission under the shadow of his Kororipo Pa. There's an ongoing campaign to have the area recognised as a Unesco World Heritage Site.

◎ Sights & Activities

★ Stone Store
& Mission House HISTORIC BUILDINGS
(www.historic.org.nz; 246 Kerikeri Rd; ☺10am-4pm) Dating from 1836, the Stone Store is NZ's oldest stone building. It sells interesting Kiwiana gifts as well as the type of goods that used to be sold in the store. Tours ($10) of the wooden Mission House, NZ's oldest building (1822), depart from here and include entry to *The Soul Trade* exhibition on the 1st floor of the store.

Just up the hill is a marked historical walk, which leads to the site of Kororipo Pa. Huge war parties led by Hika once departed from here, terrorising much of the North Island and slaughtering thousands during the Musket Wars. The role of missionaries in arming Ngapuhi remains controversial. The walk emerges near the cute wooden St James Anglican Church (1878).

Rewa's Village MUSEUM
(Landing Rd; adult/child $5/1; ☺9.30am-4.30pm) If you had a hard time imagining Kororipo Pa in its original state, take the footbridge across the river to this fascinating mock-up of a traditional Maori fishing village.

Aroha Island WILDLIFE RESERVE
(☎09-407 5243; www.arohaisland.co.nz; 177 Rangitane Rd; ☺9.30am-5.30pm) 🌿FREE Reached via a permanent causeway through the mangroves, this 5-hectare island provides a haven for the North Island brown kiwi and other native birds, as well as a pleasant

Kerikeri

Kerikeri

◎ Top Sights
1 Stone Store & Mission House D2

◎ Sights
2 Rewa's Village.....................................D2
3 Wharepuke Falls D1

🛏 Sleeping
4 Bed of Roses......................................C1
5 Pagoda Lodge D2
6 Wharepuke Subtropical
   Accommodation C1

✖ Eating
7 Cafe Jerusalem B1
8 Cafe Zest...A1
9 Fishbone..A1
Food at Wharepuke ....(see 6)
10 Kerikeri Farmers Market....................A1
11 Pear Tree...D2
The Village Cafe ....(see 7)

picnic spot for their nonfeathered admirers. It has a visitor centre, kayaks for rent, and after-dark walks to spy kiwi in the wild (per person $35) can also be arranged. You've got around a 50% chance of seeing a kiwi, and booking ahead is essential.

Kerikeri River Track　　　　　WALKING
Starting from Kerikeri Basin, this 4km-long track leads past **Wharepuke Falls** and the **Fairy Pools** to the **Rainbow Falls**, where the sheet of water encloses a moss-covered cavern. Alternatively, you can reach the Rainbow Falls from Rainbow Falls Rd, in which case it's only a 10-minute walk.

🛏 Sleeping

Relax a Lodge　　　　　HOMESTAY $
(☑09-407 6989; www.relaxalodge.co.nz; 1574 Springbank Rd/SH10; s $55, d & tw $70-90, cottages $110-135; @🛜🏊) Less a farm, more an orange grove, this quiet rural house 4km out of town sleeps just 12 people and is a cosy and welcoming place. Some newly refurbished cottages dotted around the property are also very good value.

Aroha Island　　　　　CAMPSITE $
(☑09-407 5243; www.arohaisland.co.nz; 177 Rangitane Rd; sites/units from $18/119) 🐾 Kip among the kiwi on the eco island of *aroha* (love). There's a wide range of reasonably priced options, from the peaceful campsites with basic facilities by the shelly beach to a whole house. The entire island, indoors and out, is nonsmoking.

Pagoda Lodge　　　　　LODGE, CAMPSITE $$
(☑09-407 8617; www.pagoda.co.nz; 81 Pa Rd; sites/safari tent/caravan from $40/120/130, apt $120-350; 🛜) Built in the 1930s by an oddball Scotsman with an Asian fetish, this lodge features pagoda-shaped roofs grafted onto wooden cottages. The property descends to the river and is dotted with Buddhas, gypsy caravans, and safari tents with proper beds, or you can pitch your own. To get here, take Cobham Rd, turn left into Kerikeri Inlet Rd and then left into Pa Rd.

Kauri Park　　　　　MOTEL $$
(☑09-407 7629; www.kauripark.co.nz; 512 Kerikeri Rd; units $130-170; @🛜🏊) Hidden behind tall trees on the approach to Kerikeri, this well-priced motel has a mixture of units of vary-

ing layouts – some quite stylishly furnished and others a little more old fashioned.

Wharepuke Subtropical Accommodation
CABINS $$

(☑09-407 8933; www.accommodation-bay-of-islands.co.nz; 190 Kerikeri Rd; cabins $150; ☎) Best known for its food and lush gardens, Wharepuke also rents five self-contained one-bedroom cottages hidden among the palms. They have the prefabricated look of holiday-park cabins but are a step up in terms of fixtures and space.

Bed of Roses
B&B $$$

(☑09-407 4666; www.bedofroses.co.nz; 165 Kerikeri Rd; r $295-475; @) It's all petals and no thorns at this stylish B&B, furnished with French antiques, luxe linens and comfy beds. The house has an art-deco ambience and awesome views.

Eating & Drinking

Cafe Jerusalem
MIDDLE EASTERN $

(www.cafejerusalem.co.nz; Village Mall, 85 Kerikeri Rd; snacks & mains $9-18; ⊘10am-late Mon-Sat, 5pm-late Sun in summer) Northland's best felafels and lamb kebabs, all served with a smile and a social vibe. Good salads, and wine and and beer are also available. Try the *shakshuka* (baked eggs in a spicy tomato sauce) for a hearty brunch.

Fishbone
CAFE, BAR $

(www.fishbonecafe.co.nz; 88 Kerikeri Rd; mains $10-18; ⊘8am-4pm Mon-Wed, to 8pm Thu-Fri, 8.30am-3pm Sat & Sun) Kerikeri's best brekkie spot serves excellent coffee and food. Dr Seuss fans should try the green (pesto) eggs and ham. From 4pm to 7pm on Thursdays and Fridays, Fishbone morphs into a wine bar.

The Village Cafe
CAFE $

(Village Mall, 85 Kerikeri Rd; mains $10-17; ⊘8am-4pm Mon-Fri, to 2pm Sat & Sun) This chic and cosmopolitan spot is popular with locals for good coffee, freshly prepared counter food, and a relaxed menu of brunch and lunch dishes. Grab a table outside in the Northland sunshine, and order the hearty potato hash.

Cafe Zest
CAFE, BAR $

(73 Kerikeri Rd; mains $10-19; ⊘7.30am-4pm Mon-Wed, to 8.30pm Thu-Sat, to 2pm Sun) Cute Zest serves cafe fare during the day and tapas in the evening, but the main reason to drop by is to sample wines from all of the local producers.

KERIKERI COTTAGE INDUSTRIES

You'd be forgiven for thinking that everyone in Kerikeri is involved in some small-scale artisanal enterprise, as the bombardment of craft shops on the way into town attests.

While Northland isn't known for its wine, a handful of vineyards are doing their best to change that. The little-known red grape chambourcin has proved particularly suited to the region's subtropical humidity, along with pinotage and syrah.

Look out for the *Art & Craft Trail* and *Wine Trail* brochures. Here are our tasty recommendations.

Kerikeri Farmers Market (www.boifm.org.nz; Hobson Ave; ⊘8.30am-noon Sun) From gourmet sausages to *limoncello*.

Get Fudged & Keriblue (www.getfudged.co.nz; 560 Kerikeri Rd; ⊘9am-5pm) An unusual pairing of ceramics and big, decadent slabs of fudge.

Makana Confections (www.makana.co.nz; 504 Kerikeri Rd; ⊘9am-5.30pm) Artisan chocolate factory with lots of sampling.

Marsden Estate (www.marsdenestate.co.nz; 56 Wiroa Rd; mains $19-32, platters $35; ⊘10am-5pm) Excellent wine and lunch on the deck.

Ake Ake (☑09-407 8230; www.akeakevineyard.co.nz; 165 Waimate North Rd; tastings $5, tour $5, mains $27-34, lunch platters $25-48; ⊘cellar door 10am-4.30pm Wed-Sun, restaurant noon-late Wed-Sun winter, daily summer) Vineyard tours (11.30am) and tastings, both free with lunch or purchase of wine. The swanky restaurant is open for lunch and dinner on the days the cellar door is open.

Cottle Hill (www.cottlehill.co.nz; Cottle Hill Dr; tastings $5, free with purchase.; ⊘10am-5.30pm Nov-Mar, 10am-5pm Wed-Sun Apr-Oct) Wine and port.

Fat Pig Vineyard (www.fatpig.co.nz; 177 Puketotara Rd; ⊘3-7pm Fri, 11am-7pm Sat & Sun) Wine and port.

WORTH A TRIP

PUKETI & OMAHUTA FORESTS

Inland from Kerikeri, the Puketi and Omahuta Forests form a continuous expanse of native rainforest. Logging in Puketi was stopped in 1951 to protect not only the remaining kauri but also the endangered kokako bird. Keep an eye out for this rare charmer (grey with a blue wattle) on your wanders.

The forests are reached by several entrances and contain a network of walking tracks varying in length from 15 minutes (the wheelchair-accessible Manginangina Kauri Walk) to two days (the challenging Waipapa River Track); see the DOC website for other walks.

You'll find a **DOC campsite** (☑09-407 0300; www.doc.govt.nz; Waiare Rd; sites per adult/child 6/3), two three-person cabins ($21) and a 18-bunk hut (exclusive use $62) at the Puketi Recreation Area on the forests' eastern fringe. The hut has hot showers, a kitchen and a flush toilet, while the cabins and campsite make do with cold showers.

Adventure Puketi (www.forestwalks.com; tours $75-155) leads guided ecowalks through the forest, including night-time tours to seek out the nocturnal wildlife.

Just next door the owners have opened a funky space serving freshly made waffles.

Food at Wharepuke   CAFE $$
(☑09-407 8936; www.foodatwharepuke.co.nz; 190 Kerikeri Rd; breakfast $14-22, lunch $24-38, dinner $30-40; ☺10am-10pm Tue-Sat, 9am-3pm Sun) 🍴
With one foot in Europe, the other in Thailand and its head in the lush vegetation of Wharepuke Subtropical Gardens, this is Kerikeri's most unusual and inspired eatery. On Friday nights it serves popular Thai banquets (three courses $47.50), while on Sunday afternoons it hosts live jazz. Adjacent is the interesting Wharepuke Print Studio & Gallery.

Pear Tree   RESTAURANT, BAR $$
(☑09-407 8479; www.thepeartree.co.nz; 215 Kerikeri Rd; lunch $15-20, dinner $25-32; ☺10am-2pm daily, 6pm-late Wed-Mon) Kerikeri's best-located and most upmarket restaurant occupies an old homestead right on the basin (book ahead for a table on the verandah). Mains run the gamut of bistro favourites, along with the occasional Asian dish.

ℹ Information

Procter Library (Cobham Rd; ☺8am-5pm Mon-Fri, 9am-2pm Sat, 9am-1pm Sun; 🛜) Tourist information and free internet access.

ℹ Getting There & Away

AIR

Bay of Islands (Kerikeri) Airport (☑09-407 7147; www.bayofislandsairport.co.nz; 218 Wiroa Rd) is 8km southwest of town. Air New Zealand flies from Auckland to Kerikeri. **Super Shuttle** (☑0800 748 885; www.supershuttle.co.nz; $25) operates a shuttle service from the airport to Kerikeri, Paihia, Opua and Kawakawa.

BUS

InterCity (p108) and partner buses leave from a stop at 9 Cobham Rd, opposite the library.

THE FAR NORTH

Here's your chance to get off the beaten track, even if that does mean onto unsealed roads. The far-flung Far North always play second fiddle to the Bay of Islands for attention and funding, yet the subtropical tip of the North Island has more breathtaking coastline per square kilometre than anywhere but the offshore islands. While the 'winterless north' may be a popular misnomer, summers here are long and leisurely. Note that parts of the Far North are noticeably economically depressed and in places could best be described as gritty. Online see www.topofnz.co.nz.

Matauri & Tauranga Bays

It's a short detour from SH10, but the exceptionally scenic loop route leading inland to these awesome beaches is a world away from the glitzy face presented for tourists in the Bay of Islands.

Matauri Bay is a long, sandy surf beach, 18km off SH10, with the 17 Cavalli Islands scattered offshore. **Matauri Bay Holiday Park** (☑09-405 0525; www.matauribayholiday-park.co.nz; sites from $20, units $130-140) takes up the north end of the beach and has a shop selling groceries, booze and petrol. On top of the headland above the park is a monument to the *Rainbow Warrior;* the Greenpeace ship's underwater resting place among the Cavalli Islands is a popular dive site.

DOC maintains a 12-person **hut** (☎09-407 0300; www.doc.govt.nz; adult/child $15/10) on Motukawanui Island, but you'll need a boat or kayak to reach it and you'll need to book ahead. Only water, mattresses and a composting toilet are provided; bring everything else.

Back on the main road, the route heads west, passing through pleasant Te Ngaere village and a succession of little bays before the turn-off to Tauranga Bay, a smaller beach where the sand is a peachy pink colour. **Tauranga Bay Holiday Park** (☎09-405 0436; www.taurangabay.co.nz; sites from $20, cabins $97-170; @ 🖂) has campsites and log cabins on the beachfront, but it lacks trees and bears the brunt of the weather. A minimum $59 charge per night for campsites and a seven-night minimum stay applies in January.

Down a private road leading from Tauranga Bay, **Northland Sea Kayaking** (☎09-405 0381; www.northlandseakayaking.co.nz; half-/full-day tours $75/95) leads kayak explorations of this magical coastline of coves, sea caves and islands. Accommodation is available in conjunction with tours for $25 extra per person.

There's no public transport to these parts or to neighbouring Whangaroa.

Whangaroa Harbour

Just around the headland from Tauranga Bay is the narrow entrance to Whangaroa Harbour. The small fishing village of Whangaroa is 6km from SH10 and calls itself the 'Marlin Capital of NZ'.

There are plenty of charter boats for game-fishing (December to April); prices start at around $1200 a day. If you're planning to hook a monster, insist on it being released once caught – striped marlin and swordfish are among NZ's least-sustainable fishing options.

An excellent 20-minute hike starts from the car park at the end of Old Hospital Rd and goes up **St Paul's Rock** (213m), which dominates the village. At the top you have to use a wire cable to pull yourself up, but the views make it worth the effort.

The **Wairakau Stream Track**, heading north to Pekapeka Bay, begins near the

THE BOMBING OF THE RAINBOW WARRIOR

On the morning of 10 July 1985, New Zealanders awoke to news reporting that a terrorist attack had killed a man in Auckland Harbour. The Greenpeace flagship *Rainbow Warrior* had been sunk at its anchorage at Marsden Wharf, where it was preparing to sail to Moruroa Atoll near Tahiti to protest against French nuclear testing.

A tip-off from a Neighbourhood Watch group eventually led to the arrest of two French foreign intelligence service (DGSE) agents, posing as tourists. The agents had detonated two mines on the boat in staggered explosions – the first designed to cause the crew to evacuate and the second to sink her. However, after the initial evacuation, some of the crew returned to the vessel to investigate and document the attack. Greenpeace photographer Fernando Pereira was drowned below decks following the second explosion.

The arrested agents pleaded guilty to manslaughter and were sentenced to 10 years' imprisonment. In response, the French government threatened to embargo NZ goods from entering the European Economic Community – which would have crippled NZ's economy. A deal was struck whereby France paid $13 million to NZ and apologised, in return for the agents being delivered into French custody on a South Pacific atoll for three years. France eventually paid over $8 million to Greenpeace in reparation – and the bombers were quietly freed before their sentence was served.

Initially French President François Mitterrand denied any government involvement in the attack, but following an inquiry he eventually sacked his defence minister and the head of the DGSE, Admiral Pierre Lacoste. On the 20th anniversary of the attack, *Le Monde* newspaper published a report from Lacoste dating from 1986, declaring that the president had personally authorised the operation.

The bombing left a lasting impact on NZ, and French nuclear testing at Moruroa ceased for good in 1996. The wreck of the *Rainbow Warrior* was resunk near Northland's Cavalli Islands, where, today, it can be explored by divers. The masts were bought by the Dargaville Museum and overlook the town. The memory of Fernando Pereira endures in a peaceful bird hide in Thames, while a memorial to the boat sits atop a Maori *pa* (fortified village) site at Matauri Bay, north of the Bay of Islands.

church hall on Campbell Rd in Totara North on the other side of the bay. It's an extremely beautiful, undeveloped stretch and you can cool off in swimming holes along the way. The two-hour hike passes through forest, an abandoned farm and around a steep-walled estuary before arriving at DOC's **Lane Cove Hut** (☑ 09-407 0300; www.doc.govt.nz; sole occupancy $164), which has 16 beds, plus composting toilets. Bring everything else and reserve well ahead; it's usually booked out by Kiwi families over summer.

Duke's Nose Track (1¼ hours return) starts behind the cottage and leads up Kairara Rocks; look for the Duke of Wellington's aquiline profile in the rock face. You'll need to haul yourself up a chain for the last 10m but the views are worth it. If you don't fancy walking back – or if you don't fancy walking at all – **Bushmansfriend** (☑ 09-405 1844; www.bushmansfriend.co.nz) arranges water taxis from Lane Cove ($20) and one-hour boat tours ($45).

On the other side of the harbour's north head is **Taupo Bay**, a surf beach that attracts a loyal Kiwi contingent in summer. On easterly swells, there are quality righthanders to surf at the southern end of the bay, by the rivermouth. It's reached by an 11km sealed road signposted from SH10.

Sleeping & Eating

★**Kahoe Farms Hostel**   HOSTEL $
(☑ 09-405 1804; www.kahoefarms.co.nz; dm $30, r $76-96) On SH10, 10km north of the turn-off to Whangaroa, this hostel has a deservedly great reputation – for its comfortable accommodation, for its bucolic setting, for its home-cooked Italian food, but mostly for its welcoming owners. The backpackers cottage is great, but slightly up the hill there's an even more impressive villa with excellent-value en suite rooms.

Sunseeker Lodge   HOSTEL $
(☑ 09-405 0496; www.sunseekerlodge.co.nz; Old Hospital Rd; dm/s/d/tr $25/50/66/90, units $120-150; @ 🛜) Up the hill in Whangaroa, this friendly lodge has a spa with a jaw-dropping view, hires out kayaks and motor boats, and will pick you up from Kaeo on SH10.

Marlin   PUB $$
(Whangaroa Rd; mains $15-20; ⊙ lunch & dinner) A friendly local pub with good honest tucker served from the attached cafe.

ℹ Information

Boyd Gallery (☑ 09-405 0230; Whangaroa Rd; ⊙ 8am-7pm) General store and tourist information office.

Doubtless Bay
POP 6030

The bay gets its unusual name from an entry in Cook's logbook, where he wrote that the body of water was 'doubtless a bay'. No kidding, Cap'n. It's a bloody big bay at that, with a string of pretty swimming beaches heading towards the Karikari Peninsula.

The main centre, **Mangonui** (meaning 'Big Shark'), retains a fishing-port feel, despite cafes and gift shops now infesting its well-labelled line of historical waterfront buildings. They were constructed in the days when Mangonui was a centre of the whaling industry (1792–1850) and exported flax, kauri wood and gum.

The popular holiday settlements of **Coopers Beach**, **Cable Bay** and **Taipa** are restful pockets of beachside gentrification.

◉ Sights & Activities

Grab the free *Heritage Trail* brochure from the information centre for a 3km self-guided walk that takes in 22 historic sites. Other walks lead to attractive **Mill Bay**, west of Mangonui, and **Rangikapiti Pa Historic Reserve**, which has ancient Maori terracing and a spectacular view of Doubtless Bay – particularly at sunrise and sunset. A walkway runs from Mill Bay to the *pa*, but you can also drive nearly to the top.

Butler Point Whaling Museum   MUSEUM
(www.butlerpoint.co.nz; Marant Rd, Hihi; adult/child $12/2; ⊙ by appointment) At Hihi, 15km northeast of Mangonui, this small private museum and Victorian homestead (1843) is set in lovely gardens. Its first owner, Captain Butler, left Dorset when he was 14 and at 24 was captain of a whaling ship. He settled here in 1839, had 13 children and became a trader, farmer, magistrate and Member of Parliament.

Sleeping

There's plenty of accommodation, but most is overpriced in summer. Outside the peak months things settle down considerably.

Puketiti Lodge
HOSTEL $

(☑09-406 0369; www.puketitilodge.co.nz; 10 Puketiti Dr; dm/s/d $40/100/150; @🖥) If this is what they mean by flashpacking, bring it on. For $40 you get a comfy bunk in a spacious six-person dorm that opens on to a large deck with awesome views, a locker big enough for the burliest backpack and, perhaps most surprisingly, breakfast. Turn inland at Midgley Rd, 6km south of Mangonui village, just after the Hihi turn-off.

Old Oak
BOUTIQUE HOTEL $$

(☑09-406 1250; www.theoldoak.co.nz; 66 Waterfront Dr, Mangonui; d $175-275, ste $295-325; 🖥) This atmospheric 1861 kauri inn is now an elegant boutique hotel with contemporary design and top-notch furnishings. It oozes character, not least because the building is reputedly haunted.

Mangonui Waterfront Apartments Motel
APARTMENTS $$

(☑09-406 0347; www.mangonuiwaterfront.co.nz; 88 Waterfront Dr, Mangonui; apt $120-225; @🖥) Sleeping two to eight people, these historic apartments on the Mangonui waterfront have loads of character, each one different but all with balconies, a sense of space and their own barbecue. Try to book 100-year-old Tahi.

✗ Eating

There are also cafes, takeaways and stores around the other beaches.

Mangonui Fish Shop
FISH & CHIPS $

(137 Waterfront Dr, Mangonui; fish & chips $10; ⊙10am-8pm; 🖥) Eat outdoors over the water at this chippie, which also sells smoked fish and seafood salads. Grab a crayfish salad and a beer and you'll be sorted. The other fish-and-chip shop across the road is also good.

Waterfront Cafe & Bar
CAFE $$

(Waterfront Dr, Mangonui; brunch $11-18, dinner $14-29; ⊙8.30am-late) Waterfront has water views and old-world charm. A pizza menu kicks in at lunch and extends into dinner, when it supplements bistro dishes.

Thai Chef
THAI $$

(☑09-406 1220; www.thaichef.co.nz; 80 Waterfront Dr, Mangonui; mains $18-26; ⊙5-11pm Tue-Sun) Northland's best Thai restaurant serves piquant dishes with intriguing names like The 3 Alcoholics, Spice Girls and Bangkok Showtime.

🛍 Shopping

Flax Bush
ARTS & CRAFTS

(www.flaxbush.co.nz; 50 Waterfront Dr, Mangonui; ⊙10am-5pm) Seashells, Pasifika and Maori crafts.

Exhibit A
ARTS & CRAFTS

(Old Courthouse, Waterfront Dr; ⊙10am-4.30pm) This co-op gallery showcases Far North artists.

ℹ Information

Doubtless Bay Visitor Information Centre (☑09-406 2046; www.doubtlessbay.co.nz; 118 Waterfront Dr, Mangonui; ⊙10am-4pm Mon-Sat)

ℹ Getting There & Away

InterCity buses depart near the Watefront Cafe in Mangonui, outside the wholesalers in Coopers Beach, opposite the shop in Cable Bay and outside the Shell station in Taipa. **Busabout Kaitaia** (☑09-408 1092; www.cbec.co.nz) has services to Kaitaia ($5, one hour).

Karikari Peninsula

The oddly shaped Karikari Peninsula bends into a near-perfect right angle. The result is beaches facing north, south, east and west in close proximity, so if the wind's annoying you or you want to catch some surf, a sunrise or a sunset, just swap beaches. Despite its natural assets, the sun-baked peninsula is blissfully undeveloped, with farmers well outnumbering tourist operators. There's no public transport and you won't find a lot of shops or eateries either.

◉ Sights & Activities

Tokerau Beach is the long, sandy stretch forming the western edge of Doubtless Bay. Neighbouring **Whatuwhiwhi** is smaller and more built-up, facing back across the bay. **Maitai Bay**, with its tiny twin coves, is the loveliest of them all, at the lonely end of the peninsula down an unsealed road. It's a great spot for swimming – the waters sheltered enough for the kids but with enough swell to body surf.

Rangiputa faces west at the elbow of the peninsula; the pure white sand and crystal-clear sheltered waters come straight from a Pacific Island daydream. A turn-off on the road to Rangiputa takes you to remote

Puheke Beach, a long, windswept stretch of snow-white sand dunes forming Karikari's northern edge.

Various local watersports operators can be contacted under the umbrella of **Watersports Paradise** (☑ 050 872 7234; www.watersportsparadise.co.nz).

Karikari Estate WINERY
(www.karikariestate.co.nz; Maitai Bay Rd; tastings $12; ⊙ 11am-4pm Nov-Apr) A sign of creeping gentrification is this luxury golf club and winery on the way to Maitai Bay. Impressive Karikari Estate produces acclaimed red wines and has a cafe attached – and while the wine tastings are shamelessly overpriced, at least the sublime views are free.

Airzone Kitesurfing School KITESURFING
(☑ 021 202 7949; www.kitesurfnz.com; 1-/2-/3-day course $195/350/485) The unique set-up of Karikari Peninsula makes it one of the world's premium spots for kitesurfing. Learners get to hone their skills on flat water before heading to the surf, while the more experienced can chase the wind around the peninsula.

A to Z Diving DIVING
(☑ 09-408 3336; www.atozdiving.co.nz; 13-15 Whatuwhiwhi Rd; 2 dives incl equipment $160-230) Offers PADI courses and dive trips in Doubtless Bay and to the *Rainbow Warrior*.

🛌 Sleeping

Whatuwhiwhi Top 10 Holiday Park HOLIDAY PARK $
(☑ 09-408 7202; www.whatuwhiwhitop10.co.nz; 17 Whatuwhiwhi Rd; sites from $62, units $82-385) 🐾 Sheltered by hills and overlooking the beach, this friendly complex has a great location, good facilities, free barbecues and kayaks for hire. It also offers dive fills and PADI diving instruction.

Maitai Bay DOC Campsite CAMPSITE $
(www.doc.govt.nz; Maitai Bay Rd; sites per adult/child $10/5) 🐾 A large first-in, first-served (no bookings) camping ground at the peninsula's most beautiful beach, with chemical toilets, drinking water and cold showers.

Pepper's Carrington Resort RESORT $$$
(☑ 09-408 7222; www.peppers.co.nz; r from $245; @ 🐾) 🐾 There's something very Australian-looking about this hilltop lodge with its wide verandahs and gum trees, tempered by Maori and Pacific design in the spacious rooms and villas. The view over the golf course to the dazzling white beach is exquisite.

Cape Reinga & Ninety Mile Beach

Maori consider Cape Reinga (Te Rerenga-Wairua) the jumping-off point for souls as they depart on the journey to their spiritual homeland. That makes the Aupouri Peninsula a giant diving board, and it even resembles one – long and thin, it reaches 108km to form NZ's northern extremity. On its west coast Ninety Mile Beach (Ninety Kilometre Beach would be more accurate) is a continuous stretch lined with high sand dunes, flanked by the Aupouri Forest.

◉ Sights & Activities

Cape Reinga LANDMARK
Standing at windswept **Cape Reinga Lighthouse** (a rolling 1km walk from the car park) and looking out over the ocean engenders a real end-of-the-world feeling. This is where the waters of the Tasman Sea and Pacific Ocean meet, breaking together into waves up to 10m high in stormy weather. Little tufts of cloud often cling to the ridges, giving sudden spooky chills even on hot days.

Visible on a promontory slightly to the east is a spiritually significant 800-year-old pohutukawa tree; souls are believed to slide down its roots. Out of respect to the most sacred site in Maoridom, don't go near the tree and refrain from eating or drinking anywhere in the area.

Cape Reinga Coastal Walkway TRAMPING
Contrary to expectation, Cape Reinga isn't actually the northernmost point of the country; that honour belongs to **Surville Cliffs** further to the east. A walk along **Te Werahi Beach** to **Cape Maria van Diemen** (a five-hour loop) takes you to the westernmost point of the north island. This is one of many sections of the three- to four-day, 53km Cape Reinga Coastal Walkway (from Kapowairua to Te Paki Stream) that can be tackled individually. Beautiful **Tapotupotu Bay** is a two-hour walk east of Cape Reinga, via **Sandy Bay** and the cliffs. From Tapotupotu Bay it's an eight-hour walk to **Spirits Bay**, one of NZ's most beautiful beaches. Both bays are also accessible by road.

Te Paki Recreation Reserve NATURE RESERVE
A large chunk of the land around Cape Reinga is part of the Te Paki Recreation Reserve managed by DOC. It's public land with free access; leave the gates as you found them and don't

disturb the animals. There are 7 sq km of giant sand dunes on either side of the mouth of Te Paki Stream. Clamber up to take flying leaps off the dunes or to toboggan down them. During summer, Ahikaa Adventures (p137) are on hand to rent sandboards ($15).

Great Exhibition Bay BEACH
On the east coast, Great Exhibition Bay has dazzling snow-white silica dunes. There's no public road access, but some tours pay a *koha* (donation) to cross Maori farmland or approach the sand by kayak from Parengarenga Harbour.

Nga-Tapuwae-o-te-Mangai TEMPLE
(6576 Far North Rd) With its two domed towers (Arepa and Omeka, alpha and omega) and the Ratana emblem of the star and crescent moon, you could be forgiven for mistaking this temple for a mosque. Ratana is a Maori Christian sect with more than 50,000 adherents, formed in 1925 by Tahupotiki Wiremu Ratana, who was known as 'the mouthpiece of God'. The temple is built on land where Ratana once stood, and the name translates as 'the sacred steps of the mouthpiece'. You'll pass it at Te Kao, 46km south of Cape Reinga.

Gumdiggers Park MUSEUM
(www.gumdiggerspark.co.nz; 171 Heath Rd, Waiharara; adult/child $14/7; ⊙9am-5pm) Kauri forests covered this area for 100,000 years, leaving ancient logs and the much-prized gum (used for making varnish and linoleum) buried beneath. Digging it out was the region's main industry from the 1870s to the 1920s. In 1900 around 7000 gumdiggers were digging holes all over Northland, including at this site. Start with the 15-minute video, and then walk on the bush tracks, leading past gumdiggers' huts, ancient kauri stumps, huge preserved logs, and holes left by the diggers.

Ancient Kauri Kingdom WOODTURNERS
(www.ancientkauri.co.nz; 229 Far North Rd, Awanui; ⊙8.30am-5pm; ☎) Here, 50,000-year-old kauri stumps dragged out of swamps are fashioned into furniture, woodcraft products and a fair bit of tourist tat. The large complex includes a cafe, gift shop and workshop. A huge kauri log has been transformed into an impressive spiral staircase.

⟲ Tours
Bus tours go to Cape Reinga from Kaitaia, Ahipara, Doubtless Bay and the Bay of Islands, but there's no scheduled public transport up here.

Cape Reinga Adventures 4WD TOURS
(☑09-409 8445; www.capereingaadventures.co.nz; half-/full-day 4WD trips $75/135) Runs 4WD tours (including sunset visits to the cape after the crowds have gone), plus fishing, kayaking and sandboarding as day activities or as part of overnight camping trips.

Far North Outback Adventures 4WD TOURS
(☑09-408 0927; www.farnorthtours.co.nz; price on application) Flexible, day-long tours from Kaitaia/Ahipara, including morning tea and lunch. Options include visits to remote areas such as Great Exhibition Bay.

Harrisons Cape Runner ADVENTURE TOUR
(☑0800 227 373; www.harrisonscapereingatours.co.nz; adult/child $50/25) Day trips from Kaitaia along Ninety Mile Beach that include sandboarding and a picnic lunch.

Sand Safaris ADVENTURE TOUR
(☑09-408 1778, 0800 869 090; www.sandsafaris.co.nz; adult/child $50/30) Coach trips from Ahipara and Kaitaia including sandboarding and a picnic lunch.

Ahikaa Adventures CULTURAL TOUR
(☑09-409 8228; www.ahikaa-adventures.co.nz; tours $70-190) Maori culture permeates these tours, which can include sand-surfing, kayaking, fishing and pigging out on traditional *kai* (food).

⊨ Sleeping & Eating
Unless you're a happy camper you won't find much decent accommodation up here. Pukenui – literally 'Big Stomach' – is the best place to fill yours; there's a cafe, takeaways and grocery store. Another option is the friendly fishing club at Houhora.

North Wind Lodge Backpackers HOSTEL $
(☑09-409 8515; www.northwind.co.nz; 88 Otaipango Rd, Henderson Bay; dm/s/tw/d $30/60/80/80) Six kilometres down an unsealed road on

---

SEED FOR THE FUTURE
The local Ngati Kuri, guardians of the sacred spaces around the Cape, have come up with a unique way of funding reforestation. For $20 you can assuage your carbon guilt by planting a native tree or bush of your choice – or, if you don't want to break a nail, letting the staff plant it for you; contact **Natives** (☑09-409 8482; www.natives.co.nz).

the Aupouri peninsula's east side, this unusual turreted house offers a homely environment and plenty of quiet spots on the lawn to sit with a beer and a book.

DOC Campsites
CAMPSITES $

(www.doc.govt.nz; sites per adult/child $10/5) There are spectacularly positioned sites at Kapowairua, Tapotupotu Bay and Rarawa Beach. Only water, composting toilets and cold showers are provided. Bring a cooker, as fires are not allowed, and plenty of repellent to ward off mosquitoes and sandflies. 'Freedom/Leave No Trace' camping is allowed along the Cape Reinga Coastal Walkway.

ℹ Getting There & Around

Apart from numerous tours, there's no public transport past Pukenui, which is linked to Kaitaia ($5, 45 minutes) by **Busabout Kaitaia** (☑ 09-408 1092; www.cbec.co.nz).

As well as Far North Rd (SH1), rugged vehicles can travel along Ninety Mile Beach itself. However, cars have been known to hit soft sand and be swallowed by the tides – look out for unfortunate vehicles poking through the sands. Check tide times before setting out; avoid it 2½ hours either side of high tide. Watch out for 'quicksand' at Te Paki Stream – keep moving. Many car-rental companies prohibit driving on the sands; if you get stuck, your insurance won't cover you.

Fill up with petrol before hitting the Aupouri Peninsula.

Kaitaia

POP 4900

Nobody comes to the Far North to hang out in this provincial town, but it's a handy stop if you're after a supermarket, a post office or an ATM. It's also a jumping-off point for tours to Cape Reinga and Ninety Mile Beach.

◉ Sights

Te Ahu Centre
ARTS CENTRE

(www.teahu.org.nz; Matthews Ave; 🛜) This civic and community centre features a cinema, the eclectic local-history **Te Ahu Heritage** (www.teahuheritage.co.nz; ⊙10am-4pm Mon-Fri, to 2pm Sat) `FREE` exhibits of the Far North Regional Museum, and the local i-SITE information centre. There's also a cafe and free wi-fi at the library.

Okahu Estate Winery
WINERY

(www.okahuestate.co.nz; 520 Okahu Rd; ⊙noon-5pm Thu-Sat, also open holiday weekends) Just

south of town, off the road to Ahipara, Kaitaia's only winery offers free tastings and sells local produce, including the famous Kaitaia Fire chilli sauce. Enquire about tours ($5).

🛏 Sleeping & Eating

Mainstreet Lodge
HOSTEL $

(☑ 09-408 1275; www.mainstreetlodge.co.nz; 235 Commerce St; dm $27-30, s $55-70, d & tw $64-78; @🛜) Maori carvings abound at this groovy old cottage, which has a modern purpose-built wing facing the rear courtyard. The friendly owners know the area inside-out.

Loredo Motel
MOTEL $$

(☑ 09-408 3200; www.loredomotel.co.nz; 25 North Rd; units $130-160; 🛜⛱) Opting for a breezy Spanish style, this tidy motel has well-kept units set among palm trees and lawns, with a swimming pool.

Beachcomber
RESTAURANT $$

(www.beachcomber.net.nz; 222 Commerce St; lunch $19-33, dinner $24-36; ⊙11am-3pm Mon-Fri, 5pm-late Mon-Sat) Easily the best place to eat in town, with a wide range of seafood and meaty fare and a well-stocked salad bar.

ℹ Information

Far North i-SITE (☑ 03-408 9450; www. northlandnz.com; Te Ahu Centre, cnr Matthews Ave & South Rd; ⊙8.30am-5pm)

ℹ Getting There & Away

Kaitaia Airport (www.bayofislandsairport.co.nz; Quarry Rd) is 6km north of town. **Busabout Kaitaia** (☑ 09-408 1092; www.cbec.co.nz) has services to Doubtless Bay ($5, one hour), Pukenui ($5, 45 minutes) and Ahipara ($3.50, 15 minutes). Both Air New Zealand (p108) and InterCity (p108) operate services to Kaitaia.

Ahipara

POP 1130

All good things must come to an end, and Ninety Mile Beach does at this spunky beach town. A few holiday mansions have snuck in, but mostly it's just the locals keeping it real, rubbing shoulders with visiting surfers.

The area is known for its huge sand dunes and massive gum field, where 2000 people once worked. Sandboarding and quad-bike rides are popular activities on the dunes above Ahipara and further around the Tauroa Peninsula.

◉ Sights

Shipwreck Bay   BEACH
(Wreck Bay Rd) The best surfing is at this small cove at Ahipara's western edge, so named for shipwrecks still visible at low tide.

Ahipara Viewpoint   LOOKOUT
(Gumfields Rd) This lookout on the bluff behind Ahipara is reached by an extremely rough road leading off the unsealed Gumfields Rd, which starts at the western end of Foreshore Dr.

✦ Activities

Ahipara Adventure Centre   ADVENTURE SPORTS
(☑ 09-409 2055; www.ahiparaadventure.co.nz; 15 Takahe St) Hires sand toboggans ($10 per half day), surfboards ($30 per half day), mountain bikes ($50 per day), kayaks ($25 per hour), blokarts for sand yachting ($65 per hour) and quad bikes ($95 per hour).

Tua Tua Tours   QUAD BIKES
(☑ 0800 494 288; www.ahipara.co.nz/tuatuatours; 250 Ahipara Rd; s/d rides from $100/110) Reef- and dune-rider tours, plus the Gumfields Safari (per one/two people $175/185), three hours that includes sand tobogganing.

NZ Surf Bros   SURFING
(☑ 09-945 7276; www.nzsurfbros.com; 27 Kaka St; surf lessons $60, paddle boarding $60-100) Based in a cool house with amazing views of the surf, NZ Surf Bros offer surfing and paddleboarding lessons, plus day excursions and multiday trips that take in beaches on both the west and east coasts of Northland.

Ahipara Treks   HORSE RIDING
(☑ 09-409 4122; www.ahiparahorsetreks.moonfruit.com; 1/2/3 hours $50/70/110) Offers beach canters, including some farm and ocean riding (when the surf permits).

⌂ Sleeping

★Endless Summer Lodge   HOSTEL **$**
(☑ 09-409 4181; www.endlesssummer.co.nz; 245 Foreshore Rd; dm $30, d $70-85; @) Across from the beach, this superb kauri villa (1880) has been beautifully restored and converted into an exceptional hostel. There's no TV, which encourages bonding around the long table and wood-fired pizza oven on the vine-covered back terrace. Body boards and sandboards can be borrowed and surfboards can be hired.

**90 Mile Beach
Ahipara Holiday Park**   HOLIDAY PARK **$**
(☑ 0800 888 988; www.ahiparaholidaypark.co.nz; 168 Takahe St; sites from $40, dm/r $28/95, units $75-125; @ 🛜) There's a large range of accommodation on offer at this holiday park, including cabins, motel units and a worn but perfectly presentable YHA-affiliated backpackers' lodge. The communal hall has an open fire and colourful murals.

Beachfront   APARTMENTS **$$**
(☑ 09-409 4007; www.beachfront.net.nz; 14 Kotare St; apt $175-310; 🛜) Who cares if it's a bit bourgeois for Ahipara? These two upmarket, self-contained apartments have watery views and there's direct access to the beach.

NGATI TARARA

As you're travelling around the north you might notice the preponderance of road names ending in '-ich'. The sign leading into Kaitaia proclaims, 'haere mai, dobro došli and welcome', denoting one of the more peculiar ethnic conjunctions in the country.

From the end of the 19th century, men from the Dalmatian coast of what is now Croatia started arriving in NZ looking for work. Many ended up in Northland's gum fields. Pakeha (white) society wasn't particularly welcoming to the new immigrants, particularly during WWI, as they were on Austrian passports. Not so the small Maori communities of the north. Here the immigrants found an echo of Dalmatian village life, with its emphasis on extended family and hospitality, not to mention a shared history of injustice at the hands of colonial powers.

The Maori jokingly named them Tarara, as their rapid conversation in their native tongue sounded like 'ta-ra-ra-ra-ra' to Maori ears. Many Croatian men married local wahine (women), founding clans that have left several of today's famous Maori with Croatian surnames, like singer Margaret Urlich and former All Black Frano Botica. You'll find large Tarara communities in the Far North, Dargaville and West Auckland.

✕ Eating

Bidz Takeaways   FISH & CHIPS **$**
(Takahe St; meals $6-12; ⊙ 9am-8pm; 🛜) Fresh fish for sale, and the best fish, chips and burgers in town (plus free wi-fi with purchase). There's also a small grocery store attached.

Gumdiggers Cafe   CAFE **$$**
(3 Ahipara Rd; mains $6-26; ⊙ 7am-2pm & 5-10pm) Good coffee and huge portions are the hallmarks of this friendly little cafe, serving cooked breakfasts, nachos, burgers and huge platters. Dinners are on offer from 5pm most nights.

ℹ Getting There & Around

Busabout Kaitaia (☑ 09-408 1092; www.cbec. co.nz) runs services from Kaitaia ($3.50, 15 minutes).

HOKIANGA

The Hokianga Harbour stretches out its skinny tentacles to become the fourth-biggest in the country. Its ruggedly beautiful landscape is painted in every shade of green and brown. The water itself is rendered the colour of ginger ale by the bush streams that feed it.

Of all the remote parts of Northland, this is the pocket that feels the most removed from the mainstream. Pretension has no place here. Isolated, predominantly Maori communities nestle around the harbour's many inlets, as they have done for centuries. Discovered by legendary explorer Kupe, it's been settled by Ngapuhi since the 14th century. Hippies arrived in the late 1960s and their legacy is a thriving little artistic scene.

Many of the roads remain unsealed, and, while tourism dollars are channelled eastward to the Bay of Islands, this truly fascinating corner of the country remains remarkably undeveloped, just how many of the locals like it.

See www.hokiangatourism.org.nz.

Mitimiti

The tiny community at Mitimiti, which consists of only 30 families and not even a shop, has the unspoilt 20km stretch of coast between the Hokianga and Whangape Harbours all to itself. The 40km drive from Kohukohu via Panguru (14km of it unsealed) is quite an experience: prepare to dodge cows, sheep, potholes and kids.

Sandtrails Hokianga (☑ 09-409 5035; www. sandtrailshokianga.co.nz; 32 Paparangi Dr) offers an inside perspective on Mitimiti's tight-knit Maori community, with two-hour Sandscapes dune-buggy tours, which head 12km along the beach to the giant dunes that form the harbour's north head ($155), or personally tailored tours on which you can stay overnight in the guide's house ($640 for two people).

Motuti

It's worth taking a short detour from the road to Mitimiti to visit **St Mary's Church** (Hata Maria; www.hokiangapompallier.org.nz; Motuti Rd), where NZ's first Catholic bishop is buried beneath the altar. Jean Baptiste Pompallier arrived in the Hokianga in 1838, celebrating NZ's first Mass at Totara Point. He was interred here in 2002 after an emotional 14-week pilgrimage full of Maori ceremony brought his remains back from France.

The nearby **Motuti Marae** (☑ 09-409 5545; www.motuti.co.nz; 318 Motuti Rd; tours 90min/day $36/60, stay $214) offers *marae* tours and stays, including a traditional Maori welcome and, on the longer tours, the opportunity to take part in flax-weaving, carving and stick games.

Kohukohu

POP 190

Quick, someone slap a preservation order on Kohukohu before it's too late. There can be few places in NZ where a Victorian village full of interesting kauri buildings has been so completely preserved with hardly a modern monstrosity to be seen. During the height of the kauri industry it was a busy town with a sawmill, shipyard, two newspapers and banks. These days it's a very quiet backwater on the north side of Hokianga Harbour, 4km from the Rawene car ferry (p142). There's good eating at the local pub and on the cosy deck of the **KB Cafaway** (cnr Beach Rd & Kohukohu Rd; mains $12-14; ⊙ noon-8pm Wed-Sun). **Village Arts** (www.villagearts. co.nz; 1376 Kohukohu Rd; ⊙ 10am-4pm, to 3pm winter) is an excellent little art gallery.

Tree House (☑ 09-405 5855; www.treehouse. co.nz; 168 West Coast Rd; sites/dm $19/32, s $60-70, tw & d $86; 🛜) 🍃 is the best place to stay in the Hokianga, with helpful hosts and brightly painted little cottages set among exotic fruit and nut trees. This quiet retreat is

LOCAL KNOWLEDGE

HOKIANGA

I love the north of the north island, the beaten, bloody and beautiful landscape and *wairua*. The small towns up north, where I grew up, reach out all along the moody west coast. As kids, my brother and I would sneak in to Ngawha Springs and have our mud baths in the morning – smelling of rotten eggs for the rest of the day. In Opononi we'd go crab hunting on the rocks with Uncle Rata, then take the car ferry from Rawene home. At Pawarenga – a dusty old Maori town – we'd go horse riding with the cuzzies, learn Maori with my Grandpa, eat *karahu* and oysters, and, as we grew up, drink with the aunties and uncles. We'd drive to Kaitaia to buy all our food for the next week, and hang at the local pubs. Then further north for the Mangonui fish 'n' chip shop, the best *kai* in Aotearoa. When we were tired, we'd drive to Ahipara and sleep on the beach.

Anika Moa, singer/songwriter

2km from the ferry terminus (turn sharp left as you come off the ferry).

Horeke & Around

Tiny Horeke was NZ's second European settlement after Russell. A Wesleyan mission operated here from 1828 to 1855, while, in 1840, 3000 Ngapuhi gathered here for what was the single biggest signing of the Treaty of Waitangi. The rustic **Horeke Tavern** (www.horeketavern.co.nz; 2118 Horeke Rd; ⊘1pm-late Wed-Sun, bistro Thu-Sun 5.30-8pm) is reputedly New Zealand's oldest pub – the first cold one was poured back in 1826 – and the garden bar rocks with live music on occasional weekends during summer.

Horeke is also the western end point of the Pou Herenga Tai Twin Coast Cycle Trail (p118).

◎ Sights & Activities

Mangungu Mission House   HISTORIC BUILDING
(www.historic.org.nz; Motukiore Rd; adult/child $10/free; ⊘noon-4pm Sat & Sun) Completed in 1839, this sweet wooden cottage contains relics of the missionaries who once inhabited it, and of Horeke's shipbuilding past. In the grounds there's a large stone cross and a simple wooden church. Mangungu is 1km down the unsealed road leading along the harbour from Horeke village.

Wairere Boulders Nature Park   NATURE PARK
(www.waireboulders.co.nz; McDonnell Rd; adult/child/family $15/5/35; ⊘to 5pm/7pm winter/summer) 🌀 At Wairere, massive basalt rock formations have been eroded into odd fluted shapes by the acidity of ancient kauri forests. Allow an hour for the main loop track, but wear sensible shoes and expect a few dips and climbs. An additional track leads through rainforest to a platform at the end

of the boulder valley (allow 1½ hours). The park is signposted from SH1 and Horeke; the last 3km are unsealed.

Without your own transport, get here on a Discover Hokianga tour by Fullers (p119), which departs from Paihia.

Wairere Adventure Park   QUAD BIKES, KAYAKING
(☎09-401 9544; www.waireadventurepark.co.nz; 34 McDonnell Rd; quad-bike tours $65-135, kayak hire $15) Offers quad-bike tours with harbour, bush and boulders scenery, and kayak hire to explore a scenic tidal estuary. Booking ahead for kayaks is recommended to catch the best tidal conditions.

Rawene

POP 440

Founded shortly after Horeke, Rawene was NZ's third European settlement. A surprising number of historic buildings (including six churches!) remain from a time when the harbour was considerably busier than it is now. Information boards outline a heritage trail of the main sights.

There's an ATM in the Four Square grocery store, and you can get petrol here.

◎ Sights

Clendon House   HISTORIC BUILDING
(www.historic.org.nz; Clendon Esplanade; adult/child $10/free; ⊘10am-4pm Sat & Sun Nov-Apr, Sun May-Oct) Clendon House was built in the bustling 1860s by James Clendon, a trader, shipowner and magistrate. After his death, his 34-year-old half-Maori widow Jane was left with a brood of kids and a whopping £5000 debt. She managed to clear the debt and her descendants remained in the house until 1972, when it passed to the Historic Places Trust.

🛏 Sleeping & Eating

Rawene Holiday Park
HOLIDAY PARK $

(☑09-405 7720; www.raweneholidaypark.co.nz; 1 Marmon St; dm $20, sites/units from $32/65; @🛜📶) Tent sites shelter in the bush at this nicely managed park. The cabins are simple, with one converted into a bunkroom for backpackers (linen costs extra).

Boatshed Cafe
CAFE $

(☑09-405 7728; 8 Clendon Esplanade; mains $10-20; ⊗8.30am-4pm) Eat overlooking the water at this cafe, a cute place with excellent food and a gift shop that sells local art and crafts. The cafe sometimes opens for dinner at the weekend.

ℹ Getting There & Away

There are no regular bus services to Rawene. A car ferry (☑09-405 2602; car/campervan/motorcycle $20/40/5, passenger $2; ⊗7.30am-8pm) heads to the northern side of the Hokianga, docking 4km south of Kohukohu at least hourly. You can buy your ticket for this 15-minute ride on board. It usually leaves Rawene on the half-hour and the north Kohukohu side on the hour.

Opononi & Omapere

POP 480

These tranquil settlements near the south head of Hokianga Harbour run into one another. The water's much clearer here and good for swimming, and views are dominated by the mountainous sand dunes across the water at North Head. If you're approaching Omapere from the south, the view of the harbour is nothing short of spectacular.

🏃 Activities

Hokianga Express
SANDBOARDING

(☑021 405 872; www.hokiangaexpress.webs.com; adult/child $25/15; ⊗from 10am) A boat departs from Opononi Jetty and takes you across the harbour to the large golden sand dunes, where you can sandboard down a 30m slope and skim over the water. Boats leave on the hour. Bookings essential.

Jim Taranaki's Bone Carving Studio
BONE CARVING

(☑09-405 8061; hokiangabonecarvingstudio@gmail.com; 15 Akiha St, Omapere; $60) Create your own Maori-inspired bone carving in a studio with ocean views.

Arai te Uru Heritage Walk
WALKING

Starting at the car park at the end of Signal Station Rd, this short walk (30 minutes return) follows the cliffs and passes through a tall stand of manuka before opening out to the grassy southern headland of the Hokianga and the remains of an old signal station. Built to assist ships making the treacherous passage through the harbour mouth, the station was closed in 1951 due to the decline in shipping in the harbour.

Six Foot Track
TRAMPING

The Six Foot Track at the end of Mountain Rd gives access to many Waima Forest walks.

☞ Tours

Footprints Waipoua
CULTURAL TOUR

(☑09-405 8207; www.footprintswaipoua.co.nz; adult/child $95/35) 🍃 Led by Maori guides, this four-hour twilight tour into Waipoua Forest is a fantastic introduction to both the culture and the forest giants. Tribal history and stories are shared, and mesmerising *karakia* (prayer, incantation) recited before the gargantuan trees.

Sandtrails Hokianga
DUNE BUGGY

(☑09-409 5035; www.sandtrailshokianga.co.nz) Jump off the Hokianga Express (p142) boat and into a dune buggy for a sandy ride to Mitimiti ($185, three hours), or a 70-minute Sandsecrets tour ($95).

🛏 Sleeping & Eating

Each of these neighbouring villages has its own grocery store and takeaway, and there is a good bistro and bar at the Opononi Hotel.

GlobeTrekkers Lodge
HOSTEL $

(☑09-405 8183; www.globetrekkerslodge.com; SH12, Omapere; dm/s/d $29/53/67; @) Unwind in casual style at this home-style hostel with harbour views and bright dorms. Private rooms have plenty of thoughtful touches, such as writing desks, mirrors, art and fluffy towels. There's a stereo but no TV, encouraging plenty of schmoozing in the grapevine-draped BBQ area.

Hokianga Haven
B&B $$

(☑09-405 8285; www.hokiangahaven.co.nz; 226 SH12, Omapere; r $140-200) This modern house with original Kiwi art on the walls offers spacious accommodation on the harbour's edge and glorious views of the sand dunes. Alternative healing therapies can be arranged.

Copthorne Hotel & Resort HOTEL $$
(☑09-405 8737; www.milleniumhotels.co.nz; 336 SH12, Omapere; r $140-200; ☎☒) *✿* Despite the original grand Victorian villa having been violated by aluminium joinery, this waterside complex remains an attractive spot for a summer's drink or bistro meal ($19 to $36). The more expensive rooms in the newer accommodation block have terraces and water views.

Opononi Hotel HOTEL $$
(☑09-405 8858; www.opononihotel.com; 19 SH12; r $110-130) The rooms at the old Opononi pub aren't huge but the white-paint and blond-wood makeover has left them quietly stylish. Try to grab one of the front two – they're a bit bigger and have the best views. Otherwise aim for those facing away from the pub for a quieter stay.

Kokohuia Lodge B&B $$$
(☑021 779 927; www.kokohuialodge.co.nz; d incl breakfast $295; ☎) *✿* Luxury and sustainable and ecofriendly practices combine at this new B&B, nestled in regenerating native bush high above the silvery dune-fringed expanse of the Hokianga harbour. Solar energy and organic and free-range produce all feature, but there's no trade-off for luxury in the modern and stylish accommodation.

ⓘ Information

Opononi i-SITE (☑09-405 8869; 29 SH12; ☉8.30am-5pm) Includes the Hokianga Art Gallery.

ⓘ Getting There & Away

There's no regular public transport to these parts, so you'll need to rent a car from Kerikeri or Paihia for independent exploration. Another option is a Discover Hokianga day trip (adult/child $112/56) from Paihia with Fullers (p119), taking in Opononi, Omapere and the Waiere Boulders.

Waiotemarama & Waimamaku

These neighbouring villages, nestled between the Hokianga Harbour and the Waipoua Forest, are the first of many tiny rural communities scattered along this underpopulated stretch of SH12.

Activities

Labyrinth Woodworks MAZE
(www.nzanity.co.nz; 647 Waiotemarama Gorge Rd; maze $4; ☉9am-5pm) Crack the code in the outdoor maze by collecting letters to form a word. The puzzle museum and lots of retro board games are also interesting. Nearby walks lead to a waterfall and magnificent kauri trees.

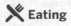
Eating

Morrell's Cafe CAFE $$
(7235 SH12, Waimamaku; mains $10-24; ☉9am-4pm) This cafe and craft shop occupies a former cheese factory. It's the last good eatery before Baylys Beach, so drop in for coffee or an eggy breakfast.

KAURI COAST

Apart from the odd bluff and river, this coast is basically unbroken and undeveloped for the 110km between the Hokianga and Kaipara Harbours. The main reason for coming here is to marvel at the kauri forests, one of the great natural highlights of NZ. You'd need 8m arms to get them around some of the big boys here.

There are few stores or eateries and no ATMs north of Dargaville, so stock up beforehand. Trampers should check DOC's website for walks in the area (www.doc.govt.nz).

For visitor information see www.kauri-coast.com.

Waipoua Forest

The highlight of Northland's west coast, this superb forest sanctuary – proclaimed in 1952 after much public pressure – is the largest remnant of the once-extensive kauri forests of northern NZ. The forest road (SH12) stretches for 18km and passes some huge trees – a kauri can reach 60m in height and have a trunk more than 5m in diameter.

Control of the forest has been returned to Te Roroa, the local *iwi* (tribe), as part of a settlement for Crown breaches of the Treaty of Waitangi. Te Roroa runs the **Waipoua Forest visitor centre** (☑09-439 6445; www.waipouakauriforest.co.nz; 1 Waipoua River Rd; ☉9am-6.30pm summer, to 4pm winter), near the south end of the park.

Another option to visit the forest is on a twilight tour, departing from Omapere with Footprints Waipoua (p142).

◉ Sights & Activities

Tane Mahuta   TREE
Near the north end of the park, not far from the road, stands mighty Tane Mahuta, named for the Maori forest god. At 51.5m, with a 13.8m girth and wood mass of 244.5 cu metres, he's the largest kauri alive, and has been holding court here for somewhere between 1200 and 2000 years.

Te Matua Ngahere,
Four Sisters & Yakas   TREE
From the Kauri Walks car park, a 20-minute (each way) walk leads past the Four Sisters, a graceful stand of four tall trees fused together at the base, to Te Matua Ngahere (the Father of the Forest). At 30m, he's shorter than Tane Mahuta, but still has a significant presence. Reinforced by a substantial girth – he's the fattest living kauri (16.4m) – the tree presides over a clearing surrounded by mature trees resembling mere matchsticks in comparison.

A 30-minute (one way) path leads from near the Four Sisters to Yakas, the seventh-largest kauri.

Lookout   LOOKOUT
For a bird's-eye view over the canopy, head to the forest lookout, near the very south end of the park. You can either drive to it (the road is well signposted but not suitable for campervans) or take the 2.5km Lookout Track from the visitor centre.

Waipoua Visitor Centre   ARTS & CRAFTS
(www.waipouakauriforest.co.nz; 1 Waipoua River Rd; ⊙9am-6.30pm summer, to 4pm winter) Interesting exhibition on the kauri forests, guided tours ($25), flax-weaving lessons ($5) and a good cafe. You can also plant your own kauri tree – complete with GPS coordinates – for $180.

🛏 Sleeping & Eating

Waipoua Forest Campground   CAMPSITE $
(☑09-439 6445; www.waipouakauriforest.co.nz; 1 Waipoua River Rd; site/unit/house from $15/20/175) Situated next to the Waipoua River and the visitor centre, this peaceful camping ground offers hot showers, flush toilets and a kitchen. The cabins are extremely spartan, with unmade squab beds

(bring your own linen or hire it). There are also whole houses for rent, sleeping 10.

Waipoua Lodge   B&B $$$
(☑09-439 0422; www.waipoualodge.co.nz; SH12; r $585) This fine old villa at the southern edge of the forest has four luxurious, spacious suites, which were originally the stables, the woolshed and the calf-rearing pen. Decadent dinners ($75) are available.

Trounson Kauri Park

The 450-hectare Trounson Kauri Park has an easy half-hour loop walk that leads from the picnic area by the road. It passes through beautiful forest with streams, some fine kauri stands, a couple of fallen trees and another Four Sisters – two pairs of trees with conjoined trunks. DOC operates a campsite (www.doc.govt.nz; sites per adult/child $10/5) at the edge of the park with a communal kitchen and hot showers.

Just 2km from SH12, Kauri Coast Top 10 Holiday Park (☑09-439 0621; www.kauricoasttop10.co.nz; Trounson Park Rd; site/unit from $42/95; @) ✿ is an attractive riverside camping ground with good facilities and a small shop. It also organises night-time nature walks (adult/child $25/15), which explain the flora and nocturnal wildlife that thrives here. This is a rare chance to see a kiwi in the wild. Trounson has a predator-eradication program and has become a mainland refuge for threatened native bird species, so you should at least hear a morepork (a native owl) or a brown kiwi.

If you're approaching from the north, it's easier to take the second turn-off to the park, near Kaihu, which avoids a rough unsealed road.

Kai Iwi Lakes

These three trout-filled freshwater lakes nestle together near the coast, 12km off SH12. The largest, Taharoa, has blue water fringed with sandy patches. Lake Waikere is popular with water-skiers, while Lake Kai Iwi is relatively untouched. A half-hour walk leads from the lakes to the coast and it's another two hours to reach the base of volcanic Maunganui Bluff (460m); the hike up and down it takes five hours.

Camping (☑09-439 0986; lakes@kaipara.govt.nz; adult/child $10/5) is permitted at the side of Lake Taharoa; cold showers, drinking water and flush toilets are provided.

Baylys Beach

A village of brightly coloured baches and a few new holiday mansions, Baylys Beach is 12km from Dargaville, off SH12. It lies on 100km-long Ripiro Ocean Beach, a surf-pounded stretch of coast that has been the site of many shipwrecks. The beach is a gazetted highway: you can drive along its hard sand at low tide, although it is primarily for 4WDs. Despite being NZ's longest drivable beach, it's less well known and hence less travelled than Ninety Mile Beach. Ask locals about conditions and check your hire-car agreement before venturing onto the sand. Quad bikes (single/double $75/95) can be hired at the holiday park. Ask there also about an equine outing with **Baylys Beach Horse Treks** (⌨ 0800 229 597; www. baylysbeachhorsetreks.webs.com; 24 Seaview Rd; 1/2/3 hours $50/70/90; ⊙ late Oct-Easter).

⌘ Sleeping

Baylys Beach Holiday Park   HOLIDAY PARK $
(⌨ 09-439 6349; www.baylysbeach.co.nz; 24 Seaview Rd; site/unit from $16/65; @⌢) Circled by pohutukawa trees, this midsized camping ground has tidy facilities and attractive cream and green units, some with funky Kiwiana decor. Options range from basic cabins to a cottage sleeping six.

Sunset View Lodge   B&B $$
(⌨ 09-439 4342; www.sunsetviewlodge.co.nz; 7 Alcemene Lane; r $175-190; @⌇) If gin-in-hand sunset-gazing is your thing, this large, modern B&B fits the bill. The upstairs rooms have terrific sea views and there's a self-service bar with an honesty box in the guest lounge.

✖ Eating

Funky Fish   CAFE, BAR $$
(⌨ 09-439 8883; www.thefunkyfish.co.nz; 34 Seaview Rd; lunch $14-22, dinner $22-32; ⊙ 11am-late Tue-Sun, reduced hours in winter) Brightly decorated with murals and mosaics, this highly popular cafe, restaurant and bar has a wonderful back garden and a wide-ranging menu, including lots of seafood. Bookings are advisable in summer. Check its Facebook page for occasional live music.

Dargaville

POP 4500

When a town proclaims itself the 'kumara capital of NZ' (it produces two-thirds of the country's sweet potatoes), you should know not to expect too much. Founded in 1872 by timber merchant Joseph Dargaville, this once-important river port thrived on the export of kauri timber and gum. As the forests were decimated, it declined, and today is a quiet backwater servicing the agricultural Northern Wairoa area.

◉ Sights & Activities

Dargaville Museum   MUSEUM
(www.dargavillemuseum.co.nz; adult/child $15/2; ⊙ 9am-4pm) The hilltop Dargaville Museum is more interesting than most regional museums. There's a large gumdigging display, plus maritime, Maori and musical-instrument sections, and a neat model railway. Outside, the masts of the *Rainbow Warrior* are mounted at a lookout near a *pa* site, and there's a re-creation of a gumdiggers' camp.

Kumara Box   FARM
(⌨ 09-439 7018; www.kumarabox.co.nz; 503 Pouto Rd; tours $20) To learn all about kumara, book ahead for Kumara Ernie's show. It's surprisingly entertaining, usually involving a journey by home-built tractor-train through the fields to 'NZ's smallest church'.

⌘ Sleeping & Eating

Campervans can stay at the Dargaville Museum car park for $15 per night.

Greenhouse Backpackers   HOSTEL $
(⌨ 09-439 6342; greenhousebackpackers@ihug. co.nz; 15 Gordon St; dm/s/d $28/45/70; @⌢) This converted 1921 schoolhouse has classrooms partitioned into a large dorm and a communal lounge, both painted with colourful murals. Better still are the cosy units in the back garden.

The Hangi Hut   MAORI $
(⌨ 09-439 4264; www.facebook.com/thehangi-hut; 1 Murdoch St; hangi $12; ⊙ 11am-6pm Tue-Sat) Opposite the information centre, The Hangi Hut does heaped plates of meat and vegies – including, of course, local kumara. Choose from lamb, pork or chicken, all served with delicious stuffing, and steamed slowly on hot volcanic rocks. Raw fish and

coconut ($5) and traditional Maori *paraoa parae* (fried bread, 50c) are also available.

Riverside Produce Market   MARKET $
(Kapia St; ⊙2.30-5.30pm Thu) Local produce and crafts.

Blah, Blah, Blah...   CAFE, BAR $$
(101 Victoria St; breakfast $12-25, lunch $13-18, dinner $22-34; ⊙9am-late Tue-Sat, to 4pm Sun-Mon) The number-one eatery in Dargaville has a garden area, hip music, deli-style snacks, a global menu including *dukkah*, pizza and steak, and beer, wine and cocktails.

❶ Information

DOC Kauri Coast Area Office (☑09-439 3450; www.doc.govt.nz; 150 Colville Rd; ⊙8am-4.30pm Mon-Fri)

Visitor Information Centre (☑09-439 4975; www.kauriinfocentre.co.nz; 4 Murdoch St; ⊙9am-5.30pm; 🛜) Operates out of the Woodturners Kauri Gallery & Studio. Books accommodation and tours.

❶ Getting There & Away

Weekday shuttle buses run by West Coaster (p108) link Dargaville with Whangarei.

Pouto Point

A narrow spit descends south of Dargaville, bordered by the Tasman Sea and Wairoa River, and comes to an abrupt halt at the entrance of NZ's biggest harbour, the Kaipara. It's an incredibly remote headland, punctuated by dozens of petite dune lakes and the lonely Kaipara Lighthouse (built from kauri in 1884). Less than 10km separates Kaipara Harbour's north and south heads, but if you were to drive between the two you'd cover 267km.

A 4WD can be put to its proper use on the ocean-hugging 71km stretch of beach from Dargaville. DOC's *Pouto Hidden Treasures* is a helpful guide for motorists, with tips for protecting both your car and the fragile ecosystem. It can be downloaded at www.doc.govt.nz.

To explore the huge expanse of sand dunes on an organised tour, contact Jock at **Poutu Sand Safaris** (☑09-439 6678; www.poutu.co.nz; per person from $35).

Matakohe

POP 400

Apart from the rural charms of this village, the key reason for visiting is the superb **Kauri Museum** (www.kaurimuseum.com; 5 Church Rd; adult/child $25/8; ⊙9am-5pm). The giant cross sections of trees are astounding, but the entire industry is brought to life through video kiosks, artefacts, fabulous furniture and marquetry, and reproductions of a pioneer sawmill, boarding house, gumdigger's hut and Victorian home. The Gum Room holds a weird and wonderful collection of kauri gum, the amber substance that can be carved, sculpted and polished to a jewel-like quality. The museum shop stocks mementoes crafted from kauri wood and gum.

Facing the museum is the tiny kauri-built **Matakohe Pioneer Church** (1867), which served both Methodists and Anglicans, and acted as the community's hall and school. Nearby, you can wander through a historic **school house** (1878) and **post office/telephone exchange** (1909).

🛏 Sleeping & Eating

Matakohe Holiday Park   HOLIDAY PARK $
(☑09-431 6431; www.matakoheholidaypark.co.nz; 66 Church Rd; site/unit from $38/65; @🛜🐾) This little park has modern amenities, plenty of space and good views of Kaipara Harbour.

Petite Provence   B&B $$
(☑09-431 7552; www.petiteprovence.co.nz; 703c Tinopai Rd; s/d $120/160) 🐾 This attractive, French-influenced B&B is a popular weekender for Aucklanders, so it pays to book ahead. Excellent dinners can be arranged for $45 per person.

Matakohe House   B&B $$
(☑09-431 7091; www.matakohehouse.co.nz; 24 Church Rd; d $160; @🛜) This B&B occupies a pretty villa with a cafe attached. The simply furnished rooms open out onto a verandah and offer winning touches like complimentary port and chocolates.

❶ Getting There & Away

No scheduled buses run to Matakohe, but return day trips from Auckland to the Kauri Museum are $149. See www.kauri-museum.com for tour bookings.

Waikato & Coromandel Peninsula

Includes ➡

Waikato......................149
Hamilton....................151
Raglan.........................157
Cambridge.................163
Matamata.................164
Te Aroha.....................165
Waitomo Caves.........169
Thames.......................178
Coromandel Town......181
Whitianga..................186
Hahei.........................189
Waihi & Around..........193

Best Outdoors

➡ New Chum's Beach (p185)

➡ Cathedral Cove (p189)

➡ Otama Beach (p185)

➡ Surfing at Manu Bay (p160)

➡ Black-water rafting at Waitomo Caves (p169)

Best Places to Stay

➡ Wairua Lodge (p186)

➡ Driving Creek Villas (p183)

➡ Purangi Garden Accommodation (p190)

➡ Solscape (p160)

Why Go?

Verdant rolling hills line New Zealand's mighty Waikato River, and adrenaline junkies can surf at Raglan, or undertake extreme underground pursuits in the extraordinary Waitomo Caves.

But this is also Tainui country. In the 1850s this powerful Maori tribal coalition elected a king to resist the loss of land and sovereignty. The fertile Waikato was forcibly taken from them, but they retained control of the rugged King Country to within a whisper of the 20th century.

To the northeast, the Coromandel Peninsula juts into the Pacific, forming the Hauraki Gulf's eastern boundary. The peninsula's east coast has some of the North Island's best white-sand beaches, and the muddy wetlands and picturesque stony bays of the west coast have long been a refuge for alternative lifestylers. Down the middle, the mountains are criss-crossed with walking tracks, allowing trampers to explore large tracts of isolated bush studded with kauri trees.

When to Go

➡ Beachy accommodation in Waihi, Whitianga, Whangamata and Raglan peaks across the summer holidays from Christmas until the end of January. New Year's Eve in particular can be very busy.

➡ Balmy February and March are much quieter around the Coromandel Peninsula with settled weather and smaller crowds. Rainfall peaks in the mountainous Coromandel region from May to September.

➡ The Waikato region can see summer droughts, but the southern area around Taumarunui is often wetter and colder.

➡ If you avoid the height of summer school holidays (Christmas to January), accommodation is plentiful in the Waikato region.

➡ Raglan's surf breaks are popular year-round.

Waikato & Coromandel Peninsula Highlights

1 Travelling remote gravel roads under a crimson canopy of ancient pohutukawa trees in **Far North Coromandel** (p184)

2 Kayaking around the hidden islands, caves and bays of **Te Whanganui-A-Hei Marine Reserve** (p190)

3 Pigging out on smoked mussels in **Coromandel Town** (p181)

4 Penetrating the mystical depths of the dense bush of **Coromandel Forest Park** (p182) and **Karangahake Gorge** (p195)

5 Watching the offshore islands glow in the dying haze of a summer sunset from **Hahei Beach** (p189)

6 Seeking subterranean stimulation in the **Waitomo Caves** (p169) – this is your chance to try black-water rafting

7 Hitting the surf (and then the pub) in unhurried **Raglan** (p157)

8 Tramping through an inland island paradise at **Sanctuary Mountain Maungatautari** (p162)

ℹ Getting There & Around

Hamilton is the region's transport hub, with its airport servicing extensive domestic routes. Buses link the city to everywhere in the North Island. Most inland towns are also well connected on bus routes, but the remote coastal communities (apart from Mokau on SH3) are less well served. See p156 for more information on transport options to Hamilton.

Options on the Coromandel Peninsula are more limited, and the beaches and coastline of the area are most rewarding with independent transport.

AIR

Sunair (☑ 0800 786 247; www.sunair.co.nz) Regional North Island airline linking Auckland, Whitianga, Hamilton, Gisborne, Napier, Tauranga, Great Barrier Island and New Plymouth.

BOAT

360 Discovery (☑ 0800 360 3472; www.360discovery.co.nz) Operates ferries to/from Auckland (one-way/return $57/92, two hours) via Orapiu on Waiheke Island (one-way/return $37/62, 70 minutes), five times per week (daily in summer). The boats dock at Hannafords Wharf, Te Kouma, where free buses shuttle passengers the 10km into Coromandel Town. It makes a great day trip from Auckland (same-day return $69), and there's a day-tour option that includes a hop-on, hop-off bus (adult/child $94).

BUS

Go Kiwi (☑ 07-866 0336; www.go-kiwi.co.nz) Has daily Auckland City–International Airport–Thames–Tairua–Whitianga shuttles year-round, with a connection to Opoutere and Whangamata. From mid-December to Easter it also runs Rotorua–Tauranga–Waihi–Whangamata–Whitianga and Coromandel Town–Whitianga shuttles.

InterCity (www.intercity.co.nz) Has two routes to/from the Coromandel peninsula: Auckland–Thames–Paeroa–Waihi–Tauranga and Hamilton–Te Aroha–Paeroa–Thames–Coromandel Town. Local routes include Thames–Coromandel Town–Whitianga and Whitianga–Tairua–Thames.

Naked Bus (www.nakedbus.com) Buses on the Auckland–Tauranga–Mt Maunganui–Rotorua–Gisborne route stop at Ngatea, where local associate Tairua Bus Company continues on to Whitianga.

Tairua Bus Company (TBC; ☑ 07-808 0748; www.tairuabus.co.nz) Local buses on the Thames–Tairua–Hahei–Whitianga–Coromandel Town route and a Hamilton–Cambridge–Te Aroha–Thames–Tairua service.

CAR

Car is the only option for accessing some of the more remote areas, but be careful to check hire agreements as there are plenty of gravel roads and a few streams to ford. Most of them are in good condition and even a small car can cope unless the weather's been particularly wet.

WAIKATO

History

By the time Europeans started to arrive, this region – stretching as far north as Auckland's Manukau Harbour – had long been the homeland of the Waikato tribes, descended from the Tainui migration. In settling this land, the Waikato tribes displaced or absorbed tribes from earlier migrations.

Initially European contact was on Maori terms and to the advantage of the local people. Their fertile land, which was already cultivated with kumara and other crops, was well suited to the introduction of new fruits and vegetables. By the 1840s the Waikato economy was booming, with bulk quantities

---

ESSENTIAL WAIKATO & COROMANDEL PENINSULA

Eat Coromandel bivalves – mussels, oysters and scallops are local specialities

Drink Local craft beer from Hamilton's Good George (p155)

Read *The Penguin History of New Zealand* (2003) by the late Michael King, an Opoutere resident

Listen to The Waikato-influenced sounds of Kimbra, the Topp Twins and the Datsuns

Watch The birds at Miranda the Firth of Thames

Festival The Coromandel Peninsula–wide **Pohutukawa Festival** (www.pohutukawafestival.co.nz)

Go green Off-the-grid tepees at Solscape (p160)

Online www.thecoromandel.com, www.hamiltonwaikato.com, www.kingcountry.co.nz

Area code ☑ 07

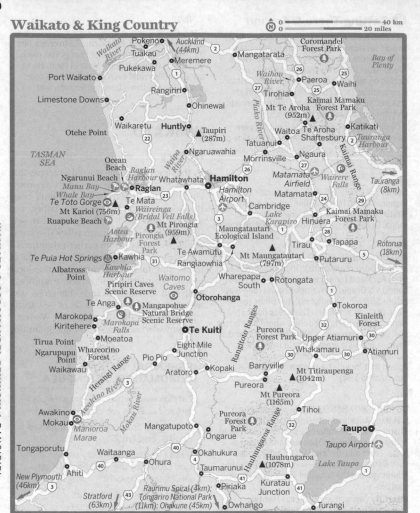

of produce exported to the settlers in Auckland and beyond.

Relations between the two cultures soured during the 1850s, largely due to the colonists' pressure to purchase Maori land. In response, a confederation of tribes united to elect a king to safeguard their interests, forming what became known as the Kingitanga (King Movement).

In July 1863 Governor Grey sent a huge force to invade the Waikato and exert colonial control. After almost a year of fighting, known as the Waikato War, the Kingites retreated south to what became branded the King Country.

The war resulted in the confiscation of 3600 sq km of land, much of which was given to colonial soldiers to farm and defend. In 1995 the Waikato tribes received a full Crown apology for the wrongful invasion and confiscation of their lands, as well as a $170 million package, including the return of land that the Crown still held.

Rangiriri

Following SH1 south from Auckland you're retracing the route of the colonial army in the spectacular land grab that was the

Waikato War. On 20 November 1863, around 1500 British troops backed by gunboats and artillery, attacked the substantial fortifications erected by the Maori king's warriors at Rangiriri. They were repulsed a number of times and lost 49 men, but overnight many of the 500 Maori defenders retreated; the remaining 183 were taken prisoner the next day after the British gained entry to the *pa* (fortified village) by conveniently misunderstanding a flag of truce.

The **Rangiriri Heritage Centre** (☑ 07-826 3663; www.nzmuseums.co.nz; 12 Rangiriri Rd; admission $3, film $5; ◔ 8am-4pm) screens a short documentary about the battle, and across the road the **Maori War & Early Settlers Cemetery** (Rangiriri Rd; ◔ 24hr) FREE houses the soldiers' graves and a mound covering the mass grave of 36 Maori warriors.

Next to the heritage centre is the historic **Rangiriri Hotel** (☑ 07-826 3467; 8 Talbot St; lunch mains $11-20, dinner $17-30; ◔ 11am-11pm), a cheery spot for lunch or a beer.

Ngaruawahia & Around

POP 4940

The headquarters of the Maori King movement, Ngaruawahia is 19km north of Hamilton on SH1. The impressive fences of **Turangawaewae Marae** (☑ 07-824 5189; 29 River Rd) maintain the privacy of this important place, but twice a year visitors are welcomed. **Regatta Day** is held in mid-March, with *waka* (canoe) races and all manner of Maori cultural activities. For a week from 15 August the *marae* (meeting house) is open to celebrate **Koroniehana**, the anniversary of the coronation of the current king, Tuheitia.

Hamilton

POP 206,400

Landlocked cities in an island nation are never going to have the glamorous appeal of their coastal cousins. Rotorua compensates with boiling mud and Taupo has its lake, but Hamilton, despite the majestic Waikato River, is more prosaic.

However, the city definitely has appeal. The main street has vibrant bars around Hood St and Victoria St, and excellent restaurants and cafes mean you're guaranteed to eat really well in the city after visiting highlights like the Hamilton Gardens.

Oddly, the great grey-green greasy Waikato River rolls right through town, but the city's layout largely ignores its presence: unless you're driving across a bridge you'll hardly know it's there.

☉ Sights

★**Hamilton Gardens** GARDENS
(www.hamiltongardens.co.nz; Cobham Dr; ◔ enclosed sector 7.30am-5pm, info centre 9am-5pm) FREE Hamilton Gardens, spread over 50

MAORI NZ: WAIKATO & COROMANDEL PENINSULA

The Waikato and King Country region remains one of the strongest pockets of Maori influence in NZ. This is the heartland of the Tainui tribes, descended from those who disembarked from the *Tainui waka* (canoe) in Kawhia in the 14th century. Split into four main tribal divisions (Waikato, Hauraki, Ngati Maniapoto and Ngati Raukawa), Tainui are inextricably linked with the Kingitanga (King Movement), which has its base in Ngaruawahia.

The best opportunities to interact with Maori culture are the Kawhia Kai Festival (p167), and Ngaruawahia's Regatta Day and Koroneihana celebrations (p151). Interesting *taonga* (treasures) are displayed at museums in Hamilton and Te Awamutu.

Reminders of the Waikato Land War can be found at Rangiriri, Rangiaowhia and Orakau. See www.waikatowar.co.nz to download maps, audio files and and a smartphone app covering various locations of the fighting from 1863 to 1864.

Dozens of *marae* (meeting-house) complexes are dotted around the countryside – including at Awakino, and at Kawhia, where the *Tainui waka* is buried. You won't be able to visit these without permission but you can get decent views from the gates. Some regional tours include an element of Maori culture, including Ruakuri Cave (p170) and Kawhia Harbour Cruises (p167).

Although it has a long and rich Maori history, the nearby Coromandel Peninsula doesn't offer many opportunities to engage with the culture. Historic *pa* (fortified village) sites are dotted around, with the most accessible being Paaku (p191). There are others at Opito Beach, Hahei and Hot Water Beach.

Hamilton

Hamilton

◎ Top Sights
1 Waikato Museum C3

◎ Sights
2 ArtsPost C3
3 Riff Raff C3
4 Waikato River C3

🛏 Sleeping
5 Anglesea Motel A1
6 Backpackers Central B1
7 City Centre B&B C4
8 Ibis Hotel B2

✕ Eating
9 Banh Mi Caphe C3
10 Chim Choo Ree C3

11 Hamilton Farmers Market C2
12 Hazel Hayes B2
13 Pak 'n Save A1
14 Palate C2
15 River Kitchen C3
16 Rocket Coffee B2
17 Scott's Epicurean C3

◉ Drinking & Nightlife
18 Good George A3
19 Gothenburg C3
20 House on Hood C3
21 Wonderhorse C3

◉ Entertainment
22 Lido Cinema B2
23 Metro by Hoyts B2

hectares, incorporates a large park, cafe, restaurant and extravagant themed enclosed gardens. There are separate Italian Renaissance, Chinese, Japanese, English, American and Indian gardens complete with colonnades, pagodas and a mini Taj Mahal. Equally interesting are the sustainable Productive Garden Collection, a fragrant herb garden and the precolonisation Maori Te Parapara garden. Look for the impressive *Nga Uri O Hinetuparimaunga* (Earth Blanket) sculpture at the main gates. The gardens are southeast of Hamilton city centre.

★ Waikato Museum MUSEUM

(www.waikatomuseum.co.nz; 1 Grantham St; free-$6.50; ☉10am-4.30pm) The excellent Waikato Museum has five main areas: an art gallery; interactive science galleries; Tainui galleries housing Maori treasures, including the magnificently carved *waka taua* (war canoe), *Te Winikawaka*; a Hamilton history exhibition entitled 'Never a Dull Moment'; and a Waikato River exhibition. The museum also runs a rigorous program of public events. Admission is charged for some exhibits.

Waikato River RIVER, PARK

Bush-covered riverside walkways run along both sides of the river and provide the city's green belt. Jogging paths continue to the boardwalk circling Lake Rotoroa, west of the centre. Memorial Park is closer to town, and has the remains of *PS Rangiriri* – an iron-clad, steam-powered gunboat from the Waikato War – embedded in the riverbank.

Riff Raff MONUMENT

(www.riffraffstatue.org; Victoria St; ☞) One of Hamilton's more unusual public artworks is a life-size statue of *Rocky Horror Picture Show* writer Richard O'Brien, aka Riff Raff, the time-warping alien from the planet Transsexual. It looks over a small park on the site of the former Embassy Theatre where O'Brien worked as a hairdresser, though it's hard to imagine 1960s Hamilton inspired the tale of bisexual alien decadence. Free wi-fi emanates from Riff Raff's three-pronged stun gun.

ArtsPost GALLERY

(www.artspost.co.nz; 120 Victoria St; ☉10am-4.30pm) FREE This contemporary gallery and gift shop is housed in a grand former post office. It focuses on the best of local art: paintings, glass, prints, textiles and photography.

Hamilton Zoo ZOO

(☏07-838 6720; www.hamiltonzoo.co.nz; 183 Brymer Rd; adult/child/family $19/9/56, tours extra; ☉9am-5pm, last entry 3.30pm) Hamilton Zoo houses 500-plus species including wily and curious chimpanzees. Guided-tour options include Eye2Eye and Face2Face opportunities to go behind the scenes to meet various animals, plus daily 'Meet the Keeper'

talks from the critters' caregivers. The zoo is 8km northwest of Hamilton city centre.

Classics Museum MUSEUM

(www.classicsmuseum.co.nz; 11 Railside Pl, Frankton; adult/child $20/8; ☉9am-4pm) Travel in time amid this collection of over 100 classic cars from the first half of the 20th century. Even if you're not a motorhead, you'll still be dazzled by the crazy Amphicar and the cool Maserati and Corvette sports cars. The museum is just off SH1 northwest of central Hamilton.

🏃 Activities

Extreme Edge ROCK CLIMBING

(☏07-847 5858; www.extremeedge.co.nz; 90 Greenwood St; day pass incl harness adult/child $18.50/14; ☉noon-9.30pm Mon-Fri, 9am-7pm Sat & Sun) Near the Frankton train station, with hyper-coloured climbing walls, 14m of which is overhanging. There's a kids' climbing zone, and free safety lessons.

Waikato River Explorer CRUISE

(☏0800 139 756; www.waikatoexplorer.co.nz; Hamilton Gardens jetty; adult/child $26/13; ☉Thu-Sun) Scenic 90-minute cruises along the Waikato River depart from the Hamilton Gardens jetty. On Sunday afternoons, three-hour wine-tasting cruises (adult/child $55/24) operate.

Kiwi Balloon Company BALLOONING

(☏021 912 679, 07-843 8538; www.kiwiballooncompany.co.nz; per person $350) Floating above lush Waikato countryside, the whole experience takes about four hours and includes a champagne breakfast and an hour's flying time.

🎊 Festivals & Events

Hamilton Gardens
Arts Festival PERFORMING ARTS

(www.hamiltongardensartsfestival.co.nz; Hamilton Gardens) Music, comedy, theatre, dance and movies, all served up alfresco in the Hamilton Gardens during the last two weeks of February.

Balloons Over Waikato SPORTS

(www.balloonsoverwaikato.co.nz) A colourful hot-air-balloon fest held in March.

🛏 Sleeping

The road into town from Auckland (Ulster St) is lined with dozens of unremarkable, traffic-noisy motels: passable for short stays.

J's Backpackers
HOSTEL $

(📞07-856 8934; www.jsbackpackers.co.nz; 8 Grey St; dm/s/d/tr $28/55/66/84; @🛜) A homely hostel occupying a characterful house near Hamilton Gardens, friendly J's offers good security, a cosy kitchen, free bikes and bright, tidy rooms. There's a barbecue out the back and a Mongolian yurt lounge-space on the front lawn.

Backpackers Central
HOSTEL $

(📞07-839 1928; www.backpackerscentral.co.nz; 846 Victoria St; dm $25, s $50-60, r $75-140; @🛜) Well-run hostel with dorms, singles, doubles and family rooms, some with en suite bathrooms and all with access to a shared kitchen and lounge. Worth considering as an alternative to a motel room if you're travelling as a couple or in a group.

Hamilton City Holiday Park
HOLIDAY PARK $

(📞07-855 8255; www.hamiltoncityholidaypark. co.nz; 14 Ruakura Rd; campsites/cabins/units from $37/47/75; @🛜) Simple cabins and leafy sites are the rule at this shady park. It's reasonably close to town (2km east of the centre) and very affordable.

City Centre B&B
B&B $$

(📞07-838 1671; www.citycentrebnb.co.nz; 3 Anglesea St; r $90-165; @🛜🏊) At the quiet riverside end of a central city street (five minutes' walk to the Victoria/Hood St action), this sparkling self-contained apartment opens on to a swimming pool. There's also a bedroom available in a wing of the main house. Self-catering breakfast is provided.

Anglesea Motel
MOTEL $$

(📞0800 426 453, 07-834 0010; www.angleseamotel.co.nz; 36 Liverpool St; units $140-300; @🛜🏊) Getting great feedback from travellers and a preferred option to anything on Ulster St's 'motel row', the Anglesea has plenty of space, friendly managers, a pool and squash and tennis courts, and not unstylish decor.

Ibis Hotel
HOTEL $$

(📞07-859 9200; www.ibis.com/hamilton; 18 Alma St; r $100-130; 🛜) The rooms are compact, but they're clean and well designed, and the riverfront Ibis is a good option if you're looking for quiet, centrally located digs just a short walk from the best of Hamilton's bars and restaurants. The shared public areas – complete with a restaurant for a good-value breakfast buffet ($20) – are spacious and colourful.

Eating

Rocket Coffee
CAFE $

(www.rocketcoffee.co.nz; 302 Barton St; coffee from $4; ⊘8am-4pm Mon-Fri) Duck down a lane off Barton St for what some locals reckon is Hamilton's hippest cafe. Rocket Coffee is a warehouselike bean barn, roasting on site and enticing caffeine fiends to the communal table strewn with newspapers. Staff spin old-school vinyl (and take requests) in between playing barista and packaging up sacks of beans for shipment.

Scott's Epicurean
INTERNATIONAL $

(📞07-839 6680; www.scottsepicurean.co.nz; 181 Victoria St; mains $11-20; ⊘7am-3pm Mon-Fri, 8.30am-4pm Sat & Sun) This gorgeous joint features swanky leather banquettes, pressed-tin ceilings, great coffee and an interesting and affordable menu: try the *pytti panna* (Swedish bubble-and-squeak) or the ever-popular *spaghetti aglio e olio*. Friendly service and fully licensed.

Banh Mi Caphe
VIETNAMESE $

(www.facebook.com/banhmicaphe; 198/2 Victoria St; snacks & mains $7-14; ⊘11am-4pm Tue, Wed, Sat & Sun, to late Thu & Fri) Fresh spring rolls, Vietnamese *banh mi* sandwiches and steaming bowls of *pho* (noodle soup) all feature at this hip spot channelling the backstreets of Hanoi. In the immediate vicinity there are plenty more tasty opportunities for ethnic dining, with Indian, Thai, Chinese, Mexican and Japanese restaurants also lining Victoria St and nearby Hood St.

Hamilton Farmers Market
MARKET $

(www.waikatofarmersmarkets.co.nz; River Rd Carpark, 204 River Rd; ⊘8am-noon Sun) Take a stroll across the Claudelands Rd bridge to this farmers market with local cheeses, baked goods and produce. A coffee from the Rocket caravan and a flash hot dog from Bangin Bangaz is our recommended breakfast combo.

Pak 'n Save
SUPERMARKET $

(Mill St; ⊘7am-10pm) North of downtown Hamilton.

Hazel Hayes
CAFE $$

(www.hazelhayes.co.nz; 587 Victoria St; mains $10-20; ⊘7am-4pm Mon-Fri, 8am-3pm Sat) This mash-up of country-kitchen decor showcases inventive cafe fare. Free range this and organic that punctuate the short, focused menu, and both the service and coffee are very good. A concise wine and beer list also focuses on quality fare, and next door the Hazel's Counter deli is also worth visiting.

River Kitchen
CAFE $$

(www.theriverkitchen.co.nz; 237 Victoria St; mains $10-18; ⊙7am-4pm Mon-Fri, 8am-4pm Sat & Sun; ⍰) River Kitchen does things with simple style: cakes, gourmet breakfasts and fresh seasonal lunches (angle for the salmon hash), and a barista who knows his beans. It's the kind of place you visit for breakfast, come back to for lunch, then consider for breakfast the next day.

★ Chim Choo Ree
MODERN NZ $$$

(☑07-839 4329; www.chimchooree.co.nz; 14 Bridge St; mains $30-34; ⊙11.30am-2pm & 5pm-late Mon-Sat) In an airy heritage building beside the river, Chim Choo Ree focuses on shared plates like tuna tartare, smoked potato ravioli and Sichuan pork belly, and larger, equally inventive mains using duck, lamb, venison and snapper. Local foodies wash it all down with a great wine list and flavourful New Zealand craft beers.

Palate
MODERN NZ, FUSION $$$

(☑07-834 2921; www.palaterestaurant.co.nz; 20 Alma St; mains $34-38; ⊙11.30am-2pm Wed-Fri, 5.30pm-late Mon-Sat) Simple, sophisticated Palate has a well-deserved reputation for lifting the culinary bar across regional NZ. The innovative menu features highlights like red roasted duck with yams, scallops, shiitake and a chilli broth. The wine selection is Hamilton's finest.

Drinking & Nightlife

The blocks around Victoria and Hood Sts make for a boozy bar-hop, with weekend live music and DJs. Friday is the big night of the week.

Wonderhorse
COCKTAIL BAR

(www.facebook.com/wonderhorsebar; 232 Victoria St; ⊙5pm-3am Wed-Sat) Look for the subtle spraypainted Wonderhorse logo on the footpath and follow the white arrow to this cool cocktail bar that also regularly features craft beers from tiny local brewers like Shunters Yard, Brewaucracy and 666. Vintage vinyl is often spinning on the turntable, and $5 cheeseburger sliders and killer cocktails complete the picture at Hamilton's best bar.

Good George
BREWERY

(☑07-847 3223; www.goodgeorge.co.nz; 32a Somerset St, Frankton; tours incl beer & food $15;

TAUPIRI

About 26km north of Hamilton on SH1 is Taupiri (287m), the **sacred mountain** of the Tainui people. You'll recognise it by the cemetery on its slopes and the honking of passing car horns – locals saying hi to their loved ones as they pass by. In August 2006 thousands gathered here as the much-loved Maori queen, Dame Te Atairangikaahu, was transported upriver by *waka* (canoe) to her final resting place, an unmarked grave on the summit.

⊙11am-late, tours from 5.30pm Mon-Thu) Channelling a cool industrial vibe, the former Church of St George is now a shrine to craft beer. Order a tasting flight of six beers ($19), and partner the hoppy heaven with wood-fired pizzas ($20 to $23), platters ($12 to $16), and larger main meals ($20 to $34). Our favourites are the zesty White Ale and the zingy Drop Hop cider. Tours must be booked ahead.

Gothenburg
BAR,

(www.gothenburg.co.nz; 15 Hood St; ⊙10.30am-late) This cosy hybrid of bar and restaurant takes a serious approach to beer and wine, with local craft brewers joined by a very impressive range of Belgian brews. Foodwise the menu steers from tapas to mains – try the Vietnamese-style pork belly or the gin-soaked salmon – and the service is a cut-above other nearby places along sometimes-rambunctious Hood St.

House on Hood
BAR

(www.houseonhood.co.nz; 27 Hood St; ⊙11am-late) House on Hood is a 1915 barn with lots of drops to slake your thirst. Beer specials, tasting sessions and meal deals abound, plus Saturday-night bands and Sunday-afternoon DJs.

☆ Entertainment

Lido Cinema
CINEMA

(www.lidocinema.co.nz; Level 1, Centre Place, 501 Victoria St; adult/child $15.50/9.50; ⊙10am-late) Art-house movies with $10 Tuesday tickets.

Metro by Hoyts
CINEMA

(www.hoyts.co.nz; Centre Place Shopping Centre, 12 Ward St; adult/child $14/10) Blockbuster flicks with $10 Tuesday tickets.

❶ Information

Anglesea Clinic (☑07-858 0800; www.angle-seamedical.co.nz; cnr Anglesea & Thackeray Sts; ⊘24hr) For accidents and urgent medical assistance.

DOC (Department of Conservation; ☑07-858 1000; www.doc.govt.nz; Level 5, 73 Rostrevor St; ⊘8am-4.30pm Mon-Fri)

Hamilton i-SITE (☑0800 242 645, 07-958 5960; www.visithamilton.co.nz; cnr Caro & Alexandra Sts; ⊘9am-5pm Mon-Fri, 9.30am-3.30pm Sat & Sun; 🛜) Accommodation, activities and transport bookings, plus free wi-fi right across Garden Pl.

Waikato Hospital (☑07-839 8899; www.waikatodhb.govt.nz; Pembroke St; ⊘24hr)

❶ Getting There & Away

AIR

Air New Zealand (☑0800 737 000; www.airnewzealand.co.nz) Regular direct flights from Hamilton to Auckland, Christchurch, Palmerston North and Wellington.

Sunair (☑0800 786 247; www.sunair.co.nz) Direct flights to Gisborne, Napier and New Plymouth.

BUS

All buses arrive and depart from the **Hamilton Transport Centre** (☑07-834 3457; www.hamilton.co.nz; cnr Anglesea & Bryce Sts; 🛜).

Waikato Regional Council's **Busit!** (☑0800 4287 5463; www.busit.co.nz) coaches serve the region, including Ngaruawahia ($3.20, 25 minutes), Cambridge ($6.70, 40 minutes), Te Awamutu ($6.70, 50 minutes) and Raglan ($8.50, one hour).

InterCity (☑09-583 5780; www.intercity.co.nz) services numerous destinations including the following:

DESTINATION	PRICE ($)	DURATION	FREQUENCY (DAILY)
Auckland	12-35	2hr	11
Cambridge	10-20	25min	9
Matamata	10-25	50min	4
Ngaruawahia	10-21	20min	9
Rotorua	14-35	1½hr	5
Te Aroha	10	1hr	2
Te Awamutu	10-22	35min	3
Wellington	27-70	5hr	3

Naked Bus (☑0900 625 33; www.nakedbus.com) services run to the following destinations (among many others):

DESTINATION	PRICE ($)	DURATION	FREQUENCY (DAILY)
Auckland	17-19	2hr	5
Cambridge	15	30min	5-7
Matamata	20	1hr	1
Ngaruawahia	15	30min	5
Rotorua	10	1½hr	4-5
Wellington	20-30	9½hr	1-2

SHUTTLE BUSES

Minibus Express (☑0800 646 428, 07-856 3191; www.minibus.co.nz) Shuttles between Hamilton and Auckland airport (one way $75).

Raglan Scenic Tours (☑021 0274 7014, 07-825 0507; www.raglanscenictours.co.nz) Shuttle linking Hamilton with Raglan (one way $35). Auckland airport service also available.

TRAIN

Hamilton is on the **Northern Explorer** (☑0800 872 467; www.kiwiscenic.co.nz) route between Auckland ($48, 2½ hours) and Wellington ($186, 9½ hours) via Otorohanga ($48, 45 minutes). Trains depart Auckland on Monday, Thursday and Saturday and stop at Hamilton's **Frankton train station** (Fraser St), 1km west of the city centre; there are no ticket sales here – see the website for ticketing details.

❶ Getting Around

TO/FROM THE AIRPORT

Hamilton International Airport (HIA; ☑07-848 9027; www.hamiltonairport.co.nz; Airport Rd) is 12km south of the city. The **Super Shuttle** (☑0800 748 885, 07-843 7778; www.super-shuttle.co.nz; one way $26) offers a door-to-door service into the city. A taxi costs around $50.

BUS

Hamilton's **Busit!** (☑0800 4287 5463; www.busit.co.nz; city routes adult/child $3.30/2.20) network services the city centre and suburbs daily from around 7am to 7.30pm (later on Friday). All buses pass through Hamilton Transport Centre. Busit! also runs a free Onboard CBD shuttle looping around Victoria, Liverpool, Anglesea and Bridge Sts every 10 minutes (7am to 6pm weekdays, 9am to 1pm Saturday).

CAR

Rent-a-Dent (☑07-839 1049; www.rentadent.co.nz; 383 Anglesea St; ⊘7.30am-5pm Mon-Fri, 8am-noon Sat) Car hire.

TAXI

Hamilton Taxis (☑0800 477 477, 07-8477 477; www.hamiltontaxis.co.nz)

Raglan

POP 2740

Laid-back Raglan may well be NZ's perfect surfing town. It's small enough to have escaped mass development, but it's big enough to exhibit signs of life including good eateries and a bar that attracts big-name bands in summer. Along with the famous surf spots to the south, the harbour just begs to be kayaked upon. There's also an excellent arts scene, with several galleries and shops worthy of perusal.

◎ Sights & Activities

Old School Arts Centre   ARTS CENTRE, GALLERY
(www.raglanartscentre.co.nz; Stewart St; ⊙10am-2pm Mon & Wed, exhibition hours vary) FREE A community hub, the Old School Arts Centre has changing exhibitions and workshops, including weaving, carving, yoga and storytelling. Movies screen here regularly through summer ($11): grab a curry and a beer to complete the experience. The hippie/artsy **Raglan Creative Market** happens out the front on the second Sunday of the month (9am to 2pm).

Raglan

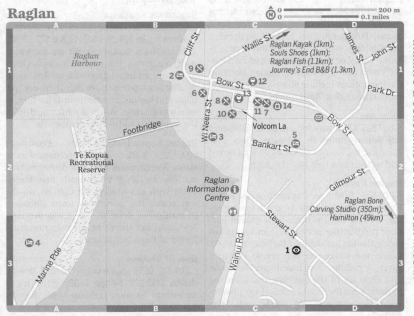

Raglan

◎ Sights
1 Old School Arts Centre C3

✦ Activities, Courses & Tours
Raglan Scenic Tours .... (see 5)

🛏 Sleeping
2 Bow St Studios B1
3 Raglan Backpackers C2
4 Raglan Kopua Holiday Park A3
5 Raglan Sunset Motel C2

✕ Eating
6 Aloha Market Place B1

7 Banteay Srey C1
8 Juantanameras C1
9 Orca B1
10 Raglan Roast C1
11 The Shack C1

🍷 Drinking & Nightlife
12 Harbour View Hotel C1
13 Yot Club C1

🛍 Shopping
14 Jet Collective C1

Raglan Surf School
SURFING

(☑ 07-825 7873; www.raglansurfingschool.co.nz; 5b Whaanga Rd; 3hr lesson incl transport from Raglan $89) Raglan Surf School prides itself on getting 95% of first-timers standing during their first lesson. Rental gear includes surfboards (from $20 per hour), body boards ($5 per hour) and wet suits ($5 per hour). It's based at Karioi Lodge in Whale Bay. It also operates **Surfdames** (www.surfdames.co.nz), offering women-only surfing experiences incorporating lessons with yoga, massage and beauty treatments.

Raglan Rock
ROCK CLIMBING, CAVING

(☑ 0800 724 7625; www.raglanrock.com; climbing half-/full day $89/119, caving $89-99, minimum 2 people) Full instruction and all equipment for climbing on the limestone cliffs of nearby Stone Valley, or the exciting 'Stupid Fat Hobbit' climb and abseil above Raglan harbour. Caving options include Stone Valley and the more challenging 'Rattlesnake'.

Solscape
SURFING

(☑ 07-825 8268; www.solscape.co.nz; 611 Wainui Rd) Supersustainable Solscape offers 2½-hour surfing lessons ($85), as well as board and wetsuit hire (per half-day $35).

Raglan Kayak
KAYAKING

(☑ 07-825 8862; www.raglaneco.co.nz; Raglan Wharf) Raglan Kayak is great for kayaking. This outfit runs three-hour guided harbour paddles (per person $75) and rents out single/double kayaks (per half-day $40/60). Learn the basics on the gentle Opotoru River, or paddle out to investigate the nooks and crannies of the pancake rocks on the harbour's northern edge. Stand up paddleboards are also available (one hour/half-day $20/40).

Raglan Bone Carving Studio
BONE CARVING

(☑ 021 0223 7233; raglanbonecarvingstudio@hotmail.com; workshops $69) Carve your own bone pendant with Rangi Wills, a reformed 'troubled teenager' who found out he was actually really good at carving things. Workshops run for four hours and Rangi can provide transport from Raglan township to his studio. Bookings essential.

☞ Tours

Raglan Scenic Tours
GUIDED TOUR

(☑ 07-825 0507; www.raglanscenictours.co.nz; 5a Bankart St) Sightseeing tours, including 2½ hours around the Raglan area (adult/child $55/20) and four hours around Mount Ka-

rioi including Bridal Veil Falls and Te Toto Gorge ($90/40). Various treks and paddleboarding instruction can be arranged, and kayaks, mountain bikes and paddle boards can be hired.

Cruise Raglan
CRUISE

(☑ 07-825 7873; www.raglanboatcharters.co.nz; adult/child $40/29) Two-hour sunset cruises around Raglan Harbour on the *Wahine Moe*, with fish and chips and a few drinks. Ninety-minute morning harbour cruises ($30/15 per adult/child) are also available.

🛏 Sleeping

Raglan Backpackers
HOSTEL $

(☑ 07-825 0515; www.raglanbackpackers.co.nz; 6 Wi Neera St; dm $27-29, s $58, tw & d $72-82; @) This laid-back hostel is right on the water, with sea views from some rooms. Other rooms are arranged around a garden courtyard or in a separate building. There are free bikes and kayaks, and surfboards for hire, or take a yoga class, strum a guitar or drip in the sauna. No wi-fi – it 'ruins the vibe'.

Raglan Kopua Holiday Park
HOLIDAY PARK $

(☑ 07-825 8283; www.raglanholidaypark.co.nz; Marine Pde; campsites from $34, dm/cabins/units from $56/85/100; @ 🛜) A neatly maintained outfit with lots of sleeping options, on the spit across the inlet from town (there's a footbridge, or drive the long way around). No shade, but there's beach swimming and plenty of room to run amok.

Bow St Studios
APARTMENTS $$

(☑ 07-825 0551; www.bowstreet.co.nz; 1 Bow St; studios $145-225, cottage $205; 🛜) With a waterfront location right in town, Bow St has self-contained studios and a historic cottage. The property is surrounded by a subtropical garden and shaded by well-established pohutukawa trees, and the cool and chic decor is stylish and relaxing.

Journey's End B&B
B&B, APARTMENTS $$

(☑ 07-825 6727; www.raglanaccommodation.co.nz; 49 Lily St; s/d $100/140, exclusive use $200; 🛜) These two attractive en suite rooms share a central modern lounge with a kitchenette and a lovely deck overlooking the wharf and harbour. You can book out the whole place, or just one of the rooms. Fifteen minutes' walk from town.

Raglan Sunset Motel
MOTEL $$

(☑ 07-825 0050; www.raglansunsetmotel.co.nz; 7 Bankart St; d from $150; 🛜) A block from Bow

St's shops and restaurants with spacious and modern units. The owners also have self-contained apartments (doubles from $160) and beach houses (four people $300) available. Bike and kayak hire is available (per half-day $30 and $45 respectively).

✗ Eating

Juantanameras SOUTH AMERICAN $
(Electric Ave, off 5 Wainui Rd; snacks $3-7; ⊙9am-5pm) Hunt down this summer-only food caravan for tasty Venezuelan *arepas* (corn cakes) or Mexican quesadillas and tacos. Get there early for *churros* (Mexican doughnuts), perfect for a local Raglan coffee just next door. It's only open Friday to Sunday in winter, and even then it can be subject to surf conditions. Welcome to laid-back Raglan.

Aloha Market Place JAPANESE $
(5 Bow St; sushi $1.20-2.20, mains $10-13; ⊙9am-5pm; ✍) Rolled-to-order sushi, udon noodles and *donburi* rice bowls, all with a touch of hip Hawaiian-Japanese surfer style. Reduced opening hours in winter.

Raglan Roast CAFE $
(www.raglanroast.co.nz; Volcom Lane; coffee $4; ⊙7am-5pm) Hole-in-the-wall coffee roaster with the best brew in town. Stop by for a cup, a cookie and a conversation. Reduced winter hours.

Raglan Fish FISH & CHIPS $
(www.facebook.com/RaglanFishShop; Raglan Wharf, 92 Wallis St; fish & chips $6-10; ⊙9am-8pm) Super-fresh fish and chips and funky decor at this locals' favourite right on Raglan's recently restored wharf. Fresh oysters, mussels and seafood salads are also available.

The Shack CAFE, INTERNATIONAL $$
(www.theshackraglan.com; 19 Bow St; tapas $6-14, mains $12-27; ⊙8am-5pm Sun-Thu, to late Fri & Sat; 🛜✍) Brunch classics – try the chickpea-and-corn fritters – and interesting shared-plate mains like tempura squid and star-anise chicken feature at the best cafe in town. A longboard strapped to the wall, wobbly old floorboards, up-tempo tunes and international staff serving Kiwi wines and craft beers complete the picture.

Banteay Srey CAMBODIAN $$
(☑07-825 0952; www.raglancambodian.weebly.net; 23 Bow St; mains $18-24; ⊙8.30am-9pm) The menu also strays into Western flavours, but the authentic Cambodian dishes are the ones to go for. Our pick is the Char Kreoung

chicken or beef with lemongrass and lime, or the delicate Amok steamed and curried fish. On Tuesdays from 6.30pm, the restaurant hosts a buffet (per person $28). Booking ahead is recommended.

Orca CAFE, MODERN NZ $$
(☑07-825 6543; www.orcarestaurant.co.nz; 2 Wallis St; breakfast $11-21, mains $19-30; ⊙10am-late Mon-Fri, 9am-late Sat & Sun) A day started at an Orca window seat, looking over the water, with some eggs Benedict and coffee, is a day well launched. Come back in the evening for salmon risotto, shared platters and live music.

⚲ Drinking & Nightlife

Yot Club BAR, LIVE MUSIC
(www.mukuna.co.nz/waikato/raglan/yot-club.htm; 9 Bow St; admission free-$25; ⊙9pm-late) Raucous, nocturnal bar with DJs and touring bands.

Harbour View Hotel PUB
(14 Bow St) Classic old pub with main-street drinks on the shaded verandah. Decent pizza too and occasional live music on weekends and during summer.

🛍 Shopping

Jet Collective ARTS & CRAFTS
(www.jetcollective.co.nz; 19a Bow St; ⊙10am-4pm Wed-Mon) Funky gallery-shop showcasing 100% Raglan artists with everything from music CDs and mixed-media pieces through to retro Kiwiana-inspired work. It's also a good spot to drop in and chat with the friendly team about Raglan's growing and diverse arts scene.

Soul Shoes SHOES, ACCESSORIES
(www.soulshoes.co.nz; Raglan Wharf, Wallis St; ⊙10am-5pm) World famous in Raglan since 1973, and in a new century, Soul Shoes' range of handmade leather footwear has been joined by equally cool satchels, backpacks and bags.

ⓘ Information

Raglan Information Centre (☑07-825 0556; www.raglan.org.nz; 13 Wainui Rd; ⊙9.30am-5pm Mon-Fri, 10am-5pm Sat, 10am-4pm Sun) Department of Conservation (DOC) brochures plus information about accommodation and activities including kitesurfing and paddle boarding. Check out also the attached museum, especially the exhibition on the history of Raglan's surfing scene.

West Coast Health Centre (📞07-825 0114; wchc@wave.co.nz; 12 Wallis St; ⊙9am-5pm Mon-Fri) General medical assistance.

❶ Getting There & Around

From Hamilton, Raglan is 48km west along SH23. Unsealed back roads connect Raglan to Kawhia, 50km south; they're slow, winding and prone to rockslides, but scenic and certainly off the beaten track. Head back towards Hamilton for 7km and take the Te Mata/Kawhia turn-off and follow the signs; allow at least an hour.

Waikato Regional Council's **Busit!** (📞0800 4287 5463; www.busit.co.nz; adult/child $8.50/5.50) heads between Hamilton and Raglan (one hour) three times daily on weekdays and twice daily on weekends.

Raglan Scenic Tours (p158) runs a Raglan–Hamilton shuttle bus (one way $35) and direct transfers to/from Auckland International Airport.

For a cab call **Raglan Taxi** (📞07-825 0506).

South of Raglan

The surf spots near Raglan – Indicators, Whale Bay and Manu Bay – are internationally famous for their point breaks. Bruce Brown's classic 1964 wave-chaser film *The Endless Summer* features Manu Bay.

Ocean Beach

Ocean Beach sits at the mouth of the harbour, 4km southwest of Raglan down Riria Kereopa Memorial Dr. It's popular for **windsurfing** and **kitesurfing**, but strong currents make it extremely treacherous for swimmers.

Ngarunui Beach

Less than 1km south of Ocean Beach, Ngarunui Beach is a great for grommets learning to surf. On the clifftop is a club-

WORTH A TRIP

RUAPEKE BEACH

Whale Bay marks the end of the sealed road, but a gravel road continues to the wild spans of Ruapuke Beach, 22km from Raglan. It's dangerous for swimmers here, but popular with surfcasting fisherfolk. The gravel road continues to Mt Karioi and rejoins the inland road at Te Mata.

house for the volunteer lifeguards who patrol part of the black-sand beach from late October until April. This is the only beach with lifeguards, and is the best ocean beach for **swimming**.

Manu Bay

A 2.5km journey from Ngarunui Beach will bring you to Manu Bay, a legendary **surf spot** said to have the longest left-hand break in the world. The elongated uniform waves are created by the angle at which the Tasman Sea swell meets the coastline (it works best in a southwesterly swell).

🛏 Sleeping

⭐ **Solscape**   HOSTEL, CABINS $
(📞07-825 8268; www.solscape.co.nz; 611 Wainui Rd; campsites from $17, caboose dm/d $30/72, teepees per person $36, cottages d $82-189; @🛜) 🌿 With a hilltop location fringed by native bush, Solscape's ecofriendly accommodation includes teepees, rammed-earth domes, railway carriages and stylish eco baches. There's room for tents and campervans, and simpler cottages are also available. Environmental impact is minimised with solar energy, and organic produce from the permaculture garden is used for guests' meals in the Conscious Kitchen cafe.

Yoga, massage and surfing lessons are all available, and Solscape is also YHA-affiliated.

Whale Bay

Whale Bay is a renowned **surf spot** 1km west of Manu Bay. It's usually less crowded than Manu Bay, but from the bottom of Calvert Rd you have to clamber 600m over the rocks to get to the break.

🛏 Sleeping

Karioi Lodge   HOSTEL $
(📞07-825 7873; www.karioilodge.co.nz; 5b Whaanga Rd; dm/d $30/75; @🛜) 🌿 Deep in native bush, Karioi Lodge offers a sauna, a flying fox, mountain bikes, bush and beach walks, sustainable gardening, tree planting and the Raglan Surf School. There are no en suites but the rooms are clean and cosy. These friendly folks also run **Sleeping Lady Lodges** (📞07-825 7873; www.sleepinglady.co.nz; 5b Whaanga Rd; lodges $175-260), a collection of six luxury self-contained houses nearby, all with ocean views.

Mt Karioi

In legend, Mt Karioi (756m), the Sleeping Lady (check out that profile), is the sister to Mt Pirongia. At its base (8km south of Whale Bay), **Te Toto Gorge** is a steep cleft in the mountainside, with a vertigo-inducing lookout perched high over the chasm.

Starting from Te Toto Gorge car park, a strenuous but scenic track goes up the western slope. It takes 2½ hours to reach a lookout point, followed by an easier hour up to the summit. From the east side, the **Wairake Track** is a steeper 2½-hour climb to the summit, where it meets the Te Toto Track.

Waireinga (Bridal Veil Falls)

Just past Te Mata (a short drive south of the main Raglan–Hamilton road) is the turn-off to the 55m Waireinga (Bridal Veil Falls), 4km from the main road. From the car park, it's an easy 10-minute walk through mossy native bush to the top of the falls (not suitable for swimming). A further 10-minute walk leads down to the bottom. Lock your car: theft is a problem here.

Magic Mountain Horse Treks (☑ 07-825 6892; www.magicmountain.co.nz; 334 Houtchen Rd, Te Mata; 1/2hr rides $50/80) runs horse treks around the hills, plus a ride to Waireinga (Bridal Veil Falls, $100).

Pirongia Forest Park

The main attraction of this 170-sq-km forest park is **Mt Pirongia** (www.mtpirongia.org.nz), its 959m summit clearly visible from much of the Waikato. The mountain is usually climbed from Corcoran Rd (three to five hours, one way) with tracks to other lookout points. Interestingly, NZ's tallest-known kahikatea tree (66.5m) grows on the mountainside. There's a six-bunk DOC hut near the summit if you need to spend the night: maps and information are available from Hamilton DOC (p156).

Te Awamutu

POP 9800

Deep into dairy-farming country, Te Awamutu (which means 'The River Cut Short'; the Waikato beyond this point was unsuitable for large canoes) is a pleasant rural service centre. With a blossom-treed main street and a good museum, TA (aka Rose Town) makes a decent overnighter.

TE AWAMUTU'S SACRED SOUND

In the opening lines of Crowded House's first single *Mean to Me*, Neil Finn single-handedly raised his sleepy home town, Te Awamutu, to international attention. It wasn't the first time it had provided inspiration – Split Enz songs *Haul Away* and *Kia Kaha*, with Neil's big bro Tim, include similar references.

Despite NZ's brilliant songwriting brothers being far from the height of their fame, Finn devotees continue to make the pilgrimage to Te Awamutu. Ask at the i-SITE about Finn postage stamps and the interesting scrapbook focused on the brothers' achievements.

◎ Sights

★**Te Awamutu Museum**   MUSEUM
(www.tamuseum.org.nz; 135 Roche St; admission by donation; ⊘ 10am-4pm Mon-Fri, 10am-1pm Sat, 1-4pm Sun) Te Awamutu Museum, 'where history never repeats', has a *True Colours*–painted shrine to local heroes Tim and Neil Finn. There are gold records, original lyrics, Finn memorabilia and oddities such as Neil's form-two exercise book. There's also a fine collection of Maori *taonga* (treasures), and an excellent display on the Waikato War. A great little museum.

Rose Garden   GARDENS
(cnr Gorst Ave & Arawata St; ⊘ 24hr) FREE The Rose Garden is next to the i-SITE and has 2500 bushes and 51 varieties with fabulously fruity names like Lady Gay and Sexy Rexy. The roses usually bloom from November to May.

🛏 Sleeping

Rosetown Motel   MOTEL $$
(☑ 07-871 5779, 0800 767 386; www.rosetownmotel.co.nz; 844 Kihikihi Rd; d $120-145; ☜ ☒) The older-style units at Rosetown have kitchens, new linen and TVs, and share a spa. A solid choice for a straight-up small-town sleep.

✖ Eating

Walton St Coffee   CAFE $
(www.facebook.com/WaltonStreetCollective; 3 Walton St; snacks $5-10; ⊘ 6.30am-2pm Mon-Fri) 🍃
In a rustic building with exposed beams and retro furniture, this combo of cafe, gallery

and performance space is Te Awamutu's top spot for a coffee. There's a strong focus on organic and gluten free with the food.

Sugoi Sushi
SUSHI $

(343 Alexandra St; sushi $8-10; ⊘7.30am-6pm) Quite probably Waikato's best sushi, with a huge selection and exemplary service.

Red Kitchen
CAFE $$

(www.redkitchen.co.nz; 51 Mahoe St; mains $14-20; ⊘7am-5.30pm Mon-Fri, 7.30am-2.30pm Sat) Excellent coffee, counter food and cosmopolitan brunches and lunches – try the macadamia and cranberry muesli – all feature at this sunny spot also incorporating a food store and a cookery school. Drop in for one of its gourmet TV dinners – actually really good – and fire up the motel microwave for your evening meal.

Redoubt Bar & Eatery
PUB $$

(www.redoubtbarandeateryta.co.nz; cnr Rewi & Alexandra Sts; mains $16-34; ⊘10am-late) A relaxed place to eat or drink, with cheap-but-potent cocktails, classic old photos of Te Awamutu sports teams on the walls, and a decent menu stretching from pasta to curry.

☆ Entertainment

Regent Theatre
CINEMA

(www.facebook.com/RegentTeawamutu; 235 Alexandra St; adult/child $15.50/9.50; ⊘10am-late) Art-deco cinema with movie memorabilia.

❶ Information

Te Awamutu i-SITE (⊘07-871 3259; www.teawamutuinfo.com; 1 Gorst Ave; ⊘9am-5pm Mon-Fri, 10am-4pm Sat & Sun) Local information and bookings.

❶ Getting There & Away

Te Awamutu is on SH3, halfway between Hamilton and Otorohanga (29km either way). The regional bus service **Busit!** (⊘0800 4287 5463; www.busit.co.nz) is the cheapest option for Hamilton (adult/child $6.70/4.50, 50 minutes, eight daily weekdays, three daily weekends).

Three daily **InterCity** (⊘09-583 5780; www.intercity.co.nz) services connect Te Awamutu with Auckland ($14 to $45, 2½ hours) and Hamilton ($21, 35 minutes).

Rangiaowhia

Before the Waikato invasion, Rangiaowhia (5km east of Te Awamutu on Rangiaowhia Rd; ask at the i-SITE for directions) was a thriving Maori farming town, exporting wheat, maize, potatoes and fruit to as far afield as Australia. It was home to thousands of inhabitants, two churches, a flour mill and a racecourse, and was the perfect model of what NZ under the Maori version of the Treaty of Waitangi had outlined for NZ – two sovereign peoples interacting to mutual advantage.

In February 1864 the settlement was left undefended while King Tawhiao's warriors held fortified positions further north. In a key tactical move, General Cameron outflanked them and took the town, killing women, children and the elderly. This was a turning point in the campaign, demoralising the Maori and drawing the warriors out of their near-impregnable *pa* fortifications.

Sadly, all that remains of the town is the cute 1854 Anglican **St Paul's Church** (⊘07-871 5568; Rangiaowhia Rd; ⊘services 9am 1st &

WORTH A TRIP

SANCTUARY MOUNTAIN MAUNGATAUTARI

Can a landlocked volcano become an island paradise? Inspired by the success of pest eradication and native-species reintroduction in the Hauraki Gulf, a community trust has erected 47km of pest-proof fencing around the triple peaks of Maungatautari (797m) to create the impressive **Sanctuary Mountain Maungatautari** (www.sanctuarymountain.co.nz; adult/child $15/6). This atoll of rainforest dominates the skyline between Te Awamutu and Karapiro and is now home to its first kiwi chicks in 100 years. The main entrance is at the visitor centre on the sanctuary's southern side.

Out in the Styx (⊘07-872 4505; www.styx.co.nz; 2117 Arapuni Rd, Pukeatua; dm/s/d $95/130/260) is near the south end of the Maungatautari guided day- and night-walk options. The three stylishly furnished themed rooms (Polynesian, African or Maori) are especially nice, plus there are bunk rooms and a spa for soothing weary legs. Prices include a four-course dinner and breakfast. It also provides a pick-up service if you wish to walk across the mountain from south to north (around six hours).

3rd Sun of month) and the Catholic mission's **cemetery**, standing in the midst of rich farming land – confiscated from the Maori and distributed to colonial soldiers.

The war ended further south at **Orakau**, where a roadside obelisk marks the site where 300 Maori, led by Rewi Maniapoto, repulsed three days of attacks against an unfinished *pa* by 1500 troops, before breaking out and retreating to what is now known as the King Country (losing 70 warriors).

Wharepapa South

A surreal landscape of craggy limestone provides some of the best **rock climbing** in the North Island. It's an area best suited to travellers with at least basic climbing skills.

Bryce's Rockclimbing (07-872 2533; www.rockclimb.co.nz; 1424 Owairaka Valley Rd; 1-day instruction for 1-2 people $440) is suited to the serious climber. On site is NZ's largest retail climbing store, selling and hiring out a full range of gear. It also has an indoor bouldering cave, free to those staying out back in the shipshape accommodation (dorm/ double $30/76). There's a licensed cafe (light meals $6 to $16, open 8am to 5pm Friday to Monday), and accommodation is also open to nonclimbers.

Cambridge

POP 15,200

The name says it all. Despite the rambunctious Waikato River looking nothing like the Cam, the good people of Cambridge have done all they can to assume an air of English gentility with village greens and tree-lined avenues.

Cambridge is famous for the breeding and training of thoroughbred horses. Equine references are rife in public sculpture, and plaques boast of past Melbourne Cup winners.

◉ Sights & Activities

Cambridge Museum MUSEUM
(www.cambridgemuseum.org.nz; 24 Victoria St; admission by donation; ⊘10am-4pm Mon-Fri, to 2pm Sun) In a former courthouse, the quirky Cambridge Museum has plenty of pioneer relics, a military-history room and a small display on the local Te Totara Pa before it was wiped out.

Jubilee Gardens GARDENS, MONUMENT
(Victoria St; ⊘24hr) Apart from its Spanish Mission town clock, Jubilee Gardens is a wholehearted tribute to the 'mother country'. A British lion guards the cenotaph, with a plaque that reads, 'Tell Britain ye who mark this monument faithful to her we fell and rest content'.

Lake Karapiro LAKE
(07-827 4178; www.waipadc.govt.nz; Maungatautari Rd) Eight kilometres southeast of Cambridge, Karapiro is the furthest downstream of a chain of eight hydroelectric power stations on the Waikato River. It's an impressive sight, especially when driving across the top of the 1947 dam. The 21km-long lake is also a world-class rowing venue.

Boatshed Kayaks KAYAKING
(07-827 8286; www.theboatshed.net.nz; 21 Amber Lane; single/double kayak for 3hr $25/50, paddle board $20; ⊘9am-5pm Wed-Sun) Located at the Boatshed Cafe with basic kayaks and paddle boards for hire. You can paddle to a couple of waterfalls in around an hour. There are also guided kayak trips at twilight (adult/child $110/40) to see a glowworm canyon up the nearby Pokewhaenua stream. Bookings are essential for these trips.

Waikato River Trails CYCLING, TRAMPING
(www.waikatorivertrails.com) Winding east from Cambridge, the 100km Waikato River Trails track is part of the **Nga Haerenga, New Zealand Cycle Trail** (www.nzcycletrail.com) project. You can either walk or cycle the five combined trails (or parts thereof), with lots of history and local landscapes en route.

Heritage & Tree Trail WALKING TOUR
This Cambridge walking tour includes the Waikato River, the 1881 St Andrew's Anglican Church (look for the Gallipoli window) and leafy Lake Ko Utu. Grab a map at the i-SITE.

Camjet JETBOATING
(0800 226 538; www.camjet.co.nz; adult/child $75/50) Exciting 35-minute spins to Karapiro dam on a jetboat. A 15-minute ride costs $45. Minimum two people.

🛏 Sleeping

Cambridge Motor Park HOLIDAY PARK $
(07-827 5649; www.cambridgemotorpark. co.nz; 32 Scott St; campsites from $17, cabins s/d from $47/57, units d $110; ⚑) A quiet,

well-maintained camping ground with lots of green, green grass. The emphasis is on tents and vans here, but the cabins and units are fine. Drive over the skinny Victoria Bridge from Cambridge town centre.

Cambridge Coach House B&B, CABIN **$$**
(📞07-823 7922; www.cambridgecoachhouse. co.nz; 3796 Cambridge Rd, Leamington; d/cottage $150/160; 🛜🍴) This farmhouse accommodation is slightly chintzy, but it's still a beaut spot to relax amid Waikato's rural splendour. There are two separate doubles and a self-contained cottage. It's a couple of kilometres south of town en route to Te Awamutu.

Cambridge Mews MOTEL **$$**
(📞07-827 7166; www.cambridgemews.co.nz; 20 Hamilton Rd; d $160-200; 🛜) All the spacious units in this chalet-style motel have double spa baths, decent kitchens and are immaculately maintained. It's a 10-minute walk to town.

✖ Eating

Boatshed Cafe CAFE **$**
(www.theboatshedkarapiro.co.nz; 21 Amber Lane, off Gorton Rd; mains $10-19; ⏱10am-3pm Thu-Sun) This stylish cafe on the edge of Lake Karapiro (heading south from Cambridge on SH1, turn right into Gorton Rd) is a top place for a leisurely brunch or lunch. Order the eggs Benedict, and grab an outside table for lake views and Waikato birdsong.

Red Cherry CAFE **$$**
(www.redcherrycoffee.co.nz; cnr SH1 & Forrest Rd; meals $16-20; ⏱7.30am-4.30pm; 🅿) With a cherry-red espresso machine working overtime, barnlike Red Cherry offers coffee roasted on site, delicious counter food and impressive cooked breakfasts. For lunch, the gourmet beef burger is hard to beat. Cambridge's best cafe is 4km from town en route to Hamilton.

Onyx CAFE, RESTAURANT **$$**
(📞07-827 7740; www.onyxcambridge.co.nz; 70 Alpha St; mains $17-30; ⏱9am-late) All-day Onyx occupies a lofty space, with onyx black furnishings and warm-toned timber floors. Wood-fired pizzas ($20 to $24) are the mainstay, plus salads, tortillas, sandwiches, steaks, cakes, organic coffee and NZ wines and beer.

ℹ Information

Cambridge i-SITE (📞07-823 3456; www. cambridge.co.nz; cnr Victoria & Queen Sts; ⏱9am-5pm Mon-Fri, 10am-4pm Sat & Sun; 🛜) Free Heritage & Tree Trail and town maps, and internet access.

ℹ Getting There & Away

Being on SH1, 22km southeast of Hamilton, Cambridge is well connected by bus. Waikato Regional Council's **Busit!** (📞0800 4287 5463; www.busit.co.nz) heads to Hamilton ($6.70, 40 minutes, seven daily weekdays, three daily weekends).

InterCity (📞09-583 5780; www.intercity. co.nz) services numerous destinations including the following:

DESTINATION	PRICE ($)	DURATION	FREQUENCY (DAILY)
Auckland	27-45	2½hr	12
Hamilton	10-25	30min	8
Matamata	10-22	30min	2
Rotorua	17-35	1¼hr	5
Wellington	28-68	8½hr	3

Naked Bus (📞0900 625 33; www.nakedbus. com) services to the same destinations are as follows:

DESTINATION	PRICE ($)	DURATION	FREQUENCY (DAILY)
Auckland	13-17	2½hr	6
Hamilton	20	30min	5
Matamata	24-25	2¼hr	1
Rotorua	10	1¼hr	4
Wellington	28	9½hr	1

Matamata

POP 7800

Matamata was just one of those pleasant, horsey country towns you drove through until Peter Jackson's epic film trilogy *Lord of the Rings* put it on the map. During filming 300 locals got work as extras (hairy feet weren't a prerequisite).

Following the subsequent filming of *The Hobbit*, the town has now ardently embraced its Middle Earth credentials, including a spooky statue of Gollum, and given the local information centre an appropriate extreme makeover.

Most tourists who come to Matamata are dedicated hobbit-botherers: for everyone else there's a great cafe, avenues of mature trees and undulating green hills.

◉ Sights & Activities

Hobbiton Movie Set Tours FILM LOCATION
(☑0508 446 224 866, 07-888 1505; www.hobbitontours.com; 501 Buckland Rd, Hinuera; adult/child $75/37.50; ☺tours 10am-4.30pm) Due to copyright, all the intricate movie sets around the country were dismantled after filming of *Lord of the Rings*, but Hobbiton's owners negotiated to keep their hobbit holes, which were then rebuilt for the filming of *The Hobbit*. Tours include a drink at the wonderful Green Dragon Inn. Free transfers leave from the Matamata i-SITE; check timings on the Hobbiton website. Booking ahead is strongly recommended.

With your own transport, head towards Cambridge from Matamata, turn right into Puketutu Rd and then left into Buckland Rd, stopping at the Shire's Rest Cafe.

Wairere Falls WATERFALL
About 15km northeast of Matamata are the spectacular 153m-high Wairere Falls (the highest on the North Island). From the car park it's a 45-minute walk through native bush to the lookout or a steep 90-minute climb to the summit.

Firth Tower MUSEUM, HISTORIC BUILDING
(www.firthtower.co.nz; Tower Rd; grounds free, tours adult/child $5/1; ☺grounds 10am-4pm daily, buildings 10am-4pm Thu-Mon) Firth Tower was built by Auckland businessman Josiah Firth in 1882. The 18m concrete tower was a fashionable status symbol, and is now filled with Maori and pioneer artefacts. Around it are 10 other historic buildings, including a schoolroom, church and jail. It's 3km east of town.

Opal Hot Springs SWIMMING
(www.opalhotsprings.co.nz; 257 Okauia Springs Rd; adult/child $8/4, 30min private spas $10/5; ☺9am-9pm) Opal Hot Springs isn't nearly as glamorous as it sounds but it does have three large thermal pools. Turn off just north of Firth Tower and follow the road for 2km. There's a holiday park here too.

🛏 Sleeping

Broadway Motel & Miro Court Villas MOTEL $$
(☑07-888 8482; www.broadwaymatamata.co.nz; 128 Broadway; s $89-145, d $99-165, 2-bedroom villa $265; @☒) This sprawling family-run motel complex has spread from a well-maintained older-style block to progressively newer and flasher blocks set back from the street. The nicest are the chic apartment-style Miro Court villas.

✖ Eating & Drinking

Workman's Cafe Bar CAFE $$
(www.matamata-info.co.nz/workmans; 52 Broadway; brunch $12-18, tapas $11, dinner $20-33; ☺9am-10pm Wed-Sun, 3-10pm Tue-Sun) Truly eccentric (old transistor radios dangling from the ceiling; a wall-full of art-deco mirrors; Johnny Cash on the stereo), this funky eatery has built itself a reputation that extends beyond Matamata. It's also a decent bar later at night.

Redoubt Bar & Eatery PUB
(www.redoubtbarandeatery.co.nz; 48 Broadway; lunch $11-20, dinner $21-34; ☺11am-late Mon-Fri, 10am-late Sat & Sun) Look forward to thin-crust pizzas named after LOTR, chowder, steaks, a winning hash stack and live music every Friday. It's also a minishrine to all things sporty and Matamata-related.

ℹ Information

Matamata i-SITE (☑07-888 7260; www.matamatanz.co.nz; 45 Broadway; ☺9am-5pm Mon-Fri, to 3pm Sat & Sun) Housed in a wonderful Hobbit gatehouse. Hobbiton tours also leave from here.

ℹ Getting There & Away

Matamata is on SH27, 20km north of Tirau.

InterCity (☑09-583 5780; www.intercity.co.nz) Runs to Cambridge ($22, 40 minutes, two daily), Hamilton ($27, one hour, three daily), Rotorua ($25, one hour, one daily) and Tauranga ($26, one hour, two daily).

Naked Bus (☑0900 625 33; www.nakedbus.com) Runs to Auckland ($13, 3½ hours, two daily), Cambridge ($20, two hours, one daily), Hamilton ($20, 3½ hours, two daily) and Tauranga ($14, one hour, one daily).

Te Aroha

POP 3800

Te Aroha has a great vibe. You could even say that it's got 'the love', which is the literal meaning of the name. Tucked under the elbow of the bush-clad Mt Te Aroha (952m), it's a good base for tramping or 'taking the waters' in the town's therapeutic thermal springs. It's also the southern trailhead on the Hauraki Rail Trail (p178).

Sights & Activities

Te Aroha Museum
MUSEUM

(www.tearoha-museum.com; Te Aroha Domain; adult/child $4/2; ⊙ 11am-4pm Nov-Mar, noon-3pm Apr-Oct) In the town's ornate former thermal sanatorium (aka the 'Treasure of Te Aroha'). Displays include quirky ceramics, old spa-water bottles, historic photos and an old printing press.

Te Aroha Mineral Spas
SPA

(☑ 07-884 8717; www.tearohamineralspas.co.nz; Boundary St, Te Aroha Domain; 30min session adult/child $18/11; ⊙ 10.30am-9pm Mon-Fri, to 10pm Sat & Sun) In the Edwardian Hot Springs Domain, this spa offers private tubs, massage, beauty therapies and aromatherapy. Also here is the temperamental Mokena Geyser – the world's only known soda geyser – which blows its top around every 40 minutes, shooting water 3m into the air (the most ardent eruptions are between noon and 2pm). Book ahead for spas and treatments.

Te Aroha Leisure Pools
SWIMMING, BATHHOUSE

(☑ 07-884 4498; www.tearohaleisurepools.co.nz; Boundary St, Te Aroha Domain; adult/child $7/5; ⊙ 10am-5.45pm Mon-Fri, to 6.45pm Sat & Sun) Outdoor heated freshwater pools, a thermal bath house and a toddlers' pool.

Mt Te Aroha
TRAMPING, MOUNTAIN BIKING

Trails up Mt Te Aroha start at the top of the domain. It's a 45-minute climb to Bald Spur/Whakapipi Lookout (350m), then another 2.7km (two hours) to the summit. Ask at the i-SITE about mountain-bike trails.

Sleeping

Te Aroha Holiday Park
HOLIDAY PARK $

(☑ 07-884 9567; www.tearohaholidaypark.co.nz; 217 Stanley Rd; campsites from $15, on-site vans s/d $30/40, cabins & units $53-90; @ 🛜 🏊) Wake up to a bird orchestra among the oaks at this site equipped with a grass tennis court, gym and hot pool, 2km southwest of town.

★ Aroha Mountain Lodge
LODGE, B&B $$

(☑ 07-884 8134; www.arohamountainlodge.co.nz; 5 Boundary St; s/d/ste/cottage $115/135/155/295) Spread over two *aroha*-ly Edwardian villas on the hillside above town, the plush Mountain Lodge offers affordable luxury (*sooo* much nicer than a regulation motel) and optional breakfast ($20 per person). The self-contained Gold Miner's Cottage sleeps six.

Te Aroha Motel
MOTEL $$

(☑ 07-884 9417; www.tearohamotel.co.nz; 108 Whitaker St; units $115-145; 🐾) Old-fashioned but reasonably priced and tidy units with kitchenettes, right in the centre of town.

Eating

Ironique
CAFE $$

(www.ironique.co.nz; 159 Whitaker St; mains $10-35; ⊙ 8am-late Mon-Fri, 4pm-late Sat & Sun) Come for a coffee and a restorative breakfast of eggs Benedict after tackling the Hauraki Rail Trail, or grilled salmon or confit duck for dinner. Don't overlook venturing to the quiet courtyard out the back for a few drinks.

Berlusconi on Whitaker
ITALIAN, TAPAS $$

(☑ 07-884 9307; www.tearoha-info.co.nz/berlusconi; 149 Whitaker St; lunch $14-20, pizza $27, dinner $33-24; ⊙ 11.30am-3.30pm Tue-Sun, plus 6pm-late Wed-Sun) We know the defunct Italian PM has his fingers in a lot of pies, but surely they don't extend to this suave upmarket wine, tapas and pizza bar in Te Aroha.

ℹ Information

Te Aroha i-SITE (☑ 07-884 8052; www.tearohanz.co.nz; 102 Whitaker St; ⊙ 9.30am-5pm Mon-Fri, to 4pm Sat & Sun)

ℹ Getting There & Away

Te Aroha is on SH26, 21km south of Paeroa and 55km northeast of Hamilton. Waikato Regional Council's **Busit!** (☑ 0800 4287 5463; www.busit.co.nz) runs to/from Hamilton (adult/child $8/4, one hour, two daily Monday to Friday). **Naked Bus** (☑ 0900 625 33; www.nakedbus.com) runs to Hamilton ($20, one hour, one daily) and Cambridge ($20, 1½ hours, one daily).

THE KING COUNTRY

Holding good claim to the title of NZ's rural heartland, this is a no-nonsense place that raises cattle and All Blacks. A bastion of independent Maoridom, it was never conquered in the war against the King Movement. The story goes that King Tawhiao placed his hat on a large map of NZ and declared that all the land it covered would remain under his *mana* (authority), and the region was effectively off limits to Europeans until 1883.

The Waitomo Caves are the area's major drawcard. An incredible natural phenomenon in themselves, they also feature lots of adrenaline-inducing activities.

Kawhia

POP 670

Along with resisting cultural annihilation, low-key Kawhia (think mafia with a K) has avoided large-scale development, retaining its sleepy fishing-village vibe. There's not much here except for the general store, a couple of takeaways and a petrol station. Even Captain Cook blinked and missed the narrow entrance to the large harbour when he sailed past in 1770.

⊙ Sights & Activities

Kayaks can be hired from Kawhia Beachside S-Cape and Kawhia Motel.

Ocean Beach   BEACH, SPRING
(Te Puia Rd) Four kilometres west of Kawhia is Ocean Beach and its high, black-sand dunes. Swimming can be dangerous, but one to two hours either side of low tide you can find the **Te Puia Hot Springs** in the sand – dig a hole for your own natural hot pool.

Kawhia Regional
Museum & Gallery   MUSEUM, GALLERY
(www.kawhiaharbour.co.nz; Omimiti Reserve, Kawhia Wharf; admission by gold coin donation; ⊙ noon-3pm Wed-Sun) Kawhia's modest waterside museum has local history, nautical and Maori artefacts, and regular art exhibitions. It doubles as the visitor information centre.

Maketu Marae   MARAE
(www.kawhia.maori.nz; Kaora St) From the wharf, a track extends along the coast to Maketu Marae, which has an impressively carved meeting house, Auaukiterangi. Two stones here – Hani and Puna – mark the burial place of the *Tainui waka*. You can't see a lot from the road, but the *marae* is private property – don't enter without permission from the **Maketu Marae Committee** (info@kawhia.maori.nz).

Kawhia Harbour Cruises   CRUISE
(✆ 021 966 754; www.kawhiaharbourcruises.co.nz; cruises per adult $35) There are some gorgeous beaches and kooky rock formations to check out around isolated Kawhia Harbour: bring your swimming gear! Minimum six adults.

Dove Charters   FISHING
(✆ 07-871 5854; www.westcoastfishing.co.nz; full day $110) Full-day fishing trips.

⚐ Festivals & Events

Kawhia Traditional Maori Kai Festival   FOOD
(www.kawhiakaifestival.co.nz; adult/child $10/2) During the annual Kai Festival in early February, over 10,000 people descend to enjoy traditional Maori *kai* (food) and catch up with *whanau* (relations). Once you've filled up on seafood, *rewana* bread and rotten corn, settle in to watch the bands and rousing *kapa haka* (traditional Maori group singing and dancing) performances.

⌷ Sleeping & Eating

Kawhia Beachside S-Cape   HOLIDAY PARK $
(✆ 07-871 0727; www.kawhiabeachsidescape.co.nz; 225 Pouewe St; campsites from $30, cabins dm/s/d from $30/40/58, cottages 165-185) This water's edge camping ground looks shabby from the road but has comfortable cottages, and cabins and camping with shared bathrooms. Two-hour kayak hire is $12 per person.

Kawhia Motel   MOTEL, RENTAL HOUSE $$
(✆ 07-871 0865; www.kawhiamotel.co.nz; cnr Jervois & Tainui Sts; d $129-169; ⧉) These six perkily

WAIKATO & COROMANDEL PENINSULA KAWHIA

KINGITANGA

The concept of a Maori people is a relatively new one. Until the mid-19th century, NZ was effectively comprised of many independent tribal nations, operating in tandem with the British from 1840.

In 1856, faced with a flood of Brits, the Kingitanga (King Movement) formed to unite the tribes to better resist further loss of land and culture. A gathering of leaders elected Waikato chief Potatau Te Wherowhero as the first Maori king, hoping that his increased *mana* (prestige) could achieve the cohesion that the British had under their queen.

Despite the huge losses of the Waikato War and the eventual opening up of the King Country, the Kingitanga survived – although it has no formal constitutional role. A measure of the strength of the movement was the huge outpouring of grief when Te Arikinui Dame Te Atairangikaahu, Potatau's great-great-great-granddaughter, died in 2006 after 40 years at the helm. Although it's not a hereditary monarchy (leaders of various tribes vote on a successor), Potatau's line continues to the present day with King Tuheitia Paki.

KAWHIA'S CANOE

The *Tainui waka* – a 14th-century ancestral canoe – made its final landing at Kawhia. The expedition leaders – Hoturoa, the chief/captain, and Rakataura, the *tohunga* (priest) – searched the west coast until they recognised their prophesied landing place. Pulling into shore, they tied the *waka* to a pohutukawa tree, naming it Tangi te Korowhiti. This unlabelled tree still stands on the shoreline between the wharf and Maketu Marae. The *waka* was then dragged up onto a hill and buried: sacred stones were placed at either end to mark its resting place, now part of the *marae*.

painted, well-kept, old-school motel units are right next to the shops. Kayak/bike hire costs $20/15 per hour.

Annie's Cafe & Restaurant CAFE, RESTAURANT $
(146 Jervois St; meals $10-22; ⊙ 7am-3pm Easter-Oct, 7am-late Nov–Easter) An old-fashioned licensed eatery in the main street, serving espresso, sandwiches and local specialities such as flounder and whitebait with kumara chips.

ⓘ Getting There & Away

Kawhia doesn't have a bus service. Take SH31 from Otorohanga (58km) or explore the scenic but rough road to Raglan (50km, 22km unsealed).

Otorohanga

POP 2700

Otorohanga's main street is festooned with images of cherished Kiwiana icons: sheep, gumboots, jandals, No 8 wire, All Blacks, pavlova, and the beloved Buzzy Bee children's toy. The town's Kiwi House is well worth a visit.

◉ Sights

**Otorohanga Kiwi House
& Native Bird Park** ZOO
(www.kiwihouse.org.nz; 20 Alex Telfer Dr; adult/child $22/7; ⊙ 9am-4.30pm Sep-May, to 4pm Jun-Aug) This bird barn has a nocturnal enclosure where you can see active kiwi energetically digging with their long beaks, searching for food. This is the only place in NZ where you

can see a great spotted kiwi, the biggest of the three kiwi species. The kiwi get fed at 1.30pm daily. Other native birds, such as kaka, kea, morepork and weka, are also on show.

Ed Hillary Walkway MEMORIAL
(⊙ 24hr) FREE As well as the Kiwiana decorating the main street, the Ed Hillary Walkway (running off Maniapoto St) has information panels on the All Blacks, Marmite and, of course, Sir Ed.

🛏 Sleeping

Otorohanga Holiday Park HOLIDAY PARK $
(☎ 07-873 7253; www.kiwiholidaypark.co.nz; 20 Huiputea Dr; campsites from $30, cabins & units $89-120; @ 🐾) It's not the most attractive locale, but this friendly park's tidy facilities include a fitness centre and sauna. And if you can't find a bed in Waitomo (it happens), Otorohanga is only 16km away.

✖ Eating & Drinking

Origin Coffee Station CAFE $
(www.origincoffee.co.nz; 7 Wahanui Cres; coffee $4-5; ⊙ 8.30am-4.30pm Mon-Fri) The folks at Origin are dead serious about coffee – sourcing, importing and roasting it themselves.

Countdown SUPERMARKET $
(www.countdown.co.nz; 123 Maniapoto St; ⊙ 7am-10pm) There's no supermarket at Waitomo Caves, so stock up en route to the caves in Otorohonga.

Thirsty Weta PUB
(www.theweta.co.nz; 57 Maniapoto St; meals $10-37; ⊙ 10am-1am) Hearty meals including pizza, steak, burgers and quesadillas; later on a pub–meets–wine bar ambience kicks off as the local musos plug in.

ⓘ Information

Otorohanga i-SITE (☎ 07-873 8951; www.otorohanga.co.nz; 27 Turongo St; ⊙ 9am-5pm Mon-Fri, 10am-2pm Sat & Sun; 🛜) Free wi-fi and local information.

ⓘ Getting There & Away

BUS

InterCity (☎ 09-583 5780; www.intercity.co.nz) Buses run from Otorohanga to Auckland ($47, 3¼ hours, four daily), Te Awamutu ($21, 30 minutes, three daily), Te Kuiti ($20, one hour, three daily) and Rotorua ($53, 2½ hours, two daily).

Naked Bus (✆0900 625 33; www.nakedbus.com) Runs one bus daily to Waitomo Caves ($20, 30 minutes), Hamilton ($25, one hour) and New Plymouth ($30, 3¼ hours).

Waitomo Shuttle (✆0800 808 279, 07-873 8279; one-way adult/child $12/7) Heads to the Waitomo Caves five times daily, coordinating with bus and train arrivals. Bookings recommended.

TRAIN

Otorohanga is on the **Northern Explorer** (✆0800 872 467; www.kiwiscenic.co.nz) train route between Auckland (from $48, 3¼ hours) and Wellington (from $99, nine hours) via Hamilton ($48, 50 minutes).

Waitomo Caves

Even if damp, dark tunnels are your idea of hell, head to Waitomo anyway. The limestone caves and glowing bugs here are one of the North Island's premier attractions.

The name Waitomo comes from *wai* (water) and *tomo* (hole or shaft): dotted across this region are numerous shafts dropping into underground cave systems and streams. There are 300-plus mapped caves in the area: the three main caves – Glowworm, Ruakuri and Aranui – have been bewitching visitors for over 100 years.

Your Waitomo experience needn't be claustrophobic: the electrically lit, cathedral-like Glowworm Cave is far from squeezy. But if it's tight, gut-wrenching, soaking-wet, pitch-black excitement you're after, Waitomo can oblige.

◎ Sights

Waitomo Caves Visitor Centre VISITOR CENTRE
(✆0800 456 922; www.waitomo.com; Waitomo Caves Rd; ⊙9am-5pm) The big-three Waitomo Caves are all operated by the same company, based at the flash Waitomo

Waitomo Caves

◎ Top Sights
1 Glowworm Cave.....................A2

◎ Sights
2 Opapake Pa.....................D1
3 Waitomo Caves Discovery Centre........B1
4 Waitomo Caves Visitor Centre.............A1

⊕ Activities, Courses & Tours
5 CaveWorld.....................B1
6 Legendary Black Water Rafting Company.....................D2
Spellbound.................... (see 13)
7 Waitomo Adventures.....................C2

⊜ Sleeping
8 Abseil Inn.....................C2
9 Kiwi Paka.....................B2
10 Waitomo Caves Guest Lodge.............B1
11 Waitomo Top 10 Holiday Park.............B1
12 YHA Juno Hall Waitomo.....................D2

⊗ Eating
13 Florence's Kitchen.....................B1
14 Huhu.....................B1
Morepork Cafe.................... (see 9)

⊖ Drinking & Nightlife
King Country Brewing Company..(see 13)

GLOWWORM MAGIC

Glowworms are the larvae of the fungus gnat. The larva glowworm has luminescent organs that produce a soft, greenish light. Living in a sort of hammock suspended from an overhang, it weaves sticky threads that trail down and catch unwary insects attracted by its light. When an insect flies towards the light it gets stuck in the threads – the glowworm just has to reel it in for a feed.

The larval stage lasts from six to nine months, depending on how much food the glowworm gets. When it has grown to about the size of a matchstick, it goes into a pupa stage, much like a cocoon. The adult fungus gnat emerges about two weeks later.

The adult insect doesn't live very long because it doesn't have a mouth. It emerges, mates, lays eggs and dies, all within about two or three days. The sticky eggs, laid in groups of 40 or 50, hatch in about three weeks to become larval glowworms.

Glowworms thrive in moist, dark caves but they can survive anywhere if they have the requisites of moisture, an overhang to suspend from and insects to eat. Waitomo is famous for its glowworms but you can see them in many other places around NZ, both in caves and outdoors.

When you come upon glowworms, don't touch their hammocks or hanging threads, try not to make loud noises and don't shine a light right on them. All of these things will cause them to dim their lights. It takes them a few hours to become bright again, during which time the grub will go hungry. The glowworms that shine most brightly are the hungriest.

Caves Visitor Centre (behind the Glowworm Cave), which incorporates a cafe and theatre. Various combo deals are available, including a Triple Cave Combo (adult/child $91/40). Try to avoid the large tour groups, most of which arrive between 10.30am and 2.30pm.

★ **Glowworm Cave** CAVE
(adult/child $48/21; ⊙45min tours every 30min 9am-5pm) The guided tour of the Glowworm Cave, which is behind the visitor centre, leads past impressive stalactites and stalagmites into a large cavern known as the Cathedral. The highlight comes at the tour's end when you board a boat and swing off onto the river. As your eyes grow accustomed to the dark you'll see a Milky Way of little lights surrounding you – these are the glowworms. Book your tour at the visitor centre.

The acoustics are so good that Dame Kiri Te Kanawa and the Vienna Boys Choir have given concerts here.

Aranui Cave CAVE
(adult/child $48/21; ⊙1hr tours 9.30am, 11am, 1pm, 2.30pm & 4pm) Three kilometres west from the Glowworm Cave is Aranui Cave. This cave is dry (hence no glowworms) but compensates with an incredible array of limestone formations. Thousands of tiny 'straw' stalactites hang from the ceiling. Book tours at the visitor centre, from where there is also transport to the cave entrance. A 15-minute bush walk is also included.

Ruakuri Cave CAVE
(☑0800 782 587, 07-878 6219; adult/child $67/26; ⊙2hr tours 9am, 10am, 11.30am, 12.30pm, 1.30pm, 2.30pm & 3pm) Ruakuri Cave has an impressive 15m-high spiral staircase, bypassing a Maori burial site at the cave entrance. Tours lead through 1.6km of the 7.5km system, taking in caverns with glowworms, subterranean streams and waterfalls, and intricate limestone structures. Visitors have described it as spiritual – some claim it's haunted – and it's customary to wash your hands when leaving to remove the *tapu* (taboo). Book tours at the visitor centre, or at the departure point, the Legendary Black Water Rafting Company.

Waitomo Caves Discovery Centre MUSEUM
(☑07-878 7640, 0800 474 839; www.waitomo-caves.com; 21 Waitomo Caves Rd; adult/child $5/free; ⊙9am-5.30pm) Adjoining the i-SITE, the Waitomo Caves Discovery Centre has excellent exhibits explaining how caves are formed, the flora and fauna that thrive in them and the history of Waitomo's caves and cave exploration.

🏃 Activities

Underground

Legendary Black Water Rafting Company
CAVING, ADVENTURE TOUR

(📞0800 782 5874; www.waitomo.com; 585 Waitomo Caves Rd; ☺ Black Labyrinth tour 9am, 10.30am, noon, 1.30pm & 3pm, Black Abyss tour 9am & 2pm, Black Odyssey tour 10am & 2.30pm) The Black Labyrinth tour (three hours, $125) involves floating in a wetsuit on an inner tube down a river that flows through Ruakuri Cave. The highlight is leaping off a small waterfall and then floating through a long, glowworm-covered passage. The trip ends with showers, soup and bagels in the cafe. The more adventurous Black Abyss tour (five hours, $225) includes a 35m abseil into Ruakuri Cave, a flying fox and more glowworms and tubing.

Recently launched, the Black Odyssey tour (four hours, $175) is a challenging dry caving adventure including flying foxes and negotiating high wires. Minimum ages apply for all tours, and there are 10% discounts if you prebook online.

Spellbound
CAVING, GUIDED TOUR

(📞0800 773 552, 07-878 7622; www.glowworm. co.nz; 10 Waitomo Caves Rd; adult/child $73/26; ☺ 3hr tours 10am, 11am, 2pm & 3pm, closed Jun) Spellbound is a good option if you don't want to get wet, are more interested in glowworms than an 'action' experience, and want to avoid the big groups in the main caves. Small-group tours access parts of the heavily glowworm-dappled Mangawhitiakau cave system, 12km south of Waitomo (...and you still get to ride in a raft!).

Waitomo Adventures
CAVING, ADVENTURE TOUR

(📞07-878 7788, 0800 924 866; www.waitomo. co.nz; 654 Waitomo Caves Rd) Waitomo Adventures offers various cave adventures, with discounts for combos and advance bookings. The Lost World trip ($340/490, four/seven hours) combines a 100m abseil with walking, rock climbing, wading and swimming. Haggas Honking Holes ($260, four hours) includes three waterfall abseils, rock climbing and a subterranean river. TumuTumu Toobing ($180, four hours) is a walking, climbing, swimming and tubing trip. St Benedict's Cavern ($180, three hours) includes abseiling and a subterranean flying fox.

Green Glow Eco-Adventures
CAVING, ADVENTURE TOUR

(📞0800 476 459; www.greenglow.co.nz; 1117 Oparure Rd, Te Kuiti; 6hr tours per person $220) Green Glow Eco-Adventures runs customised, small-group Waitomo tours, putting a caving, rock-climbing, photographic or glowworm spin on your day. It's based in Te Kuiti, 20 minutes from Waitomo.

CaveWorld
CAVING, ADVENTURE TOURS

(📞0800 228 338, 07-878 6577; www.caveworld. co.nz; cnr Waitomo Caves Rd & Hotel Access Rd) CaveWorld runs the Tube It ($139, two hours) black-water rafting trip through glowworm-filled Te Anaroa. Also available are a glowworm-illuminated night abseil down a 45m crevice called the Glowworm Canyon ($199, two hours), or the Footwhistle Glowworm Cave Tour ($55, one hour).

Kiwi Cave Rafting
CAVING, ADVENTURE TOUR

(📞07-873 9149, 0800 228 372; www.caveraft.com; 95 Waitomo Caves Rd) These small-group expeditions (five hours, $225) start with abseil training, followed by a 27m descent into a natural cave, and then a float along a subterranean river on an inner tube with plenty of glowworms. After some caving, a belayed rock climb up a 20m cliff brings you to the surface. A three-hour dry tour ($125) without the inner-tube adventure is also available.

LOCAL KNOWLEDGE

WAITOMO CAVES

The best way to experience the Waitomo glowworm caves is via black-water rafting. It's an exhilarating experience and involves getting dressed up in a wetsuit (laughing at how funny everyone looks is half the fun), choosing an inflatable inner tube to sit in (another hilarious experience) and travelling through the limestone caves with two guides, your wits, and the glowworms. It is a real hands-on experience and requires some agility and the guts to jump backwards down some small waterfalls as you make your way through the tunnels. You finish off the trip quietly drifting through the caves in your tube, looking at the glowworms with your head lamp turned off.

Dr Farah Rangikoepa Palmer,
former captain of the Black Ferns (NZ's women's rugby team)

Tramping

The Waitomo i-SITE has free pamphlets on walks in the area. The walk from **Aranui Cave** to **Ruakuri Cave** is an excellent short path. From the Waitomo Caves Visitor Centre, the 5km, three-hour-return **Waitomo Walkway** takes off through farmland, following Waitomo Stream to the **Ruakuri Scenic Reserve**, where a 30-minute return walk passes by a natural limestone tunnel. There are glowworms here at night – drive to the car park and bring a torch to find your way. Near Waitomo Adventures a steep 20-minute walk leads through bush then along farmland to the abandoned **Opapake Pa**, where terraces and kumara pits are visible.

Dundle Hill Walk TRAMPING
(☑0800 924 866, 07-878 7788; www.dundlehillwalk.com; adult/child $75/35) The self-guided privately run Dundle Hill Walk is a 27km, two-day/one-night loop walk through Waitomo's bush and farmland, including overnight bunkhouse accommodation high up in the bush.

🛌 Sleeping

Waitomo Top 10 Holiday Park HOLIDAY PARK $
(☑0508 498 666, 07-878 7639; www.waitomopark.co.nz; 12 Waitomo Caves Rd; campsites from $23, cabins $70-130, units $150-180; @ 🕏 🛜 🌊) This lovely holiday park in the heart of the village has spotless facilities, modern cabins and plenty of outdoor distractions to keep the kids busy.

Kiwi Paka HOSTEL $
(☑07-878 3395; www.waitomokiwipaka.co.nz; Hotel Access Rd; dm/s/d $32/65/70, chalets s/d/tw/q $95/100/110/160; @ 🕏) This purpose-built, alpine-style hostel has four-bed dorms in the main lodge, plus separate peak-roofed chalets, Morepork Cafe on site and super-tidy facilities. Popular with big groups.

YHA Juno Hall Waitomo HOSTEL $
(☑07-878 7649; www.junowaitomo.co.nz; 600 Waitomo Caves Rd; campsites from $17, dm $30, d with/without bathroom $84/74; @ 🕏 🛜 🌊) A slick purpose-built hostel 1km from the village with a warm welcome, a warmer wood fire in the woody lounge area, and an outdoor pool and tennis court.

Abseil Inn B&B $$
(☑07-878 7815; www.abseilinn.co.nz; 709 Waitomo Caves Rd; d from $150; 🕏) A *veeery* steep driveway takes you to this delightful B&B with four themed rooms, great breakfasts and witty hosts. The biggest room has a double bath and valley views.

Waitomo Caves Guest Lodge B&B $$
(☑0800 465 762, 07-878 7641; www.waitomocavesguestlodge.co.nz; 7 Te Anga Rd; s $90, d incl breakfast $110-130; 🕏) Bag your own cosy little hillside en suite cabin at this central operation with a sweet garden setting. The top cabins have valley views. Large continental breakfast and friendly resident dog included.

🍴 Eating & Drinking

The general store in Waitomo sells the basics, but it's cheaper to stock up in Otorohanga or Te Kuiti before you visit.

★**Huhu** CAFE, MODERN NZ $$
(☑07-878 6674; www.huhucafe.co.nz; 10 Waitomo Caves Rd; small plates $11-17, mains $19-33; ☺noon-late; 🕏) Slick and modern Huhu has great views from the terrace and sublime contemporary NZ food. Sip a strong coffee or Kiwi craft beer, or graze through a seasonal tapas-style menu of delights like slow-cooked lamb, teriyaki salmon and organic Scotch fillet steak.

Florence's Kitchen CAFE $$
(www.facebook.com/WaitomoGeneralStore; Waitomo General Store, 15 Waitomo Caves Rd; snacks & mains $12-20; ☺7.30am-10pm) In the Waitomo general store with a wide range of pre- and postcaving sustenance.

Morepork Cafe CAFE, PIZZERIA $$
(Kiwi Paka, Hotel Access Rd; breakfast & lunch $10-18, dinner $15-27; ☺8am-10.30pm; 🕏) At the Kiwi Paka backpackers is this cheery joint, a jack-of-all-trades eatery serving breakfast, lunch and dinner either inside or out on the deck. The 'Caveman' pizza is a definite winner.

King Country Brewing Company BREWERY
(www.facebook.com/kingcountrybrewingcompany; Waitomo General Store, 15 Waitomo Caves Rd) This craft brewery does four top drops – an IPA, a pale ale, a wheat beer and a cider – and features occasional guest beers from other smaller Kiwi breweries. Grab a tasting rack of all four for $16.

ℹ Information

There's no petrol in town, but there's an ATM at Kiwi Paka.

Waitomo i-SITE (☑07-878 7640, 0800 474 839; www.waitomocaves.com; 21 Waitomo Caves Rd; ☺9am-5.30pm) Internet access, post office and booking agent.

❶ Getting There & Away

Naked Bus (📞0900 625 33; www.nakedbus. com) Runs once daily to Otorohanga ($20, 20 minutes), Hamilton ($25, 1¼ hours) and New Plymouth ($30, three hours).

Waitomo Shuttle (📞0800 808 279, 07-873 8279; waikiwi@ihug.co.nz; one-way adult/child $12/7) Heads to the caves five times daily from Otorohanga (15 minutes away), coordinating with bus and train arrivals.

Waitomo Wanderer (📞03-477 9083, 0800 000 4321; www.travelheadfirst.com) Operates a daily return services from Rotorua or Taupo, with optional caving, glowworm and tubing add-ons (packages from $133). Shuttle-only services are $99 return.

Waitomo to Awakino

This obscure route, heading west of Waitomo on Te Anga Rd, is a slow but fascinating alternative to SH3 if Taranaki's your goal. Only 12km of the 111km route remains unsealed, but it's nearly all winding and narrow. Allow around two hours (not including stops) and fill up with petrol.

Walks in the **Tawarau Forest**, 20km west of the Waitomo Caves, are outlined in DOC's *Waitomo & King Country Tracks* booklet ($1, available from DOC in Hamilton or Te Kuiti), including a one-hour track to the Tawarau Falls from the end of Appletree Rd.

The **Mangapohue Natural Bridge Scenic Reserve**, 26km west of Waitomo, is a 5.5-hectare reserve with a giant natural limestone arch. It's a five-minute walk to the arch on a wheelchair-accessible pathway. On the far side, big rocks full of 35-million-year-old oyster fossils jut up from the grass, and at night you'll see glowworms.

About 4km further west is **Piripiri Caves Scenic Reserve**, where a five-minute walk leads to a large cave containing fossils of giant oysters. Bring a torch and be prepared to get muddy after heavy rain. Steps wind down into the gloom...

The impressively tiered, 30m **Marokopa Falls** are 32km west of Waitomo. A short track (15 minutes return) from the road leads to the bottom of the falls.

Just past Te Anga you can turn north to Kawhia, 59km away, or continue southwest to **Marokopa** (population 1560), a small black-sand village on the coast with some scarily big new mansions starting to appear. The whole Te Anga/Marokopa area is riddled with caves.

Marokopa Campground (📞07-876 7444; marokopacampground@xtra.co.nz; Rauparaha St; campsites from $24, dm/van d $18/45) ain't flash but it's in a nice spot, close to the coast. There's a small shop for grocery basics.

The road heads south to **Kiritehere**, through idyllic farmland to **Moeatoa** then turns right (south) into Mangatoa Rd. Now you're in serious backcountry, heading into the dense **Whareorino Forest**. For trampers, the 16-bunk DOC-run **Leitch's Hut** (📞07-878 1050; www.doc.govt.nz; per adult $5) has a toilet, water and a wood stove.

At **Waikawau** take the 5km detour along the unsealed road to the coast near **Ngarupupu Point**, where a 100m walk through a dank tunnel opens out on an exquisitely isolated stretch of black-sand beach. Think twice about swimming here as there are often dangerous rips in the surf.

The road then continues through another twisty 28km, passing lush forest and the occasional farm before joining SH3 east of Awakino (p174).

Te Kuiti

POP 4380

Cute Te Kuiti sits in a valley between picturesque hills. Welcome to the shearing capital of the world, especially if you visit for the annual Great New Zealand Muster.

◎ Sights

Big Shearer   LANDMARK
(Rora St) This 7m, 7½-tonne Big Shearer statue is at the southern end of town.

Te Kuititanga-O-Nga-Whakaaro   MONUMENT
(Rora St) Te Kuititanga-O-Nga-Whakaaro (The Gathering of Thoughts and Ideas) is a beautiful pavilion of etched-glass, *tukutuku* (woven flax panels) and wooden carvings that celebrates the town's history.

✯ Festivals & Events

Great New Zealand Muster   CULTURE, FOOD
(www.waitomo.govt.nz/events/the-great-nz-muster) The highlight of the Great New Zealand Muster is the legendary **Running of the Sheep**: when 2000 woolly demons stampede down Te Kuiti's main street. The festival in late March/early April includes sheep-shearing championships, a parade, Maori cultural performances, live music, barbecues, *hangi* and market stalls.

🛏 Sleeping & Eating

Waitomo Lodge Motel
MOTEL $$

(☑ 07-878 0003; www.waitomo-lodge.co.nz; 62 Te Kumi Rd; units $125-140; 🛜) At the Waitomo end of Te Kuiti, this motel's modern rooms feature contemporary art, flat-screen TVs and little decks overlooking Mangaokewa Stream in the units at the back.

Simply the Best B&B
B&B $$

(☑ 07-878 8191; www.simplythebestbnb.co.nz; 129 Gadsby Rd; s/d incl breakfast $70/110) It's hard to argue with the immodest name when the prices are this reasonable, the breakfast this generous, and the hosts this charming.

New World
SUPERMARKET $

(www.newworld.co.nz; Te Kumi Rd; ⊘8am-8pm) Waitomo-bound self-caterers should stock up.

Bosco Cafe
CAFE $

(theteam@boscocafe.co.nz; 57 Te Kumi Rd; mains $10-20; ⊘8am-5pm; 🛜🍴) This excellent industrial-chic cafe offers great coffee and tempting food (try the bacon-wrapped meatloaf with greens). Free wi-fi with purchase.

ℹ Information

DOC (Department of Conservation; ☑ 07-878 1050; www.doc.govt.nz; 78 Taupiri St; ⊘8am-4.30pm Mon-Fri)

Te Kuiti i-SITE (☑ 07-878 8077; www.waitomo.govt.nz; Rora St; ⊘9am-5pm Mon-Fri, 10am-2pm Sat) Internet access and visitor information.

ℹ Getting There & Away

BUS

InterCity (☑ 09-583 5780; www.intercity.co.nz) buses run daily to the following destinations (among others):

DESTINATION	PRICE ($)	DURATION (HR)	FREQUENCY (DAILY)
Auckland	28-58	3½	3
Mokau	30	1	2
New Plymouth	30	2½	2
Otorohanga	20	¾	3
Taumarunui	34	1¼	1

Naked Bus (☑ 0900 625 33; www.nakedbus.com) runs once daily to Auckland ($35, four hours), Hamilton ($25, 1½ hours), New Plymouth ($30, 2¼ hours) and Otorohanga ($20, 30 minutes).

Te Kuiti to Mokau

From Te Kuiti, SH3 runs southwest to the coast before following the rugged shoreline to New Plymouth. Detour at Pio Pio northwest to the Mangaotaki valley and **Hairy Feet Waitomo** (☑ 07-877 8003; www.hairyfeetwaitomo.co.nz; 1411 Mangaotaki Rd, Pio Pio; adult/child $50/25; ⊘10am & 1pm), one of NZ's newest Middle Earth–themed film-location attractions. Scenes from *The Hobbit* were filmed here with a background of towering limestone cliffs.

Along this scenic route the sheep stations sprout peculiar limestone formations before giving way to lush native bush as the highway winds along the course of the Awakino River.

The Awakino River spills into the Tasman at **Awakino** (population 60), a small settlement where boats shelter in the estuary while locals find refuge at the rustic **Awakino Hotel** (☑ 06-752 9815; www.awakinohotel.co.nz; SH3; meals $11-20; ⊘7am-11pm).

A little further south the impressive **Maniaroa Marae** dominates the cliff above the highway. This important complex houses the anchor stone of the *Tainui waka* which brought this region's original people from their Polynesian homeland. You can get a good view of the intimidatingly carved meeting house, Te Kohaarua, from outside the fence – don't cross into the *marae* unless someone invites you.

Five kilometres further south, as Mt Taranaki starts to emerge on the horizon, is the village of **Mokau** (population 400). It offers a fine black-sand beach and good surfing and fishing. From August to November the Mokau River (the second longest on the North Island) spawns whitebait and subsequent swarms of territorial whitebaiters. The town's interesting **Tainui Historical Society Museum** (☑ 06-752 9072; mokaumuseum@vodafone.co.nz; SH3; admission by donation; ⊘10am-4pm) has old photographs and artefacts from when this once-isolated outpost was a coal and lumber shipping port for settlements along the river. **Mokau River Cruises** (☑ 0800 665 2874; www.mokaurivercruises.co.nz; adult/child $50/15) operates a three-hour river cruise with commentary onboard the historic MV *Cygnet*. Twilight cruises are also avialable.

Just north of Mokau, **Seaview Holiday Park** (☑ 0800 478 786; seaviewhp@xtra.co.nz; SH3; campsites from $14, d cabins/units from $65/90) is rustic, but it's right on an expansive beach. Above the village the **Mokau Motel** (☑ 06-752 9725; www.mokaumotels.co.nz; SH3; s/d/ste from $95/110/125; ⏴) offers fishing advice, self-contained units and three luxury suites.

Taumarunui

POP 5140

Taumarunui on a cold day can feel a bit miserable, but this town in the heart of the King Country has potential. The main reason to stay here is to kayak on the Whanganui River or as a cheaper base for skiing in Tongariro National Park, and there are some beaut walks and cycling tracks around town.

For details on the Forgotten World Highway between Taumarunui and Stratford, see Taranaki (p210). For details on canoeing and kayaking on the Whanganui River, see Whanganui National Park (p221).

◉ Sights & Activities

The 3km **Riverbank Walk** along the Whanganui River runs from Cherry Grove Domain, 1km south of town, to Taumarunui Holiday Park. **Te Peka Lookout**, across the Ongarue River on the western edge of town, is a good vantage point.

Hakiaha Street   STREET
At the street's eastern end is **Hauaroa Whare**, a beautifully carved house. At the western end **Te Rohe Potae** memorialises King Tawhiao's assertion of his *mana* (authority) over the King Country in a sculpture of a top hat on a large rock.

Raurimu Spiral   RAILWAY
The Raurimu Spiral, 30km south of town, is a unique feat of railway engineering that was completed in 1908 after 10 years' work. Rail buffs can experience the spiral by catching the *Northern Explorer* train linking Auckland and Wellington to National Park township (around $96 return from Otorohonga). Unfortunately this train ceased stopping in Taumarunui in 2012.

Forgotten World Adventures   TOUR
(☑ 0800 7245 2278; www.forgottenworldadventures.co.nz; 1 Hakiaha St; 1/2 days $285/495; ◷ booking office 9am-2pm) Ride the rails on quirky converted former golf carts on the railway line linking Taumarunui to the tiny hamlet of Whangamomona in the Taranaki region. The spectacular trip takes in 20 tunnels, and other options include a rail and jet-boat combo, and longer two-day excursions covering the full 140km from Taumarunui to Stratford (including an overnight stay in

---

PUREORA FOREST PARK & THE TIMBER TRAIL

Fringing the western edge of Lake Taupo, the 78,000-hectare Pureora Forest is home to NZ's tallest totara tree. Logging was stopped in the 1980s after a long campaign by conservationists, and the subsequent regeneration is impressive. Hiking routes through the park include tracks to the summits of **Mt Pureora** (1165m) and the rock pinnacle of **Mt Titiraupenga** (1042m). A 12m-high tower, a short walk from the Bismarck Rd car park, provides a canopy-level view of the forest for birdwatchers.

To stay overnight in one of three standard **DOC huts** (adult/child $5/2.50) you'll need to buy hut tickets in advance, unless you have a Backcountry Hut Pass. The three **campsites** (adult/child $6/3) have self-registration boxes. Hut tickets, maps and information are available from DOC.

Awhina Wilderness Experience (www.awhinatours.co.nz; per person $90) offers five-hour walking tours with local Maori guides through virgin bush to the summit of Titiraupenga, their sacred mountain. Farmstay accommodation is also available.

Another option is to ride the spectacular **Timber Trail** from Pureora village in the north of the forest southwest for 85km to Ongarue. Accommodation and shuttle transport is available at **Pa Harakeke** (☑ 07-929 8708; www.paharekeke.co.nz; 138 Maraeroa Rd; d $150), an interesting Maori-operated initiative near Pureora village, and **Black Fern Lodge** (☑ 07-894 7677; www.blackfernlodge.co.nz; Ongarue Stream Rd, Waimiha; per person from $58) at Waimiha gets rave reviews for its home cooking.

See www.thetimbertrail.com for maps, shuttle and bike-hire information and route planning.

Whangamomona). For more information, see p210.

Taumarunui Jet Tours
JETBOATING

(☑ 0800 853 886, 07-896 6055; www.taumarunui-jettours.co.nz; Cherry Grove Domain; 30/60min tour from $60/100) High-octane jetboat trips on the Whanganui River.

🛏 Sleeping & Eating

Taumarunui Holiday Park
HOLIDAY PARK $

(☑ 07-895 9345; www.taumarunuiholidaypark.co.nz; SH4; campsites from $16, d cabin & cottage $65-85; @ 🛜) On the banks of the Whanganui River, 4km east of town, this shady camping ground offers safe river swimming and clean facilities. The friendly owners have lots of ideas on what to see and do.

Twin Rivers Motel
MOTEL $$

(☑ 07-895 8063; www.twinrivers.co.nz; 23 Marae St; units $90-215; 🛜) The 12 units at Twin Rivers are spick and span, and bigger units sleep up to seven.

Jasmine's Cafe & Thai Restaurant
CAFE, THAI $$

(43 Hakiaha St; mains $10-16; ⊗ 7am-9pm) Robust all-day breakfasts, decent coffee and stonking toasted sandwiches, before morphing tastily into a Thai restaurant. Lunch specials ($10 to $13) are good value.

ℹ Information

Taumarunui i-SITE (☑ 07-895 7494; www.visitruapehu.com; 116 Hakiaha St; ⊗ 9am-5pm) Visitor information and internet access.

ℹ Getting There & Away

Taumarunui is on SH4, 81km south of Te Kuiti and 41km north of National Park township.

InterCity (☑ 0508 353 947; www.intercity.co.nz) buses head to Auckland ($29 to $61, 4½ hours, one daily) via Te Kuiti ($14 to $30, one hour), and to Palmerston North ($29 to $61, 4¾ hours, one daily) via National Park ($21, 30 minutes).

Owhango

POP 210

A pint-sized village where all the street names start with 'O', Owhango makes a cosy base for walkers, mountain bikers (the **42 Traverse** ends here) and skiers who can't afford to stay closer to the slopes in Tongariro National Park. Take Omaki Rd for a two-hour loop walk through virgin forest in **Ohinetonga Scenic Reserve**.

🛏 Sleeping & Eating

Forest Lodge
LODGE $

(☑ 07-895 4854; www.owhangohotel.co.nz/forest-lodge; 12 Omaki Rd; dm/d $25/60; motel d $80; @ 🛜) A snug backpackers with comfortable, clean rooms and good communal spaces. For privacy junkies there's a separate self-contained motel next door. Mountain-bike rental and bike-shuttle services for the 42 Traverse are also available.

Blue Duck Station
LODGE, HOSTEL $$

(☑ 07-895 6276; www.blueduckstation.co.nz; RD2, Whakahoro; dm/d $45/195) 🌿 Overlooking the Retaruke River 36km southwest of Owhango (take the Kaitieke turn-off 1km south of town), this eco-savvy place is actually various lodges, offering accommodation from dorms in an old shearers' quarters to a self-contained family cottage sleeping eight. The owners are mad-keen conservationists, restoring native-bird habitats and historic buildings.

Cafe 39 South
CAFE $

(☑ 07-895 4800; www.facebook.com/cafe39south; SH4; meals $9-20; ⊗ 8am-3pm Mon-Thu, to 4pm Sat & Sun) The food is delicious – try the sweet-corn fritters – the coffee is excellent, and the electric fire and daily soup specials will make you want to linger on cold days. The 39° South latitude marker is just across the road.

ℹ Getting There & Away

Owhango is 14km south of Taumarunui on SH4. All the **InterCity** (☑ 0508 353 947; www.intercity.co.nz) buses that stop in Taumarunui also stop here.

COROMANDEL

History

This whole area, including the peninsula, the islands and both sides of the gulf, was known to the Maori as Hauraki. Various *iwi* (tribes) held claim to pockets of it, including the Pare Hauraki branch of the Tainui tribes and others descended from Te Arawa and earlier migrations. Polynesian artefacts and evidence of moa hunting have been found, pointing to around 1000 years of continuous occupation.

The Hauraki *iwi* were some of the first to be exposed to European traders. The region's proximity to Auckland, safe anchorages and ready supply of valuable timber initially led to a booming economy. Kauri logging was big business on the peninsula. Allied to the

Coromandel Peninsula

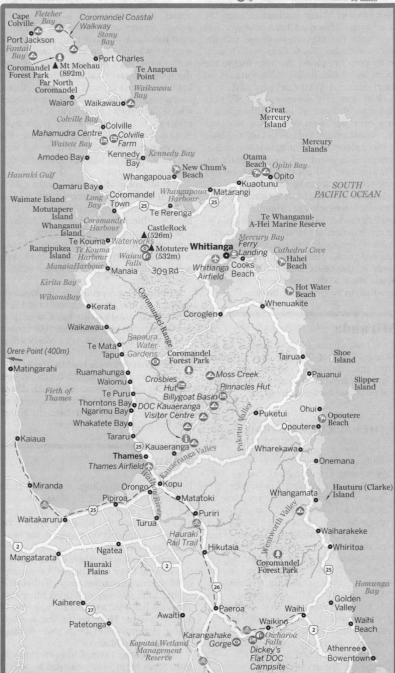

N

0 — 20 km
0 — 10 miles

Cape Colville
Fletcher Bay
Coromandel Coastal Walkway
Stony Bay
Port Jackson
Fantail Bay
Coromandel Forest Park
Mt Moehau (892m)
Port Charles
Te Anaputa Point
Far North Coromandel
Waikawau Bay
Waiaro
Waikawau
Colville Bay
Mahamudra Centre
Colville
Waitete Bay
Colville Farm
Kennedy Bay
Kennedy Bay
Great Mercury Island
Mercury Islands
Amodeo Bay
Whangapoua
New Chum's Beach
Otama Beach
Opito Bay
Opito
Hauraki Gulf
Oamaru Bay
Long Bay
Coromandel Town
Whangapoua Harbour
Matarangi
Kuaotunu
SOUTH PACIFIC OCEAN
Waimate Island
Motutapere Island
Whanganui Island
Te Rerenga
Coromandel Harbour
CastleRock (526m)
Te Whanganui-A-Hei Marine Reserve
Rangipukea Island
Te Kouma
Te Kouma Harbour
Waterworks
Motutere (532m)
Waiau Falls
Whitianga
Ferry Landing
Mercury Bay
Cathedral Cove
Hahei Beach
Manaia Harbour
Manaia
309 Rd
Whitianga Airfield
Cooks Beach
Kirita Bay
WilsonsBay
Kerata
Hot Water Beach
Whenuakite
Waikawau
Coroglen
Orere Point (400m)
Te Mata
Tapu
Rapaura Water Gardens
Coromandel Forest Park
Tairua
Shoe Island
Matingarahi
Ruamahunga
Waiomu
Crosbies Hut
Moss Creek
Pinnacles Hut
Pauanui
Slipper Island
Firth of Thames
Te Puru
Thorntons Bay
Ngarimu Bay
Billygoat Basin
DOC Kauaeranga Visitor Centre
Puketui
Ohui
Opoutere Beach
Whakatete Bay
Tararu
Puketui
Opoutere
Kaiaua
Kauaeranga
Thames
Thames Airfield
Kauaeranga Valley
Puketui Valley
Wharekawa
Onemana
Miranda
Orongo
Kopu
Matatoki
Puriri
Whangamata
Hauturu (Clarke) Island
Pipiroa
Waitakaruru
Turua
Hauraki Rail Trail
Hikutaia
Wentworth Valley
Waiharakeke
Whiritoa
Ngatea
Hauraki Plains
Coromandel Forest Park
Mangatarata
Homunga Bay
Kaihere
Awaiti
Paeroa
Waihi
Golden Valley
Patetonga
Karangahake Gorge
Waikino
Ohharoa Falls
Dickey's Flat DOC Campsite
Waihi Beach
Koputai Wetland Management Reserve
Athenree
Bowentown

timber trade was shipbuilding, which took off in 1832 when a mill was established at Mercury Bay. Things got tougher once the kauri around the coast became scarce and the loggers had to penetrate deeper into the bush for timber. Kauri dams, which used water power to propel the huge logs to the coast, were built. By the 1930s virtually no kauri remained and the industry died.

Gold was first discovered in NZ near Coromandel Town in 1852. Although this first rush was short-lived, more gold was discovered around Thames in 1867 and later in other places. The peninsula is also rich in semiprecious gemstones, such as quartz, agate, amethyst and jasper. A fossick on any west-coast beach can be rewarding.

Despite successful interactions with Europeans for decades, the Hauraki *iwi* were some of the hardest hit by colonisation. Unscrupulous dealings by settlers and government to gain access to valuable resources resulted in the Maori losing most of their lands by the 1880s. Even today there is a much lower Maori presence on the peninsula than in neighbouring districts.

Miranda

It's a pretty name for a settlement on the swampy Firth of Thames, just an hour's drive from Auckland. The two reasons to come here are splashing around in the thermal pools and **bird-watching**.

THE HAURAKI RAIL TRAIL

The cycle trail running from Thames south to Paeroa, and then further south to Te Aroha, or east to Waihi, the Hauraki Rail Trail, is growing in popularity due to its proximity to the bigger cities of Auckland and Hamilton. Two- and three-day itineraries are most popular, but shorter sections of the trail can be very rewarding too. The spur from Paeroa east through the Karangahake Gorge via Waikino to Waihi is spectacular as it skirts a picturesque river valley. The key centres of Thames, Paeroa, Te Aroha and Waihi have an expanding range of related services including bike hire, shuttles and accommodation. See www.haurakirailtrail.co.nz for detailed information including trail maps and recommendations for day rides.

This is one of the most accessible spots for studying waders or shorebirds all year round. The vast mudflat is teeming with aquatic worms and crustaceans, which attract thousands of Arctic-nesting shorebirds over the winter – 43 species of wader have been spotted here. The two main species are the bar-tailed godwit and the lesser or red knot, but it isn't unusual to see turnstones, sandpipers and the odd vagrant red-necked stint. One godwit tagged here was tracked making an 11,570km nonstop flight from Alaska. Short-haul travellers include the pied oystercatcher and the threatened wrybill from the South Island, and banded dotterels and pied stilts.

The **Miranda Shorebird Centre** (☑ 09-232 2781; www.miranda-shorebird.org.nz; 283 East Coast Rd; ☉ 9am-5pm) has bird-life displays, hires out binoculars and sells useful bird-watching pamphlets ($2). Nearby are a **hide** and several **walks** (30 minutes to two hours). The centre offers clean bunk-style accommodation (dorm beds/rooms $25/95) with a kitchen.

Miranda Hot Springs (www.mirandahotsprings.co.nz; Front Miranda Rd; adult/child $13/6; ☉ 9am-9.30pm), 5km south, has a large thermal swimming pool (reputedly the largest in the southern hemisphere), a toasty sauna pool and private spas ($10 extra).

Next door is **Miranda Holiday Park** (☑ 07-867 3205; www.mirandaholidaypark.co.nz; 595 Front Miranda Rd; campsites per adult/child $23/11, units $89-189; @ 🛜 🏊) 🐾, with sparkling-clean units and facilities, its own thermally heated pool and a floodlit tennis court.

Thames

POP 6800

Dinky wooden buildings from the 19th-century gold rush still dominate Thames, but grizzly prospectors have long been replaced by alternative lifestylers. It's a good base for tramping or canyoning in the nearby Kauaeranga Valley.

Captain Cook arrived here in 1769, naming the Waihou River the 'Thames' 'on account of its bearing some resemblance to that river in England'; you may well think otherwise. This area belonged to Ngati Maru, a tribe of Tainui descent. Their spectacular meeting house, Hotunui (1878), holds pride of place in the Auckland Museum.

After opening Thames to gold-miners in 1867, Ngati Maru were swamped by 10,000

Thames

Thames

Top Sights
1 Goldmine Experience A1

Sights
2 Historical Museum A2
3 School of Mines &
   Mineralogical Museum A2

Activities, Courses & Tours
4 Karaka Bird Hide A2
5 Paki Paki Bike Shop B3
6 Thames Small Gauge Railway A2

Sleeping
7 Gateway Backpackers B4
8 Ocean View on Thames A1
9 Sunkist Backpackers A1

Eating
10 Cafe Melbourne............................. A2
11 Coco Espresso A2
12 Nakontong A2
   Organic Co-op .... (see 12)
13 The Wharf Coffee House & Bar.......... B4

Drinking & Nightlife
14 Junction Hotel.............................. A2
15 Rick's Wine & Brew A2

Entertainment
16 Multiplex Cinemas A2

Shopping
17 Grahamstown Market B2

European settlers within a year. When the initial boom turned to bust, a dubious system of government advances resulted in Maori debt and forced land sales.

Sights

★ **Goldmine Experience**   MINE
(www.goldmine-experience.co.nz; cnr Moanataiari Rd & Pollen St; adult/child $15/5; ⊙10am-4pm daily Jan-Mar, to 1pm Apr, May & Sep-Dec) Walk through a mine tunnel, watch a stamper battery crush rock, learn about the history of the Cornish miners and try your hand at panning for gold ($2 extra).

**School of Mines &
Mineralogical Museum**   MUSEUM
(www.historicplaces.org.nz; 101 Cochrane St; adult/child $5/free; ⊙11am-3pm Wed-Sun Mar-Dec, daily Jan-Feb) The Historic Places Trust runs tours of these buildings, which house an extensive collection of NZ rocks, minerals and

fossils. The oldest section (1868) was part of a Methodist Sunday school, situated on a Maori burial ground. The Trust has a free self-tour pamphlet taking in Thames' significant buildings.

Butterfly & Orchid Garden   GARDENS
(www.butterfly.co.nz; Victoria St; adult/child $12/6; ⊙9.30am-4.30pm) Around 3km north of town within the Dickson Holiday Park is this enclosed jungle full of hundreds of exotic flappers.

Historical Museum   MUSEUM
(cnr Cochrane & Pollen Sts; adult/child $5/2; ⊙1-4pm) Pioneer relics, rocks and old photographs of the town.

🏃 Activities

Karaka Bird Hide   BIRDWATCHING
🏷FREE Built with compensation funds from the *Rainbow Warrior* bombing, this hide can be reached by a boardwalk through the mangroves just off Brown St.

**Thames Small
Gauge Railway**   NARROW-GAUGE RAILWAY
(Brown St; tickets $2; ⊙11am-3pm Sun) Young
'uns will enjoy the 900m loop ride on this
cute-as-a-button train.

Canyonz   CANYONING
(☑0800 422 696; www.canyonz.co.nz; trips $360)
🏊 All-day canyoning trips to the Sleeping
God Canyon in the Kauaeranga Valley. Expect a vertical descent of over 300m, requiring abseiling, water-sliding and jumping.
Trips leave from Thames at 8.30am, and
7am pick-ups from Hamilton are also available. Note that Thames is only 90 minutes'
drive from central Auckland, so with your
own transport a day trip from Auckland is
possible.

Eyez Open   CYCLING
(☑07-868 9018; www.eyezopen.co.nz) Rents out
bikes ($30 per day) and organises small-
group cycling tours of the Coromandel Peninsula (one- to three-day tours from $150
to $660).

Paki Paki Bike Shop   BICYCLE RENTAL
(☑07-867 9026; 535 Pollen St; 9am-5pm Mon-Fri,
to 1pm Sat) Rents out bikes ($25 per day) and
performs repairs.

🛏 Sleeping

Sunkist Backpackers   HOSTEL $
(☑07-868 8808; www.sunkistbackpackers.com;
506 Brown St; dm $26-29, s/d $55/70; @ 🖥) This
hostel in a character-filled 1860s heritage
building has spacious dorms and a sunny
garden. It also offers 4WD and car hire and
shuttles to the Kauaeranga Valley ($35 re-
turn). Bikes can also be hired and shuttle
transport arranged if you're keen on exploring the Hauraki Rail Trail.

Gateway Backpackers   HOSTEL $
(☑07-868 6339; overend@xtra.co.nz; 209 Mackay
St; dm $25-27, s $53, d $62-72; @) Generations
of Kiwis grew up in state houses just like
this, giving this relaxed, friendly hostel a
homely feel. Bathrooms are in short supply
but there are pleasant rooms, a nice garden
and free laundry facilities.

Cotswold Cottage   B&B $$
(☑07-868 6306; www.cotswoldcottage.co.nz; 46
Maramarahi Rd; r $180-210; 🖥) 🏊 Looking over
the river and racecourse, 3km southeast of
town, this pretty villa features luxuriant
linen and an outdoor spa pool. The comfy
rooms all open onto a deck.

Ocean View on Thames   B&B $$
(☑07-868 3588; www.retreat4u.co.nz; 509 Up-
per Albert St; ste $160-180, apt $180-200; 🖥)
Aside from the expansive views, it's the
little touches that make this place so special – such as fresh flowers and, in the two-
bedroom apartment downstairs, a fridge
stocked with cost-price beverages offered on
an honesty system.

Coastal Motor Lodge   MOTEL $$
(☑07-868 6843; www.stayatcoastal.co.nz; 608
Tararu Rd; units $150-179; 🖥) Motel and
chalet-style accommodation is provided
at this smart, welcoming place, 2km north
of Thames. It overlooks the sea, making it
a popular choice, especially in the summer
months.

Grafton Cottage & Chalets   CHALET $$
(☑07-868 9971; www.graftoncottage.co.nz; 304
Grafton Rd; units $140-220; @ 🖥 🏊) Perched on
a hill, most of these attractive wooden chalets have decks with awesome views. The
hospitable hosts provide free internet access
and breakfast, as well as use of the pool, spa
and barbecue areas.

Brunton House B&B   B&B $$
(☑07-868 5160; www.bruntonhouse.co.nz; 210
Parawai Rd; r $160-180, tr $195; @ 🖥 🏊) This im-
pressive two-storey kauri villa (1875) has a
modern kitchen and bathrooms, while stay-
ing true to the building's historic credentials
(there are no en suites). Guests can relax in
the grounds, by the pool, in the designated
lounge or on the upstairs terrace.

🍴 Eating

Cafe Melbourne   CAFE $
(www.facebook.com/CafeMelbourneGrahamsTown;
715 Pollen St; mains $12-19; ⊙8am-5pm Mon-Thu,
8am-9pm Fri, 9am-4pm Sat & Sun) Stylish and
spacious, this cafe definitely channels the
cosmopolitan vibe of a certain Australian
city. Chic industrial furniture and shared ta-
bles promote a convivial ambience, and the
menu travels from brunchy ricotta pancakes
to beef sliders and fish curry for lunch.

The Wharf Coffee House & Bar   CAFE, BAR $
(www.facebook.com/TheWharfCoffeehouseandbar;
Shortland Wharf, Queen St; snacks & mains $10-18;
⊙9am-3pm Mon, to 8pm Tue, Wed & Sun, to 9pm
Thu-Sat) Perched beside the water, this rus-
tic wood-lined pavilion does great fish and
chips. Grab a table outside with a beer or a
wine to understand why the Wharf is a firm
local favourite.

Coco Espresso
CAFE $

(661 Pollen St; snacks from $4.50; ⊗8am-2.30pm Tue-Fri, to noon Sat) Occupying a corner of an old villa, this chic little cafe serves excellent coffee and enticing pastries and cakes.

Organic Co-op
SELF-CATERING $

(736 Pollen St; ⊗9am-5pm Mon-Fri, to noon Sat; ✎) ✐ A good source of planet-friendly vegetables, nuts, bread, eggs and meat.

Nakontong
THAI $$

(☎07-868 6821; www.nakontong.com; 728 Pollen St; mains $16-21; ⊗11am-2.30pm Mon-Fri, 5-10pm daily; ✎) This is the most popular restaurant in Thames by a country mile. Although the bright lighting may not induce romance, the tangy Thai dishes will provide a warm glow.

☙ Drinking & Entertainment

Rick's Wine & Brew
WINE BAR

(746 Pollen St; ⊗4pm-late Wed-Sun) With art-deco chandeliers, zany wallpaper and regular live music, Rick's is the sort of place where a solo traveller of any gender can chill out over a glass of wine.

Junction Hotel
PUB

(www.thejunction.net.nz; 700 Pollen St; pizza $16-22, mains $15-30; ⊗10am-late) Serving thirsty gold-diggers since 1869, the Junction is the archetypal slightly rough-around-the-edges, historic, small-town pub. Live music attracts a younger crowd on the weekends, while families head to the corner-facing Grahamstown Bar & Diner for hearty pub grub.

Multiplex Cinemas
CINEMA

(www.cinemathames.co.nz; 708 Pollen St; adult/child $15/10) Recent blockbusters with cheaper $11 tickets on Wednesdays.

🔒 Shopping

Pollen St has stores selling local art and craft.

Grahamstown Market
MARKET

(Pollen St; ⊗8am-noon Sat) ✐ On Saturday mornings the Grahamstown Market fills the street with organic produce and handicrafts.

❶ Information

Thames i-SITE (☎07-868 7284; www.thames-info.co.nz; 206 Pollen St; ⊗9am-5pm)

❶ Getting There & Around

InterCity (☎09-583 5780; www.intercity.co.nz), **Tairua Bus Company** (☎07-808 0748;

www.tairuabus.co.nz) and **Go Kiwi** (☎0800 446 549; www.go-kiwi.co.nz) all run bus services to Thames.

Thames to Coromandel Town

Narrow SH25 snakes along the coast past pretty little bays and rocky beaches. Sea birds are plentiful, and you can fish, dig for shellfish and fossick for quartz, jasper and even gold-bearing rocks. The landscape turns crimson when the pohutukawa (often referred to as the 'New Zealand Christmas tree') blooms in December.

A handful of stores, motels, B&Bs and camping grounds are scattered around the picturesque bays. For backpackers, **Wolfie's Lair** (☎07-868 2777; 11 Firth View Rd, Te Puru; d & tw $54), a tidy house in **Te Puru**, has three rooms to rent. Just north of Te Puru, stop at the colourful **Waiomu Beach Cafe** (62 Thames Coast Rd, Waiomu Bay; mains $10-23; ⊗7am-6pm) for gourmet pizza, freshly squeezed juices and healthy salads.

At **Tapu** turn inland for a mainly sealed 6km drive to the **Rapaura Water Gardens** (☎07-868 4821; www.rapaurawatergardens.co.nz; 586 Tapu-Coroglen Rd; adult/child $15/6; ⊗9am-5pm), combining water, greenery and sculpture. There's accommodation (cottage/lodge $165/275) and a cafe (mains $14 to $29).

From **Wilsons Bay** the road heads away from the coast and climbs over several hills and valleys before dropping down to Coromandel Town, 55km from Thames. The view looking towards the island-studded Coromandel Harbour is exquisite.

Coromandel Town

POP 1480

Crammed with heritage buildings, Coromandel Town is a thoroughly quaint little place. Its natty cafes, interesting art stores, excellent sleeping options and delicious smoked mussels could keep you here longer than you expected.

Gold was discovered at Driving Creek in 1852. Initially the local Patukirikiri *iwi* kept control of the land and received money from digging licences. After initial financial success the same fate befell them as the Ngati Maru in Thames. By 1871, debt had forced them to sell all but 778 mountainous acres of their land. Today, fewer than 100 people remain who identify as part of this *iwi*.

COROMANDEL FOREST PARK

More than 30 walks criss-cross the Coromandel Forest Park, spread over several major blocks throughout the centre of the Coromandel Peninsula. The most popular hike is the challenging six- to eight-hour return journey up to the **Pinnacles** (759m) in the Kauaeranga Valley behind Thames. Other outstanding tramps include the **Coromandel Coastal Walkway** in Far North Coromandel, from Fletcher Bay to Stony Bay, and the **Puketui Valley** walk to abandoned gold mines.

The **DOC Kauaeranga Visitor Centre** (Department of Conservation; ☑ 07-867 9080; www.doc.govt.nz; Kauaeranga Valley Rd; ⊗ 8.30am-4pm) has maps, information and interesting displays about the kauri forest and its history. The centre is 14km off SH25; it's a further 9km along a gravel road to the start of the trails. Ask at Thames hostels about shuttles.

The DOC **Pinnacles Hut** (adult/child $15/7) has 80 beds, gas cookers, heating, toilets and cold showers. The 10-bunk **Crosbies Hut** (adult/child $15/7.50) is a four- to six-hour tramp from Thames or the Kauaeranga Valley, and booking in advance is required. There are also four basic **backcountry campsites** (adult/child $6/3) in this part of the park: one near each hut and others at Moss Creek and Billygoat Basin; expect only a toilet. A further eight **conservation campsites** (adult/child $10/5) are accessible from Kauaeranga Valley Rd. Bookings must be made online for the huts and some of the campsites.

Note that Coromandel Town is just one part of the entire Coromandel Peninsula, and its location on the peninsula's west coast means means it is not a good base for visiting Cathedral Cove and Hot Water Beach on the peninsula's east coast.

⊙ Sights

Many historic sites are featured in the Historic Places Trust's *Coromandel Town* pamphlet.

Coromandel Goldfield Centre & Stamper Battery HISTORIC BUILDING (☑ 021 0232 8262; www.coromandelstamperbattery.weebly.com; 360 Buffalo Rd; adult/child $10/5; ⊗ 10am-4pm, tours hourly 10am-3pm) The rock-crushing machine clatters into life during the informative tours of this 1899 plant. You can also try panning for gold ($5). Outside of tours stop to see NZ's largest working waterwheel.

Coromandel Mining & Historic Museum MUSEUM (841 Rings Rd; adult/child $5/free; ⊗ 10am-4pm daily mid-Dec–Jan, to 1pm Sat & Sun Feb–mid-Dec) Small museum with glimpses of pioneer life.

🏃 Activities

★ **Driving Creek Railway & Potteries** NARROW-GAUGE RAILWAY (☑ 07-866 8703; www.drivingcreekrailway.co.nz; 380 Driving Creek Rd; adult/child $25/10; ⊗ 10.15am & 2pm) 🖉 A lifelong labour of love for its conservationist owner, this unique train runs up steep grades, across four trestle bridges, along two spirals and a double switchback, and through two tunnels, finishing at the 'Eye-full Tower'. The hour-long trip passes artworks and regenerating native forest – more than 17,000 natives have been planted, including 9000 kauri. It's worth lingering for the video about the extraordinary guy behind it all, well-known potter Barry Brickell. Booking ahead is recommended in summer.

Coromandel Kayak Adventures KAYAKING (☑ 07-866 7466; www.kayakadventures.co.nz) Paddle-powered tours including half-day ecotours (from $150) and fishing trips (half-/full day $200/340).

Mussel Barge Snapper Safaris FISHING (☑ 07-866 7667; www.musselbargesafaris.co.nz; adult/child $50/25) Fishing trips with a local flavour and lots of laughs.

☞ Tours

Tri Sail Charters SAILING (☑ 0800 024 874; www.trisailcharters.co.nz; half-/full day $55/110) Cruise the Coromandel Harbour with your mates (minimum of four) on an 11.2m trimaran.

Coromandel Adventures DRIVING TOUR (☑ 07-866 7014; www.coromandeladventures.co.nz; adult/child $25/15) Various trips including a hop-on, hop-off service around Coromandel Town and transfers to Whangapoua Beach.

🛏 Sleeping

Anchor Lodge
MOTEL, HOSTEL $

(☎07-866 7992; www.anchorlodgecoromandel.co.nz; 448 Wharf Rd; dm $26, r $55-75, units $165-350; @🛜⛱) This upmarket backpacker-motel combo has its own gold mine, glow-worm cave, heated swimming pool and spa. The 2nd-floor units have harbour views.

Lion's Den
HOSTEL $

(☎07-866 8157; www.lionsdenhostel.co.nz; 126 Te Tiki St; dm/r $27/62; 🛜) Chill out to the hippy boho vibe in this magical place. A tranquil garden with fish pond, fairy lights and wisteria, an on-site massage therapist, and a relaxed collection of comfy rooms make for a soothing stay.

Coromandel Motel & Holiday Park
HOLIDAY PARK $

(☎07-866 8830; www.coromandelholidaypark.co.nz; 636 Rings Rd; campsites from $44, units $65-210; @🛜⛱) Well-kept and welcoming, with nicely painted cabins and manicured lawns, this large park includes the semi-separate Coromandel Town Backpackers. It gets busy in summer, so book ahead. Also hires bikes ($20 per day).

Tui Lodge
HOSTEL $

(☎07-866 8237; www.coromandeltuilodge.co.nz; 60 Whangapoua Rd; campsites from $15, dm $28-31, r $70-90; @🛜) Pleasantly rural, this cheery backpackers has plenty of trees, free bikes, fruit (in season) and straight-up rooms. The pricier ones have en suites.

Hush Boutique Accommodation
STUDIOS $$

(☎07-866 7771; www.hushaccommodation.co.nz; 425 Driving Creek Rd; campervans $35, cabins & studios $120-199) Rustic but stylish studios are scattered throughout a stand of native bush at this easygoing spot. Lots of honey-coloured natural wood creates a warm ambience, and the shared Hush Alfresco area with kitchen facilities and a barbecue is a top spot to catch up with fellow travellers.

Jacaranda Lodge
B&B $$

(☎07-866 8002; www.jacarandalodge.co.nz; 3195 Tiki Rd; s $85, d $140-170; 🛜) 🌿 Located among 6 hectares of farmland and rose gardens, this two-storey cottage is a relaxing retreat. Look forward to excellent breakfasts from the friendly owner, often using produce – plums, almonds, macadamia nuts and citrus fruit – from the property's spray-free orchard. Some rooms share bathrooms.

Little Farm
APARTMENTS $$

(☎07-866 8427; www.thelittlefarmcoromandel.co.nz; 750 Tiki Rd; r $115-130; 🛜) Overlooking a private wetland reserve at the rear of a fair-dinkum farm, these three comfortable units offer plenty of peace and quiet. The largest has a full kitchen and superb sunset views.

Green House
B&B $$

(☎07-866 7303; www.greenhousebandb.co.nz; 505 Tiki Rd; r $160-170; @🛜) Good old-fashioned hospitality and smartly furnished rooms are on offer here. The downstairs room opens onto the host's lounge, so it's worth paying $15 more for an upstairs room with a view.

Coromandel Accommodation Solutions
ACCOMMODATION SERVICE $$

(☎07-866 8803; www.accommodationcoromandel.co.nz; 265 Kapanga Rd; unit & apt $120-250) Booking service for cottages and rental houses around the Coromandel region; an excellent opportunity for coastal scenery. It also has two stylish apartments centrally located in Coromandel Town.

★Driving Creek Villas
COTTAGES $$$

(☎07-866 7755; www.drivingcreekvillas.com; 21a Colville Rd; villa $325; 🛜) This is the posh, grown-up's choice – three spacious, self-contained, modern, wooden villas with plenty of privacy. The Polynesian-influenced interior design is slick and the bush setting, complete with bubbling creek, sublime.

🍴 Eating & Drinking

Driving Creek Cafe
VEGETARIAN $

(180 Driving Creek Rd; mains $9-16; ⏱9.30am-5pm; 🛜🌿) 🌿 Vegetarian, vegan, gluten-free, organic and fair-trade delights awaits at this funky mudbrick cafe. The food is beautifully presented, fresh and healthy. Once sated, the kids can play in the sandpit while the adults check their email.

> ### ⓘ SENSIBLE CYCLISTS' LEAPFROG
>
> There's no charge for carrying your bike on a 360 Discovery (p149) ferry. Touring cyclists can avoid Auckland's traffic fumes and treacherous roads completely by catching the ferry at Gulf Harbour (north of Auckland) to Auckland's ferry terminal, and then leapfrogging directly to Coromandel Town.

The Chai Tea House
CAFE $

(www.facebook.com/ChaiTeaHouse; 24 Wharf Rd; snacks $6-12; ⊙10am-5pm Tue-Sun; ☑) ◢ Welcoming cafe with a bohemian New Age bent serving up lots of organic, vegan and vegetarian goodies. The outdoor garden is a very relaxing space, and is also used for occasional live-music gigs.

Mussel Kitchen
SEAFOOD $$

(www.musselkitchen.co.nz; cnr SH25 & 309 Rd; mains $9-18; ⊙9am-3.30pm & 6-10pm Jan & Feb) This cool cafe-bar sits among fields 3km south of town. Mussels are served either with Thai- and Mediterranean-tinged sauces, or grilled on the half-shell. In summer the garden bar is perfect for a mussel-fritter burger and a frosty beer. Smoked and chilli mussels are available for take away.

Pepper Tree
MODERN NZ $$

(☑07-866 8211; www.peppertreerestaurant.co.nz; 31 Kapanga Rd; lunch $18-26, dinner $26-36; ⊙10am-9pm; ☎) Coromandel Town's most upmarket option dishes up generously proportioned meals with an emphasis on local seafood. On a summer's evening, the courtyard tables under the shady tree are the place to be.

Umu
CAFE $$

(www.facebook.com/umucafe; 22 Wharf Rd; breakfast $11-18, lunch $12-25, dinner $14-32; ⊙9am-9pm; ☎) Classy cafe fare, including pizza, counter food (tarts and quiches around $7), superb coffee and tummy-taming breakfasts.

Coromandel Smoking Co
SEAFOOD

(www.corosmoke.co.nz; 70 Tiki Rd; fish $5-15; ⊙9am-5pm) Smoked fish and seafood for cooking and snacking.

Coromandel Oyster Company
SEAFOOD

(1611 Tiki Rd; fish $5-25; ⊙9am-5pm) Briny-fresh mussels, scallops, oysters and cooked crayfish.

Star & Garter Hotel
PUB

(www.starandgarter.co.nz; 5 Kapanga Rd; ⊙11am-late) Making the most of the simple kauri interior of an 1873 building, this smart pub has pool tables, decent sounds and a roster of live music and DJs on the weekends. The beer garden is smartly clad in corrugated iron.

🛍 Shopping

The Source
ARTS & CRAFTS

(31 Kapanaga Rd; ⊙10am-4pm) Creative showcase of more than 30 local artists.

ℹ Information

Coromandel Town Information Centre (☑07-866 8598; www.coromandeltown.co.nz; 85 Kapanga Rd; ⊙10am-4pm)

ℹ Getting There & Away

The best way to Coromandel Town from Auckland is on a 360 Discovery (p149) ferry. The town is also serviced by **InterCity** (☑09-583 5780; www.intercity.co.nz), **Tairua Bus Company** (☑07-808 0748; www.tairuabus.co.nz; advance fares from $1) and **Go Kiwi** (☑0800 446 549; www.go-kiwi.co.nz) buses.

Far North Coromandel

Supremely isolated and gobsmackingly beautiful, the rugged tip of the Coromandel Peninsula is well worth the effort required to reach it. The best time to visit is summer, when the gravel roads are dry, the pohutukawa trees are in their crimson glory and camping's an option (there isn't much accommodation up here).

The 1260-hectare **Colville Farm** (☑07-866 6820; www.colvillefarmholidays.co.nz; 2140 Colville Rd; campsites/units from $12/75, dm/s/d $25/38/76; @☎) has accommodation including bare-basics bush lodges and self-contained houses. Guests can try their hands at farm work (including milking) or go on horse treks ($40 to $150, one to five hours).

The nearby **Mahamudra Centre** (☑07-866 6851; www.mahamudra.org.nz; campsite/dm/s/tw $15/28/45/70) is a serene Tibetan Buddhist retreat with a stupa, a meditation hall and regular meditation courses. The simple accommodation is in a parklike setting.

Another kilometre on is the tiny settlement of **Colville** (25km north of Coromandel Town). It's a remote rural community by a muddy bay and a magnet for alternative lifestylers. There's not much here except for the **Green Snapper Cafe** (☑07-866 6697; www.greensnapper.co.nz; 2312 Colville Rd; mains $13-22; ⊙8am-3pm daily, 6-10pm Fri), which does great wood-fired pizza on Friday nights, and the quaint **Colville General Store** (☑07-866 6805; Colville Rd; ⊙8.30am-5pm), selling everything from organic food to petrol (warning: this is your last option for either).

Three kilometres north of Colville the sealed road turns to gravel and splits to straddle each side of the peninsula. Following the west coast, ancient pohutukawa spread overhead as you pass turquoise waters and stony beaches. The small DOC-run **Fantail Bay campsite** (adult/child $9.20/2), 23km north of Colville, has running water and a couple of long-drop toilets under the shade of puriri trees. Another 7km brings you to the **Port Jackson campsite** (adult/child $9.20/2), a larger DOC site right on the beach.

There's a spectacular lookout about 4km further on, where a metal dish identifies the various islands on the horizon. Great Barrier Island is only 20km away, looking every part the extension of the Coromandel Peninsula that it once was.

The road stops at **Fletcher Bay** – a magical land's end. Although it's only 37km from Colville, allow an hour for the drive. There's another **DOC campsite** (adult/child $10/5) here, as well as **Fletcher Bay Backpackers** (☑07-866 6685; www.doc.govt.nz; dm $26) – a simple affair with four rooms with four bunks in each. Bring sheets and food.

The **Coromandel Coastal Walkway** is a scenic, 3½-hour one-way hike between Fletcher Bay and **Stony Bay**. It's a relatively easy walk with great coastal views and an ambling section across farmland. If you're not keen on walking all the way back, **Coromandel Discovery** (☑07-866 8175; www.coromandeldiscovery.co.nz; adult/child $125/70) will drive you from Coromandel Town up to Fletcher Bay and pick you up from Stony Bay four hours later.

At Stony Bay, where the east-coast road terminates, there's another **DOC campsite** (adult/child $10/5) and a small DOC-run bach (holiday home) that sleeps five ($77). Heading south there are a couple of nice beaches peppered with baches on the way to the slightly larger settlement of **Port Charles**.

Tangiaro Kiwi Retreat (☑07-866 6614; www.kiwiretreat.co.nz; 1299 Port Charles Rd; units $220-350; ☜) offers eight very comfortable one- or two-bedroom self-contained wooden cottages. There's a bush-fringed spa, an in-house masseuse ($70 per hour) and, in summer, a cafe and licensed restaurant.

Another 8km brings you to the turn-off leading back to Colville, or you can continue south to **Waikawau Bay**, where there's a large **DOC campsite** (☑07-866 1106; adult/child $10/5) which has a summer-only store. The road then winds its way south past **Kennedy Bay** before cutting back to come out near the Driving Creek Railway.

Book DOC campsites at www.doc.govt.nz.

Coromandel Town to Whitianga

There are two routes from Coromandel Town southeast to Whitianga. The main road is the slightly longer but quicker SH25, which enjoys sea views and has short detours to pristine sandy beaches. The other is the less-travelled but legendary 309 Rd, an unsealed, untamed route through deep bush.

State Highway 25

SH25 starts by climbing sharply to an incredible lookout before heading steeply down. The turn-off at Te Rerenga follows the harbour to **Whangapoua**. There's not much at this beach except for holiday homes, but you can walk along the rocky foreshore to the remote, beautiful and often-deserted and undeveloped **New Chum's Beach** (30 minutes), regarded as one of the most beautiful in the country. Back in Te Rerenga on SH25, the **Castle Rock Cafe** (www.castlerockcafe.co.nz; 1242 Whangapoua Rd, Te Rerenga; mains $15-32; ☺9am-3pm Sun-Thu, to 8.30pm Fri & Sat) offers cafe dining, good takeaway pizzas and gourmet burgers, and its own range of jams, dressings and sauces.

Continuing east on SH25 you soon reach **Kuaotunu**, a more interesting holiday village on a beautiful stretch of white-sand beach, with a cafe-gallery, a store and an ancient petrol pump. **Black Jack Lodge** (☑07-866 2988; www.black-jack.co.nz; 201 SH25; dm $35, s/tw/d from $55/80/90; ☜) has a prime position directly across from the beach. It's a lovely little hostel with smart facilities and bikes and kayaks for hire. In Kuaotunu village, **Luke's Kitchen** (www.lukeskitchen.co.nz; 20 Blackjack Rd, Kuaotunu; pizza $12-28; ☺9am-late daily) has a rustic surf-shack ambience, cold beer and wood-fired pizzas. Occasional live music, local seafood and creamy fruit smoothies make Luke's an essential stop, though hours are reduced outside of summer. For more luxury, head along the beach to **Kuaotunu Bay Lodge** (☑07-866 4396; www.kuaotunubay.co.nz; SH25; s/d $270/295; ☜), an elegant B&B set among manicured gardens, offering a small set of spacious sea-gazing rooms.

Heading off the highway at Kuaotunu takes you (via an unsealed road) to one of Coromandel's best-kept secrets. First the long stretch of **Otama Beach** comes into view – deserted but for a few houses and farms. There's extremely basic camping (think long-drop toilet in a corrugated shack) in a farmer's field at **Otama Beach Camp** (07-866 2362; www.otamabeachcamp. co.nz; 400 Blackjack Rd; campsites per adult/child $10/5, cottages $220-260). Down by the beach they've also built a couple of self-contained, ecofriendly cottages (sleeping four to six), with solar power, a composting waste-water system and ocean views.

Continue along the narrowing road, the sealed road finally starts again and you reach **Opito**, a hidden-away enclave of 250 flash properties (too smart to be called baches), of which only 16 have permanent residents. From this magical beach, you can walk to the Ngati Hei *pa* (fortified village) site at the far end.

At Opito, **Leighton Lodge** (07-866 0756; www.leightonlodge.co.nz; 17 Stewart Pl; s $135-145, d $175-195; @) is a smart B&B with friendly owners, a self-contained flat downstairs, and an upstairs room with a view-hungry balcony.

309 Road

Starting 3km south of Coromandel Town, the 309 cuts through the Coromandel Range for 21km (most of which is unsealed but well maintained), rejoining SH25 7km south of Whitianga. The wonderfully bizarre **Waterworks** (www.thewaterworks.co.nz; 471 309 Rd; adult/child $20/15; 10am-6pm Nov-Apr, to 4pm May-Oct), 5km from SH25, is filled with whimsical water-powered amusements made from old kitchen knives, washing machines, bikes and toilets.

Two kilometres on there's a two-minute walk through bush to the 10m-high **Waiau Falls**. A further 500m on, an easy 10-minute bush walk leads to an amazing kauri grove. This stand of 600-year-old giants escaped the carnage of the 19th century, giving a majestic reminder of what the peninsula once looked like. The biggest tree has a 6m circumference.

If you enjoy the remoteness and decide to linger, **Wairua Lodge** (07-866 0304; www. wairualodge.co.nz; 251 Old Coach Rd; r $150-235) is a peaceful B&B with charming hosts, nestled in the bush towards the Whitianga end of the 309. There's a riverside swimming hole on the property, a barbecue, a spa and a romantic outdoor bathtub.

Whitianga

POP 3800

Whitianga's big attractions are the sandy beaches of Mercury Bay and the diving, boating and kayaking opportunities afforded by the craggy coast and nearby Te Whanganui-A-Hei Marine Reserve. The pretty harbour is a renowned base for game-fishing (especially marlin and tuna, particularly between January and March). Fishing charters start at around $500 and head into the thousands. If you snag an overfished species, consider releasing your catch.

The legendary Polynesian explorer and seafarer Kupe is believed to have landed near here sometime around AD 950. The name Whitianga is a contraction of Te Whitianga a Kupe (the Crossing Place of Kupe).

◉ Sights & Activities

Buffalo Beach stretches along Mercury Bay, north of Whitianga Harbour. A five-minute ferry ride (p189) will take you across the harbour to **Ferry Landing**. From here you can walk to local sights like Whitianga Rock Scenic & Historical Reserve, a park with great views over the ocean, and the **Shakespeare Cliff Lookout**. Further afield are Hahei Beach (13km), Cathedral Cove (15km) and Hot Water Beach (18km, one hour by bike). Look forward to relatively flat terrain – with a few hills – if you're keen on riding from Ferry Landing to these other destinations.

Mercury Bay Museum MUSEUM
(www.mercurybaymuseum.co.nz; 11a The Esplanade; adult/child $5/50c; 10am-4pm) A small but interesting museum focusing on local history – especially Whitianga's most famous visitors, Kupe and Cook.

Lost Spring SPA
(www.thelostspring.co.nz; 121a Cook Dr; per hr/day $35/60; 11am-6pm Sun-Fri, to 8pm Sat) This expensive but intriguing Disney-meets-Rotorua thermal complex comprises a series of hot pools in a lush junglelike setting, complete with an erupting volcano. Children under 14 aren't permitted, leaving the grown-ups to marinate themselves in tropical tranquility, cocktail in hand. There's also a day spa and cafe.

Dive Zone DIVING
(07-867 1580; www.divethecoromandel.co.nz; 7 Blacksmith Lane; trips $150-225) Shore, kayak and boat dives.

Twin Oaks Riding Ranch
HORSE RIDING
(☑ 07-866 5388; www.twinoaksridingranch.co.nz; 927 Kuaotunu-Wharekaho Rd; 2hr trek $60) Trek over farmland and through bush on horseback, 9km north of Whitianga.

Highzone
ROPES COURSE
(☑ 07-866 2113; www.highzone.co.nz; 49 Kaimarama Rd; activities $10-70) Hit the ropes for high adventure, including a trapeze leap, high swing and flying fox. It's located 7km south of Whitianga, just off the main road. Call for opening hours.

The Bike Man
BICYCLE RENTAL
(☑ 07-866 0745; thebikeman@xtra.co.nz; 16 Coghill St; per day $25; ☺ 9am-5pm Mon-Fri, to 1pm Sat) Rent a bike to take across on the ferry and journey to Hahei and Hot Water Beach.

Windborne
SAILING
(☑ 027 475 2411; www.windborne.co.nz; day sail $95) Day sails in a 19m 1928 schooner from December to April, and also departures to the Mercury Islands ($150) in February and March.

☞ Tours

There are a baffling number of tours to **Te Whanganui-A-Hei Marine Reserve**, where you'll see interesting rock formations and, if you're lucky, dolphins, fur seals, penguins and orcas. Some are straight-out cruises while others offer optional swims and snorkels.

Banana Boat
CRUISE
(☑ 07-866 5617; www.whitianga.co.nz/bananaboat; rides $10-35; ☺ Dec 26-Jan 31) Monkey around in Mercury Bay on the bright-yellow motorised Banana Boat – or split to Cathedral Cove.

Cave Cruzer
CRUISE
(☑ 07-866 0611; www.cavecruzer.co.nz) A rigid-hull inflatable offering a one-hour (adult/child $50/30) or two-hour (adult/child $75/40) tour.

Ocean Leopard
BOAT TOUR
(☑ 0800 843 8687; www.oceanleopardtours.co.nz; adult/child $70/40; ☺ tours 8am, 10.30am, 1.30pm & 4pm) Two-hour trips around coastal scenery, naturally including Cathedral Cove. The boat has a handy canopy for sun protection, and a one-hour 'Whirlwind Tour' (adult/child $50/30) is also on offer.

Glass Bottom Boat
CRUISE
(☑ 07-867 1962; www.glassbottomboatwhitianga.co.nz; adult/child $95/50) Two-hour bottom-gazing tours.

Whitianga Adventures
CRUISE
(☑ 0800 806 060; www.whitianga-adventures.co.nz; adult/child $65/40) A two-hour Sea Cave Adventure in an inflatable.

Whitianga

Whitianga

◉ **Sights**
1 Mercury Bay Museum B2

➌ **Activities, Courses & Tours**
2 Dive Zone A2
3 Lost Spring A1
4 The Bike Man A2

🛌 **Sleeping**
5 Beachside Resort A1
6 Cat's Pyjamas A2
7 Mercury Bay Holiday Park A3

🍴 **Eating**
8 Cafe Nina A2
9 Coghill House A2
10 Monk St Market B2
11 Motu Kitchen A2
12 Squids B2

🍷 **Drinking & Nightlife**
13 Bay Brewery Bistro A2
14 Blacksmith Bar B2

🎭 **Entertainment**
15 Mercury Twin Cinemas A2

✹ Festivals & Events

Coromandel Gold Festival   MUSIC
(www.coromandelgold.co.nz; Ohuka Farm, Buffalo Beach Rd; 2-day pass $169) Top NZ and international bands feature at this two-day festival culminating in the early hours of New Year's Day. The festival didn't take place in 2013, but was planned to return for New Year's Eve 2014. Check the website.

Scallop Festival   FOOD
(www.scallopfestival.co.nz) In early September, the Scallop Festival provides a week of food and entertainment.

🛏 Sleeping

On the Beach Backpackers Lodge   HOSTEL $
(☎07-866 5380; www.coromandelbackpackers. com; 46 Buffalo Beach Rd; dm/s/d $26/41/80; @) Brightly painted and beachside, this large YHA-affiliate has a wide range of rooms, including some with sea views and en suites. It provides free kayaks, boogie boards and spades (for Hot Water Beach). Camping ($15) and bikes ($20) are also available.

Cat's Pyjamas   HOSTEL $
(☎07-866 4663; www.cats-pyjamas.co.nz; 12 Albert St; dm $25, d $60-70; @🛜) Perfectly positioned between the pubs and the beach, this converted house offers bunk-filled dorms as well as private rooms, some with their own bathroom.

Mercury Bay Holiday Park   HOLIDAY PARK $
(☎07-866 5579; www.mercurybayholidaypark. co.nz; 121 Albert St; campsites from $18, units $75-160; @🛜🏊) 🐾 Strangely planted in a suburban neighbourhood, this small holiday park is comfortable and clean, with playgrounds, trampoline, swimming pool and pool table.

Pipi Dune B&B   B&B $$
(☎07-869 5375; www.pipidune.co.nz; 5 Pipi Dune; r $160; 🛜) This attractive B&B in a quiet cul-de-sac has guest lounges, kitchenettes, laundries and free wi-fi. To get here, head north on Cook Dr, turn left onto Surf St and then take the first right.

Beachside Resort   MOTEL $$
(☎07-867 1356; www.beachsideresort.co.nz; 20 Eyre St; units $175-225; 🛜🏊) Attached to the sprawling Oceans Resort, this modern motel has tidy units with kitchenettes and, on the upper level, balconies. Despite the name, it's set back from the beach but it does have a heated pool.

Within the Bays   B&B $$$
(☎07-866 2848; www.withinthebays.co.nz; 49 Tarapatiki Dr; r $295; @) It's the combination of charming hosts and incredible views that make this B&B set on a hill overlooking Mercury Bay worth considering. It's extremely well set up for guests with restricted mobility – there's even a wheelchair-accessible bush track on the property.

🍴 Eating

Coghill House   CAFE $
(www.thecog.co.nz; 10 Coghill St; mains $8-17; ⊙8am-3pm) Get an early start on the sunny terrace of this side-street cafe, where good counter food is partnered by huge cornfritter stacks and plump tortilla wraps.

Cafe Nina   CAFE $
(20 Victoria St; mains $8-20; ⊙8am-3pm) Barbecue for breakfast? Why the hell not. Too cool to be constricted to four walls, the kitchen grills bacon and eggs on an outdoor hotplate while the punters spill out onto tables in the park. Other dishes include robust Greek salads and tasty quesadillas.

Monk St Market   DELI $
(1 Monk St; ⊙10am-6pm Mon-Sat) 🐾 Self-catering foodies should head here for deli goods, imported chocolate and organic produce.

Squids   SEAFOOD $$
(☎07-867 1710; www.squids.co.nz; 15/1 Blacksmith Lane; mains $15-29; ⊙11am-2.30pm & 5.30pm-late) On a corner facing the harbour, this informal restaurant offers good-value seafood meals in a prime location. Steamed mussels, smoked seafood platters, and chowder combine with occasional Asian touches, and the steaks are also good.

Motu Kitchen   MODERN NZ $$$
(www.motukitchen.co.nz; 2 Mill Rd; small plates $10-15, mains $26-37; ⊙4pm-late Tue-Sat) This Mediterranean-style villa – complete with a garden shaded by palm trees – is the most stylish eatery in town. Menu highlights include locally sourced scallops, Coromandel oysters and interesting spins on beef, lamb and duck. Smaller shared plates include mushroom arancini and felafel, and from 4pm to 6pm, craft beers from the Hot Water Brewing Co are just $5. Dinner available from 6pm.

🍷 Drinking & Entertainment

Bay Brewery Bistro PUB
(www.baybrew.co.nz; 25 Coghill St; ⊘5pm-late Sun-Fri, from noon Sat) Good English-style beers – brewed up by Toby, an entertainingly friendly ex-journalist – and decent pub food ($21 to $24) including top-notch fish and chips and burgers. Plan your next Coromandel detour in the attached garden bar.

Blacksmith Bar PUB
(www.blacksmithbar.co.nz; 1 Blacksmith Lane; ⊘10.30am-late) On the weekends, live bands keep the punters pumping until the wee hours (well, 1am). It's the kind of small-town pub and beer garden that attracts all ages, styles and dancing abilities.

Mercury Twin Cinemas CINEMA
(⊘07-867 1001; www.flicks.co.nz; Lee St; adult/child $15/10) Latest-release films.

ℹ️ Information

Whitianga i-SITE (⊘07-866 5555; www.whitianga.co.nz; 66 Albert St; ⊘9am-5pm Mon-Fri, to 4pm Sat & Sun) Information and internet access. Hours are extended in summer.

ℹ️ Getting There & Around

Sunair (⊘0800 786 247; www.sunair.co.nz) operates flights linking Whitianga to Auckland, Great Barrier Island and Tauranga. Bus services are offered by InterCity (p149), **Tairua Bus Company** (⊘07-864 7770; www.tairuabus.co.nz) and Go Kiwi (p149).

The **passenger ferry** (⊘07-866 5472; www.whitiangaferry.co.nz; adult/child/bicycle $3/1.50/1.50; ⊘7.30am-6.30pm Easter-late Oct, to 10.30pm late Oct-Easter) links Buffalo Beach with Ferry Landing.

Coroglen & Whenuakite

The blink-and-you'll-miss-them villages of Coroglen and Whenuakite are on SH25, south of Whitianga and west of Hot Water Beach. The legendary **Coroglen Tavern** (www.coroglentavern.com; 1937 SH25) is the archetypal middle-of-nowhere country pub that attracts big-name Kiwi bands in summer.

Running from Labour Day (late October) to Queen's Birthday (early June), **Coroglen Farmers Market** (SH25; ⊘9am-1pm Sun) sells a bit of everything local from vegetables to compost. Nearby, the folks at **Rangihau Ranch** (⊘07-866 3875; www.rangihauranch.co.nz; Rangihau Rd, Coroglen; rides per hr $40) will lead you on horseback up a historic packhorse track, through beautiful bush to spectacular views.

Located at the friendly **Seabreeze Holiday Park** (⊘07-866 3050; www.seabreezeholidaypark.co.nz; 1043 SH25, Whenuakite; campsites from $36, dm $30, units $75-195; 🛜), **Hot Water Brewing Co** (www.hotwaterbrewingco.com; 1043 SH25, Whenuakite; 11am-late) is a modern craft brewery with lots of outdoor seating. Standout brews include the hoppy Kauri Falls Pale Ale and the robust Walkers Porter. Platters and pizzas ($18 to $35) all make it easy to order another beer. Better than your average highway stop, **Colenso** (www.colensocafe.co.nz; SH25, Whenuakite; mains $7-14; ⊘10am-5pm) has excellent fair-trade coffee, scones, cakes and light snacks, as well as a shop selling homewares and gifts.

Hahei

POP 270 (7000 IN SUMMER)

A legendary Kiwi beach town, little Hahei balloons to bursting in summer but is nearly abandoned otherwise – apart from the busloads of tourists doing the obligatory stop off at Cathedral Cove. It's a charming spot and a great place to unwind for a few days, especially in the quieter months. It takes its name from Hei, the eponymous ancestor of the Ngati Hei people, who arrived in the 14th century on the Te Arawa canoe.

◉ Sights

Cathedral Cove BEACH
Beautiful Cathedral Cove, with its famous gigantic stone arch and natural waterfall shower, is best enjoyed early or late in the day – avoiding the worst of the hordes.

From the car park, a kilometre north of Hahei, it's a rolling walk of around 30 to 40 minutes. On the way there's rocky **Gemstone Bay** (which has a snorkelling trail where you're likely to see big snapper, crayfish and stingrays) and sandy **Stingray Bay**. The walk from Hahei Beach to Cathedral Cove takes about 70 minutes. Another option is a 10-minute ride in a water taxi (p190).

Hahei Beach BEACH
Long, lovely Hahei Beach is made more magical by the view to the craggy islands in the distance. From the southern end of Hahei Beach, it's a 15-minute walk up to Te Pare, a *pa* site with splendid coastal views.

🏃 Activities

Cathedral Cove Sea Kayaking KAYAKING
(☑07-866 3877; www.seakayaktours.co.nz; 88 Hahei Beach Rd; half-/full day $95/160; ☻9am & 2pm) This outfit runs guided kayaking trips around the rock arches, caves and islands in the Cathedral Cove and Mercury Bay area. The Remote Coast Tour heads the other way when conditions permit, visiting caves, blowholes and a long tunnel.

Cathedral Cove Dive & Snorkel DIVING
(☑07-866 3955; www.hahei.co.nz/diving; 48 Hahei Beach Rd; dives from $85) Takes daily dive trips and rents out scuba gear, snorkelling gear ($20), bikes ($20) and boogie boards ($20). A Discover Scuba half-day beginners' course costs $195 including all the gear.

Hahei Explorer BOAT TOUR
(☑07-866 3910; www.haheiexplorer.co.nz; adult/child $70/40) Hour-long jetboat rides touring the coast.

🛏 Sleeping

Tatahi Lodge HOSTEL, MOTEL $
(☑07-866 3992; www.tatahilodge.co.nz; Grange Rd; dm $30, r $88-123, units $150-275; @🛜) A wonderful place where backpackers are treated with at least as much care and respect as the lush, bromeliad-filled garden. The dorm rooms and excellent communal facilities are just as attractive as the pricier motel units.

⭐**Purangi Garden Accommodation** COTTAGES $$
(☑07-866 4038; www.purangigarden.co.nz; Lees Rd; d $170-190) On a quiet cove on the Purangi River, this relaxing spot has accommodation ranging from comfortable chalets through to larger houses and a spacious, self-contained yurt. Well-established gardens and rolling lawns lead to the water – perfect for swimming and kayaking – and don't be surprised if the friendly owners drop off some organic fruit or freshly baked bread.

Hahei and Hot Water Beach are both a short drive away.

Church COTTAGE $$
(☑07-866 3533; www.thechurchhahei.co.nz; 87 Hahei Beach Rd; cottages $130-250; @🛜) 🖋 Set within a subtropical garden, these beautifully kitted-out, rustic timber cottages have plenty of character. The ultracharming wooden church at the top of the drive is Hahei's swankiest eatery with excellent Mediterranean- and Asian-inspired dishes

made to be shared, and a stellar, if pricey, selection of Kiwi craft beers.

🍴 Eating & Drinking

Hahei really does have a 'gone fishing' feel in the off-season. The local store remains open and the eateries take it in turns so that there's usually one option open every evening.

Mercury Bay Estate WINERY $$
(www.mercurybayestate.co.nz; 761a Purangi Rd, Cooks Beach; platters $18-35, wine tasting $8-12) Repurposed timber and corrugated iron feature at this rustic but chic vineyard en route from Ferry Landing to Cooks Beach. Local artwork is for sale, and seafood, cheese and charcuterie platters team well with wines like the excellent Lonely Bay chardonnay.

The Pour House PUB
(www.coromandelbrewingcompany.co.nz; 7 Grange Rd; ☻11am-11pm) Home base for the Coromandel Brewing Company, this pub and bistro features its five beers alongside regular guest taps from other Kiwi craft breweries. Platters of meat, cheese and local seafood combine with decent pizzas in the beer garden, and our favourite brew is the Cloud 9 Belgian-style wheat beer. Reduced hours outside of summer.

ℹ Getting There & Around

Tairua Bus Company (p149) has bus connections to Hahei. In the height of summer the council runs a bus service from the Cooks Beach side of the ferry landing to Hot Water Beach, stopping at Hahei (adult/child $3/2). Another option on the same route is the **Cathedral Cove Shuttle** (☑027 422 5899; www.cathedralcoveshuttles. co.nz; up to 5 passengers $30).

Cathedral Cove Water Taxi (☑027 919 0563; www.cathedralcovewatertaxi.co.nz; return/one way adult $25/15, child $15/10, every 30 min) Has water taxis from Hahei to Cathedral Cove.

Hot Water Beach

Justifiably famous, Hot Water Beach is quite extraordinary. For two hours either side of low tide, you can access an area of sand in front of a rocky outcrop at the middle of the beach where hot water oozes up from beneath the surface. Bring a spade, dig a hole and voila, you've got a personal spa pool. Surfers stop off before the main beach to access some decent breaks. The headland between the two beaches still has traces of a Ngati Hei *pa*.

Spades ($5) can be hired from the **Hot Water Beach Store** (Pye Pl; ⊙9am-5pm), which also has Hottie's Cafe attached.

Near the beach, **Moko** (www.moko.co.nz; 24 Pye Pl; ⊙10am-5pm) has art, sculpture and jewellery with a modern Pasifika/Maori bent.

🛏 Sleeping & Eating

Hot Water Beach Top 10 Holiday Park HOLIDAY PARK $
(☑07-866 3116; www.hotwaterbeachholidaypark. com; 790 Hot Water Beach Rd; campsites from $18, dm $30, units $70-200; @ 🛜) Bordered by tall bamboo and gum trees, this is a very well-run holiday park with everything from grassy campsites, through to a brand-new and spotless backpackers lodge, and stylish villas with arched ceilings crafted from New Zealand timber.

Hot Water Beach B&B B&B $$$
(☑07-866 3991; www.hotwaterbedandbreakfast. co.nz; 48 Pye Pl; r $260) This hillside pad has priceless views, a spa bath on the deck, and attractive living quarters.

Hot Waves CAFE $
(8 Pye Pl; mains $12-26; ⊙8.30am-4pm, to 8.30pm Fri & Sat Dec-Feb) In summer everyone wants a garden table at this excellent cafe. It also hires spades for the beach ($5). Ask about occasional Sunday-afternoon music sessions from 1pm.

ℹ Getting There & Away

The Hahei bus services Tairua Bus Company (p149) and Cathedral Cove Shuttle (p190) stop here, but usually only on prebooked requests.

Tairua
POP 1270

Tairua and its twin town Pauanui sit either side of a river estuary that's perfect for wind-surfing or for little kids to splash about in. Both have excellent surf beaches (Pauanui's is probably a shade better), but that's where the similarity stops. Where Tairua is a functioning residential town (with shops, ATMs and a choice of eateries), Pauanui is an upmarket refuge for wealthy Aucklanders. Friendly Tairua knows how to keep it real. Both are ridiculously popular in the summertime.

◉ Sights & Activities

Various operators offer fishing charters and sightseeing trips, including **Pauanui Charters** (☑07-864 9262; www.pauanuicharters.co.nz) and **Epic Adventures** (☑021-227 4354; www. epicadventures.co.nz).

Paaku MOUNTAIN
Around seven million years ago Paaku was a volcanic island but now it forms the north head of Tairua's harbour. Ngati Hei had a *pa* here before being invaded by Ngati Maru in the 17th century. It's a steep 15-minute walk to the summit from the top of Paku Dr, with the pay-off being amazing views over Tairua, Pauanui and the Alderman Islands. Plaques along the way detail Tairua's colonial history, with only one rather dismissive one devoted to its long Maori occupation.

Tairua Dive & Marine DIVING
(☑07-864 8800; www.tairuadiveandmarine.co.nz; 7 The Esplanade; boat dives from $200, PADI Discovery $25; ⊙7.30am-5pm) A solid operator with reliable service. Also hires snorkelling gear, kayaks and paddle-boards ($25 to $40 per hour).

🛏 Sleeping

Tairua Beach Villa Backpackers HOSTEL $
(☑07-864 8345; www.tairuabackpackers.co.nz; 200 Main Rd; dm $25-28, s $60-73, d $70-86; @ 🛜) Rooms are homely and casual at this estuary-edge hostel in a converted house, and the dorm scores great views. Guests can help themselves to fishing rods, kayaks, sail-boards and bikes.

Pacific Harbour Lodge HOTEL $$
(☑07-864 8581; www.pacificharbour.co.nz; 223 Main Rd; chalets $144-233; @ 🛜) This 'island-style' resort in the town centre has spacious self-contained chalets, with natural wood and Gauguin decor inside and a South Seas

garden outside. Discount packages are usually available online.

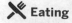 Eating

Old Mill Cafe CAFE $
(www.theoldmillcafe.co.nz; 1 The Esplanade; mains $12-33; ⊙ 8am-4pm daily, from 5.30pm Fri & Sat) Zooshed up with bright-pink feature walls and elegant verandah furniture, Old Mill Cafe serves interesting cafe fare as well as dinner on Friday and Saturday. There's sometimes live music on Friday nights too.

Manaia Kitchen & Bar CAFE $$
(☑ 07-864 9050; 228 Main Rd; breakfast $11-17, lunch $17-24, dinner $24-33; ⊙ 8.30am-late) With courtyard seating for lazy summer brunches and a burnished-copper bar to prop yourself up on later in the night, Manaia is the most cosmopolitan spot on the Tairua strip. New owners have revitalised the place, and interesting menu options now include a scallop tortilla and prawn naan pizza.

ⓘ Information

Tairua Information Centre (☑ 07-864 7575; www.tairua.info; 223 Main Rd; ⊙ 9am-5pm)

ⓘ Getting There & Around

InterCity, Tairua Bus Company and Go Kiwi all run bus services to Tairua.

Tairua and Pauanui are connected by a **passenger ferry** (☑ 027-497 0316; one-way/return $3/5; ⊙ daily Dec-Jan), which departs every two hours from 9am to 5pm (until 11pm in January). In other months the ferry offers a water-taxi service.

Puketui Valley

Located 12km south of Tairua is the turn-off to Puketui Valley and the historic **Broken Hills gold-mine workings**, which are 8km from the main road along a mainly gravel road. There are short walks up to the sites of stamper batteries, but the best hike is through the 500m-long **Collins Drive mine tunnel**. After the tunnel, keep an eye out for the short 'lookout' side trail which affords panoramic views. It takes about three hours return; remember to take a torch and a jacket with you.

There's a basic **DOC campsite** (www.doc. govt.nz; adult/child $10/5) located in a pretty spot by the river. This is a wilderness area so take care and be properly prepared. Water from the river should be boiled before drinking.

Opoutere

File this one under Coromandel's best-kept secrets. Apart from a cluster of houses there's nothing for miles around. Swimming can be dangerous, especially near Hikinui Islet, which is close to the beach. On the sand spit is the **Wharekawa Wildlife Refuge**, a breeding ground for the endangered New Zealand dotterel.

⌖ Sleeping

YHA Opoutere HOSTEL $
(☑ 0800 278 299, 07-865 9072; www.yha.co.nz; 389 Opoutere Rd; dm $30-33, r $80-110) ⚲ Housed partly in the historic Opoutere Native School, this wonderful get-away-from-it-all hostel resounds with birdsong. Kayaks, hot-water bottles, alarm clocks, stilts and hula hoops can all be borrowed.

Copsefield B&B $$
(☑ 07-865 9555; www.copsefield.co.nz; 1055 SH25; r $100-200) On SH25 but closer to Opoutere than it is to Whangamata, Copsefield is a peaceful country-style villa set in attractive, lush gardens with a spa and a riverside swimming hole. The house has three attractive B&B rooms, while cheaper accommodation is offered in a separate bach-style cottage.

ⓘ Getting There & Away

The **Go Kiwi** (☑ 0800 446 549; www.go-kiwi. co.nz) seasonal Auckland–Whitianga shuttle stops in Opoutere on request.

Whangamata

POP 3560
When Auckland's socially ambitious flock to Pauanui, the city's young and horny head to Whangamata to surf, get stoned and hook up. It can be a raucous spot over New Year, when the population swells to more than 40,000. It's a true summer-holiday town, but in the off-season there may as well be tumbleweeds rolling down the main street.

⭍ Activities

Besides **fishing** (game-fishing runs from January to April), **snorkelling** near Hauturu (Clarke) Island, **surfing**, **kayaking**, **orienteering** and **mountain biking**, there are excellent walks. A popular destination for kayaking and paddle boarding is Whenuakura (Donut Island), around 1km from the beach. Note that in an effort to boost the islands' status as wildlife sanctuaries, it's not permitted to land on them. Boating around the islands is allowed.

The **Wentworth Falls walk** takes 2½ hours (return); it starts 3km south of the town and 4km down the unsealed Wentworth Valley Rd. A further 3km south of Wentworth Valley Rd is Parakiwai Quarry Rd, at the end of which is the **Wharekirauponga walk**, a sometimes muddy 10km return track (allow 3½ to four hours) to a mining camp, battery and waterfall that passes unusual hexagonal lava columns and loquacious bird life.

SurfSup　　　BICYCLE RENTAL, PADDLE BOARDING
(⌨07-865 8096; www.pedalandpaddelnz.com; 703 Port Rd) Bike hire (half-/full day $15/30), kayak hire (half-/full day from $30/50) and paddle-board hire (one/two hours $20/30). Paddle boarding lessons ($99) and kayaking and paddle-boarding tours are also available.

Kiwi Dundee Adventures　　　HIKING
(⌨07-865 8809; www.kiwidundee.co.nz) ⟋ Styling himself as a local version of Crocodile Dundee, Doug Johansen offers informative one- to 16-day wilderness walks and guided tours in the Coromandel Peninsula and countrywide.

🛏 Sleeping

Wentworth Valley Campsite　　　CAMPSITE $
(⌨07-865 7032; www.doc.govt.nz; 474 Wentworth Valley Rd; adult/child $10/5) ⟋ More upmarket than most DOC camping grounds, this campsite is accessed from the Wentworth Falls walk and has toilets, showers and gas barbecues.

Southpacific Accommodation　　　MOTEL $$
(⌨07-865 9580; www.thesouthpacific.co.nz; 249 Port Rd; units $130-216; @ 🖥) This hard-to-miss corner-hogging complex consists of a cafe and warmly decorated, self-contained motel units. Facilities are clean and modern; bikes and kayaks are available for hire.

Breakers　　　MOTEL $$
(⌨07-865 8464; www.breakersmotel.co.nz; 324 Hetherington Rd; units $175-230; 🖥🏊) Facing the marina on the Tairua approach to Whangamata, this newish motel compensates for saggy beds with an enticing swimming pool and spa pools on the decks of the upstairs units.

🍴 Eating

Lazy Lizard　　　CAFE $
(427 Port Rd; mains $10-20; ⊘7.30am-3.30pm Tue-Sun) Winning points for bizarre hand-shaped stools, this funky lizard does delicious counter food, cooked breakfasts, bagels and salads. We're big fans of the 'It's a Wrap' breakfast tortilla.

Soul Burger　　　BURGERS $
(www.soulburger.co.nz; 441 Port Rd; burgers $10-15; ⊘5-9pm Thu, 8am-9pm Fri-Sun Easter–late Oct, 5pm-late Wed-Sun late Oct–Easter) Serving audacious burgers with names like Soul Blues Brother and Vegan Vibe, this hip corner joint is also licensed so you can have an ice-cold beer with your burger.

The Lincoln　　　CAFE, PUB $$
(www.thelincolnbar.co.nz; 501 Port Rd; mains $17-34) Part bar, part bistro, part cafe and all-round good times feature at this versatile spot on Whangamata's main drag. DJs kick in on summer weekends.

ⓘ Information

Whangamata i-SITE (⌨07-865 8340; www. whangamatainfo.co.nz; 616 Port Rd; ⊘9am-5pm Mon-Fri, 9.30am-3.30pm Sat & Sun)

ⓘ Getting There & Away

Go Kiwi (⌨0800 446 549; www.go-kiwi.co.nz) has a shuttle service to Whangamata.

Waihi & Around
POP 4500 & 1800

Gold and silver have been dragged out of Waihi's **Martha Mine**, NZ's richest, since 1878. The town formed quickly thereafter and blinged itself up with grand buildings and a show-offy avenue of phoenix palms, now magnificently mature.

After closing down in 1952, open-cast mining restarted in 1988, and current proposals to harness the potential of other nearby mines forecast mining to continue to around 2020. Another more low-key bonanza is also taking place with Waihi an integral part of the excellent Hauraki Rail Trail (p178).

While Waihi is interesting for a brief visit, it's **Waihi Beach** where you'll want to linger. The two places are as dissimilar as surfing is from mining, separated by 11km of farmland. The long sandy beach stretches 9km to Bowentown, on the northern limits of Tauranga Harbour, where you'll find sheltered harbour beaches such as beautiful **Anzac Bay**. There's a very popular 45-minute walk north through bush to pristine **Orokawa Bay**, which has no road access.

⦿ Sights

Waihi's main drag, Seddon St, has interesting sculptures, information panels about Waihi's golden past and roundabouts that look like squashed daleks. Opposite the visitor centre, the skeleton of a derelict **Cornish Pumphouse** (1904) is the town's main landmark, atmospherically lit at night. From here the **Pit Rim Walkway** has fascinating views into the 250m-deep Martha Mine. If you want to get down into it, the mining company runs 1½-hour **Waihi Gold Mine Tours** (www.waihigoldminetours.co.nz; adult/child $28/14; ⊘ 10am & 12.30pm Mon-Sat), departing from the Waihi Visitor Centre.

The *Historic Hauraki Gold Towns* pamphlet (free from the visitor centre) outlines walking tours of both Waihi and Paeroa.

Athenree Hot Springs　　THERMAL POOLS
(www.athenreehotsprings.co.nz; 1 Athenree Rd, Athenree; adult/child $7/4.50; ⊘ 10am-7.30pm) 🌿 In cooler months, retreat to these two small but blissful outdoor hot pools, hidden within a holiday park.

Waihi Arts Centre & Museum　　MUSEUM
(www.waihimuseum.co.nz; 54 Kenny St, Waihi; adult/child $5/3; ⊘ 10am-3pm Thu & Fri, noon-3pm Sat-Mon) The Waihi Arts Centre & Museum has an art gallery and displays focusing on the region's gold-mining history. Prepare to squirm before the collection of miners' chopped-off thumbs preserved in glass jars.

✦ Activities

Goldfields Railway　　RAILWAY
(☑ 07-863 8251; www.waihirail.co.nz; 30 Wrigley St, Waihi; adult/child return $18/10, bikes extra $2; ⊘ daily Sep-Mar, Fri-Mon Apr-Aug) Vintage trains depart Waihi for a 7km, 30-minute scenic journey to Waikino. It's possible to take bikes on the train so they can be used to further explore the Karangahake Gorge section of the Hauraki Rail Trail. The timetable varies seasonally so check the website.

Dirtboard Waihi　　DIRTBOARDING
(☑ 021 244 1646; www.dirtboard.co.nz; off Orchard Rd, Waihi; per hr $30) Hit the slopes on a mutant snowboard-skateboard.

Waihi Bicycle Hire　　BICYCLE RENTAL
(☑ 07-863 8418; www.waihibicyclehire.co.nz; 25 Seddon St, Waihi; bike hire half-/full day from $25/40; ⊘ 8am-5pm) Bike hire and loads of information on the Waihi end of the Hauraki Rail Trail.

Bularangi Motorbikes　　MOTORBIKE TOURS
(☑ 07-863 6069; www.motorbikesnz.co.nz) Based in Waihi, Bularangi Motorbikes offers Harley Davidson rentals and one- to 21-day guided tours throughout the country.

🛏 Sleeping

Bowentown Beach Holiday Park　　HOLIDAY PARK $
(☑ 07-863 5381; www.bowentown.co.nz; 510 Seaforth Rd, Waihi Beach; campsites from $44, units $72-195; @ 🛜) Having nabbed a stunning stretch of sand, this impressively maintained holiday park makes the most of it with first-rate motel units and campers' facilities.

Athenree Hot Springs & Holiday Park　　HOLIDAY PARK $
(☑ 07-863 5600; www.athenreehotsprings.co.nz; 1 Athenree Rd, Athenree; campsites from $44, units $70-175; @ 🛜 🌊) 🌿 Harbour-hugging Athenree has smart accommodation and friendly owners. Entry to the thermal pools is free for guests, making this a top choice for the winter months.

Waihi Beach Top 10 Holiday Resort　　HOLIDAY PARK $
(☑ 0800 924 448; www.waihibeachtop10.co.nz; 15 Beach Rd, Waihi Beach; campsites from $27, units $110-220; @ 🛜 🌊) This massive, resort-style holiday park is pretty darn flash, with a pool, gym, spa, beautiful kitchen and a smorgasbord of sleeping options.

Westwind B&B　　B&B $
(☑ 07-863 7208; westwindgarden@xtra.co.nz; 58 Adams St, Waihi; s/d $50/90) Run by a charming couple who are inveterate travellers themselves, this old-fashioned homestay B&B has two comfortable rooms with a shared bathroom.

Beachfront B&B　　B&B $$
(☑ 07-863 5393; www.beachfrontbandb.co.nz; 3 Shaw Rd, Waihi Beach; r $140) True to its name with absolute beachfront and spectacular sea views, this comfortable downstairs flat has a TV, fridge and direct access to the surf.

Manawa Ridge　　LODGE $$$
(☑ 07-863 9400; www.manawaridge.co.nz; 267 Ngatitangata Rd, Waihi; r $850) 🌿 The views from this castlelike eco-retreat, perched on a 310m ridge 6km northeast of Waihi, take in the entire Bay of Plenty. Made of recycled railway timber, mudbrick and lime-plastered straw walls, the rooms marry earthiness with sheer luxury.

✕ Eating

Ti-Tree Cafe & Wine Bar CAFE $
(14 Haszard St, Waihi; mains $12-20; ⊙9am-4pm; 🤶) Housed in a cute little wooden building with punga-shaded outdoor seating, Ti-Tree serves fair-trade organic coffee, cooked breakfasts and delicious fruit sorbets and ice cream during summer. Occasional live music on Sunday afternoons.

Porch CAFE, BAR $$
(23 Wilson Rd, Waihi Beach; brunch $14-20, dinner $29-36; ⊙9am-3pm Mon & Tue, to 1am Wed-Sun) Waihi Beach's coolest chow-down spot, serving sophisticated, substantial mains.

Waitete CAFE, ICE CREAM $$
(📞07-863 8980; www.waitete.co.nz; 31 Orchard Rd; mains $10-34; ⊙11am-3pm & 6pm-late daily, 8.30am-11am Sat & Sun) Delicious ice cream – try the licorice or fig and honey – and a wide menu with a few tasty German and European touches feature at this eatery just off SH2 west of Waihi.

Flatwhite CAFE $$
(www.flatwhitecafe.co.nz; 21 Shaw Rd, Waihi Beach; brunch $14-24, dinner $20-33; ⊙8am-late; 🤶) Funky, licensed and right by Waihi Beach, Flatwhite has a lively brunch menu and also serves decent pizzas and flash burgers.

🛍 Shopping

Artmarket ARTS & CRAFTS
(www.artmarket.co.nz; 65 Seddon St, Waihi; ⊙10am-5pm) Local arts and crafts.

ℹ Information

Waihi Visitor Centre (📞07-863 6715; www.waihi.org.nz; 126 Seddon St, Waihi; ⊙9am-5pm) Local information and the interesting Waihi Gold Discovery Centre, a modern and interactive showcase of the gold-flecked past, present and future of the Waihi region.

ℹ Getting There & Away

Waihi is serviced by **InterCity** (www.intercity.co.nz) buses and seasonal **Go Kiwi** (📞0800 446 549; www.go-kiwi.co.nz) shuttles.

Karangahake Gorge

The road between Waihi and Paeroa, through the bush-lined ramparts of the Karangahake Gorge, is one of the best short drives in the country. Walking and biking tracks take in old Maori trails, historic mining and rail detritus, and spookily dense bush. In Maori legend the area is said to be protected by a *taniwha*, a supernatural creature. The local *iwi* managed to keep this area closed to miners until 1875, aligning themselves with the militant Te Kooti.

The very worthwhile 4.5km **Karangahake Gorge Historic Walkway** takes 1½ hours (each way) and starts from the car park 14km west of Waihi. It follows the disused railway line and the Ohinemuri River Waikino station, where you can pick up the vintage train to Waihi, stopping in at **Waikino Station Cafe** (SH2; mains $10-18; ⊙9.30am-3pm) while you wait. The eastern spur of the Hauraki Rail Trail also passes through, and it's possible to combine a ride on the train from Waihi with a spin on the trail through the most spectacular stage of the gorge. Bikes can also be rented from the Waikino Station Cafe (per day $45). Across the river from the cafe, the **Victoria Battery Tramway & Museum** (www.vbts.org.nz; ⊙10am-3pm Wed & Sun) is the former site of the biggest quartz-ore processing plant in Australasia. There's a dinky tram ride and guided tours of the underground kilns.

A few kilometres further west, Waitawheta Rd leads across the river from SH2 to **Owharoa Falls**. Opposite the falls the **Bistro at The Falls Retreat** (www.fallsretreat.co.nz; 25 Waitawheta Rd; pizza $20, mains $20-36; ⊙10am-10pm) is located in a wooden cottage under a shaded canopy of trees. Gourmet pizzas and rustic meat dishes emerge from the wood-fired oven on a regular basis, and there's a great little playground for the kids.

There are a range of shorter walks and loop tracks leading from the main car park at Karangahake Gorge; bring a torch as some pass through tunnels. A two-hour tramp will bring you to Dickey's Flat, where there's a free **DOC campsite** (Dickey's Flat Rd) and a decent swimming hole. River water will need to be boiled for drinking. You'll find DOC information boards about the walks and the area's history at both the station and the main car park.

Across from the car park, **Golden Owl Lodge** (📞07-862 7994; www.goldenowl.co.nz; 3 Moresby St; dm $29, r $62-100; @🤶) is a homely, handy tramping base, sleeping only 12. Allow $5 extra for linen in the dorm rooms.

Further up the same road, **Ohinemuri Estate Winery** (📞07-862 8874; www.ohinemuri.co.nz; Moresby St; mains $19-32; ⊙10am-4pm Wed-Sun, daily Dec-Feb) has Latvian-influenced architecture and serves excellent lunches. You'd be right if you thought it was an unusual site for growing grapes – the fruit is imported from other regions. Tastings are $5, refundable with purchase. If you imbibe too much, snaffle the chalet-style hut ($135 per night) and revel in the charming atmosphere of this secluded place.

Paeroa

POP 3980

Paeroa is the birthplace of Lemon & Paeroa (L&P), an icon of Kiwiana that markets itself as 'world famous in NZ'. Ironically, the fizzy drink is now owned by global monster Coca-Cola Amatil and produced in Auckland. Still,

generations of Kiwi kids have pestered their parents to take this route just to catch a glimpse of the giant L&P bottles.

The small **museum** (37 Belmont Rd; adult/child $2/1; ◷ noon-3pm Mon-Fri) has a grand selection of Royal Albert porcelain and other pioneer and Maori artefacts. Paeroa is also known for its antique stores.

At the **L&P Cafe & Bar** (www.lpcafe.co.nz; SH2; mains $7-20; ◷ 8.30am-3pm Mon-Wed, to 8pm Thu-Sun) you can order L&P fish and chips or an L&P brekkie, washed down with the lemony lolly water itself. The cafe shares the space with the **information centre** (☏ 07-862 8636; www.paeroa.org.nz; ◷ 9am-4pm), where you can also rent bikes ($45 per day) to take on the Hauraki Rail Trail (p178).

Taranaki & Whanganui

Includes ➡

New Plymouth...........200

Mt Taranaki (Egmont National Park) 207

Surf Highway 45.........211

Whanganui 213

Whanganui National Park...............219

Palmerston North 224

Manawatu Gorge & Around 228

Best Outdoors

➡ New Plymouth's Coastal Walkway (p203)

➡ Surfing along Surf Highway 45 (p211)

➡ Walking on Mt Taranaki (p207)

➡ Canoeing the Whanganui River (p219)

➡ Tramping in Whanganui National Park (p219)

Best Places to Stay

➡ Fitzroy Beach Motel (p205)

➡ Ahu Ahu Beach Villas (p211)

➡ Anndion Lodge (p216)

➡ Plum Trees Lodge (p226)

Why Go?

Halfway between Auckland and Wellington, Taranaki (aka 'the 'Naki') is the Texas of New Zealand: oil and gas stream in from offshore rigs, plumping the region with enviable affluence. New Plymouth is the regional hub, home to an excellent art gallery and provincial museum, and enough decent espresso joints to keep you humming.

Behind the city, the moody volcanic cone of Mt Taranaki demands to be visited. Taranaki also has a glut of black-sand beaches: surfers and holidaymakers swell summer numbers.

Further east the history-rich Whanganui River curls its way through Whanganui National Park down to Whanganui city, a 19th-century river port that's ageing with artistic grace.

Palmerston North, the Manawatu's main city, is a town of two peoples: tough-talkin' country fast-foodies in hotted-up cars and caffeinated Massey University literati. Beyond the city the region blends rural grace with yesterday's pace: you might even find time for a little laziness!

When to Go

➡ Mt Taranaki is one of NZ's wettest spots, and frequently cops snowfalls, even in summer: weather on the mountain can be extremely changeable. Ironically, New Plymouth frequently tops the North Island's most-sunshine-hours list. Expect warm summers and cool winters.

➡ Over in Whanganui the winters are milder, but they're chillier on the Palmerston North plains. Sunshine is abundant hereabouts too – around 2000 hours per year!

Taranaki & Whanganui Highlights

1 Walking up or around the massive cone of **Mt Taranaki** (p207)

2 Riding the big breaks along **Surf Highway 45** (p211)

3 Getting experimental at New Plymouth's **Govett-Brewster Art Gallery** (p200)

4 Bouncing from bean to bean in **New Plymouth's cafes** (p205)

5 Watching a glass-blowing demonstration at one of **Whanganui's glass studios** (p214)

6 Redefining serenity on a canoe or kayak trip on the **Whanganui River** (p220)

7 Traversing the rainy **Whanganui River Road** (p219) by car or bike – it's all about the journey, not how fast you get there

8 Flexing your All Blacks spirit at Palmerston North's **New Zealand Rugby Museum** (p224)

ℹ️ Getting There & Around

In Taranaki, Air New Zealand (p207) has domestic flights to/from New Plymouth. Naked Bus (p207) and InterCity (p207) bus services also service New Plymouth. Shuttle services run between Mt Taranaki, New Plymouth and surrounding towns.

Whanganui and Palmerston North airports are also serviced by Air New Zealand, and both cities are on the radar for InterCity and Naked Bus services. KiwiRail Scenic Journeys (p228) trains stop in Palmerston North too, travelling between Auckland and Wellington.

New Plymouth

POP 53,400

Dominated by Mt Taranaki and surrounded by lush farmland, New Plymouth is the only international deep-water port in this part of New Zealand. The city has a bubbling arts scene, some fab cafes and a rootsy, outdoorsy focus, with surf beaches and Egmont National Park a short hop away.

History

Local Maori *iwi* (tribes) have long contested Taranaki lands. In the 1820s they fled to the Cook Strait region to escape Waikato tribes, who eventually took hold of the area in 1832. Only a small group remained, at Okoki Pa (New Plymouth). When European settlers arrived in 1841, the coast of Taranaki seemed deserted and there was little opposition to land claims. The New Zealand Company bought extensive tracts from the remaining Maori.

When other members of local tribes returned after years of exile, they fiercely objected to the land sale. Their claims were upheld by Governor Fitzroy, but the Crown gradually acquired more land from Maori, and European settlers sought these fertile lands. The settlers forced the government to abandon negotiations with Maori, and war erupted in 1860. By 1870 over 500 hectares of Maori land had been confiscated.

Ensuing economic growth was largely founded on dairy farming. The 1959 discoveries of natural gas and oil in the South Taranaki Bight have kept the province economically healthy in recent times.

◎ Sights

◎ In Town

⭐ **Puke Ariki** MUSEUM
(www.pukeariki.com; 1 Ariki St; ⊙9am-6pm Mon, Tue, Thu & Fri, to 9pm Wed, to 5pm Sat & Sun) FREE Translating as 'Hill of Chiefs', Puke Ariki is home to the i-SITE (p207), a museum, a library, a cafe and the fabulous Arborio (p205) restaurant. The excellent museum has an extensive collection of Maori artefacts, plus colonial, mountain geology and wildlife exhibits (we hope the shark suspended above the lobby isn't life-size).

⭐ **Pukekura Park** GARDENS
(www.pukekura.org.nz; Liardet St; ⊙7.30am-6pm, to 8pm Nov-Mar) The pick of New Plymouth's parks, Pukekura has 49 hectares of gardens, playgrounds, trails, streams, waterfalls, ponds and display houses. **Rowboats** ($10 per half-hour, December and January only) meander across the main lake (full of arm-sized eels), next to which the **Tea House** (Liardet St; snacks $4-9, mains $10-12; ⊙9am-4pm Mar-Nov, 9am-late Dec-Feb) serves light meals (and fudge!). The technicoloured Festival of Lights (p204) here draws the summer crowds, as does the classically English **cricket oval**.

⭐ **Govett-Brewster Art Gallery** GALLERY
(☏06-759 6060; www.govettbrewster.com; 42 Queen St; ⊙10am-5pm) FREE Arguably the country's best regional art gallery. Presenting contemporary – often experimental – local and international shows, it's most

---

ESSENTIAL TARANAKI & WHANGANUI

Eat In one of Palmerston North's hip George St eateries

Drink A bottle of Mike's Pale Ale from Mike's Organic Brewery

Read The *Wanganui Chronicle*, NZ's oldest newspaper

Listen to The rockin' album *Back to the Burning Wreck* by Whanganui riff-monsters The Have

Watch *The Last Samurai*, co-starring Tom Cruise (Mt Taranaki gets top billing)

Go green Paddle a stretch of the Whanganui River, an awe-inspiring slice of NZ wilderness

Online www.taranaki.co.nz; www.wanganui.com; www.ourregion.co.nz

Area code ☏06

MAORI NZ: TARANAKI & WHANGANUI

Ever since Mt Taranaki fled here to escape romantic difficulties, the Taranaki region has had a turbulent history. Conflicts between local *iwi* (tribes) and invaders from the Waikato were followed by two wars with the government – first in 1860–61, and then again in 1865–69. Following the wars there were massive land confiscations and an extraordinary passive-resistance campaign at Parihaka.

Further east, a drive up the Whanganui River Rd takes you into traditional Maori territory, passing the Maori villages of Atene, Koriniti, Ranana and Hiruharama along the way. In Whanganui itself, run your eyes over amazing indigenous exhibits at the Whanganui Regional Museum (p214), and check out the superb Maori carvings in Putiki Church (p215).

Over in Palmerston North, Te Manawa (p224) museum has a strong Maori focus, while the New Zealand Rugby Museum (p224) pays homage to Maori All Blacks, without whom the team would never have become a world force.

famous for its connection with famous NZ sculptor, filmmaker and artist Len Lye (1901–80). There's a cool cafe here too. It was closed temporarily for earthquake proofing when we visited: call or check the website for updates.

Puke Ariki Landing   SCULPTURE PARK
(St Aubyn St) Along the city waterfront is Puke Ariki Landing, a historic area studded with sculptures, including Len Lye's wonderfully eccentric **Wind Wand** (www.windwand.co.nz), a kooky kinetic sculpture.

Paritutu   HILL
(Centennial Dr) Just west of town is Paritutu, a steep-sided, craggy hill (154m) whose name translates appropriately as 'Rising Precipice'. From the summit you can see for miles around: out to the Sugar Loaves, down to the town and to the mountain beyond. It's a 20-minute scramble to the top.

Sugar Loaf Islands Marine Park   ISLAND
(www.doc.govt.nz) A refuge for sea birds and over 400 NZ fur seals 1km offshore, these rugged islets (Nga Motu in Maori) are eroded volcanic remnants. Most seals come here from June to October but some stay all year round. Learn more about the marine park at the tiny interpretation booth on the Breakwater Bay waterfront, or take a tour (p204).

Real Tart Gallery   GALLERY
(www.tact.org.nz; 19 Egmont St; ⊙10am-5pm Mon-Fri, 10am-3pm Sat & Sun, closed Mon Jun-Aug) FREE
To see what local artists have to offer, visit this 100-year-old reconstructed warehouse. Exhibitions change regularly and most works are for sale. Don't miss the old graffiti preserved under perspex!

Brooklands Park   PARK
(www.newplymouthnz.com; Brooklands Park Dr; ⊙daylight hr) Adjoining Pukekura, Brooklands Park is home to the **Bowl of Brooklands** (www.bowl.co.nz; Brooklands Park Dr), a world-class outdoor sound-shell, hosting festivals such as WOMAD (p204) and old-school rockers like Fleetwood Mac. Park highlights include a 2000-year-old puriri tree, a 300-variety rhododendron dell and the farmy **Brooklands Zoo** (www.newplymouthnz.com; Brooklands Park Dr; ⊙9am-5pm) FREE.

Taranaki Cathedral   CHURCH
(www.taranakicathedral.org.nz; 37 Vivian St; ⊙services daily) The austere Church of St Mary (1846) is NZ's oldest stone church and its newest cathedral! Its graveyard has the headstones of early settlers and soldiers who died during the Taranaki Land Wars, as well as those of several Maori chiefs. Check out the fabulous vaulted timber ceiling inside.

New Plymouth Observatory   OBSERVATORY
(☑021 751 524; www.sites.google.com/site/astronomynp; Marsland Hill, Robe St; adult/child/family $5/3/10; ⊙7.30-9.30pm Tue Mar-Oct, 8.30-10pm Tue Nov-Feb) Atop Marsland Hill (great views!) is this wee observatory. Also on the hill is the cacophonous 37-bell **Kibby Carillon**, a huge automated glockenspiel-like device that tolls out across the New Plymouth rooftops.

◉ South of Town

Pukeiti   GARDENS
(www.pukeiti.org.nz; 2290 Carrington Rd; ⊙9am-5pm) FREE This 4-sq-km garden, 20km south of New Plymouth, is home to masses of rhododendrons and azaleas. The flowers

TARANAKI & WHANGANUI NEW PLYMOUTH

New Plymouth

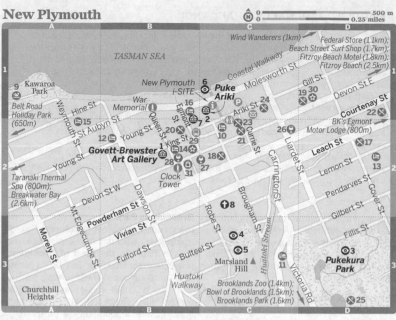

New Plymouth

◉ Top Sights
1 Govett-Brewster Art Gallery	B2
2 Puke Ariki	C1
3 Pukekura Park	D3

◉ Sights
4 Kibby Carillon	C3
5 New Plymouth Observatory	C3
6 Puke Ariki Landing	C1
7 Real Tart Gallery	B2
8 Taranaki Cathedral	C2
Wind Wand	(see 6)

◉ Activities, Courses & Tours
9 Todd Energy Aquatic Centre	A1

◉ Sleeping
10 Ariki Backpackers	C2
11 Carrington Motel	C3
12 Dawson Motel	B2
13 Ducks & Drakes	D2
14 King & Queen Hotel Suites	B2
15 Seaspray House	A2
16 Waterfront	B1

◉ Eating
17 Andre's Pies & Patisserie	D2
Arborio	(see 2)
18 Chaos	C2
19 Elixir	D1
20 Frederic's	B2
21 Laughing Buddha	C2
22 Pak 'n Save	D1
23 Petit Paris	C2
24 Portofino	C1
25 Tea House	D3

◉ Drinking & Nightlife
26 Hour Glass	C2
27 Mayfair	C2
28 Snug Lounge	B2

◉ Entertainment
29 Basement	B2
30 Event Cinemas	D1

◉ Shopping
31 Kina	B2

bloom between September and November, but it's worth a visit any time. The drive here passes between the Pouakai and Kaitake Ranges, both part of Egmont National Park. There's a cafe here too.

Tupare HISTORIC BUILDING, GARDENS

(www.tupare.info; 487 Mangorei Rd; ⏱9am-5pm Apr-Oct, to 8pm Nov-Mar, tours 11am Fri-Mon Oct-Mar) **FREE** Tupare is a Tudor-style house designed by the renowned architect James

Chapman-Taylor. It's as pretty as a picture, but the highlight of this 7km trip south of New Plymouth will likely be the rambling 3.6 hectare garden surrounding it. Bluebells and birdsong under the boughs...picnic paradise.

Hurworth Cottage   HISTORIC BUILDING
(www.historic.org.nz; 906 Carrington Rd; adult/child/family $5/2/10; ☉11am-3pm Sat & Sun) This 1856 cottage, 8km south of New Plymouth, was built by four-time NZ prime minister Harry Atkinson. The cottage is the sole survivor of a settlement abandoned at the start of the Taranaki Land Wars: a rare window into the lives of early settlers.

Taranaki Aviation, Transport & Technology Museum   MUSEUM
(TATATM; http://tatatm.tripod.com/museum; cnr SH3 & Kent Rd; adult/child/family $7/2/16; ☉10.30am-4.30pm Sat & Sun) Around 9.5km south of New Plymouth is this roadside museum, with ramshackle displays of old planes, trains, automobiles and general household miscellany. Ask to see the stuff made by the amazing bee guy (hexagons ahoy!).

◉ North via SH3

Heading north from New Plymouth along SH3 are various seaward turn-offs to high sand dunes and surf beaches. **Urenui**, 16km past Waitara, is a summer hot spot.

About 5km past Urenui is arguably the highlight of North Taranaki: **Mike's Organic Brewery** (☑06-752 3676; www.organicbeer.co.nz; 487 Mokau Rd; tastings/tours $15/25; ☉10am-6pm), which offers tours (book ahead), takeaways, tastings of the legendary Mike's Pale Ale (the pilsener and lager are ace, too), and an Oktoberfest party every (you guessed it) October. A little further on is the turn-off to **Pukearuhe** and **White Cliffs**, huge precipices resembling their Dover namesakes. From Pukearuhe boat ramp you can tackle the **White Cliffs Walkway**, a three-hour loop walk with mesmerising views of the coast and mountains (Taranaki and Ruapehu). The tide can make things dicey along the beach: walk between two hours either side of low tide.

Continuing north towards **Mokau**, stop at the **Three Sisters** rock formation signposted just south of the Tongaporutu Bridge – you can traverse the shore at low tide. Two sisters stand somewhat forlornly off the coast: their other sister collapsed in a heap

10 years ago, but check the progress of a new sis emerging from the eroding cliffs.

Activities

Surfing

Taranaki's black, volcanic-sand beaches are terrific for surfing. Close to the eastern edge of town are **Fitzroy Beach** and **East End Beach** (allegedly the cleanest beach in Oceania). There's also decent surf at **Back Beach**, near Paritutu, at the western end of the city. Otherwise, head for Surf Hwy 45 (p211).

Beach Street Surf Shop   SURFING
(☑06-758 0400; beachstreet@xtra.co.nz; 39 Beach St; 90min lesson $75; ☉10am-5pm Mon-Thu, to 6pm Fri, to 3pm Sat & Sun) Close to Fitzroy Beach, this surf shop offers lessons, gear hire (surfboard/wetsuit per hour $10/5) and surf tours.

Tarawave Surf School   SURFING
(☑021 119 6218; www.tarawavesurfschool.com; 90min lesson $75) Based 15km south of town at Oakura, on Surf Hwy 45.

Tramping

The i-SITE stocks the *Taranaki: A Walker's Guide* booklet, including coastal, local reserve and park walks. The excellent **Coastal Walkway** (11km) from Bell Block to Port Taranaki gives you a surf-side perspective on New Plymouth and crosses the sexily engineered **Te Rewa Rewa Bridge**. **Huatoki Walkway** (5km), following Huatoki Stream, is a rambling walk into the city centre. Alternatively, the **New Plymouth Heritage Trail** brochure, taking in historic hot spots, is a real blast from the past.

Other Activities

Taranaki Thermal Spa   SPA, MASSAGE
(☑06-759 1666; www.windwand.co.nz/mineral-pools; 8 Bonithon Ave; treatments $13-245; ☉10am-5pm Mon & Tue, 10am-9pm Wed-Fri, 3-9pm Sat & Sun) The warm mineral water filling the tanks at Taranaki Thermal Spa was discovered during the search for oil around 1910. The private baths are filled on arrival, and there's a suite of massage and beauty therapies available. An absolute tonic.

Todd Energy Aquatic Centre   SWIMMING
(☑06-759 6060; www.newplymouthnz.com; Tisch Ave, Kawaroa Park; adult/child $4.50/3.50, waterslide $3.50; ☉6am-8.15pm Mon-Fri, 7am-6.45pm Sat & Sun) Just west of town in grassy Kawaroa Park is the Todd Energy Aquatic

Centre, which has a waterslide, outdoor pool and indoor pool.

Wind Wanderers
BICYCLE RENTAL

(☑ 027 358 1182; www.windwanderer.co.nz; Nobs Line car park, East End Reserve; bike hire single/tandem per hr $10/15; ⊙ 9am-5pm) Bike hire on New Plymouth's excellent Coastal Walkway. Quirky side-by-side two-seaters also available.

☞ Tours

Chaddy's Charters
BOAT TOUR

(☑ 06-758 9133; www.chaddyscharters.co.nz; Ocean View Pde; adult/child $35/10) Take a trip out to visit the Sugar Loaf Islands with Chaddy: expect at least four laughs a minute on a one-hour bob around on the chop. Departs daily from Breakwater Bay, tide and weather permitting. You can also hire kayaks (single/double per hour $15/30) and bikes ($10 per hour) here.

Canoe & Kayak Taranaki
KAYAKING

(☑ 06-769 5506; www.canoeandkayak.co.nz; half-day incl hire $95) Paddle out to the Sugar Loaf Islands or over the gentle Waitara River rapids.

☆ Festivals & Events

Festival of Lights
CULTURAL

(www.festivaloflights.co.nz) Complete with live music and costumed characters roaming the undergrowth, this colourful display lights up Pukekura Park from late December to late January.

WOMAD
MUSIC, CULTURAL

(World of Music Arts & Dance; www.womad.co.nz) A diverse array of local and international artists perform at the Bowl of Brooklands each March. Hugely popular, with music fans trucking in from across NZ.

Taranaki International Arts Festival
ARTS

(www.taft.co.nz/artsfest) The regional big-ticket arts fest happens in August: theatre, dance, music, visual arts, parades and plenty of food and wine.

Taranaki Garden Spectauclar
HORTICULTURAL

(www.taft.co.nz/gardenfestnz) A long-running NZ flower fest, held in early November each year: more rhododendrons than you'll ever see in one place again.

⌂ Sleeping

Seaspray House
HOSTEL $

(☑ 06-759 8934; www.seasprayhouse.co.nz; 13 Weymouth St; dm/s/d $31/54/74; ⊙ closed Jun-Aug; @☎) A big 100-year-old house with gloriously high ceilings, Seaspray has had a recent makeover inside but remains relaxed, spacey and affordable, with well-chosen retro and antique furniture. Fresh and arty, it's a rare bunk-free backpackers with no TV (conversation encouraged).

Ariki Backpackers
HOSTEL $

(☑ 06-769 5020; www.arikibackpackers.com; cnr Ariki & Brougham Sts; dm $27-30, d $70-90; @☎) Upstairs at the old Royal Hotel (Queen Liz stayed here once!), welcoming Ariki offers downtown hostelling with funky carpets, a roomy lounge area with retro couches, and a fantastic roof terrace looking across the park to Puke Ariki. Most rooms have their own shower and toilet. Bikes and surfboards for hire.

Ducks & Drakes
HOSTEL, HOTEL $

(☑ 06-758 0404; www.ducksanddrakes.co.nz; 48 Lemon St; hostel dm/s/d $30/63/84, hotel r from $125; @☎) The hostel here occupies a labyrinthine 1920s heritage building with stripy wallpaper and fancy timberwork, brimming with character. The upstairs rooms are the pick: secluded, quiet and catching the morning sun. Next door is a pricier (newer) hotel wing with snazzy studios and one-bedroom suites.

Belt Road Holiday Park
HOLIDAY PARK $

(☑ 06-758 0228, 0800 804 204; www.beltroad. co.nz; 2 Belt Rd; campsites from $20, cabins $70-140; @☎) ⊘ This environmentally attuned, pohutukawa-covered holiday park sits atop a bluff overlooking the increasingly interesting Breakwater Bay area, about a 10-minute walk from town. The half-dozen best cabins have million-dollar views. 'Recycle – that's what Kiwis do!', says the manager.

Egmont Eco Lodge
HOSTEL $

(☑ 06-753 5720; www.yha.co.nz; 12 Clawton St; dm/d from $29/75; @☎) An immaculate YHA in a glade with chirping birds and a chuckling creek (with eels!). Mixed dorms in the main lodge; smaller pinewood cabins down below (sleeping four). It's a hike uphill from town, but the prospect of free nightly Egmont cake will put a spring in your step.

New Plymouth Top 10 Holiday Park
HOLIDAY PARK $

(☑ 06-758 2566, 0800 758 256; www.nptop10. co.nz; 29 Princes St; campsites/cabins from $20/80, units $95-180; @☎) Sequestered in Fitzroy, 3.5km east of town and a seven-minute walk to the beach, this quaint, family-run Top 10 feels a bit like a school camp, with a dinky little row of units, life-sized chess set, trampoline, laundry and spacious kitchen.

★ Fitzroy Beach Motel
MOTEL $$

(✆06-757 2925; www.fitzroybeachmotel.co.nz; 25 Beach St; 1-/2-bedroom units from $155/190; 🛜) This quiet, old-time motel (just 160m from Fitzroy Beach) has been thoroughly re-deemed with a major overhaul and extension. Highlights include quality carpets, double glazing, lovely bathrooms, LCD TVs and an absence of poky studio-style units (all one- or two-bedroom). Free bikes too. Winner!

Dawson Motel
MOTEL $$

(✆06-758 1177; www.thedawsonmotel.co.nz; 16 Dawson St; d from $150, 1-/2-bedroom units from $180/210; 🛜) Just a couple of years old, the corporate Dawson is a sharp-looking, two-storey number – all white, red and black inside – with sea and mountain views from the top-floor rooms. The location is primo: a five-minute walk into town and 50m to the Coastal Walkway.

BK's Egmont Motor Lodge
MOTEL $$

(✆0800 115 033, 06-758 5216; www.egmontmotor-lodge.co.nz; 115 Coronation Ave; d $130-200; 🅿🛜) Opposite the racecourse, low-slung BK's has ground-floor units and oceans of parking. Rooms are smart, comfortable and clean, and the managers (travellers too) read-ily share a laugh with the cleaners (a good sign). Free wi-fi and DVDs.

Carrington Motel
MOTEL $$

(✆0800 779 431, 06-757 9431; www.carringtonmo-tel.co.nz; 61 Carrington St; s/d/f from $89/98/155; 🛜) Sixteen old but tidy units close to Puke-kura Park and a 10-minute walk to town. It's very family friendly and great value (espe-cially in winter), but noisy when the hoons careen up Carrington St. Wildly eclectic fur-nishings and tsunami-like showers.

★ King & Queen Hotel Suites
BOUTIQUE HOTEL $$$

(✆06-757 2999; www.kingandqueen.co.nz; cnr King & Queen Sts; ste $200-400) The new kid on the New Plymouth accommodation block is this regal boutique hotel on the corner of King and Queen Sts (get it?). Run by unerringly professional staff, it's an interesting 17-room affair over two levels. Each suite features an-tique Moroccan and Euro furnishings, plush carpets, lustrous black tiles, hip art, retro leather couches and *real* flowers. Cafe-bean roastery on site. Nice one!

Waterfront
HOTEL $$$

(✆06-769 5301; www.waterfront.co.nz; 1 Egmont St; r $190-550; @🛜) Sleek and snazzy, Water-front is the place to stay if the boss is pay-ing. The minimalist studios are pretty flash, while the penthouses steal the show with big TVs and little balconies. It's got terrific views from some – but not all – rooms, but certain-ly from the curvy-fronted bar and restaurant.

✗ Eating

Chaos
CAFE $

(36 Brougham St; meals $8-16; ⏲7.30am-3.30pm Mon-Fri, 8.30am-3pm Sat, 9am-2pm Sun; ✍) Not so much chaotic as endearingly boho, Chaos is a dependable spot for a coffee and a zingy breakfast. Beans with bacon, avocado and sour cream, background jazz, smiley staff and arty interior design – hard to beat! Plen-ty of vegetarian and gluten-free options, too. Love the graffiti-covered side wall.

Petit Paris
BAKERY $

(www.petitparis.co.nz; 34 Currie St; lunches $8-15; ⏲7.30am-4.30pm Mon-Fri, to 2.30pm Sat & Sun) *Ooh-la-la!* Lashings of buttery treats! Fly-ing the tricolour with pride, Petit Paris is a boulangerie and patisserie turning out crispy baguettes and *tart au citron* (lemon tart), or an omelette or *croque-monsieur* for lunch.

Andre's Pies & Patisserie
BAKERY $

(44 Leach St; pies $4-8; ⏲6am-3.30pm Mon-Fri) Expanding waistlines since 1972, this is an easy pull-over off the main road through town. Hefty pies, buns, sandwiches and calo-rific slabs of cake.

Pak 'n Save
SUPERMARKET $

(www.paknsave.co.nz; 53 Leach St; ⏲8am-11pm) Just east of downtown NP.

★ Federal Store
CAFE $$

(440 Devon St E; mains $10-20; ⏲7am-5pm Mon-Fri, 9am-5pm Sat & Sun; ✍) Super-popular and crammed with retro furniture, Federal con-jures up a 1950s corner-store vibe. Switched-on staff in dinky head scarves take your coffee order as you queue to order at the counter, keeping you buoyant until your hot cakes, New Yorker sandwich or spicy beans arrive. Terrific cakes, tarts and pre-made counter food (love the vegie frittata), and very kid-friendly, too.

Arborio
MEDITERRANEAN $$

(✆06-759 1241; www.arborio.co.nz; Puke Ariki, 1 Ariki St; mains $13-34; ⏲9am-late) Despite looking like a cheese grater, Arborio, in the Puke Ariki building, is the star of New Plymouth's food show. It's airy, arty and modern, with sea views and faultless service. The Med-influenced menu ranges from an awesome tandoori chicken pizza to pastas, risottos and spicy calamari with garlic and coriander. Cocktails and NZ wines available.

Elixir   CAFE $$
(www.elixircafe.co.nz; 117 Devon St E; brunch $8-18, dinner $18-31; ⊙7am-4.30pm Mon, 7am-late Tue-Sat, 8am-4pm Sun) Behind a weird louvered wall facing onto Devon St, Elixir fosters an American-diner vibe, serving up everything from coffee, cake, bagels and eggs on toast, through to more innovative evening fare. Below a wall of rock posters, sexy staff give the coffee machine a serious work-out.

Bach on Breakwater   CAFE, RESTAURANT $$
(☑06-769 6967; www.bachonbreakwater.co.nz; Ocean View Pde; brunch $11-24, dinner $27-38; ⊙9.30am-10pm Wed-Sun; ☑) Constructed from weighty recycled timbers, this cool cafe-bistro in the emerging Breakwater Bay precinct looks like an old sea chest washed up after a storm. Expect plenty of seafood and steak, sunny outdoor tables and killer coffee. The seafood chowder is a real winter warmer. Lots of gluten-free and vegetarian options.

Frederic's   TAPAS $$
(www.frederics.co.nz; 34 Egmont St; plates $12-19, mains $18-25; ⊙11am-late) Freddy's is a fab gastro-bar with quirky interior design (rusty medieval chandeliers, peacock-feather wallpaper, religious icon paintings), serving generous share plates. Order some lemon-crusted calamari, or green-lipped mussels with coconut cream, chilli and coriander to go with your Monteith's pale ale.

Portofino   ITALIAN $$
(☑06-757 8686; www.portofino.co.nz; 14 Gill St; mains $20-49; ⊙5pm-late Tue-Sun) This discreet little family-run eatery has been here for years, serving old-fashioned Italian pasta and pizza just like nonna used to make. The rigatoni Portofino is a knockout (spinach, feta, garlic and sun-dried tomatoes).

Laughing Buddha   CHINESE $$
(☑06-759 2065; www.facebook.com/laughingbuddha2009; cnr Devon St E & Currie St; mains $12-19; ⊙dinner Tue-Sat) Red-glowing windows and a rather menacing-looking Buddha sign suggest 'nightclub'...but a wander upstairs delivers you instead to New Plymouth's best Chinese restaurant. Load up on entree plates ($4 to $8; try the pork buns), or order a steaming main course (the sliced beef with cumin and chilli is magic). Great for groups.

🍷 Drinking & Nightlife

Hour Glass   BAR
(www.facebook.com/thehourglass49; 49 Liardet St; ⊙4pm-12.30am Tue-Sat) On an unremarkable rise of Liardet St is this new late-night tapas bar, with richly brocaded crimson drapes, straight-backed wooden chairs and interesting timber paneling. Upwards of 30 craft beers, killer cocktails and zingy tapas: New Plymouth can't get enough!

Snug Lounge   COCKTAIL BAR
(www.snuglounge.co.nz; cnr Devon St W & Queen St; ⊙4pm-late Tue-Thu & Sat, noon-late Fri) This savvy new speakeasy on the downtown fringe is the classiest place in town for a drink. Dress to the nines, order a Lychee Long Time (sake, vodka, apple juice and rosewater) and act like you own this town. A few excellent Japanese share plates will ensure you stay vertical.

Mayfair   BAR, LIVE MUSIC
(www.themayfair.co.nz; 69 Devon St W; ⊙11am-late) This old theatre has expanded into the adjoining shopfronts to become the Mayfair, a fairly mainstream but always busy bar/restaurant/live-music space. Everyone from rock bands to jazz trios, stand-up comedy acts, DJs and chamber orchestras play the main room out the back; the front bar offers pizzas, shared platters and a decent wine list.

☆ Entertainment

Basement   LIVE MUSIC, COMEDY
(www.facebook.com/thebasementnightclub; cnr Devon St W & Egmont St) Underneath a regulation Irish pub, the grungy Basement is the best place in town to catch up-and-coming live bands, broadly sheltering under a rock, metal and punk umbrella. Opening hours vary with gigs.

Event Cinemas   CINEMA
(www.eventcinemas.co.nz; 119 Devon St E; adult/child $14/9; ⊙10am-late) Mainstream, mainstreet megaplex, the carpet a sea of popcorn. All tickets $8.50 on Tuesdays.

🛍 Shopping

Kina JEWELLERY, DESIGN
(www.kina.co.nz; 101 Devon St W; ⊙9am-5.30pm Mon-Fri, 9.30am-4pm Sat, 11am-4pm Sun) Fabulous Kiwi crafts, jewellery, art and design in a lovely shopfront on the main drag, plus regular gallery exhibitions. The perfect spot to pick up an authentic NZ souvenir.

ℹ Information

DOC (Department of Conservation; ☑06-759 0350; www.doc.govt.nz; 55a Rimu St; ⊙8am-4.30pm Mon-Fri)

New Plymouth i-SITE (☑06-759 6060; www.taranaki.co.nz; Puke Ariki, 1 Ariki St; ⊙9am-6pm Mon-Tue & Thu-Fri, to 9pm Wed, to 5pm Sat & Sun) Situated in the Puke Ariki building, with a fantastic interactive tourist-info database.

Phoenix Urgent Doctors (☑06-759 4295; www.phoenixdoctors.co.nz; 95 Vivian St; ⊙8.30am-8pm) Doctors by appointment and urgent medical help.

Post Office (21 Currie St; ⊙8.30am-5pm Mon-Fri, 9am-1pm Sat) Foreign exchange is available at the local post office.

Taranaki Base Hospital (☑06-753 6139; www.tdhb.org.nz; David St; ⊙24hr) Accident and emergency.

ℹ Getting There & Away

AIR

New Plymouth Airport (www.newplymouthairport.com; Airport Dr) is 11km east of the centre off SH3. **Air New Zealand** (☑06-757 3300; www.airnewzealand.co.nz; 12-14 Devon St E; ⊙9am-5pm Mon-Fri) Daily direct flights to/from Auckland, Wellington and Christchurch, with onward connections.

BUS

Services run from the **bus centre** (cnr Egmont & Ariki Sts).

InterCity (www.intercity.co.nz) services include the following:

DESTINATION	PRICE ($)	DURATION (HR)	FREQUENCY (DAILY)
Auckland	73	6	2
Hamilton	49	4	2
Palmerston North	35	4	1
Wellington	45	7	1
Whanganui	29	2½	1

Naked Bus (www.nakedbus.com) services ply similar routes:

DESTINATION	PRICE ($)	DURATION (HR)	FREQUENCY (DAILY)
Auckland	30	6	1
Hamilton	30	4	1
Palmerston North	23	3½	1
Wellington	20	6¼	1
Whanganui	18	2½	1

ℹ Getting Around

Citylink (www.taranakibus.info; adult/child $3.50/2.10) Services run Monday to Friday around town, as well as north to Waitara and south to Oakura. Buses depart from the bus centre.

Chaddy's Charters (☑06-758 9133; www.windwand.co.nz/chaddiescharters; Ocean View Pde; per 30min $10) Bicycle rental.

Cycle Inn (☑06-758 7418; www.cycleinn.co.nz; 133 Devon St E; per 2hr/day $10/20; ⊙8.30am-5pm Mon-Fri, 9am-4pm Sat, 10am-2pm Sun) Bike rental.

Energy City Cabs (☑06-757 5580)

Rent-a-Dent (☑06-757 5362, 0800 736 823; www.rentadent.co.nz; 592 Devon St E; ⊙8am-5pm Mon-Fri, to noon Sat) Cheap car hire.

Scott's Airport Shuttle (☑0800 373 001, 06-769 5974; www.npairportshuttle.co.nz; adult from $25) Operates a door-to-door shuttle to/from the airport.

Mt Taranaki (Egmont National Park)

A classic 2518m volcanic cone dominating the landscape, Mt Taranaki is a magnet to all who catch his eye. Geologically, Taranaki is the youngest of three large volcanoes – Kaitake and Pouakai are the others – which stand along the same fault line. With the last eruption over 350 years ago, experts say that the mountain is overdue for another go. But don't let that put you off – this mountain is an absolute beauty and the highlight of any visit to the region.

Access points for the mountain are North Egmont, Dawson Falls and East Egmont. There are DOC info centres at North Egmont and Dawson Falls; for accommodation and supplies head to Stratford and Inglewood.

History

According to Maori legend, Taranaki belonged to a tribe of volcanoes in the middle of the North Island. However, he was forced to depart rather hurriedly when he was caught with Pihanga, the beautiful volcano near Lake Taupo and the lover of Mt Tongariro. As he fled south (some say in disgrace; others say to keep the peace), Taranaki gouged out a wide scar in the earth (now the Whanganui River) and finally settled in the west in his current position. He remains here in majestic isolation, hiding his face behind a cloud of tears.

🏃 Activities

Tramping

Due to its accessibility, Mt Taranaki ranks as the 'most climbed' mountain in NZ. Nevertheless, tramping on this mountain is dangerous and should not be undertaken lightly. It's *crucial* to get advice before departing and to leave your intentions with a Department of Conservation (DOC) visitor centre or i-SITE.

Most walks are accessible from North Egmont, Dawson Falls or East Egmont. Check out DOC's collection of detailed walk pamphlets ($1 each) or the free *Taranaki: A Walker's Guide* booklet for more info.

From North Egmont, the main walk is the scenic **Pouakai Circuit**, a two- to three-day, 25km loop through alpine, swamp and tussock areas with awesome mountain views. Short, easy walks from here include the **Ngatoro Loop Track** (one hour), **Veronica Loop** (two hours) and **Nature Walk** (15-minute loop). The **Summit Track** also starts from North Egmont. It's a 14km poled route taking eight to 10 hours return, and

should not be attempted by inexperienced people, especially in icy conditions and snow.

East Egmont has the **Potaema Track** (wheelchair accessible; 30 minutes return) and **East Egmont Lookout** (10 minutes return); a longer walk is the steep **Enchanted Track** (two to three hours return).

At Dawson Falls you can do several short walks including **Wilkies Pools Loop** (1¼ hours return) or the excellent but challenging **Fanthams Peak Return** (five hours return), which is snowed-in during winter. The **Kapuni Loop Track** (one hour) runs to the impressive 18m **Dawson Falls** themselves. You can also see the falls from the visitor centre via a 10-minute walk to a viewpoint.

The difficult 55km **Around-the-Mountain Circuit** takes three to five days and is for experienced trampers only. There are a number of huts en route, tickets for which should be purchased in advance.

The **York Loop Track** (three hours), accessible from York Rd north of Stratford, is a fascinating walk following part of a disused railway line.

You can tramp without a guide from February to March when snowfalls are low, but at other times inexperienced climbers can check with DOC for details of local clubs and guides. It costs around $300 per day to hire a guide. Reliable operators include Mt Taranaki Guided Tours, and the following:

Adventure Dynamics   MOUNTAINEERING
(☑ 06-751 3589; www.adventuredynamics.co.nz)

Top Guides   MOUNTAINEERING
(☑ 021 838 513, 0800 448 433; www.topguides.co.nz)

Skiing

Manganui Ski Area   SKIING
(☑ ski lodge 06-765 5493, snow phone 06-759 1119; www.skitaranaki.co.nz; daily lift pass adult/child $40/25) From Stratford take Pembroke Rd up to Stratford Plateau, from where it's a 1.5km (20 minute) walk to the small Manganui Ski Area. The Stratford i-SITE (p210) has daily weather and snow reports; otherwise ring the snow phone or check the webcam online.

👉 Tours

Mt Taranaki Guided Tours   GUIDED HIKE
(☑ 027 441 7042; www.mttaranakiguidedtours.co.nz) Guided hikes on the mountain from one to three days, with the appropriately named Ian McAlpine. Price on application.

ℹ DECEPTIVE MOUNTAIN

Mt Taranaki might look like an easy peak to bag, but this cute cone has claimed more than 60 lives. The mountain microclimate changes fast: from summery to white-out conditions almost in an instant. There are also precipitous bluffs and steep icy slopes.

There are plenty of short walks here, safe for much of the year, but for adventurous trampers January to March is the best time to go. Take a detailed topographic map (the Topo50 1:50,000 *Mt Taranaki or Mt Egmont* map is good) and consult a DOC officer for current conditions. You *must* also register your tramping intentions with the DOC visitor centre (p209), i-SITE (p210) or online via www.adventuresmart.org.nz.

Taranaki Tours GUIDED TOUR
(☑ 0800 886 877, 06-757 9888; www.taranakitours.
com; per person from $130) Runs an around-
the-mountain day tour, strong on Maori culture and natural history.

Heliview SCENIC FLIGHTS
(☑ 0800 767 886, 06-753 0123; www.heliview.co.nz;
flights from $149) A 25-minute 'Port to Peak'
summit flight costs $249 per passenger.

🛏 Sleeping & Eating

Several DOC huts are scattered about the
mountain, accessible by tramping tracks.
Most cost $15 per night (Syme and Kahui
cost $5); purchase hut tickets in advance
from DOC. BYO cooking, eating and sleeping
gear, and bookings are not accepted – it's first
come, first served. There are also sleeping options in nearby Stratford and Inglewood.

Camphouse HOSTEL $
(☑ 06-278 6523; www.mttaranaki.co.nz; Egmont Rd,
North Egmont; dm/d/f $38/90/225) Bunkhouse-
style accommodation behind the North
Egmont visitor centre in a historic 1850
corrugated-iron building, complete with
gun slots in the walls (through which settlers fired at local Maori during the Taranaki
Land Wars). Horizon views from the porch.
Day use $20 per walker (hot showers).

EcoInn HOSTEL $
(☑ 06-752 2765; www.ecoinnovation.co.nz; 671 Kent
Rd; s/tw/d $35/70/70; @ 🛜) 🍴 About 6.5km
up the road from the turn-off at the Aviation, Transport & Technology Museum, this
ecofriendly place is made from recycled timber and runs on solar, wind and hydropow-
er. There's a spa and pool table, too. Good
group rates.

Konini Lodge LODGE $
(☑ 06-756 0990; www.doc.govt.nz; Manaia Rd,
Dawson Falls; dm $25) Basic bunkhouse accom-
modation 100m downhill from the Dawson
Falls visitor centre. Six dorm rooms feed off
a huge communal space and kitchen.

Mountain House LODGE $$
(☑ 06-765 6100; www.stratfordmountainhouse.
co.nz; 998 Pembroke Rd; d $155, extra person $20)
This upbeat lodge, on the Stratford side of the
mountain (15km from the SH3 turn-off and
3km to the Manganui Ski Area), has recently
renovated motel-style rooms and a mod
Euro-style **restaurant-cafe** (brunch $13-38,
dinner $34-42; ⊙ 9am-late Wed-Sun). Dinner plus
B&B packages available (from $295).

Mountain Cafe CAFE $
(www.mttaranaki.co.nz; Egmont Rd; meals $10-18;
⊙ 9am-3pm Dec-Feb, 10am-3pm Mar-Nov) Inside
the North Egmont Visitor Centre.

ℹ Information

Dawson Falls Visitor Centre (☑ 027 443
0248; www.doc.govt.nz; Manaia Rd; ⊙ 9am-
4pm Thu-Sun, daily school holidays) On the
southeastern side of the mountain, fronted by
an awesome totem pole.
MetPhone (☑ 0900 999 06) Mountain weather
updates.
North Egmont Visitor Centre (☑ 06-756
0990; www.doc.govt.nz; Egmont Rd; ⊙ 8am-
4.30pm) Current and comprehensive national
park info.

ℹ Getting There & Away

There are three main entrance roads to Egmont
National Park, all of which are well signposted
and either pass by or end at a DOC visitor centre.
Closest to New Plymouth is North Egmont: turn
off SH3 at Egmont Village, 12km south of New
Plymouth, and follow Egmont Rd for 14km. From
Stratford, turn off at Pembroke Rd and continue
for 15km to East Egmont and the Manganui Ski
Area. From the southeast, Manaia Rd leads up to
Dawson Falls, 23km from Stratford.

There are no public buses to the national park
but numerous shuttle-bus/tour operators will
gladly take you there for around $40/55 one-
way/return (usually cheaper for groups).
Cruise NZ Tours (☑ 0800 688 687) Mountain
shuttle bus departing New Plymouth 7.30am
for North Egmont; returns 4.30pm. Other
pick-ups/drop-offs by arrangement. Tours also
available.
Eastern Taranaki Experience (☑ 06-765
7482; www.eastern-taranaki.co.nz) Shuttle
services as well as tours and accommodation
in Stratford.
Outdoor Gurus (☑ 027 270 2932, 06-758 4152;
www.outdoorgurus.co.nz) Pick-up points (New
Plymouth) and times to suit; gear hire available.
Taranaki Tours (☑ 06-757 9878, 0800 886
877) Offers New Plymouth to North Egmont
return.

Around Mt Taranaki

Inglewood
POP 3250
Handy to the mountain on SH3, the lit-
tle main-street town of Inglewood is an
adequate stop for supermarket supplies and
a noteworthy stop for a steak-and-egg pie at

Nelsons Bakery (06-756 7123; 45 Rata St; pies $3-4; 6am-4.30pm Mon-Fri, 7am-4pm Sat). Inglewood's other shining light is the cute **Fun Ho! National Toy Museum** (06-756 7030; www.funhotoys.co.nz; 25 Rata St; adult/child $6/3; 10am-4pm), exhibiting (and selling) old-fashioned sand-cast toys. It doubles as the local visitor information centre; online, www.inglewood.co.nz is a good source of information.

On the road into town from New Plymouth, **White Eagle Motel** (06-756 8252; www.whiteeaglemotel.co.nz; 87b Rata St; s/d from $90/105, extra person $20;) is an old-school motel but tidy and quiet with blooming flower boxes. The two-bedroom units feel bigger than they are.

Inside a fire-engine-red 1878 heritage building, **Caffe Windsor** (06-756 6665; www.caffewindsor.co.nz; 1 Kelly St; brunch $9-23, dinner $23-30; 8.30am-5pm Mon-Wed, to late Thu-Sat, to 3pm Sun) sells super-sized custard squares and coffee during the day and Thai chicken curry at night (among other things). Nearby, **Funkfish Grill** (06-756 7287; www.funkfishgrill.co.nz; 32 Matai St; takeaways $5-10, mains $23-36; 4pm-late) is a hip pizzeria and fish-and-chippery doing eat-in and take-away meals, and doubles as a bar at night. Try the tempura scallops.

Stratford

POP 5470

Forty kilometres southeast of New Plymouth on SH3, Stratford plays up its namesake of Stratford-upon-Avon, Shakespeare's birthplace, by naming its streets after bardic characters. Stratford also claims NZ's first **glockenspiel**. Four times daily (10am, 1pm, 3pm and 7pm) this clock doth chime out Shakespeare's greatest hits with some fairly wooden performances.

Stratford i-SITE (06-765 6708, 0800 765 6708; www.stratford.govt.nz; Prospero Pl, Broadway S; 8.30am-5pm Mon-Fri, 10am-3pm Sat & Sun) also houses the **Percy Thomson Gallery** (06-765 0917; www.percythomsongallery.org.nz; Prospero Pl; 10.30am-4pm Mon-Fri, to 3pm Sat & Sun) FREE, a community gallery (named after the former mayor) displaying eclectic local and touring art shows.

One kilometre south of Stratford on SH3, the **Taranaki Pioneer Village** (06-765 5399; www.pioneervillage.co.nz; adult/child $12/5; 10am-4pm) is a 4-hectare outdoor museum housing 40 historic buildings. It's very bygone-era (and more than a little bit spooky).

Seemingly embalmed in calamine lotion, the old-fashioned **Stratford Top Town Holiday Park** (0508 478 728, 06-765 6440; www.stratfordtoptownholidaypark.co.nz; 10 Page St; campsites/dm/cabins/units from $16/20/40/98;) is a trim caravan park offering one-room cabins, motel-style units and backpackers' bunks.

All stone-clad columns, jaunty roof angles, timber louvres and muted cave-colours, the newish **Amity Court Motel** (06-765 4496; www.amitycourtmotel.co.nz; 35 Broadway N; d & apt $130-200;) has upped the town's accommodation standings 100%.

OFF THE BEATEN TRACK

FORGOTTEN WORLD HIGHWAY

The 155km road between Stratford and Taumarunui (SH43) has become known as the Forgotten World Hwy. The drive winds through hilly bush country with just a short section (around 11km) of unsealed road, passing Maori pa (fortified villages), abandoned coal mines and memorials to those long gone. Allow four hours and plenty of stops, and fill up with petrol at either end (there's no petrol along the route itself). Pick up a pamphlet from i-SITEs or DOC visitor centres in the area.

The town of **Whangamomona** (population 30) is a highlight. This quirky village declared itself an independent republic in 1989 after disagreements with local councils. The town celebrates Republic Day in January every odd-numbered year, with a military-themed extravaganza. In the middle of town is the unmissable grand old **Whangamomona Hotel** (06-762 5823; www.whangamomonahotel.co.nz; 6018 Forgotten World Hwy; accommodation per person incl breakfast $75, mains $16-35; 11am-late), a pub offering simple accommodation and big country meals.

If you're not driving, **Eastern Taranaki Experience** (06-765 7482, 027 471 7136; www.eastern-taranaki.co.nz; day trips per person from $60) runs tours through the area. See also Forgotten World Adventures (p175).

PARIHAKA

From the mid-1860s Parihaka, a small Maori settlement east of SH45 near Pungarehu, became the centre of a peaceful resistance movement, one which involved not only other Taranaki tribes, but Maori from around the country. Its leaders, Te Whiti-o-Rongomai and Tohu Kakahi, were of both Taranaki and Ati-Awa descent.

After the Land Wars, confiscation of tribal lands was the central problem faced by Taranaki Maori, and under Te Whiti's leadership a new approach to this issue was developed: resisting European settlement through nonviolent methods.

When the government started surveying confiscated land on the Waimate plain in 1879, unarmed followers of Te Whiti, wearing the movement's iconic white feather in their hair and in good humour, obstructed development by ploughing troughs across roads, erecting random fences and pulling survey pegs. Many were arrested and held without trial on the South Island, but the protests continued and intensified. Finally, in November 1881 the government sent a force of over 1500 troops to Parihaka. Its inhabitants were arrested or driven away, and the village was later demolished. Te Whiti and Tohu were arrested and imprisoned until 1883. In their absence Parihaka was rebuilt and the ploughing campaigns continued into the 1890s.

In 2006 the NZ government issued a formal apology and financial compensation to the tribes affected by the invasion and confiscation of Parihaka lands.

Te Whiti's spirit lives on at Parihaka, with annual meetings of his descendants and a public music-and-arts **Parihaka International Peace Festival** held early each year. For more info see www.parihaka.com.

Surf Highway 45

Sweeping south from New Plymouth to Hawera, the 105km-long SH45 is known as Surf Highway 45. There are plenty of black-sand beaches dotted along the route, but don't expect to see waves crashing ashore the whole way. The drive generally just undulates through farmland – be ready to swerve for random tractors and cows. Pick up the *Surf Highway 45* brochure at visitor centres.

Oakura

POP 1380

From New Plymouth, the first cab off the rank is laid-back Oakura, 15km southwest on SH45. Its broad sweep of beach is hailed by waxheads for its right-hander breaks, but it's also great for families (take sandals – that black sand gets scorching hot). A surf shop on the main road, **Vertigo** (☑ 06-752 7363; www.vertigosurf.com; lessons from $80; ☺ 9am-5pm Mon-Fri, 10am-4pm Sat), runs surfing and stand-up paddle-boarding lessons. See also Tarawave Surf School (p203).

🛏 Sleeping

Wave Haven   HOSTEL $
(☑ 06-752 7800; www.thewavehaven.co.nz; cnr Lower Ahu Ahu Rd & SH45; dm/s/d from $25/50/60; @�🎅) A surfie backpackers close

to the big breaks, this colonial charmer has a coffee machine, a large deck to chill out on, surfboards, a couple of affable Newfoundland dogs and empty wine bottles strewn about the place.

Oakura Beach Holiday Park   HOLIDAY PARK $
(☑ 06-752 7861; www.oakurabeach.com; 2 Jans Tce; campsites from $20, cabins $70-140; @☎) Squeezed between the cliffs and the sea, this classic beachside park caters best to caravans but has simple cabins and well-placed spots to pitch a tent (absolute beachfront!).

Oakura Beach Motel   MOTEL $$
(☑ 06-752 7680; www.oakurabeachmotel.co.nz; 53 Wairau Rd; d from $115, extra person $20; ☎) A very quiet, seven-unit motel set back from the main road, just three minutes' walk to the beach. It's a '70s number, but the Scottish owners keep things shipshape, and there are 300 DVDs to choose from.

★ **Ahu Ahu Beach Villas**   BOUTIQUE HOTEL $$$
(☑ 06-752 7370; www.ahu.co.nz; 321 Lower Ahu Ahu Rd; d from $270; ☎) Pricey, but pretty amazing. Set on a knoll overlooking the big wide ocean, these luxury, architect-designed villas are superbly eccentric, with huge recycled timbers, bottles cast into walls, lichen-covered French tile roofs and polished-concrete floors with inlaid paua. A new lodge addition sleeps four. Rock stars stay here!

✖ Eating

Carriage Café
CAFE $

(☎06-752 7226; 1143 SH45; meals $10-20; ☺8.30am-3pm) Housed in a very slow-moving 1914 railway carriage set back from the main street, this is an unusual stop for good-value breakfast stacks, bacon-and-egg pies and cheese scones. Good coffee, too.

Cafe Mantra
INDIAN $$

(☎06-752 7303; www.cafemantra.co.nz; 1131 SH45; mains $14-23; ☺7.30am-2pm & 4.30-10pm) 'Let the good times roll' is the mantra at this roadside Indian cafe, which treads cross-cultural lines between curries, burgers, wood-fired pizzas, sandwiches, muffins, cakes and coffee. Closed Monday in winter.

Oakura to Opunake

From Oakura, SH45 veers inland, with detours to sundry beaches along the way. On the highway near Okato the buttermilk-coloured, 130-year-old **Stony River Hotel** (☎06-752 4253; www.stonyriverhotel.co.nz; 2502 SH45; tw/d/tr incl breakfast $95/120/150, mains $10-28; ☺lunch 10am-2pm Wed-Sun; ☐) has simple country-style en-suite rooms and a straight-up public bar.

Just after Warea is **Stent Rd**, a legendary shallow reef break suitable for experienced surfers (look for the painted-boulder sign: the street sign kept being stolen). Another famous spot is **Kumara Patch**, down Komene Rd west of Okato, which is a fast 150m left-hander.

A coastward turn-off at **Pungarehu** leads 3km to **Cape Egmont Lighthouse**, a photogenic cast-iron lighthouse moved here from Mana Island near Wellington in 1881. Abel Tasman sighted this cape in 1642 and called it 'Nieuw Zeeland'. There's a replica lighthouse off Bayly Rd a bit further west around the coast, built to house the original Cape

---

Egmont Lighthouse light after it was automated in 1986.

The road to Parihaka (p211) leads inland from this stretch of SH45.

Opunake

POP 1335

A summer town and the surfie epicentre of the 'Naki, Opunake has a sheltered family beach and plenty of challenging waves further out. **Dreamtime Surf Shop** (☎06-761 7570; www.opunakesurf.co.nz; cnr Tasman & Havelock Sts; surfboards/bodyboards/wetsuits per half-day $30/20/10; ☺9am-5pm, closed Sun Jun-Aug) has internet access and surf-gear hire.

⌁ Sleeping

Opunake Beach Holiday Park
HOLIDAY PARK $

(☎0800 758 009, 06-761 7525; www.opunake-beachnz.co.nz; Beach Rd; campsites/cabins/cottages $38/70/105; @☐) Opunake Beach Holiday Park is a mellow spot behind the surf beach. Sites are grassy, the camp kitchen is big, the amenities block is cavernous and the waves are just a few metres away.

Opunake Motel
& Backpackers
MOTEL, HOSTEL $

(☎06-761 8330; www.opunakemotel.co.nz; 36 Heaphy Rd; dm/s/d/f from $30/95/110/130; ☐) On the edge of some sleepy fields, Opunake Motel & Backpackers is a low-key, back-steet operation, with old-style motel rooms and a funky dorm lodge (a triumph in genuine retro).

Headlands
HOTEL $$

(☎06-761 8358; www.headlands.co.nz; 4 Havelock St; d $120-250) Just 100m back from the beach, Headlands is a new(ish) operation encompassing a mod, airy bistro (mains $10 to $35; open 8.30am to late) and an upmarket, three-storey accommodation tower. The best rooms snare brilliant sunsets. B&B and DB&B packages available.

✖ Eating

★Sugar Juice Café
CAFE $$

(42 Tasman St; snacks $4-10, mains $10-34; ☺9am-late Tue-Sat, to 4pm Sun; ☐) Sugar Juice Café has the best food on SH45. It's buzzy and brimming with delicious, homemade, filling things (try the crayfish-and-prawn ravioli or cranberry lamb shanks). Terrific coffee, salads, wraps, tarts, cakes and big brekkies too – don't pass it by. Also open Mondays in summer.

TARANAKI & WHANGANUI SURF HIGHWAY 45

> ## SNELLY!
>
> Opunake isn't just about the surf – it's also the birthplace of iconic middle-distance runner Peter Snell (b 1938), who showed his rivals a clean set of heels at the 1960 Rome and 1964 Tokyo Olympics. Old Snelly won the 800m gold in Italy, then followed up with 800m and 1500m golds in Japan. Legend! Check out his funky running statue outside the library.

ℹ️ Information

Opunake Library (📞0800 111 323; opunakel@ stdc.govt.nz; Tasman St; ⊙9am-5pm Mon-Fri, 9.30am-1pm Sat; 📶) Doubles as the local visitor information centre, with a couple of internet terminals and free 24-hour wi-fi in the forecourt.

Hawera

POP 11,100

Don't expect much urban virtue from agricultural Hawera, the largest town in South Taranaki. Still, it's a good pit stop for supplies, to stretch your legs, or to bed down for a night. And don't miss Elvis!

👁️ Sights & Activities

⭐ **KD's Elvis Presley Museum**   MUSEUM
(📞06-278 7624; www.elvismuseum.co.nz; 51 Argyle St; admission by donation) Elvis lives! At least he does at Kevin D Wasley's astonishing museum, which houses over 10,000 of the King's records and a mind-blowing collection of Elvis memorabilia collected over 50 years. 'Passion is an understatement', says KD. Just don't ask him about the chubby Vegas-era Elvis: his focus is squarely on the rock 'n' roll King from the '50s and '60s. Admission is by appointment, phone ahead.

Hawera Water Tower   TOWER, LOOKOUT
(www.southtaranaki.com; 55 High St; adult/child/ family $2.50/1/6; ⊙10am-2pm) The austere, 54.21m Hawera Water Tower beside the i-SITE is one of the coolest things in Hawera. Grab the key from the i-SITE, ascend the 215 steps, then scan the horizon for signs of life (you can see the coast and Mt Taranaki on a clear day).

Tawhiti Museum   MUSEUM
(www.tawhitimuseum.co.nz; 401 Ohangai Rd; adult/ child $12/6; ⊙10am-4pm Fri-Mon Feb-May & Sep-Dec, Sun only Jun-Aug, daily Jan) The excellent Tawhiti Museum houses a collection of exhibits, dioramas and creepily lifelike human figures modelled on people from the region. A large collection of tractors pays homage to rural heritage; there's also a bush railway and a 'Traders & Whalers' boat ride here (extra charges for both). It's near the corner of Tawhiti Rd, 4km north of town.

🛏️ Sleeping

Wheatly Downs Farmstay   FARMSTAY $
(📞06-278 6523; www.mttaranaki.co.nz; 484 Ararata Rd; campsites from $20, dm/s/tw $30/75/75, d with/without bathroom $130/75; 📶) Set in a

rural idyll, this heritage building is a classic, with its clunky wooden floors and no-nonsense fittings. Host Gary is an affable bloke, and might show you his special pigs. To get there, head past the turn-off to Tawhiti Museum and continue on Ararata Rd for 5.5km. Pick-ups by arrangement.

Hawera Central Motor Lodge   MOTEL $$
(📞06-278 8831; www.haweracentralmotorlodge. co.nz; 53 Princes St; d $140-175; 📶) The pick of the town's motels (better than any of those along South Rd), the shiny Hawera Central does things with style: grey-and-eucalypt colour scheme, frameless-glass showers, big flat-screen TVs, good security, DVD players, free movie library and free wi-fi.

🍴 Eating

Indian Zaika   INDIAN $$
(📞06-278 3198; www.indianzaika.co.nz; 91 Princes St; mains $17-20; ⊙11am-2pm Tue-Sat, 5pm-late daily; 🍴) For a fine lunch or dinner, try this spicy-smelling, black-and-white diner, serving decent curries in upbeat surrounds. The $10 takeaway lunches are a steal.

ℹ️ Information

South Taranaki i-SITE (📞06-278 8599; www. southtaranaki.com; 55 High St; ⊙8.30am-5pm Mon-Fri, 9.30am-4pm Sat & Sun) The South Taranaki low-down. Reduced winter weekend hours.

Whanganui

POP 42,150

With rafts of casual Huck Finn sensibility, Whanganui is a raggedy historic town on the banks of the wide Whanganui River. The local arts community is thriving: old port buildings are being turned into glass-art studios, and the town centre has been rejuvenated – there are few more appealing places to while away a sunny afternoon than beneath Victoria Ave's leafy canopy.

History

Maori settlement at Whanganui dates from around 1100. The first European on the river was Andrew Powers in 1831, but Whanganui's European settlement didn't take off until 1840 when the New Zealand Company could no longer satisfy Wellington's land demands – settlers moved here instead.

When the Maori understood that the gifts the Pakeha settlers had given them were in

Whanganui

Whanganui

◉ Top Sights
1 Sarjeant Gallery C2
2 Whanganui Regional Museum C2
3 Whanganui Riverboat Centre C3

◉ Sights
4 Chronicle Glass Studio C3
5 Durie Hill Elevator D3
6 War Memorial Tower D3

◉ Activities, Courses & Tours
7 Waimarie Paddle-Steamer
   Tours C3

◉ Sleeping
8 151 on London Motel A2
9 Aotea Motor Lodge A1
10 Astral Motel B1
11 Braemar House YHA B1
12 Grand Hotel B3
13 Riverview Motel C2
14 Siena Motor Lodge A2

15 Tamara Backpackers Lodge C2

◉ Eating
Big Orange .... (see 16)
16 Ceramic Lounge C3
17 Jolt Coffee House C3
18 New World A2
19 Spice Guru C3
20 Stellar C3
21 WA Japanese Kitchen C2
22 Yellow House Café B1

◉ Drinking & Nightlife
Grand Irish Pub .... (see 12)
23 Spirit'd B2

◉ Entertainment
24 Embassy 3 Cinemas C3

◉ Shopping
25 River Traders Market C3

permanent exchange for their land, they were understandably irate, and seven years of conflict ensued. Thousands of government troops occupied the Rutland Stockade in Queens Park. Ultimately, the struggle was settled by arbitration; during the Taranaki Land Wars the Whanganui Maoris assisted the Pakeha.

◉ Sights & Activities

★ **Whanganui Regional Museum** MUSEUM
(www.wrm.org.nz; Watt St, Queens Park; ⊘10am-4.30pm) FREE The Whanganui Regional Museum is one of NZ's better natural-history museums. Maori exhibits include the carved

Te Mata o Hoturoa war canoe and some vicious-looking *mere* (greenstone clubs). The colonial and wildlife installations are first rate, and there's plenty of button-pushing and drawer-opening to keep the kids engaged.

⭐ **Sarjeant Gallery** GALLERY
(☑06-349 0506; www.sarjeant.org.nz; Queens Park; ⊙10.30am-4.30pm) FREE About to temporarily relocate for earthquake-proofing when we visited, the elegant neoclassical Sarjeant Gallery covers the bases from historic to contemporary with its extensive permanent art exhibition and frequent special exhibits (including glass from the annual Wanganui Festival of Glass). Call or check the website to find out if the renovations are complete: if not, you can see selected works in gallery spaces above the i-SITE and nearby at 38 Taupo Quay.

⭐ **Whanganui Riverboat Centre** MUSEUM
(www.riverboats.co.nz; 1a Taupo Quay; ⊙10am-4pm) FREE The historical displays are interesting, but everyone's here for the *Waimarie*, the last of the Whanganui River paddle steamers. In 1900 she was shipped from England and paddled the Whanganui until she sank ingloriously at her mooring in 1952. Submerged for 41 years, she was finally raised, restored, then relaunched on the first day of the 21st century. She now offers two-hour tours along the Whanganui.

Chronicle Glass Studio GALLERY
(www.chronicleglass.co.nz; 2 Rutland St; ⊙9am-5pm Mon-Fri, 10am-3pm Sat & Sun) FREE The pick of Whanganui's many glass studios is the Chronicle Glass Studio where you can watch glass-blowers working, check out the gallery, take a weekend glass-blowing course ($390) or a one-hour 'Make a Paperweight' lesson ($100), or just hang out and warm up on a chilly afternoon.

Durie Hill Elevator TOWER
(www.wanganui.govt.nz; Anzac Pde; adult/child one-way $2/1; ⊙8am-6pm Mon-Fri, 10am-5pm Sat & Sun) Across City Bridge from downtown Whanganui, this elevator was built with grand visions for Durie Hill's residential future. A tunnel burrows 213m into the hillside, from where a 1919 elevator rattles 65.8m to the top. At the summit you can climb the 176 steps of the **War Memorial Tower** and scan the horizon for Mt Taranaki and Mt Ruapehu.

Putiki Church CHURCH
(20 Anaua St; per person $2, plus deposit $20; ⊙services 9am Sun) Across the City Bridge from town and 1km towards the sea is the Putiki Church (aka St Paul's Memorial Church). It's unremarkable externally but, just like the faithful pew-fillers, it's what's inside that counts: the interior is magnificent, completely covered in Maori carvings and *tukutuku* (woven panels). Show up for Sunday service, or borrow a key from the i-SITE.

Kai Iwi Beach BEACH
Kai Iwi Beach is a wild ocean frontier, strewn with black sand and masses of broken driftwood. To get here follow Great North Rd 4km north of town, then turn left onto Rapanui Rd and head seawards for 10km.

Splash Centre SWIMMING
(www.splashcentre.co.nz; Springvale Park, London St; adult/child $4.50/3, waterslide $3; ⊙6am-8pm Mon-Fri, 8am-6pm Sat & Sun) If the sea is angry, try the Splash Centre for a safe swim.

☞ Tours

Whanganui National Park has canoe, kayak and jetboat tours on the Whanganui River.

Waimarie Paddle-Steamer Tours BOAT TOUR
(☑06-347 1863, 0800 783 2637; www.riverboats. co.nz; 1a Taupo Quay; adult/child/family $39/15/89; ⊙tours 10am Oct-Mar; ☎) Take a two-hour trip up ol' man Whanganui on the historic PS *Waimarie*, the last of the river paddle steamers.

Wanganui City Guided Walking Tours WALKING TOUR
(☑06-349 3258; per person $10; ⊙10am & 2pm Sat) Sign up for one of two 90-minute guided tours through old Whanganui, giving your feet a workout as you pass historic sights. Tours depart the i-SITE (book tickets inside).

★ Festivals & Events

Vintage Weekend CULTURAL
(www.vintageweekend.co.nz) Time-travelling cars, clothes, music and architecture, and good times over three January days by the Whanganui River.

Wanganui Festival of Glass ARTS
(www.wanganuiglass.co.nz) Classy glass fest in September. Plenty of open studios, demonstrations and workshops.

WHANGANUI OR WANGANUI?

Yeah, we know, it's confusing. Is there a 'h' or isn't there? Either way, the pronunciation is identical: 'wan-ga', not (as in the rest of the country) 'fan-ga'.

Everything was originally spelled Wanganui, because in the local dialect *whanga* (harbour) is pronounced 'wan-ga'. However, in 1991 the New Zealand Geographic Board officially adopted the correct Maori spelling (with a 'h') for the Whanganui River and Whanganui National Park. This was a culturally deferential decision: the Pakeha-dominated town and region retained the old spelling, while the river area – Maori territory – adopted the new.

In 2009 the Board assented that the town and region should also adopt the 'h'. This caused much community consternation, opinions on the decision split almost evenly (outspoken mayor Michael Laws was particularly anti-'h'). Ultimately, NZ Minister for Land Information Maurice Williamson decreed that either spelling was acceptable, and that adopting the querulous 'h' is up to individual businesses or entities. A good old Kiwi compromise! Whanderful...

Whanganui Literary Festival CULTURAL
(www.facebook.com/whanganuiliteraryfestival) Thoughts, words, and thoughts about words. Every second September (odd-numbered years).

Cemetery Circuit Motorcycle Race SPORTS
(www.cemeterycircuit.co.nz) Pandemonic motorcycle race around Whanganui's city streets on Boxing Day. The southern hemisphere's version of the Isle of Man TT?

🛏 Sleeping

Anndion Lodge HOSTEL $
(📞06-343 3593, 0800 343 056; www.anndionlodge.co.nz; 143 Anzac Pde; s/d/f/ste from $75/88/105/135; @🎖🏊) Hell-bent on constantly improving and expanding their fabulous hyper-hostel, hosts Ann and Dion (Anndion, get it?) go to enormous lengths to make things homey: stereo systems, big TVs, spa, swimming pool, barbecue area, restaurant, bar, courtesy van etc. 'No is not in our vocabulary', says super-helpful Ann.

Tamara Backpackers Lodge HOSTEL $
(📞06-347 6300; www.tamaralodge.com; 24 Somme Pde; dm/s from $28/53, d & tw with/without bathroom $84/70; @🎖) Tamara is a photogenic, maze-like, two-storey heritage house with a wide balcony, lofty ceilings (people weren't taller in 1904 were they?), kitchen, TV lounge, free bikes and a leafy, hammock-hung back garden. Ask for one of the beaut doubles overlooking the river.

Braemar House YHA HOSTEL $
(📞06-348 2301; www.braemarhouse.co.nz; 2 Plymouth St; dm/s/d/tw $30/50/75/75, f $96-130, guesthouse incl breakfast s/d $95/130; @🎖) Riverside Braemar brings together an 1895 Victorian B&B guesthouse and a reliable YHA backpackers. Centrally heated guesthouse rooms are floral and fancy; airy dorms conjure up a bit more fun out the back. Chooks patrol the back yard.

Whanganui River
Top 10 Holiday Park HOLIDAY PARK $
(📞06-343 8402, 0800 272 664; www.wrivertop10.co.nz; 460 Somme Pde; campsites/cabins/units from $21/72/135; @🎖🏊) This tidy Top 10 park sits on the Whanganui's west bank 6km north of Dublin Bridge. Facilities (including pool, games room and jumping pillow) are prodigious. Kayak hire also available: the owners shuttle you upriver then you paddle back to camp. The budget cabins by the river have big-dollar views. Self-catering or dining in town is your best bet foodwise. Horizons (p219) buses go past here.

Aotea Motor Lodge MOTEL $$
(📞06-345 0303; www.aoteamotorlodge.co.nz; 390 Victoria Ave; d from $150, 1-bedroom ste from $190; 🎖) It gladdens the heart to see a job done well, and the owners of one of Whanganui's newest motels have done just that. On the upper reaches of Victoria Ave, this flashy, two-storey motel features roomy suites, lavish linen, leather chairs, dark timbers and plenty of marble and stone – classy stuff.

Kembali B&B B&B $$
(📞06-347 1727; www.bnb.co.nz/kembali.html; 26 Taranaki St, St Johns Hill; s/d incl breakfast from $110/125) Up on leafy St Johns Hill on the way to Taranaki, this home-spun B&B has two private upstairs guest rooms sleeping four, available on an exclusive-use basis. It's a sedate

place overlooking some wetlands, all achirp with tuis, pukekos and native whistling frogs.

151 on London Motel
MOTEL **$$**

(☑0800 151 566, 06-345 8668; www.151onlondon.co.nz; 151 London St; d $115-160, apt $200-280; 🛜) This five-year-old, snappy-looking spaceship of a motel wins plenty of fans with its architectural angles, quality carpets and linen, natty lime/silver/black colour scheme and big TVs. At the top of the price tree are some excellent upstairs/downstairs apartment-style units sleeping six: about as ritzy as Whanganui accommodation gets.

Siena Motor Lodge
MOTEL **$$**

(☑06-345 9009, 0800 888 802; www.siena.co.nz; 335 Victoria Ave; d $130-160; 🛜) Aiming for Tuscany but hitting Taranaki, the compact rooms here are four-star and spotless. Business travellers enjoy double glazing, a DVD library, gym passes, heated towel rails, coffee plungers and real coffee.

Riverview Motel
MOTEL **$$**

(☑06-345 2888, 0800 102 001; www.wanganuimotels.co.nz; 14 Somme Pde; d $98-150; 🛜) Take your pick from one of 10 older-but-updated kitchenette units in the main block, or the five spa suites out the back. Super-clean, affordable and central, with a charming Irish host.

Grand Hotel
HOTEL **$$**

(☑0800 843 472, 06-345 0955; www.thegrandhotel.co.nz; cnr St Hill & Guyton Sts; s/d/ste from $79/99/130; 🛜) If you can't face another soulless motel room, rooms at this stately old-school Whanganui survivor (built 1927) have a bit more personality (and all have bathrooms). Singles and doubles are basic but good value; suites are spacious. The Grand Irish Pub and a restaurant are downstairs.

Astral Motel
MOTEL **$$**

(☑06-347 9063, 0800 509 063; www.astralmotel.co.nz; 46 Somme Pde; s/d/f from $85/95/110; 🛜🎫) Astrally aligned with the very terrestrial Dublin Bridge nearby, rooms here are a bit dated and a tad noisy but are well serviced and good bang for your buck. There's also a pool and 24-hour check-in if you're rolling in off the midnight highway.

✖ Eating

Jolt Coffee House
CAFE **$**

(19 Victoria Ave; items $3-8; ⊙7am-4.30pm Mon-Fri, 7.30am-1pm Sat, 8am-1pm Sun) Give your morning a jolt at this hip coffee house inside a 105-year-old former pharmacy. There's not much on the menu (muffins, caramel slice, chocolate croissants): the focus is squarely on fair-trade caffeine. Pretend you're Bob Dylan at acoustic music nights on the second Friday of each month.

WA Japanese Kitchen
JAPANESE **$**

(☑06-345 1143; www.facebook.com/wa.wanganui; Victoria Court, Victoria Ave; sushi $2-3, mains $7-14; ⊙10am-5pm Mon & Tue, 10am-8pm Wed-Fri, 11am-8pm Sat) Duck into the quiet Victoria Court mini-mall on the main street and discover this sweet little Japanese restaurant, serving great-value sushi, bento boxes and donburi rice bowls.

Yellow House Café
CAFE **$** ✓

(cnr Pitt & Dublin Sts; meals $10-18; ⊙8am-4pm daily; 🖉) Take a walk away from the main drag for funky tunes, buttermilk pancakes, local art and courtyard tables beneath a chunky-trunk cherry blossom tree. Ooh look! Marmalade and almond tart! Actually, it's more of a taupe colour...

Big Orange
CAFE **$**

(www.facebook.com/bigorangecafe; 51 Victoria Ave; meals $9-22; ⊙7.30am-5pm Mon-Fri, 9am-late Sat, 9am-5pm Sun; 🛜) Inside a gorgeous old Whanganui red-brick building, Big Orange is a babbling espresso bar serving gourmet burgers, big breakfasts, muffins, cakes and sandwiches (try the BLT). The outdoor tables go berserk during summer.

New World
SUPERMARKET **$**

(www.newworld.co.nz; 374 Victoria Ave; ⊙7am-9pm) Self-catering option.

Spice Guru
INDIAN **$$**

(☑06-348 4851; www.spiceguru.co.nz; 23a Victoria Ave; mains $17-25; ⊙11am-2pm Tue-Sat, 5pm-late daily; 🖉) There are a few Indian joints in the River City (an affinity with the Ganges, perhaps?), but the Guru takes the cake for its charismatic black-and-chocolate-coloured interior, attentive service and flavoursome dishes (the chicken tikka masala is great). Plenty of vego options.

Ceramic Lounge
CAFE, LOUNGE **$$**

(www.facebook.com/ceramicloungebar; 51 Victoria Ave; mains $9-33; ⊙4pm-late Tue-Sat; 🛜) In a split-business arrangement with adjacent Orange, Ceramic takes over for the dinner shift, serving upmarket cafe food (killer quesadillas) in a low-lit, rust-coloured interior. Occasional DJs ooze tunes across the tables to cocktail-sipping seducers.

Stellar
CAFE, BAR $$

(www.stellarwanganui.co.nz; 2 Victoria Ave; mains $15-33; ⊙11am-late Mon-Fri, 9am-late Sat & Sun; ☎) Stellar is a buzzy bar-cum-restaurant in a stellar location on the corner of the main street and Taupo Quay. Inside, try to ignore the gaming machines and tuck into pizzas, steaks, big salads and cold beers.

 Drinking & Nightlife

Check out Stellar and Ceramic Lounge, too.

Grand Irish Pub
IRISH PUB

(www.thegrandhotel.co.nz; cnr St Hill & Guyton Sts; ⊙11am-late) Siphoning into NZ's insatiable (and, it has to be said, annoying) passion for Irish pubs, the Grand Hotel's version is as good a spot as any to elbow down a few pints of Guinness on a misty river afternoon. Good pub meals too.

Spirit'd
BAR

(75 Guyton St; ⊙10am-late) Pool tables, happy hours, Jack Daniels, Metallica on the jukebox and local young bucks trying to out-strut each other – just like 1989 minus the cigarettes.

☆ **Entertainment**

Embassy 3 Cinemas
CINEMA

(☑06-348 7958; www.embassy3.co.nz; 34 Victoria Ave; adult/child from $12.50/9, Tue from $9; ⊙11am-midnight) Nightly new-release blockbusters selling out faster than you can say 'bored Whanganui teenagers'.

🛍 **Shopping**

River Traders Market
FARMERS MARKET

(www.therivertraders.co.nz; Moutoa Quay; ⊙9am-1pm Sat) The Saturday-morning River Traders Market, next to the Riverboat Centre, is crammed with local crafts and organic produce.

ℹ **Information**

DOC (Department of Conservation; ☑06-349 2100; www.doc.govt.nz; 34-36 Taupo Quay; ⊙8.30am-4.30pm Mon-Fri)
Post Office (115 Victoria Ave; ⊙8.30am-5pm Mon-Fri, 9am-1pm Sat)
Whanganui Hospital (☑06-348 1234; www.wdhb.org.nz; 100 Heads Rd; ⊙24hr) Accident and emergency.
Whanganui i-SITE (☑06-349 0508; www.whanganuinz.com; 31 Taupo Quay; ⊙8.30am-5pm Mon-Fri, 9am-3pm Sat & Sun; ☎) Tourist and DOC information (if the DOC office across the street is closed) in an impressive renovated riverside building (check out the old floorboards!). Internet access available.

ℹ **Getting There & Away**

AIR

Whanganui Airport (www.wanganuiairport.co.nz; Airport Rd) is 4km south of town, across the river towards the sea.
Air New Zealand (☑06-348 3500; www.airnewzealand.co.nz; 133 Victoria Ave; ⊙9am-5pm Mon-Fri) Daily direct flights to/from Auckland and Wellington, with onward connections.

BUS

InterCity (www.intercity.co.nz) buses operate from the **Whanganui Travel Centre** (☑06-345 7100; 160 Ridgeway St; ⊙8.15am-5.15pm Mon-Fri). Some destinations:

DESTINATION	PRICE ($)	DURATION (HR)	FREQUENCY (DAILY)
Auckland	65	8	1
Hamilton	58	5½	1
New Plymouth	29	2½	1
Palmerston North	48	2¾	3
Wellington	39	4	3

Naked Bus (www.nakedbus.com) departs from Whanganui i-SITE to most North Island centres, including the following:

DESTINATION	PRICE ($)	DURATION (HR)	FREQUENCY (DAILY)
Auckland	39	9	1
Hamilton	32	7	1
New Plymouth	18	2½	1
Palmerston North	25	1½	1
Wellington	20	4	1

ℹ **Getting Around**

BICYCLE

Bike Shed (☑06-345 5500; www.bikeshed.co.nz; cnr Ridgway & St Hill Sts; ⊙8am-5.30pm Mon-Fri, 9am-2pm Sat) Hires out bikes from $35 per day, including helmet and lock. Also a good spot for info on the Mountains to Sea (p222) bike trail from Mt Ruapehu to Whanganui, which is part of the **Nga Haerenga, New Zealand Cycle Trail** (www.nzcycletrail.com).

BUS

Horizons (www.horizons.govt.nz; tickets adult/child $2.50/1.50) Operates four looped council-run bus routes departing Trafalgar Square shopping centre on Taupo Quay, including orange and purple routes past the Whanganui River Top 10 Holiday Park in Aramoho.

TAXI

Rivercity Cabs (☑06-345 3333, 0800 345 3333; www.wanganui.bluebubbletaxi.co.nz)

Whanganui National Park

The Whanganui River – the lifeblood of Whanganui National Park – curls 290km from its source on Mt Tongariro to the Tasman Sea. It's the longest navigable river in NZ, and today conveys canoes, kayaks and jetboats, its waters shifting from deep mirror greens in summer to turbulent winter browns.

The native bush here is thick podocarp broad-leaved forest interspersed with ferns. Occasionally you'll see poplar and other introduced trees along the river, remnants of long-vanished settlements. Traces of Maori settlements also appear, with old *pa* (fortified village) and *kainga* (village) sites, and Hauhau *niu* (war and peace) poles at the convergence of the Whanganui and Ohura Rivers at Maraekowhai.

The impossibly scenic Whanganui River Rd, a partially unsealed river-hugging road from Whanganui to Pipiriki, makes a fabulous alternative to the faster but less magical SH4.

History

In Maori legend the Whanganui River was formed when Mt Taranaki, after brawling with Mt Tongariro over the lovely Mt Pihanga, fled the central North Island for the sea, leaving a long gouge behind him. He turned west at the coast, finally stopping at his current address. Mt Tongariro sent cool water to heal the gouge – thus the Whanganui River was born.

Kupe, the great Polynesian explorer, is believed to have travelled 20km up the Whanganui around AD 800; Maori lived here by 1100. By the time Europeans put down roots in the late 1830s, Maori settlements lined the river valley. Missionaries sailed upstream and their settlements – at Hiruharama, Ranana, Koriniti and Atene – have survived to this day.

Paddle steamers first tackled the river in the mid-1860s. In 1886 a Whanganui company established the first commercial steamer transport service. Others soon followed, utilising the river between Whanganui and Taumarunui.

NZ's contemporary tourism leviathan was seeded here. Internationally advertised trips on the 'Rhine of Maoriland' became so popular that by 1905, 12,000 tourists a year were making the trip upriver from Whanganui to Pipiriki or downriver from Taumarunui. The engineering feats and skippering ability required on the river became legendary.

From 1918 land upstream of Pipiriki was granted to returning WWI soldiers. Farming here was a major challenge, with many families struggling for years to make the rugged land productive. Only a few endured into the early 1940s.

The completion of the railway from Auckland to Wellington and the improving roads ultimately signed river transport's death warrant; 1959 saw the last commercial riverboat voyage. Today, just one old-fleet vessel cruises the river – the PS *Waimarie* (p215).

◉ Sights

The scenery along the **Whanganui River Road** en route to Pipiriki is camera conducive – stark, wet mountain slopes plunge into lazy jade stretches of the Whanganui River.

From **Aramoana Hill** near the southern end of the road there's a terrific view: peaks, paddocks, poplars and the curling river. The Maori villages of **Atene**, **Koriniti**, **Ranana** and **Hiruharama** crop up as you travel upstream – ask a local before you go sniffing around. You can wander around **Koriniti Marae** (☑06-342 8198; www.koriniti.com; Koriniti Pa Rd), between the road and the river (look for the signs), unless there's a *marae* function happening.

A French Catholic mission led by Suzanne Aubert established the Daughters of Our Lady of Compassion in Jerusalem in 1892. Around a corner in the road, the picture-perfect spire of **St Joseph's Church** stands tall on a spur of land above a deep river bend. Other sights along the road include the restored 1854 **Kawana Flour Mill** (www.historic.org.nz; ☉dawn-dusk) **FREE** near Matahiwi, **Operiki Pa** and other *pa* sites.

Pipiriki is beside the river at the north end of Whanganui River Rd. It's a rainy river town without much going on (no shops or petrol), but was once a humming

Whanganui National Park Area

holiday hot spot serviced by river steamers and paddleboats. Seemingly cursed, the old **Pipiriki Hotel**, formerly a glamorous resort full of international tourists, burned to the ground twice. Recent attempts to rebuild it have stalled due to funding issues; it's been vandalised and stripped of anything of value, leaving a hollow brick husk riddled with potential. Pipiriki is the end point for canoe trips coming down the river and the launching pad for jetboat rides.

Standing in mute testimony to the optimism of the early settlers is the **Bridge to Nowhere**, built in 1936. The lonesome bridge – once part of a long-lost 4.5m-wide roadway from Raetihi to the river – is on the Mangapurua Track (p223), or it's a 40-minute walk from Mangapurua Landing upstream from Pipiriki, accessible by jetboat.

🏃 Activities

Canoeing & Kayaking

The most popular stretch of river for canoeing and kayaking is the 145km downstream run from Taumarunui to Pipiriki. This has been added to the NZ Great Walks system as the **Whanganui Journey**. It's a Grade II river – easy enough for the inexperienced,

Whanganui National Park Area
⊙ **Sights**
1 Aramoana Hill..............................C5
2 Bridge to Nowhere.......................B2
3 Downes Hut.................................C4
4 John Coull Hut.............................B1
5 Kawana Flour Mill........................C3
6 Koriniti Marae..............................C4
7 Operiki Pa...................................C4
8 St Joseph's Church.......................C3
9 Tieke Kainga...............................C2
10 Whakahoro Bunkroom...................C1

🛏 **Sleeping**
11 Bridge to Nowhere Lodge..............B2
12 Flying Fox..................................C4
13 Kohu Cottage..............................C4
14 Rivertime Lodge...........................C4
   St Joseph's Church.................(see 8)
15 Te Punga Homestead.....................C4

with enough moiling rapids to keep things interesting. If you need a Great Walks Ticket you must arrange one before you start paddling; see p222.

Taumarunui to Pipiriki is a five-day/four-night trip; **Ohinepane to Pipiriki** is a four-day/three-night trip; and **Whakahoro to Pipiriki** is a three-day/two-night trip. **Taumarunui to Whakahoro** is a popular overnight trip, especially for weekenders, or you can do a one-day trip from **Taumarunui to Ohinepane** or **Ohinepane to Whakahoro**. From Whakahoro to Pipiriki, 87km downstream, there's no road access so you're wed to the river for a few days. Most canoeists stop at Pipiriki.

The season for canoe trips is usually from September to Easter. Up to 5000 people make the river trip each year, mostly between Christmas and the end of January. During winter the river is almost deserted – cold currents run swift and deep as wet weather and short days deter potential paddlers.

To hire a two-person Canadian canoe for one/three/five days costs around $80/200/250 per person not including transport (around $50 per person). A single-person kayak costs about $60 per day. Operators provide you with everything you need, including life jackets and waterproof drums (essential if you go bottom-up).

You can also take guided canoe or kayak trips – prices start at around $350/850 per person for a two-/five-day guided trip.

Operators include the following:

Awa Tours CANOEING, KAYAKING
(☎027 698 5135; www.awatours.co.nz; Raetihi)

Blazing Paddles CANOEING, KAYAKING
(☎07-895 5261, 0800 252 946; www.blazingpaddles.co.nz; Taumarunui)

Canoe Safaris CANOEING, KAYAKING
(☎0800 272 335, 06-385.9237; www.canoesafaris.co.nz; Ohakune)

Taumarunui Canoe Hire CANOEING, KAYAKING
(☎07-895 7483, 0800 226 6348; www.taumarunui-canoehire.co.nz; Taumarunui)

Unique Whanganui River Experience CANOEING, KAYAKING
(☎06-323 9842, 027 245 2567; www.unique-whanganuiriver.co.nz; Feilding)

Whanganui River Canoes CANOEING, KAYAKING
(☎06-385 4176, 0800 408 888; www.whanganui-rivercanoes.co.nz; Raetihi)

Wades Landing Outdoors CANOEING, KAYAKING
(☎027 678 6461, 07-895 4854; www.whanganui.co.nz; Raurimu)

Yeti Tours CANOEING, KAYAKING
(☎06-385 8197; www.canoe.co.nz; Ohakune)

Jetboating

Hold onto your hats – jetboat trips give you the chance to see parts of the river that would otherwise take you days to paddle through. Jetboats depart from Pipiriki and Whanganui; four-hour tours start at around $125 per person. The following operators can also provide transport to the river ends of the Matemateaonga and Mangapurua Tracks.

Bridge to Nowhere Tours JETBOATING, CANOEING
(☎06-385 4622, 0800 480 308; www.bridgetonowhere.co.nz) Canoe trips also available.

Whanganui River Adventures JETBOATING, CANOEING
(☎0800 862 743; www.whanganuiriveradventures.co.nz; Pipiriki) Canoe trips and camping at Pipiriki also available.

Whanganui Scenic Experience Jet JETBOATING, CANOEING
(☎06-342 5599, 0800 945 335; www.whanganui-scenicjet.com) Canoe trips also available.

Tramping

Bridge to Nowhere Track TRAMPING
The most popular track in Whanganui National Park is the 40-minute walk from Mangapurua Landing to the Bridge to Nowhere

(p220), 30km upstream from Pipiriki by jetboat. Contact jetboat operators for transport (around $100 per person one-way).

Atene Viewpoint Walk & Atene Skyline Track
TRAMPING

At Atene, on the Whanganui River Rd about 22km north of the SH4 junction, you can tackle the short Atene Viewpoint Walk, about a one-hour ascent. The track travels through native bush and farmland along a 1959 roadway built by the former Ministry of Works and Development during investigations for a Whanganui River hydroelectric scheme (a dam was proposed at Atene that would have flooded the river valley almost as far as Taumarunui). Expect great views across the national park.

From the Viewpoint Walk you can continue along the circular 18km Atene Skyline Track. The track takes six to eight hours, showcasing native forest, sandstone bluffs and the Taumata Trig (523m), with its broad views as far as Mt Ruapehu, Mt Taranaki and the Tasman Sea. The track ends back on the Whanganui River Rd, 2km downstream from the starting point.

Matemateaonga Track
TRAMPING

Three to four days from end to end, the 42km Matemateaonga Track gets kudos as one of NZ's best walks. Probably due to its remoteness, it doesn't attract the hordes of trampers that amass on NZ's more famous tracks. Penetrating deep into wild bush and hill country, it follows the crest of the Matemateaonga Range along the route of the Whakaihuwaka Rd, started in 1911 to create a more direct link from Stratford to the railway at Raetihi. WWI interrupted planning and the road was never finished.

On a clear day, a 1½-hour side trip to the top of Mt Humphries (730m) rewards you with sigh-inducing views all the way to Mt Taranaki and the volcanoes of Tongariro. There's a steep section between the Whanganui River (75m above sea level) and the Puketotara Hut (427m above sea level), but mostly it's easy walking. There are four DOC backcountry huts along the way: Omaru (eight bunks), Pouri (12 bunks), Ngapurua (10 bunks) and Puketotara (12 bunks); hut tickets cost $15 per person per night. There's road access at the track's western end.

Mangapurua/Kaiwhakauka Track
TRAMPING

The Mangapurua/Kaiwhakauka Track is a 40km trail between Whakahoro and the Mangapurua Landing, both on the Whanganui River. The track runs along the Mangapurua and Kaiwhakauka Streams (both Whanganui River tributaries). Between these valleys a side track leads to the 663m Mangapurua Trig, the area's highest point, from which cloudless views extend to the Tongariro and Egmont National Park volcanoes. The route also passes the Bridge to Nowhere (p220). Walking the track takes 20 hours (three to four days). The Whakahoro Bunkroom at the Whakahoro end of the track is the only hut ($10), but there's plenty of good camping (free to $10). There's road access to the track both at the Whakahoro end and from a side track from the end of the Ruatiti Valley–Ohura Rd (from Raetihi).

Mountain Biking

The Whanganui River Rd and Mangapurua/Kaiwhakauka Track have been incorporated into the 317km Mountains to Sea (www.mountainstosea.co.nz) Mt Ruapehu–Whanganui bike track, part of the Nga Haerenga, New Zealand Cycle Trail (www.nzcycletrail.com) project. As part of the experience, from Mangapurua Landing on the Whanganui River near the Bridge to Nowhere, you catch a (prebooked) jetboat downstream to Pipiriki, then continue riding down the Whanganui River Rd. For bike hire and track info try Bike Shed in Whanganui.

Tours

See also Activities (p220) for info on canoe and jetboat tours on the Whanganui River.

---

① CAMPING & HUT PASSES

Great Walk Tickets are required in Whanganui National Park from 1 October to 30 April for the use of huts (adult/child $32/free) and campsites (adult/child $14/free) between Taumarunui and Pipiriki. Outside the main season you'll only need a Backcountry Hut Pass (adult/child 1 year $122/61, 6 months $92/46), or you can pay on a night-by-night basis (adult/child $5/free). Passes and tickets can be purchased online (www.greatwalks.co.nz), via email (greatwalks@doc.govt.nz) or by phone (☎ 0800 694 732); or at DOC offices in Whakapapa, Taumarunui, Ohakune or Whanganui.

Whanganui Tours GUIDED TOUR
(☎06-345 3475; www.whanganuitours.co.nz) Join the mailman on the Whanganui River Rd to Pipiriki ($63; departs 7am) with lots of social and historical commentary. Returns mid-afternoon. Ask about transport/cycling options from Jerusalem back down the road to Whanganui.

Whanganui River Road Tours GUIDED TOUR
(☎0800 201 234; www.whanganuiriverroad.com; per person $80) Take a five-hour minibus ride up the River Rd with lots of stops and commentary. Or, you can take a truncated tour up to Pipiriki then cycle back to Whanganui ($100 per person; bikes supplied). Minimum four people on both tours.

🛏 Sleeping

🛏 Whanganui National Park

The park has a sprinkling of huts, a lodge and numerous camping grounds. Along the Taumarunui–Pipiriki section are three huts classified as Great Walks Huts during summer and Backcountry Huts in the off-season: **Whakahoro Bunkroom**, **John Coull Hut** and **Tieke Kainga Hut**, which has been revived as a *marae* (you can stay here, but full *marae* protocol must be observed). On the lower part of the river, **Downes Hut** is on the west bank, opposite Atene. See the boxed text for booking info.

Bridge to Nowhere Lodge LODGE $
(☎0800 480 308; www.bridgetonowhere.co.nz; dm/d $50/100) Across the river from the Tieke Kainga *marae*, this remote lodge lies deep in the national park, 21km upriver from Pipiriki near the Matemateaonga Track. The only way to get here is by jetboat from Pipiriki or on foot. It has a licensed bar, and meals are quality home-cooked affairs. The lodge also runs jetboat, canoe and mountain-bike trips. Transport/accommodation/meals packages available.

🛏 Whanganui River Road

There's a free informal campsite with toilets and cold water at Pipiriki, and another one (even less formal) just north of Atene. There's also a campsite at Pipiriki run by Whanganui River Adventures (p221) – call for info.

From south to north, non-camping accommodation (book in advance) includes the following:

REMOTE TRACK ACCESS

The Matemateaonga and Mangapurua/Kaiwhakauka Tracks are brilliant longer tramps (DOC booklets $1, or see www.doc.govt.nz for up-to-date track info). Both are one-way tracks beginning (or ending) at remote spots on the river, so you have to organise jetboat transport to or from the river trailheads – ask any jetboat operator. Between Pipiriki and the Matemateaonga Track is around $50 per person; for the Mangapurua Track it's around $100.

Rivertime Lodge LODGE $$
(☎06-342 5599; www.rivertimelodge.co.nz; 1569 Whanganui River Rd; d $160, extra person $35) A rural idyll: grassy hills folding down towards the river and the intermittent bleating of sheep. Rivertime is a simple riverside farmhouse with two bedrooms, a laundry, a wood heater, a lovely deck and no TV! Sleeps five; meals available.

Te Punga Homestead LODGE $$
(☎06-342 8239; www.tepunga.co.nz; 2929 Whanganui River Rd; campsites $25, d $150, extra person $25; 🗻) A basic self-contained cottage next to the owner's house, just south of Atene. You can also park your campervan or pitch a tent in the adjacent paddock. Sleeps five.

Flying Fox LODGE, B&B $$
(☎06-342 8160; www.theflyingfox.co.nz; Whanganui River Rd; campsites $20, d $100-200; 🗻) 🍃 This eco-attuned getaway is on the riverbank across from Koriniti. You can self-cater in the Brewers Cottage, James K or Glory Cart (self-contained cottages), opt for B&B ($120 per person) or pitch a tent in a bush clearing. Access is by jetboat; otherwise you can park across the river from the accommodation then soar over the river on the flying fox.

Kohu Cottage RENTAL HOUSE $
(☎06-342 8178; kohu.cottage@xtra.co.nz; 3154 Whanganui River Rd; d from $70) A snug little cream-coloured weatherboard cottage (100 years old) above the road in Koriniti, sleeping three bods. There's a basic kitchen and a wood fire for chilly riverside nights.

St Joseph's Church HOSTEL $
(☎06-342 8190; www.compassion.org.nz; Whanganui River Rd; dm adult/child $25/15, linen $10) Taking in bedraggled travellers and offering

20 dorm-style beds and a simple kitchen, the sisters at St Joe's await to issue your deliverance – book ahead for the privilege. Moutoa Island, site of a historic 1864 battle, is just downriver.

❶ Information

For national park information, try the affable Whanganui (p218) or Taumarunui (p176) i-SITEs, or check out www.doc.govt.nz or www.whanganuiriver.co.nz. Otherwise, a more tangible resource is the NZ Recreational Canoeing Association's *Guide to the Whanganui River* ($10). The **Wanganui Tramping Club** (⌀ 06-346 5597; www.wanganuitrampingclub.org.nz) puts out the quarterly *Wanganui Tramper* magazine.

There's no mobile-phone coverage along the River Rd, and no petrol or shops. There are a couple of takeaway food vans in Pipiriki open during summer, plus the casual cafe **Matahiwi Gallery** (⌀ 06-342 8112; www.matahiwigallery. com; 3925 Whanganui River Rd; snacks $3-5; ☉ 9am-3.30pm Thu-Sun) in Matahiwi (call ahead to ensure it's open).

❶ Getting There & Away

From the north, there's road access to the Whanganui River at Taumarunui, Ohinepane and Whakahoro, though the latter is a long, remote drive on mostly unsealed roads. Roads to Whakahoro lead off from Owhango and Raurimu, both on SH4. There isn't any further road access to the river until Pipiriki.

From the south, the Whanganui River Rd veers off SH4 14km north of Whanganui, rejoining it at Raetihi, 91km north of Whanganui. It takes about two hours to drive the 79km between Whanganui and Pipiriki. The full circle from Whanganui through Pipiriki and Raetihi and back along SH4 takes four hours minimum (longer if you want to stop and look at some things). Alternatively, take a River Rd tour from Whanganui.

Note that the River Rd is unsealed between Ranana and 4km south of Pipiriki, although road crews are making steady progress in sealing the entire route.

Palmerston North

POP 83,800

The rich sheep- and dairy-farming Manawatu region embraces the districts of Rangitikei to the north and Horowhenua to the south. The hub of it all, on the banks of the Manawatu River, is Palmerston North, with its moderate high-rise attempts reaching up from the plains. Massey University, NZ's largest, informs the town's cultural and social structures. As a result 'Palmy' has an open-minded, rurally bookish vibe.

None of this impressed a visiting John Cleese who scoffed, 'If you ever do want to kill yourself, but lack the courage, I think a visit to Palmerston North will do the trick.' The city exacted revenge by naming a rubbish dump after him.

⊙ Sights

★ **New Zealand Rugby Museum**   MUSEUM
(www.rugbymuseum.co.nz; Te Manawa Complex, 326 Main St; adult/child/family $12.50/5/30; ☉ 10am-5pm) Fans of the oval ball holler about the New Zealand Rugby Museum, an amazing space overflowing with rugby paraphernalia, from a 1905 All Blacks jumper to a scrum machine and the actual whistle used to start the first game of every Rugby World Cup. Of course, NZ won the 2011 Rugby World Cup: quiz the staff about the All Blacks' 2015 prospects.

★ **Te Manawa**   MUSEUM
(www.temanawa.co.nz; 326 Main St; ☉ 10am-5pm) FREE Te Manawa merges a museum and art gallery into one experience. Vast collections join the dots between 'life, art and mind'. The museum has a strong Maori focus, while the gallery's exhibits change frequently. Kids will get a kick out of the hands-on exhibits and interactive play area. The New Zealand Rugby Museum is in the same complex.

The Square   LANDMARK
(The Square) Taking the English village green concept to a whole new level, the Square is Palmy's heart and soul. Seven spacey hectares, with a clock tower, duck pond, giant chess, Maori carvings, statues and trees of all seasonal dispositions. Locals eat lunch on the manicured lawns in the sunshine.

🏃 Activities

Swing into the i-SITE and pick up the *Discover City Walkways* booklet and the *Cycling the Country Road Manawatu* brochure.

Lido Aquatic Centre   SWIMMING
(www.lidoaquaticcentre.co.nz; 50 Park Rd; adult/child $4/3, hydroslide $5; ☉ 6am-8pm Mon-Thu, 6am-9pm Fri, 8am-8pm Sat & Sun) When the summer plains bake, dive into the Lido Aquatic Centre. It's a long way from Lido Beach in Venice, but it has a 50m pool, waterslides, a cafe and a gym.

Palmerston North

Palmerston North

Top Sights
1 New Zealand Rugby
  Museum B3
2 Te Manawa B3

Sights
3 Square C2

Sleeping
4 @ the Hub B2
5 Bentleys Motor Inn C3
6 Café de Paris B3
7 Fitzherbert Castle Motel C3
8 Peppertree Hostel C1

Eating
9 Café Cuba B2
10 Halikarnas C2
11 Indian2nite B2
12 Pak 'n Save C3
13 Tomato Cafe B2

Drinking & Nightlife
14 Brewer's Apprentice B3
15 Celtic Inn C1
16 Fish C1

Entertainment
17 Centrepoint Theatre B3
18 CinemaGold C2
   Downtown Cinemas ....(see 18)

Manawatu Gorge Experience Jet JETBOATING
(📞06-342 5599, 0800 945 335; www.manawatugorgejet.com; 25min tours per person from $75) Jetboat rides through gorgeous Manawatu Gorge, about 25 minutes from Palmy.

☞ Tours

Feilding Saleyard Tours CULTURAL TOUR
(📞06-323 3318; www.feilding.co.nz; Feilding; tours $10; ⏰11am Fri) Local farmers instruct you in the gentle art of selling livestock at this small town north of the city centre. Farmers market from 9am to 2pm every Friday.

Tui Brewery Tours GUIDED TOUR
(📞06-376 0815.; www.tuibrewery.co.nz; SH2, Mangatainoka; 35min tours per person $20; ⏰11am & 2pm) Even if you're more of a craft-beer fan than a drinker of ubiquitous Tui, this boozy tour is a worthwhile outing. Check out the interesting brewery and museum and taste a Tui or three. About 30 minutes east of Palmerston North; bookings essential.

✲✲ Festivals & Events

Festival of Cultures CULTURAL, FOOD & WINE
(www.foc.co.nz) Massive arts/culture/lifestyle festival in late March, with a food-and-craft market in the Square.

International Jazz & Blues Festival MUSIC
(www.jazzandblues.co.nz) All things jazzy, bluesy and swingin' in late May/early June, including plenty of workshops.

Manawatu Wine & Food Festival FOOD & WINE
(www.mwff.co.nz) Mid-June weekend fiesta of culinary creations and the best local drops.

Manawatu Harvest Festival FOOD, CULTURE
(www.maifarm.org.nz) 🖉 Showcases local harvest delights and sustainable living practices in October.

🛏 Sleeping

Peppertree Hostel HOSTEL $
(☑06-355 4054; www.peppertreehostel.co.nz; 121 Grey St; dm/s/d $30/53/72; @🖙) Inexplicably strewn with green-painted boots, this endearing 100-year-old house is the best budget option in town. Mattresses are thick, the kitchen will never run out of spatulas, and the piano and wood fire make things feel downright homey. Doubles off the kitchen are a bit noisy – angle for one at the back.

@ the Hub HOTEL, HOSTEL $
(☑06-356 8880; www.atthehub.co.nz; 10 King St; r per night/week from $85/350; 🖙) There are lots of students in Palmy, and lots of them stay here during the term. But plenty of rooms are usually available for travellers too. Book a serviced en-suite double unit with kitchenette, or a simple student shoebox (also with en suite). Great location, great value.

**Palmerston North
Holiday Park** HOLIDAY PARK $
(☑06-358 0349; www.palmerstonnorthholidaypark.co.nz; 133 Dittmer Dr; campsites/cabins from $35/45, d unit $80; 🖙) About 2km from the Square, off Ruha St, this shady park with daisy-speckled lawns has a bit of a bootcamp feel to it, but it's quiet, affordable and right beside Victoria Esplanade gardens. Great for kids.

Café de Paris HOTEL $
(☑06-355 2130; www.cafedeparisinn.co.nz; 267 Main St; s/d $60/80; ℗) It ain't Montmartre, but this friendly, 1893 boozer three minutes' walk from the Square has a warren of surprisingly decent pub rooms upstairs, all with TV, en suite and rather kooky furnishings. Good value! Limited off-street parking.

★Plum Trees Lodge LODGE $$
(☑06-358 7813; www.plumtreeslodge.co.nz; 97 Russell St; s/d incl breakfast from $150/185; 🖙) In a flat-grid town with more motels than seems plausible, this secluded lodge comes as sweet relief. It's brilliantly designed using recycled timbers from demolition sites, with raked timber ceilings punctuated with skylights, and a balcony set among swaying boughs. Romantic nights slide lazily into breakfast – a sumptuous hamper of fresh fruit, croissants, jams, eggs, cheese, coffee and juice.

Fitzherbert Castle Motel MOTEL $$
(☑06-358 3888, 0800 115 262; www.fitzcastlemotel.co.nz; 124 Fitzherbert Ave; d $110-195; 🖙) It looks unapologetically like a Tudor castle from outside, but inside it's more like an intimate hotel. Fourteen immaculate rooms with cork-tiled bathroom floors and quality carpets, plenty of trees, friendly staff and small kitchens in some units. Free wi-fi and laundry.

Bentleys Motor Inn MOTEL, APARTMENT $$
(☑06-358 7074, 0800 2368 5397; www.bentleysmotorinn.co.nz; cnr Linton & Chaytor Sts; ste $155-320) Putting a corporate spin on the motel theme, Bentleys' five-star apartments are worth the investment. Inside are new appliances, DVD player, spa, stereo, contemporary furnishings and Sky TV; outside are a full-blown gym, squash court and sauna. You could stay here for weeks...

🍴 Eating

Pak 'n Save SUPERMARKET $
(www.paknsave.co.nz; 335 Ferguson St; ⊙8am-10pm) Cheap and cheerful.

★Tomato Cafe CAFE, BISTRO $$
(☑06-357 6663; www.tomatocafe.co.nz; 72 George St; brunch $7-30, dinner $16-30; ⊙7am-4pm Sun-Wed, to 9pm Thu-Sat) This brilliant new cafe is a buzzy yellow box plastered with 'Kiwiana': retro NZ album covers, photos, prints and canvases. Infused with entrepreneurial spirit, the boss gets up at 5am to make the daily dough. His enthusiasm is infectious: happy staff deliver beaut salads, pizzas, croissant BLTs and excellent eggs Benedict. Friday-evening happy hour; occasional live jazz. Winner!

Izakaya Yatai
JAPANESE $$

(06-356 1316; www.yatai.co.nz; 316 Featherston St; mains $16-30; noon-2pm Tue-Fri, 6-9pm Tue-Sat) Simple, fresh, authentic Japanese food cooked by Atsushi Taniyama in an unpretentious suburban house with empty sake bottles lining the window sills. Front-of-house host Barbara comes with a big personality. Set menus available.

Indian2nite
INDIAN $$

(06-353 7400; www.indian2nite.com; 22 George St; mains $10-19; 10.30am-3pm & 5pm-late daily;) With just the right touch of Bollywood schmaltz, this reasonably upmarket place smells enticing and certainly won't break the bank. Behind George St picture windows and tucked under a curved wall-cum-ceiling, northern Indian curries are served by super-polite waiting staff. Try the *dahl makhani*.

Café Cuba
CAFE $$

(www.cafecuba.co.nz; cnr George & Cuba Sts; brunch $9-26, dinner $26-31; 7am-10pm Sun-Tue, to late Wed-Sat;) Need a sugar shot? Proceed to day-turns-to-night Café Cuba – the cakes here are for professional chocoholics only. Supreme coffees and cafe fare (risottos, salads, curries, corn fritters) also draw the crowds. The kumara cakes with avocado, sweet chilli and cream are magic. Live music Friday nights.

Halikarnas
TURKISH $$

(06-357 5777; www.halikarnas.co.nz; 15 Fitzherbert Ave; mains $18-25; noon-2pm Tue-Fri, 5pm-late daily) Angling for an Ali-Baba-and-the-Forty-Thieves vibe, with magic carpets, brass hookahs and funky trans-Bosphorus beats, Halikarnas plates up generous Turkish delights, from lamb shish kebabs to felafels and kick-arse Turkish coffee. Takeaway kebabs next door.

Drinking & Nightlife

Fish
COCKTAIL BAR

(Regent Arcade; 4-11pm Wed, to 1am Thu, to 3am Fri & Sat) A progressive, stylish, Pacifically hewn cocktail bar, the Fish has got its finger firmly on the Palmy pulse. DJs smooth over your problems on Thursday and Friday nights as a sexy, urbane crew sips Manhattans and Tamarillo Mules (yes, they kick).

Brewer's Apprentice
PUB

(www.brewersapprentice.co.nz; 334 Church St; 4pm-late Mon-Wed, from 11am Thu-Sun) What was once a grungy student pub is now a slick Monteith's-sponsored bar. Business crowds flock for meals (brunch and lunch $8 to $18, dinner $23 to $29), and drinkers over 25 fill the beer terrace after dark. Live music Friday nights. You have been warned: 'No untidy shoes.'

Celtic Inn
IRISH PUB

(www.celticinn.co.nz; Regent Arcade; 11am-late Mon-Sat, 4pm-11am Sun) The Celtic expertly offsets the Fish bar nearby with good old-fashioned pub stuff, labourers, travellers and students bending elbows with a few tasty pints of the black stuff. Friendly staff, live music, red velvet chairs, kids darting around parents' legs – it's all here.

☆ Entertainment

CinemaGold
CINEMA

(www.cinemagold.co.nz; Downtown Shopping Arcade, Broadway Ave; adult/child $17/12; 10am-midnight) In the same complex as the more mainstream Downtown Cinemas (www.dtcinemas.co.nz; adult/child $16/10; 10am-midnight), CinemaGold ups the ante with plush seats and a booze licence to enhance art-house classics and limited-release screenings.

Centrepoint Theatre
THEATRE

(www.centrepoint.co.nz; 280 Church St; box office 9am-5pm Mon-Fri) A mainstay of the simmering Palmerston North theatre scene, Centrepoint serves up big-name professional shows, theatre sports and seasonal plays.

ℹ Information

DOC (Department of Conservation; 06-350 9700; www.doc.govt.nz; 717 Tremaine Ave; 8am-4.30pm Mon-Fri) DOC information 3km north of the Square.

Palmerston North Hospital (06-356 9169; www.midcentraldhb.govt.nz; 50 Ruahine St; 24hr) Accident and emergency assistance.

Palmerston North i-SITE (06-350 1922; www.manawatunz.co.nz; The Square; 9am-5pm Mon-Fri, 10am-2pm Sat & Sun;) A super-helpful source of tourist information; free wi-fi throughout the Square.

Post Office (cnr Main St & The Square; 8am-5.30pm Mon-Fri, 9am-5.30pm Sat)

Radius Medical, The Palms (06-354 7737; www.radiusmedical.co.nz; 445 Ferguson St; 8am-7pm Mon-Fri, 9am-6pm Sat & Sun) Urgent medical help, plus doctors by appointment and a pharmacy.

⊕ Getting There & Away

AIR

Palmerston North Airport (www.pnairport. co.nz; Airport Dr) is 4km north of the town centre. Air New Zealand runs daily direct flights to Auckland, Christchurch and Wellington.

BUS

InterCity (www.intercity.co.nz) buses operate from the **Palmerston North Travel Centre** (⊠ 06-355 4955; cnr Main & Pitt Sts; ⊘ 8.45am-5pm Mon-Thu, 8.45am-7.45pm Fri, 9am-2.45pm & 3.45-5pm Sat, 9am-2.45pm & 3.45-7.15pm Sun). Destinations include the following:

DESTINATION	PRICE ($)	DURATION (HR)	FREQUENCY (DAILY)
Auckland	72	9	2
Napier	29	3½	2
Taupo	35	4	2
Wellington	35	2¼	7
Whanganui	25	1½	3

Naked Bus (www.nakedbus.com) services depart from the i-SITE and outside the courthouse in Main St. Destinations include the following:

DESTINATION	PRICE ($)	DURATION (HR)	FREQUENCY (DAILY)
Auckland	25	9	2
Napier	18	3	1
Taupo	24	4¼	2
Wellington	15	2¼	4
Whanganui	13	1¼	1

TRAIN

KiwiRail Scenic Journeys (⊠ 04-495 0775, 0800 872 467; www.kiwirailscenic.co.nz) runs long-distance trains between Wellington and Auckland, stopping at the retro-derelict **Palmerston North Train Station** (Mathews Ave), off Tremaine Ave about 2.5km north of the Square. From Palmy to Wellington, take the *Northern Explorer* ($48, 2½ hours) departing at 4.20pm Monday, Thursday and Saturday; or the *Capital Connection* ($30.50, two hours) departing Palmy at 6.15am Monday to Friday. To Auckland, the *Northern Explorer* ($198, nine hours) departs at 10am on Tuesday, Friday and Sunday. Buy tickets from KiwiRail Scenic Journeys directly, or on the train for the *Capital Connection* (no ticket sales at the station).

⊕ Getting Around

TO/FROM THE AIRPORT

There's no public transport between the city and airport, but taxis abound or **Super Shuttle** (⊠ 09-522 5100, 0800 748 885; www.super-shuttle.co.nz; tickets $16) can whiz you into town in a minivan (prebooking required). A city-to-airport taxi costs around $20.

BICYCLE

Crank It Cycles (⊠ 06-358 9810; www.crank-itcycles.co.nz; 244 Cuba St; ⊘ 8am-5.30pm Mon-Fri, 10am-3pm Sat, 10am-2pm Sun) Hires out city bikes from $20/30 per half/full day, including helmet and lock (deposit $50).

BUS

Horizons (www.horizons.govt.nz; tickets adult/child $2.50/1.50) Runs daytime buses departing from the Main St bus stop on the east side of the Square. Bus 12 goes to Massey University; none go to the airport.

TAXI

Gold & Black Taxis (⊠ 0800 351 2345, 06-351 2345; www.facebook.com/taxisgoldblack) Family-run local outfit.

Around Palmerston North

Just south of 'Student City' in the underrated Horowhenua district, **Shannon** (population 1250) and **Foxton** (population 2650) are sedentary country towns en route to Wellington.

Our fine feathered friends at **Owlcatraz** (⊠ 06-362 7872; www.owlcatraz.co.nz; SH57, Shannon; adult/child incl 2hr tour $25/10; ⊘ 9am-5pm) have obligingly adopted oh-so-droll names like Owlvis Presley and Owl Capone. It's a 30-minute drive south from Palmerston North.

Foxton Beach is one of a string of broad, shallow Tasman Sea beaches along this stretch of coast – brown sand, driftwood and holiday houses proliferate. Other worthy beaches include **Himatangi**, **Hokio** and **Waikawa**.

The town of **Levin** (population 19,550) is more sizeable, but suffers from being too close to both Wellington and Palmerston North to warrant the through-traffic making a stop.

Manawatu Gorge & Around

About 15km northeast of Palmerston North, SH2 dips into Manawatu Gorge. Maori named the gorge Te Apiti (the Narrow Passage), believing the big reddish rock near the centre of the gorge was its guardian spirit. The rock's colour is said to change intensity when a prominent Rangitane tribe member dies or sheds blood. It takes around four hours to walk through the gorge from either end, or you can see it via jetboat (p225).

On the southwestern edge of the gorge, about 40 minutes' drive from Palmerston North, is the **Tararua Wind Farm** (www.trustpower.co.nz), allegedly the largest wind farm in the southern hemisphere. From Hall Block Rd there are awesome views of the turbines. Spinning similarly, north of the gorge is **Te Apiti Wind Farm** (www.meridianenergy.co.nz). There are great views from Saddle Rd – ask the Palmerston North **i-SITE** (☑06-350 1922, 0800 626 292; www.manawatunz.co.nz; The Square; ☺9am-5pm Mon-Fri, 10am-2pm Sat & Sun; ☎) for directions to both farms.

Alternatively, flee the city with a visit to **Timeless Horse Treks** (☑06-376 6157; www.timelesshorsetreks.co.nz; Gorge Rd, Ballance; 1-/2-hr rides from $45/75). Gentle trail rides take in the Manawatu River and surrounding hills, or saddle up for an overnight summertime trek ($225). Palmerston North pick-up/drop-off available.

Taupo & the Central Plateau

Includes ➡

Taupo 232
Turangi & Around 243
The Central Plateau .. 246
Tongariro
National Park............. 246
Whakapapa Village 250
National Park Village .. 251
Ohakune 253
Waiouru 256
Taihape & Around 256

Best Places to Eat

➡ Lakeland House (p245)

➡ L'Arté (p241)

➡ Station (p252)

➡ Piccolo (p241)

➡ Bearing Point (p255)

Best Places to Stay

➡ Station Lodge (p255)

➡ Powderhorn Chateau (p255)

➡ Creel Lodge (p245)

➡ Reef Resort (p240)

➡ Lake Taupo Top 10 Holiday Resort (p240)

Why Go?

From river deep to mountain high, New Zealand's geology takes centre stage in this diverse region – and boy, does it shoot for the moon. Much of the drama happens along the Taupo Volcanic Zone – a line of geothermal activity that stretches via Rotorua to Whakaari (White Island) in the Bay of Plenty. It's the commotion below the surface that has gifted the region with some of the North Island's star attractions, including the country's largest lake and the three hot-headed peaks of Tongariro National Park.

And the thrills don't stop there: this area rivals Queenstown for outdoor escapades. How about hooning on a jet-boat up to a waterfall, bouncing on a bungy over a river, skydiving or skiing fresh powder? Or maybe you'd rather take it easy, soaking in thermal baths or frittering away a day or two with some fly-fishing. If so, mark Taupo and the Central Plateau as a must-do on your North Island itinerary.

When to Go

➡ Equally popular in winter and summer; there's not really a bad time to visit the centre of NZ.

➡ The ski season runs roughly from July to October, but storms and freezing temperatures can occur at any time on the mountains, and above 2500m there is a small permanent cap of snow.

➡ Due to its altitude, the Central Plateau has a generally cool climate, with average high temperatures ranging from around 3°C in winter to around 24°C in summer.

➡ Lake Taupo is swamped with Kiwi holidaymakers from Christmas to late January, so it pays to book ahead for accommodation during this time.

Taupo & the Central Plateau Highlights

① Exploring fascinating volcanic terrain while tramping the **Tongariro Alpine Crossing** (p248)

② Rediscovering the 'lost valley' of **Orakei Korako** (p237)

③ Hurtling to earth strapped to a complete stranger above the world's skydiving capital, **Taupo** (p232)

④ Carving fresh powder on **Mt Ruapehu** (p246)

⑤ Mountain biking over the 284m Hapuawhenua Viaduct on the **Ohakune Old Coach Road** (p254)

⑥ Paddling Lake Taupo to check out the modern **Maori carvings** (p233)

⑦ Rocketing up the Waikato River to the base of **Huka Falls** (p233) in a jetboat

⑧ Soaking in the healing geothermal waters of the **Wairakei Terraces** (p235) hot pools

ⓘ Getting There & Away

AIR

Air New Zealand (☑0800 737 000; www.airnz.co.nz) The national carrier has daily direct flights to Taupo from Auckland and Wellington.

BUS

InterCity (☑07-348 0366; www.intercitycoach.co.nz) Taupo is a hub for Intercity coach services, with regular services running through on direct routes to Auckland (via Rotorua and Hamilton), Tauranga (via Rotorua), Napier and Hastings, and Wellington via Turangi, Waiouru, Taihape, Palmerston North and Kapiti Coast towns. The Palmerston North–Auckland service passes through Whanganui before skirting the western edge of Tongariro National Park via Ohakune and National Park before heading north via Taumaranui, Te Awamutu and Hamilton.

Naked Bus (www.nakedbus.com) Naked Bus services extend from Taupo to Auckland via Hamilton as well as Rotorua and Tauranga, Gisborne via Rotorua, Napier and Hastings, and Wellington via Turangi, Waiouru, Taihape, Palmerston North and Kapiti Coast towns. Other destinations are serviced by Naked Bus affiliates and can therefore be booked through its website.

TRAIN

KiwiRail Scenic (☑04-495 0775, 0800 872 467; www.kiwirailscenic.co.nz) The

---

ESSENTIAL TAUPO & THE CENTRAL PLATEAU

Eat Trout; but you'll have to catch it first!

Drink A mouthful of water from the Waikato River as you bungy over it

Read *Awesome Forces* by Hamish Campbell and Geoff Hicks – the geological story of NZ in explosive detail

Listen to The sonorous chirruping of tui along the Tongariro River Trail

Watch *The Lord of the Rings* and *The Hobbit* movies, and spot Tongariro's movie-star mountains

Pedal Lake Taupo Cycle Challenge

Explore Tongariro National Park's alpine flora and geological oddities

Online www.greatlaketaupo.com; www.visitruapehu.com; www.nationalpark.co.nz; www.visitohakune.co.nz

Area code ☑07

Northern Explorer services stop at National Park, Ohakune and Taihape on the Auckland–Hamilton–Palmerston North–Wellington route.

LAKE TAUPO REGION

NZ's largest lake, Lake Taupo, sits in the caldera of a volcano that began erupting about 300,000 years ago. The caldera was formed by a collapse during the Oruanui eruption about 26,500 years ago, which threw out 750 cu km of ash and pumice, making Krakatoa (8 cu km) look like a pimple.

The last major cataclysm was in AD 180, shooting up enough ash into the atmosphere for the red skies to be noted by the ancient Romans and Chinese. The area is still volcanically active and, like Rotorua, has fascinating thermal hot spots.

Today the 622-sq-km lake and its surrounding waterways are serene enough to attract fishing enthusiasts from all around the world. Well positioned by the lake, both Taupo and Turangi are popular tourist centres. Taupo, in particular, has plenty of activities and facilities catering to families and independent travellers alike.

Taupo

POP 26,100

With a postcard-perfect setting on the northeastern shores of the lake, Taupo now rivals Rotorua as the North Island's premier resort town. There's an abundance of adrenaline-pumping activities on offer but for those with no appetite for white knuckles and churned stomachs, there's plenty of enjoyment to be had simply strolling by the lake and enjoying the views, which on clear days encompass the snowy peaks of Tongariro National Park. It's also a magnet for outdoor athletes and is emerging as one of NZ's greatest cycling destinations, both on- and off-road.

NZ's longest river, the Waikato, originates from Lake Taupo at the township, before crashing its way through the Huka Falls and Aratiatia Rapids and then settling down for a sedate ramble to the west coast, just south of Auckland.

History

When Maori chief Tamatea-arikinui first visited this area, his footsteps reverberated, making him think the ground was hollow;

MAORI NZ: THE CENTRAL PLATEAU

The North Island's central region is home to a group of mountains that feature in several Maori legends of lust and betrayal, which end with a few mountains fleeing to other parts of the island (refer to Mt Taranaki's sad tale).

Long after all that action was over, the *tohunga* (priest) Ngatoro-i-rangi, fresh off the boat from Hawaiki, explored this region and named the mountains that remained. The most sacred was Tongariro, consisting of at least 12 volcanic cones, seen as the leader of all the other mountains.

The major *iwi* (tribe) of the region is **Ngati Tuwharetoa** (www.tuwharetoa.co.nz), one of the few *iwi* in NZ that has retained an undisputed *ariki* (high chief). The current *ariki* is Sir Tumu Te Heuheu Tukino VIII, whose great-great-grandfather, Te Heuheu Tukino IV (a descendent of Ngatoro-i-rangi), gifted the mountains of Tongariro to NZ in 1887.

To discover the stories of local Maori and their ancestors, visit Taupo Museum (p233), the carved cliff faces at Mine Bay (p233), or Wairakei Terraces (p235).

he therefore dubbed the area Tapuaeharuru (Resounding Footsteps). The modern name, however, originates from the story of Tia. After Tia discovered the lake and slept beside it draped in his cloak, the area became known as Taupo Nui a Tia (The Great Cloak of Tia).

Europeans settled here in force during the East Coast Land War (1868–72), when it was a strategic military base. A redoubt was built in 1869 and a garrison of mounted police remained until the defeat of Te Kooti later that year.

In the 20th century the mass ownership of the motorcar saw Taupo grow from a lakeside village of about 750 people to a large resort town, easily accessible from most points on the North Island. Today the population increases considerably at peak holiday times, when New Zealanders and international visitors alike flock to the 'Great Lake'.

◉ Sights

Many of Taupo's attractions are outside the town, with a high concentration around Wairakei Park to the north.

★ Taupo Museum   MUSEUM
(Map p236; www.taupo.govt.nz/museum; Story Pl; adult/child $5/free; ◷10am-4.30pm) With an excellent Maori gallery and quirky displays, which include a 1960s caravan set up as if the occupants have just popped down to the lake, this little museum makes an interesting rainy-day diversion. The centrepiece is an elaborately carved Maori meeting house, Te Aroha o Rongoheikume. Set up in a courtyard, the 'Ora Garden of Wellbeing' is a re-creation of NZ's gold-medal-winning entry into the 2004 Chelsea Flower Show. Historical displays cover local industries, a

mock-up of a 19th-century shop and a moa skeleton, and there's also a gallery devoted to local and visiting exhibitions. Don't miss the rose garden alongside.

Maori Rock Carvings   CARVINGS
Accessible only by boat, these 10m-high carvings were etched into the cliffs near Mine Bay by carver Matahi Whakataka-Brightwell in the late 1970s. They depict Ngatoro-i-rangi, the visionary Maori navigator who guided the Tuwharetoa and Te Arawa tribes to the Taupo area a thousand years ago. See the Watersports section (p237) and Tours section (p239) for companies that arrange trips.

★ Huka Falls   WATERFALL
(Map p234; Huka Falls Rd) FREE Clearly signposted and with a car park and kiosk alongside, these falls mark the spot where NZ's longest river, the Waikato is slammed into a narrow chasm, making a dramatic 10m drop into a surging pool. As you cross the footbridge, you can see the full force of this torrent that the Maori called Hukanui (Great Body of Spray). On sunny days the water is crystal clear and you can take great photographs from the lookout on the other side of the footbridge. You can also take a few short walks around the area or pick up the Huka Falls Walkway (p236) back to town, or the Aratiatia Rapids Walking/Cycling Track to the rapids.

Aratiatia Rapids   WATERFALL
(Map p234) FREE Two kilometres off SH5, this was a spectacular part of the Waikato River until the government plonked a hydroelectric dam across the waterway, shutting off the flow. But the spectacle hasn't disappeared completely, with the floodgates opening from October to March at 10am,

Taupo & Wairakei

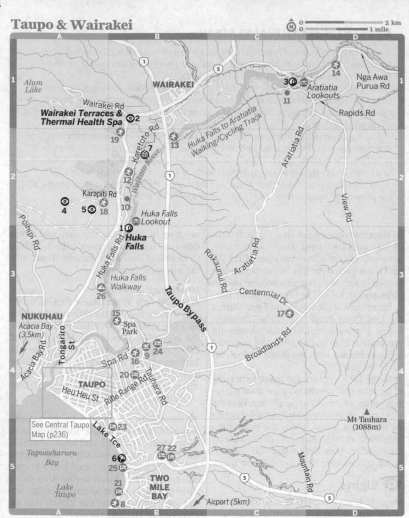

noon, 2pm and 4pm, and from September at 10am, noon and 2pm. You can see the water surge through the dam from two good vantage points. Drive here or take a leisurely four-hour return (30km) bike ride along the river from town.

Geothermal Area

Volcanic Activity Centre   MUSEUM
(Map p234; www.volcanoes.co.nz; Karetoto Rd; adult/child $10/6; ⊙9am-5pm Mon-Fri, 10am-4pm Sat & Sun) What's with all the geothermal activity around Taupo? This centre has the an-

swers, with excellent, if text-heavy, displays on the region's geothermal and volcanic activity, including a live seismograph keeping a watch on what's currently going on. A favourite exhibit with kids is the Earthquake Simulator, a little booth complete with teeth-chattering shudders and jarring wobbles. You can also configure your own tornado then watch it wreak havoc, or see a simulated geyser above and below ground. A small theatre screens footage of local eruptions and a 10-minute film of the 2011 Christchurch earthquake.

Taupo & Wairakei

◎ **Top Sights**
1 Huka Falls..B3
2 Wairakei Terraces & Thermal
    Health Spa...B1

◎ **Sights**
3 Aratiatia Rapids.................................C1
4 Craters of the Moon.........................A2
5 Craters of the Moon MTB Park.........A2
6 Hot Water Beach................................B5
7 Volcanic Activity Centre....................B2

◎ **Activities, Courses & Tours**
8 2 Mile Bay Sailing & Watersports
    Centre...B5
9 AC Baths...B4
10 Heli Adventure Flights.......................B2
11 Huka Falls River Cruise......................C1
12 Huka Honey Hive...............................B2
13 Huka Prawn Park...............................B2
    Hukafalls Jet.............................(see 13)

Rapid Sensations & Kayaking
    Kiwi.......................................(see 10)
14 Rapids Jet...D1
    Rock'n Ropes...........................(see 12)
15 Spa Park Hot Spring..........................B3
16 Taupo Bungy.......................................B4
    Taupo DeBretts Hot Springs.......(see 27)
17 Taupo Gliding Club..............................C3
18 Taupo Horse Treks.............................A2
19 Wairakei Golf & Sanctuary................B2

◎ **Sleeping**
20 All Seasons Kiwi Holiday Park............B4
21 Cottage Mews.....................................B5
22 Hilton Lake Taupo..............................B5
23 Lake..B5
24 Lake Taupo Top 10 Holiday
    Resort...B4
25 Reef Resort...B5
26 Reid's Farm Recreation
    Reserve...A3
27 Taupo DeBretts Spa Resort...............B5

Craters of the Moon   THERMAL AREA

(Map p234; www.cratersofthemoon.co.nz; Karapiti Rd; adult/child $8/4; ⊙ 8.30am-5.30pm) This lesser-known geothermal area sprang to life as a result of the hydroelectric tinkering that created the power station. When underground water levels fell and pressure shifted, new steam vents and bubbling mud pools sprang up. The perimeter loop walk takes about 45 minutes and affords great views down to the lake and mountains beyond. There's a kiosk at the entrance, staffed by kindly volunteers who keep an eye on the car park. It's signposted from SH1, about 5km north of Taupo.

★ Wairakei Terraces & Thermal Health Spa   HOT POOLS

(Map p234; ☑ 07-378 0913; www.wairakeiterraces.co.nz; Wairakei Rd; thermal walk adult/child $18/9, pools $25, massage from $80; ⊙ 8.30am-7pm) 🖉 At our pick of the region's hot pools, mineral-laden waters from the nearby Wairakei geothermal steamfield cascade over silica terraces into pools (open to those 14 years and over) nestled in serene native gardens. Take a therapeutic soak and a self-guided tour on the **Terraces Walkway**. On this you'll find a re-created Maori village, carvings depicting the history of NZ, Maori and local *iwi* Ngati Tuwahretoa, and artificially made geysers and silica terraces, that re-create, on a smaller scale, the famous Pink and White Terraces, which were destroyed by the Tarawera eruption in 1886.

The nighttime **Maori Cultural Experience** (adult/child $98/49) – which includes a traditional challenge, welcome, concert, tour and *hangi* meal – gives an insight into Maori life in the geothermal areas.

🏃 Activities

Tramping & Cycling

Obtain trail maps and hire bikes from **Pack & Pedal** (Map p236; ☑ 07-377 4346; taupo@packandpedal.co.nz; 5 Tamamutu St; full day $35) or **Cornershop Cycles** (Map p236; ☑ 07-378 7381; craig@cornershop.co.nz; cnr Horomatangi & Ruapehu Sts; half/full day $35/50).

Great Lake Walkway   WALKING, CYCLING

This pleasant path follows the Taupo lakefront south to Five Mile Bay (10km). It's flat, easy walking or cycling along public-access beaches.

Great Lake Trail   TRAMPING, CYCLING

(www.greatlaketrail.com) A purpose-built 71km track from Whakaipo Bay to Waihaha in the remote northwestern reaches of the lake. The **W2K** section between Whakaipo and Kinloch has splendid views across the lake to Tongariro National Park. If you are looking for more challenging off-road riding, look up **Craters of the Moon MTB Park** (Map p234; www.biketaupo.org.nz; Craters Rd).

Central Taupo

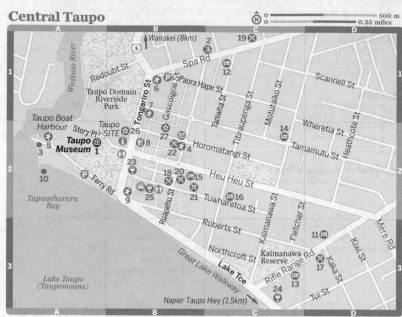

Central Taupo

◎ Top Sights
1 Taupo Museum A2

◎ Activities, Courses & Tours
Big Sky Parasail ....(see 5)
Boating Lake Taupo ....(see 3)
2 Canoe & Kayak................................C1
3 Chris Jolly Outdoors.......................A2
4 Cornershop Cycles B2
Ernest Kemp Cruises ....(see 5)
5 Fish Cruise Taupo A2
6 Greenstone Fishing B1
7 Pack & Pedal...................................B1
8 Pointons...B2
Sail Barbary ....(see 5)
9 Taupo Rod & Tackle B2
10 Taupo's Floatplane A2

◎ Sleeping
11 Beechtree Suites D3
12 Blackcurrant Backpackers..............C1

13 Catelli's of Taupo...........................C3
14 Silver Fern Lodge...........................C2
15 Taupo Urban Retreat......................B2
16 Tiki Lodge.......................................C2

◎ Eating
17 Brantry..D3
18 Indian Affair...................................B2
19 Merchant..C1
20 Piccolo..B2
21 Plateau...B2
22 Saluté...B2

◎ Drinking & Nightlife
23 Finn MacCuhal's..............................B2
24 Jolly Good Fellows.........................C3
25 Vine Eatery & Bar...........................B2

◎ Entertainment
26 Great Lake Centre...........................B2
27 Starlight Cinema Centre.................B2

Huka Falls Walkway
WALKING, CYCLING

Starting from the Spa Park car park at the end of County Ave (off Spa Rd), this scenic, easy walk takes just over an hour to reach the falls, following the east bank of the Waikato River. Continuing on from the falls is the 7km **Huka Falls to Aratiatia Rapids Walking Track** (another two-plus hours). The Taupo–Huka Falls–Aratiatia loop bike ride will take around four hours in total.

Hot Springs

Combine a soak in the hot pools with a walk around a fascinating thermal area at Wairakei Terraces (p235).

Spa Park Hot Spring
HOT POOLS

(Map p234; Spa Park) FREE The hot thermal waters of the Otumuheke Stream meet the bracing Waikato River at this pleasant and well-worn spot under a bridge, creating a free natural spa bath. Take care: people have been known to drown while trying to cool off in the fast-moving river. It's near the beginning of the Huka Falls Walkway, about 20 minutes from the centre of town.

Taupo DeBretts Hot Springs
HOT POOLS

(Map p234; ☎ 07-377 6502; www.taupodebretts. com; 76 Napier Taupo Hwy; adult/child $20/10; ⊙ 8.30am-9.30pm) ✐ A variety of mineral-rich indoor and outdoor thermal pools are on offer. The kids will love the giant dragon waterslide, while the adults can enjoy a wide choice of treatments, such as massage and body scrubs.

Water Sports

Lake Taupo is famously chilly, but in several places, such as Hot Water Beach (Map p234), immediately south of the centre, there are thermal springs just below the surface. You can swim right in front of the township, but Acacia Bay, 5km west, is a particularly pleasant spot. Even better and quieter is Whakaipo Bay, another 7km further on, an undeveloped waterfront reserve perfect for a lazy day.

Canoe & Kayak
CANOEING, KAYAKING

(Map p236; ☎ 07-378 1003, 0800 529 256; www. kayaktoursnz.co.nz; 54 Spa Rd; ⊙ 9am-5pm Mon-Sat) Instruction and boat hire, as well as guided tours, including a two-hour trip on the Waikato River ($49) or a half-day to the Maori carvings (p233) for $95.

Rapid Sensations & Kayaking Kiwi
KAYAKING, RAFTING

(Map p234; ☎ 07-374 8117, 0800 35 34 35; www.rapids.co.nz; 413 Huka Falls Rd) Offers kayak trips to the Maori carvings (four hours, $98), a gentle paddle along the Waikato (two hours, $48), white-water rafting on the Tongariro River ($88 to $115), guided mountain-bike rides ($90) and bike hire (half/full day $45/60).

Taupo Kayaking Adventures
KAYAKING

(☎ 07-376 8981, 0274 801 231; www.tka.co.nz; Acacia Bay) Runs guided kayaking trips from its base in Acacia Bay to the Maori carvings, with the return trip taking around four hours ($100; includes refreshments). Longer trips and walk/bike combos also available.

2 Mile Bay Sailing & Watersports Centre
SAILING, KAYAKING

(Map p234; ☎ 0274 967 350, 0275 886 588; www. sailingcentre.co.nz; Lake Tce; ⊙ 9am-10pm) Has a lakeside cafe-bar and hires out paddle boards ($30), kayaks (from $30), canoes (from $30), windsurfers (from $55), sailboats ($75) and catamarans (from $65); rates are per hour.

AC Baths
SWIMMING, CLIMBING

(Map p234; www.taupodc.govt.nz; 26 AC Baths Ave; adult/child $7/3, slides $5, climbing wall adult/child $14/10; ⊙ 6am-9pm, climbing wall hours vary) At the Taupo Events Centre, about 2km east of town, this complex has three heated pools, two waterslides, private mineral pools and a sauna. There's also a climbing wall and gym.

Adventure & Adrenaline

More than 30,000 jumps a year are made over Taupo, which makes it the skydiving capital of the world. It's certainly a terrific

TAUPO & THE CENTRAL PLATEAU TAUPO

WORTH A TRIP

ORAKEI KORAKO

A bit off the beaten track, Orakei Korako (www.orakeikorako.co.nz; 494 Orakeikorako Rd; adult/child $36/15) gets fewer visitors than other thermal areas. Yet, since the destruction of the Pink and White Terraces, it is arguably the best thermal area left in NZ, even though two-thirds of the original site now lies beneath a dammed section of the Waikato River.

A walking track follows stairs and boardwalks around the colourful silica terraces for which the park is famous, and passes geysers and Ruatapu Cave (allow 1½ hours). This impressive natural cave has a jade-green pool, thought to have been used as a mirror by Maori women preparing for rituals (Orakei Korako means 'The Place of Adorning'). Entry includes the boat ride across the lake from the pleasant visitor centre and cafe.

It's about 30 minutes to Orakei Korako from Taupo. Take SH1 towards Hamilton for 23km, and then travel for 14km from the signposted turn-off. From Rotorua the turn-off is on SH5, via Mihi. You can also arrive via the NZ River Jet (p238).

spot to do it with the deep blue lake and snowcapped volcanic peaks of Tongariro National Park providing epic, dizzying views. Just remember to keep your eyes open. Taupo Airport is 8km south of town (free pick-ups available).

Taupo Tandem Skydiving
SKYDIVING

(☑ 07-377 0428, 0800 826 336; www.taupotandemskydiving.com; Anzac Memorial Dr; 12,000/15,000ft $249/339) Various packages that include DVDs, photos, T-shirts etc ($388 to $679); bungy combo available.

Skydive Taupo
SKYDIVING

(☑ 07-378 4662, 0800 586 766; www.skydivetaupo.co.nz; Anzac Memorial Dr; 12,000ft/15,000ft $249/339) Packages available (from $439) including a reduced-price second jump for altitude junkies.

Taupo Bungy
BUNGY JUMPING

(Map p234; ☑ 07-377 1135, 0800 888 408; www.taupobungy.co.nz; 202 Spa Rd; solo/tandem $169/338; ⊙ 9am-5pm, extended hrs in summer) On a cliff high above the Waikato River, this picturesque bungy site is the North Island's most popular, with plenty of vantage points for the chickens. The courageous will be led onto a platform jutting 20m out over the cliff, where they can throw themselves off the edge for a heart-stopping 47m plunge. Tandem leaps are available, as they are for the Cliffhanger giant swing (solo/tandem $119/238).

Hukafalls Jet
JETBOATING

(Map p234; ☑ 07-374 8572, 0800 485 253; www.hukafallsjet.com; 200 Karetoto Rd; adult/child $109/65) ✐ This 30-minute thrill ride takes you up the river to the spray-filled foot of the Huka Falls and down to the Aratiatia Dam, all the while dodging daringly and doing acrobatic 360-degree turns. Trips run all day (prices include shuttle transport from Taupo).

Rapids Jet
JETBOATING

(Map p234; ☑ 07-374 8066, 0800 727 437; www.rapidsjet.com; Nga Awa Purua Rd; adult/child $110/65) This sensational 35-minute ride shoots along the lower part of the Aratiatia Rapids – rivalling the Huka Falls trip for thrills. The boat departs from the end of the access road to the Aratiatia lookouts. Go down Rapids Rd and then turn into Nga Awa Purua Rd.

NZ River Jet
JETBOATING

(☑ 07-333 7111, 0800 748 375; www.riverjet.co.nz; Mihi Bridge, SH5; 1½hr ride incl entry to Orakei Korako adult/child $159/79) NZ River Jet will zip you to Orakei Korako (p237) in thrilling fashion along the Waikato River and through the 50m-high Tutukau Gorge. It also offers the Squeeze jetboat ride, where you disembark in warm water and edge your way through a crevice to a concealed natural thermal waterfall surrounded by native bush (adult/child $145/79), and a 1¼-hour Scenic Safari ($125/79).

Taupo Horse Treks
HORSE RIDING

(Map p234; ☑ 0274 786 104, 0800 244 398; www.taupohorsetreks.co.nz; Karapiti Rd; per hr $70, pony ride $30) Leads treks through mature forest offering views over the Craters of the Moon, Waikato River and beyond.

Big Sky Parasail
PARASAILING

(Map p236; ☑ 0800 724 4759; www.bigskyparasail.co.nz; Taupo Boat Harbour, Redoubt St; trips $95; ⊙ 9am-6pm Dec-Apr) Lofty parasailing flights from the lakefront; bookings essential. Early-bird special $85.

Rock'n Ropes
ROPES COURSE

(Map p234; ☑ 07-374 8111, 0800 244 508; www.rocknropes.co.nz; 65 Karetoto Rd; giant swing $20, adrenaline combo $40, half-day $65) A vertiginous and challenging high-ropes course that includes balancing in teetering 'treetops', negotiating a tricky two-wire bridge and scaling ropes. The combo includes the swing, high beam and trapeze.

Taupo Gliding Club
GLIDING

(Map p234; ☑ 07-378 5627; www.taupoglidingclub.co.nz; Centennial Dr; flights $160-205) Flights daily by appointment (weather permitting).

Pointons
SKIING, WATERSPORTS

(Map p236; ☑ 07-377 0087; www.pointons.co.nz; 57 Tongariro St; ski/snowboard hire $35/45; ⊙ 7am-7pm Jun-Sep, 9am-5pm Oct-May) Pointons hires ski gear in winter, and water-sports equipment such as wetsuits come summertime.

Fishing

Fish Cruise Taupo
FISHING

(Launch Office; Map p236; ☑ 07-378 3444; www.fishcruisetaupo.co.nz; Taupo Boat Harbour, Redoubt St; ⊙ 9am-5pm Oct-Mar, 9.30am-3pm Apr-Sep) Representing a collective of 13 local boats, this booking office can hook you up with private charters whether you're looking for fishing on a small runabout or a leisurely cruise on a yacht.

Boating Lake Taupo
KAYAKING, SAILING

(Map p236; ☑ 0800 262 833; www.boatinglaketaupo.co.nz; Marina) Located five minutes' walk

TAUPO & THE CENTRAL PLATEAU TAUPO

from the town centre at the marina, this outfit hires out single/double kayaks ($20/30), paddle boards ($25), and self-drive motor boats ($90 to $95), and can take you out for waterskiing and wakeboarding ($180 to $220); all prices are per hour.

Greenstone Fishing   FISHING
(Map p236; ☑07-378 3714; www.greenstonefishingtaupo.co.nz; 147 Tongariro St; fishing rod hire from $20; ☺8am-5pm Mon-Sat, 9am-3pm Sun) Central fishing shop that sells licences, hires gear and arranges guided trips (half-day trips from $250).

Taupo Rod & Tackle   FISHING
(Map p236; ☑07-378 5337; www.tauporodandtackle.co.nz; 7 Tongariro St; gear hire $20-35; ☺8am-6pm, to 8pm Fri) Rental gear, fishing guides and boat charters.

Other Activities

Huka Prawn Park   AQUARIUM
(Map p234; www.hukaprawnpark.co.nz; Karetoto Rd; adult/child $26/15; ☺9.30am-4pm) One of the world's only geothermally heated freshwater prawn farms, this place offers a surprising cocktail of activities, including prawn 'fishing', Killer Prawn Golf and an interactive walk around the prawn ponds. And, of course, there's a restaurant.

Huka Honey Hive   FOOD
(Map p234; www.hukahoneyhive.com; 65 Karetoto Rd; ☺10am-5pm) This sweet spot has a glass-enclosed viewing hive, honey tastings and a cafe, and sells all manner of bee products – edible, medicinal and cosmetic – and mead.

Wairakei Golf & Sanctuary   GOLF
(Map p234; ☑07-374 8152; www.wairakeigolfcourse.co.nz; SH1; 18 holes $160) 🏌 Surrounded by a 2m-high, 5km-long pest-proof fence, this challenging, beautiful golf course doubles as a native bird sanctuary.

⌖ Tours

Huka Falls River Cruise   BOAT TOUR
(Map p234; ☑0800 278 336; www.hukafallscruise.co.nz; Aratiatia Dam; adult/child $37/15; ☺10.30am, 12.30pm & 2.30pm year-round, plus 4.30pm Dec-Feb) 🏌 For a photo-friendly ride, this boat offers a relaxed jaunt (80 minutes) from Aratiatia Dam to Huka Falls.

Sail Barbary   BOAT TOUR
(Map p236; ☑07-378 5879; www.sailbarbary.com; Taupo Boat Harbour, Redoubt St; adult/child $44/16; ☺10.30am & 2pm year-round, plus 5pm

Dec-Feb) 🏌 A classic 1926 yacht offering 2½-hour cruises to the Maori rock carvings every day. Enquire about the popular movie and music charter cruises in summer.

Chris Jolly Outdoors   BOAT TOUR, FISHING
(Map p236; ☑07-378 0623, 0800 252 628; www.chrisjolly.co.nz; Taupo Boat Harbour, Ferry Rd) Operates the *Cruise Cat,* a large, modern launch that offers fishing trips and daily cruises to the Maori carvings (adult/child $44/16; 10.30am, 1.30pm and 5pm). Sunday brunch trips (adult/child $62/34) are also worthwhile. Charter, and guided hiking and mountain-biking trips also available.

Ernest Kemp Cruises   BOAT TOUR
(Map p236; ☑07-378 3444; www.ernestkemp.co.nz; Taupo Boat Harbour, Redoubt St; adult/chid $40/10; ☺10.30am, 2pm, 5.30pm Dec-Feb) Board the *Ernest Kemp* replica steamboat for a two-hour cruise to view the Maori carvings, Hot Water Beach, lakefront and Acacia Bay. Lively commentary and complimentary tea and coffee. Book at Fish Cruise Taupo).

Helipro   HELICOPTER
(☑07-377 8805, 0800 435 4776; www.helipro.co.nz; Anzac Memorial Dr; flights $99-1250) Specialises in heli-tours, which include alpine and landings, as well as shorter scenic flights over the town, lake and volcanoes.

Heli Adventure Flights   HELICOPTER
(Map p234; ☑07-374 8680, 0508 435 474; www.helicoptertours.co.nz; 415 Huka Falls Rd; flights $99-740) Offers a variety of scenic helicopter flights, from 10 minutes to 1½ hours. Combine a flight with the Hukafalls Jet in the Helijet combo ($189). Helibiking and hunting adventures also available.

Taupo's Floatplane   SCENIC FLIGHTS
(Map p236; ☑07-378 7500; www.tauposfloatplane.co.nz; Taupo Boat Harbour, Ferry Rd; flights $105-790) Located near the marina, the floatplane offers a variety of trips, including quick flights over the lake and longer forays over Mt Ruapehu or White Island. Their three-hour 'Taupo Trifecta' ($505) combines a scenic flight, visit to Orakei Korako and jetboat ride.

Paradise Tours   BUS TOUR
(☑07-378 9955; www.paradisetours.co.nz; adult/child $99/45) Three-hour tours to the Aratiatia Rapids, Craters of the Moon and Huka Falls. Also offers day tours to Tongariro National Park, Orakei Korako, Rotorua, Hawke's Bay and Waitomo Caves.

TAUPO & THE CENTRAL PLATEAU TAUPO

✽✦ Festivals & Events

Heralding itself as the events capital of NZ, Taupo plays host to numerous shindigs throughout the year, many of them of a sporting nature – and plenty you can participate in. See www.greatlaketaupo.com and www.eventpromotions.co.nz for more details.

Ironman New Zealand   SPORTS
(www.ironman.co.nz) Bring a magnet, as buns of steel are plentiful during this pimped-up triathlon. Held in early March, it attracts some of the world's finest athletes.

Erupt Festival   ARTS
(www.erupt.co.nz) Biennial arts festival, which is held over 11 days in May on even-numbered years.

Winterfest   FAMILY
Billed as a festival of old-fashioned family fun, held around town over three days in August.

Lake Taupo Cycle Challenge   SPORTS
(www.cyclechallenge.com) One of NZ's biggest annual cycling events, the 160km Lake Taupo Cycle Challenge, sees around 10,000 people pedalling around the lake on the last Saturday in November.

🛏 Sleeping

Taupo has plenty of accommodation, all of which is in hot demand during late December and January and during major sporting events. Book ahead during these times. Self-contained campervan travellers can camp for free at 'Freedom Camp' between 5pm and 10am in a car park along Ferry Rd; non-self-contained vans have the option of **Reid's Farm Recreation Reserve** (Map p234; Huka Falls Rd), a scruffy spot beside the Waikato River.

★ Lake Taupo Top 10
Holiday Resort   HOLIDAY PARK $
(Map p234; ☑07-378 6860, 0800 332 121; www.taupotop10.co.nz; 41 Centennial Dr; campsites from $48, units $97-306; ☜❋) ✔ This slick 8-hectare park about 2.5km from the i-SITE has all mod cons, including heated swimming pool, tennis courts and an on-site shop. Manicured grounds, swish new accommodation options and spotless facilities help make it a contender for camp of the year.

Blackcurrant Backpackers   HOSTEL $
(Map p236; ☑07-378 9292; www.blackcurrantbp.co.nz; 20 Taniwha St; dm/s/d $27/60/78; ☜)

Fashioned from an ageing motel, our favourite Taupo hostel has private rooms with en suites and super-comfy beds. The staff rival the cartoon blackcurrants in the Ribena ads for chirpiness.

Taupo Urban Retreat   HOSTEL $
(Map p236; ☑07-378 6124, 0800 872 261; www.tur.co.nz; 65 Heu Heu St; dm $25-29, d $75; ☜) A younger crowd gravitates to this hostel, attracted by its pub-like hub (with retractable roof) and carefree style. It's refreshingly modern in design with a beach-house feel, despite being on a busy road.

Silver Fern Lodge   HOSTEL $
(Map p236; ☑07-377 4929; www.silverfernlodge.co.nz; cnr Tamamutu & Kaimanawa Sts; dm $28-30, d $85-99; ☜) Rooms range from five-bed dorms to studio en-suite units in this large, custom-built complex, trimmed in shiny corrugated steel yet still strangely lifeless, decor-wise. There's a large communal kitchen and lounge.

Tiki Lodge   HOSTEL $
(Map p236; ☑07-377 4545, 0800 845 456; www.tikilodge.co.nz; 104 Tuwharetoa St; dm $27, d $76-80; ☜) This hostel has lake and mountain views from the balcony, a spacious kitchen, comfy lounges, Maori artwork and a spa pool out back. Scooters and bikes for hire.

All Seasons Kiwi Holiday Park HOLIDAY PARK $
(Map p234; ☑07-378 4272, 0800 777 272; www.taupoallseasons.co.nz; 16 Rangatira St; campsites from $25, dm $47, units $75-160; ☜) ✔ A pleasant holiday park, with lovely staff; well-established trees and hedgerows between sites; a playground; games room; thermal pool; bike hire; and good kitchen facilities. Lots of accommodation options from lodge rooms and cabins to self-contained motels. It's a 20-minute walk downhill to town.

Taupo DeBretts Spa Resort   HOLIDAY PARK $
(Map p234; ☑07-378 8559; www.taupodebretts.com; 76 Napier Taupo Hwy; campsites from $22, units $95-285; ☜) ✔ More a trim holiday park than a flashy resort, DeBretts offers everything from hedged tent sites to motel units. The five-minute drive from downtown is well worth the hop for the indulgent thermal pools on site (half-price entry for guests).

★ Reef Resort   APARTMENTS $$
(Map p234; ☑0800 733 378, 07-378 5115; www.accommodationtaupo.com; 219 Lake Tce; d $150-250; ☜❋) This smart complex stands out amongst Taupo's waterfront apartment

complexes for its classy, well-priced one- to three-bedroom apartments, centred upon an appealing pool patio.

Lake
MOTEL $$
(Map p234; ☑ 07-378 4222; www.thelakeonline.co.nz; 63 Mere Rd; d $130-200; ☎) A reminder that 1960s and '70s design wasn't all Austin Powers–style groovaliciousness, this distinctive boutique motel is crammed with furniture from the era's signature designers. The four one-bedroom units all have kitchenettes and dining-living areas, and everyone has use of the pleasant garden out back.

Waitahanui Lodge
MOTEL $$
(☑ 07-378 7183, 0800 104 321; www.waitahanui-lodge.co.nz; 116 SH1, Waitahanui; d $119-179; ☎) Ten kilometres south of Taupo, this enclave of genuine retro bach-style units are ideally positioned for swimming, fishing and superb sunsets. Pick of the bunch are the two absolute-lakefront units, but all have lake access, sociable communal areas plus free rowboat and kayaks.

Cottage Mews
MOTEL $$
(Map p234; ☑ 07-378 3004, 0800 555 586; www.cottagemews.co.nz; 311 Lake Tce, Two Mile Bay; d $115-130, q $150; ☎) Few motels muster much charm, but this cute gable-roofed block, festooned with hanging flowers, manages to seem almost rustic. Some units have lake views, most have spa baths and all have a small private garden. Bikes and kayaks for hire.

Catelli's of Taupo
MOTEL $$
(Map p236; ☑ 07-378 4477, 0800 884 477; www.catellis.co.nz; 23-27 Rifle Range Rd; d $135-165, q $230; ☎) ✿ The exterior is all hobbitish '80s curves, sloping roofs and nipple-pink trim, but these orderly motel units have a fresh feel inside. In summer it's worth paying extra for a garden studio.

Beechtree Suites
MOTEL $$
(Map p236; ☑ 0800 233 248, 07-377 0181; www.beechtreemotel.co.nz; 56 Rifle Range Rd; apt $145-380; ☎) The Beechtree offers classy rooms, fresh and modern in design with neutral-toned decor, large windows, ground-floor patios and upstairs balconies.

Acacia Cliffs Lodge
B&B $$$
(☑ 07-378 1551; www.acaciacliffslodge.co.nz; 133 Mapara Rd, Acacia Bay; d $700; ☎) ✿ This luxurious B&B, high above Acacia Bay, offers four comtemporarily and artfully designed suites, three with grand lake views and one

that compensates for the lack of them with a curvy bath and a private garden ($595). The chef-owner dishes up high-quality fare, with dinner available. Tariff includes breakfast, pre-dinner drinks, canapes and Taupo airport transfer.

Hilton Lake Taupo
HOTEL $$$
(Map p234; ☑ 07-378 7080; www.hilton.com/lake-taupo; 80-100 Napier Rd; from $220; ☎ ☒) Occupying the historic Terraces Hotel (1889) and a modern extension, this large complex offers the expected Hilton standard of luxury including swish suites, an outdoor heated pool, and Bistro Lago, the decent in-house restaurant. It's a little out of town but is handy for the DeBretts thermal complex.

✖ Eating

★ L'Arté
CAFE $
(www.larte.co.nz; 255 Mapara Rd, Acacia Bay; snacks $4-9, mains $10-19; ☉ 9am-4pm Wed-Sun, daily Jan) Lots of mouth-watering treats are made from scratch at this fantastically artful cafe on the hill that backs Acacia Bay. Brunch in the sunshine, then check out the sculpture garden and gallery.

Merchant
DELI $
(Map p236; www.themerchant.co.nz; 114 Spa Rd; ☉ 9am-7pm Mon-Sat, 10am-5pm Sun) Championing NZ artisan producers and importing specialities from abroad, this grocery on the town fringe is a fruitful stop for those looking to stock up on supplies ranging from cheese to chocolate to craft beer.

★ Piccolo
CAFE $$
(Map p236; www.taupocafe.co.nz; 41 Ruapehu St; mains $12-24; ☉ 7am-4pm; ☎🖉) This sharp, modern cafe is well tuned, offering a cabinet-load of pastries, sandwiches and salads, with great value wines by the glass should you feel inclined. Excellent coffee, and sublime home-baked sweets.

Saluté
CAFE, DELI $$
(Map p236; www.salutedelicatessen.co.nz; 47 Horomatangi St; snacks $3-9, mains $10-20; ☉ 8am-5pm Mon-Fri, 9am-5pm Sat, 9am-4pm Sun; 🖉) Bellissimo deli-cafe with operatic soundtrack, Taupo's best espresso and what everyone needs: a walk-in cheese fridge. The Mediterranean-flavoured menu includes pizzas, fresh homemade pasta and aromatic pork *carzuela,* plus a counterful of quality nibbly treats like bagels, slices, cakes and naughty-but-nice cronuts. Picnic supplies aplenty.

Indian Affair
INDIAN $$

(Map p236; ☑ 07-378 2295; www.indianaffair.co.nz; cnr Ruapehu & Tuwharetoa Sts; mains $16-29; ⊙ lunch Mon-Fri, dinner daily; 🖉) Eschewing the staid, traditional curry-house vibe in favour of bold, floral feature walls and high-back leather chairs, this thoroughly modern Indian restaurant serves up spicy classics (try the tikka lamb chops and chicken *jalfrezi*) with warm service. Alfresco tables bask in late sun; good whiskies.

Plateau
PUB $$

(Map p236; www.plateautaupo.co.nz; 64 Tuwharetoa St; mains $20-35; ⊙ 11.30am-late; 🐾) An ambient place for a handle or two of the Monteith's range, popular Plateau delivers in the food department, too. Its menu of modern pub classics features the likes of smoked salmon salad with corn cakes, and an artful steak sandwich.

Brantry
MODERN NZ $$$

(Map p236; ☑ 07-378 0484; www.thebrantry.co.nz; 45 Rifle Range Rd; mains $30, 2-/3-course set menu $45/55; ⊙ dinner) Operating out of an unobtrusive 1950s house, the Brantry continues its reign as one of the best in the region for its well-executed, good-value offerings centred on meaty mains turned out in classical style. Book-ending with entrée and dessert is highly recommended.

Drinking & Nightlife

Things get lively in the height of summer when the town swells. The rest of the year it might pay to take a newspaper to read over your pint.

Vine Eatery & Bar
TAPAS, WINE BAR

(Map p236; www.vineeatery.co.nz; 37 Tuwharetoa St; tapas $9-20; ⊙ 9am-late) The clue's in the name at this wine bar sharing its barn-like home with the Scenic Cellars wine store. Share traditional tapas alongside larger divisible dishes, accompanied by your choice of an expansive array of wines at keen prices. This is Taupo's best bet for a sophisticated nibble and natter amongst the town's well-heeled.

Jolly Good Fellows
PUB

(Map p236; www.jollygoodfellows.co.nz; 80 Lake Tce; ⊙ 11am-late) Corr 'blimey, Guvnor! You ain't seen a rubber-dub-dub like this since Old Blighty, with lashings of colonial cliches and the likes of London Pride on tap, plus a couple of NZ craft beers. Solid service, square meals, outside seating, lake views – she's pukka!

Finn MacCuhal's
IRISH PUB

(Map p236; www.finns.co.nz; cnr Tongariro & Tuwharetoa Sts; ⊙ 11am-late) With Irish ephemera nailed to the walls and a backpackers next door, you can be sure that there will be plenty of craic here. A host of locals get in on the action, likely to involve bands, DJs and dancing, and a bonanza of well-managed bacchanalia.

☆ Entertainment

Great Lake Centre
CONCERT VENUE

(Map p236; www.taupovenues.co.nz; Tongariro St) Hosts performances, exhibitions and conventions. Ask at the i-SITE for the current program.

Starlight Cinema Centre
CINEMA

(Map p236; www.starlightcinema.co.nz; Starlight Arcade, off Horomatangi St; adult/child $14.50/10) Screens the latest Hollywood blockbusters.

🛈 Information

Taupo i-SITE (Map p236; ☑ 07-376 0027, 0800 525 382; www.greatlaketaupo.com; Tongariro St; ⊙ 8.30am-5pm) Handles bookings for accommodation, transport and activities; dispenses cheerful advice; and stocks Department of Conservation (DOC) maps and town maps.

🛈 Getting There & Away

Taupo Airport (☑ 07-378 7771; www.taupoairport.co.nz; Anzac Memorial Dr) is 8km south of town. InterCity and Naked Bus services (see p232) stop outside the i-SITE, where bookings can be made.

🛈 Getting Around

Local buses are run by **Busit!** (☑ 0800 4287 5463; www.busit.co.nz), including the Taupo North service running as far as Huka Falls and Wairakei, twice daily Monday to Friday.

Hotbus (☑ 0508 468 287; www.alpinehotbus.co.nz) is a hop-on, hop-off minibus service around the town's key attractions. **Great Lake Shuttles** (☑ 021 656 424; www.greatlakeshuttles.co.nz) offers charter services around the area, and can hook you up with bike hire.

Taxi companies include **Taupo Taxi** (☑ 07-378 5100; www.taupotaxi.co.nz) and **Top Cabs** (Map p236; ☑ 07-378 9250; 23 Tuwharetoa St). Expect to pay about $25 for a cab from the airport to the centre of town.

There are plenty of shuttle services operating year-round to Turangi and Tongariro National Park. Ask at the i-SITE who will best suit your needs as services vary according to season (ski or hike).

Turangi & Around

POP 3000

Once a service town for the nearby hydroelectric power station, sleepy Turangi's claim to fame nowadays is as the 'Trout Fishing Capital of the World' and as one of the country's premier white-water-rafting destinations. Set on the Tongariro River, the town is a shortish hop for snow bunnies from the ski fields and walking tracks of Tongariro National Park.

◉ Sights & Activities

The Tongariro River Trail offers enjoyable walks from the centre of town. Further afield, good leg-stretchers include **Hinemihi's Track**, near the top of Te Ponanga Saddle, 8km west of Turangi on SH47 (15 minutes return); **Maunganamu Track**, 4km west of Turangi on SH41 (40 minutes return); and **Tauranga–Taupo River Walk** (30 minutes), which starts at Te Rangiita, 12km north of Turangi on SH1.

The Tongariro River has some superb Grade III rapids for **river rafting**, as well as Grade I stretches suitable for beginners in the lower reaches during summer.

It's also a likely spot for **trout fishing**, as evident by anglers stationed on every bend of the river.

Tongariro National Trout Centre   AQUARIUM
(www.troutcentre.com; SH1; adult/child $10/free; ⊙10am-3pm) The DOC-managed trout hatchery has polished educational displays, a collection of rods and reels dating back to the 1880s and freshwater aquariums displaying river life, both nasty and nice. A gentle stroll along the landscaped walkway leads to the hatchery, keeping ponds, an underwater viewing chamber, the Tongariro River and a picnic area.

★**Tongariro River Trail**   WALKING, CYCLING
(www.tongariroriveririvertrail.co.nz) Should you have at least half a day to spare around Turangi, the must-do is the picturesque Tongariro River Trail, a 16km dual-use walking and cycling loop track starting from town and heading upriver to the Red Hut suspension bridge, taking in the National Trout Centre along the way. It takes around four hours to walk the entire loop, and around two hours to cycle on easy terrain; hire bikes from Tongariro River Rafting who offer a $35 bike-hire and trout centre entry package. Shorten your outing by crossing at Major Jones Bridge – a circuit known as the **Tongariro River Lookout Track** which is a 1½-hour riverside amble passing lookout points to Mt Pihanga.

Tongariro River Rafting   RAFTING
(☑07-386 6409, 0800 101 024; www.trr.co.nz; Atirau Rd) ✒ Test the white waters with a Gentle Family Float (adult/child $75/65), splash straight into the Grade III rapids (adult/child $115/105), or try a more physical kayaking trip ($129). Raft fishing available in summer (price on enquiry). Turangi's original rafting company also hires out mountain bikes and

Turangi   ⓝ 0 ——— 500 m
                    0 ——— 0.25 miles

Turangi

◉ **Activities, Courses & Tours**

Creel Tackle House & Cafe	(see 6)
1	Greig's Sporting World	A1
2	Rafting NZ	B1
3	Sporting Life	A2
4	Tongariro River Rafting	A3
5	Tongariro River Trail	B3

🛏 **Sleeping**

6	Creel Lodge	B2
7	Extreme Backpackers	B1
8	Judges Pool Motel	B2
9	Riverstone Backpackers	B1
10	Sportmans Lodge	B1
11	Turangi Kiwi Holiday Park	A2

✗ **Eating**

12	Grand Central Fry	B1

runs guided trips around local rides including the 42 Traverse, Tongariro River Trail, Tree Trunk Gorge and Fishers Track. Ask about multi-activity combos.

Rafting NZ RAFTING
(☑07-386 0352, 0800 865 226; www.rafting-newzealand.com; 41 Ngawaka Pl) The main trips offered by this slick outfit are a four-hour, Grade III trip on the Tongariro River with an optional waterfall jump (adult/child $129/119) and a family fun run over more relaxed rapids (Grade II, three hours, adult/child $85/75). Groups of four or more can tackle a two-day trip overnighting at a riverside camp (Grade III-plus, $350 per person).

Motuoapa Hire Boats BOATING
(☑0275 303 333; Motuoapa Esplanade; kayak hire per hr $20-25) Hires kayaks, paddle boards and small motorboats from its launchpad 10km northeast of Turangi.

Tokaanu Thermal Pools HOT POOLS
(www.tokaanuthermalpools.co.nz; Mangaroa St, Tokaanu; adult/child $6/4, private pools per 20min $10/6; ☉10am-9pm) Soak in thermally heated

---

ABOUT TROUT

Early European settlers, wishing to improve NZ's farming, hunting and fishing opportunities, were responsible for the introduction of such ghastly wreckers as possums and rabbits. One of their more benign introductions was that of trout – brown and rainbow – released into NZ rivers in the second half of the 19th century.

Today they are much prized by sports anglers, whom you may stumble across flicking their flies, thigh-deep in limpid rivers or on the edge of deep green pools. While this pastime, nay obsession, remains a mystery to the authors of this book, it is apparent that it brings much unbridled joy and satisfaction to the lives of its patrons. To quote NZ author and poet Kevin Ireland in his illuminating book *How to Catch a Fish*, 'It has as much to do with simple stubbornness and personal compulsion as it does with any complex notions of happiness and mystical fulfilment. The last thing to which it has any reasonable relationship is success.'

The Tongariro River is the largest and most important spawning river in the Taupo district, and well known all over the world for its fish. Tall tales boast of Taupo trout weighing more than a sack of spuds and measuring the length of a surfboard. Truth be told, more than 28,000 legal trout are bagged annually, by both domestic and international fishing enthusiasts.

Trout fishing is highly regulated, with plenty of rules regarding where and how, and licences most certainly required. Read more at **Fish & Game New Zealand** (www.fishandgame.org.nz), but our best advice is to seek out a guide. Most offer flexible trips, with $250 for a half-day a rough ballpark. Local experts include the following:

Creel Tackle House & Cafe (☑07-386 7929; www.creeltackle.com; 183 Taupahi Rd) Fishing equipment, tips, guiding and coffee.

Bryce Curle Fly Fishing (☑07-386 6813; www.brycecurleflyfishing.com) Turangi-based guide.

Fish Tongariro (☑07-386 7775) Turangi-based guide, Peter Canziani.

Flyfishtaupo (☑07-377 8054; www.flyfishtaupo.com) Guide Brent Pirie offers a range of fishing excursions, including seniors-focused 'Old Farts & Tarts' trips.

Greig's Sporting World (☑07-386 6911; www.greigsports.co.nz; 59 Town Centre) Hires and sells gear and handles bookings for guides and charters.

Sporting Life (www.sportinglife-turangi.co.nz; Town Centre) Sports store laden with fishing paraphernalia. Its website details the latest fishing conditions.

AJ Charters (☑07-386 7992; www.ajtaupocharters.com) Turangi-based fishing trips plus scenic lake cruises on a 38ft catamaran.

Ian & Andrew Jenkins (☑07-386 0840; www.tui-lodge.co.nz) Father and son fly-fishing guides.

Central Plateau Fishing (☑07-378 8192, 027 681 4134; www.cpf.net.nz) Turangi-based guide, Brett Cameron.

water at this unpretentious, family-orientated facility, 5km northwest of Turangi. A 10-minute stroll along the boardwalk (wheelchair accessible) showcases boiling mud pools, thermal springs and a trout-filled stream.

🛏 Sleeping

Extreme Backpackers   HOSTEL $

(☑07-386 8949; www.extremebackpackers.co.nz; 22 Ngawaka Pl; dm $25-27, s $46-56, d $62-72; 🛜) Crafted from native timber and corrugated iron, this modern backpackers has the bonus of a climbing wall and cafe, a lounge with an open fire and a sunny courtyard with hammocks. Dorms range from four to eight beds and the pricier private rooms have en suites. Staff will happily help with arrangements for the Alpine Crossing and other activites.

Turangi Kiwi Holiday Park   HOLIDAY PARK $

(☑07-386 8754, 0800 386 875; www.turangiholidaypark.com; 13 Te Reiti Tamara Grove; campsites per person from $18, d $50-120; 🛜) Roomy, suburban holiday park with established leafy grounds, five minutes' walk from the town centre. Facilities and cabins are old, but clean and continuingly being upgraded by friendly, hard-working owners. Sweet alcoves for campervans and tents.

Riverstone Backpackers   HOSTEL $

(☑07-386 7004; www.riverstonebackpackers.com; 222 Tautahanga Rd; dm $26-28, r $64-85; 🛜) This homely backpackers resides in a refitted house close to the town centre. Along with an enviable kitchen and comfortable lounge, it sports a stylish landscaped yard with a pizza oven.

Sportmans Lodge   LODGE $

(☑07-386 8150, 0800 366 208; www.sportmanslodge.co.nz; 15 Taupahi Rd; r $80, cottage $115; 🛜) Backing on to the river, this lodge is a hidden bargain for trout-fishing folk unbothered by punctuation. Tidy, compact rooms share a lounge with open fire and a well-equipped kitchen. The self-contained cottage sleeps four.

★Creel Lodge   LODGE $$

(☑07-386 8081, 0800 273 355; www.creel.co.nz; 183 Taupahi Rd; units $130-150; 🛜) 🍃 Set in green and peaceful grounds, this heavenly hideaway backs onto a fine stretch of the Tongariro River. Spacious units have separate lounges, kitchens, soothing patios for sundowners and free use of barbecues. Creel Tackle House & Cafe on site.

Judges Pool Motel   MOTEL $$

(☑07-386 7892, 0800 583 439; www.judgespoolmotel.co.nz; 92 Taupahi Rd; d $110; 🛜) This older motel has tidy, spacious rooms with kitchenettes. All one-bedroom units have outdoor decks for relaxing beers, although the barbecue area is the best place to talk about the one that got away. Free-range eggs from the owners' chooks sold cheap.

Oreti Village   APARTMENTS $$$

(☑07-386 7070; www.oretivillage.com; Mission House Dr, Pukawa; apt $220-280; 🛜) This enclave of smart self-contained apartments sits high over the lake surrounded by bird-filled native bush and landscaped with colourful rhododendrons. Gaze at blissful lake views from the balcony, undertaking a spot of tennis or taking a dip in the indoor pool. Take SH41 for 15km, heading northwest of Turangi, and turn right into Pukawa Rd.

🍴 Eating

Grand Central Fry   FAST FOOD $

(8 Ohuanga Rd; meals $3-8; ⊙11am-8.30pm) A local mainstay serving top fish and chips, plus burgers and anything else fryable. Erratic opening hours.

Licorice   CAFE $

(57 SH1, Motuoapa; mains $9-17; ⊙8am-4pm Mon-Sat, 9am-3pm Sun) Look for the giant licorice allsort on the roof of this roadside cafe, 8km north of Turangi. It's better than any of the cafes in the town itself, with fine coffee and baking.

★Lakeland House   INTERNATIONAL $$

(☑07-386 6442; 88 Waihi Rd, Waihi; brunch $16-25, dinner $23-42; ⊙10am-3pm & 6pm-late) Destination dining at the southern end of Lake Taupo, with generous pastas, salads and chowder dominating the daytime menu. Come evening, meat lovers can salivate over a rack of lamb with tamarillo and plum compote, rounded off with a toothsome passion-fruit meringue gateau. Six kilometres from Turangi, just off SH41.

ℹ Information

Turangi i-SITE (☑07-386 8999, 0800 288 726; www.greatlaketaupo.com; Ngawaka Pl; ⊙8.30am-5pm; 🛜) A good stop for information on Tongariro National Park, Kaimanawa Forest Park, trout fishing, and snow and road conditions. It issues DOC hut tickets, ski passes and fishing licences, and makes bookings for transport, accommodation and activities.

ⓘ Getting There & Away

Both InterCity and Naked Bus (p232) coaches stop outside the i-SITE.

THE CENTRAL PLATEAU

Tongariro National Park

Tongariro National Park (797 sq km) lies in the heart of the North Island. Its major landmarks are three active volcanoes – Ruapehu, Ngauruhoe and Tongariro. These form the southern end of a chain that extends northwest through the heart of the North Island, past Taupo and Rotorua, to finally reach Whakaari (White Island). The volcanic nature of the region is responsible for Tongariro's hot springs, boiling mud pools, fumaroles and craters.

Geologically speaking, the Tongariro volcanoes are relatively young. Both Ruapehu and Tongariro are less than 300,000 years old. They were shaped by a mixture of eruptions and glacial action, especially in the last ice age. At one time, glaciers extended down Ruapehu to below 1300m, leaving polished rock far below their present snouts.

Mt Ruapehu (www.mtruapehu.com), at 2797m, is the highest mountain on the North Island. It is also one of the world's most active volcanoes. One eruption began in March 1945 and continued for almost a year, spreading lava over Crater Lake and sending huge dark clouds of ash as far away as Wellington. No wonder, then, that the mountain's name translates as 'pit of sound'.

Ruapehu rumbled in 1969 and 1973, but its worst disaster was on Christmas Eve 1953, when a crater lake lip collapsed. An enormous lahar swept down the mountainside, taking everything in its path, including a railway bridge. Moments later a crowded train plunged into the river, killing 151 people; it was one of NZ's worst tragedies.

Ruapehu hasn't let up, with significant eruptions occurring with suspicious frequency. In 2007 a primary-school teacher had a lucky shave when a rock was propelled through the roof of a trampers' shelter, crushing his leg.

Ongoing rumbles are reminders that these volcanoes in the area are very much in the land of the living. The last major event was in 2012 when Mt Tongariro – the northernmost and lowest peak in the park

(1967m) – gave a couple of good blasts from its northern craters, causing a nine-month partial closure of the famous Alpine Crossing track. (To see video of recent eruptions, visit www.doc.govt.nz/eruption.)

Northeast of Ruapehu is Mt Ngauruhoe, at 2287m, the youngest of the three volcanoes. Its first eruptions are thought to have occurred 2500 years ago. Until 1975 Ngauruhoe had erupted at least every nine years, including a 1954 eruption that lasted 11 months and disgorged 6 million cu metres of lava. In contrast to the others, which have multiple vents, Ngauruhoe is a conical, single-vent volcano with perfectly symmetrical slopes – the reason that it was chosen to star as Mt Doom in Peter Jackson's *Lord of the Rings*.

Tongariro was NZ's first national park, established in 1887. The previous year, in the aftermath of the New Zealand Wars (Land Wars), the Native Land Court met to determine the ownership of the land around Tongariro. Ngati Tuwharetoa chief Horonuku Te Heuheu Tukino IV pleaded passionately for the area to be left intact, mindful of Pakeha eyeing it up for grazing. 'If our mountains of Tongariro are included in the blocks passed through the court in the ordinary way,' said the chief, 'what will become of them? They will be cut up and sold, a piece going to one Pakeha and a piece to another.'

In 1887 chief Horonuku ensured the land's everlasting preservation when he presented the area to the Crown for the purpose of a national park, the first in NZ and only the fourth in the world. With incredible vision for a man of his time, the chief realised that Tongariro's value lay in its priceless beauty and heritage, not as another sheep paddock.

Development of the national park was slow, and it was only after the main trunk railroad reached the region in 1909 that visitors arrived in significant numbers. Development mushroomed in the 1950s and 1960s as roads were sealed, tracks cut and more huts built.

Today the park is the most popular in NZ, receiving around one million visitors per annum. Many visitors come to ski – Ruapehu's snowfields being the only legitimate ski area north of Wellington – but more people arrive each summer to tramp up, down and around the mountains. The park can get busy, most noticeably on the popular day walks, but most visitors consider this a small price to pay for the chance to experience its magic.

The most popular tramps in the park are the Alpine Crossing and Northern Circuit, but there are plenty more besides. These range from short ambles to excellent day walks such as the Whakapapa Valley and Tama Lakes tracks, both of which begin from the National Park Visitor Centre at Whakapapa. There are also various challenging routes that should only be attempted by the fit, experienced and well equipped. One of these is the Round the Mountain Track, a remote, 71km, four- to six-day tramp circuiting Mt Ruapehu.

🏃 Activities

Tramping

The DOC and i-SITE visitor centres at Whakapapa (p251), Ohakune (p256) and Turangi (p245) have maps and information on walks in the park, as well as current track and weather conditions. Each January, DOC offers an excellent guided-walks program in and around the park; ask at DOC centres for information or book online.

The safest and most popular time to tramp in the national park is December to March, when the tracks are normally clear of snow and the weather is more settled. In winter many of the tracks become full alpine adventures, requiring mountaineering experience, an ice axe and crampons.

Scattered around the park's tramping tracks are 10 huts, most of which are rated Standard ($5). However, as the Tongariro Northern Circuit is a Great Walk, Mangatepopo, Oturere and Waihohonu huts are designated Great Walk huts ($32) during the Great Walk season (mid-October to 30 April). Each hut has gas cookers, heating, cold running water and good old long-drop toilets, along with communal bunk rooms with mattresses. Campsites are located next to the huts; the $15 fee allows campers use of the hut facilities.

Great Walk hut tickets must be obtained in advance, either from the Tongariro National Park Visitor Centre (p251), **Great Walks Bookings** (📞0800 694 732; www.greatwalks.co.nz), or DOC visitor centres nationwide. It will pay to book early during the Great Walk season. In the off-season, the huts become Standard huts ($5), the gas cookers are removed, and fees can be paid with Backcountry Hut Passes and tickets.

Tongariro Northern Circuit   TRAMPING

Circumnavigating Ngauruhoe, this four-day, 50km track is a Great Walk for a number of good reasons. The route can be easily walked in four days from Whakapapa Village, Mangatepopo Rd or Ketetahi Rd, all regularly serviced by shuttle services. Although there is some moderate climbing, the track is well marked and well maintained, putting it within the ability of people of medium fitness and tramping experience.

The Northern Circuit passes plenty of the spectacular and colourful volcanic features that have earned the park its Unesco World Heritage Area status. Highlights include craters, including the South Crater, Central Crater and Red Crater; brilliantly colourful lakes, including the Emerald Lakes, Blue Lake and the Upper and Lower Tama Lakes; the cold Soda Springs; and various other formations, including cones, lava flows and glacial valleys. Optional side trips include the summits of Ngauruhoe and Tongariro, both of which lie along the Tongariro Alpine Crossing, part of which makes up a leg of this circuit.

The traditional place to start and finish the tramp is Whakapapa Village, the site of the park's visitor information centre. However, many trampers begin at Mangatepopo Rd to ensure they have good weather for the tramp's most dramatic day. This reduces it to a three-day tramp, with stays at Oturere and Waihohonu Huts, ending at Whakapapa Village.

ROUTE	ESTIMATED SUMMER WALK TIME (HR)
Whakapapa Village to Mangatepopo Hut	3-5
Mangatepopo Hut to Oturere Hut	5-6
Oturere Hut to Waihohonu Hut	3
Waihohonu Hut to Whakapapa Village	5-6

ℹ️ MOUNTAIN SAFETY

Many visitors to NZ come unstuck in the mountains. The weather can change more quickly than you expect, and rescues (and fatalities) are not uncommon. When heading out on remote tracks, you must be properly equipped and take safety precautions, including leaving your itinerary with a responsible person. Appropriate clothing is paramount. Think wool, and several layers of it, topped with a waterproof jacket. Gloves and a hat are good too, even in summer. And don't even think about wearing anything other than sturdy boots. Take plenty of water and sunscreen, especially on hot days.

TAUPO & THE CENTRAL PLATEAU TONGARIRO NATIONAL PARK

See Turangi Map (p243)

Warning
Desert Rd may be closed in severe conditions

TAUPO & THE CENTRAL PLATEAU TONGARIRO NATIONAL PARK

★ **Tongariro Alpine Crossing**   HIKING
This legendary crossing is often lauded as NZ's finest one-day walk. It's certainly the most popular, with 60,000 to 70,000 trampers completing it every year. It's

no wonder. Very few day walks offer such thrilling scenery. Among its highlights are steaming vents and springs, crazy rock formations and peculiar moonscape basins, impossible scree slopes and vast views in

Tongariro National Park & Around

◉ Sights
1 Lake Rotokura B6
2 National Army Museum C6
3 Tongariro National Trout Centre D2

◎ Activities, Courses & Tours
4 Mountain Air B3
5 Ruapehu Homestead A6
6 Tokaanu Thermal Pools D1
7 Tukino Ski Area C4

8 Wades Landing Outdoors A3

◉ Sleeping
9 Discovery Lodge B3
10 Mangahuia DOC Campsite B3
11 Oreti Village D1
12 Tongariro Family Holiday Park C2

⊗ Eating
13 Lakeland House D1

almost every direction. Along the way it passes diverse vegetation zones from alpine scrub and tussock to higher zones with no plant life at all.

This is a fair-weather tramp. In poor conditions it is little more than an arduous up-and-down, with only orange-tipped poles to mark the passing of the day. Should strong winds be blowing on top, you'll be practically crawling along the ridge of Red Crater, the high point of the trek.

This is an alpine crossing, and it needs to be treated with respect. You need not only a reasonable level of fitness, you should be prepared for all types of weather. Shockingly ill-equipped trampers are legendary on this route – stupid shoes, no rain jackets, blue jeans soaked to the skin – we've seen it all. As well as proper gear, you'll need plenty of water, as there is none available between Mangatepopo and Ketetahi.

The most crowded times on the track are the first nice days after Christmas and Easter, when there can easily be more than 1000 people strung out between the two road ends. The upside of this popularity is excellent shuttle connections, with plenty of operators offering round-trip transport. Be sure to book your ride in advance, and keep an eye on your progress so you don't miss your ride.

The Crossing starts at Mangatepopo Rd car park, off SH47, and finishes at Ketetahi Rd, off SH46. It takes takes seven to eight hours to make the 19.4km journey, although this will vary significantly if you decide to take side-trips up to the summits of Ngauruhoe or Tongariro – both very worthwhile and taking around two and three hours respectively. A word of warning: if you summit Ngauruhoe, keep an eagle-eye out for dislodged boulders careening down the slopes. Injuries do occur.

ROUTE	ESTIMATED SUMMER WALK TIME (HR)
Mangatepopo Rd end to Mangatepopo Hut	¼
Mangatepopo Hut to South Crater	1½-2
South Crater to Mt Ngauruhoe summit (side trip)	2-3 (return)
Red Crater to Tongariro summit (side trip)	1½ (return)
South Crater to Emerald Lakes	1-1½
Emerald Lakes to Ketetahi Shelter	1½
Ketetahi Shelter to road end	1½

Crater Lake   HIKING

The unmarked rugged route up to Ruapehu's Crater Lake (seven hours return) is a good one, allowing you to see the acidic lake up close. This moderate-to-difficult walk begins at Iwikau Village at the top of the Bruce Rd. You can cut three hours off it by catching the **chairlift** (adult/child $30/17; ☺ 9am-3.30pm mid-Dec–April) from Whakapapa Ski Area. **Guided walks** (☑ 0508 782 734; www.mtruapehu.com; adult/child incl lift pass $145/95) to Crater Lake are hosted by Safety & Mountaineering Guides along with local Ngati Hikairo cultural guides, and run from mid-December to May, weather dependent. Like most of the walks in Tongariro, check conditions before heading out and don't attempt it in winter unless you're a mountaineer.

Other Activities

Whakapapa & Turoa

Ski Areas   SKIING, SNOWBOARDING

(☑ Turoa 06-385 8456, Whakapapa 07-892 4000; www.mtruapehu.com; day pass adult/child $97/58) These linked resorts straddle either side of

Mt Ruapehu and are NZ's two largest ski areas. Each offers similar skiing at an analogous altitude (around 2300m), with areas to suit each level of experience – from beginners' slopes to black-diamond runs for the pros. The same lift passes cover both ski areas.

The only accommodation at the Whakapapa ski field is in private lodges (mainly owned by ski clubs), so most visitors stay at Whakapaka or National Park Villages. Turoa is only 16km from Ohakune, which has the best après-ski scene.

Tukino Ski Area
SKIING, SNOWBOARDING

(☑06-387 6294, 0800 885 466; www.tukino.co.nz; day pass adult/child $50/30) Club-operated Tukino is on Mt Ruapehu's east, 46km from Turangi. It's quite remote, 14km down a gravel road from the sealed Desert Rd (SH1), and you need a 4WD vehicle to get in. It offers uncrowded, backcountry runs, mostly beginner and intermediate.

Mountain Air
SCENIC FLIGHTS

(☑0800 922 812; www.mountainair.co.nz; junction SH47 & SH48; 15/25/35min $120/185/225) Offers scenic flights from its base halfway between Whakapapa and National Park Villages. Turangi and Taupo departures also available.

Whakapapa Village

POP 100 (SUMMER), 300 (WINTER)

Located within the bounds of Tongariro National Park on the lower slopes of Mt Ruapehu, Whakapapa Village (pronounced 'fa-ka-pa-pa'; altitude 1140m) is the gateway to the park, home of the park's visitor centre, and the starting point for numerous walking tracks.

🏃 Activities

Whakapapa Nature Walk
WALKING

Suitable for wheelchairs, this 15-minute loop track begins about 250m above the visitor centre, passing through beech forest and gardens typical of the park's vegetation zones.

Ridge Track
HIKING

A 30-minute return walk from the village that climbs through beech forest to alpine-shrub areas for views of Ruapehu and Ngauruhoe.

Taranaki Falls Track
HIKING

A two-hour, 6km loop track heads from the village to Taranaki Falls, which plunge 20m

over an old lava flow into a boulder-ringed pool.

Silica Rapids Track
HIKING

From Whakapapa Village this 2½-hour, 7km loop track leads to the Silica Rapids, named for the silica mineral deposits formed there by rapids on the Waikare Stream.

Tama Lakes Track
HIKING

Part of the Tongariro Northern Circuit, starting at Whakapapa Village, this 17km return track leads to the Tama Lakes, on the Tama Saddle between Ruapehu and Ngauruhoe (five to six hours return). The upper lake affords fine views of Ngauruhoe and Tongariro.

Edge to Edge
EQUIPMENT HIRE

(☑0800 800 754; www.edgetoedge.co.nz; Skotel Alpine Resort; 1-day full ski gear $35-65, 1-day snowboard gear $43-71) Stocks an extensive range of skiing, climbing and alpine gear for hire.

🛏 Sleeping & Eating

Whakapapa Village has limited accommodation, and during ski season prices hit their peak. A greater range of options can be found in National Park Village and Ohakune, with the latter offering the most in the way of eating and shopping.

Whakapapa Holiday Park
HOLIDAY PARK $

(☑07-892 3897; www.whakapapa.net.nz; campsites from $19, dm $25, units $69-149; ☎) This popular DOC-associated park beside Whakapapanui Stream has a wide range of accommodation options, including campervan sites perched on the edge of beautiful beech forest, a 32-bed backpackers lodge (linen required), cabins (linen required) and a self-contained unit. The camp store stocks basic groceries.

Mangahuia DOC Campsite
CAMPING GROUND $

(www.doc.govt.nz; sites per adult/child $6/3) Situated between National Park Village and the SH48 turn-off heading to Whakapapa, this basic roadside DOC campsite has bushy nooks, cold water and pit toilets for self-contained campers only.

Skotel Alpine Resort
HOSTEL $

(☑07-892 3719, 0800 756 835; www.skotel.co.nz; Ngauruhoe Pl; s/tw/tr without bathroom $40/55/75, r with bathroom $110-185, cabins $185; ☎) If you think of it more as a hostel than a hotel, you'll excuse the odd bit of stained carpet or cheap lino, and enjoy the timber-lined alpine ambience and decidedly non-hostel-like facilities: free sauna, spa pool and gym, and ski hire, restaurant and bar.

Tongariro Family
Holiday Park HOLIDAY PARK $
(☑ 07-386 8062; www.thp.co.nz; SH47; campsites per person unpowered/powered $18/20, cabins $60-90, units from $130; 🛜) Conveniently situated for Alpine Crossing trampers, halfway along the highway between the start and finish points, this wee gem is in the middle of nowhere and everywhere at the same time. It's a welcoming camp – simple, sunny and surrounded by forest, with plenty of grass, trees and a playground. Communal facilities, cabins and self-contained units are unflashy but well tended. It's 24km to both Whakapapa Village and Turangi.

Bayview Chateau Tongariro HOTEL $$$
(☑ 07-892 3809, 0800 242 832; www.chateau. co.nz; Whakapapa Village; d $155-355; 🛜 ⊠) With its sublime setting and manor house grandeur, this iconic hotel promises as much as it did when it opened its doors in 1929. Step inside, however, and you will see that its many charms are somewhat faded. But the Chateau remains one of NZ's most romantic hotels, complete with high tea in the library, aperitifs in the elegant foyer bar, and evening dining in the grand **Ruapehu Room** (mains $32-38; ⊘ dinner). Other facilities include two cafes, indoor pool, cinema and nine-hole golf course. Choose from rooms in either the historic hotel (with greater charm) or the adjacent modern wing.

Tussock PUB $
(Whakapapa Village; meals $5-18; ⊘ 3pm-late; 🛜) An agreeable hybrid of the back-blocks Kiwi pub and ski club rooms, Tussock is a warm and comfortable place to eat a basic meal (bacon and egg muffins, pizza, burgers), play pool, watch the big game, or admire the view from the large windows.

❶ Information

Further national park information is available from the i-SITEs in Ohakune (p256), Turangi (p245) and Taupo (p242).
Tongariro National Park Visitor Centre
(☑ 07-892 3729; www.doc.govt.nz; Whakapapa Village; ⊘ 8am-5pm) Has maps and info on all corners of the park, including walks, huts and current skiing, track and weather conditions. Its exhibits on the geological and human history of the area should keep you busy for a couple of hours on a rainy day. The *Walks in and around Tongariro National Park* brochure

provides a helpful overview of 30 walks and tramps in the park ($3).

❶ Getting There & Around

BUS
Tongariro National Park is well serviced by shuttle operators, which service Whakapapa Village, National Park Village, Ohakune, Taupo and Turangi, as well as popular trailheads. In summer, tramping trips are their focus, but in winter most offer ski-field shuttles. Book your bus in advance to avoid unexpected strandings.

Many shuttle-bus operators are offshoots or affiliates of accommodation providers so ask about transport when you book your stay. Otherwise, try Taupo-based **Tongariro Expeditions** (☑ 0800 828 763; www.tongariroexpeditions. com), Turangi-based **Turangi Alpine Shuttles** (☑ 0272 322 135, 07-386 8226; www.turangi-rentals.co.nz) and Whakapapa Village-based **Roam** (☑ 021 588 734, 0800 762 612; www. roam.net.nz).

National Park Village
POP 200
This small sprawl of a town lies at the junction of SH4 and SH47 at 825m above sea level, 15km from the hub of Whakapapa Village. In ski season the township is packed, but in summer it's sleepy despite being a handy base for activities in and around the park.

As you'll discover, it's railway country around here. About 20km south on SH4 at **Horopito** is a monument to the Last Spike, the spike that marked the completion of the Main Trunk Railway Line between Auckland and Wellington in 1908 (although Horopito is better known for Smash Palace, NZ's most famous car graveyard). Five kilometres north from National Park, at **Raurimu**, is evidence of the engineering masterpiece that is the 'spiral'. Trainspotters will marvel, while non-trainspotters will probably wonder what the hell they're looking at it (there's not much to see).

🏃 Activities
There's little to do in the village itself, its major enticement being its proximity to national-park tramps, mountain-bike trails (p254), canoe trips on the Whanganui River, and winter skiing. Most accommodation in town offers packages for lift passes and ski hire, sparing you the steeper prices further up the mountain. Ski gear can be hired from **Eivins** (☑ 07-892 2843; www.eivins.co.nz; Carroll

St), **Snow Zone** (07-892 2757; www.snowzone.co.nz; 25-27 Buddo St) and **Ski Biz** (07-892 2717; www.skibiz.co.nz; 10 Carroll St).

Daily shuttles leave from here to the Tongariro Alpine Crossing and Whakapapa Village in summer, and the ski area in winter.

Adrift Guided Outdoor Adventures
CANOEING, HIKING

(07-892 2751, 0800 462 374; www.adriftnz.co.nz; 3 Waimarino-Tokaanu Road) Runs guided canoe trips on the Whanganui River (one to six days, $245 to $999), as well as freedom canoe hire (three to five days, $185 to $205) and all necessary transfers. It also offers guided tramps in Tongariro National Park (two hours to three days, $95 to $850).

Wades Landing Outdoors
CANOEING, KAYAKING

(07-895 4854; www.whanganui.co.nz; 11 Kaitieke Rd, Raurimu) Offers freedom kayak and canoe hire for one- to five-day Whanganui River expeditions, including jetboat/road transfers to trailheads ($150 to $190). Also mountain-biking shuttles, Alpine Crossing transport ($35), *Lord of the Rings* tours and a 'prehistoric driftwood sculpture park'.

Kiwi Mountain Bikes
MOUNTAIN BIKING

(0800 562 4537; www.kiwimountainbikes.co.nz; 54 Carroll St) Affable Rick rents mountain bikes (half/full day from $40/65) and provides bike transport to the 17km (mostly) downhill Fishers Track and 42 Traverse ($35), as well as information and transport for other trails in the area.

Climbing Wall
CLIMBING

(www.npbp.co.nz; 4 Findlay St; adult/child $15/10; 9am-8pm) For rainy days there's an 8m-high indoor climbing wall at National Park Backpackers. Outdoor climbers with their own gear can find spots near Manataupo Valley and Whakapapa Gorge.

Sleeping

National Park is a town of budget and mid-range accommodation. This makes sense, as you'll probably spend most of your time in the great outdoors.

The following listings give summer prices; be warned that when the ski season is in full swing, accommodation is tight and bookings are essential.

Plateau
LODGE, HOSTEL $

(07-892 2993; www.plateaulodge.co.nz; 17 Carroll St; dm $30, d $70-110, apt from $160;) Family-friendly Plateau has cosy rooms, some with

en suite and TV, as well as an attractive communal lounge, kitchen and hot tub. The dorms don't get bigger than two sets of bunks and there are two-bedroom apartments sleeping up to six. Local shuttle services available.

National Park Backpackers
HOSTEL $

(07-892 2870; www.npbp.co.nz; 4 Findlay St; dm $26-29, d $62-86;) This big, old board and batten YHA hostel has a large garden for lounging, a well-equipped kitchen and standard rooms. It's a good one-stop shop for booking activities in the area, and is home to the Climbing Wall for when the weather turns to custard. Small shop on site.

Tongariro Crossing Lodge
LODGE $$

(07-892 2688; www.tongarirocrossinglodge.com; 27 Carroll St; s $115-125, d $155-165;) As pretty as a picture, this white weatherboard cottage is decorated with a baby-blue trim and rambling blooms in summer. Cosy accommodation ranges from standard doubles to larger self-contained apartments, and is dotted with period furniture. Breakfast is optional ($17 to $26) but wi-fi and use of the barbecue and sunny patio are free.

Adventure Lodge & Motel
LODGE, MOTEL $$

(07-892 2991; www.adventurenationalpark.co.nz; 21 Carroll St; d/tw $50/70, units from $110;) This place caters particularly to Tongariro Alpine Crossing trampers, offering accommodation and transfers, with all-inclusive packages available (two nights' accommodation, breakfasts, lunch, dinner, T-shirt and transport for $170 to $265). Chill out post-walk in the relaxing lounge, spa pool or barbecue area. The motel units are clean but unspectacular.

Discovery Lodge
LODGE $$

(07-892 2744; www.discovery.net.nz; SH47; cabins per person $30, units d $145-225) Midway between the village and the Whakapapa turn-off, this complex has a range of rooms from basic cabins and beige motel room, to upmarket chalets sleeping four people. An onsite restaurant has views of Ruapehu, plus there's a large deck, bar and comfy lounge. The zealous owner is keen to help you discover his world; shuttles available.

Eating & Drinking

★ Station
CAFE $$

(07-892 2881; www.stationcafe.co.nz; cnr Findlay St & Station Rd; lunch $9-18, dinner $29-38; 9am-late Wed-Mon, to 3pm Tue) Count your blessings ye who find this little railway station along the line, a lovely old dear, restored with care and now serving eggy brunches, sandwiches, coffee and yummy cakes, plus an impressive à la carte evening menu. Sunday roasts ($35) and Curry Thursdays ($16) are dinnertime highlights.

Four Square Supermarket SELF-CATERING $
(cnr SH4 & Waimarino-Takaanu Rd; ⊙7am-7pm) This shop-cum-service-station stocks groceries, tramping food and a cornucopia of other useful wares.

Schnapps PUB
(www.schnappsbarruapehu.com; Findlay St; meals $14-28; ⊙noon-late) This popular pub has a meat-fest menu, open fire, big screen, pool table and a handy ATM. Things crank up on wintry weekends.

ⓘ Information

There's no i-SITE in the village, so visit www.nationalpark.co.nz and www.visitruapehu.com for info.

ⓘ Getting There & Away

Passing through are buses run by **InterCity** (✆06-835 4326; www.intercity.co.nz) and **Naked Bus** (www.nakedbus.com), as well as *The Northerner* train run by KiwiRail Scenic (p232).

Ohakune

POP 1000

Expect to see carrots crop up all over Ohakune, for this is indisputably the country's carrot capital. Carrots were first grown in the area during the 1920s by Chinese settlers, who cleared the land by hand and explosives. Today, the venerable vegetable is celebrated during the annual **Carrot Carnival** (www.carrotcarnival.org.nz), and immortalised in a roadside tribute – the impossible-to-miss **Big Carrot** (Rangataua Rd), erected in 1984.

But locals needn't mention liver cleansing and eyesight improvement to win us over to the charms of this little town. A pretty retreat in the summer offering outdoor adventure galore, Ohakune springs to life in winter when the snow drifts down on Turoa Ski Area and the snow bunnies invade.

There are two distinct parts to the town: the commercial hub is strung along the highway, but in winter the northern end around the train station, known as the Junction, is the epicentre of the action. The two are linked by the **Mangawhero River Walkway**, a leafy amble taking around 25 minutes on foot.

🏃 Activities

There are several scenic walks near the town, many starting from the Ohakune Mountain Rd, which stretches 17km from Ohakune to the Turoa Ski Area (p249) on Mt Ruapehu. The handy DOC brochure *Walks in and Around Tongariro National Park* ($3), available from the i-SITE, is a good starting point.

The Tongariro Alpine Crossing is readily accessible via regular shuttle services from Ohakune, while the **Round the Mountain** (www.doc.govt.nz) track can be accessed by continuing on the Waitonga Falls track.

Mangawhero Forest Walk WALKING
An easy stroll starting near the beginning of Ohakune Mountain Rd (one-hour loop, 3km), taking in native forest and the Mangawhero River. It is well graded and suitable for wheelchairs and pushchairs.

Waitonga Falls &
Lake Surprise Tracks HIKING
The path to Waitonga Falls (1½ hours return, 4km), Tongariro's highest waterfall (39m), offers magnificent views of Mt Ruapehu. A more challenging walk climbs to shallow Lake Surprise (five hours return, 9km). Both tracks start from Ohakune Mountain Rd.

Mountain Bike Station MOUNTAIN BIKING
(✆06-385 8797; www.mountainbikestation.co.nz; 60 Thames St) Rents mountain bikes (half/full day from $35/50) and provides transfers to local mountain-biking routes, including the Ohakune Old Coach Road (p254) for $20; bike and transport packages are available. Its subsidiary, Ski & Board Station, rents ski and snowboard gear (from $25).

TCB EQUIPMENT HIRE
(✆06-385 8433; www.tcbskiandboard.co.nz; 29 Ayr St) A good source of information about local mountain-biking routes, TCB publishes a free bike trail map and rents mountain bikes (half/full day $35/50) and skiing/boading gear (from $35/40).

Ski Shed EQUIPMENT HIRE
(✆06-385 9173; www.skished.com; 71 Clyde St) Hires skiing/boarding gear (from $35/43), and snow-appropriate clothing.

MOUNTAIN BIKING THE OLD COACH ROAD

The **Ohakune Old Coach Road** (www.ohakunecoachroad.co.nz) is a fantastic adventure for moderately fit cyclists, with local operators offering all the gear and transport to make things easy.

An excellent example of restoration for recreation, the dual-use (walking and cycling) track follows the original 15km coach track from Ohakune to Horopito. Dating from 1886, it was built largely by hand by workers who lived in canvas tents and endured harsh winter conditions. The track was gradually upgraded to carry passengers and goods, and used until 1909 when SH49 opened. Largely forgotten and overgrown, the Old Coach Road was resurrected by the locals and restored to glory.

And glorious it is. One of the most enjoyable half-day (three to four hours) cycle rides in NZ, the gently graded route passes a number of unique engineering features, including the historic Hapuawhenua and Toanui viaducts – the only two remaining curved viaducts in the southern hemisphere. It also passes through ancient forest of giant rimu and totara that survived the Taupo blast of AD 180, being in the lea of Ruapehu. Views extend over the odd-shaped hillocks and mesa around the foot of the volcano.

Cyclists are best to start at Horopito (where you can check out the car graveyard known as 'Smash Palace'), as this gives you more downhill, overall. The odd push uphill may well be required, but you'll get sufficient in-the-saddle time to justify the effort – especially on some of the sweeping downhills underlaid with historic cobblestones. This is wobbly, freewheeling fun for the whole family.

And this is just the tip of the Central Plateau's mountain-biking iceberg. The Old Coach Road is the start of the **Mountains to Sea Trail** (Nga Ara Tuhono; www.mountainstosea.co.nz), a 317km route from Mt Ruapehu to Whanganui. This epic also encompasses the improving Mangapurua and Kaiwhakauka Tracks, easily accessible from Ohakune and National Park and set to challenge the long-established **42 Traverse** and **Fishers Track** as the must-do day-rides in the area.

For bike hire and shuttles, visit TCB (p253) and Mountain Bike Station (p253) in Ohakune, and Kiwi Mountain Bikes (p252) in National Park.

SLR   EQUIPMENT HIRE, CLIMBING
(☑06-385 9018; www.slr.co.nz; Goldfinch St) As well as ski/board hire (from $25), SLR runs **Vertigo Climbing Centre** (www.vertigoclimbing.co.nz), a climbing wall behind the shop ($15).

Powderhorn Snow Centre   EQUIPMENT HIRE
(☑06-385 9100; www.snowcentre.co.nz; 194 Mangawhero Tce) Sells and hires snow gear and mountain bikes (half/full day $35/55).

Ruapehu Homestead   HORSE RIDING
(☑027-267 7057; www.ruapehuhomestead.co.nz; cnr Piwara St & SH49, Rangataua; 30min-3hr adult $30-120, child $15-90) Located 4km east of Ohakune (near Rangataua), Ruapehu Homestead offers guided treks around its paddocks, as well as longer rides along the river and on backcountry trails with views of the mountain.

Canoe Safaris   CANOEING, RAFTING
(☑06-385 9237, 0800 272 3353; www.canoesafaris.co.nz; 6 Tay St) Offers guided canoeing trips on the Whanganui River (one to five days, $175 to $995) and Rangitikei River (one to four days, $175 to $875), plus guided rafting trips on the Mohaka River (two to four days, $425 to $950). Canoe and kayak hire (two to five days $170 to $205).

Yeti Tours   CANOEING, KAYAKING
(☑06-385 8197, 0800 322 388; www.yetitours.co.nz; 61 Clyde St; guided tours 2-6 days $365-895, 2-6 day hire $175-210) Leads guided canoeing safaris on the Whanganui and Mokau Rivers, and hires canoes and kayaks.

Heliview   HELICOPTER
(☑0800 435 426; www.heliview.co.nz; Ohakune Airfield, SH49; flights 35/45mins $329/439) Offers scenic helicopter flights including the 35-minute 'Carrot to Crater' flight over the summit of Ruapehu, or the 45-minute 'Three Peaks' over the park's mountain trio.

🛏 Sleeping

The prices listed are for summer; expect to pay up to twice as much in winter and book ahead. Savings can be made on winter rates by booking midweek.

★ Station Lodge
HOSTEL $

(☑ 06-385 8797; www.stationlodge.co.nz; 60 Thames St; dm $27, r $54, unit $100-200; ☎) ⬤ Housed in a lovely old villa with wooden floors and high ceilings, this excellent YHA hostel has a well-equipped kitchen, comfortable lounge, spa pool, and tidy garden with a pizza oven. If you're after privacy, separate chalets and apartments are available. The clued-up owners also run Mountain Bike Station and Ski & Board Station.

Ohakune Top 10
HOLIDAY PARK $

(☑ 06-385 8561, 0800 825 825; www.ohakune.net. nz; 5 Moore St; campsites $42, units $68-135; ☎) ⬤ A bubbling stream borders this holiday park, which has a wide range of accommodation including tidy motel units. Extras include a playground, barbecue area and private spa bath.

Mountain View
MOTEL $

(☑ 06-385 8675; www.mountain-viewmotel.co.nz; 2 Moore St; units $75-100; ☎) In this old, vaguely Tudor-styled motel, rooms are basic but clean, quiet and good value. Most have kitchen facilities and there's also a spa pool.

Snowhaven
APARTMENTS, B&B $$

(☑ 06-385 9498; www.snowhaven.co.nz; 92 Clyde St; apt $95-125, r $195, townhouse from $195; ☎) A tasty trio is on offer here: modern studio apartments in a slate-fronted block on the main drag; three self-contained, three-bedroom townhouses by the Junction; or luxury B&B rooms somewhere between the other two. All are top, well-priced options.

Peaks Motor Inn
MOTEL $$

(☑ 06-385 9144, 0508 843 732; www.thepeaks. co.nz; cnr Mangawhero Tce & Shannon St; units $99-124; ☎) This well-kept motel offers spacious rooms with good bathrooms and full kitchens. Communal facilities include grassy lawns, a basic gym, large outdoor spa, and sauna.

★ Powderhorn Chateau
HOTEL $$$

(☑ 06-385 8888; www.powderhorn.co.nz; cnr Thames St & Mangawhero Tce; r from $215; ☎ ☒) Enjoying a long-standing reputation as the hub of activity during the ski season, the Powderhorn has a Swiss-chalet feel with woody interiors, slate floors and exposed rafters. The spa-temperature indoor pool is a relaxing way to recover from the slopes before enjoying revelry in the popular in-house establishments.

✖ Eating & Drinking

The Junction is the après-ski place to be, but in summer most of the action drifts to the other end of town. Many hotels sprout restaurants during the ski season.

New World
SUPERMARKET $

(12 Goldfinch St; ⊙ 7am-7pm) Self-caterers should head for New World, your best bet for stocking up before heading to National Park or Whakapapa.

★ Bearing Point
INTERNATIONAL $$

(☑ 06-385 9006; www.thebearingpointrestaurant. co.nz; Clyde St; mains $26-36; ⊙ 6pm-late Tue-Sat) Hearty, accomplished fare is offered at this surprisingly chic establishment. Warm your cockles with a venison hot pot, maple-glazed salmon, aged steaks or spicy Thai curry.

OCR
CAFE $$

(☑ 06-385 8322; www.ocrcafe.co.nz; 2 Tyne St; mains $10-29; ⊙ 9am-late Fri & Sat, 9am-3pm Sun) Housed in a spacious old bungalow, this groovy cafe has limited opening hours but remains a favourite among locals and visitors alike. Burgers, sandwiches, salads and hearty breakfasts are made with care as are the home-baked cakes and slices. A rootsy soundtrack and wood burner lend a rustic vibe.

Powderkeg & Matterhorn
BAR, RESTAURANT $$

(☑ 06-385 8888; www.powderhorn.co.nz; cnr Thames St & Mangawhero Tce; bar menu $11-22, à la carte menu $22-36; ⊙ 4pm-late) The Powderkeg is the party bar of the Powderhorn Chateau, with DJs in winter, regular dancing on the tables and a notable craft beer selection. Upstairs is the swankier Matterhorn,

WORTH A TRIP

LAKE ROTOKURA

Rotokura Ecological Reserve (www.doc.govt.nz) is 14km southeast of Ohakune, at Karioi, just off SH49 (*karioi* means 'places to linger'). There are two lakes here: the first is Dry Lake, actually quite wet and perfect for picnicking; the furthest is Rotokura, *tapu* (sacred) to Maori, so eating, fishing and swimming are prohibited. The round-trip walk will take you 45 minutes; longer if you linger to admire the ancient beech trees and waterfowl such as dabchicks and paradise ducks.

serving cocktails and an à la carte menu of meaty mains and decadent desserts. In summer the Matterhorn closes and its menu descends to the Powderkeg.

Cyprus Tree ITALIAN $$
(19a Goldfinch St; mains $23-32; ⊗9am-late) Open all year round, this restaurant and bar serves up a tasty mix of Italian and Kiwi-influenced dishes: think pasta, risotto and sumac lamb. The high-season chaos is tempered by a friendly team, cocktails, and quality wines and beer.

Mountain Rocks BAR, CAFE
(www.themountainrocks.co.nz; cnr Clyde & Goldfinch Sts; mains $14-33; ⊗8am-late) A log-cabin-like space with a nod to the all-American diner. Join the locals for cheap beers and a no-surprises selection of big-portion burgers, lamb shanks, steaks, and fish and chips. Buzzy garden bar with a big screen for the big games.

ⓘ Information

Ohakune Public Library (☎06-385 8364; 37 Ayr St; ⊗8am-5pm Mon-Fri; 🕾) Offers free internet access.

Ruapehu i-SITE (☎06-385 8427; www.visitruapehu.com; 54 Clyde St; ⊗9am-5pm) Can make bookings for activities, transport and accommodation; DOC officers are usually on hand from 10am to 4.30pm most days.

Visit Ohakune (www.visitohakune.co.nz) Useful website for 'The Mountain Town' and around.

ⓘ Getting There & Around

Passing through are buses run by **InterCity** (www.intercity.co.nz) and **Naked Bus** (www.nakedbus.com), as well as *The Northerner* train run by KiwiRail Scenic (p232).

Matai Shuttles (☎06-385 8724; www.mataishuttles.co.nz) is based in Ohakune, offering services around the Central Plateau.

Waiouru

POP 740

At the junction of SH1 and SH49, 27km east of Ohakune, Waiouru (altitude 792m) is primarily an army base and a refuelling stop for the 56km-long Desert Rd leading to Turangi. A barren landscape of reddish

sand with small clumps of tussock, **Rangipo Desert** isn't actually a desert. This unique landscape is in fact the result of two million years of volcanic eruptions – especially the Taupo eruption about 2000 years ago which coated the land with thick deposits of pumice and destroyed all vegetation. In winter, the road occasionally closes due to snow.

Housed in a large, concrete bunker at the south end of the township, the **National Army Museum** (www.armymuseum.co.nz; adult/child $15/5; ⊗9am-4.30pm) 🍃 preserves the history of the NZ army and its various campaigns, from colonial times to the present. Moving stories are told through displays of arms, uniforms, medals and memorabilia.

Taihape & Around

POP 1500

Taihape, 20km south of Waiouru, enjoys the dubious distinction of being the Gumboot Capital of the World, celebrated with – you guessed it – a giant corrugated gumboot on the main road. It is also the access point for **Mokai Gravity Canyon** (☎06-388 9109, 0800 802 864; www.gravitycanyon.co.nz; 332 Mokai Rd; ⊗9am-5pm), 20km southeast, where adrenaline-junkies can take a 1km, 170m-high flying-fox ride at speeds of up to 160km/h ($155); dive from the North Island's highest bridge bungy (80m, $179); or freefall for 50m on a tandem swing ($159). Multi-thrill packages are available.

Taihape is also the nearest town to **River Valley** (☎06-388 1444; www.rivervalley.co.nz), an adventure centre and lodge 32km to the northeast (follow the signs from Taihape's Gretna Hotel). Their popular half-day white-water rafting trip takes in the thrilling Grade V rapids of the Rangitikei River ($175). Free-style horse treks are also offered, which take in views of Mt Ruapehu, the Ruahine Range and the Rangitikei River (two hours $109, half-day $175). Lodge accommodation (from $31) is also offered, as are meals in the on-site restaurant, featuring fresh ingredients from the lodge's gardens.

For more information, visit www.taihape.co.nz.

Rotorua & the Bay of Plenty

Includes ➡

Rotorua...................... 259

Tauranga.................... 276

Mt Maunganui 284

Katikati 288

Te Puke 289

Whakatane 289

Whakaari
(White Island)............294

Ohope 295

Opotiki 295

Best Outdoors

➡ Rotorua Canopy Tours (p262)

➡ Surfing at Mt Maunganui (p282)

➡ Redwoods Whakarewarewa Forest (p273)

➡ Waikite Valley Thermal Pools (p276)

Best Places to Stay

➡ Regent of Rotorua (p269)

➡ Warm Earth Cottage (p288)

➡ Captain's Cabin (p292)

➡ Opotiki Beach House (p296)

Why Go?

Captain Cook christened the Bay of Plenty when he cruised past in 1769, and plentiful it remains. Blessed with sunshine and sand, the bay stretches from Waihi Beach in the west to Opotiki in the east, with the holiday hubs of Tauranga, Mt Maunganui and Whakatane in between.

Offshore from Whakatane is New Zealand's most active volcano, Whakaari (White Island). Volcanic activity defines this region, and nowhere is this subterranean sexiness more obvious than in Rotorua. Here the daily business of life goes on among steaming hot springs, explosive geysers, bubbling mud pools and the billows of sulphurous gas responsible for the town's 'unique' eggy smell.

Rotorua and the Bay of Plenty are also strongholds of Maori tradition, presenting many opportunities to engage with NZ's rich indigenous culture: check out a power-packed concert performance, chow down at a *hangi* (Maori feast) or skill-up with some Maori arts-and-crafts techniques.

When to Go

➡ The Bay of Plenty is one of NZ's sunniest regions: Whakatane records a brilliant 2350 average hours of sunshine per year! In summer (December to February) maximums hover between 20°C and 27°C. Everyone else is here too, but the holiday vibe is heady.

➡ Visit Rotorua any time: the geothermal activity never sleeps, and there are enough beds in any season.

➡ The mercury can slide below 5°C overnight here in winter, although it's usually warmer on the coast (and you'll have the beach all to yourself).

Rotorua & the Bay of Plenty Highlights

① Watching Rotorua's geysers blow their tops at **Te Puia** (p259) or **Whakarewarewa Thermal Village** (p260)

② Ogling kaleidoscopic colours and bubbling mud pools at **Wai-O-Tapu Thermal Wonderland** (p276)

③ Mountain biking in the **Redwoods Whakarewarewa Forest** (p273)

④ Carving up the surf over NZ's first artificial reef at **Mt Maunganui** (p282)

⑤ Flying or boating out to NZ's only active marine volcano, **Whakaari** (p293)

⑥ Kicking back for a few days in **Whakatane** (p289) – NZ's most underrated seaside town?

⑦ Swimming with dolphins at **Tauranga** (p276)

⑧ Drinking in **Mt Maunganui** (p286) after a beach afternoon

⑨ Climbing the pohutukawa-studded flanks of **Mauao** (Mt Maunganui; p284)

ℹ Getting There & Around

Air New Zealand (www.airnewzealand.co.nz) has direct flights from Tauranga and Rotorua to Auckland, Wellington and Christchurch, plus Rotorua to Sydney (every Tuesday and Saturday) and Whakatane to Auckland.

InterCity (www.intercity.co.nz) and **Naked Bus** (www.nakedbus.com) services connect Tauranga, Rotorua and Whakatane with most other main cities in NZ. **Bay Hopper** (☑ 0800 422 928; www.baybus.co.nz) bus services run between Tauranga, Whakatane and Opotiki. **Twin City Express** (☑ 0800 422 928; www.baybus.co.nz) buses link Tauranga and Rotorua.

ROTORUA

POP 65,280

Catch a whiff of Rotorua's sulphur-rich, asthmatic airs and you've already got a taste of NZ's most dynamic thermal area, home to spurting geysers, steaming hot springs and exploding mud pools. The Maori revered this place, naming one of the most spectacular springs Wai-O-Tapu (Sacred Waters). Today 35% of the population is Maori, with their cultural performances and traditional *hangi* as big an attraction as the landscape itself.

Despite the pervasive eggy odour, 'Sulphur City' is one of the most touristed spots on the North Island, with nearly three million visitors annually. Some locals say this steady trade has seduced the town into resting on its laurels, and that socially Rotorua lags behind more progressive towns such as Tauranga and Taupo. And with more motels than nights in November, the urban fabric of 'RotoVegas' isn't particularly appealing... but still, where else can you see a 30m geothermal geyser!

History

The Rotorua area was first settled in the 14th century when the canoe *Te Arawa,* captained by Tamatekapua, arrived from Hawaiki at Maketu in the central Bay of Plenty. Settlers took the tribal name Te Arawa to commemorate the vessel that had brought them here.

In the next few hundred years, subtribes spread and divided through the area, with conflicts breaking out over limited territory. A flashpoint occurred in 1823 when the Arawa lands were invaded by tribes from the Northland in the so-called Musket Wars. After heavy losses on both sides, the Northlanders eventually withdrew.

During the Waikato Land War (1863–64) Te Arawa threw in its lot with the government against its traditional Waikato enemies, gaining troop support and preventing East Coast reinforcements getting through to support the Kingitanga movement.

With peace in the early 1870s, word spread of scenic wonders, miraculous landscapes and watery cures for all manner of diseases. Rotorua boomed. Its main attraction was the fabulous Pink and White Terraces, formed by volcanic silica deposits. Touted at the time as the eighth natural wonder of the world, they were destroyed in the 1886 Mt Tarawera eruption.

◉ Sights

Te Puia   GEYSER, CULTURAL TOUR
(Map p274; ☑ 07-348 9047, 0800 837 842; www.tepuia.com; Hemo Rd; tours adult/child $48.50/24.50, daytime tour & performance combo $60.50/30.50, evening tour, performance & hangi combo $150/75; ⊙ 8am-6pm Nov-Apr, to 5pm May-Oct) Rotorua's main drawcard is Te Whakarewarewa (pronounced 'fa-ka-re-wa-re-wa'), a thermal reserve 3km south of the city centre. There are more than 500 springs here, the most famous of which is **Pohutu** ('Big Splash' or 'Explosion'), a geyser which erupts up to 20 times a day, spurting hot water up to 30m skyward. You'll

---

ESSENTIAL ROTORUA & THE BAY OF PLENTY

Eat A buttery corn cob in Rotorua, cooked in a thermal *hangi* at Whakarewarewa Thermal Village (p260)

Drink Croucher Brewing Co's pale ale, brewed in Rotorua

Read *How to Watch a Bird,* an exposition on the joys of avian observation, written by Mt Maunganui schoolboy Steve Braunias

Listen to *Kora,* the eponymous rootsy album from Whakatane's soulful sons

Watch Maori TV and Te Reo, NZ's two Maori TV stations

Go green See www.sustainablenz.com for tips on how to make your Rotorua visit more ecofriendly

Online www.rotoruanz.com; www.bayofplenty.co.nz

Area code ☑ 07

Rotorua

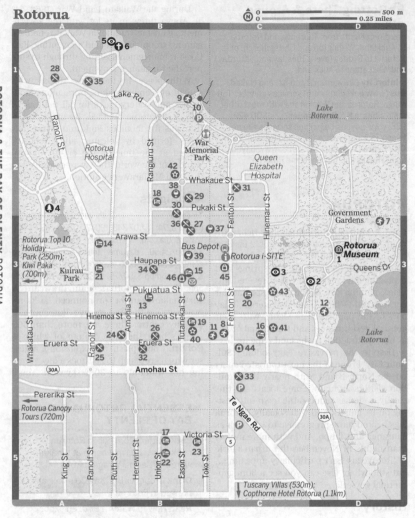

know when it's about to blow because the adjacent **Prince of Wales' Feathers** geyser will start up shortly before. Both these geysers form part of Te Puia, the most polished of NZ's Maori cultural attractions. Also here is the National Carving School and the National Weaving School, where you can discover the work and methods of traditional Maori woodcarvers and weavers, plus a carved meeting house, a cafe, galleries, a kiwi reserve and a gift shop.

Tours take 1½ hours and depart hourly from 9am (the last tour an hour before closing). Daytime 45-minute cultural performances start at 10.15am, 12.15pm and 3.15pm; nightly three-hour Te Po indigenous concerts and *hangi* feasts start at 6pm (following on from a 4.30pm tour in a combo package).

Whakarewarewa Thermal Village
THERMAL RESERVE, CULTURAL TOUR

(Map p274; ☏ 07-349 3463; www.whakarewarewa. com; 17 Tyron St; tour & cultural performance adult/ child $35/15; ⊙ 8.30am-5pm) Whakarewarewa Thermal Village is a living village where *tangata whenua* (the locals) still reside, as they have for centuries. The villagers show

Rotorua

◎ **Top Sights**
1 Rotorua Museum.....................................D3

◎ **Sights**
2 Blue Baths..D3
3 Government Gardens.............................C3
4 Kuirau Park...A2
5 Ohinemutu..A1
6 St Faith's Anglican Church...................B1

◉ **Activities, Courses & Tours**
7 Ballbusters..D3
8 Bike Barn...C4
9 Kawarau Jet...B1
 Lakeland Queen...............................(see 10)
10 Mana Adventures....................................B1
 Mokoia Island Wai Ora
 Experiences...................................(see 9)
11 O'Keefe's Fishing Specialists................C4
12 Polynesian Spa.......................................D3
 The Wall...(see 19)
 Volcanic Air Safaris.......................(see 10)

◉ **Sleeping**
13 Astray..B3
14 Base Rotorua...A3
15 Blarney's Rock...B3
16 Crash Palace...C4
17 Funky Green Voyager.............................B5
 Millennium Hotel...........................(see 41)
18 Regent of Rotorua..................................B2
19 Rock Solid Backpackers.......................B4
20 Rotorua Central
 Backpackers...C3

21 Rotorua YHA..A3
22 Six on Union..B5
23 Victoria Lodge...B5

⊗ **Eating**
24 Abracadabra Cafe Bar...........................B4
25 Bistro 1284...A4
26 Capers Epicurean..................................B4
27 Fat Dog Cafe & Bar.................................B3
28 Fish & Chip Shop....................................A1
29 Indian Star..B2
30 Leonardo's...B2
31 Lime Caffeteria.......................................C2
32 Mistress of Cakes..................................B4
33 Pak 'n Save...C4
34 Sabroso..B3
35 Third Place Cafe.....................................A1
36 Weilin's Noodle House...........................B3

◉ **Drinking & Nightlife**
37 Belgian Bar..C3
38 Brew...B2
39 Pig & Whistle..B3

◉ **Entertainment**
40 Basement Cinema..................................B4
41 Millennium Hotel Rotorua....................C4
42 Novotel Rotorua.....................................B2
43 Tamaki Maori Village..............................C3

◉ **Shopping**
44 Mountain Jade...C4
45 Out of New Zealand...............................C3
46 Rotorua Night Market.............................B3

you around and tell you the stories of their way of life and the significance of the steamy bubbling pools, the silica terraces and the geysers that, although inaccessible from the village, are easily viewed from vantage points (the view of Pohutu is just as good from here as it is from Te Puia, and considerably cheaper).

The village shops sell authentic arts and crafts, and you can learn more about Maori traditions such as flax weaving, carving, and *ta moko* (tattooing). Nearby you can eat tasty, buttery sweetcorn ($2) pulled straight out of the hot mineral pool – the only genuine geothermal *hangi* in town. There are cultural performances at 11.15am and 2pm, and guided tours at 9am, 10am, 11am, noon, 1pm, 3pm and 4pm.

★ **Rotorua Museum**   MUSEUM, GALLERY
(Map p260; ☏ 07-351 8055; www.rotoruamuseum. co.nz; Queens Dr, Government Gardens; adult/child $20/8; ◷ 9am-5pm, to 6pm Dec-Feb, tours hourly 10am-4pm plus 5pm Dec-Feb) This outstanding museum occupies a grand Tudor-style edifice. It was originally an elegant spa retreat called the Bath House (1908): displays in the former shower rooms give a fascinating insight into some of the eccentric therapies once administered here, including 'electric baths' and the Bergonie Chair.

A gripping 20-minute film on the history of Rotorua, including the Tarawera eruption, runs every 20 minutes from 9am (not for small kids – the eruption noises are authentic!). The fabulous **Don Stafford Wing** houses eight object-rich galleries dedicated to Rotorua's Te Arawa people, featuring woodcarving, flax weaving, jade, interactive audiovisual displays and the stories of the revered WWII 28 Maori Battalion. Also here are two **art galleries** (with air swabbed clean of hydrogen sulphide) and a cool cafe with garden views (although the best view in town can be had from the **viewing platform** on the roof).

MAORI NZ: ROTORUA & THE BAY OF PLENTY

The Bay of Plenty's traditional name, Te Rohe o Mataatua, recalls the ancestral *Mataatua* canoe, which arrived here from Hawaiki to make an eventful landfall at Whakatane. The region's history stretches back further than that, though, with the Polynesian settler Toi setting up what's claimed to be Aotearoa's first settlement in about AD 800.

Major tribal groups in the region are the **Ngati Awa** (www.ngatiawa.iwi.nz) of the Whakatane area, **Whakatohea** (www.whakatohea.co.nz) of Opotiki, **Ngai Te Rangi** (www.ngaiterangi.org.nz) of Tauranga, and **Te Arawa** (www.tearawa.iwi.nz) of Rotorua. Tribes in this region were involved on both sides of the Land Wars of the late 19th century, with those fighting against the government suffering considerable land confiscations that have caused legal problems right up to the present day.

There's a significant Maori population around the region, and many ways for travellers to engage with Maori culture. Opotiki has Hiona St Stephen's Church (p295) – the death here of government spy Reverend Carl Volkner in 1865 inspired the charming eyeball-eating scene in *Utu*. Whakatane has a visitor-friendly main-street *marae* (p289) (meeting house complex) and Toi's Pa, perhaps NZ's oldest *pa* (fortified village) site. Rotorua has traditional Maori villages, *hangi* and cultural performances aplenty.

Lake Rotorua   LAKE

FREE Lake Rotorua is the largest of the district's 16 lakes and is – underneath all that water – a spent volcano. Sitting in the lake is Mokoia Island, which has for centuries been occupied by various subtribes of the area. The lake can be explored by boat, with several operators situated at the lakefront.

Kuirau Park   PARK

(Map p260; cnr Ranolf & Pukuatua Sts) **FREE** Want some affordable geothermal thrills? Just west of central Rotorua is Kuirau Park, a volcanic area you can explore for free. In 2003 an eruption covered much of the park (including the trees) in mud, drawing crowds of spectators. It has a crater lake, pools of boiling mud and plenty of huffing steam. Take care – the pools here are boiling, and accidents have happened.

Government Gardens   GARDENS

(Map p260; Hinemaru St) **FREE** The manicured English-style Government Gardens surrounding the Rotorua Museum are pretty as a picture, with roses aplenty, steaming thermal pools dotted about and civilised amenities such as croquet lawns and bowling greens. Also here is the upmarket Polynesian Spa and Ballbusters golf.

Blue Baths   BATHHOUSE

(Map p260; ☑07-350 2119; www.bluebaths.co.nz; Government Gardens; adult/child/family $11/6/30; ⊙noon-6pm Apr-Oct, 10am-6pm Nov-Mar) The gorgeous Spanish Mission–style Blue Baths opened in 1933 (and, amazingly, were closed from 1982 to 1999). If you feel like taking a

dip, the **heated pool** awaits. Ask about occasional **dinner-and-cabaret shows** (from $80 per person).

Ohinemutu   MAORI VILLAGE

(Map p260) **FREE** Ohinemutu is a ramshackle lakeside Maori village (access via Kiharoa, Haukotuku or Korokai Sts off Lake St, north of Rotorua Hospital) that traces the fusing of European and Maori cultures. Highlights include the sacred 1905 **Tama-te-kapua Meeting House** (not open to visitors), plenty of steaming volcanic vents, and the historic timber **St Faith's Anglican Church** (Map p260; ☑07-348 2393; cnr Mataiawhea & Korokai Sts; admission by donation; ⊙8am-6pm, services 9am Sun & 10am Wed), which features intricate Maori carvings, *tukutuku* (woven panels) and a stained-glass window of Christ wearing a Maori cloak as he walks on the waters of Lake Rotorua.

Be respectful if you're visiting the village: this is private land, and locals don't appreciate loud, nosy tourists wandering around taking photos.

🏃 Activities

Extreme Sports

Rotorua Canopy Tours   EXTREME SPORTS

(Map p274; ☑07-343 1001, 0800 226 679; www.canopytours.co.nz; 173 Old Taupo Rd; 3hr tours per adult/child/family $129/85/399; ⊙8am-8pm Oct-Apr, 8am-6pm May-Sep) Explore a 1.2km web of bridges, flying foxes, ziplines and platforms, 22m high in a lush native forest canopy 10 minutes out of town (...they say that rimu tree is 1000 years old!). Plenty of native birds to keep you company. Free pick-ups available.

Agroventures
EXTREME SPORTS

(Map p274; ☑ 07-357 4747, 0800 949 888; www.agroventures.co.nz; Western Rd, off Paradise Valley Rd, Ngongotaha; 1/2/4/8 rides $49/75/99/179; ☺9am-5pm) Agroventures is a hive of action, 9km north of Rotorua on SH5 (shuttles available). Start off with the 43m **bungy** and the **Swoop**, a 130km/h swing that can be enjoyed alone or with friends. If that's not enough, try **Freefall Xtreme**, which simulates skydiving by blasting you 3m into the air on a column of wind. Also here is the **Shweeb**, a monorail velodrome from which you hang in a clear capsule and pedal yourself along recumbently at speeds of up to 60km/h. Alongside is the **Agrojet**, allegedly NZ's fastest jetboat, splashing around a 1km course.

Zorb
EXTREME SPORTS

(Map p274; ☑ 07-357 5100, 0800 227 474; www.zorb.com; cnr Western Rd & SH5, Ngongotaha; 1/2/3 rides $45/70/90; ☺9am-5pm, to 7pm Dec-Mar) The Zorb is 9km north of Rotorua on SH5 – look for the grassy hillside with large, clear, people-filled spheres rolling down it. Your eyes do not deceive you! There are three courses: 150m straight, 180m zigzag or 250m 'Drop'. Do your zorb strapped in and dry, or freestyle with water thrown in.

Ogo
EXTREME SPORTS

(Map p274; ☑ 07-343 7676, 0800 646 768; www.ogo.co.nz; 525 Ngongotaha Rd; rides from $45; ☺9am-5pm, to 6.30pm Dec-Feb) Similar to the Zorb, the Ogo (about 5km north of town) involves careening down a grassy hillside in a big bubble, with water or without. Silly? Fun? Terrifying? All of the above...

The Wall
ROCK CLIMBING

(Map p260; ☑ 07-350 1400; www.thewall.co.nz; 1140 Hinemoa St; adult/child incl harness $16/12, shoe hire $5; ☺noon-10pm Mon-Fri, 10am-10pm Sat & Sun) Get limbered up at the Wall, a three-storey indoor climbing wall with overhangs aplenty.

Skyline Rotorua
EXTREME SPORTS

(Map p274; ☑ 07-347 0027; www.skyline.co.nz; Fairy Springs Rd; adult/child gondola $25/12.50, luge 3 rides $42/32, sky swing $63/53; ☺9am-11pm) This gondola cruises up Mt Ngongotaha, about 3km northwest of town, from where you can take in panoramic lake views or ride a speedy luge back down on three different tracks. For even speedier antics, try the Sky Swing, a screaming swoosh through the air at speeds of up to 160km/h. Also at the top are a restaurant, a cafe and walking tracks.

Kawarau Jet
JETBOATING

(Map p260; ☑ 07-343 7600, 0800 538 7746; www.kjetrotorua.co.nz; Lakefront; 30min adult/child $74/54; ☺9am-6pm) Speed things up on a

---

HINEMOA & TUTANEKAI

Hinemoa was a young woman of a *hapu* (subtribe) that lived on the western shore of Lake Rotorua, while Tutanekai was a young man of a Mokoia Island *hapu*. The pair met and fell in love during a regular tribal meeting. While both were of high birth, Tutanekai was illegitimate, so marriage between the two was forbidden.

Home on Mokoia, the lovesick Tutanekai played his flute for his love, the wind carrying the melody across the water. Hinemoa heard his declaration, but her people took to tying up the canoes at night to ensure she wouldn't go to him.

Finally, Tutanekai's music won her over. Hinemoa undressed and swam the long distance from the shore to the island. When she arrived on Mokoia, Hinemoa found herself in a quandary. Shedding her clothing in order to swim, she could hardly walk into the island's settlement naked. She hopped into a hot pool to think about her next move.

Eventually a man came to fetch water from a cold spring beside the hot pool. In a deep man's voice, Hinemoa called out, 'Who is it?' The man replied that he was Tutanekai's slave on a water run. Hinemoa grabbed the slave's calabash and smashed it to pieces. More slaves came, but she smashed their calabashes too, until finally Tutanekai came to the pool and demanded that the interloper identify himself – imagine his surprise when it turned out to be Hinemoa. He secreted her into his hut.

Next morning, after a suspiciously long lie-in, a slave reported that someone was in Tutanekai's bed. The two lovers were rumbled, and when Hinemoa's superhuman efforts to reach Tutanekai had been revealed, their union was celebrated.

Descendants of Hinemoa and Tutanekai still live around Rotorua today.

ROTORUA IN...

Two Days

Order breakfast at **Third Place Cafe** after which stroll back into town via steamy **Kuirau Park**. Next stop is the fabulous **Rotorua Museum**, followed by a soak at the **Blue Baths**. In the evening, catch a *hangi* and concert at **Tamaki Maori Village** or **Mitai Maori Village**.

Start the second day with a tour of **Whakarewarewa Thermal Village** and watch Pohutu geyser blow its top. From here, it's a quick hop to the **Redwoods Whakarewarewa Forest** for a couple of hours' mountain biking. More forest action awaits in the afternoon courtesy of **Rotorua Canopy Tours**, or pay a visit to the swooping falcons at the **Wingspan National Bird of Prey Centre**.

Four Days

Too much geothermal excitement is barely enough! Explore the hot spots to the south: **Waimangu Volcanic Valley** and **Wai-O-Tapu Thermal Wonderland**. The nearby **Waikite Valley Thermal Pools** are perfect for an end-of-day plunge.

On your last day, head southeast and visit the **Buried Village**, swim in **Lake Tarawera**, or take a long walk on one of the tracks at nearby **Lake Okataina**. Back in town, cruise the restaurants and bars on **Tutanekai St** (aka 'Eat Street) and toast your efforts with a few cold beers at **Brew**.

---

jetboat ride with Kawarau Jet, which tears around the lake. Parasailing (30 minutes tandem/solo $80/115) and fishing trips (from $170 per hour) also available.

Mountain Biking

On the edge of town is the Redwoods Whakarewarewa Forest (p273), home to some of the best mountain-bike trails in the country. There are close to 100km of tracks to keep bikers of all skill levels happy for days on end. Note that not all tracks in the forest are designated for bikers, so adhere to the signposts. Pick up a trail map at the forest visitor centre.

Also here is the **Te Ara Ahi** ride, one of the **New Zealand Cycle Trail** (www.nzcycletrail.com) 'Great Rides'. It's an intermediate, two-day, 66km ride heading south of town to Wai-O-Tapu Thermal Wonderland and beyond.

For more information, the Rotorua i-SITE stocks the *Get on Your Bike* Rotorua cycle map. Online, see the Cycling/Mountain Biking info at www.rotoruanz.com/visit/to-do.

Mountain Bike Rotorua　　BICYCLE RENTAL
(Map p274; ☑0800 682 768; www.mtbrotorua.
co.nz; Waipa State Mill Rd; mountain bikes per 2hr/
day from $35/45, guided half-/full-day rides from
$130/275; ☺9am-5pm) This outfit hires out
bikes at the Waipa Mill car park entrance
to the Redwoods Whakarewarewa Forest,
the starting point for the bike trails. There's

also a satellite bike depot across the forest at the visitor centre, so you can ride through the trees one-way then catch a shuttle back.

Planet Bike　　BICYCLE RENTAL
(Map p274; ☑027 280 2817; www.planetbike.
co.nz; Waipa Bypass Rd; mountain bikes per 2hr/
day $35/60) Bike hire and guided rides (two
hours/half-day from $75/115) in the Redwoods Whakarewarewa Forest.

Bike Barn　　BICYCLE RENTAL
(Map p260; ☑07-347 1151; www.bikebarn.co.nz;
1275 Fenton St; mountain bikes per half-/full day
from $45/60; ☺8.30am-5.30pm Mon-Fri, 9am-
4.30pm Sat, 10am-4.30pm Sun) Bike hire and
repairs in downtown Rotorua.

White-Water Rafting, Sledging & Kayaking

There's plenty of kayaking and white-water action around Rotorua with the chance to take on the Grade V **Kaituna River**, complete with a startling 7m drop at Okere Falls. Most of these trips take a day. Some companies head further out to the **Rangitaiki River** (Grade III–VI) and **Wairoa River** (Grade V), raftable only when the dam is opened every second Sunday. Sledging (in case you didn't know) is zooming downriver on a body board. Most operators can arrange transport.

River Rats　　RAFTING, KAYAKING
(☑07-345 6543, 0800 333 900; www.riverrats.
co.nz) Takes on the Wairoa ($129), Kaituna

($105) and Rangitaiki ($139), and runs a scenic trip on the lower Rangitaiki (Grade II) that is good for youngsters (adult/child $139/110). Kayaking options include freedom hire ($40/60 per half-/full day) and guided four-hour Lake Rotoiti trips ($110).

Wet 'n' Wild　　　　　　　　RAFTING
(☑ 07-348 3191, 0800 462 7238; www.wetnwildrafting.co.nz) Runs trips on the Kaituna ($99), Wairoa ($110) and Mokau ($160), as well as easy-going Rangitaiki trips (adult/child $130/110) and longer trips to remote parts of the Motu and Mohaka (two to five days, $650 to $1095).

Raftabout　　　　　　　　RAFTING, SLEDGING
(☑ 07-343 9500, 0800 723 822) Rafting trips on the Kaituna ($105), Rangitaiki ($139) and Wairoa ($129), plus sledging on the Kaituna ($119).

Kaituna Cascades　　　　　RAFTING, KAYAKING
(☑ 07-345 4199, 0800 524 8862; www.kaitunacascades.co.nz) Rafting on the Kaituna ($84), Rangitaiki ($118) and Wairoa ($108), plus kayaking options and combos.

Go Wild Adventures　　　　　　KAYAKING
(☑ 07-533 2926; www.adventurekayaking.co.nz) Takes trips on Lakes Rotorua, Rotoiti, Tarawera and Okataina (per two hours/half-day/full day from $80/95/130). Also offers freedom hire (from $50 per day).

Kaitiaki Adventures　　　RAFTING, SLEDGING
(☑ 07-357 2236, 0800 338 736; www.kaitiaki.co.nz) Offers white-water rafting trips on the Kaituna ($95), Wairoa ($99) and Rangitaiki ($125), plus sledging on the Wairoa ($299) and a Grade III section of the Kaituna ($109).

Kaituna Kayaks　　　　　　　KAYAKING
(☑ 07-362 4486; www.kaitunakayaks.co.nz; half-day trips from $199, lessons per half-/full day from $199/299) Guided tandem trips and kayaking lessons (cheaper for groups) on the Kaituna River.

Thermal Pools & Massage

Spa/pool complexes in the area include Hells Gate & Wai Ora Spa (p273), 16km northeast of Rotorua, and Waikite Valley Thermal Pools (p276), around 35km south.

Polynesian Spa　　　　　　SPA, MASSAGE
(Map p260; ☑ 07-348 1328; www.polynesianspa.co.nz; 1000 Hinemoa St; adults-only pools $25, private pools per 30min adult/child from $18/6.50, family

pool adult/child/family $14.50/6.50/36, spa therapies from $85; ☺ 8am-11pm, spa therapies 10am-7pm) A bathhouse opened at these Government Gardens springs in 1882, and people have been swearing by the waters ever since. There is mineral bathing (36°C to 42°C) in several picturesque pools at the lake's edge, marble-lined terraced pools and a larger, main pool. Also here are luxury therapies (massage, mud and beauty treatments) and a cafe.

Tramping

There are plenty of opportunities to stretch your legs around Rotorua, with day walks a speciality. The booklet *Walks in the Rotorua Lakes Area* ($2.50), available from the i-SITE, showcases town walks, including the popular lakefront stroll (20 minutes). See also www.doc.govt.nz.

The **Eastern Okataina Walkway** (three hours one way) goes along the eastern shoreline of Lake Okataina to Lake Tarawera and passes the Soundshell, a natural amphitheatre that has *pa* (fortified village) remains and several swimming spots. The **Western Okataina Walkway** (five hours one way) mimics this route on the western side of the lake.

The **Northern Tarawera Track** (three hours one way) connects to the Eastern Okataina Walkway, creating a two-day walk from either Ruato or Lake Okataina to Lake Tarawera with an overnight camp at either Humphries Bay (sites free) or Tarawera Outlet (sites per adult/child $6/3). From Tarawera Outlet you can walk on to the 65m **Tarawera Falls** (four hours return). There's a forestry road into Tarawera Outlet from Kawerau, a grim timber town in the shadow of Putauaki (Mt Edgecumbe), off the road to Whakatane; access costs $5, with permits available from the **Kawerau visitor centre** (☑ 07-323 6300; www.kawerauonline.com; Plunkett St bus terminal; ☺ 8am-6pm Dec-Mar, 8am-4pm Apr-Nov).

The **Okere Falls** are about 21km northeast of Rotorua on SH33, with an easy track (30 minutes return) past the 7m falls (popular for rafting), through native podocarp (conifer) forest and along the Kaituna River. Along the way is a lookout over the river at Hinemoa's Steps.

Just north of Wai-O-Tapu on SH5, the **Rainbow Mountain Track** (1½ hours one way) is a strenuous walk up the peak known to Maori as Maungakakaramea (Mountain of Coloured Earth). There are spectacular views from the top towards Lake Taupo and Tongariro National Park.

For a short stroll try **Hamurana Springs** (Map p274) on the northern edge of Lake Rotorua – a sacred place for Ngati Rangiwewehi Maori – where there's a 1.5km loop walk alongside gin-clear springs through a redwood grove.

There are also a couple of good walks at Mt Ngongotaha, 10km northwest of Rotorua: the easy 3.2km **Nature Walk** loop through native forest, and the steep 5km return **Jubilee Track** to the (viewless) summit. See www.ngongotaha.org.

Fishing

There's always good trout fishing to be had somewhere around Rotorua. Hire a guide or go solo: either way a licence (per day/half-season/full season $23/73/121) is essential, available from **O'Keefe's Fishing Specialists** (Map p260; ☑ 07-346 0178; www.okeefesfishing.co.nz; 1113 Eruera St; ☉ 8.30am-5pm Mon-Fri, 9am-2pm Sat, 9am-1pm Sun). You can fish Rotorua's lakefront with a licence, though not all lakes can be fished year-round; check with O'Keefe's or the i-SITE.

Trout Man FISHING

(☑ 07-357 5255, 0800 876 881; www.waiteti.com; 2hr/day trips from $40/140) Learn to fish from experienced angler Harvey Clark, from a couple of hours to multiday trips.

Clark Gregor FISHING

(☑ 07-347 1123; www.troutnz.co.nz; per hr $105) Fly- and boat fishing.

Gordon Randle FISHING

(☑ 07-349 2555; www.rotoruatrout.co.nz; half-/full-day charters $370/750) Reasonable hourly rates also available.

Horse Riding

Farmhouse HORSE RIDING

(Map p274; ☑ 07-332 3771; www.thefarmhouse.co.nz; 55 Sunnex Rd, off Central Rd; 30/60/120min $26/42/74) North of Lake Rotorua at the Farmhouse you can saddle up for a short horse-riding trip for beginners, or a longer trek for experienced riders.

Golf

Ballbusters GOLF

(Map p260; ☑ 07-348 9126; www.ballbusters.co.nz; Queens Dr, Government Gardens; ☉ 7.30am-8pm) Ballbusters has a nine-hole course (adult/child $18/12), minigolf ($11/8) and driving range (80 balls $11). A $40 golf package includes clubs, green fees, balls and tees. There's also a baseball batting cage (bucket of balls $10).

☞ Tours

Happy Ewe Tours CYCLING

(☑ 022 622 9252; www.happyewetours.com; per person $35; ☉ 10am & 2pm) Saddle up for a three-hour, small-group bike tour of Rotorua, wheeling past 20 sights around the city. It's all flat and slow-paced, so you don't need to be at your physical peak (you're on holiday after all).

Foris Eco Tours RAFTING, TRAMPING

(☑ 0800 367 471; www.foris.co.nz; adult/child $169 /99) ✐ Check out some ancient rainforest on a one-hour walk in Whirinaki Forest Park then raft along the easy-going Rangitaiki River on this full-day trip. Full-day walks also available. Includes lunch, pick-up/drop-off and lots of wildlife-spotting.

Rotorua Paddle Tours PADDLE BOARDING

(☑ 0800 787 768; www.rotoruapaddletours.co.nz; tours from $90; ☉ 10am & 3pm) Keen to try stand-up paddle boarding without any waves to contend with? This outfit runs three-hour trips on Lake Rotoiti, Blue Lake and Lake Tarawera, with boundless beautiful scenery. No experience required.

Geyser Link Shuttle SIGHTSEEING

(☑ 03-477 9083, 0800 304 333; www.travelheadfirst.com/local-legends/geyser-link-shuttle) Tours of some of the major sights, including Wai-O-Tapu (half-day adult/child $70/35) or Waimangu (half-day adult/child $70/35), or both (full day $120/60). Transport-only options available too.

Rotorua Duck Tours SIGHTSEEING

(☑ 07-345 6522; adult/child/family $68/38/175; ☉ tours 11am, 1pm & 3.30pm Oct-Apr, 11am & 2.15pm May-Sep) Ninety-minute trips in an amphibious biofuelled vehicle taking in the major sights around town and heading out onto three lakes (Rotorua, Okareka and Tikitapu/Blue). Longer Lake Tarawera trips also available.

Elite Adventures SIGHTSEEING

(☑ 07-347 8282; www.eliteadventures.co.nz; tours adult/child half-day $145/100, full day $240/170) Small-group tours covering a selection of Rotorua's major cultural and natural highlights.

Thermal Land Shuttle SIGHTSEEING

(☑ 0800 894 287; www.thermalshuttle.co.nz; tours adult/child from $33/65) Daily scheduled morning, afternoon and night tours around a selection of key sights, including Waimangu, Wai-O-Tapu, Te Puia and Rainbow Mountain. Transport-only options also available.

Mana Adventures
CRUISE, KAYAKING

(Map p260; ☑07-348 4186, 0800 333 660; www.manaadventures.co.nz; Lakefront; ☺9am-5pm) Down at the lake, Mana Adventures offers (weather permitting) rental pedal boats ($9/6 per adult/child per 20 minutes) and kayaks ($50/75 per hour/half-day). It also runs low-key, one-hour lake cruises ($55/39 per adult/child), trout-fishing charters and three-hour tours to Manupirua Hot Pools on nearby Lake Rotoiti ($95/75 per adult/child).

Volcanic Air Safaris
SCENIC FLIGHTS

(Map p260; ☑0800 800 848, 07-348 9984; www.volcanicair.co.nz; Lakefront; trips $95-915) A variety of floatplane and helicopter flights taking in Mt Tarawera and surrounding geothermal sites including Hell's Gate, the Buried Village and Waimangu Volcanic Valley. A 3¼-hour Whakaari (White Island)/Mt Tarawera trip tops the price list.

Helipro
SCENIC FLIGHTS

(Map p274; ☑0800 435 477, 07-357 2515; www.helipro.co.nz; Hemo Rd; flights $99-940) Helipro plies the skies over Rotorua in nippy little red choppers (eight-minute city sightseeing flights $99), also extending to Mt Tarawera and as far as Whakaari (White Island). Landings in various places cost extra.

Lakeland Queen
CRUISE

(Map p260; ☑07-348 0265, 0800 572 784; www.lakelandqueen.com; Lakefront) The *Lakeland Queen* paddle steamer offers sedate one-hour Lake Rotorua breakfast cruises (adult/child $38/22.50), lunch cruises ($55/22.50) and Saturday-night summer dinners for big groups ($59/30).

Mokoia Island
Wai Ora Experiences
CRUISE, CULTURAL TOUR

(Map p260; ☑07-349 0976; www.mokoiaisland.co.nz; Lakefront; tours adult/child $75/38; ☺9.30am & 2pm) Visit Mokoia Island in the middle of Lake Rotorua on a 2½-hour Ultimate Island Experience tour, with wildlife-spotting, tales of the island, and a dip in the hot pool of Hinemoa. Minimum numbers may apply.

🛏 Sleeping

Rotorua has plenty of holiday parks and an ever-changing backpacker scene. Generic motels crowd Fenton St: better and more interesting rooms are away from the main drag.

★ Funky Green Voyager
HOSTEL $

(Map p260; ☑07-346 1754; www.funkygreenvoyager.co.nz; 4 Union St; dm from $25, d with/without bathroom $68/59; @🛜) 🌿 Green on the outside and the inside – due to several cans of paint and a dedicated environmental policy – the shoe-free Funky GV features laid-back tunes and plenty of sociable chat among a spunky bunch of guests and worldly-wise owners, who know what you want when you travel. The best doubles have bathrooms; dorms are roomy with quality mattresses and solid timber beds.

Rotorua Central Backpackers
HOSTEL $

(Map p260; ☑07-349 3285; www.rotoruacentralbackpackers.co.nz; 1076 Pukuatua St; dm from $25, tw & d $62; @🛜) This heritage hostel was built in 1936 and retains historic features including dark-wood skirting boards and door frames, deep bath-tubs and geothermally powered radiators. Dorms have no more than six beds (and no bunks), plus there's a spa pool and barbecue. Perfect if you're not looking to party.

Waiteti Trout
Stream Holiday Park
HOLIDAY PARK $

(Map p274; ☑0800 876 881, 07-357 5255; www.waiteti.com; 14 Okona Cres, Ngongotaha; campsites $36, dm from $25, d cabin/motel from $58/110; @🛜) This well-maintained park is a great option if you don't mind the 8km drive into town. Set in two tidy garden acres abutting a trout-filled stream, it's a cute classic with character-filled motel units, compact cabins, a tidy backpackers lodge and beaut campsites by the stream. Free kayaks and dinghies; fly-fishing lessons from $30. And no sulphur smell!

Blarney's Rock
HOSTEL $

(Map p260; ☑07-343 7904; www.blarneysrock.com; 1210 Tutanekai St; dm $20-27, d $50-60; @🛜) You might expect a backpackers above an Irish pub to be effervescing with drunken antics. Sorry to disappoint: this one's quiet, clean and comfy, with live-in managers who ensure the party stays downstairs. It's a small, homey affair, with a sunny deck, free wi-fi, free apple pie twice weekly and hot water bottles in your bed on chilly nights.

Rotorua YHA
HOSTEL $

(Map p260; ☑07-349 4088; www.yha.co.nz; 1278 Haupapa St; dm $26-35 d with/without bathroom $90/70; @🛜) Bright and sparkling clean, this classy, purpose-built hostel is great for those wanting to get outdoors, with staff eager to assist with trip bookings, and storage for bikes and kayaks. Pricier rooms come with bathroom, and there's a barbecue area and deck for hanging out on (though this ain't a party pad). Off-street parking a bonus.

Crash Palace HOSTEL $
(Map p260; ☑0800 892 727, 07-348 8842; www.
crashpalace.co.nz; 1271 Hinemaru St; dm/s/d/f from
$22/45/65/95; @🛜) Crash occupies a big, mus-
tard-coloured 1930s hotel near Government
Gardens. The atmosphere strikes a balance between party and pristine, without too much of
either. The nicest rooms have floorboards, and
there's lots of art on the walls, a pool table and
DJ console in the lobby, and a beaut terrace
out the back. Limited off-steet parking.

Astray MOTEL, HOSTEL $
(Map p260; ☑0800 481 200, 07-348 1200; www.
astray.co.nz; 1202 Pukuatua St; dm/s/d from
$24/40/60, f $95-150; @🛜) Even if you are
6'3", Astray – a 'micro motel' that would
probably be more at home in Tokyo than
Rotorua – is a decent bet. Clean, tidy, quiet,
friendly and central: just don't expect acres
of space. Free wi-fi a bonus.

**Rotorua Thermal
Holiday Park** HOLIDAY PARK $
(Map p274; ☑07-346 3140; www.rotoruathermal.
co.nz; 463 Old Taupo Rd; sites from $32, d cabins/
units from $51/98; @🛜♨) This super-friendly
holiday park on the edge of town sits deep
in the leisure groove, with barbecues, a playground, campsites galore, a shop and a cafe.
There's plenty of room and lots of trees and
open grassy areas, plus hot mineral pools to
soak the day away. Bike hire available.

Rock Solid Backpackers HOSTEL $
(Map p260; ☑07-282 2053; www.rocksolidrotorua.
co.nz; 1140 Hinemoa St; dm $19-25, d & tw $58;
@🛜) Cavernous, locally owned Rock Solid
occupies a former shopping mall: you might
be bunking down in a florist or a delicatessen.
Dorms over the street are sunny, and there's
a big, bright kitchen. Downstairs is the Wall
rock-climbing facility and the art-house Basement Cinema. Free wi-fi and pool table.

Rotorua Top 10 Holiday Park HOLIDAY PARK $
(Map p274; ☑0800 223 267, 07-348 1886; www.
rotoruatop10.co.nz; 1495 Pukuatua St; campsites
from $38, d cabin/motel from $80/125; @🛜♨) A
small but perfectly formed holiday park with
a continual improvement policy that has seen
a new playground, shower/toilet blocks and
mineral hot pools installed. Cabins are in
good nick and have small fridges and micro-
waves. Shrubberies and picnic tables aplenty.

Kiwi Paka HOSTEL $
(Map p274; ☑07-347 0931; www.kiwipaka.co.
nz; 60 Tarewa Rd; campsites from $15, dm/s/d

$29/60/64, chalets with bathroom d/tr/q
$87/107/147; @🛜♨) This rambling complex
is a 10-minute walk through Kuirau Park to
town. The vibe is a bit 'school camp', with acceptable amenities and a range of accommodation from campsites to plain dorms, lodge
rooms, three kitchens and two-storey pine-
clad chalets. There's a cafe and bar on site.

Base Rotorua HOSTEL $
(Map p260; ☑0800 227 369, 07-348 8636; www.
stayatbase.co.nz; 1286 Arawa St; dm/s/d from
$25/70/70; @🛜) A link in the Base chain,
this huge hostel is ever-popular with partying backpackers who love the trashy Lava
Bar (cheap meals, toga parties, wet T-shirt
comps etc). Dorms can be tight (up to 12
beds), but extras such as girls-only rooms,
en suites in most rooms, a thermally heated
pool and campervan parking ($9 per person)
compensate.

Tuscany Villas MOTEL $$
(Map p274; ☑0800 802 050, 07-348 3500; www.
tuscanyvillasrotorua.co.nz; 280 Fenton St; d from
$145; 🛜) With its Italian-inspired architec-
ture and pointy conifers, this family-owned
eye-catcher is the pick of the Fenton St
motels. It pitches itself at both corporate
and leisure travellers, all of who appreciate
the plush furnishings, multiple TVs, DVD
players and deep spa baths. Free wi-fi.

Six on Union MOTEL $$
(Map p260; ☑0800 100 062, 07-347 8062; www.
sixonunion.co.nz; 6 Union St; d/f from $105/145;
🛜♨) Hanging baskets ahoy! This modest
place is an affordable bonanza with pool
and spa, and small kitchenettes in all units.
Rooms are functional, and the new owners
(from Yorkshire) keep the swimming-pool
area in good nick. It's away from traffic
noise, but still an easy walk into town.

Sandi's Bed & Breakfast B&B $$
(Map p274; ☑07-348 0884, 0800 726 3422; www.
sandisbedandbreakfast.co.nz; 103 Fairy Springs Rd;
s/d/f incl breakfast $85/130/160; 🛜♨) A friend-
ly, family B&B run by the well-humoured
Sandi who offers local advice with a ready
smile. It's on a busy road a couple of kilo-
metres north of town, so the best bets are
the two bohemian chalets out the back with
TV and plenty of room to move.

Victoria Lodge MOTEL $$
(Map p260; ☑0800 100 039, 07-348 4039; www.
victorialodge.co.nz; 10 Victoria St; d/apt from
$115/160; 🛜) The friendly Vic has seen a lot

of competitors come and go, maintaining its foothold in the market with individual-feeling apartments and studios with thermally heated plunge pools. Fully equipped, freshly painted apartments can squeeze in seven, though four would be comfortable.

Ann's Volcanic Motel
MOTEL $$

(Map p274; ☑ 0800 768 683, 07-347 1007; www.rotoruamotel.co.nz; 107 Malfroy Rd; d/1-bedroom/2-bedroom from $95/129/209; ☎) Ann's is an affordable motel with an ever-friendly host offering loads of local advice. Larger rooms feature courtyard spas and facilities for travellers with disabilities, with a house next door available for big groups (sleeps nine). Rooms close to the street can be a tad noisy.

★ Regent of Rotorua
BOUTIQUE HOTEL $$$

(Map p260; ☑ 0508 734 368, 07-348 4079; www.regentrotorua.co.nz; 1191 Pukaki St; d/ste from $169/239; ☎☎☎) Wow! It's about time Rotorua showed some slumbering style, and the Regent (a renovated 1960s motel) delivers. 'The '60s were a glamorous time to travel,' say the owners: the decor follows suit, with hip black-and-white tones, funky mirrors, retro wallpaper and colourful splashes. There's a pool and restaurant, the Tutanekai St eateries are an amble away, and there's a whole new wing of rooms next door. Terrific value.

Millennium Hotel
HOTEL $$$

(Map p260; ☑ 07-347 1234; www.millenniumrotorua.co.nz; cnr Eruera & Hinemaru Sts; d from $200; @☎☎) The slick Maori-inspired lobby sets the scene for this elegant five-storey motel. Lakefront rooms afford excellent views as does the club lounge, popular with the suits and internationalists swanning about. The poolside *hangi* is fab, as is the in-house restaurant Nikau. Advance booking rates slip into midrange territory.

✗ Eating

The lake end of Tutanekai St – known as **Eat Street** – has a strip of eateries beneath a new roof, but there are plenty of other options around town.

Mistress of Cakes
BAKERY $

(Map p260; www.mistressofcakes.co.nz; 1224 Eruera St; items $4-8; ☺ 7.30am-2.30pm Mon-Fri) 'Food that your grandmother made' is the slogan here, but we bet your Grandma couldn't bake a lemon passionfruit meringue like the ones the Mistress makes! Fab muffins, slices, biscuits, scones and quiches too, all home-made with local ingredients.

Fish & Chip Shop
FISH & CHIPS $

(Map p260; ☑ 07-343 7400; 47 Lake Rd; meals $5-15; ☺ 11am-8pm Mon-Thu, 11am-8.30pm Fri-Sun) What you see is what you get: top-notch takeaway fish and chips from this little sky-blue shopfront out near Ohinemutu.

Weilin's Noodle House
NOODLES, CHINESE $

(Map p260; ☑ 07-343 9998; 1148 Tutanekai St; mains $9-25; ☺ noon-3pm & 5-9pm Wed-Mon) A neat and tidy shop serving traditional (and refreshingly un-fatty/salty/stodgy) Chinese dumplings and oodles of noodles in soups and stir-fries. Eat in or take away. Try the noodles with spicy pork and peanuts.

Pak 'n Save
SUPERMARKET $

(Map p260; www.paknsave.co.nz; cnr Fenton & Amohau Sts; ☺ 7.30am-10pm) On the downtown fringe.

★ Third Place Cafe
CAFE $$

(Map p260; ☑ 07-349 4852; www.thirdplacecafe.co.nz; 36 Lake Rd; mains $12-18; ☺ 8am-4pm Mon-Fri, 8am-3pm Sat) A really interesting cafe away from the hubbub, Third Place has leap-frogged into first by our reckoning. All-day breakfast/brunch sidesteps neatly between chicken jambalaya, fish and chips, and an awesome 'mumble jumble' of crushed kumara (sweet potato), green tomatoes and spicy chorizo topped with bacon, poached egg and hollandaise sauce. Hangover? What hangover? Slide into a red-leather couch or score a window seat overlooking Ohinemutu.

Abracadabra Cafe Bar
MIDDLE EASTERN, CAFE $$

(Map p260; ☑ 07-348 3883; www.abracadabracafe.com; 1363 Amohia St; mains $19-30; ☺ 8.30am-11pm Tue-Fri, 9am-11pm Sat, 9am-3pm Sun) Wedged somewhere between Mexico and Morocco, Abracadabra is a magical cave of spicy delights, from beef-and-apricot tagine to king-prawn fajitas and Tijuana pork chilli. Conjure up your own 'Day of the Dead' (tomorrow) with a tour though the dedicated tequila menu. Beaut beer terrace out the back.

Sabroso
LATIN AMERICAN $$

(Map p260; ☑ 07-349 0591; www.sabroso.co.nz; 1184 Haupapa St; mains $18-29; ☺ 5-9pm Thu-Mon) What a surprise! This modest Latin American cantina – adorned with sombreros, guitars, hessian tablecloths and salt-and-pepper shakers made from Corona bottles – serves adventurous south-of-the-border fare to spice up bland Kiwi palates. The black-bean chilli is a knockout (as are the margaritas).

Lime Caffeteria
CAFE **$$**

(Map p260; ☑ 07-350 2033; cnr Fenton & Whakaue Sts; mains $13-24; ☺ 7.30am-4.30pm; ☞) Occupying a quiet corner near the lake, this zesty cafe offers alfresco breakfasts and dishes with a welcome twist: try the chicken-and-chorizo salad or prawn-and-salmon risotto in lime sauce. Classy counter snacks and excellent coffee, too. 'This is the best lunch I've had in ages', says one happy punter.

Indian Star
INDIAN **$$**

(Map p260; ☑ 07-343 6222; www.indianstar.co.nz; 1118 Tutanekai St; mains $14-22; ☺ 11am-2pm & 5pm-late; ☞) This is one of several Indian eateries around town, elevating itself above the competition with immaculate service and marvellous renditions of subcontinental classics. It has sizeable portions and good vegetarian selections (try the chickpea masala). Book for dinner.

Leonardo's
ITALIAN **$$**

(Map p260; ☑ 07-347 7084; www.leonardospureitalian.nznic.biz; 1176 Pukaki St; mains $22-32.50; ☺ 5-10pm Mon-Thu, 11.30am-2pm & 5-10pm Fri-Sun) Not far from the lake in an unpretentious shopfront, Leonardo's goes heavy on the hokey 'just like mama used to make' marketing, but what comes out of the kitchen is far from kitsch. Try the simple but perfect gnocchi with tomato, mozzarella and pesto, or the angel-hair pasta with mussels and anchovies.

Capers Epicurean
CAFE, DELICATESSEN **$$**

(Map p260; ☑ 07-348 8818; www.capers.co.nz; 1181 Eruera St; mains breakfast & lunch $7-23, dinner $27-32; ☺ 7.30am-9pm; ☞) This slick, barn-like cafe is perennially busy, with diners perusing cabinets full of delicious gourmet sandwiches, pastries, salads and cakes, and the excellent blackboard menu of breakfasts and other tasty hot foods (try the pork belly with pumpkin dumplings). The deli section is stocked with olive oils, marinades, relishes, jams and chocolates.

Urbano Bistro
MODERN NZ, CAFE **$$**

(Map p274; ☑ 07-349 3770; www.urbanobistro.co.nz; cnr Fenton & Grey Sts; mains breakfast & lunch $14-21, dinner $24-43; ☺ 9am-11pm Mon-Sat, to 3pm Sun) This hip suburban diner, with mega-checkerboard carpet and curvy wallpaper, is a bold move by reputable local restaurateurs. Try the beef, pineapple and kumara curry – rich in flavour and well executed. Fine wines and five-star service to boot.

Fat Dog Cafe & Bar
CAFE **$$**

(Map p260; ☑ 07-347 7586; 1161 Arawa St; mains breakfast & lunch $12-23, dinner $28-30; ☺ 7am-9pm; ☞) With paw prints and silly poems painted on the walls, this is the town's friskiest and most child-friendly cafe. During the day it dishes up burgers (try the Dogs Bollox version), nachos, salads and sandwiches; in the evening it's candlelit lamb and venison. Takeway caffeine in the shopfront next door.

Bistro 1284
MODERN NZ **$$$**

(Map p260; ☑ 07-346 1284; www.bistro1284.co.nz; 1284 Eruera St; mains $35-39; ☺ 5pm-late) A fine-dining hot spot on an unremarkable stretch of Eruera St, this intimate place (all chocolate and mushroom colours) serves stylish NZ cuisine with an Asian influence. The lamb is always good, but be sure to leave room for the delectable desserts.

 ## Drinking & Entertainment

Brew
BAR, CRAFT BEER

(Map p260; www.brewpub.co.nz; 1103 Tutanekai St; ☺ 4pm-late Mon-Thu, noon-late Fri, 11am-late Sat & Sun) Run by the lads from Croucher Brewing Co, Rotorua's best microbrewers, Brew sits in a sunny spot on Rotorua's main eat-street. Sip down a pint of fruity pale ale, aromatic drunken hop bitter or malty pilsener and wonder how you'll manage a sleep-in tomorrow morning. Good coffee and pizzas, plus Friday DJs and Tuesday open-mike nights.

Pig & Whistle
PUB, BREWERY

(Map p260; www.pigandwhistle.co.nz; cnr Haupapa & Tutanekai Sts; ☺ 11am-late) Inside a former police station, this busy microbrewery-pub serves up Swine lager, big-screen TVs, a beer garden and live music Thursday to Saturday, plus solid grub (mains $19 to $32). The menu runs the gamut from crispy pork-belly salad to burgers and vegetarian nachos.

Belgian Bar
BAR, LIVE MUSIC

(Map p260; www.facebook.com/pages/belgian-bar/137762819598058; 1151 Arawa St; ☺ 4pm-late Tue-Fri, 2pm-late Sat & Sun) The best bar in town for lovers of gigs and good beer. Half a dozen Euro-beers on tap and 42 in the bottle accompany regular blues and acoustic acts ('Clapton is God' is spraypainted behind the stage). Garden bar out the back.

Basement Cinema
CINEMA

(Map p260; ☑ 07-350 1400; www.basementcinema.co.nz; 1140 Hinemoa St; tickets $14.50; ☺ noon-

DON'T MISS

MAORI CONCERTS & HANGI

Maori culture is a big-ticket item in Rotorua and, although it is commercialised, it's a great opportunity to learn about the indigenous culture of NZ. The two big activities are concerts and *hangi* feasts, often packaged together in an evening's entertainment featuring the famous *hongi* (Maori greeting; the pressing of foreheads and noses, and sharing of life breath) and *haka* and *poi* dances.

An established favourite, **Tamaki Maori Village** (Map p260; ✆ 07-349 2999; www. maoriculture.co.nz; booking office 1220 Hinemaru St; adult/child/family $110/20-60/250; ⊗ tours depart 5pm, 6.15pm & 7.30pm Nov-Apr, 6.15pm May-Oct) does an excellent twilight tour to a *marae* (meeting house) and Maori village 15km south of Rotorua. Buses collect from the Hinemaru St booking office and local accommodation. The experience is very hands-on, taking you on an interactive journey through Maori history, arts, traditions and customs from pre-European times to the present day. The concert is followed by an impressive *hangi*.

The family-run **Mitai Maori Village** (Map p274; ✆ 07-343 9132; www.mitai.co.nz; 196 Fairy Springs Rd; adult/child/family $111/21.50-55/290; ⊗ 6.30pm) offers a popular three-hour evening event with a concert, *hangi* and glowworm bushwalk. The experience can be combined with a tour (adult/child $150/75) of Hells Gate thermal reserve (p273) , or a tour ($126/67) of Ohinemutu (p262) Maori village. Pick-ups available.

Te Puia (p259) and Whakarewarewa Thermal Village (p260) also put on shows, and many of the big hotels offer mainstream Maori concerts and *hangi,* including the following:

Copthorne Hotel Rotorua (Map p274; ✆ 07-348 0199; www.millenniumhotels.co.nz; 328 Fenton St; concert adult/child $25/15, incl hangi $55/25.25)

Holiday Inn Rotorua (Map p274; ✆ 0800 476 488, 07-348 1189; www.holidayinnrotorua. co.nz/cultural-show.php; cnr Froude & Tryon Sts; concerts & hangi adult/child $69/34.50)

Millennium Hotel Rotorua (Map p260; ✆ 07-347 1234; www.millenniumrotorua.co.nz; cnr Eruera & Hinemaru Sts; concerts adult/child $30/15, incl hangi $70/35)

Novotel Rotorua (Map p260; ✆ 07-346 3888; www.novotelrotorua.co.nz; 11 Tutanekai St; concerts adult/child $39/18, incl hangi $69/19)

10pm Mon-Fri, 10am-10pm Sat & Sun) Part of the same complex as the Wall rock-climbing gym, the Basement screens offbeat, foreign-language and art-house flicks.

🛍 Shopping

South of town, Te Puia and Whakarewarewa Thermal Village have excellent selections of genuine Maori-made arts.

Rotorua Night Market　　　MARKET
(Map p260; www.rotoruanightmarket.co.nz; Tutanekai St; ⊗ 5pm-late Thu) Tutanekai St is closed off on Thursday nights between Haupapa and Pukuatua Sts to allow the Rotorua Night Market to spread its wings. Expect local arts and crafts, souvenirs, cheesy buskers, coffee, wine and plenty of deli-style food stalls for dinner.

Mountain Jade　　ARTS & CRAFTS, JEWELLERY
(Map p260; www.mountainjade.co.nz; 1288 Fenton St; ⊗ 9am-6pm) High-end hand-crafted greenstone jewellery and carvings. You

can watch the carvers at work through the streetside window.

Out of New Zealand　　ARTS & CRAFTS, JEWELLERY
(Map p260; 1189 Fenton St; ⊗ 10am-6pm, to 9pm Dec-Mar) Stocks NZ-made craft and gifts including carvings, ceramics and jewellery: affordable, packable souvenirs.

ℹ Information

There are plenty of ATMs around town. Most banks offer currency exchange.

Lakes Care Medical (✆ 07-348 1000; 1165 Tutanekai St; ⊗ 8am-10pm) Urgent medical care.

Police (✆ 111, non-emergency 07-349 9400; 1190 Fenton St; ⊗ 24hr)

Post Office (Map p260; cnr Tutanekai & Pukuatua Sts; ⊗ 8am-5.30pm Mon-Fri, 9am-1pm Sat)

Rotorua Hospital (✆ 07-348 1199; www. lakesdhb.govt.nz; Arawa St; ⊗ 24hr) Round-the-clock medical care.

Rotorua i-SITE (Map p260; ✆ 0800 768 678, 07-348 5179; www.rotoruanz.com; 1167 Fenton

St; ☺7.30am-7pm Sep-May, reduced hours Jun-Aug) The hub for travel information and bookings, including Department of Conservation (DOC) walks. Also has an exchange bureau, a cafe, showers and lockers.

❶ Getting There & Away

AIR

Rotorua Airport (Map p274; ☎07-345 8800; www.rotorua-airport.co.nz; SH30; ☎) is 10km northeast of town. **Air New Zealand** (☎07-343 1100; www.airnewzealand.co.nz; 1267 Tutanekai St; ☺9am-5pm Mon-Fri) has direct flights between Rotorua and Auckland, Wellington and Christchurch, plus Sydney (every Tuesday and Saturday).

BUS

All the major bus companies stop outside the Rotorua i-SITE, from where you can arrange bookings.

InterCity destinations include the following:

DESTINATION	PRICE ($)	DURATION (HR)	FREQUENCY (DAILY)
Auckland	55	3½	7
Gisborne	64	4½	1
Hamilton	40	1½	5
Napier	60	4	1
Taupo	32	1	4
Tauranga	25	1½	2
Wellington	65	7	5
Whakatane	35	1½	1

Naked Bus services include the following:

DESTINATION	PRICE ($)	DURATION (HR)	FREQUENCY (DAILY)
Auckland	15	4	3
Gisborne	19	4¾	1
Hamilton	10	1½	3
Napier	18	3	3
Taupo	10	1	3
Tauranga	10	1½	3
Wellington	19	8	1
Whakatane	14	1½	1

Twin City Express buses run twice daily Monday to Friday between Rotorua and Tauranga/Mt Maunganui via Te Puke ($11.60, 1½ hours).

White Island Shuttle (☎0800 733 529, 07-308 9588; www.whiteisland.co.nz; one way/return $35/60), run by White Island Tours in Whakatane, operates return shuttles to Whakatane from Rotorua. It's ostensibly for tour customers, but you can use the service without taking the tour.

❶ Getting Around

TO/FROM THE AIRPORT

Super Shuttle (☎0800 748 885, 09-522 5100; www.supershuttle.co.nz) offers a door-to-door airport service for $21 for the first person then $5 per additional passenger. **Baybus** (☎0800 422 928; www.baybus.co.nz) runs a daily airport bus service ($2.50). A taxi to/from the city centre costs about $25.

BUS

Many local attractions offer free pick-up/drop-off shuttle services. Shuttle services are also available to/from outlying attractions – see p266.

Baybus operates local bus services around town, and also to Ngongotaha (route 1, $2.50) and the airport (route 10, $2.50).

CAR

The big-name car-hire companies vie for your attention at Rotorua Airport. Otherwise, try **Rent a Dent** (☎07-349 3993; 39 Fairy Springs Rd; ☺8am-5pm Mon-Fri, 8am-noon Sat).

TAXI

Rotorua Taxis (☎07-348 1111; www.rotoruataxis.co.nz)

AROUND ROTORUA

North of Rotorua

◉ Sights & Activities

Rainbow Springs WILDLIFE RESERVE
(Map p274; ☎0800 724 626; www.rainbowsprings.co.nz; 192 Fairy Springs Rd; 24hr pass adult/child/family $40/20/99; ☺8.30am-late) About 3km north of central Rotorua, Rainbow Springs is a family-friendly winner. The natural springs here are home to wild trout and eels, which you can peer at through an underwater viewer. There are interpretive walkways, a new 'Big Splash' water ride, and plenty of animals, including tuatara (a native lizard) and native birds (kea, kaka and pukeko).

A highlight is the **Kiwi Encounter**, which offers a rare peek into the lives of these endangered birds: excellent 30-minute tours (an extra $10 per person) have you tiptoeing through incubator and hatchery areas.

Wingspan National Bird of Prey Centre
WILDLIFE CENTRE

(Map p274; ☑ 07-357 4469; www.wingspan.co.nz; 1164 Paradise Valley Rd, Ngongotaha; adult/child $25/8; ⊙ 9am-3pm) Wingspan is dedicated to conserving three threatened NZ birds: the falcon, the hawk and the owl. Learn about the birds in the museum display, then take a sneaky peek into the incubation area before walking through the all-weather aviary. Don't miss the 2pm flying display.

Paradise Valley Springs
WILDLIFE RESERVE

(☑ 07-348 9667; www.paradisevalleysprings.co.nz; 467 Paradise Valley Rd; adult/child $30/15; ⊙ 8am-dusk) In Paradise Valley at the foot of Mt Ngongotaha, 8km from Rotorua, is Paradise Valley Springs, a 6-hectare park with trout springs, big slippery eels and various land-dwelling animals such as deer, alpacas, possums and a pride of lions (fed at 2.30pm). There's also a coffee shop and an elevated treetop walkway.

Agrodome
AGRICULTURAL

(Map p274; ☑ 07-357 1050; www.agrodome.co.nz; 141 Western Rd, Ngongotaha; 1hr tour adult/child/family $41/20/84.50, 1hr show $31/15.50/79.50, tour & show $51/25.50/118.50; ⊙ 8.30am-5pm, shows 9.30am, 11am & 2.30pm, tours 10.40am, 12.10pm, 1.30pm & 3.40pm) Learn everything you need to know about sheep at the educational Agrodome. Shows include a parade of champion rams, a livestock auction, and shearing and doggy displays. The tour lets you check out farm animals including, among others, sheep. Other agro-attractions include a shearing-shed museum and cafe.

aMAZEme
MAZE

(Map p274; ☑ 07-357 5759; www.amazeme.co.nz; 1335 Paradise Valley Rd, Ngongotaha; adult/child/family $16/9/45; ⊙ 9am-5pm) This amazing 1.4km maze is constructed from immaculately pruned, head-high escallonia hedge. Lose yourself (or the kids) in the endless spirals.

Northeast of Rotorua

◉ Sights & Activities

Hells Gate & Wai Ora Spa
VOLCANIC AREA, SPA

(Map p274; ☑ 07-345 3151; www.hellsgate.co.nz; SH30, Tikitere; admission adult/child/family $35/17.50/85, mud bath & spa $75/35/185, massage per 30/60min $85/130; ⊙ 8.30am-8.30pm) Known as Tikitere to the Maori, Hells Gate is an impressive geothermal reserve 16km

northeast of Rotorua on the Whakatane road (SH30). Tikitere is an abbreviation of *Taku tiki i tere nei* (My youngest daughter has floated away), remembering the tragedy of a young girl jumping into a thermal pool. The English name originates from a 1934 visit by George Bernard Shaw. The reserve covers 10 hectares, with a 2.5km walking track to the various attractions, including a hot thermal waterfall. You can also see a master woodcarver at work, and learn about flax weaving and other Maori traditions.

Long regarded by Maori as a place of healing, Tikitere also houses the Wai Ora Spa, where you can get muddy with a variety of treatments. A courtesy shuttle to/from Rotorua is available.

Southeast of Rotorua

◉ Sights & Activities

Redwoods Whakarewarewa Forest
FOREST

(Map p274; www.redwoods.co.nz; Long Mile Rd, off Tarawera Rd; ⊙ 5.30am-8.30pm) **FREE** This magical forest park is 3km southeast of town

---

WORTH A TRIP

WHIRINAKI FOREST PARK

This lush podocarp (conifer) forest park is 90km southeast of Rotorua off SH38, en route to Te Urewera National Park (take the turn-off at Te Whaiti to Minginui). Also here are canyons, waterfalls, lookouts and streams, plus the **Oriuwaka Ecological Area** and **Arahaki Lagoon**.

Walking tracks here vary in length and difficulty: the DOC booklet *Walks in Whirinaki Forest* ($2.50) details walking and camping options. Pick one up at DOC's **Murupara visitor centre** (☑ 07-366 1080; www.doc.govt.nz; SH38, Murupara; ⊙ 9am-5pm Mon-Fri).

A good short walk is the **Whirinaki Waterfalls Track** (four hours return), which follows the Whirinaki River. Longer walks include the **Whirinaki Track** (two days), which can be combined with **Te Hoe Track** (four days). There's also a rampaging 16km **mountain bike track** here.

There are several accessible camping areas and 10 backcountry huts (free to $15) in the park; pay at the DOC office.

Around Rotorua

Around Rotorua

Tauranga (56km)

Kaituna River

Lake Rotoehu

Okere Falls

Okere Falls

Te Waerenga Rd

Otopi Rd

15

Central Rd

Lake Rotoiti

Whakatane (50km)

16

Hamurana Rd

Ruato

Tikitere (Hells Gate)

22 1 32

Ngongotaha

Te Ngae

3

Lake Rotokawau

12

13

Lake Rotorua

Mokoia Island

Lake Okataina

4

Paradise Valley Rd

Western Okataina Walkway

29

20

Rotorua Airport

26

See Rotorua Map (p260)

Mt Ngongotaha (757m)

Rotorua

Eastern Okataina Walkway

28

19 23

Te Ngae Rd

Lake Okataina

31

33

Tarawera Rd

Lake Okareka DOC campsite

Northern Tarawera Track

Tarawera River

27 7 11

5

Millar Rd

Tarawera Falls

18 6

Lake Okareka

17

Redwoods Whakarewarewa Forest

24

Tarawera Outlet

30

Lake Tikitapu (Blue Lake)

Lake Tarawera

Mt Tarawera (erupted 1886; 1110m)

2 14

8

Lake Tarawera Water Taxi & Eco Tours

Crater

Chasm

Lake Rotokakahi (Green Lake)

Turinui Rd

25

Lake Rotomahana

Patiti Island

Ash Pit Road DOC campsite

Waimangu Rd

Waimangu

9

Lake Okaro

Lake Rerewhakaaitu

Brett Road DOC Campsite

21

Rainbow Mountain (743m)

Lake Ohakuri

Waikite Valley

Waikite Valley Rd

Lake Ngapouri

Wai-O-Tapu

Yankee Rd

Te Kopia Rd

10

Paeroa Range

Taupo (46km)

38

Around Rotorua

◎ **Sights**
1 Agrodome A3
2 Buried Village C5
3 Hells Gate & Wai Ora Spa C2
4 Rainbow Springs A3
5 Redwoods Gift Shop & Visitor
  Centre B4
6 Redwoods Whakarewarewa Forest B4
7 Te Puia A4
8 The Landing C4
9 Waimangu Volcanic Valley C6
10 Wai-O-Tapu Thermal Wonderland C7
11 Whakarewarewa Thermal Village B4
12 Wingspan National Bird of Prey
   Centre A3

◎ **Activities, Courses & Tours**
   Agroventures .... (see 13)
13 aMAZEme A3
14 Clearwater Cruises C5
15 Farmhouse A2
16 Hamurana Springs A2
   Helipro .... (see 7)
17 Mountain Bike Rotorua A4
   Ogo .... (see 20)
18 Planet Bike B4

19 Rotorua Canopy Tours A4
20 Skyline Rotorua A3
21 Waikite Valley Thermal Pools B6
22 Zorb A3

◎ **Sleeping**
23 Ann's Volcanic Motel A4
24 Blue Lake Top 10 Holiday Park B4
25 Hot Water Beach Campsite D5
26 Kiwi Paka A3
27 Rotorua Thermal Holiday Park A4
28 Rotorua Top 10 Holiday Park A3
29 Sandi's Bed & Breakfast A3
30 Tarawera Outlet Campsite D4
31 Tuscany Villas A4
32 Waiteti Trout Stream Holiday
   Park A3

◎ **Eating**
   Urbano Bistro .... (see 31)

◎ **Entertainment**
33 Copthorne Hotel Rotorua A4
   Holiday Inn Rotorua .... (see 33)
   Mitai Maori Village .... (see 20)

on Tarawera Rd. It was originally home to over 170 tree species (a few less now), planted from 1899 to see which could be grown successfully for timber. Radiata pine proved a hit (as evident throughout NZ), but it's the mighty Californian redwoods that give the park its grandeur today.

Clearly signposted walking tracks range from a half-hour wander through the Redwood Grove to an enjoyable whole-day route to the Blue and Green Lakes. Most walks start from the **Redwoods Gift Shop & Visitor Centre** (Map p274; ☑07-350 0110; www.redwoods.co.nz; Long Mile Rd, off Tarawera Rd; ☺8.30am-5.30pm Mon-Fri, 10am-5pm Sat & Sun Oct-Mar, 8.30am-4.30pm Mon-Fri, 10am-4pm Sat & Sun Apr-Sep), where you can get maps and view displays about the forest. Aside from walking, the park is great for picnics and acclaimed for its accessible **mountain biking**. Mountain Bike Rotorua (p264) and Planet Bike (p264) offer bike hire, across the park off Waipa State Mill Rd.

Buried Village   ARCHAEOLOGICAL SITE, MUSEUM
(Map p274; ☑07-362 8287; www.buriedvillage.co.nz; 1180 Tarawera Rd; adult/child/family $35/10/66; ☺9am-5pm Nov-Mar, to 4.30pm Apr-Oct) Fifteen kilometres from Rotorua on Tarawera Rd, beyond the pretty Blue and

Green Lakes, is the buried village of Te Wairoa, interred by the eruption of Mt Tarawera in 1886. Te Wairoa was the staging post for travellers coming to see the Pink and White Terraces. Today a museum houses objects dug from the ruins, and guides in period costume escort groups through the excavated sites. There's also a walk to the 30m **Te Wairoa Falls** and a teahouse if you're feeling more sedate.

Lake Tarawera   LAKE
(www.doc.govt.nz; Tarawera Rd) Tarawera means 'Burnt Spear', named by a visiting hunter who left his bird spears in a hut and on returning the following season found both the spears and hut had been burnt. The lake is picturesque and good for swimming, fishing, cruises and walks.

A good place to access the lake is at the **Landing** (Map p274), about 2km past the Buried Village. Here you'll find **Clearwater Cruises** (Map p274; ☑027 362 8590, 07-345 6688; www.clearwater.co.nz; per hr cruise vessel/self-drive runabout $550/140), which runs scenic cruises and self-drive boat options aboard a variety of vessels. Also here is the **Landing Café** (www.thelandinglaketarawera.co.nz; mains $15-30; ☺10am-late), serving hearty mains like lamb rump and seafood chowder with beaut lake views. Also at the Landing is **Lake Tarawera Water Taxi & Eco Tours** (Map p274; ☑07-362 8080; www. ecotoursrotorua.co.nz; 1375 Tarawera Rd; from $55), which can take you anywhere on the lake, at any time: a trip to Hot Water Beach is $55.

There's a privately run camping ground (boat access only; bookings required) at **Hot Water Beach** (Map p274; ☑07-349 3463; www. whakarewarewa.com/tarawera; adult/child $10/5), and a DOC-managed site at **Tarawera Outlet** (Map p274; ☑07-323 6300; www.doc.govt.nz; adult/child $6/3). The **Blue Lake Top 10 Holiday Park** (Map p274; ☑0800 808 292, 07-362 8120; www.bluelaketop10.co.nz; 723 Tarawera Rd; campsites from $21, cabins $73-120, units $125-180; @ ⬦) offers camping next to the Blue Lake (good for swimming and kayaking), 6km before you get to Lake Tarawera; well run, it has spotless facilities and a handy range of cabins.

South of Rotorua

⊙ Sights & Activities

Waimangu

Volcanic Valley   VOLCANIC AREA, SPRING
(Map p274; ☑07-366 6137; www.waimangu. com; 587 Waimangu Rd; adult/child walking tour $34.50/11, boat cruise $42.50/11; ⊙8.30am-5pm daily, to 6pm Jan, last admission 3.30pm, 4.30pm Jan) This interesting thermal area was created during the eruption of Mt Tarawera in 1886 – geologically young! Waimangu (Black Water) refers to the dark, muddy colour of much of the water here.

The easy downhill stroll through the valley passes spectacular thermal and volcanic features, including **Inferno Crater Lake**, where overflowing water can reach 80°C, and **Frying Pan Lake**, the largest hot spring in the world. The walk continues down to Lake Rotomahana (meaning 'Warm Lake'), from where you can either get a shuttle ride back up to where you started or take a 45-minute boat trip on the lake, past steaming cliffs and the former site of the Pink and White Terraces.

Waimangu is 20 minutes south of Rotorua, 14km along SH5 (towards Taupo) and then 6km from the marked turn-off.

Wai-O-Tapu Thermal
Wonderland   VOLCANIC AREA, GEYSER
(Map p274; ☑07-366 6333; www.waiotapu.co.nz; 201 Waiotapu Loop Rd, off SH5; adult/child/family $32.50/11/80; ⊙8.30am-5pm, last admission 3.45pm) Wai-O-Tapu (Sacred Waters) is a fairly commercial operation with a lot of interesting geothermal features packed into a small area, including the boiling, multi-hued **Champagne Pool**, bubbling **mud pool**, stunning **mineral terraces** and **Lady Knox Geyser**, which spouts off (with a little prompting from an organic soap) punctually at 10.15am and gushes up to 20m for about an hour (be here by 9.45am to see it).

Wai-O-Tapu is 27km south of Rotorua along SH5 (towards Taupo), and a further 2km from the marked turn-off.

Waikite Valley Thermal Pools   SWIMMING
(Map p274; ☑07-333 1861; www.hotpools.co.nz; 648 Waikite Valley Rd; public pools adult/child/family $15/8/38, private pools 40min $18; ⊙10am-9pm) Around 35km south of Rotorua are these excellent open-air pools, formalised in the 1970s but utilised for centuries before then. There are four main pools, two more relaxing, smaller pools, and four private spas, all ranging from 35°C to 40°C. There's also a cafe and camping (adult/child unpowered sites $20/10, powered sites $22/12; pools free for campers).

To get here, turn right off SH5 opposite the Wai-O-Tapu turn-off, and continue 6km (worth the drive if only for the gorgeous valley view as you come over the hill).

BAY OF PLENTY

The Bay of Plenty stretches along the pohutukawa-studded coast from Waihi Beach to Opotiki and inland as far as the Kaimai Range. This is where New Zealanders have come on holiday for generations, lapping up salt-licked activities and lashings of sunshine.

Tauranga

POP 114,800

Tauranga (pronounced 'toe-rung-ah') has been booming since the 1990s and remains one of NZ's fastest-growing cities. It's also NZ's busiest port – with petrol refineries and mountains of coal and lumber – but it's beach-seeking holidaymakers who have seen the old workhorse reborn as a show pony. Restaurants and bars line the vamped-up waterfront, fancy hotels rise high, and the once-sleepy burbs of Mt Maunganui and Papamoa have woken up to new prosperity. This is about as Riviera as NZ gets. Online, www.downtowntauranga.co.nz is a commercial but useful resource.

Tauranga

◉ Top Sights
1 Tauranga Art Gallery B3

◉ Sights
2 Brain Watkins House..........................A4
3 Elms Mission House A1
4 Mission Cemetery...............................B1
5 Monmouth Redoubt............................B2
6 Robbins Park.......................................B2

◉ Activities, Courses & Tours
7 Dive Zone..A4

◉ Sleeping
8 City Suites...A2
9 Harbour City Motor Inn......................A3
10 Harbourside City Backpackers...........B3
11 Hotel on Devonport............................B4
12 Loft 109..B4
13 Roselands Motel.................................A1
14 Trinity Wharf......................................B1

◉ Eating
15 City Markets..B3
16 Collar & Thai.......................................B4
17 Elizabeth Cafe & Larder......................A4
18 Fresh Fish Markets..............................B2
19 Harbourside...B4
20 Mediterraneo Café..............................B4
21 Shima...B3
22 Zeytin on the Strand...........................B3

◉ Drinking & Nightlife
23 Brew...B3
24 Crown & Badger..................................B3
25 Phoenix..B3

◉ Entertainment
Rialto Cinemas ....(see 16)

◉ Sights

★**Tauranga Art Gallery**   GALLERY
(☑07-578 7933; www.artgallery.org.nz; cnr Wharf & Willow Sts; ◷10am-4.30pm) **FREE** The Tauranga Art Gallery presents historic and contemporary art, and houses a permanent collection along with frequently changing local and visiting exhibitions. The building itself is a former bank, although you'd hardly know it – it's an altogether excellent space with no obvious compromise (cue applause). Touring the ground-floor and mezzanine galleries will take an hour or so.

Elms Mission House   HISTORIC BUILDING
(www.theelms.org.nz; 15 Mission St; house adult/child $5/50c, gardens free; ◷house 2-4pm Wed, Sat & Sun, gardens 9am-5pm daily) Built in 1847, Elms Mission House is the oldest building in the Bay of Plenty. Furnished in period style, it sits among other well-preserved mission buildings in leafy gardens. The spooky

Mission Cemetery (cnr Marsh St & Dive Cres; ◷24hr) lies not far away – a shady tangle of trees and headstones.

Classic Flyers NZ   MUSEUM
(☑07-572 4000; www.classicflyersnz.com; 8 Jean Batten Dr; adult/child/family $10/5/25; ◷10am-4pm) Out near the airport, Classic Flyers NZ is an interesting aviation museum (biplanes, retired US Airforce jets, helicopters etc) with a buzzy on-site cafe.

Monmouth Redoubt ARCHAEOLOGICAL SITE, PARK
(Monmouth St; ◷24hr) **FREE** Shaded by huge pohutukawa trees, spooky Monmouth Redoubt was a fortified site during the Maori Wars. Next door is **Robbins Park** (Cliff Rd), a verdant pocket of roses with sweeping views across to Mt Maunganui. At the foot of the

Redoubt on the end of the Strand is **Te Awa nui Waka**, a replica Maori canoe, on display in an open-sided building.

Minden Lookout
LOOKOUT

(Minden Rd) From Minden Lookout, about 10km west of Tauranga towards Katikati, there's a superb view back over the cranes in Tauranga Harbour and across the Bay of Plenty. To get there, take SH2 to Te Puna and turn off south on Minden Rd; the lookout is about 3km up the road.

Brain Watkins House
HISTORIC BUILDING

(✐ 07-578 1835; www.taurangahistorical.blogspot. co.nz; 233 Cameron Rd; adult/child/family $4/2/10; ☉ 2-4pm Sun) A demure Victorian villa stranded on a hill as the roads around it grew, Brain Watkins House (no, not Brian) was built in 1881 from kauri (wood) and remains one of Tauranga's best-preserved colonial homes.

Mills Reef Winery
WINERY

(✐ 07-576 8800; www.millsreef.co.nz; 143 Moffat Rd, Bethlehem; ☉ 10am-5pm) Stately Mills Reef, 7km from the town centre at Bethlehem, has tastings of its award-winning wines (dig the chardonnay) and a refined restaurant (read: great food but not much fun) that's open for lunch daily and dinner by reservation (mains $25 to $39).

Huria Marae
MARAE

(✐ 07-578 7838; www.huriamarae.co.nz; Te Kaponga St, Judea) FREE Huria Marae is on a nondescript suburban street, but has sensational carvings both inside and out. Call to organise permission to visit, or to book a cultural experience (large groups only).

🏃 Activities

The free *Tauranga City Walkways* pamphlet (from the i-SITE) details walks around Tauranga and Mt Maunganui. History buffs should pick up the free *Historic Tauranga* brochure and stroll around the town's cache of historic sites.

Adventure Bay of Plenty
KAYAKING, MOUNTAIN BIKING

(✐ 0800 238 267; www.adventurebop.co.nz; 2hr/ half-day/full-day tours from $95/125/180) Offers an enticing array of adventure tours by kayak, mountain bike and horse. Half-day paddles around Mt Maunganui with a stop on Matakana Island cost $150/125 per adult/ child. A two-to-three hour cycle around Tauranga costs $95.

Adrenalin Forest
EXTREME SPORTS

(✐ 07-929 8724; www.adrenalin-forest.co.nz; Upper Pyes Pa Rd, TECT All Terrain Park; adult/ child $42/27; ☉ 10am-2.30pm daily, closed Mon & Tue Jun-Aug) About 26km from Tauranga en route to Rotorua is this heart-starter: a series of high-wires, flying foxes, platforms and rope bridges strung through a grove of tall conifers. There are six different routes of increasing difficulty to test your nerve.

Waimarino Adventure Park
KAYAKING, WATER SPORTS

(✐ 0800 456 996, 07-576 4233; www.waimarino. com; 36 Taniwha Pl; kayak tours from $65, kayak hire per hr/day $26/55, park day-pass adult/child $40/32; ☉ 10am-6pm Sep-Apr, 10am-5pm May-Aug) On the banks of the Wairoa River 8km west of town, Waimarino offers freedom kayak hire, self-guided kayak tours, sea kayaking trips and a magical Glowworm Tour ($120 per person) at McLaren Falls Park. The adventure park here has all kinds of watery distractions: a kayak slide, a diving board, a ropes course, water-walking zorbs, warm pools, and a human catapult called 'The Blob' – intense!

Kaimai Mamaku Forest Park
TRAMPING

(www.doc.govt.nz; SH29) FREE The backdrop to the Western Bay of Plenty is the rugged 70km-long Kaimai Mamaku Forest Park, 35km southwest of Tauranga, with tramps for the intrepid and huts (per person per night $5 to $15) and campsites ($6). For more info see DOC's pamphlet *Kaimai to Coast* ($2.50), or contact **Kaimai New Zealand Tours** (✐ 07-552 5257; www.kaimai-new-zealand-tours.com) to arrange a guided tramp.

Dolphin Blue
WILDLIFE TOUR

(✐ 027 666 8047; www.dolphinblue.co.nz; day trips adult/child $150/100; ☉ departs 8.30am) 🐾 Unhurried, small-group (15 people maximum) day trips across Tauranga Harbour and out onto the Bay of Plenty in pursuit of pods of dolphins. When you find them, you can jump in and splash around with them.

Dolphin Seafaris
WILDLIFE TOUR

(✐ 0800 326 8747, 07-577 0105; www.nzdolphin. com; half-day trip adult/child $140/95; ☉ departs Tauranga 8am, Mt Maunganui 8.15am) 🐾 Eco-attuned dolphin-spotting trips where you can get into the water and swim with the big fish (...sorry, mammals).

Blue Ocean Charters FISHING
(☑0800 224 278, 07-544 3072; www.blueocean.
co.nz; trips from $120) Fishing, diving and
sightseeing trips (including one to Tuhua
Island) on the TS *Ohorere*, MV *Te Kuia* and
MV *Ratahi*.

Dive Zone DIVING
(☑07-578 4050; www.divezone.co.nz; 213 Cameron
Rd; trips/courses from $120/600; ⊘8am-6pm
Mon-Fri, 7.30am-4pm Sat, 7.30am-2pm Sun) PADI-
qualifying courses or trips to local wrecks
and reefs, plus gear rental.

Elements Watersports WATER SPORTS
(☑0800 486 729; www.elementsonline.co.nz; lessons from $20) If you're new to the sea and
want to splash safely into the big blue, Elements Watersports runs sailing, windsurfing
and jetskiing lessons, and has gear for hire.

Tauranga Tandem Skydiving SKYDIVING
(☑07-574 8533; www.tandemskydive.co.nz; 2
Kittyhawk Way, Tauranga Airport; jumps
8000/10,000/12,000ft $285/325/375) Tauranga
Tandem Skydiving offers jumps from three
different heights, with views of Whakaari
(White Island), Mt Ruapehu and across the
Bay of Plenty on the way down.

☞ Tours

Tauranga Tasting Tours GUIDED TOUR
(☑07-544 1383; www.tastingtours.co.nz; tours
$130) Whips around a local brewery, Mills
Reef and Morton Estate wineries, and back
to town for cocktails.

No.8 Farm Tours GUIDED TOUR
(☑07-579 3981; www.no8farmtours.co.nz; tours
adult/child from $89/69) Half-day Tauranga
tours, plus 4WD tours of a working NZ farm,
featuring shearing, milking, sheep dogs,
deer and morning tea.

Aerius Helicopters SCENIC FLIGHTS
(☑0800 864 354; www.aerius.co.nz; flights from $65)
Local flights and aerial excursions as far away
as Lake Tarawera, Rotorua and Whakaari
(White Island), departing Tauranga.

Gyrate SCENIC FLIGHTS
(☑021 038 0760, 0800 3592 4976; www.gyrate.
co.nz; flights from $135) Scenic flights around
Tauranga/Mt Maunganui in a gyroplane
(the jetski of the sky).

Shore Trips & Tours GUIDED TOUR
(☑07-574 1779; www.shoretripsandtours.com;
half-/full-day tours from $49/90) Trips around

Tauranga's sights and enticements aimed
at cruise-boat passengers finding their land
legs. Longer tours to Rotorua also available.

✯ Festivals & Events

National Jazz Festival MUSIC, FOOD & WINE
(www.jazz.org.nz) An Easter extravaganza of
big blowers and scoobee-doobee-doo, with
concerts and food and wine galore.

Tauranga Arts Festival ARTS
(www.taurangafestival.co.nz) Kicking off on Labour weekend in October (in odd-numbered
years), showcasing dance, comedy, plays and
other things arty.

🛏 Sleeping

Harbourside City Backpackers HOSTEL $
(☑07-579 4066; www.backpacktauranga.co.nz; 105
The Strand; dm/tw/d from $29/74/74; @🛜) Soak
up the sea airs at this sociable hostel (a former
hotel), deliciously handy to the Strand's bars
and restaurants. Rooms are smallish but
clean, and you'll spend more time on the awesome roof terrace anyway. There's no parking,
but down the road is a public car park that
empties out at the right time.

Loft 109 HOSTEL $
(☑07-579 5638; www.loft109.co.nz; 109 Devonport
Rd, upstairs; dm/d/tr from $28/76/90; @🛜) This
small, central hostel feels like somebody's flat,
with an intimate kitchen-lounge and a cute
little balcony over Devonport St. It's bright,
with plenty of skylights and a gas fire for
colder days. Super-relaxed without being lax
about things like security or boozy badness.

Tauranga YHA HOSTEL $
(☑07-578 5064, 0800 278 299; www.yha.co.nz; 171
Elizabeth St; dm from $29, d with/without bathroom
$110/90; @🛜) 🍃 A well-kept, deceptively big
YHA on the edge of town, with a large grassy
backyard and a nearby mangrove swamp
boardwalk to explore. Inviting dorms have
individual lockers, and there's info available
on local walking trails and a noticeboard for
all things green.

Just the Ducks
Nuts Backpackers HOSTEL $
(☑07-576 1366; www.justtheducksnuts.co.nz; 6
Vale St; dm from $27, with/without bathroom s
$66/56, d $78/70; @🛜) Just out of the town
centre, this friendly place has colourful
rooms, a fulsome library, TVs strewn about
and quirky touches like flowers planted in
a bath-tub and duck-themed toilets – like

a university share-house minus the parties. Free shuttles to/from the bus stop; self-contained flats also available.

Tauranga Tourist Park HOLIDAY PARK $

(✆07-578 3323; www.taurangatouristpark.co.nz; 9 Mayfair St; unpowered/powered sites from $30/35, cabins from $55; @☎) The layout at this harbourside holiday park feels a bit tight (don't expect rolling acres), but it's well maintained, clean and tidy. Aim for a site down by the bay under the pohotukawa trees.

Roselands Motel MOTEL $$

(✆07-578 2294, 0800 363 093; www.roselands. co.nz; 21 Brown St; d/ste from $110/135; ☎) Tarted up with splashes of orange paint and new linen, this sweet, old-style motel is in a quiet but central location. Expect spacious units (all with kitchenettes), friendly first-name-basis hosts and new TVs. Nice one.

Harbour City Motor Inn MOTEL $$

(✆07-571 1435, 0800 253 525; www.tauranga-harbourcity.co.nz; 50 Wharf St; d/1-bedroom from $150/170; ☎) With a winning location right in the middle of town (and plenty of parking), this newish, lemon-yellow motor inn has all the mod cons. There are spa baths in each room, and friendly staff who can offer sound advice on your itinerary.

City Suites HOTEL $$

(✆07-577 1480; www.citysuites.co.nz; 32 Cameron Rd; r from $155; ☎�) The spacious rooms here (all with either terrace or balcony) have a rather regal feel, with king-sized beds and full kitchens. A swimming pool, free wi-fi and secure parking complete the list of essentials for wandering business bods.

Ambassador Motor Inn MOTEL $$

(✆0800 735 294, 07-578 5665; www.ambassador-motorinn.co.nz; 9 Fifteenth Ave; d/f from $110/175; ☎swim) This tidy motel on the edge of town has noise-reducing glass for peaceful sleeps. Some rooms have spa baths; all have kitchen facilities. It's not overtly ambassadorial and a bit out of the way, but it's spotlessly clean and the new owners are keen to make a good impression.

Hotel on Devonport HOTEL $$$

(✆07-578 2668; www.hotelondevonport.net.nz; 72 Devonport Rd; d/ste from $165/205; @☎) City-centre Devonport is top of the town, with bay-view rooms, noise-reducing glass, slick interiors and sassy staff, all of which appeal to business travellers and upmarket weekenders. Help yourself to the bowl of apples in the lobby.

Trinity Wharf HOTEL $$$

(✆07-577 8700, 0800 577 8700; www.trinitywharf. co.nz; 51 Dive Cres; d from $180; @☎swim) This blocky three-storey number near the harbour bridge has a slick, contemporary lobby – all white tiles and spiky pot plants – leading to the upmarket in-house restaurant Halo (mains $15 to $36). Rooms are supersized and luxurious in tones *au naturel*. Amenities include an underutilised gym, infinity-edge swimming pool and free wi-fi. Very flashy.

✕ Eating

★ Grindz Café CAFE $

(✆07-579 0017; www.facebook.com/pages/grindz-cafe/110512979024824; 50 First Ave; meals $5-15; ⊙7am-4pm Mon-Fri, 8am-3.30pm Sat, 8am-3pm Sun; ☎✆) The undisputed highlight of wide-open First Ave is Grindz, a hip cafe with scattered footpath tables. Inside it's a roomy, split-level affair, with funky wallpaper, antiques and retro relics. Bagels, vegie stacks, muffins, cakes and salads are the order of the day, plus creative coffee (try 'The Trough' if you're sleepy: a four-shot soup bowl of caffeine heaven). Free wi-fi too.

Fresh Fish Markets FISH & CHIPS $

(✆07-578 1789; 1 Dive Cres; meals from $6; ⊙11am-8pm) A local legend serving up fresh fish and chips, with hexagonal outdoor tables on the water's edge and plenty of seagulls to keep you company.

Mediterraneo Café CAFE, MEDITERRANEAN $

(The Med; ✆07-577 0487; www.mediterraneocafe. co.nz; 62 Devonport Rd; mains $8-20; ⊙7am-4pm Mon-Fri, 7.30am-4pm Sat, 8am-4pm Sun; ✆) A hot spot reeling with regulars enjoying terrific coffee and scrumptious all-day breakfasts. Order from the blackboard or from the cabinet crammed with sandwiches, salads, flans and cakes. Lunchtime crowds can be frantic (but the chicken salad is worth it). Cute staff, and plenty of gluten-free and vegetarian options.

City Markets SELF CATERING $

(cnr Willow & Hamilton Sts; ⊙9am-5pm Mon-Fri, to noon Sat) For fresh fundamentals (fruit and veg, bread, eggs, milk), City Markets is a block back from the Strand.

Pak 'n Save SUPERMARKET $

(www.paknsave.co.nz; 476 Cameron Rd; ⊙8am-10pm) A short drive south of town.

Elizabeth Cafe & Larder MODERN NZ, BAR $$
(☑07-579 0950; www.elizabethcafe.co.nz; 247 Cameron Rd; mains breakfast & lunch $10-20, dinner $24-34; ☺7am-4pm Mon & Tue, 7am-5pm Wed, 7am-9pm Thu & Fri, 8am-9pm Sat, 8am-4pm Sun) 'Eat, drink, enjoy' at Elizabeth, a hip new cafe-bar on the ground floor of a four-storey downtown office block. Predictably, many of the customers drift down from upstairs, but you don't need a suit to enjoy a knockout Moroccan lamb salad with a glass of Central Otago pinot gris. Interesting industrial aesthetics and Peroni on tap.

Zeytin on the Strand TURKISH $$
(☑07-579 0099; www.zeytin.co.nz; 83 The Strand; mains $20-30; ☺11.30am-3pm & 4.30pm-late Tue-Sun; ☑) Ask the locals to name their favourite restaurant, and odds-on they'll name Zeytin – a Turkish delight. Authentic Turkish fare, with something for everyone: kebabs, delicious homemade breads, dips, healthy salads, wood-fired pizza and a few exotic surprises.

Collar & Thai THAI $$
(☑07-577 6655; www.collarandthai.co.nz; Goddards Centre, 21 Devonport Rd; mains lunch $14-17, dinner $21-32; ☺11.30am-2pm Mon-Sat, 5-10pm daily) No tie required at this upstairs eatery that artfully elaborates on Thai standards and uses plenty of fresh seafood. Perfect for a pre-movie meal (the Rialto Cinemas are right next door). Good-value lunch specials, too.

Shima JAPANESE, KOREAN $$
(☑07-571 1382; www.nzshima.co.nz; 15 Wharf St; mains $12-30; ☺noon-3pm & 6pm-late) There are flashier Japanese joints in town, but Shima endures as a simple, unpretentious sushi and sashimi bar, hung with fans, umbrellas and lanterns. Bento boxes and set-price menus are great bang for your buck.

★**Harbourside** MODERN NZ $$$
(☑07-571 0520; www.harbourside.co.nz; Railway Bridge, The Strand; mains $26-38; ☺11.30am-2.30pm & 5.30pm-late) In a marvellously atmospheric 100-year-old boathouse at the end of the Strand, Harbourside is the place for a romantic dinner, with lapping waves and the overhead railway bridge arching out over the harbour. The roast duck with Chinese cabbage, lime and chilli is hard to beat, or you can just swing by for a moody pre-dinner drink.

Somerset Cottage MODERN NZ $$$
(☑07-576 6889; www.somersetcottage.co.nz; 30 Bethlehem Rd, Bethlehem; mains $30-40; ☺11.30am-2.30pm Wed-Fri, 6-9pm Mon-Sat) The most awarded restaurant in the Bay, Somerset Cottage is a simple-but-elegant venue for that special treat. The food is highly seasonal, made from the best NZ ingredients and impressively executed without being too fussy. Standout dishes include baked cheese soufflé, duck with coconut kumara and the famous liquorice ice cream.

🍸 Drinking & Entertainment

Brew CRAFT BEER, PUB
(www.brewpub.co.nz; 107 The Strand; ☺4pm-late Mon-Thu, 11am-late Wed-Sun) The long concrete bar here has room for plenty of elbows, and plenty of glasses of Croucher's crafty seasonal ales, pilseners and stouts (pray the Ethiopian coffee stout is on tap). The vibe is social, with communal tables and plates of bar food designed to share ($8 to $28). And no TV! Winner.

Phoenix PUB
(www.thephoenixtauranga.co.nz; 67 The Strand; ☺10.30am-late Mon-Fri, 8.30am-late Sat & Sun) Rising phoenix-like from the northern end of the Strand, this sprawling new gastropub pours fine Monteith's beers (once niche, now mainstream) and serves meaty pub meals (mains $20 to $34; try the pork ribs). Dressed-up drinkers; Red Hot Chilli Peppers on the stereo.

Crown & Badger PUB
(www.crownandbadger.co.nz; cnr The Strand & Wharf St; ☺9am-late) A particularly convincing black-painted Brit boozer that does pukka pints of Tennent's and Guinness, and food along the lines of bangers-and-mash and BLTs (mains $17 to $29). Things get more energetic on weekends with live bands.

Rialto Cinemas CINEMA
(☑07-577 0445; www.rialtotauranga.co.nz; Goddards Centre, 21 Devonport Rd; tickets adult/child $18.50/12.50; ☺opens 30min before screenings) Home to the Tauranga Film Society, the Rialto is the best spot in town to catch a flick: classic, offbeat, art-house and international. And you can sip a coffee or a glass of wine in the darkness.

ℹ Information

Paper Plus (17 Grey St; ☺8.30am-5.30pm Mon-Fri, 9am-4pm Sat, 10am-3pm Sun) The local NZ Post branch.

Tauranga Hospital (☎07-579 8000; www. bopdhb.govt.nz; 375 Cameron Rd; ⊙24hr) A couple of kilometres south of town.

Tauranga i-SITE (☎07-578 8103; www.bayof-plentynz.com; 8 Wharf St; ⊙8.30am-5.30pm, reduced winter hours; 🕾) Local tourist information, bookings, InterCity bus tickets and DOC maps.

ℹ Getting There & Away

AIR

Air New Zealand (☎07-577 7300; www. airnewzealand.co.nz; cnr Devonport Rd & Elizabeth St; ⊙9am-5pm Mon-Fri, 10am-1pm Sat) Has daily direct flights to Auckland, Wellington and Christchurch.

BUS

Twin City Express buses run twice daily Monday to Friday between Tauranga/Mt Maunganui and Rotorua via Te Puke ($11.60, 1½ hours).

InterCity tickets and timetables are available at the i-SITE. Destinations include the following:

DESTINATION	PRICE ($)	DURATION (HR)	FREQUENCY (DAILY)
Auckland	46	4	3
Hamilton	33	2	2
Rotorua	32	1½	2
Taupo	52	3	2
Wellington	55	9	1

Naked Bus offers substantial fare savings when you book in advance. Destinations include the following:

DESTINATION	PRICE ($)	DURATION (HR)	FREQUENCY (DAILY)
Auckland	16	3¼	3
Hamilton	10	3	2
Napier	35	5	2
Rotorua	10	1	3
Taupo	15	3	2
Wellington	23	9	1
Whakatane	18	3	1

Shuttle Bus

A couple of companies can pick you up at Auckland or Rotorua airports and bus you to Tauranga (though you'll pay upwards of $100 for the privilege).

Luxury Airport Shuttles (☎07-547 4444; www.luxuryairportshuttles.co.nz) Also shunts travellers between Tauranga Airport and Tauranga (from $10).

Apollo Connect Shuttles (☎07-218 0791; www.taurangashuttles.co.nz)

CAR

If you're heading to Hamilton on route K, the toll road costs $1.50 (pay at the toll booth).

ℹ Getting Around

BICYCLE

Cycle Tauranga (☎0800 253 525, 07-571 1435; www.cycletauranga.co.nz; Harbour City Motor Inn, 50 Wharf St; per half-/full day $29/49) Has hybrid road-trail bikes for hire, including helmets, locks, saddle bags and maps. Tours also available.

BUS

Tauranga's bright yellow Bay Hopper buses run to most locations around the area, including Mt Maunganui ($3, 15 minutes) and Papamoa ($3, 30 minutes). There's a central stop on Wharf St; timetables available from the i-SITE.

CAR

Numerous car-rental agencies have offices in Tauranga, including **Rent-a-Dent** (☎0800 736 823, 07-578 1772; www.rentadent.co.nz; 19 Fifteenth Ave; ⊙8am-5pm Mon-Fri, 8am-noon Sat).

TAXI

A taxi from the centre of Tauranga to the airport or Mt Maunganui costs around $20. Call **Tauranga Mount Taxis** (☎07-578 6086; www. taurangataxis.co.nz).

Mt Maunganui

POP 30,400

Named after the hulking 232m hill that punctuates the sandy peninsula occupied by the township, up-tempo Mt Maunganui is often just called 'the Mount', or Mauao, which translates as 'caught by the light of day'. It's considered part of greater Tauranga, but really it's an enclave unto itself, with great cafes and restaurants, hip bars and fab beaches. Sun-seekers flock to the Mount in summer, supplied by an increasing number of 10-storey apartment towers studding the spit. Online, see www.mountmaunganui. org.nz for information.

◉ Sights & Activities

The Mount lays claim to being NZ's premier **surfing** city (they teach surfing at high school!). You can carve up the waves at **Mount Beach**, which has lovely beach

Mt Maunganui

ROTORUA & THE BAY OF PLENTY MT MAUNGANUI

Mt Maunganui

◎ Top Sights
1 Mauao...A1

✪ Activities, Courses & Tours
2 Mount Hot Pools.............................A1
3 Mount Surfshop..............................B2
4 Rock House......................................C4

🛏 Sleeping
5 Beachside Holiday Park...................B1
6 Belle Mer...C2
7 Mission Belle Motel........................B2
8 Mount Backpackers........................B2
9 Mt Maunganui B&B.........................C4
10 Pacific Coast Lodge &
Backpackers................................C3
11 Seagulls Guesthouse B&B..............C3
12 Westhaven Motel............................B2

🍴 Eating
Drawing Room..........................(see 15)
13 Kwang Chow....................................B2
14 Mount Bistro...................................B2
15 Mount Mainstreet Farmers
Market...B2
16 New World.......................................D4
17 Providores Urban Food Store........B2
18 Slowfish..B1
19 Thai Khan Koon...............................B3

🍷 Drinking & Nightlife
20 Astrolabe..B2
21 Latitude 37......................................B2
22 Major Tom's....................................B3

🎭 Entertainment
23 Bay City Cinemas...........................B2

breaks and a 100m artificial surf reef not far offshore. Learn-to-surf operators include **Hibiscus** (027 279 9687, 07-575 3792; www.surfschool.co.nz; 2hr/2-day lesson $85/165), **Discovery Surf School** (027 632 7873; www.discoverysurf.co.nz; 2hr lesson $90, 4 lessons $320) and **Mount Surfshop** (07-575 9133; www.mountsurfshop.co.nz; 96 Maunganui Rd; rental per hr wetsuit/bodyboard/surfboard/paddleboard from $5/5/10/20, 2hr lesson $80; ⊙ 9am-5pm Mon-Sat, 10am-5pm Sun).

⭐ Mauao   MOUNTAIN, LOOKOUT

Explore Mauao (Mt Maunganui) itself on the walking trails winding around it and leading up to the summit. The steep **summit walk** takes about an hour return (with a rest at the top). You can also clamber around the rocks on **Moturiki Island**, which adjoins the peninsula. The island and the base of Mauao comprise the **Mauao Base Track** (3½km, 45 minutes), wandering through magical groves of pohutukawa trees that bloom between November and January. Pick up the *Mauao* map from the info desk at Beachside Holiday Park.

Mount Hot Pools   SWIMMING

(www.tcal.co.nz; 9 Adams Ave; adult/child/family $11/8/31; ⊙ 6am-10pm Mon-Sat, 8am-10pm Sun) If you've worked up a sweat walking up and down Mauao, take a long relaxing soak at these hotwater pools at the foot of the hill.

Canoe & Kayak   KAYAKING

(07-574 7415; www.canoeandkayak.co.nz; 3/5 MacDonald St; tours per person from $99) Canoe & Kayak runs 2½-hour kayaking trips around Mauao checking out seals and rock formations and hearing local legends, plus three-hour nocturnal glowworm paddles in nearby McLarens Falls Park.

Rock House   ROCK CLIMBING

(www.therockhouse.co.nz; 9 Triton Ave; adult/child $16.50/14.50, gear hire extra; ⊙ noon-9pm Tue-Fri, 10am-6pm Sat & Sun) Try rock climbing at the Rock House, a huge blue steel shed with huge blue climbing walls inside it.

Baywave   SWIMMING

(07-575 0276; www.tcal.co.nz; cnr Girven & Gloucester Rds; adult/child $7.50/5, hydroslide $4.60; ⊙ 5.30am-9pm Mon-Fri, 7am-7pm Sat & Sun) For unsalted swimming-pool action plus NZ's biggest wave pool, a hydroslide and aqua aerobics, visit Baywave.

🛏 Sleeping

Seagulls Guesthouse B&B   B&B, HOSTEL $

(07-574 2099; www.seagullsguesthouse.co.nz; 12 Hinau St; dm/s/d/f from $30/65/85/110; @ 🛜) Can't face another crowded, alcohol-soaked

---

THE WRECK OF THE RENA

On 5 October 2011, the 47,000-tonne cargo ship MV *Rena*, loaded with 1368 containers and 1900 tonnes of fuel oil, ran aground on Astrolabe Reef, 22km off the coast of Mt Maunganui. The ship had been attempting to enter Tauranga Harbour, NZ's busiest port, but inexplicably hit one of the most consistently charted obstacles in the way. Pitched acutely on the reef with a rupturing hull, the *Rena* started spilling oil into the sea and shedding containers from its deck. Over subsequent days, disbelieving locals watched as oil slicks, containers and dead fish and seabirds washed up on their glorious beaches.

The blame game began: the captain? The owners? The company that chartered the vessel? Thousands of volunteers pitched in to help with the clean-up. Salvors eventually managed to remove most of the oil from the ship, but on 8 January 2012 the *Rena* finally broke in two, spilling remnant oil and dozens more containers into the sea. The stern section subsequently slipped below the surface.

With the initial focus on preventing an oil spill, the elephant in the corner of the room – the *Rena* herself – seemed a problem too large. With refloating the ship no longer an option, debate raged on what to do: drag the bow section off the rocks too? A future dive site for the Bay of Plenty? At the time of writing the plan was to cut the bow section down to 1m below the water line, and remove the four-storey accommodation tower from the submerged stern.

The grounding has been an environmental and economic disaster, but long-term impacts are hard to gauge: local businesses suffered at the time but are back in full swing, and the beautiful beaches are clean again. See www.renaproject.co.nz for updates, or ask a local for their take on the situation (a sure-fire converstaion starter!).

hostel? On a quiet street not far from town, Seagulls is a gem: an immaculate, upmarket backpackers where the emphasis is on peaceful enjoyment of one's surrounds rather than wallowing in the excesses of youth (not that there's anything wrong with that). The best rooms have bathrooms and TVs. Free wi-fi.

Pacific Coast Lodge & Backpackers
HOSTEL $

(✆0800 666 622, 07-574 9601; www.pacificcoast-lodge.co.nz; 432 Maunganui Rd; dm/d from $27/78; @🛜) Not far from the action, this efficiently run, sharp-looking hostel is sociable but not party-focused, with drinkers gently encouraged to migrate into town after 10pm. Purpose-built bunkrooms are spacious and adorned with beachy murals. Free bikes and surfboards.

Beachside Holiday Park
HOLIDAY PARK $

(✆07-575 4471; www.mountbeachside.co.nz; 1 Adams Ave; campsites from $35, on-site vans $60-90, cabins $80-130; @) With three different camping areas nooked into the foot of Mt Maunganui itself, this community-run park has spectacular camping with all the requisite facilities, plus it's handy to the Mount Hot Pools (discounts for campers) and a strip of good eateries. Reception is the local info centre.

Mount Backpackers
HOSTEL $

(✆07-575 0860; www.mountbackpackers.co.nz; 87 Maunganui Rd; dm/tw/tr from $25/80/90; @🛜) A tidy hostel on the main drag, bolstered by location – close to the beach and a mere stagger from the Mount's best restaurants and bars – plus extras like cheap surfboard and bike hire and discounted surf lessons.

Cosy Corner Holiday Park
HOLIDAY PARK $

(✆07-575 5899, 0800 684 654; www.cosycorner.co.nz; 40 Ocean Beach Rd; campsites from $40, cabins & flats $70-120; @🛜☒) This compact, spartan camping ground has a sociable feel, with barbecues, trampolines and a games room. Handy to the beach, too (access via a little path just across the road). New hot tub!

Mission Belle Motel
MOTEL $$

(✆0800 202 434, 07-575 2578; www.missionbelle-motel.co.nz; cnr Victoria Rd & Pacific Ave; d/f from $130/190; 🛜) With a distinctly Tex-Mex exterior (like something out of an old Clint Eastwood movie), this family-run motel goes all modern inside, with especially good two-storey family rooms with large bathtubs, plus sheltered barbecue and courtyard areas.

Westhaven Motel
MOTEL $$

(✆07-575 4753; www.westhavenmotel.co.nz; 27a The Mall; units $100-210; 🛜) The 1969 architecture here is funky, but the new owners are modernising things room-by-room (get in now if you're a retro fan!). Full kitchens are perfect for self-caterers, and it's an easy walk to the shops and restaurants. The most affordable motel in miles.

Mt Maunganui B&B
B&B $$

(✆07-575 4013; www.mountbednbreakfast.co.nz; 463 Maunganui Rd; s/d incl cooked breakfast from $70/100; @🛜) This good-value five-room B&B on the main road into town offers a cosy guest lounge, basic shared kitchen, pool table, barbecue and cable TV. The two rooms at the front cop a bit of traffic noise, but the rest are fine. Good for groups.

Belle Mer
HOTEL, APARTMENTS $$$

(✆07-575 0011, 0800 100 235; www.bellemer.co.nz; 53 Marine Pde; apt $190-450; 🛜☒) A flashy beachside complex of one-, two- and three-bedroom apartments, some with seaview balconies and others opening onto private courtyards (though you'll more likely head for the resort-style pool terrace). Rooms are tastefully decorated in warm tones with soft edges, and have everything you need for longer stays, with full kitchens and laundries.

🍴 Eating

Providores Urban Food Store
CAFE, DELICATESSEN $

(✆07-572 1300; 19a Pacific Ave; meals $5-22; ⊙7.30am-5pm, closed Mon & Tue Apr-Oct; 🖉) Mexican rugs and comfy couches set the mood here as your eyes peruse fresh-baked breads, buttery croissants, home-smoked meats and cheeses, organic jams and free-range eggs – perfect ingredients for a bang-up breakfast or a hamper-filling picnic on the beach. Superb.

Mount Mainstreet Farmers Market
MARKET $

(www.mountmaunganui.org.nz; Phoenix Car Park, Maunganui Rd; ⊙9am-1pm Sun) Roll up to the local farmers market for a Sunday morning fix-me-up: fresh fruit and vegies, coffee, pastries, honey, cheese, juices... Arts and crafts are banned!

New World
SUPERMARKET $

(www.newworld.co.nz; cnr Tweed St & Maunganui Rd; ⊙7am-9pm) A haven for self-caterers.

Slowfish
CAFE $$

(07-574 2949; www.slowfish.co.nz; Shop 5, Twin Towers, Marine Pde; mains $15-24; 7am-4.30pm;) There's no slacking off in the kitchen of this eco-aware cafe, which promotes the art of savouring fine, locally sourced food. It's a hit with the crowds: you'll have to crowbar yourself in the door or pounce on any available alfresco seat, but it's worth it for its free-range bacon and eggs, Greek salads and fish cakes with chilli jam.

Thai Khan Koon
THAI $$

(07-574 8500; www.thaikhankoon.co.nz; 277 Maunganui Rd; mains $15-19; 11am-10pm Mon, Wed-Fri & Sun, 5-10pm Tue, 11am-late Sat) A couple of flapping Thai flags herald this low-key eatery on an unsexy part of the Mount's main street. But don't let the location, the faux orchids or shiny food photos put you off – the cooking here is the real deal. Try the *gaeng dang bhed* (red duck curry) or classic Thai fish cakes.

Kwang Chow
CHINESE $$

(07-575 5063; 241 Maunganui Rd; lunch/dinner $15/20; 11.30am-10pm Tue-Sun) This all-you-can-eat Chinese place is a local favourite for a bargain bite that maintains tasty flavours rather than resorting to a bland melange. And great puddings. Cavernous interior with floorboards and refreshingly little gold/crimson/mirror festoonery.

★ Drawing Room
MODERN NZ, FRENCH $$$

(07-575 0096; www.thedrawingroom-nz.tumblr.com; 107 Maunganui Rd; mains $34; 6pm-late Mon-Sat Apr-Oct, 3pm-late daily Nov-Mar) This outstanding new Frenchy food room fills a niche: upmarket but totally unpretentious, with a commitment to local produce and local art (the window mural changes monthly). Design-wise it's leather banquettes and timber floorboards; booze-wise it's NZ craft beers, single malts and an inspired selection of Kiwi and French wines. Order the pan-fried scallops, and leave room for a secret dessert!

Mount Bistro
MODERN NZ $$$

(07-575 3872; www.mountbistro.co.nz; 6 Adams Ave; mains $26-64; 5.30-9pm Tue-Sun) The buttermilk-coloured Mount Bistro, an unpretentious fine-dining experience at the foot of Mauao, is onto a good thing: quality local meats (fish, lamb, beef, crayfish, chicken, duck) creatively worked into classic dishes (lamb shanks, seafood chowder) and served with élan. Makes for a classy night out.

Drinking & Entertainment

★ Major Tom's
BAR, LIVE MUSIC

(www.majortomsbar.com; 297 Maunganui Rd; 4-11pm Sun-Tue, 5-11pm Wed & Thu, 4pm-1am Fri & Sat) A funky little bar set back from the main drag in what looks like Major Tom's spaceship. Inside it's all kooky antiques, vintage couches, dangling inverted desk lamps and prints of Elvis, the *Mona Lisa* and (of course) David Bowie. Fabulous streetside terrace, cool tunes, free wi-fi and occasional live acts. Everybody sing: 'Planet Earth is blue, and there's nothing I can do...'

Astrolabe
PUB

(07-574 8155; www.astrolabe.co.nz; 82 Maunganui Rd; 10am-1am) Run by Mac's brewery, Astrolabe conjures up a funky-retro 'bach' vibe, with floral carpet, bookshelves jammed with old novels, beach umbrellas, battered suitcases and vintage placemats. If all that doesn't float your holiday boat, a few pilseners and some blackened fish tacos just might (mains $15 to $25).

Latitude 37
BAR

(www.37.co.nz; 181 Maunganui Rd; 4pm-1am Mon, noon-1am Tue-Sun;) A slick, upmarket bar with stone-faced walls, fold-back windows and flaming torches out the front. A lot of folk come here to eat (mains $22 to $39... oh, the smoked bourbon mussels!), but it's also a beaut spot for a cold Heineken after a day in the surf.

Bay City Cinemas
CINEMA

(07-572 3311; www.baycitycinemas.co.nz; 249 Maunganui Rd; tickets adult/child $16/10; 10am-late) Mainstream offerings.

Information

The reception desk at Beachside Holiday Park doubles as an informal info centre for the Mount; open 8.30am to 7pm.

Getting There & Around

BUS

InterCity and Naked Bus services visiting Tauranga also stop at Mt Maunganui, with fares similar to those to/from Tauranga. Buses stop on Salisbury Ave.

CAR

Mt Maunganui is across the harbour bridge from Tauranga, or accessible from the south via Te Maunga on SH2. For car hire, try **Rite Price Rentals** (07-575 2726, 0800 250 251; www.ritepricerentals.co.nz; 63 Totara St; 8am-5pm).

Papamoa

POP 20,100

Papamoa is a burgeoning 'burb next to Mt Maunganui, separated now by just an empty paddock or two, destined for subdivision. With big new houses on pristine streets, parts of Papamoa have the air of a gated community, but the beach beyond the sheltering dunes is awesome – you can't blame folks for moving in.

Back a few kilometres from the beach, **Blo-kart Heaven** (☑07-572 4256; www.blokartheaven.co.nz; 176 Parton Rd; blokarting 1hr $50; ☺10am-4.30pm) is the place to attempt land-sailing around a custom-built speedway (blokarts are like seated windsurfers on wheels).

The sprawling **Papamoa Beach Top 10 Holiday Resort** (☑07-572 0816, 0800 232 243; www.papamoabeach.co.nz; 535 Papamoa Beach Rd; campsites from $40, villas & units $98-275; @☎) is a spotless, modern park, primed and priced beyond its caravan-park origins, with fab self-contained villas behind the dunes (*shhhh*, listen to the surf).

With its angular corrugated-iron exterior and tasteful caneware furnishings, **Beach House Motel** (☑07-572 1424, 0800 429 999; www.beachhousemotel.co.nz; 224 Papamoa Beach Rd; d from $130; ☎☒) offers an immaculate, upmarket version of the Kiwi bach holiday, relaxed and close to the beach. There's a pool if the beach is too windy, and orange daisies poking up through rock gardens.

Bluebiyou (☑07-572 2099; www.bluebiyou.co.nz; 559 Papamoa Beach Rd; mains $15-38; ☺noon-2.30pm & 5.30pm-late Wed & Thu, noon-late Fri & Sat, 10am-late Sun) is a casual, breezy restaurant riding high on the dunes, serving big brunches and seafood specialities. The prawn Benedict is a sure-fire Sunday morning start-me-up. Open seven days in summer.

Matakana Island

About 24km long and forming the seaward side of Tauranga Harbour, privately owned Matakana is laced with secluded white-sand surf beaches on its eastern shore (experienced surfers only). The community lifestyle here is laid-back and beachy, but the only way you can visit is on a kayak tour with Adventure Bay of Plenty (p278).

Katikati

POP 4060

'Katikat' to the locals, this busy little town was the only planned Ulster settlement in the world, and celebrates this history with a series of colourful **murals**. The **Mural Town Information Centre** (☑07-549 1658; www.katikati.org.nz; 36 Main Rd; ☺8am-5pm Mon-Fri, 9am-2pm Sat, 10am-2pm Sun; ☎) sells a guide to the murals ($2.50), or you can take a small-group **guided tour** (☑07-549 2977; per person $5).

◉ Sights & Activities

Katikati Heritage Museum   MUSEUM
(☑07-549 0651; www.katikatiheritagemuseum.co.nz; 3 Wharawhara Rd; adult/child $7.50/5; ☺9am-4pm) This rusty old museum traces local history with an engaging mix of Maori artefacts and Ulster history, some moa bones, old flat-tyre tractors and reputedly the largest bottle collection in the southern hemisphere.

Haiku Pathway   WALKWAY
(www.katikati.co.nz; ☺24hr) FREE Kicking off just near the information centre, the Haiku

---

OFF THE BEATEN TRACK

TUHUA (MAYOR ISLAND)

Commonly known as Mayor Island, this dormant volcano is 35km north of Tauranga. It's a privately owned island noted for its black, glasslike obsidian rock and **birdlife**, including a clutch of kiwi, introduced to the predator-free isle in 2006. Walking tracks cut through the overgrown crater valley, and the northwest corner is a **marine reserve**.

You need permission to visit from the island's *kaitiaki* (guardians), via the **Tuhua Trust Board** (☑07-577 0942). There's a $5 landing fee, and visitors must observe strict quarantine regulations. Accommodation is limited to basic camping/cabins ($10/30); bring your own food and water (no fridges). The landing fee is included in accommodation costs. Several boat-charter companies will take you to Tuhua, including Blue Ocean Charters (p279). Contact **DOC** (☑07-578 7677; taurangainfo@doc.govt.nz) in Tauranga for more info.

Pathway rambles along the Uretara River past boulders inscribed with haiku verses. A serene scene.

Katikati Bird Gardens
WILDLIFE RESERVE

(☑07-549 0912; www.birdgardens.co.nz; 263 Walker Rd E; adult/child/family $9.50/5/25; ⊙10am-4.30pm) About 7km south of town, the 4-hectare Katikati Bird Gardens is aflap with native birdlife (ever seen a kawaupaka?). There's a cafe and gallery here, plus boutiquey cottage accommodation (double B&B $160).

Morton Estate
WINERY

(www.mortonestatewines.co.nz; 2389 SH2; ⊙9.30am-5pm) The monastic-looking Morton Estate, one of NZ's bigger wineries, squats on SH2 8km south of Katikati. It's open for tastings and stock-ups: try the smooth-as-cream chardonnay.

🛏 Sleeping

Kaimai View Motel
MOTEL $$

(☑07-549 0398; www.kaimaiview.co.nz; 84 Main Rd; d from $120; 🛜🐾) Beyond a funky mural on the streetside wall, this jaunty, mod motel offers neat rooms (all named after NZ native trees) with CD player, kitchenette and, in larger rooms, spa. The namesake views extend over the back fence.

★ Warm Earth Cottage
CABIN, B&B $$$

(☑07-549 0962; www.warmearthcottage.co.nz; 202 Thompsons Track; d $220) Reignite your romance or simmer in simple pleasures at this rural idyll, 5km south of town then 2km west of SH2. Two pretty, electricity-less cottages sit by the swimmable Waitekohe River. Fire up the barbecue (generous barbecue packs $85), melt into a wood-fired outdoor bath, or chew through a book in the lovely guest lounge/library. Big DIY breakfasts are included in the price.

Eating

Ambria
MODERN NZ $$

(☑07-549 2272; www.ambria.co.nz; 5/62 Main Rd; mains lunch $15-19, dinner $24-36) Surprisingly atmospheric, Ambria is a hip bar-eatery in a nondescript shopping strip on the eastern side of town. Order a glass of Kiwi wine to wash over your pork belly stuffed with sage, apple and streaky bacon.

Talisman Hotel & Landing Restaurant
PUB $$

(☑07-549 2218; www.facebook.com/talisman-hotel; 7 Main Rd; mains $18-30; ⊙11.30am-2.30pm & 5-9pm) The Talisman is the local boozer, with occasional live music (including 'Sing For Your Supper' nights – bring your guitar!) and the Landing Restaurant serving pubby standards: pizzas, steaks, lamb Wellington, pan-fried salmon and surf 'n' turf.

Te Puke

POP 7500

Welcome to the 'Kiwifruit Capital of the World', a busy town during the picking season when there's plenty of work around. The **Te Puke Visitor Information Centre** (☑07-573 9172; www.tepuke.co.nz; 130 Jellicoe St; ⊙8am-5pm Mon-Fri, 9am-noon Sat; 🛜) is in the same building as the public library (staff will confirm that 'Puke' rhymes with cookie, not fluke).

For the low-down on all things kiwifruit, swing into **Kiwi360** (☑0800 549 4360, 07-573 6340; www.kiwi360.com; 35 Young Rd, off SH2; admission free, tour adult/child/family $20/6/46; ⊙9am-5pm) at the turn-off for Maketu. Sitting among orchards of nashi pears, citrus, avocados and (you guessed it) kiwifruit, this visitor centre peels off a range of attractions including a 35-minute 'kiwicart' orchard

---

HOT FUZZ: KIWIFRUIT

The humble kiwifruit earns NZ more than a billion dollars every year, and with the Bay of Plenty in the thick of the action, it's no wonder the locals are fond of them.

The fruit's origins are in China, where it was called the monkey peach (they were considered ripe when the monkeys munched them). As they migrated to NZ, they were renamed the Chinese gooseberry – they were a lot smaller then, but canny Kiwis engineered them to more generous sizes and began exporting them in the 1950s. The fruit was then sexily rebranded as the Zespri. Today the Zesprians grow two types of kiwifruit: the common fuzzy-covered green fruit, and the gold fruit with its smooth complexion. To learn more about the kiwifruit, visit Kiwi360 in Te Puke.

For visitors after a dollar or two, there's always kiwifruit-picking work around the area, most of it during harvest (May and June): don't expect to make much more than $14 an hour. Enquire at regional i-SITEs, or check online at www.picknz.co.nz.

tour, kiwifruit viewing tower (not much of a view) and a cafe serving kiwifruit delights.

After something sweeter? About 10km south of Te Puke in Paengaroa, **Comvita** (☑ 0800 493 782, 07-533 1987; www.experience-comvita.com; 23 Wilson Rd S, Paengaroa; admission free, guided tours adult/child/family $22.50/11/64; ☺ 8.30am-5pm Mon-Fri, 9.30am-5pm Sat & Sun) **FREE** is home to NZ's most famous honey- and bee-derived health-care products. A big new visitor centre was being built when we visited: expect a cafe, shop and guided tours. Grab a pot of vitamin E cream with bee pollen and manuka honey on your way out.

Not far from Comvita, **Kaituna Jet** (☑ 0800 867 386; www.jetboating.co.nz; 316 SH33, Paengaroa; adult/child/family $104/49/277; ☺ 9am-4pm) puts a few ripples on the surface of an otherwise tranquil stretch of the Kaituna River. Also nearby is **Briars Horse Trek** (☑ 07-533 2582; www.briarshorsetrek.co.nz; 540 SH33, Paengaroa; 1hr/2hr/4hr treks from $65/110/195), offering horse rides taking in the local forests and rivers.

Homestays and farmstays dapple the Te Puke area: ask the visitor centre for a list. For fruit-pickers and doyens of dorm-life there's basic hostel accommodation at **Hairy Berry** (☑ 07-573 8015; www.hairyberrynz.com; 2 No 1 Rd; dm/tw/d from $25/60/60; @ �🖥), a sociable, barn-like affair on the Whakatane side of town with a roomy communal space and small, tidy bedrooms.

Whakatane

POP 18,950

A true pohutukawa paradise, Whakatane (pronounced 'fokka-*tar*-nay') sits on a natural harbour at the mouth of the river of the same name. It's the hub of the Rangitaiki agricultural district, but there's much more to Whakatane than farming – blissful beaches, a sunny main-street vibe and volcanic Whakaari (White Island) for starters. And (despite Nelson's protestations) it's officially NZ's sunniest city.

⊙ Sights

Te Manuka Tutahi Marae   MARAE
(☑ 07-308 4271; www.mataatua.com; 105 Muriwai Dr; ☺ 9am-4pm Dec-Feb, reduced hours Mar-Nov) **FREE** The centrepiece of this recently opened Ngati Awa *marae* isn't new: **Mataatua Wharenui** (The House That Came Home) is a fantastically carved 1875

WORTH A TRIP

PADDLES & PIES: MAKETU

Take SH2 through Te Puke then turn left onto Maketu Rd, and you'll find yourself deposited at this seaside town which, although historic, has seen better days.

Maketu (population 1240) played a significant role in NZ's history as the landing site of *Te Arawa* canoe in 1340, commemorated with a somewhat underwhelming 1940 monument on the foreshore. Arguably, though, the town is more famous for **Maketu Pies** (☑ 07-533 2358; www.maketupies.co.nz; 6 Little Waihi Rd; ☺ 9am-3.30pm Mon-Fri), baked fresh daily here and employing a good proportion of the population. You can buy a pie, hot from the oven, at the factory shopfront, or from the shop next door if you're here on a weekend (go for the legendary lamb and mint).

meeting house. In 1879 it was dismantled and shipped to Sydney, before spending 71 years in the Otago Museum from 1925. It was returned to the Ngati Awa in 1996. You can check out Mataatua Wharenui from the outside for free (behave respectfully), or book an excellent 90-minute cultural tour (adult/child $49/15).

★ **Whakatane District Museum**   MUSEUM, GALLERY
(☑ 07-306 0509; www.whakatanemuseum.org.nz; Esplanade Mall, Kakahoroa Dr; admission by donation; ☺ 9am-5pm Mon-Fri, 10am-2pm Sat & Sun) This impressive new museum-gallery in the library building has artfully presented displays on early Maori and European settlement in the area: Maori *taonga* (treasures) trace a lineage back to the *Mataatua* canoe. Other displays focus on Whakaari (White Island) and Motuhora (Whale Island). The gallery section presents a varied program of NZ and international exhibitions.

Wairere Falls   WATERFALL
(Toroa St) Tumbling down the cliffs behind the town, picture-perfect Te Wairere (Wairere Falls) occupies a deliciously damp nook, and once powered flax and flour mills and supplied Whakatane's drinking water. It's a gorgeous spot, and goes almost completely unheralded: in any other country there'd be a ticket booth, interpretive audiovisual displays and a hotdog van!

Whakatane

Whakatane

◎ Top Sights
1 Whakatane District Museum................ B2

◎ Sights
2 Muriwai's Cave.................................... D1
3 Papaka Pa... B2
4 Pohaturoa.. B2
5 Puketapu Pa.. C2
6 Te Manuka Tutahi Marae.....................C1
7 Wairere Falls....................................... C2

◎ Activities, Courses & Tours
8 Dive White Island................................ B2
9 Diveworks Dolphin & Seal
   Encounters...................................... B2
10 Whakatane Observatory.....................C3
   White Island Tours........................(see 14)

◎ Sleeping
11 Motuhora Rise B&B............................ B3
12 Tuscany Villas C2

13 Whakatane Hotel................................ B2
14 White Island Rendezvous.....................C1
15 Windsor Backpackers...........................A3

◎ Eating
16 Cafe Coco.. B2
17 Countdown... B3
18 L'Epicerie... B1
19 Niko Niko.. B2
20 Roquette...C1
21 Wally's on the Wharf C1

◎ Drinking & Nightlife
Craic...(see 13)
Detour..(see 22)
22 Office.. B1

◎ Entertainment
23 Boiler Room B2
24 WhakaMax Movies B2

Pohaturoa   LANDMARK, MONUMENT
(cnr The Strand & Commerce St) Beside a round-about on the Strand is Pohaturoa, a large *tapu* (sacred) rock outcrop, where baptism, death, war and *moko* (tattoo) rites were performed. The Treaty of Waitangi was signed here by Ngati Awa chiefs in 1840; there's

a monument to the Ngati Awa chief Te Hurinui Apanui here too.

Muriwai's Cave   CAVE
(Muriwai Dr) The partially collapsed Te Ana o Muriwa (Muriwai's Cave) once extended 122m into the hillside and sheltered 60 people, including Muriwai, a famous seer

and aunt of Wairaka. Along with Wairere Falls and a rock in the harbour mouth, the cave was one of three landmarks Toroa was told to look for by his father Irakewa, when he arrived in the *Mataatua* canoe.

Te Papaka & Puketapu ARCHAEOLOGICAL SITES, LOOKOUTS

On the clifftops behind the town are two ancient Ngati Awa *pa* sites – Te Papaka and Puketapu – both of which offer sensational (and very defendable) outlooks over Whakatane.

🏃 Activities

Feel like a stroll? The **Kohi Point Walkway** is highly recommended: a bushy four-hour, 5.5km track with panoramic clifftop views and a genuine 'gasp' moment when you set eyes on Otarawairere Bay. A short detour rewards you with amazing views from Toi's Pa (Kapua te rangi), reputedly the oldest *pa* site in NZ. You can also get to Toi's Pa by a partly unsealed access road off the Whakatane–Ohope road. From Ohope, you can catch the bus back to Whakatane if there aren't any more kilometres in your legs. Ask the i-SITE for a walk map.

A flatter option is the **River Walk** (two to three hours), following the Whakatane River past the Botanical Gardens, Muriwai's Cave and on to Wairaka's statue.

See p293 for info on boat and helicopter tours out to the explosive Whakaari (White Island) and p294 for trips to Motuhora (Whale Island).

Diveworks Dolphin & Seal Encounters DIVING, WILDLIFE TOUR

(☑ 0800 354 7737, 07-308 2001; www.whale-islandtours.com; 96 The Strand; dolphin & seal swimming adult/child $160/130, diving incl gear from $215) This dive/ecotour company runs dolphin- and seal-swimming trips from Whakatane (cheaper if you're just watching from the boat), plus guided tours of Motuhora (Whale Island; adult child $120/85) and diving at Whakaari (White Island; two dives including gear $275). Fishing trips also available.

Whakatane Observatory ASTRONOMY

(☑ 07-308 6495; www.whakatane.info/business/whakatane-astronomical-society; 22 Hurinui Ave; adult/child/family $15/5/35; ☺ 7.30pm Tue & Fri) Up on a hilltop behind the town, Whakatane Observatory offers some plentiful Bay of Plenty star-spotting when the sky is clear.

Whakatane District Aquatic Centre SWIMMING

(www.tlc.net.nz; 28 Short St; adult/child/family $4/2.20/11.50; ☺ 6am-8pm Mon-Fri, 7am-6pm Sat & Sun) Indoor and outdoor pools, spa pools and a tubular yellow worm of a waterslide ($4.50).

Tui Glen Farm HORSE RIDING

(☑ 027 232 5367, 07-323 6457; www.tuiglenfarm.com; Kawerau Loop Rd, Kawerau; 30min rides adult/child $35/25, 1hr ride $60/45) Close to Kawerau about 35km from Whakatane off SH30 to Rotorua, Tui Glen Farm offers horse treks through bush and farm for beginners and the adventurous. Basic dorm accommodation costs $35 per person; camping $10.

🛏 Sleeping

Whakatane Hotel HOTEL $

(☑ 07-307 1670; www.whakatanehotel.co.nz; 79 The Strand; dm/s $25/40, d with/without bathroom from $75/55; ☏) This lovely old art-deco classic has 27 basic (but very decent) rooms upstairs in two wings. Clean shared bathrooms, high celings, communal kitchen... great value for money. Some rooms cop a bit of noise from the pub downstairs, but the owners try to shuffle people around to dodge the din.

Windsor Backpackers HOSTEL $

(☑ 07-308 8040; www.windsorlodge-backpackers.co.nz; 10 Merritt St; dm/s/d from $27/48/66; @☏) Whakatane's best backpackers occupies a converted funeral parlour...so expect a restful sleep! Excellent rooms range from

---

WAKA LIKE A MAN

Whakatane's name originated some eight centuries ago, 200 years after the original Maori settlers arrived here. The warrior Toroa and his family sailed into the estuary in a huge ocean-going *waka* (canoe), the *Mataatua*. As the men went ashore to greet local leaders, the tide turned, and the *waka* – with all the women on board – drifted out to sea. Toroa's daughter, Wairaka, cried out *'E! Kia whakatane au i ahau!'* (Let me act as a man!) and, breaking the traditional *tapu* (taboo) on women steering a *waka*, she took up the paddle and brought the boat safely ashore. A whimsical **statue of Wairaka** stands proudly atop a rock in Whakatane's harbour in commemoration of her brave deed.

serviceable dorms to a couple of motel-standard doubles out the front. The communal kitchen, lounge and barbecue courtyard are spacious and tidy.

Awakeri Hot Springs
HOLIDAY PARK $

(☑07-304 9117; www.awakerisprings.co.nz; SH30; campsites $36, d cabins/flats/units $70/85/95; ☏) About 16km from Whakatane on the road to Rotorua (SH30) you'll come to the immaculate Awakeri Hot Springs, an old-fashioned holiday park complete with (as the name suggests) hot springs (adult/child $7.50/5), picnic areas and a bed for every budget.

Captain's Cabin
APARTMENT $$

(☑07-308 5719; www.captainscabin.co.nz; 23 Muriwai Dr; d from $125, extra person $25) On the serene side of town with sparkling water views, this homely self-contained unit is perfect if you're hanging round for a few days (cheaper for two nights or more). A cosy living area cleverly combines bedroom, lounge, kitchen and dining, with a second smaller room and bijou bathroom – all sweetly decorated along nautical lines. Sleeps three.

White Island Rendezvous
HOTEL, B&B $$

(☑0800 733 529, 07-308 9500; www.whiteisland. co.nz; 15 The Strand E; d $100-160, apt from $200, B&B $190; ☏) An immaculate 28-room complex run by the on-the-ball White Island Tour people (cheaper rates for tour-goers). Lots of balcony and deck space for inhaling the sea air, while interiors are decked out with timber floors for a nautical vibe. Deluxe rooms come with spas; disabled-access facilities available. The B&B next door includes cooked breakfast.

Tuscany Villas
MOTEL $$

(☑07-308 2244; www.tuscanyvillas.co.nz; 57 The Strand E; d $155-200; ☏) This mod motel may be a long way from Florence, but still offers a few rays of Italian sunshine with interesting architecture, wrought-iron balconies and floral plantings wherever there's room. Rooms are luxurious and comfy, with super-king beds and spa pools.

Livingston Motel
MOTEL $$

(☑0800 770 777, 07-308 6400; www.livingston. co.nz; 42 Landing Rd; d/f $130/220; ☏) It's a bit of a hike into town, but this spotless, ranch-style motel is the pick of the half-dozen dotted along the Landing. Expect spacious, well-kept units, comfy beds and large spas in executive suites.

Motuhora Rise B&B
B&B $$$

(☑07-307 0224; www.motuhorarise.com; 2 Motuhora Rise; s/d/tr incl breakfast $205/230/350; ☏) At the top of the town in both senses (steep driveway!), this jaunty hilltop spot feels vaguely Rocky Mountains, and affords a distant glimpse of Motuhora (Whale Island). Expect a gourmet cheeseboard on arrival, along with other extras such as a home theatre, outdoor spa, and fishing rods and golf clubs. Kid-free zone.

✗ Eating

Wally's on the Wharf
FISH & CHIPS $

(☑07-307 1100; www.whakatane.info/business/ wallys-wharf; 2 The Strand; meals $6-19; ☺11am-7pm) Wally knows a thing or two about fish and chips: hoki, snapper, flounder, john dory and tarakihi – done in the deep fry, on the grill or in terrific fish burgers. Whitebait fritters in season, and chips that score well on the crispometer. The reconstituted squid rings are a tad disappointing (but the seagulls don't seem to mind).

L'Epicerie
CAFE, FRENCH $

(☑07-308 5981; www.lepicerie.co.nz; 73 The Strand; mains $10-16; ☺7.30am-3.30pm Mon-Fri, 8am-4pm Sat, 8.30am-2.30pm Sun) *Ooh-la-la!* This classic French cafe in downtown Whakatane is a real surprise, serving terrific omelettes, croissants, crêpes and *croque-monsieurs* at communal tables. Fabulous coffee and deli shelves crammed with preserves, breads, mustards and deliciously stinky French cheeses complete a very Franco scene.

Niko Niko
JAPANESE $

(https://foursquare.com/v/niko-niko-sushi/; 43 Kakahoroa Dr; sushi $2-3; ☺9am-7pm) Quick-fire sushi joint tucked between the Strand and the waterfront. Order a couple of gorgeously presented chilli chicken rolls and hit the sunny outdoor tables.

Cafe Coco
CAFE $

(☑07-308 8337; www.whakatane.info/business/cafe-coco; 10 Richardson St; mains $8-19; ☺7.30am-4.30pm Mon-Fri, 8.30am-2pm Sat) Coco is a hip, L-shaped corner spot serving bright, fresh cafe fare: bagels, panini, corn fritters, fresh juices, French toast, cakes, organic fair-trade coffee, eggs any which way…and the 'Crepe of the Week'. Very kid-friendly, too.

Countdown
SUPERMARKET $

(www.countdown.co.nz; 105 Commerce St; ☺7am-10pm) Stock up on supplies.

Roquette
MODERN NZ, MEDITERRANEAN $$$

(07-307 0722; www.roquette-restaurant.co.nz; 23 Quay St; mains lunch $20-34, dinner $30-36; 10am-late Mon-Sat) A modern waterside restaurant on the ground floor of one of the town's big new apartment building, ritzy Roquette serves up refreshing Mediterranean-influenced fare with lots of summery salads, risotto and fish dishes. Laid-back tunes, lots of glass and mosaics, good coffee and sexy staff to boot. Try the char-grilled lamb salad.

🍷 Drinking & Entertainment

Craic
IRISH PUB

(www.whakatanehotel.co.nz; Whakatane Hotel, 79 The Strand; 11am-2am) The Craic is a busy locals' boozer of the Irish ilk, good for a pint or two, or a mug of hot chocolate if you're feeling sub-par. Fantastic streetside terrace for sunny afternoons, and solid pub grub (mains $13 to $22).

Office
BAR

(www.whakatane.info/business/office-bar-grill; 82 The Strand; 11am-late) The sporty Office does what it does well: beer, big meals with chips and salad all over (mains $18 to $32), and live bands and/or DJs Thursday to Saturday nights. Next door is Detour (www.whakatane. info/business/detour-bar-lounge; 84 The Strand; noon-late), a classier lounge bar run by the same folks, serving tapas and cocktails to an over-25s crowd.

Boiler Room
CLUB, LIVE MUSIC

(www.whakatanehotel.co.nz; Whakatane Hotel, 79 The Strand; 10pm-2.30am Fri & Sat) Whakatane's only club is next door to the Craic at the Whakatane Hotel – a cavernous, hedonistic space dotted with pool tables. DJs and live bands engage your ears and feet, often for free.

WhakaMax Movies
CINEMA

(07-308 7623; www.whakamax.co.nz; 99 The Strand; tickets adult/child $14/9; 10am-late) Right in the middle of the Strand, WhakaMax screens new-release movies. Cheaper tickets before 4.30pm and on Tuesdays.

ℹ Information

Post Office (197 The Strand; 8.30am-5pm Mon-Fri, 9am-noon Sat) Also has foreign exchange.

Whakatane Hospital (07-306 0999; www.bopdhb.govt.nz; cnr Stewart & Garaway Sts; 24hr) Emergency medical treatment.

Whakatane i-SITE (0800 924 528, 07-306 2030; www.whakatane.com; cnr Quay St & Kakahoroa Dr; 8am-5pm Mon-Fri, 10am-4pm Sat & Sun;) Free internet access (including 24-hour wi-fi on the terrace outside the building), tour bookings, accommodation and general DOC enquiries.

ℹ Getting There & Around

AIR

Air New Zealand (0800 737 000, 07-308 8397; www.airnewzealand.com) has daily flights linking Whakatane to Auckland.

BICYCLE

Explore the area on two wheels with a hybrid road/trail bike from **Barringtons Bike Hire** (0800 830 130, 07-308 4273; www.barringtonsmotorlodge.co.nz; 34 Landing Rd; bike hire per half-/full day $30/40, tandems $40/50).

BUS

InterCity buses stop outside the i-SITE and connect Whakatane with Rotorua ($20, 1½ hours, one daily), Tauranga ($30, eight hours, one daily via Rotorua) and Gisborne ($46, three hours, one daily via Opotiki), with onward connections.

Naked Bus destinations include the following:

DESTINATION	PRICE ($)	DURATION (HR)	FREQUENCY (DAILY)
Auckland	35	6	1
Gisborne	20	3¼	1
Hamilton	25	2½	1
Rotorua	19	1½	1
Tauranga	18	4	1
Wellington	65	10	1

Local Bay Hopper buses run to Ohope ($3, 45 minutes, six daily), Opotiki ($8.60, one hour, two daily Monday and Wednesday) and Tauranga ($13.70, two hours, one daily Monday to Saturday).

Shuttle Bus

White Island Shuttle (07-308 9588, 0800 733 529; www.whiteisland.co.nz; one way/return $60/35), run buy White Island Tours in Whakatane, drives the Rotorua–Whakatane route and can be used by nontour travellers.

Whakaari (White Island)

NZ's most active volcano (it last erupted in 2013) lies 49km off the Whakatane coast. The small island was originally formed by three separate volcanic cones of different

MOTUHORA (WHALE ISLAND)

Nine kilometres off Whakatane is Motuhora (Whale Island) – so-called because of its leviathan shape. This island is yet another volcano along the Taupo Volcanic Zone but is much less active, although there are hot springs along its shore. The summit is 353m high and the island has several historic sites, including an ancient *pa* (fortified village) site, a quarry and a camp.

Whale Island was originally home to a Maori settlement. In 1829 Maori massacred sailors from the trading vessel *Haweis* while it was anchored at Sulphur Bay. In 1867 the island passed into European ownership and remains privately owned, although since 1965 it has been a DOC-protected wildlife refuge for seabirds and shorebirds.

The island's protected status means landing is restricted, with tours running only from January to March. Operators include White Island Tours (p294), Diveworks Dolphin & Seal Encounters (p291) and KG Kayaks (p294).

ages. The two oldest have been eroded, while the younger cone has risen up between them. Mt Gisborne is the highest point on the island at 321m. Geologically, Whakaari is related to Motuhora (Whale Island) and Putauaki (Mt Edgecumbe), as all lie along Taupo Volcanic Zone.

The island is dramatic, with hot water hissing and steaming from vents over most of the crater floor. Temperatures of 600°C to 800°C have been recorded.

The island is privately owned so you can only visit it with a licensed tour operator. Fixed-wing air operators run flyover tours only, while boat and helicopter tours will usually include a walking tour around the island including a visit to the ruins of the sulphur-mining factory – an interesting story in itself. Most tours depart Whakatane; scenic flights are also possible ex-Tauranga and Rotorua.

🎫 Tours

White Island Tours   BOAT TOUR
(📞 0800 733 529, 07-308 9588; www.whiteis-land.co.nz; 15 The Strand, Whakatane; 6hr tours adult/child $199/130; ⏰ departures btwn 7am & 12.30pm) The only official boat trip to Whakaari (on board the good ship *Pee Jay*), with dolphin-spotting en route and a two-hour tour of the island. Moutohora (Whale Island) tours adult/child $90/60.

White Island Flights   SCENIC FLIGHTS
(📞 0800 944 834; www.whiteislandflights.co.nz; Whakatane Airport; flights per person $249) Fixed-wing scenic flights over Whakaari, with lots of photo opportunities. A Whakaari/Mt Tarawera combo flight costs $339.

Dive White Island   DIVING
(📞 0800 348 394, 07-307 0714; www.divewhite. co.nz; 186 The Strand, Whakatane; snorkelling per person $225, 2hr dive with gear $395) Full-day snorkelling and diving trips with lunch and gear provided; underwater volcanic terrain and lots of fish to look at.

Frontier Helicopters   SCENIC FLIGHTS
(📞 0800 804 354, 07-308 4188; www.vulcanheli. co.nz; Whakatane Airport; flights per person from $650) A two-hour trip to Whakaari (departing from Whakatane) that includes a one-hour guided walk on the volcano.

Ohope

POP 2760

Just 7km over the hill from Whakatane, Ohope has great beaches, perfect for lazing or surfing, and is backed by sleepy **Ohiwa Harbour**.

🤸 Activities

KG Kayaks   KAYAKING
(📞 07-315 4005, 027 272 4073; www.kgkayaks. co.nz; tours $85-150, 2hr hire s/d $50/70) Explore Ohiwa Harbour with KG Kayaks, which offers freedom hire and 2½-hour guided tours ($85), plus four-hour kayak trips around Motuhora (Whale Island), which involves a boat trip initially ($150).

By Salt Spray Surf School   SURFING
(📞 0211 491 972, 07-312 4909; www.facebook.com/ bysaltspraysurfschool; 2hr lesson from $90) If you want to splash around in the Ohope Beach surf, get some lessons from Beaver at By Salt Spray Surf School, which provides all gear and offers discounts for groups.

🛏 Sleeping

Aquarius Motel   MOTEL $
(☑ 07-312 4550; www.aquariusmotorlodge.co.nz;
103 Harbour Rd; d $85-150; 🛜) For a quiet, afford-
able motel-style option, roll into Aquarius, a
basic complex with various room configurations, all with kitchens and just 100m from
the beach (you don't need a swimming pool).

**Ohope Beach
Top 10 Holiday Park**   HOLIDAY PARK $$
(☑ 07-312 4460, 0800 264 673; www.ohopebeach.
co.nz; 367 Harbour Rd; unpowered/powered sites
per person from $24/26, cabins/units/apts from
$150/230/300; @ 🛜 ⚝) The Ohope Beach Top
10 Holiday Park is the very model of a mod-
ern holiday park, with a raft of family-friendly
facilities: sports courts, minigolf, pool, plus
some apartments peeking over the dunes at
the Bay of Plenty. Busy as a woodpecker in
summer (with prices to match).

🍴 Eating

Ohiwa Oyster Farm   SEAFOOD, FAST FOOD $
(☑ 07-312 4566; www.whakatane.info/business/
ohiwa-oyster-farm; 111 Wainui Rd; meals $5-14;
⊙ 9am-8pm Nov-Feb, to 7pm Mar-Oct) Poised
over a swampy back-reach of Ohiwa Har-
bour (serious oyster territory), this classic
roadside fish shack is perfect for a fish-and-
chip (and oyster) picnic.

Hui Bar & Grill   MODERN NZ $$
(☑ 07-312 5623; www.huibarandgrill.com; 19 Po-
hutukawa Ave; mains lunch $10-25, dinner $29-35;
⊙ 10am-late, closed Mon & Tue Jun-Aug) With
polished concrete floors, white leather
banquettes and fold-back windows, Hui
is a ritzy new bar-grill making a splash in
little Ohope's shopping strip. Try some pan-
seared scallops with chorizo and watercress,
or chipotle mussels with garlic and herbs.
NZ wines; live music Friday nights and Sunday afternoons. Classy stuff.

Opotiki
POP 8440

The Opotiki area was settled from at least
1150, some 200 years before the larger 14th-
century Maori migration. Maori traditions
are well preserved here, with the work of
master carvers lining the main street and
the occasional facial *moko* passing by. The
town acts as a gateway to the East Coast,
and has excellent beaches – Ohiwa and Wai-
otahi – and an engaging museum.

⊙ Sights & Activities

Pick up the *Historic Opotiki* brochure from
the i-SITE (or download from www.opo
tikinz.com) for the low-down on the town's
heritage buildings.

Opotiki Museum   MUSEUM
(www.opotikimuseum.org.nz; 123 Church St; adult/
child/family $10/5/25; ⊙ 10am-4pm Mon-Fri,
10am-2pm Sat) Run by volunteers, Opotiki's
excellent museum has interesting heritage
displays including Maori *taonga*, militaria,
re-created shopfronts (a barber, carpenter,
printer…) and agricultural items including
tractors and a horse-drawn wagon. Admission to the Shalfoon & Francis Museum is
included in the ticket price.

Shalfoon & Francis Museum   MUSEUM
(www.opotikinz.com/archive/129271.html; 129
Church St; adult/child/family $10/5/25; ⊙ 10am-
4pm Mon-Fri, 10am-2pm Sat) Opotiki's original
general store has been born again, with
shelves piled high with old grocery and
hardware products. Handbags, sticky-tape
dispensers, sets of scales, books – you name
it, they had it. An amazing collection. Admission is included in your ticket to the
main Opotiki Museum.

Hiona St Stephen's Church   CHURCH
(www.opotikinz.com/archive/129305.html; 128
Church St; ⊙ services 8am & 9.30am Sun, 10am
Thu) White-weatherboard St Stephen's (1862)
is an Anglican church with a perfectly proportioned timber-lined interior. Reverend
Carl Volkner, known by the local Whakatohea tribe to have acted as a government
spy, was murdered here in 1865. In 1992 the
Governor-General granted Mokomoko, the
man who hanged for the crime, a full par-
don, which hangs in the lobby.

Hukutaia Domain   FOREST, ARCHAEOLOGICAL SITE
(☑ 07-315 3030; www.opotikinz.com/ar-
chive/129054.html; Woodlands Rd; ⊙ daylight
hours) **FREE** Around 8km south of town is
Hukutaia Domain, home to one of the finest collections of native plants in NZ. In the
centre is Taketakerau, a 23m puriri tree estimated to be more than 2000 years old and
a burial place for the distinguished dead of
the Upokorehe *hapu* (subtribe) of Whakatohea. The remains have since been reinterred
elsewhere.

Motu Trails   MOUNTAIN BIKING
(☑ 04-472 0030; www.motutrails.co.nz) One of
the New Zealand Cycle Trail's 'Great Rides'

(see p36), Motu Trails comprises three trails around Opotiki – the easy 19km Dunes Trail, intermediate 78km Motu Road Trail and advanced 44km Pakihi Track – parts of which combine to form the 91km Loop Trail. See the website for details. For bike hire and shuttle services see www.motucycletrails.com or www.hireandshuttle.co.nz.

Motu River Jet Boat Tours   JETBOATING
(☑07-325 2735; www.motujet.co.nz; trips from adult/child $90/50) Runs as many as three 1½-hour trips on the Motu River (which runs through the Raukumara Ranges near Opotiki) every day through summer. Winter trips by arrangement.

Wet 'n' Wild   RAFTING
(☑07-348 3191, 0800 462 7238; www.wetnwildrafting.co.nz; trips from $995) Offers 100km multi-day rafting and camping adventures on the Motu River (Grade III–IV rapids) near Opotiki.

✨ Festivals & Events

Opotiki Rodeo   RODEO
(www.opotikirodeo.co.nz) Dust off your spurs and cowboy hat for the annual Opotiki Rodeo in December. Giddyup.

🛏 Sleeping

⭐ Opotiki Beach House   HOSTEL $
(☑07-315 5117; www.opotikibeachhouse.co.nz; 7 Appleton Rd; dm/s/d from $30/48/66; 🛜) A cruisy, shoe-free beachside pad with a sunny, hammock-hung deck, sea views and a *very* wide sandy backyard. Beyond the dorms and breezy lounge are decent doubles and a quirky caravan (sleeps two) for those who want a real taste of the Kiwi summer holiday. About 5km west of town; sleeps 14.

Central Oasis Backpackers   HOSTEL $
(☑07-315 5165; www.centraloasisbackpackers.co.nz; 30 King St; dm/d from $22/54; 🛜) Inside a late-1800s kauri (timber) house, this central backpackers is run by a super-laid-back German dude a long way from home. It's a snug spot with spacious rooms, a crackling fire and a big front yard to hang out in. Max the dog patrols the front yard.

Capeview Cottage   COTTAGE $$
(☑0800 227 384, 07-315 7877; www.capeview.co.nz; 167 Tablelands Rd; d $150, extra person $30; 🛜) Surrounded by chirruping birds and kiwifruit orchards, this serene, self-contained cottage has two bedrooms, a barbecue and a brilliant outdoor spa from which you can soak up some rather astonishing coastal views. Weekly rates available.

Eastland Pacific Motor Lodge   MOTEL $$
(☑07-315 5524, 0800 103 003; www.eastlandpacific.co.nz; cnr Bridge & St John Sts; d from $110, 1-/2-bedroom from $130/150; 🛜) Bright, clean Eastland is a well-kept motel with new carpets and TVs, spa baths as standard, and a wing of five new units out the back. The two-bedroom units are top value (extra person $30).

✕ Eating

⭐ Two Fish   CAFE $
(102 Church St; snacks $5-10, mains $7-21; ⊙8am-4pm Mon-Fri, 8.30am-2pm Sat) Decent eating options are thin on the ground in Opotiki, so what a surprise to discover the best cafe this side of Tauranga! Serving up hefty homemade burgers, chowder, toasties, steak sandwiches, fab muffins and salads, plus a jumbo selection in the cabinet, Two Fish has happy staff, Cuban tunes and a retro-groovy interior and courtyard. And super coffee! Nice one.

New World   SUPERMARKET $
(www.newworld.co.nz; 19 Bridge St; ⊙7am-9pm) Self-catering supplies.

☆ Entertainment

De Luxe Cinema   CINEMA
(☑07-314 5344; www.odc.govt.nz/visiting/the-movies; 127 Church St; tickets adult/child $14/7; ⊙10am-late, reduced hours Jun-Aug) The beguiling old De Luxe shows recent movies and hosts the odd brass-band concert. Check the window for upcoming events, including the annual **Silent Film Festival** (www.silentfilmfest.org.nz) in September.

ℹ Information

DOC (☑07-315 1001; www.doc.govt.nz; 70 Bridge St; ⊙8am-noon Mon-Fri) In the same building as the i-SITE.

Opotiki i-SITE (☑07-315 3031; www.opotikinz.com; 70 Bridge St; ⊙9am-4.30pm Mon-Fri, 9am-1pm Sat & Sun; 🛜) The fancy new Opotiki i-SITE takes bookings for activities and transport and stocks the indispensable free East Coast booklet *Pacific Coast Highway*.

ℹ Getting There & Away

BUS

Travelling east from Opotiki there are two routes: SH2, crossing the spectacular Waioeka

Gorge, or SH35 around East Cape. The SH2 route offers some day walks in the Waioeka Gorge Scenic Reserve, with the gorge getting steeper and narrower as you travel inland, before the route crosses typically green, rolling hills, dotted with sheep, on the descent to Gisborne.

Buses pick up/drop off at the Hot Bread Shop on the corner of Bridge and St John Sts, though tickets and bookings are made through the i-SITE or **Travel Shop** (☏ 07-315 8881; www. travelshop.co.nz; 104 Church St; ☺9am-4pm Mon-Fri). The Travel Shop also rents out bikes (per half-/full day $30/50).

InterCity has daily buses connecting Opotiki with Whakatane ($22, 45 minutes), Rotorua ($36, 2½ hours) and Auckland ($72, 7½ hours).

Heading south, daily buses connect Opotiki with Gisborne ($36, two hours).

Naked Bus runs daily services to destinations including the following:

DESTINATION	PRICE ($)	DURATION (HR)
Auckland	31	6
Gisborne	19	2½
Rotorua	23	2½
Tauranga	20	5
Wellington	45	11

The local Bay Hopper bus runs to Whakatane ($8.60, 1¼ hour, two daily Monday and Wednesday).

The East Coast

Includes ➡

East Cape 299

Pacific Coast
Highway 299

Gisborne 305

Te Urewera
National Park 312

Hawke's Bay 314

Napier 315

Hastings, Havelock
North & Around 323

Cape Kidnappers 327

Kaweka &
Ruahine Ranges 329

Best Outdoors

➡ Cape Kidnappers (p327)

➡ Cooks Cove Walkway
(p304)

➡ Hawke's Bay Trails (p315)

➡ Surfing in Gisborne (p308)

➡ Lake Waikaremoana Track
(p313)

Best Places to Stay

➡ Stranded in Paradise
(p304)

➡ Clive Colonial Cottages
(p325)

➡ Millar Road (p325)

➡ Seaview Lodge B&B (p320)

Why Go?

New Zealand is known for its mix of wildly divergent land-scapes, but on the East Coast it's the sociological contours that are most pronounced. From the earthy settlements of the East Cape to Havelock North's monied, wine-soaked streets, there's a full spectrum of NZ (New Zealand) life.

Maori culture is never more visible than on the East Coast. Exquisitely carved *marae* (meeting-house complexes) dot the landscape, and *te reo* and *tikanga* (the language and customs) are alive and well.

Intrepid types will have no trouble losing the tourist hordes – along the Pacific Coast Hwy (State Hwy 35; SH35), through rural back roads, on remote beaches, or in the mystical wilderness of Te Urewera National Park. And when the call of the wild gives way to caffeine withdrawal, you can get a quick fix in Gisborne and Napier. You'll also find plenty of wine here: the Hawke's Bay region is striped with vine-rows.

When to Go

➡ The East Coast basks in a warm, mainly dry climate. Summer temperatures around Napier and sunny Gisborne nudge 25°C, rarely dipping below 8°C in winter.

➡ The Hawke's Bay region basks in mild, dry, grape-growing conditions year-round, with an average annual rainfall of just 800mm. Harvest time is Autumn (March to May).

➡ In winter, heavy downpours sometimes wash out sections of the Pacific Coast Hwy around the East Cape: check road conditions at either end (Opotiki or Gisborne) before making the trip.

ⓘ Getting There & Around

The region's only airports are in Gisborne and Napier. **Air New Zealand** (www.airnewzealand. co.nz) flies to both towns from Auckland and Wellington, and also to Napier from Christchurch. **Sunair Aviation** (www.sunair.co.nz) flies direct from Gisborne to Rotorua, Tauranga and Napier; and from Napier to Gisborne and Hamilton, with onward connections.

Regular **Intercity** (www.intercity.co.nz) and **Naked Bus** (www.nakedbus.com) services ply State Hwy 2 (SH2) and State Hwy 5 (SH5), connecting Gisborne, Opotiki, Wairoa, Napier and Hastings with all the main centres.

Transport is limited around East Cape and Te Urewera National Park. **Bay Hopper** (www.baybus.co.nz) runs between Opotiki and Potaka/ Cape Runaway on Tuesdays and Thursdays ($15, two hours). **Cooks Passenger & Courier Services** (☑ 06-864 4711, 021 371 364) runs between Te Araroa and Gisborne ($50, 3½ hours) Monday to Saturday. Otherwise, bring your own wheels.

EAST CAPE

The slow-paced East Cape is a unique and special corner of NZ. It's a quiet place, where everyone seems to know everyone, their community ties built on rural enterprise and a shared passion for the ocean. Horseback riding, tractors on the beach, fresh fish for dinner – it's all part of daily life here.

Inland, the wild Raukumara Range forms the Cape's jagged spine. Near the edge of the sea, the 323km Pacific Coast Hwy (SH35) runs from Opotiki to Gisborne. Lonely shores lie strewn with driftwood, while picture-postcard sandy bays lure just a handful of visitors.

Pacific Coast Highway

The long and winding road around the North Island's easternmost point has long been a rite of road-trip passage for New Zealanders. And if you like scenic drives and don't mind attractions that are few and far between, you'll likely find the journey intrepid and captivating.

If you're short on time, head for Gisborne via SH2 from Opotiki – a 144km alternative via the **Waioeka Gorge** and the two- to three-hour walk leading off from the historic **Tauranga Bridge**. The route takes about 2½ hours to drive, although you could easily make a day of it.

Both routes are covered in the excellent *Pacific Coast Highway Guide,* available at Gisborne and Opotiki i-SITEs. Set off with a full petrol tank, and stock up on snacks and groceries – shops and petrol stations are in short supply. Sleeping and eating options are pretty spread out: we've listed them in the order you'll find them, heading east from Opotiki.

Opotiki to Te Kaha

The first leg offers hazy views across to Whakaari (White Island), a chain-smoking active volcano. The desolate beaches at **Torere**, **Hawai** and **Omaio** are steeply shelved and littered with flotsam. Check out the magnificent *whakairo* (carving) on the Torere school gateway. Hawai marks the boundary of the Whanau-a-Apanui tribe whose *rohe* (traditional land) extends to Cape Runaway.

About 42km east of Opotiki the road crosses the broad pebbly expanse of the **Motu River**, the first river in NZ to be designated as a protected wilderness area. Departing from the Motu bridge on the highway, Motu River Jet Boat Tours (p296) blats up the river all year round, weather permitting. **Wet 'n' Wild Rafting** (☑ 0800 462 7238; www. wetnwildrafting.co.nz; 2-5 days $995-1095) offers multiday excursions, with the longest taking

THE EAST COAST PACIFIC COAST HIGHWAY

ESSENTIAL EAST COAST

Eat Delicious fresh produce from the Hastings Farmers Market (p323)

Drink Hawke's Bay chardonnay

Read Witi Ihimaera's 1987 novel *Whale Rider,* then watch the powerful 2002 movie adaptation

Listen to Uawa FM (88.5FM, 88.8FM, 99.3FM) in Tolaga Bay

Watch *Boy* (2010), Taika Waititi's record-breaking and hilarious film, shot at Waihau Bay

Go green Millton (p305) vineyard – organic, biodynamic, and delicious to boot

Online www.hawkesbaynz.com; www. gisbornenz.com; www.lonelyplanet. com/new-zealand/the-east-coast

Area code Opotiki east to Hicks Bay ☑ 07; rest of the region ☑ 06

East Coast Highlights

1 Time-warping to the 1930s surrounded by art-deco delights in **Napier** (p316)

2 Sniffing and sipping your way around the wineries of **Hawke's Bay** (p326) or **Gisborne** (p305)

3 Losing yourself in the mighty forests and Maori culture of **Te Urewera National Park** (p312)

4 Counting off the landmarks as you cruise the coast: **Cape Kidnappers**, (p327), **Tolaga Bay**, (p304), **Tokomaru Bay** (p303) and the **East Cape Lighthouse** (p303)

5 Sliding a surfboard into the East Coast waves near **Gisborne** (p308)

6 Searching for wood nymphs among the magical forest paths of **Eastwoodhill Arboretum** (p307)

SOUTH
PACIFIC
OCEAN

Maungawhio Lagoon
Morere
Mahia
Nuhaka
Mahia Beach
Mahia Peninsula
Fraser town
Lake Whakaki
Wairoa
Hawke Bay
Mohaka Viaduct
Mohaka River
Boundary Stream, Bellbird Bush & Opouahi Reserve
Waipatiki Scenic Reserve
Tangoio Falls Scenic Reserve
Lake Tutira
Tutira
Te Pohue
White Pine Bush Scenic Reserve
Bay View
Eskdale
Napier Airport
Napier
Taradale
Clifton
Cape Kidnappers
Havelock North
Ocean Beach
Te Mata Peak (399m)
Waimarama Beach
Kairakau Beach
Mangakuri Beach
Pourerere
Aramoana Beach
Te Angiangi Marine Reserve
Porangahau
Taumatawhakatangihangakoauauotamateaturipukakapikimaungahoronukupokaiwhenuakitanatahu
Cape Turnagain
Hawke's Bay
Flaxmere
Hastings
Omahu
Clive
Waipawa
Waipukurau
Wanstead
Blackhead Beach
Ahimanawa Range
Tutaekuri River
Kaweka Range
Mohaka River
Kaweka (1724m)
Kaweka Forest Park
Kuripapango
Gentle Annie Rd
Otamauri
Ngaruroro River
Kuripapango
Ruahine Forest Park
Tikokino
Ongaonga
Norsewood
Dannevirke

MAORI NZ: THE EAST COAST

The main *iwi* (tribes) in the region are Te Whanau-a-Apanui (www.apanui.co.nz; west side of East Cape), Ngati Porou (www.ngatiporou.com; east side of East Cape), Ngati Kahungunu (www.kahungunu.iwi.nz; the coast from Hawke's Bay down) and Ngati Tuhoe (www.ngaituhoe.iwi.nz; inland in Te Urewera).

Ngati Porou and Ngati Kahungunu are the country's second- and third-biggest *iwi*. In the late 19th century they produced the great leaders James Carroll (the first Maori cabinet minister) and Apirana Ngata (who was briefly acting prime minister). Ngata, whose face adorns NZ's $50 note, worked tirelessly in parliament to orchestrate a cultural revival within Maoridom. The region's magnificent carved meeting houses are part of his legacy.

Maori life is at the forefront around the East Cape, in sleepy villages centred upon the many *marae* (meeting houses) that dot the landscape. Living in close communities, drawing much of their livelihoods off the sea and the land, the *tangata whenua* (local people) of the Cape offer a fascinating insight into what life might have been, had they not been so vigorously divested of their land in the 19th century.

You will meet Maori wherever you go. For accommodation with a distinctly Maori flavour, consider Maraehako Bay Retreat or Hikihiki's Inn (p314). For an intimate introduction to *Maoritanga* (things Maori), take a guided tour with Long Island Guides (p324) or Waimarama Tours (p324).

For a more passive brush with the culture, visit Gisborne's Tairawhiti Museum (p305), Otatara Pa (p318) in Napier, and Tikitiki's St Mary's Church.

you 100km down the river. The two-day tour requires you to be helicoptered in, therefore costing as much as the five-day trip.

Twenty-five kilometres further along, the fishing town of **Te Kaha** once sounded the death knell for passing whales. There's a shop here, a holiday park, and the welcoming B&B **Tui Lodge** (☑07-325 2922; www. tuilodge.co.nz; 200 Copenhagen Rd, Te Kaha; s/d incl breakfast $135/160; @). This five-room guesthouse sits on groomed 3-acre gardens, irresistible to tui and many other birds. Meals are available by arrangement, as are horse-trekking, fishing and diving trips. For a meal, try your luck at the mod waterside **Te Kaha Beach Resort** (☑07-325 2830; www. tekahabeachresort.com; 3 Hotel Rd, Te Kaha; mains $25-35; ☺3-9pm; ☎).

Te Kaha to Whangaparaoa (Cape Runaway)

A succession of sleepy bays extends from Te Kaha. Towards **Whanarua Bay**, the magical **Waikawa B&B** (☑07-325 2070; www.waikawa. net; 7541 SH35, Te Kaha; d/units from $110/130, extra person $35; @) sits in a private rocky cove with views of the sunset and White Island. The artful buildings blend weathered timber, corrugated iron and paua inlay to great effect. There are two double B&B rooms, and a two-bedroom self-contained bach, perfect for two to four people.

Nearby, heaven is a tub of homemade macadamia and honey ice cream at **Pacific Coast Macadamias** (☑07-325 2960; www. macanuts.co.nz; SH35, Whanarua Bay; snacks $3-9; ☺10am-3pm, extended hours Dec-Feb), with views along one of the most spectacular parts of the coast. Toasted sandwiches and nutty sweet treats make this a great lunch stop. Opening hours can be sketchy – call ahead.

Intertwined with ancient pohutukawa trees, the absolute seafront **Maraehako Bay Retreat** (☑07-325 2648; www.maraehako.co.nz; SH35, Maraehako Bay; dm/s/d $28/43/66; @) is a hostel that looks like it was cobbled together from flotsam and jetsam washed up in the craggy cove. It's rustic, but unique: what it lacks in crossed Ts and dotted Is it more than makes up for in *manaakitanga* (hospitality). Enjoy a spa under the stars ($5), free kayaks, as well as fishing charters, *marae* tours and guided walks (and no TV!), all at reasonable prices. Run by the same *hapu* (subtribe) as the retreat, **Maraehako Camping Ground** (☑07-325 2901; SH35, Maraehako Bay; sites per adult/child $12/8) offers clean toilets, showers, pohutukawa trees and beachfront nirvana.

At **Papatea Bay** stop to see the gateway of **Hinemahuru Marae**, intricately carved with images of WWI Maori Battalion soldiers. Nearby **Christ Church Raukokore** (1894) is a sweet beacon of belief on a lonely promontory. There are services at 11am on

Sundays, or the door is usually open at other times (look for the mouse on high).

Waihau Bay has a petrol pump at its western end, alongside the **Waihau Bay Lodge** (☑ 07-325 3805; www.thewaihaubaylodge.co.nz; Orete Point Rd, Waihau Bay; mains $25-35; ☺ 4pm-late Sun-Wed, 2pm-late Thu-Sat), an old two-storey timber pub by the pier, serving hefty meals and with accommodation ranging from campsites ($15) to dorms ($35) and en suite units sleeping eight (double $185, extra person $25). There is also accommodation at **Oceanside Apartments** (☑ 07-325 3699; www.waihaubay.co.nz; 10932 SH35, Waihau Bay; d from $110; @), comprising two nicely kept motel units and a next-door bach (holiday home). Meals by arrangement.

Some 17km beyond Waihau Bay, **Whangaparaoa (Cape Runaway)**, where kumara was first introduced to NZ, can only be reached on foot.

Whangaparaoa (Cape Runaway) to East Cape

The road heads inland from Whangaparaoa, crossing into hilly Ngati Porou territory before hitting the coast at **Hicks Bay**, a real middle-of-nowhere settlement with a grand beach. Brilliant views distract from the barrack ambience at the 50-year-old **Hicks Bay Motel Lodge** (☑ 06-864 4880; www.hicksbaymotel.co.nz; 5198 SH35, Hicks Bay; dm $23, d $75-130, 2-bedroom units $165; ☎ ☀), squatting high above the bay. The old-fashioned rooms are nothing flash, although the restaurant (mains $21 to $35, open for breakfast and dinner), shop, pool and glowworm grotto compensate.

Nearly 10km further is **Te Araroa**, a lonedog village with two shops, a petrol station, takeaway and beautifully carved *marae*. The geology changes here from igneous outcrops to sandstone cliffs: the dense bush backdrop doesn't seem to mind which it grows on. More than 350 years old, 20m high and 40m wide, **Te-Waha-O-Rerekohu**, allegedly NZ's largest pohutukawa tree, stands in Te Araroa schoolyard. The progressive **East Cape Manuka Company** (☑ 06-864 4824; www.eastcapemanuka.co.nz; 4464 Te Araroa Rd, Te Araroa; ☺ 8.30am-4.30pm daily Nov-Apr, Mon-Fri only May-Oct) is here too, selling soaps, oils, creams and honey made from potent East Cape manuka. It's a good stop for coffee, a cooked breakfast or a smoothie (meals and snacks $5 to $20). Check out the busy bees at work in the wall display. There's basic backpacker

accommodation in a 135-year-old house at **Te Araroa Backpackers** (☑ 06-864 4896; www.teararoabackpackers.com; 57 Waione Rd, Te Araroa; dm from $25).

From Te Araroa, drive out to see the **East Cape Lighthouse**, the easterly tip of mainland NZ. It's 21km (30 minutes) east of town along a mainly unsealed road, with a 25-minute climb (750 steps!) to the lighthouse. Set your alarm and get up there for sunrise.

East Cape to Tokomaru Bay

Heading through farmland south of Te Araroa, the first town you come to is **Tikitiki**. If you haven't yet made it onto a *marae,* you'll get a fair idea of what you're missing out on by visiting the extraordinary **St Mary's Church** (1924). It's nothing special from the outside, but step inside for a sensory overload. There are woven *tukutuku* (flax panels) on the walls, geometrically patterned stained-glass windows, painted beams and amazing carvings – check out the little guys holding up the pulpit. A stained-glass crucifixion scene behind the pulpit depicts WWI Maori Battalion soldiers in attendance.

Amid the farming sprawl of **Rangitukia**, 8km down towards the coast from Tikitiki, **Eastender Horse Treks** (☑ 06-864 3033; www.eastenderhorsetreks.co.nz; 836 Rangitukia Rd, Rangitukia; 2/4hr treks $85/120) runs horse rides along the beach and can hook you up with bone-carving lessons (from $60). Note that the beach here is dicey for swimming.

FREEDOM TO CAMP

Gisborne District Council (GDC; ☑ 0800 653 800; www.gdc.govt.nz/freedom-camping) is one of the few authorities to permit freedom camping (extremely cheap informal camping), but only at a handful of designated sites between Te Araroa and Gisborne from the end of September to early April. You can apply for a permit online for two, 10 or 28 consecutive nights at a cost of $10, $25 and $60 respectively. Freedom camping is a privilege, so please follow the requirements in the GDC *Freedom Camping* leaflet, available online or at visitor centres. Your own gas cooker, chemical toilet and water supply are obligatory.

MURRAY BALL: THE BALLAD OF FOOTROT FLATS

Where the black Raukumara Ranges

Lie out east of everywhere,

The land's been stripped by sun and rain,

Until its bones are bare.

In this land of snarl-lipped razor backs

Of possums, deer and rats,

They talk a lot of working dogs

And the man from Footrot Flats.

Mt Hikurangi (1752m), jutting out of the Raukumara Range, is the highest non-volcanic peak on the North Island and the first spot on Earth to see the sun each day. According to local tradition it was the first piece of land dragged up when Maui snagged the North Island. The Ngati Porou version of the Maui story has his canoe and earthly remains resting here on their sacred mountain.

Continuing south, the road passes **Ruatoria** (shop, petrol and general desolation) and **Te Puia Springs** (ditto). Along this stretch a 14km loop road offers a rewarding detour to **Waipiro Bay**.

Eleven kilometres south of Te Puia is **Tokomaru Bay**, perhaps the most interesting spot on the entire route, with its broad beach framed by sweeping cliffs. The town has weathered hard times since the freezing works closed in the 1950s, but it still sports several attractions including good beginner surfing, swimming and **Te Puka Tavern** (☑ 06-864 5465; www.tepukatavern.co.nz; 135 Beach Rd, Tokomaru Bay; meals $10-27; ⊙ 11am-late; ☎). This well-run pub with cracker ocean views is a cornerstone of the community, keeping everyone fed and watered, and offering visitors a place to stay (units $140 to $180). You'll also find a supermarket, takeaway and post office here (...and a B&B in the former post office), plus some crumbling surprises at the far end of the bay. Up on the hill, 12-bed **Stranded in Paradise** (☑ 06-864-5870; www.bbh.co.nz; 21 Potae St; campsites per person $15, dm/s/d $28/45/66; ☎) scores the awards for views, eco-loos and free wi-fi. There are two tricky loft rooms for sharing, a double downstairs and three wave-shaped cabins. Tenters have a panoramic knoll (astonishing views!) on which to pitch.

Tokomaru Bay to Gisborne

After a bucolic 22km of highway is the turn-off to **Anaura Bay**, 6km away. It's a definite 'wow' moment when it springs into view far below. Captain Cook arrived here in 1769 and commented on the 'profound peace' in which the people were living and their 'truly astonishing' cultivations. **Anaura Bay Walkway** is a two-hour, 3.5km ramble through steep bush and grassland, starting at the northern end of the bay. There's a standard Department of Conservation (DOC) **campsite** here (adult/child $6/3; fully self-contained campers only).

Campers are catered for best around these parts, although a few B&Bs come and go in the midst. Grassy **Anaura Bay Family Motor Camp** (☑ 06-862 6380; www.gisbornenz.com/accommodation/view/401; Anaura Bay Rd; sites per adult/child from $18/9; ☎) is all about the location – right on the beachfront by the little stream where James Cook once stocked up with water. There's a decent kitchen, showers and toilets.

Back on the highway it's 14km south to **Tolaga Bay**, East Cape's largest community (population 765). There's an **information desk** (☑ 06-862 6826; uawafm@xtra.co.nz; 55 Cook St; ⊙ 9am-5pm Mon-Fri) in the foyer of the local radio station (Uawa FM; 88.5FM). Just off the main street, **Tolaga Bay Cashmere Company** (☑ 06-862 6746; www.cashmere.co.nz; 31 Solander St; ⊙ 10am-4pm Mon-Fri) inhabits the art-deco former council building. Watch the knitters knit, then perhaps purchase one of their delicate works: call to check they're open.

Tolaga is defined by its amazing **historic wharf**. Built in 1929 and commercially functional until 1968, it's the longest in the southern hemisphere (660m), and is caught somewhere between rusty decay and dedicated (expensive!) efforts to preserve it. Nearby is **Cooks Cove Walkway** (⊙ closed Aug-Oct), an easy 5.8km, 2½-hour loop through farmland and native bush to another cove where the captain landed. At the northern end of the beach is the **Tatarahake Cliffs Lookout**, a sharp 10-minute walk to an excellent vantage point.

Tolaga Bay Holiday Park (☑ 06-862 6716; www.tolagabayholidaypark.co.nz; 167 Wharf Rd, Tolaga Bay; sites from $16, cabins $40-100) is right next to the wharf. The stiff ocean breeze tousles Norfolk Island pines, and open lawns bask in the sunshine: it's a pretty special spot. Back in town, the 1930s faux-Tudor **To-**

laga Inn (☑06-862 6856; www.tolagainn.co.nz; 12 Cook St; dm/s/d $25/60/80) has basic but clean pub rooms upstairs, cheap bar meals downstairs ($6 to $10).

Around 16km north of Gisborne, the DOC-managed **Te Tapuwae o Rongokako Marine Reserve** is a 2450-hectare haven for many species of marine life including fur seals, dolphins and whales. Get out amongst it with **Dive Tatapouri** (☑06-868 5153; www.dive-tatapouri.com; 532 SH35, Tatapouri Beach), which offers dive trips, surf lessons, snorkel hire, a reef ecology tour and even shark-cage diving.

Gisborne

POP 34,800

'Gizzy' to her friends, Gisborne (pronounced Gis-born, not Gis-bun) is a pretty thing, squeezed between surf beaches and a sea of chardonnay, and proudly claims to be the first city on Earth to see the sun. It's a good place to put your feet up for a few days, hit the beach and sip some wine.

History

The Gisborne region has been settled for over 700 years. A pact between two migratory *waka* (canoe) skippers, Paoa of the *Horouta* and Kiwa of the *Takitimu*, led to the founding of Turanganui a Kiwa (now Gisborne). Kumara flourished in the fertile soil and the settlement blossomed.

In 1769 this was the first part of NZ sighted by Cook's expedition. Eager to replenish supplies and explore, they set ashore, much to the amazement of the locals. Setting an unfortunate benchmark for intercultural relations, the crew opened fire when the Maori men performed their traditional blood-curdling challenge, killing six of them.

The *Endeavour* set sail without provisions. Cook, perhaps in a fit of petulance, named the area Poverty Bay as 'it did not afford a single item we wanted'.

European settlement began in 1831 with whaling and farming, with missionaries following. In the 1860s battles between settlers and Maori erupted. Beginning in Taranaki, the Hauhau insurrection spread to the East Coast, culminating in the battle of Waerenga a Hika in 1865.

To discover Gisborne's historical spots, pick up the *Historic Walk* pamphlet from the i-SITE.

⊙ Sights

★**Tairawhiti Museum**   MUSEUM
(www.tairawhitimuseum.org.nz; Kelvin Rise, Stout St; adult/child $5/free, Mon free; ⊘10am-4pm

---

GISBORNE WINERIES

With hot summers and fertile loam soils, the Waipaoa River valley to the northwest of Gisborne is one of New Zealand's foremost grape-growing areas. The region is traditionally famous for its chardonnay but is increasingly noted for gewürztraminer and pinot gris. See www.gisbornewine.co.nz for a cellar-door map. Opening hours scale back out of peak season. Five of the best:

Bushmere Estate (☑06-868 9317; www.bushmere.com; 166 Main Rd, Matawhero; ⊘11am-5pm Wed-Sun) Great chardonnay, gewürztraminer, cafe lunches at the Bond Room (lunch mains $8 to $18, dinner Friday and Saturday only $16 to $28), and live music on summer Sundays.

Kirkpatrick Estate (☑06-862 7722; www.kew.co.nz; 569 Wharekopae Rd, Patutahi; ⊘11am-4pm) Sustainable winery with lovely wines across the board, including a delicious malbec. Enjoy an antipasto platter in the sun.

Matawhero (☑06-867 6140; www.matawhero.co.nz; Riverpoint Rd, Matawhero; ⊘11am-5pm Thu-Mon, daily Jan) Home of a particularly buttery chardy. Enjoy your picnic in bucolic splendour, accompanied by a flight of fine wines.

Millton (☑06-862 8680; www.millton.co.nz; 119 Papatu Rd, Manutuke; ⊘by appointment Feb-Nov, 10am-5pm daily Dec & Jan) Sustainable, organic and biodynamic to boot. Bring a picnic and kick back surrounded by sturdy-trunked vines.

Gisborne Wine Centre (☑06-867 4085; www.gisbornewine.co.nz; Shed 3, 50 The Esplanade; ⊘10am-5pm Sun-Wed, to 7pm Thu-Sat) Harbourside spot with a wide selection of the region's vino to sample (...the pervasive sea-scent may be hard to reconcile with the chardy on your palate).

Gisborne

Gisborne

◎ Top Sights
1 Tairawhiti Museum D2

◎ Sights
2 Captain Cook Statue C4
3 Cook Monument C4
4 Cook Observatory D4
5 Cook's Plaza C4
6 Gisborne Botanic Gardens C1
7 Gisborne Farmers Market D2
8 Gisborne Wine Centre D3
9 Statue of Young Nick C4
10 Sunshine Brewing Company B2
11 Te Tauihu Turanga Whakamana D3
12 Titirangi Lookout D4
13 Titirangi Park D4

➕ Activities, Courses & Tours
14 Olympic Pool A3

🛏 Sleeping
15 Captain Cook Motor Lodge C3
16 Gisborne YHA D3

17 Pacific Harbour Motor Inn C3
18 Quality Hotel Emerald D3
19 Teal Motor Lodge B1
20 Waikanae Beach Top 10 Holiday
   Park C3

✖ Eating
Cafe 1874 .... (see 29)
21 Morrell's Artisan Bakery B1
22 Muirs Bookshop & Café C3
23 Pak N Save C2
24 USSCO Bar & Bistro C3
25 Villaggio C1
26 Yoko Sushi C2
27 Zest C3

🍷 Drinking & Nightlife
Rivers .... (see 18)
28 Smash Palace A3

✦ Entertainment
29 Dome Cinema C3
   Poverty Bay Club .... (see 29)

Mon-Sat, 1.30-4pm Sun) The Tairawhiti Museum, with its new gallery extension, focuses on East Coast Maori and colonial history. It is Gisborne's arts hub, with rotating exhibits, and excellent historic photographic displays. There's also a maritime wing, with displays on *waka*, whaling and Cook's Poverty Bay, although these pale in comparison to the vintage surfboard collection.

There's a shop and tearoom-style cafe overlooking Kelvin Park, while outside is the reconstructed **Wyllie Cottage** (1872), Gisborne's oldest house.

Titirangi Park   PARK

High on Kaiti Hill overlooking the city, Titirangi was once a *pa* (fortified village). You can reach it by driving or walking up Queens Dr, or pick up the walking track at the Cook Monument. Near the summit is **Titirangi Lookout** and yet another Cook edifice, **Cook's Plaza**. Due to a cock-up of historic proportions, the Cook statue here looks nothing like Cap'n Jim. A plaque proclaims, 'Who was he? We have no idea!' Adjacent is a modest pohutukawa tree planted by Princess Di in 1983. Further on is the **Cook Observatory** (www.possumobservatory.co.nz/astrogas/cook_observatory01.htm; public viewing $5; ⊙ viewing 8.30pm Tue), the world's easternmost star-gazing facility.

Eastwoodhill Arboretum   GARDENS

(☑ 06-863 9003; www.eastwoodhill.org.nz; 2392 Wharekopae Rd, Ngatapa; adult/child/family $15/2/34; ⊙ 9am-5pm) Arboreal nirvana, Eastwoodhill Arboretum is the largest collection of northern hemisphere trees and shrubs in the southern hemisphere. It's staggeringly beautiful, and you could easily lose a day wandering around the 25km of themed tracks in this pine-scented paradise. It's well signposted, 35km northwest of Gisborne. There's also accommodation (p309) here.

Gisborne Farmers Market   MARKET

(www.gisbornefarmersmarket.co.nz; cnr Stout & Fitzherbert Sts; ⊙ 9.30am-12.30pm Sat) Stock up on fresh fruit, macadamia nuts (and macadamia nut paste!), smallgoods, honey, herbs, coffee, wine, bread, pastries, fish, cheese...all of it locally grown or procured.

Cook Monument   MONUMENT

At the foot of Titirangi Park is the spot where Cook first got NZ dirt on his boots. Little more than a patch of lawn with a grim obelisk, the scrappy site was also the landing point of the *Horouta waka*. Join the sweaty joggers on the steep track up Kaiti Hill, which starts near the monument.

Statue of Young Nick   MONUMENT

There's no let-up in Gisborne's *Endeavour* endeavours: in the riverside park is a dynamic statue of Nicholas Young, Cook's cabin boy, whose eagle eyes were the first to spot NZ (the white cliffs at Young Nick's Head). There's another **Captain Cook statue** nearby, erected on a globe etched with his roaming routes.

Gisborne Botanic Gardens   GARDENS

(www.gdc.govt.nz/botanical-gardens; Aberdeen Rd; ⊙ 24hr) FREE The town gardens are sitting pretty beside the Taruheru River – a beaut spot for a picnic. Wiggle through the NZ native **Bushland Walkway**.

Te Tauihu Turanga Whakamana   MONUMENT

(The Canoe Prow; cnr Gladstone Rd & Customhouse St) Like a giant sundial, Te Tauihu Turanga Whakamana is a large modern sculpture in the shape of a *tauihu* (canoe prow) that celebrates early Maori explorers.

East Coast Museum of Technology   MUSEUM

(ECMOT; www.ecmot.org.nz; SH2, Makaraka; adult/child $5/2; ⊙ 10am-4pm Mon-Sat, 1-4pm Sun) Think analogue, rather than digital; old age rather than space age. About 5km west of the town centre, this improbable medley of farm equipment, fire engines and sundry appliances has found an appropriate home in a motley old milking barn and surrounding outhouses. Oh, the irony of the welcome sign...

Matawhero Church   CHURCH

(www.standrewsgis.org.nz/faith.html; Church Lane, off Saleyard Rd, Matawhero; ⊙ 9am-5pm) Some 7km west of the centre in the suburb of Matawhero, this historic Presbyterian church is the only building in the village to have survived Te Kooti's 1868 raid. It's a sweet timber affair with a bell turret and lovingly tended gardens.

Sunshine Brewing Company   BREWERY

(☑ 06-867 7777; www.gisbornegold.co.nz; 109 Disraeli St; ⊙ 9am-6pm Mon-Sat) FREE Sunshine Brewing Company, Gisborne's own natural brewery, offers four quality beers including the famous Gisborne Gold and its big brother Green. Free tours and tastings by arrangement.

TE KOOTI

Maori history is littered with mystics, prophets and warriors, one of whom is the legendary Te Kooti (rhymes with naughty, not booty).

In 1865 he fought with the government against the Hauhau (adherents of the Pai Marire faith, founded by another warrior-prophet) but was accused of being a spy and imprisoned on the Chatham Islands without trial.

While imprisoned, Te Kooti studied the Bible and claimed to receive visions from the archangel Michael. His charismatic preaching and 'miracles' – including producing flames from his hands (his captors claimed he used phosphorus from the head of matches) – helped win over the Pai Marire to his distinctly Maori take on Christianity.

In 1867 Te Kooti led an astounding escape from the Chathams, hijacking a supply ship and sailing to Poverty Bay with 200 followers. En route he threw a doubter overboard as a sacrifice. Upon their safe arrival, Te Kooti's disciples raised their right hands in homage to God rather than bowing submissively; *ringa tu* (upraised hand) became the name of his church.

Te Kooti requested a dialogue with the colonial government but was once again rebuffed, with magistrate Reginald Biggs demanding his immediate surrender. Unimpressed by Pakeha (European New Zealander) justice, Te Kooti commenced a particularly effective guerrilla campaign – starting by killing Biggs and around 50 others (including women and children, Maori and Pakeha) at Matawhero near Gisborne.

A four-year chase ensued. Eventually Te Kooti took refuge in the King Country, the Maori king's vast dominion where government troops feared to tread.

Proving the pointlessness of the government's approach to the whole affair, Te Kooti was officially pardoned in 1883. By this time his reputation as a prophet and healer had spread and his Ringatu Church was firmly established, and today claims more than 16,000 adherents.

🏃 Activities

Water Sports

Surfing is mainstream in Gisborne, with the teenage population looking appropriately shaggy. **Waikanae Beach** and **Roberts Road** are good for learners; experienced surfers get tubed south of town at the **Pipe**, or east at **Sponge Bay** and **Tuamotu Island**. Further east along SH35, **Wainui** and **Makorori** also have quality breaks. There's safe swimming between the flags at Waikanae and **Midway Beach**.

Surfing With Frank   SURFING
(☏06-867 0823, 021 119 0971; www.surfingwithfrank.com; lessons $50-75) Surfing with Frank offers lessons at Wainui, as well as tours of the best East Coast and Taranaki breaks. Three-hour board and wetsuit hire $30.

Rere Rockslide   SWIMMING
(Wharekopae Rd; ⊙daylight hours) FREE This natural phenomenon occurs in a section of the Rere River, 50km northwest of Gisborne along Wharekopae Rd. Grab a tyre tube or boogie board to cushion the bumps and slide down the 60m-long rocky run into the pool at the bottom. Three kilometres down-

river, the **Rere Falls** send a 20m-wide curtain of water over a 5m drop; you can walk behind it if you don't mind getting wet.

Olympic Pool   SWIMMING
(Centennial Marine Pde, Midway Beach; adult/child $3.80/2.80; ⊙6am-8pm daily, from 8am Sat & Sun May-Aug) Gisborne's big pool is a tepid 50m indoor/outdoor affair with a wormlike waterslide.

Surfit Charters   DIVING
(☏06-867 2970; www.surfit.co.nz; per person from $310) Awaken your sense of mortality with a shark-cage dive with Surfit Charters. Tamer fishing and snorkelling trips also available.

Walking

There are many kilometres of walks to tackle around Gisborne, starting with a gentle stroll along the river. The i-SITE can provide you with brochures for the *Historic Walk* and the *Walking Trails of Gisborne City*.

Winding its way through farmland and forest with commanding views, the **Te Kuri Walkway** (two hours, 5.6km, closed August to October) starts 4km north of town at the end of Shelley Rd.

☞ Tours

Gisborne Cycle Tour Company CYCLING
(☏ 06-927 7021; www.gisbornecycletours.co.nz;
half-/full-day tours from $100/200, freedom hire
per day from $50) Half-day to multiday guided
cycle tours around local sights and further
afield including wineries and Eastwoodhill
Aboretum. Cheaper rates for multiday freedom bike hire (maps and advice on tap).

✯ Festivals & Events

Feast Gisborne FOOD, WINE
(www.feastgisborne.co.nz) On October's Labour
Day weekend, local winemakers and foodies
pool talents for Gisborne's food-and-wine
fest, held at a local vineyard. Top NZ musical
talent usually makes an appearance. Over-
18s only.

Rhythm & Vines MUSIC, WINE
(www.rhythmandvines.co.nz) A huge event on
the music calendar, R&V is a three-day festival leading up to New Year's Eve, featuring
big-time local and international bands and
DJs. Local accommodation feels the sqeeze.

🛏 Sleeping

Gisborne YHA HOSTEL $
(☏ 06-867 3269; www.yha.co.nz; 32 Harris St; dm/
s/d/f $30/50/66/108; @ 🛜) A short wander
across the river from town, this rambling
1925 charmer houses a well-kept hostel. The
rooms are large and comfy (even the 10-bed
dorm in the roof space), while outside the
deck and lawns entice conversations. Family en suite unit and surfboard and bike hire
also available.

Waikanae Beach Top
10 Holiday Park HOLIDAY PARK $
(☏ 06-867 5634, 0800 867 563; www.waikanae-
beachtop10.co.nz; 280 Grey St; sites from $22, cab-
ins & units $70-155; @ 🛜) Right by the beach
and an easy 10-minute walk to town, this
grassy holiday park offers good-value cabins and units, and grassy lanes for pitching
tents and parking vans. Some of the cheaper
cabins could use some TLC. Surfboards and
bikes for hire.

Teal Motor Lodge MOTEL $$
(☏ 06-868 4019, 0800 838 325; www.teal.co.nz;
479 Gladstone Rd; d $125-175, f $195-245; @ 🛜 ▧)
With super street appeal on the main drag
(500m into town), the vaguely alpine Teal
boasts a solid offering of tidy, family-friendly
units plus a saltwater swimming pool and immaculate lawns to run around on. Free wi-fi.

Eastwoodhill Arboretum LODGE $$
(☏ 06-863 9003; www.eastwoodhill.org.nz; 2392
Wharekopae Rd, Ngatapa; dm/tw/d incl garden admission $35/80/120) The bunks and private
rooms at Eastwoodhill Arboretum (p307)
are basic, but once you're here, endless
woody delights can fill your days and nights.
Meals available by arrangement, or you can
use the fully equipped kitchen (BYO food as
there aren't any shops nearby).

Pacific Harbour Motor Inn MOTEL $$
(☏ 06-867 8847; www.pacific-harbour.co.nz; 24
Reads Quay; d $125-195; @ 🛜) Overlooking the
harbour, this two-tier motel offers well-kept
units with kitchenettes and dinky little bal-
conies. A tad classier than your average motel (black leather couches!). The best rooms
face the river and get all-day sun.

Quality Hotel Emerald HOTEL $$
(☏ 06-868 8055; www.emeraldhotel.co.nz; 13 Gladstone Rd; r $140-280; @ 🛜 ▧) With allegedly
the largest hotel rooms in NZ, the contemporary Emerald revolves around its swimming-
pool area – a reasonable impersonation of
a foxy international. Surrounding it are 48
plush suites along epic corridors connecting
various wings (much nicer inside than out).
Free wi-fi; off-street parking.

Captain Cook Motor Lodge MOTEL $$
(☏ 0800 227 826; www.captaincook.co.nz; cnr Grey
St & Awapuni Rd; d from $125, 1-/2-bedroom units
from $145/165; 🛜) It's not the architecture
you're here for – 36 rooms strung along a
vast carpark – but the location, a quick dash
to the Waikanae Beach on the other side of
the adjacent holiday park.

Knapdale Eco Lodge LODGE $$$
(☏ 06-862 5444; www.knapdale.co.nz; 114 Snowsill
Rd, Waihirere; d incl breakfast from $398; @ 🛜) ✍
Indulge yourself at this rural idyll, complete
with lake, farm animals and home-grown
produce. The mod lodge is filled with international artwork, its glassy frontage flowing
out to an expansive patio with brazier, barbecue and pizza oven. Five-course dinner by
arrangement ($85). To get here head 10km
northwest of Gisborne, via Back Ormond Rd.

✗ Eating

Cafe 1874 CAFE $
(☏ 06-863 3165; www.1874.co.nz; 38 Childers Rd;
meals $7-22; ⊙ 7am-3pm Mon-Fri, 9am-2pm Sat; ✍)
The creaky grandeur of the Poverty Bay gen-
tleman's club (1874) is reason enough to visit.
This cafe within it certainly adds impetus:

appealing counter food, all-day brunch, pizza, blackboard specials and reasonable prices. Love the big pew along the outside wall.

Zest
CAFE $

(📞 06-867 5787; www.zestcafe.co.nz; 22 Peel St; mains $8-16; ⊙ 6am-4pm Mon-Sat) Pop quiz: how many cafes are there in the Western world called 'Zest'? Plenty. But unoriginality aside, this is one of the East Coast's best, offering pizzas, pastas, big breakfasts, salads, wraps, waffles and smoothies. Again, nothing too original, but perfectly executed, affordable and superfresh. Hope the regular knitting group isn't taking up all the seats.

Muirs Bookshop & Café
CAFE $

(www.muirsbookshop.co.nz; 62 Gladstone Rd; meals $8-13; ⊙ 9am-3.30pm Mon-Fri, to 3pm Sat) Situated above Muirs Bookshop, a beloved, age-old independent in a lovely heritage building, this simple cafe offers a small but sweet selection of counter food and excellent salads. Fans of fine espresso coffee and literature may need to be forcibly removed. Over-street balcony for balmy days.

Morrell's Artisan Bakery
BAKERY $

(www.facebook.com/morrellsartisanbakery; 437 Gladstone Rd; items $4-9; ⊙ 7am-2pm Tue-Sat; 📷) Artisan bakers with killer pies, wholesome bread, delicious pastries and cookies, all made on site. Don't overlook the coconut and passionfruit custard slice.

Yoko Sushi
SUSHI $

(📞 06-868 6400; www.yokosushi.co.nz; 87 Grey St; sushi $5-12; ⊙ 8am-5pm Mon-Sat) If you're into sushi, Yoko will surely lure you in (even if your name's not John). Commendable sushi, along with the usual miso-lany of extras including beaut bento boxes.

Pak N Save
SUPERMARKET $

(274 Gladstone Rd; ⊙ 7am-9pm) Fill up the trolley, and don't forget your Gisborne oranges.

Villaggio
CAFE $$

(📞 06-863 3895; villagio@threechefs.co.nz; 57 Ballance St; mains lunch $18-26, dinner $28-36; ⊙ 8am-4pm Sun-Wed, to late Thu-Sat) North of the river, push through the gate of this old art-deco house which has been stripped back to supersmart red, white and wood fundamentals. The menu offers fresh takes on classics (seafood chowder; fish and chips), plus colourful Med-style dishes (spaghetti with tomato, goat cheese and herbs; Moroccan vegetable tagine). Loiter in the garden over lunchtime wines.

★ USSCO Bar & Bistro
MODERN NZ $$$

(📞 06-868 3246; www.ussco.co.nz; 16 Childers Rd; mains $30-42; ⊙ 4.30pm-late) Housed in the restored Union Steam Ship Company building (USSCO – get it?), this place is all class. Silky kitchen skills shine in a highly seasonal menu featuring the likes of soy-glazed pork belly with caramelized yams, parsnip puree and toasted nut salad. Devilishly good desserts, plus plenty of local wines and NZ craft beers. Generous portions, multicourse deals and live piano tunes.

🍷 Drinking & Entertainment

Smash Palace
BAR

(📞 06-867 7769; 24 Banks St; ⊙ 3pm-late Mon-Thu, 2pm-late Fri, noon-late Sat, 2-11pm Sun) Get juiced at the junkyard: an iconic drinking den in Gisborne's industrial wastelands, full to the gunwales with ephemera and its very own DC3 crash-landed in the beer garden. Occasional live music.

Rivers
PUB

(cnr Gladstone Rd & Reads Quay; ⊙ 11am-late Mon-Sat, from noon Sun) This well-run, British-style pub does the business, offering steak-and-ale pie, proper pudding, big-screen telly and pool. It's also family friendly and cosy, with some choice artefacts adding a convincing veneer of history. Quiz nights Tuesdays.

Poverty Bay Club
LIVE MUSIC, CINEMA

(📞 06-863 2006; www.thepovertybayclub.co.nz; 38 Childers Rd; ⊙ 5pm-late Wed-Fri, 8pm-late Sat, 5.30pm-late Sun) Sharing this lovely old historic building with a cafe and art shop is **Winston's Bar**, where occasional live music and vintage board games transpire, as well as the bean-baggy **Dome Cinema** (📞 08-324 3005; www.domecinema.co.nz; tickets $15; ⊙ from 5.30pm Wed-Sun), which screens art-house flicks.

ⓘ Information

DOC (Department of Conservation; 📞 06-869 0460; www.doc.govt.nz; 63 Carnarvon St; ⊙ 8am-4.30pm Mon-Fri) Tourist information.

Gisborne Hospital (📞 06-869 0500; www.tdh. org.nz; Ormond Rd; ⊙ 24hr)

Gisborne i-SITE (📞 06-868 6139; www.gisbornenz.com; 209 Grey St; ⊙ 8.30am-5.30pm Mon-Fri, 9am-5pm Sat, 10am-4pm Sun; 📶) Beside a doozy of a Canadian totem pole, this information centre has all and sundry, as well as a travel desk, internet access and toilets.

Police Station (📞 06-869 0200; www.police. govt.nz; cnr Gladstone Rd & Customhouse St; ⊙ 24hr)

Post Office (www.nzpost.co.nz; 127 Gladstone Rd; ⊘8.30am-5pm Mon-Fri, 9am-noon Sat)

ⓘ Getting There & Around

The i-SITE handles bookings for many local and national transport services.

AIR

Gisborne Airport (www.eastland.co.nz/gisborne-airport; Aerodrome Rd) is 3km west of the city. Air New Zealand flies to/from Auckland and Wellington, with onward connections. Sunair Aviation flies direct from Gisborne to Rotorua, Tauranga and Napier.

BUS

InterCity buses depart daily from the i-SITE for Napier ($47, four hours) via Wairoa ($30, 1½ hours); and Auckland ($85, 10 hours) via Opotiki ($36, two hours) and Rotorua ($64, five hours).

Naked Bus daily destinations include Taupo ($24, 5½ hours) via Opotiki ($17, two hours) and Rotorua ($25, 4½ hours).

For courier services from Gisborne to Opotiki travelling via East Cape's scenic SH35, see p299.

CAR

Gisborne Airport Car Rental (⌨1300 350 401; www.gisborneairportcarhire.co.nz) is an agent for seven car-hire companies including the big brands and local outfits.

TAXI

A city-to-airport taxi fare costs about $20.
Gisborne Taxis (⌨06-867 2222)

Gisborne to Hawke's Bay

From Gisborne, heading south towards Napier you're confronted with a choice: follow SH2, which runs closer to the coast, or take SH36 inland via Tiniroto. Either way you'll end up in Wairoa.

The coastal route is a marginally better choice, being quicker and offering occasional views out to sea. However, SH36 (**Tiniroto Road**) is also a pleasant drive (or bike route) with several good stopping points along the way. **Doneraille Park**, 49km from Gisborne, is a peaceful bush reserve with a frigid river to jump into and freedom camping for self-contained vehicles (see p303). Tree lovers might like to check out **Hackfalls Arboretum** (⌨06-863 7083; www.hackfalls.org.nz; 187 Berry Rd, Tiniroto; adult/child $10/free; ⊘9am-5pm), a 3km detour from the turn-off at the Tiniroto Tavern. The snow-white cascades of **Te Reinga Falls**, 12km further south, are well worth a stop.

WORTH A TRIP

MAHIA PENINSULA

The Mahia Peninsula's eroded hills, sandy beaches and vivid blue sea make it a mini-ringer of the Coromandel, without the tourist hordes and fancy subdivisions, and with the bonus of dramatic Dover-ish cliffs. It's an enduring holiday spot for East Coasters, who come largely for boaty, beachy stuff, and you can easily get in on the action if you have your own transport. A day or two could easily be spent visiting the scenic reserve and the bird-filled Maungawhio Lagoon, hanging out at the beach (Mahia Beach at sunset can be spectacular) or even playing a round of golf.

Mahia has several small settlements offering between them a couple of guesthouses, a campsite, a decent pub and a dairy. See www.voyagemahia.co.nz for peninsular info.

The busier SH2 route heads inland and soon enters the **Wharerata State Forest** (beware of logging trucks). Just out of the woods, 55km from Gisborne, **Morere Hot Springs** (⌨06-837 8856; www.morerehotsprings.co.nz; SH2, Morere; adult/child $10/5; ⊘10am-5pm, extended hours Dec-Feb) burble up from a fault line in the **Morere Springs Scenic Reserve**. Have a dip, or tackle a bush walk (20 minutes to three hours) before taking the plunge. The main pool is near the entrance, or a five-minute walk through virgin rainforest leads to the Nikau Pools.

Also at Morere is the **Morere Tearooms & Camping Ground** (⌨06-837 8792; www.morereaccommodation.co.nz; SH2, Morere; campsites from $17, d $60-90), where you can get a respectable toasted sandwich and avail yourself of lovely campsites and basic cabins alongside the babbling Tunanui Stream. Just over the stream is **Morere Hot Springs Lodge & Cabins** (⌨06-837 8824; www.morerelodge.co.nz; SH2, Morere; d $80-120, extra adult/child $20/10), a farmy enclave with accommodation in a classic 1917 farmhouse and two cute self-contained cabins.

From Gisborne on SH2, keep an eye out for the brightly painted **Taane-nui-a-Rangi Marae** on the left. You can get a decent view from the road; don't enter unless invited.

SH2 continues south to Nuhaka at the northern end of Hawke Bay. From here it's west to Wairoa or east to the salty **Mahia**

Peninsula. Not far from the Nuhaka round-about is **Kahungunu Marae** (www.visitwai-roa.co.nz/pages/kahungunu_marae; cnr Ihaka & Mataira Sts). From the roadside, check out the carving at the house's apex: a standing warrior holding a *taiaha* (spear), less stylised than most traditional carving.

Te Urewera National Park

Shrouded in mist and mysticism, Te Urewera National Park is the North Island's largest, encompassing 2127 sq km of virgin forest cut with lakes and rivers. The highlight is Lake Waikaremoana (Sea of Rippling Waters), a deep crucible of water encircled by the Lake Waikaremoana Track, one of NZ's Great Walks. Rugged bluffs drop away to reedy inlets, the lake's mirror surface disturbed only by mountain zephyrs and the occasional waterbird taking to the skies.

The name Te Urewera still has the capacity to make Pakeha (white) New Zealanders feel slightly uneasy – and not just because it translates as 'The Burnt Penis'. There's something primal and untamed about this wild woodland, with its rich history of Maori resistance.

Lake Waikaremoana Track

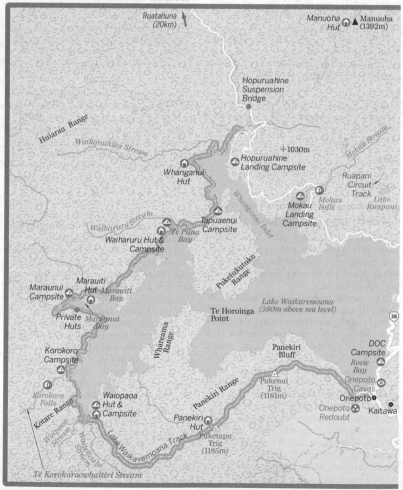

The local Tuhoe people – prosaically known as the 'Children of the Mist' – never signed the Treaty of Waitangi and fought with Rewi Maniapoto at Orakau during the Waikato Wars. The army of Te Kooti took refuge here during running battles with government troops. The claimant of Te Kooti's spiritual mantle, Rua Kenana, led a thriving community beneath the sacred mountain Maungapohatu (1366m) from 1905 until his politically motivated 1916 arrest. This effectively erased the last bastion of Maori independence in the country. Maungapohatu never recovered, and only a small settlement remains. Nearby, Ruatahuna's extraordi-nary Mataatua Marae celebrates Te Kooti's exploits.

Tuhoe remain proud of their identity and traditions, with around 40% still speaking *te reo* (the language) on a regular basis.

🏃 Activities

Lake Waikaremoana Track

This 46km, three- to four-day tramp scales the spectacular Panekiri Bluff (1180m), with open panoramas interspersed with fern groves and forest. The walk is rated as moderate with the only difficult section being the Panekiri ascent, and during summer it can get busy.

Although it's a year-round track, winter rain deters many people and makes conditions much more challenging. At this altitude (580m above sea level), temperatures can drop quickly, even in summer. Walkers should take portable stoves and fuel as there are no cooking facilities en route.

There are five **huts** (adult/child $32/free) and **campsites** (per night adult/child $14/free) spaced along the track, all of which must be prebooked through DOC, regardless of the season. Book at regional DOC offices, i-SITEs or online at www.greatwalks.co.nz.

If you have a car, it is safest to leave it at the Lake Waikaremoana Motor Camp or Big Bush Holiday Park then take a water taxi to the trailheads. Alternatively, you can take the fully catered, three-night guided tour offered by the enthusiastic and experienced **Walking Legends** (📞07-312 5297, 0800 925 569; www.walkinglegends.com; tours $1390).

Propel yourself onto the trail either clockwise from just outside **Onepoto** in the south or anticlockwise from **Hopuruahine Suspension Bridge** in the north.

Estimated walking times:

ROUTE	DURATION (HR)
Onepoto to Panekiri Hut	5
Panekiri Hut to Waiopaoa Hut	3-4
Waiopaoa Hut to Marauiti Hut	5
Marauiti Hut to Waiharuru Hut	2
Waiharuru Hut to Whanganui Hut	2½
Whanganui Hut to Hopuruahine Suspension Bridge	2

Other Walks

There are dozens of walks within the park's vast boundaries, most of which are outlined in DOC's *Lake Waikaremoana Walks* and *Recreation in Northern Te Urewera* pamphlets ($2.50). Plenty of short walks kick off

Map:
0 – 5 km
0 – 2.5 miles
N

Manuoha Track

Te Urewera National Park

Sandy Bay Hut

Lake Waikareiti (892m above sea level)

Day Shelter
Lake Waikareiti Track
+1061m
Aniwaniwa Stream

Papakorito Falls

ℹ Te Urewera National Park Visitor Centre

Lake Waikaremoana Motor Camp

Te Urewera National Park
Ngamoko (1099m)
Ngamoko Range

Lake Kaitawa
Big Bush Holiday Park
Tuai
Lake Whakamarino

Hikihiki's Inn
National Park Entrance
38
Wairoa (49km)

from the visitor centre and Lake Waikaremoana Motor Camp.

With its untouched islands, **Lake Waikareiti** is an enchanting place. Starting nearby the Te Urewera National Park Visitor Centre, it's an hour's walk to its shore. Once you're there you can explore it in a rowboat (keys from the visitor centre $20).

Accessed from the track to Lake Waikareiti, the more challenging **Ruapani Circuit Track** (six hours) passes through wetlands and dense virgin forest.

🛏 Sleeping & Eating

DOC has more than 30 huts and campsites within the park, most of which are very basic.

**Lake Waikaremoana
Motor Camp**   HOLIDAY PARK $
(☑06-837 3826; www.holidayparks.co.nz; SH38, Lake Waikaremoana; sites per adult/child from $15/8, d cabins/units from $120/190) Right on the shore, this place has Swiss-looking chalets, fisher's cabins and campsites, most with watery views. The on-site shop is full of essentials (hot pies, chocolate, fishing flies...) and has a petrol pump.

Big Bush Holiday Park   HOLIDAY PARK $
(☑06-837 3777, 0800 525 392; www.lakewaikaremoana.co.nz; SH38; sites/s/d from $15/30/60) About 4km from the Onepoto trailhead, Big Bush offers tent sites, trim cabins and backpacker rooms. Transfers to/from Wairoa, pick-ups/drop-offs around the lake, water taxis and storage also available.

Hikihiki's Inn   B&B $$
(☑06-837 3701; www.hikihiki.co.nz; 9 Rotten Row, Tuai; s $80-120, d $160-240) In the sweet little settlement of Tuai, 6km from Onepoto, this little weatherboard gem serves as a B&B run by '100% Kiwi' hosts. Prices include continental breakfast; other meals at additional cost (24 hours notice required). Sleeps six.

ⓘ Information

The DOC-run **Te Urewera National Park Visitor Centre** (☑06-837 3803; www.doc.govt.nz; Aniwaniwa; ☉8am-4.45pm) has weather forecasts, accommodation information and hut or campsite passes for the Lake Waikaremoana Track.

ⓘ Getting There & Around

Lake Waikaremoana is about an hour from Wairoa on SH38, which continues through to Rotorua. Around 95km of the entire 195km Wairoa-to-Rotorua route is unsealed: it's a four-hour bone-rattling ride.

Big Bush Water Taxi (☑06-837 3777, 0800 525 392; www.lakewaikaremoana.co.nz) will ship you to either Onepoto or Hopuruahine trailhead ($50 return), with hut-to-hut pack transfers for the less gung-ho. It also runs shuttles to and from Wairoa ($50 one way).

HAWKE'S BAY

Hawke Bay, the name given to the body of water that stretches from the Mahia Peninsula to Cape Kidnappers, looks like it's been bitten out of the North Island's eastern flank. Add an apostrophe and an 's' and you've got a region that stretches south and inland to include fertile farmland, surf beaches, mountainous ranges and forests. With food, wine and architecture the prevailing obsessions, it's smugly comfortable but thoroughly appealing, and is best viewed through a rosé-tinted wineglass.

Wairoa to Napier

The small town of **Wairoa** (population 7900) is trying hard to shirk its rough-edged rep. Not scintillating enough to warrant an extended stay, the town has a couple of points of interest, including an exceptional (and exceptionally early-opening) pie shop called **Oslers** (☑06-838 8299; 116 Marine Pde; pies $3.50-4.50, meals $7-15; ☉4.30am-4.30pm Mon-Fri, 6am-3pm Sat & Sun). Nonconsumable attractions include the plaque-studded **River Walkway**, the **Wairoa Museum** (☑06-838 3108; www.wairoamuseum.org.nz; 142 Marine Pde; ☉10am-4pm Tue-Fri,to noon Sat) **FREE** inside an old bank, and a couple of motels if you're caught short. The **Wairoa i-SITE** (☑06-838 7440; www.visitwairoa.co.nz; cnr SH2 & Queen St; ☉8am-5pm Mon-Fri, 10am-4pm Sat & Sun) is the spot for local info, including advice on Lake Waikaremoana.

The stretch of highway between Wairoa and Napier traipses through unphotogenic farmland and forestry blocks for much of its 117km. Most of it follows a railway line, currently only used for freight – you'll realise what a travesty this is when you pass under the **Mohaka viaduct** (1937), the highest rail viaduct in Australasia (97m).

Occupied by early Maori, **Lake Tutira** has walkways and a bird sanctuary. At Tutira village, just north of the lake, Pohokura Rd leads to the wonderful **Boundary Stream Scenic Reserve**, a major conservation area. Three loop tracks start from the road, ranging in length from 40 minutes to three hours. Also along this road you'll find the **Opouahi** and **Bellbird Bush Scenic Reserves**, which both offer rewarding walks. See www.doc.govt.nz for info on all of these reserves.

Off Waipatiki Rd, 34km outside Napier, Waipatiki Beach is a beaut spot boasting a low-key campsite and the 64-hectare **Waipatiki Scenic Reserve**. Further down the line, **White Pine Bush Scenic Reserve**, 29km from Napier on SH2, bristles with kahikatea and nikau palms. **Tangoio Falls Scenic Reserve**, 27km north of Napier, has Te Ana Falls, stands of wheki-ponga (tree ferns) and native orchids. Again, www.doc.govt.nz has the low-down on these reserves. Between White Pine and Tangoio Reserves the **Tangoio Walkway** (three hours return) follows Kareaara Stream.

The highway surfs the coast for the last 25km, with impressive views towards Napier. Hawke's Bay wine country starts in earnest at the mouth of the Esk River.

Napier

POP 57,240

The Napier of today – a charismatic, sunny, composed city with the air of an affluent English seaside resort – is the silver lining of the dark cloud that was the deadly 1931 earthquake. Rebuilt in the popular architectural styles of the time, the city retains a unique concentration of art-deco buildings. Don't expect the Chrysler Building – Napier is resolutely low-rise – but you will find intact 1930s facades and streetscapes, which can provoke a *Great Gatsby* swagger in the least romantic soul.

History

The area has been settled since around the 12th century and was known to Maori as Ahuriri. By the time James Cook eyeballed it in October 1769, Ngati Kahungunu was the dominant tribe, controlling the coast to Wellington.

In the 1830s whalers malingered around Ahuriri, establishing a trading base in 1839. By the 1850s the Crown had purchased – by often dubious means – 1.4 million acres of

---

CYCLE THE BAY

The 180km network of **Hawke's Bay Trails** (www.nzcycletrail.com/hawkes-bay-trails) – part of the national Nga Haerenga, New Zealand Cycle Trails project – offers cycling opportunities from short city scoots to hilly, single-track shenanagins. Dedicated cycle trails encircle Napier, Hastings and the coastline, with landscape, water and wine themes. Pick up the *Hawke's Bay Trails* brochure from the i-SITE or online.

Napier itself is very cycle friendly, particularly along Marine Pde where you'll find **Fishbike** (Map p318; ☑ 06-833 6979; www.fishbike.co.nz; 22 Marine Pde; bike hire per half-/full day $35/50, tandems $70/90; ⊙ 9am-5pm) renting comfortable bikes – including tandems for those willing to risk divorce.

Mountain bikers head to **Eskdale Mountain Bike Park** (Map p316; ☑ 06-873 8793; www.hawkesbaymtb.co.nz; 3-week permit $10) for a whole lot of fun in the forest: see the website or call for directions. Hire mountain bikes from **Pedal Power** (Map p316; ☑ 06-844 9771; www.pedalpower.co.nz; 340 Gloucester St, Taradale; half-/full day from $30/60; ⊙ 8am-5.30pm Mon-Fri, 9am-3pm Sat, 10am-3pm Sun), just out of the city centre in Taradale.

Given the conducive climate, terrain and multitudinous tracks, it's no surprise that numerous cycle companies pedal fully geared-up tours around the Bay, with winery visits near mandatory. Operators include the following:

Bike About Tours (☑ 06-845 4836; www.bikeabouttours.co.nz; tours half-/full day from $35/45)

Bike D'Vine (☑ 06-833 6697; www.bikedevine.com; tours adult/child from $35/15)

On Yer Bike Winery Tours (☑ 06-650 4627; www.onyerbikehb.co.nz; full day with/without lunch $60/50)

Takaro Trails (☑ 06-835 9030; www.takarotrails.co.nz; day rides from $40, 3-/5-day rides incl accommodation from $479/899)

Hawke's Bay

Hawke's Bay land, leaving Ngati Kahungunu with less than 4000 acres. The town of Napier was planned in 1854 and obsequiously named after the British general and colonial administrator Charles Napier.

At 10.46am on 3 February 1931, the city was levelled by a catastrophic earthquake (7.9 on the Richter scale). Fatalities in Napier and nearby Hastings numbered 258. Napier suddenly found itself 40 sq km larger, as the earthquake heaved sections of what was once a lagoon 2m above sea level (Napier's airport was once more 'port', less 'air'). A fevered rebuilding program ensued, constructing one of the world's most uniformly art-deco cities.

◉ Sights

If you haven't got time for a guided or self-guided art-deco walking tour, just take to the streets – particularly Tennyson and Emerson. Remember to look up!

Deco Centre   TOURIST INFORMATION

(Map p318; www.artdeconapier.com; 7 Tennyson St; ☉9am-5pm) The relocated and revamped Deco Centre is the place to start your explorations. Its one-hour guided deco walk ($17) departs the i-SITE daily at 10am; the two-hour version ($20) leaves the Centre at 2pm daily. There's also a lovely little shop here, and brochures for the excellent self-guided *Art Deco Walk* ($7.50), *Art Deco Scenic Drive* ($5) and *Marewa Meander* ($3). You can also take a self-guided bike tour ($50, four hours), vintage car tour ($75, one hour), or kids' art-deco treasure hunt ($4).

★ Daily Telegraph Building   ARCHITECTURE

(Map p318; 49 Tennyson St) The Daily Telegraph is one of the stars of Napier's art-deco show, with superb zigzags, fountain shapes and ziggurat aesthetic. If the front doors are open, nip inside and ogle at the painstakingly restored foyer.

Hawke's Bay

◎ Sights
1 Black Barn Vineyards.............................C4
2 Crab Farm Winery................................B1
3 Craggy Range......................................C4
4 Hastings Farmers Market.....................B3
5 Mission Estate Winery.........................B2
6 National Tobacco Company
   Building...D2
7 Otatara Pa...B3
8 Te Mata Estate....................................C4
9 Te Mata Peak Lookout..........................C4
10 Westshore Beach.................................C1

◎ Activities, Courses & Tours
11 Eskdale Mountain Bike Park................B1
12 Gannet Beach Adventures..................C4
13 Gannet Safaris....................................C4
14 Pandora Kayaks..................................D2
15 Pedal Power.......................................B2
16 Splash Planet......................................B4

◎ Sleeping
17 Clive Colonial Cottages.......................C3
18 Crown Hotel.......................................D2
19 Eco Lodge Pakowhai...........................B3
20 Hastings Top 10 Holiday Park.............B4
21 Havelock North Motor Lodge..............B4

22 Kennedy Park Resort...........................C2
23 Mangapapa Petit Hotel........................C4
24 Millar Road...C4
25 Rocks Motorlodge...............................D2

◎ Eating
26 Bay Espresso......................................B4
   Deliciosa.......................................(see 21)
   Diva..(see 21)
   Pipi...(see 21)
27 Westshore Fish Café............................C2

◎ Drinking & Nightlife
28 Filter Room...B2
29 Gintrap...D2
   Loading Ramp................................(see 21)
   Rose & Shamrock............................(see 21)
   Thirsty Whale.................................(see 29)

◎ Entertainment
   Globe Theatrette.............................(see 18)

◎ Shopping
30 Arataki Honey.....................................C4
31 Silky Oak Chocolate Company.............B3
   Strawberry Patch...........................(see 21)
32 Telegraph Hill.....................................B4

★ **MTG Hawke's Bay**   MUSEUM, THEATRE
(Museum Theatre Gallery; Map p318; ☑ 06-835 7781; www.mtghawkesbay.com; 1 Tennyson St; adult/child $15/free; ⊙10am-6pm) The beating cultural heart of Napier is the newly renovated MTG. It's a gleaming-white museum-theatre-gallery space by the water, bringing together live performances, film screenings and regularly changing gallery and museum displays with touring and local exhibitions.

National Tobacco
Company Building   ARCHITECTURE
(Map p316; cnr Bridge & Ossian Sts, Ahuriri) Around the shore at Ahuriri, the National Tobacco Company Building is arguably the region's deco masterpiece, combining art-deco forms with the natural motifs of art nouveau. Roses, raupo (bulrushes) and grapevines frame the elegantly curved entrance. During business hours, pull on the leaf-shaped brass door handles and enter the first two rooms.

Marine Parade   STREET
Napier's elegant seaside avenue is lined with huge Norfolk Island pines, and dotted with motels and charming timber villas. Along its length are parks, quirky **sunken gardens** (Map p318), a minigolf course, skate park, sound shell, swim centre and aquarium.

Near the north end of the parade is the **Tom Parker Fountain** (Map p318), best viewed at night when it's lavishly lit. Next to it is the **Pania of the Reef** (Map p318) sculpture, with her dubious boobs.

National Aquarium
of New Zealand   AQUARIUM
(Map p318; www.nationalaquarium.co.nz; 546 Marine Pde; adult/child/family $20/10/54; ⊙9am-5pm, feedings 10am & 2pm) Inside this modern complex with its stingray-inspired roof are piranhas, terrapins, eels, kiwi, tuatara and a whole lotta fish. Snorkellers can swim with sharks ($80), or sign up for a Little Penguin Close Encounter ($60).

Bluff Hill Lookout   LOOKOUT
(Map p318; Lighthouse Rd; ⊙24hr) The convoluted route to the top of Bluff Hill (102m) goes up and down like an elevator on speed (best to drive), but rewards with expansive views across the port. Bring a picnic or some fish and chips.

Napier Urban Food Market   MARKET
(Map p318; www.hawkesbayfarmersmarket.co.nz; Lower Emerson St; ⊙9am-1pm Sat) Score some superfresh local produce: fruit, veggies, bread, coffee, dairy products, honey wine...

Napier

0   500 m
0   0.25 miles

Globe Theatrette (600m);
Crown Hotel (620m)

National Tobacco
Company Building
(920m); Gintrap (1.1km);
Thirsty Whale (1.1km)

Kennedy Park
Resort (1.1km)

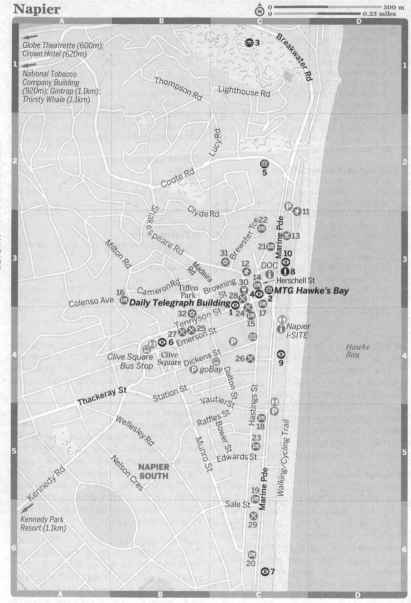

THE EAST COAST NAPIER

Napier Prison   HISTORIC BUILDING
(Map p318; ☏06-835 9933; www.napierprison.
com; 55 Coote Rd; adult/family $20/50; ⊙9am-
5pm) On the run from the law? Assuage
your guilt with a tour of the grim 1906 Napier Prison on the hill behind the town. It's
a self-guided audio set-up, available in 16
languages.

Otatara Pa   ARCHAEOLOGICAL SITE
(Map p316; www.doc.govt.nz; ⊙24hr) FREE
Wooden palisades, carved *pou* (memorial

Napier

⦿ **Top Sights**
1 Daily Telegraph Building.....................C3
2 MTG Hawke's Bay...............................C3

⦿ **Sights**
3 Bluff Hill Lookout C1
4 Deco Centre.......................................C3
5 Napier Prison......................................C2
6 Napier Urban Food Market.................B4
7 National Aquarium of New
    Zealand.. C6
8 Pania of the Reef...............................C3
9 Sunken Gardens C4
10 Tom Parker Fountain C3

⦿ **Activities, Courses & Tours**
11 Fishbike..C3
12 New Zealand Wine Centre C3
13 Ocean Spa...C3

⦿ **Sleeping**
14 Archie's Bunker..................................C3
15 Criterion Art Deco
    Backpackers.................................. C4
16 Green House on the Hill B3
17 Masonic Hotel C3
18 Napier YHA...C5
19 Nautilus..C5
20 Pebble Beach Motor Inn C6
21 Scenic Hotel Te Pania C3
    Sea Breeze B&B.......................... (see 18)
22 Seaview Lodge B&B C3
23 Stables Lodge Backpackers...............C5

⦿ **Eating**
24 Café Ujazi C4
25 Groove Kitchen Espresso B4
26 Kilim...C4
27 Kitchen Table B4
28 Mister D...C3
29 Restaurant Indonesia........................ C6

⦿ **Drinking & Nightlife**
    Emporium.....................................(see 17)
30 Guffle Bar..C3

⦿ **Entertainment**
31 Cabana Bar..C3
32 Napier Municipal Theatre B4

posts) and a carved gate help bring this *pa* site to life. An hour-long loop walk across grassy hills passes barely discernible archaeological remains but affords terrific views of the surrounding countryside. From the city head southwest on Taradale Rd and Gloucester St. Turn right into Springfield Rd just before the river.

🏃 Activities

Napier's pebbly beach isn't safe for swimming; locals head north of the city to **Westshore** (Map p316) or to the surf beaches south of Cape Kidnappers.

Pandora Kayaks   KAYAKING
(Map p316; ☎ 06-835 0684; www.pandorakayaks. co.nz; 53 Pandora Rd; single/double kayaks per hour $15/22, bikes per day $40; ◎ 9am-5pm) On the shore of Pandora Pond, these folks hire out kayaks, surfboards, windsurfers, stand-up paddle boards, small yachts and bikes. Windsurfing and sailing lessons available.

Ocean Spa   SWIMMING
(Map p318; www.oceanspa.co.nz; 42 Marine Pde; adult/child $10.50/7.90, private pools 30min adult/ child $12.50/9.50; ◎ 6am-9.45pm Mon-Sat, 8am-9.45pm Sun) A spiffy waterfront pool complex that features a lane pool, hot pools, a beauty spa and a gym.

New Zealand Wine Centre   WINE TASTING
(Map p318; ☎ 06-835 5326; www.nzwinecentre. co.nz; 1 Shakespeare Rd; tastings 3/6 wines $16/29; ◎ 10am-6pm daily, closed Sun Jun-Aug) No time for a full-blown Hawke's Bay winery tour? Swing by the NZ Wine Centre for a taste of region's best drops on 'Wine Tasting Adventures'.

Mountain Valley   ADVENTURE SPORTS
(☎ 06-834 9756; www.mountainvalley.co.nz; 408 McVicar Rd, Te Pohue; horse treks/rafting/fishing per person from $30/60/250) Sixty kilometres north of Napier on SH5, Mountain Valley is a hub of outdoorsy action: horse trekking, white-water rafting, kayaking and fly fishing. There's also accommodation on site (sites/dorms/doubles from $12/22/70).

☞ Tours

See also p315 for bike-tour info.

Absolute de Tours   BUS TOUR
(☎ 06-844 8699; www.absolutedetours.co.nz) Bus tours of the city, Marewa and Bluff Hill ($40) in conjunction with the Deco Centre, plus half-day tours of Napier and Hastings ($60).

Ferg's Fantastic Tours   GUIDED TOUR, WINE
(☎ 0800 428 687; www.fergstours.co.nz; tours $40-120) Tours from two to seven hours, exploring Napier and surrounding areas: wineries, Te Mata Peak, lookouts and foodie stops.

Hawke's Bay Scenic Tours   GUIDED TOUR
(☎ 06-844-5693; www.hbscenictours.co.nz; tours from $50) A grape-coloured bunch of tour

options including the 'Napier Whirlwind' and wineries.

Bay Tours & Charters
GUIDED TOUR, WINE

(206-845 2736; www.baytours.co.nz; tours from $40) Family-friendly tours, including a two-hour 'Napier Highlights' tour and a three-hour 'Best of the Bay' jaunt.

Packard Promenade
GUIDED TOUR

(206-835 0022; www.packardpromenades.co.nz; tours up to 4 people from $150) Offers deco and wine tours in a sassy 1939 Packard Six vintage car.

Festivals & Events

Art Deco Weekend
CULTURE

(www.artdeconapier.com) In the third week of February, Napier and Hastings cohost the sensational Art Deco Weekend. Around 200 events fill the week (dinners, picnics, dances, balls, bands, Gatsby-esque fancy dress), many of which are free. Bertie, Napier's art-deco ambassador, is omnipresent.

Sleeping

Napier YHA
HOSTEL $

(Map p318; 206-835 7039; www.yha.co.nz; 277 Marine Pde; dm/s/d from $26/45/69; @🛜) Napier's friendly YHA is housed in a lovely old timber beachfront villa with a seemingly endless ramble of rooms. There's a fabulous overhanging reading nook and a sunny rear courtyard. Staff can help with bookings and local info. A solid choice.

Criterion Art Deco Backpackers
HOSTEL $

(Map p318; 206-835 2059; www.criterionartdeco.co.nz; 48 Emerson St; dm/d/f from $26/85/120; @🛜) New owners are spending a lot of money sprucing up this 1st-floor, ruby-red downtown hostel – Napier's best Spanish Mission specimen – which has a beaut little balcony over Emerson St and an amazing old fireplace in the lounge area. A super-charming hostel on the way back up.

Kennedy Park Resort
HOLIDAY PARK $

(Map p316; 206-843 9126, 0800 457 275; www.kennedypark.co.nz; 1 Storkey St; sites from $46, cabins & units $61-227; @🛜🏊) Less a camping ground and more an entire suburb of holidaymakers, this complex is top dog on the Napier camping scene. It's the closest camping ground to town (2.5km out, south-west of the centre) and has every facility imaginable, and a swath of cabin and unit configurations. And a karaoke machine!

Archie's Bunker
HOSTEL $

(Map p318; 20800 272 443, 06-833 7990; www.archiesbunker.co.nz; 14 Herschell St; dm/s/d from $25/35/62; @🛜) One street back from the foreshore, Archie's is a shipshape modern hostel filling an old office building. It's a quiet and secure arrangement with friendly owners and bike hire. A few rooms are windowless, but well ventilated. Massive DVD library for quiet nights in.

Stables Lodge Backpackers
HOSTEL $

(Map p318; 206-835 6242; www.stableslodge.co.nz; 370 Hastings St; dm/s/d from $25/55/69; 🛜) Formerly an actual stables, this is an atmospheric, affable place to get off your horse, with hippie vibes, a barbecue courtyard, murals, saddles festooned around the place and free wi-fi.

★ Seaview Lodge B&B
B&B $$

(Map p318; 206-835 0202; www.aseaviewlodge.co.nz; 5 Seaview Tce; s $130-140, d $170; 🛜) This grand Victorian villa (1890) is queen of all she surveys – which is most of the town and a fair bit of ocean. The elegant rooms have tasteful period elements and either bathroom or en suite. It's hard to resist a sunset tipple on the verandah, which opens off the relaxing guest lounge. Free wi-fi and off-street parking a bonus.

Pebble Beach Motor Inn
MOTEL $$

(Map p318; 20800 723 224, 06-835 7496; www.pebblebeach.co.nz; 445 Marine Pde; d/f from $145/165; 🛜) Unlike the majority of NZ motels, this one is owner-operated (they own the building, rather than lease it from a higher power) – so maintenence and service top the list of staff priorities. There are 25 immaculate rooms over three levels, all with kitchens, spas, balconies and ocean views. Full to capacity most nights.

Green House on the Hill
B&B $$

(Map p318; 206-835 4475; www.the-green-house.co.nz; 18b Milton Rd; s/d $110/135; 🛜) This meat-free '70s B&B is up a steep hill and rewards with leafy surrounds and magical city 'n' sea views. The guest floor has two bedrooms, one with an en suite and one with a private (but separate) bathroom. Home-baked goodies and fine herbal teas are likely to make an appearance. Great value. Free wi-fi, too.

Masonic Hotel
HOTEL $$

(Map p318; 206-835 8689; www.masonic.co.nz; cnr Tennyson St & Marine Pde; r $179-499; 🛜) The art-deco Masonic is arguably the heart of the old town, its accommodation, restaurants and bars taking up most of a city block. It's undergoing a gradual but much-needed refurb, and is shaping up nicely around its charming old bones. The cheaper 'original' rooms are unrefurbished, but still decent. Good online discounts and free wi-fi.

Rocks Motorlodge
MOTEL $$
(Map p316; ☑06-835 9626; www.therocksmotel. co.nz; 27 Meeanee Quay, Westshore; units $110-180; ☎) Just 80m from the beach, the Rocks has corrugated and mosaic stylings that have raised the bar on Westshore's motel row. Interiors are plush with colour splashes: some have spa baths, others clawfoot baths. Free internet, free gym, and a laundry for grubby road warriors.

Nautilus
HOTEL $$
(Map p318; ☑06-974 6550, 0508 628 845; www. nautilusnapier.co.nz; 387 Marine Pde; d/apt from $175/300; ☎) A newish, two-storey waterfront number with views from every room, kitchenettes, mod-deco decor, spa baths, private balconies and an in-house restaurant (not that you'll need it in Napier). Apartments sleep up to six.

Sea Breeze B&B
B&B $$
(Map p318; ☑06-835 8067; www.seabreezebnb. co.nz; 281 Marine Pde; s/d from $100/110; ☎) Inside this Victorian seafront earthquake survivor (1906) are three richly coloured themed rooms (Chinese, Indian and Turkish), decorated with a cornucopia of artefacts. A tad over-the-top perhaps, but there's free wi-fi and the price and location are right. Self-serve continental breakfast is included.

Scenic Hotel Te Pania
HOTEL $$$
(Map p318; ☑06-833 7733; www.scenichotels. co.nz; 45 Marine Pde; d/1-bedroom/2-bedroom from $185/255/400; @☎) Looking like a mini UN HQ by-the-sea, the refurbished, curvilicious, six-storey Te Pania has instant retro appeal. Rooms are far from retro, however, with designer linen, leather lounges and floor-to-ceiling windows that slide open for chestfuls of sea air.

Crown Hotel
HOTEL $$$
(Map p316; ☑06-833 8300; www.thecrownnapier.co.nz; cnr Bridge St & Hardinge Rd, Ahuriri; d/1-bedroom/apt from $189/199/400; @☎) The conversion of this 1932 pub into a ritzy apartment-style hotel must have broken a few fishermen's hearts. The new wing features muted tones, nice wallpaper and linen and super sea views. Bike hire available.

🍴 Eating

Groove Kitchen Espresso
CAFE $
(Map p318; www.groovekitchen.co.nz; 112 Tennyson St; meals $9-19; ☺8am-2pm Mon-Fri, 8.30am-2pm Sat & Sun; ☑) A sophisticated cafe squeezed into small, groovy space where the turntable spins and the kitchen cranks out A1 brunch along with trendsetting wraps, baps, salads and killer coffee. With a bit of luck you'll be around for one of the intermittent Thursday-night gigs.

Café Ujazi
CAFE $
(Map p318; www.facebook.com/ujazicafe; 28 Tennyson St; snacks $4-10, meals $9-19; ☺8am-5pm; ☑) The most bohemian of Napier's cafes, Ujazi folds back its windows and lets the alternative vibes spill out onto the pavement. It's a long-established, consistent performer offering blackboard meals and hearty counter food. Try the classic *rewana* special – a big breakfast on traditional Maori bread. Impressive tea menu.

Kitchen Table
CAFE $
(Map p318; www.pghb.co.nz/page/cafe; 138 Tennyson St; brunch $8-19; ☺breakfast & lunch; ☎) Sharing an airy gallery space with a local photography studio, this colourful and crafty cafe produces classic fare ('homemade loveliness'), traipsing from scones to goats' cheese salad. Plenty to inspire, both on the walls and on the menu. Love the tattoo-esque sign and kooky internal ephemera. Free wi-fi.

Westshore Fish Café
FISH & CHIPS $
(Map p316; ☑06-834 0227; 112 Charles St, Westshore; takeaway $7-12, meals $14-28; ☺5-8pm Tue & Wed, 11.30am-2pm & 5-8pm Thu-Sun) If you're the type who needs cutlery, sit-down meals are served in the dining room here. Otherwise, grab some takeaway fish and chips and attract gulls down at the beach.

Kilim
TURKISH $
(Map p318; ☑06-835 9100; 193 Hastings St; meals $10-17; ☺11am-9pm Sun-Thu, to 9.30pm Fri & Sat; ☑) An authentic Turkish cafe, adorned with suitably Ottoman cushions and wall hangings. The kebabby, felafelly, saladly meals are fresh and tasty, but service can be a tad sluggish. Hair-straightening Turkish coffee.

★ Mister D
MODERN NZ $$
(Map p318; ☑06-835 5022; www.misterd.co.nz; 47 Tennyson St; mains lunch $15-29, dinner $25-29;

⊘7.30am-4pm Sun-Wed, to late Thu-Sun) This long, floorboardy room with its green-tiled bar is the pride of the Napier foodie scene. Hip and stylish but not unaffordable, with quick-fire service delivering the likes of pulled pork with white polenta or chunky corn fritters with bacon and maple syrup. Novelty of the Year award: donuts served with syringes full of chocolate, jam or custard (DIY injecting). Superpopular – bookings essential.

Restaurant Indonesia   INDONESIAN $$
(Map p318; ☑06-835 8303; www.restaurantindonesia.co.nz; 409 Marine Pde; mains $20-27; ⊘5.30-9pm; ⊘) Crammed with Indonesian curios, this intimate space oozes authenticity. Lip-smacking Indo-Dutch *rijsttafel* smorgasbords are the house speciality (14 dishes, $30 to $36) – a romantic option for those in the mood. Bookings advisable.

🍷 Drinking & Nightlife

★Emporium   BAR
(Map p318; www.emporiumbar.co.nz; Masonic Hotel, cnr Tennyson St & Marine Pde; ⊘7am-late; 🛜) Napier's most civilised bar, Emporium, with it' marble-topped bar, fab art-deco details and old-fashioned relics strewn about, is super-atmospheric. Brisk staff, creative cocktails, good coffee, NZ wines, bistro fare (plates $15 to $30) and prime location seal the deal.

Guffle Bar   BAR
(Map p318; www.guffle.co.nz; 29A Hastings St; ⊘4pm-late Tue-Fri, 6pm-late Sat) Cool tunes, stylin' drinks, genial pros behind the bar, and an on-display window seat: ingredients that lure Napier's nocturnal sophisticates through the doors.

Gintrap   PUB
(Map p316; www.gintrap.co.nz; 64 West Quay, Ahuriri; ⊘11am-late Mon-Fri, 9.30am-late Sat & Sun) The pick of the big rambling restaurant-bars out on the Ahuriri waterfront, where the city council is endeavouring to isolate noisy after-dark crowds. Seafood in the sunshine (mains $19 to $32).

Thirsty Whale   BAR
(Map p316; www.thethirstywhale.co.nz; 62 West Quay, Ahuriri; ⊘11am-late Mon-Fri, 9am-late Sat & Sun; 🛜) Does a whale drink? Or just filter krill? Either way, this big dockside bar is a sporty spot to join some fellow mammals for a brew or a bite (mains $14 to $34). Becomes a dance club on Friday and Saturday nights.

☆ Entertainment

Napier Municipal Theatre   THEATRE
(Map p318; ☑06-835 1059; www.napiermunicipaltheatre.co.nz; 119 Tennyson St; ⊘box office 9am-5pm Mon-Fri, to 12.30pm Sat) Not only the city's largest venue for the likes of rock concerts, dance and drama (1000 seats), but also one of the world's few working art-deco theatres. Worth going for the original foyer lighting alone! Box office on site.

Globe Theatrette   CINEMA
(Map p316; ☑06-833 6011; www.globenapier.co.nz; 15 Hardinge Rd, Ahuriri; tickets $16; ⊘1pm-late Wed-Sun, plus 6pm-late Tue Dec-Feb) A vision in purple, this boutique 45-seat cinema screens art-house flicks in a sumptuous cinema lounge with ready access to upmarket snacks and drinks.

Cabana Bar   LIVE MUSIC
(Map p318; ☑06-835 1102; www.cabana.net.nz; 11 Shakespeare Rd; ⊘6pm-late Wed-Sat) This legendary music venue of the '70s, '80s and '90s died in 1997, but thanks to some forward-thinking, toe-tapping folk, it's risen from the grave to save the day for Napier's gig lovers.

ℹ Information

DOC (Department of Conservation; Map p318; ☑06-834 3111; www.doc.govt.co.nz; 59 Marine Pde; ⊘9am-4.15pm Mon-Fri) Maps, advice and passes.

Napier Health Centre (☑06-878 8109; www.hawkesbay.health.nz; 76 Wellesley Rd; ⊘24hr) Round-the-clock medical assistance.

Napier i-SITE (Map p318; ☑06-834 1911; www.napiernz.co.nz; 100 Marine Pde; ⊘9am-5pm, extended hours Dec-Feb; 🛜) Handy and helpful.

Napier Police Station (☑06-831 0700; www.police.govt.nz; 77 Station St; ⊘24hr)

Napier Post Office (Map p318; www.nzpost.co.nz; Shop 9-12 Ocean Boulevard, Dickens St; ⊘9am-5pm Mon-Fri, 9am-4pm Sat, 10am-2pm Sun)

ℹ Getting There & Away

AIR

Hawke's Bay Airport (Map p316; www.hawkes-bay-airport.co.nz) is 8km north of the city.

Air New Zealand (☑06-833 5400; www.airnewzealand.co.nz; cnr Hastings & Station Sts; ⊘9am-5pm Mon-Fri, to noon Sat) runs direct flights to/from Auckland, Wellington and Christchurch. Sunair Aviation has direct weekday flights between Napier, Gisborne and Hamilton

BUS

InterCity buses can be booked online or at the i-SITE, and depart from the **Clive Square Bus Stop** (Map p318). Services run daily to Auckland ($82, 7½ hours) via Taupo ($33, two hours); Gisborne ($43, four hours) via Wairoa ($27, 2½ hours); and Wellington ($40, 5½ hours); plus four daily services to Hastings ($22, 30 minutes).

Naked Bus daily destinations include Wellington ($20, 5½ hours) via Palmerston North ($10, 2½ hours); and Auckland ($25, eight hours) via Taupo ($10, two hours).

ℹ Getting Around

Most key sights in the city are reachable on foot, or you can speed things up by hiring a bicycle from Fishbike (p315).

BUS

goBay (Map p318; ☑ 06-878 9250; www.hbrc. govt.nz) local buses (fitted with bike racks!) run many times daily between Napier, Hastings and Havelock North. Napier to Hastings (adult/ child $5.20/2.80) takes 30 minutes (express) or 55 minutes (all stops). Buses depart Dalton St Bus Stop.

CAR

See www.rentalcars.com for car-hire deals with companies at Hawke's Bay Airport, including the big brands and local outfits. **Rent-a-Dent** (☑ 0800 736 823, 06-834 0688; www. napiercarrentals.co.nz; Hawke's Bay Airport; ☺ 8am-5pm Mon-Fri, to 1pm Sat) is also at the airport.

TAXI

A city-to-airport taxi costs around $22.
Hawke's Bay Combined Taxis (☑ 0800 627 437, 06-835 7777; www.hawkes-bay.blue-bubbletaxi.co.nz)
Super Shuttle (☑ 06-835 0055, 0800 748 885; www.supershuttle.co.nz; 1 way $20, extra person $5) Airport to Napier door-to-door.

Hastings, Havelock North & Around

POP 73,250

Positioned at the centre of the Hawke's Bay fruit bowl, busy Hastings is the commercial hub of the region, 20km south of Napier. A few kilometres of orchards still separate it from Havelock North, with its prosperous village atmosphere and the towering backdrop of Te Mata Peak.

◉ Sights & Activities

As with Napier, Hastings was similarly devastated by the 1931 earthquake and also boasts some fine art-deco and Spanish Mission buildings, built in the aftermath. Main-street highlights include the **Westerman's Building** (Map p324; cnr Russell & Heretaunga St E, Hastings), arguably the Bay's best example of the Spanish Mission style, although there are myriad architectural gems here. The i-SITE stocks the *Art Deco Hastings* brochure ($1), detailing two self-guided walks.

Te Mata Peak　　　　　　　　　　PARK
(www.tematapark.co.nz) Rising melodramatically from the Heretaunga Plains 16km south of Havelock North, Te Mata Peak (399m) is part of the 98-hectare **Te Mata Trust Park**. The summit road passes sheep trails, rickety fences and vertigo-inducing stone escarpments, cowled in a bleak, lunar-meets-Scottish-Highland atmosphere. From the **lookout** (Map p316) on a clear day, views fall away to Hawke Bay, Mahia Peninsula and distant Mt Ruapehu.

The park's trails offer walks from 30 minutes to two hours: pick up the *Te Mata Trust Park* brochure from local i-SITEs.

Hastings City Art Gallery　　　　GALLERY
(HCAG; Map p324; www.hastingscityartgallery.co.nz; 201 Eastbourne St E, Hastings; ☺ 10am-4.30pm) **FREE** The city's gallery presents contemporary NZ and international art in a bright, purpose-built space. Expect some wacky stuff (much wackier than Hastings itself...).

Hastings Farmers Market　　FARMERS MARKET
(Map p316; www.hawkesbayfarmersmarket.co.nz; Showgrounds, Kenilworth Rd; ☺ 8.30am-12.30pm Sun) If you're around on Sunday, the Hastings market is mandatory. Bring an empty stomach, some cash and a roomy shopping bag.

Splash Planet　　　　　　　SWIMMING
(Map p316; ☑ 06-873 8033; www.splashplanet. co.nz; Grove Rd, Hastings; adult/child $26/18; ☺ 10am-5.30pm Nov-Feb) A massive, watery wonderland with myriad pools, slides and aquatic distractions.

Airplay Paragliding　　　　PARAGLIDING
(☑ 06-845 1977; www.airplay.co.nz; 1-day courses $220) Te Mata Peak is a paragliding hot spot, with updraughts aplenty. Airplay offers full-day beginners' courses if you're keen to take the drop.

Hastings

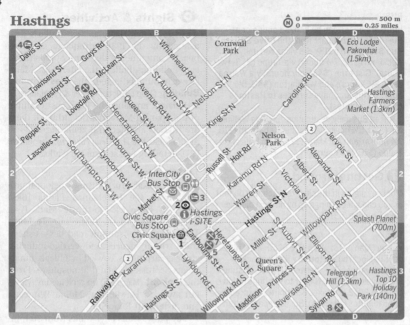

Hastings

◎ Sights
1 Hastings City Art Gallery B3
2 Westerman's Building B2

🛏 Sleeping
3 Rotten Apple..B2
4 Sleeping Giant A1

✕ Eating
5 Opera Kitchen C3
6 Rush Munro's A1
7 Taste Cornucopia C3
8 Vidal...D3

☞ Tours

See p315 for two-wheeled tours around the area.

Long Island Guides   GUIDED TOUR
(☏06-874 7877; www.longislandtoursnz.com; half-day from $180) Customised tours across a wide range of interests including Maori culture, bush walks, kayaking, horse riding and, inevitably, food and wine.

Prinsy's Tours   WINE
(☏0800 004 237, 06-845 3703; www.prinsyexperience.co.nz; half-/full-day tours from $60/85) Affable half- or full-day wine jaunts, with layman's-lingo explanations at four or five wineries.

Waimarama Tours   CULTURAL TOUR
(☏021 057 0935; www.waimaramaori.com; 2-4hr tours from $70) Maori-run tours of Te Mata Peak, with plenty of cultural insights en route.

Grape Escape   WINE
(☏0800 100 489; www.grapeescape.net.nz; tours from $70) Half-day winery tours, visiting four or five cellar doors, or six hours with a lunch stop ($90). Ask about beer tours if you're more of an ale hound.

✲ Festivals & Events

Hastings Blossom Festival   CULTURE
(www.blossomfestival.co.nz) The Hastings Blossom Festival is a petalled spring fling, infamous for its 12-person 'riot' in 1960. The flowery insubordination happens in the second half of September: parades, arts, crafts and visiting artists.

🛏 Sleeping

Hastings Top 10 Holiday Park   HOLIDAY PARK $
(Map p316; ☏06-878 6692; www.hastingstop10.co.nz; 610 Windsor Ave, Hastings; sites from $44, units $78-160, apt $300; @🐾🛜🏊) Putting the 'park' back into holiday park, within its leafy

confines are sycamore hedges, a topiary 'welcome' sign, stream, ducks and accessible serenity. The pool and spa complex satisfies young and old. New tennis court.

Eco Lodge Pakowhai
HOSTEL $

(Map p316; ☎06-876 6997, 027 298 8910; www.ecolodge-pakowhai.co.nz; 1000 Pakowhai Rd; sites/dm/tw $20/25/60, d with/without bathroom $75/60; 🛜) 🐾 The same family have tilled this land since 1885, but the attitude here is very forward-thinking. The talkative owner cuts carbon with solar panels, rainwater-collection systems, worm farms, double-glazing...and is expert at finding farm work for travellers. Accommodation comprises neat new cabins or dorms in an old farmhouse. Good weekly rates; free wi-fi and laundry.

Rotten Apple
HOSTEL $

(Map p324; ☎06-878 4363; www.rottenapple.co.nz; 114 Heretaunga St E, Hastings; dm/s/d $26/50/70; @🛜) The central city, 1st-floor option and a fairly fruity affair, with orchard workers settled in paying weekly rates. There's a bit of deck, a decent kitchen and sociable vibes, and staff can help you find work (sorting the rotten apples from the good ones).

Sleeping Giant
HOSTEL $

(Map p324; ☎06-878 5393; www.hastingsbackpackers.co.nz; 109 Davis St, Hastings; dm/tw/d $20/50/60; @🛜) A messy-but-homey backpackers in a suburban house, a 10-minute walk to town. A posse of tanned, wiry agricultural workers ensures a sociable atmosphere in the fairly close communal confines. Pool table in the shed.

★Clive Colonial Cottages
RENTAL HOUSE $$

(Map p316; ☎06-870 1018; www.clivecolonialcottages.co.nz; 198 School Rd, Clive; d from $135; 🛜) A two-minute walk to the beach and almost equidistant from Hastings, Napier and Havelock, these three tasteful kitchen cottages encircle a courtyard garden on a 2-acre spread. Communal areas include barbecue, giant chess set and snooker room. Bikes on site; trail on doorstep.

Havelock North Motor Lodge
MOTEL $$

(Map p316; ☎06-877 8627; www.havelocknorthmotorlodge.co.nz; 7 Havelock Rd, Havelock North; units $135-195; 🛜) Smack-bang in the middle of Havelock North, this modern motel is a cut above the rest. Tidy one- and two-bedroom units feature spa baths, nice art and kitchenettes. Is the new Mexican joint across the street open yet?

Millar Road
RENTAL HOUSE $$$

(Map p316; ☎06-875 1977; www.millarroad.co.nz; 83 Millar Rd, Hastings; villas/houses from $400/650; 🛜❄) Set in the Tuki Tuki Hills with vineyard and bay views, Millar Road is architecturally heaven-sent. Two plush villas (each sleep four) and a superstylish house (sleeps eight) are filled with NZ-made furniture and local artworks. Explore the 20-hectare grounds or look cool by the pool.

Mangapapa Petit Hotel
BOUTIQUE HOTEL $$$

(Map p316; ☎06-878 3234; www.mangapapa.co.nz; 466 Napier Rd, Havelock North; d incl breakfast $450-1500; @🛜❄) A five-minute drive from Hastings, this heritage home (1885), surrounded by leafy gardens, a tennis court, swimming pool and short golf course, has been sympathetically adapted into a boutique hotel. Twelve suites offer period-style luxury; a restaurant and day spa up the indulgence stakes. 'Good afternoon Sir', says the dapper doorman.

✕ Eating

Taste Cornucopia
CAFE $

(Map p324; www.tastecornucopia.co.nz; 219 Heretaunga St E, Hastings; meals $7-22; ⊙7.30am-4pm Mon-Fri, 6.30pm-late Fri; 🍴) 🐾 An award-winning, high-ceilinged organic cafe in central Hastings, serving filling 'abundant' breakfasts, organic coffee, smoked-fish pies, curries, vegtarian lasagne and amazing 'marshmallows' that look like giant blobs of extruded toothpaste. Super NZ wine list, too. Tasty dinners Friday nights.

Bay Espresso
CAFE $

(Map p316; 19 Middle Rd, Havelock North; mains $10-19; ⊙7.30am-4pm Mon-Fri, 8am-4pm Sat & Sun) On Middle Rd in the middle of Havelock, this enduringly popular cafe is far from middling, serving up house-roasted organic coffee, handsome counter food and reasonable brunch. Blaring Freddie Mercury and blueberry pancakes – a winning combo.

Rush Munro's
ICE CREAM $

(Map p324; www.rushmunro.co.nz; 704 Heretaunga St W, Hastings; ice cream $3-8; ⊙11am-6pm Mon-Fri, to 7pm Sat & Sun, reduced winter hours) Rush Munro's is a Hastings icon, serving locally made ice cream since 1926. Try the maple walnut.

★Opera Kitchen
CAFE $$

(Map p324; www.operakitchen.co.nz; 312 Eastbourne St E, Hastings; mains $9-25; ⊙7.30am-4pm

Mon-Fri, 9am-3pm Sat & Sun; 🎵) Set your rudder right with some whiskey porridge with cream and giant oats at this mod, stylish cafe abutting Hawke's Bay Opera House. For a more practical start to the day, the farmers breakfast is also a winner. Heavenly baked goods, great coffee and snappy staff. Eat in, or outside in the suntrap courtyard.

Deliciosa
TAPAS **$$**

(Map p316; 📞 06-877 6031; www.deliciosa.co.nz; 21 Napier Rd, Havelock North; tapas $8-19; ⏱ 4pm-late Mon & Tue, 11am-late Wed-Sat) Great things come in small packages at this rosy little tapas bar, run by a displaced Seattleite. The kitchen delivers sassy, locally sourced edibles like pork belly with pomegranate jus and salt-and-pepper squid with orange and parsley, while the wine list roams from Spain to Italy and back. Terrific beer list, too.

Pipi
PIZZERIA **$$**

(Map p316; 📞 06-877 8993; www.pipicafe.co.nz; 16 Joll Rd, Havelock North; mains $16-28; ⏱ 4-10pm Tue-Sun) Shockingly pink with candy stripes and mismatched furniture, Pipi cheekily thumbs its nose at small-town conventionality. The food focus is on simple pasta dishes and Roman-style thin-crusted pizza. Pipi **Bar** is across the street if you're waiting for a table, and **Pipi Truck** randomly turns up around the Bay, taking the food to the streets (check Facebook for locations).

Diva
MODERN NZ **$$**

(Map p316; 📞 06-877 5149; www.divabar.co.nz; 10 Napier Rd, Havelock North; mains lunch $16-20, dinner $22-35; ⏱ 11.30am-2.30pm Tue-Fri, 5.30pm-late Tue-Sat) A sexy fusion of orange, black and chocolately timber, Diva offers good-value lunches (from paua bugers to steaks) and bistro-style dinners featuring fresh seafood and seasonal specialities. Eat in the flashy dining room, at the groovy bar (small plates $5 to $17) or chatty pavement tables.

Vidal
MODERN NZ **$$$**

(Map p324; 📞 06-872 7440; www.vidal.co.nz; 913 St Aubyn St E, Hastings; mains lunch $25-29, dinner $28-36; ⏱ 11.30am-3pm & 6pm-late) There's nothing suburban about this winery restaurant on the backstreets of Hastings. The warm, wood-lined dining room is a worthy setting for such elegant food: order the annual signature dish (2013 market fish, 2014 venison), sip some syrah and feel your holiday come to fruition.

HAWKE'S BAY WINERIES

Once upon a time, this district was most famous for its orchards. Today it's vines that have top billing, with Hawke's Bay now NZ's second-largest wine-producing region. Expect excellent Bordeaux-style reds, syrah and chardonnay. Pick up the *Hawke's Bay Winery Guide* map from the i-SITE, or download it from www.winehawkesbay.co.nz. A few of our faves:

Black Barn Vineyards (Map p316; 📞 06-877 7985; www.blackbarn.com; Black Barn Rd, Havelock North; ⏱ 9am-5pm Mon-Fri, 10am-5pm Sat & Sun) Hip, inventive winery with a bistro, gallery, Saturday farmers market (one of NZ's first) and an amphitheatre for concerts and movie screenings. Try the flagship chardonnay.

Crab Farm Winery (Map p316; 📞 06-836 6678; www.crabfarmwinery.co.nz; 511 Main North Rd, Bay View; ⏱ 10am-5pm daily, 6pm-late Fri) Decent, reasonably priced wines and a great cafe with regular live troubadors and relaxed, rustic vibes. A good stop for lunch or a glass of rosé (or both).

Mission Estate (Map p316; 📞 06-845 9354; www.missionestate.co.nz; 198 Church Rd, Taradale; ⏱ 9am-5pm Mon-Sat, 10am-4.30pm Sun) NZ's oldest winery (1851!). Follow the *looong* tree-lined drive up to the restaurant and cellar door, inside a magnificently restored seminary.

Te Mata Estate (Map p316; www.temata.co.nz; 349 Te Mata Rd, Havelock North; ⏱ 8.30am-5pm Mon-Fri, 10am-5pm Sat) 🍷 The legendary Coleraine red at this unpretentious, old-school, family-run winery is worth the trip alone.

Craggy Range (Map p316; 📞 06-873 0141; www.craggyrange.com; 253 Waimarama Rd, Havelock North; ⏱ 10am-6pm, closed Mon & Tue Apr-Oct) Inside a cathedral-like 'wine barrel', the restaurant here, called Terroir, is one of the region's most consistent fine-dining experiences. Photogenic views of craggy Te Mata Peak.

🍷 Drinking

Loading Ramp
BAR

(Map p316; www.loadingramp.co.nz; 8 Treachers Lane, Havelock North; ⊙3pm-late Tue-Sat) This lofty timber space pulls a mixed crowd of young 'uns and seasoned drinkers, here to watch the All Blacks on the big screen, sip Monteith's or chew tapas (or all three). Also offers big pubby meals (mains $22 to $30).

Filter Room
BREWERY

(Map p316; www.thefilterroom.co.nz; Awatoto Rd, Meeanee; ⊙10am-5pm Sun-Thu, to 7pm Fri & Sat) Surrounded by orchards, these folks proffer impressive craft beers and ciders, brewed on site, plus tasting trays and belly-filling food.

Rose & Shamrock
PUB

(Map p316; www.roseandshamrock.co.nz; cnr Napier Rd & Porter Dr, Havelock North; ⊙10.30am-late) A carpeted, dark-wood, Brit-style boozer complete with 27 globe-trotting beers on tap (*oooh*, Coopers Sparkling Ale from South Australia!) and hearty pub grub (mains $14 to $26).

🛍 Shopping

The Hastings area appears to exist largely for the satisfaction of our appetites, with a plethora of boutique food producers.

Strawberry Patch
FOOD

(Map p316; www.strawberrypatch.co.nz; 76 Havelock Rd, Havelock North; ⊙9am-5.30pm) Pick your own berries in season (late November through summer), or visit year-round for fresh produce, picnic supplies, coffee and real fruit ice cream ($4).

Arataki Honey
FOOD

(Map p316; www.aratakihoneyhb.co.nz; 66 Arataki Rd, Havelock North; ⊙9am-5pm) 🐝 Stock up on buzzy by-products for your toast or your skin at family-run Arataki. Hands-on displays outline the whole sticky cycle from flower to jar. Free tastings.

Telegraph Hill
FOOD

(Map p316; www.telegraphhill.co.nz; 1279 Howard St, Hastings; ⊙9am-5pm Mon-Fri, plus 10am-3pm Sat Oct-Mar) A passionate producer of olives, oils and sundry Mediterranean-inspired gourmet treats. Four-person picnic baskets ($40) available for on-site indulgence.

Silky Oak Chocolate Company
FOOD

(Map p316; www.silkyoakchocs.co.nz; 1131 Links Rd, Napier; ⊙9am-5pm Mon-Thu, 9am-4pm Fri, 10am-4pm Sat & Sun) Watch the chocolatiers at work while deliberating over mouthwatering truffles and chocolate rugby balls. The museum (adult/child $8/5) offers a cocoa-drenched history and the odd ancient Mayan artefact. There's a cafe here too.

ℹ Information

Hastings i-SITE (Map p324; ☑06-873 0080; www.visithastings.co.nz; Westermans Bldg, cnr Russell St & Heretaunga St E; ⊙9am-5pm Mon-Fri, 9am-3pm Sat, 10am-2pm Sun; 🛜) Internet access, free maps, trail brochures and bookings.

Havelock North i-SITE (Map p316; ☑06-877 9600; www.havelocknorthnz.com; cnr Te Aute & Middle Rds, Havelock North; ⊙10am-5pm Mon-Fri, to 4pm Sat, to 3pm Sun; 🛜) Local info in a cute little booth.

Hawke's Bay Hospital (☑06-878 8109; www.hawkesbay.health.nz; Omahu Rd; ⊙24hr)

Police Station (☑06-873 0500; www.police.govt.nz; 205 Railway Rd; ⊙24hr)

Post Office (Map p324; www.nzpost.co.nz; 100 Market St; ⊙8.30am-5pm Mon-Fri, 9am-noon Sat)

ℹ Getting There & Away

Napier's Hawke's Bay Airport (p322) is a 20-minute drive away. **Air New Zealand** (☑06-873 2200; www.airnewzealand.co.nz; 117 Heretaunga St W; ⊙9am-5pm Mon-Fri) has an office in central Hastings.

Hastings' **InterCity Bus Stop** (Map p324) is on Russell St. Book InterCity and Naked Bus buses online or at the i-SITE.

ℹ Getting Around

goBay (☑06-878 9250; www.hbrc.govt.nz) ocal buses (with bike racks) run between Hastings, Havelock North and Napier. Daily Hastings to Napier buses (adult/child $5.20/2.80) take 30 minutes (express) or 55 minutes (all stops). Hastings to Havelock North buses run Monday to Saturday (adult/child $3.40/1.80, 35 minutes). Buses depart Hastings' **Civic Square Bus Stop** (Map p324).

Hastings Taxis (☑06-878 5055) is the local cab service.

Cape Kidnappers

From mid-September to late April, Cape Kidnappers (named when local Maori tried to kidnap Cook's Tahitian servant boy) erupts with squawking gannets. These big birds usually nest on remote islands but here they settle for the mainland, completely unfazed by human spectators.

The birds nest as soon as they arrive, and eggs take about six weeks to hatch, with chicks arriving in early November. In March the gannets start their migration; by May they're gone.

Early November to late February is the best time to visit. Take a tour or the walkway to the colony: it's about five hours return from the Clifton Reserve car park ($1) at the Clifton Motor Camp. En route are interesting cliff formations, rock pools, a sheltered picnic spot, and the gaggling gannets themselves. The walk is tide dependent: leave no earlier than three hours after high tide; start back no later than 1½ hours after low tide.

No regular buses go to Clifton, but the tour operators will transport you for an additional fee, or you could bike.

⛟ Tours

Gannet Beach Adventures   ECOTOUR
(Map p316; ☑ 06-8750 898, 0800 426 638; www.gannets.com; 475 Clifton Rd, Clifton; adult/child $42/24) Ride along the beach on a tractor-pulled trailer before wandering out on the Cape for 90 minutes. A good-fun, guided return trip over four hours, departing Clifton Reserve.

Gannet Safaris   ECOTOUR
(Map p316; ☑ 06-875 0888, 0800 427 232; www.gannetsafaris.co.nz; 396 Clifton Rd, Te Awanga; adult/child $60/30) Overland 4WD trips across farmland into the gannet colony. Three-hour tours depart at 9.30am and 1.30pm. Pick-ups from Napier and Hastings cost extra.

Central Hawke's Bay

Grassy farmland stretches south from Hastings, dotted with the grand homesteads of Victorian pastoralists. It's an untourioned area (aka 'Lamb Country'), rich in history and deserted beaches. **Waipukurau** (aka 'Wai-puk'), the main town, isn't exactly thrilling but it's worth calling in to the extremely helpful **Central Hawke's Bay Information Centre** (☑ 06-858 6488; www.lambcountry.co.nz; Railway Esplanade; ☻ 8.30am-4.30pm Mon-Fri, 10am-3pm Sat) in the old railway station.

◉ Sights & Activities

There are no fewer than six windswept beaches along the coast here: **Kairakau, Mangakuri, Pourerere, Aramoana, Blackhead** and **Porangahau**. The first five are good for swimming, and between the lot they offer a range of sandy, salty activities including surfing, fishing and driftwoody, rock-pooly adventures. Between Aramoana and Blackhead Beach lies the DOC-managed **Te Angiangi Marine Reserve** – bring your snorkel.

It's a nondescript hill in the middle of nowhere, but the place with the world's longest name is good for a photo op. Believe it or not, **Taumatawhakatangihangakoauauotamateaturipukakapikimaungahoronukupokaiwhenuakitanatahu** is the abbreviated form of 'The Brow of a Hill Where Tamatea, the Man with the Big Knees, Who Slid, Climbed, and Swallowed Mountains, Known as Land Eater, Played his Flute to his Brother'. To get there, fuel-up in Waipukurau and drive 40km to the Mangaorapa junction on route 52. Turn left and go 4km towards Porangahau. At the intersection with the signposts, turn right and continue 4.3km to the sign.

Ongaonga, a historic village 16km west of Waipawa, has interesting Victorian and Edwardian buildings. Pick up a pamphlet for a self-guided walking tour from the info centre in Waipukurau.

The **Central Hawke's Bay Settlers Museum** (www.chbsettlersmuseum.co.nz; 23 High St, Waipawa; adult/child $2/free; ☻ 10am-4pm) in **Waipawa** has pioneer artefacts, informative 'homestead' displays and a good specimen of a river *waka* (canoe).

⌂ Sleeping

Lochlea Backpacker Farmstay   FARMSTAY, HOSTEL $
(☑ 06-855 4816; www.bbh.co.nz; 344 Lake Rd, Wanstead; dm/s/d/f from $26/37/56/137; ☏ ☒) Far removed from urban stress, this working sheep and cattle farm has breezy stands of trees on grazing slopes. Rooms are simple but the communal lounge is cosy. There's a pool, a tennis court and endless paddocks in which to act sheepish. Free pick-ups from Waipukurau Monday to Friday.

Gwavas Garden Homestead   B&B $$
(☑ 06-856 5810; www.gwavasgarden.co.nz; 5740 SH50, Tikokino; d incl breakfast $160-180; ☏) Six kilometres from Tikokino, this grand 1890 Cornish homestead has enjoyed a faithful room-by-room renovation with floral wallpaper, period furnishings, portraits eyeballing you from the walls and heavy linens. Have breakfast on the veranda before a spot of lawn tennis or a wander through the bird-biased garden.

✖ Eating

Paper Mulberry Café CAFE $
(www.papermulberrycafe.co.nz; SH2, Pukehou; meals $8-17; ⊘7am-4pm Wed-Mon) Halfway between Waipukurau and Hastings, this retro cafe-gallery in a 100-year-old, aquamarine-coloured church serves excellent coffee, smoothies and home-spun food (unbeatable fudge). Well worth a stop for a chomp and a browse.

Misty River Café CAFE $$
(☑06-857 8911; 12 High St, Waipawa; mains $10-20; ⊘9am-4pm Wed-Sun) A little bit of upmarket vintage on the functional high street, this jade-coloured cafe plates up lip-smacking salads as well as corn fritters, pastas, nachos and other faves. Drop-dead-gorgeous baking (try the coconut and lime cake).

❶ Getting There & Away

InterCity and Naked Bus pass through Waipawa and Waipukurau on their Wellington–Napier routes.

Kaweka & Ruahine Ranges

The remote Kaweka and Ruahine ranges separate Hawke's Bay from the Central Plateau. These forested wildernesses offer some of the North Island's best tramping.

See the DOC pamphlets *Kaweka Forest Park & Puketitiri Reserves* and *Eastern Ruahine Forest Park* for details of tracks and huts (both available online at www.doc.govt.nz).

An ancient 136km Maori track, now know as the **Gentle Annie Road**, runs inland from Omahu near Hastings to Taihape, via Otamauri and Kuripapango (where there's a basic but charming DOC campsite, adult/child $6/3). This isolated route takes around three hours (or a couple of days by bike).

Kaweka J, the highest point of the range (1724m), can be reached by a three-to-five-hour tramp from the end of Kaweka Rd; from Napier take Puketitiri Rd then Whittle Rd. The drive is worthwhile in itself; it's partly unsealed and takes three hours return.

Enjoy a soak in natural hot pools before or after the three-hour walk on **Te Puia Track**, which follows the picturesque **Mohaka River**. From Napier, take Puketitiri Rd, then Pakaututu Rd, then Makahu Rd to the road-end **Mangatutu Hot Pools** (www.doc.govt.nz). Parts of the road can be dicey – bring a 4WD if you've got one.

The Mokaha can be rafted with **Mohaka Rafting** (☑06-839 1808; www.mohakarafting.com; from $95).

Wellington Region

Includes ➡

Wellington 332
Kapiti Coast 353
Paekakariki 354
Waikanae & Around ... 355
The Wairarapa 356
Martinborough 357
Cape Palliser 358
Greytown 359
Masterton &
Around 360

Best Places to Eat

➡ Ortega Fish Shack (p347)

➡ Logan Brown (p347)

➡ Ombra (p347)

➡ Duke Carvell's (p347)

➡ Nikau Cafe (p346)

Best Places to Drink

➡ Goldings Free Dive (p348)

➡ Hawthorn Lounge (p349)

➡ Little Beer Quarter (p348)

➡ Havana (p349)

➡ Micro Wine Bar (p358)

Why Go?

If your New Zealand travels thus far have been all about the great outdoors and sleepy rural towns, Wellington will blow the cobwebs away. Art-house cinemas, funky boutiques, hip bars, theatres and lashings of restaurants – all can be found in the 'cultural capital'.

As the crossing point between the North and South Islands, travellers have long been passing through these parts. The likes of Te Papa and Zealandia now stop visitors in their tracks, and even a couple of days' pause will reveal myriad other attractions – a windswept and interesting harbour with a walkable waterfront, hillsides clad in pretty weatherboard houses, ample inner-city surprises and some of the freshest city air on the planet.

Less than an hour away to the north, the Kapiti Coast has a slower, beachy vibe, with Kapiti Island nature reserve a highlight. An hour away over the Rimutaka Range, the Wairarapa farm plains are dotted with quiet towns and famed wineries, hemmed in by a rugged, wild coastline.

When to Go

➡ The capital has its fair share of blustery, cold, grey days, but such conditions prevail only part of the time. 'Windy Welly' breaks out into blue skies and T-shirt temperatures at least several days a year, when you'll hear folk exclaim 'You can't beat Wellington on a good day'.

➡ November to April are the warmer months, with average maximums hovering around 20°C. From May to August it's colder and wetter – daily temperatures lurk around 12°C.

➡ The Kapiti Coast and Wairarapa are a different story – they are both warmer, less windy, with more blue-sky days.

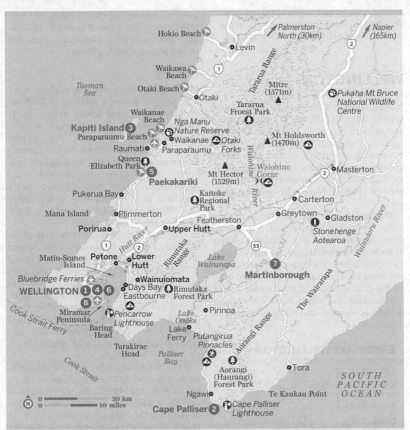

WELLINGTON REGION

Wellington Region Highlights

1 Getting interactive at NZ's finest museum, Wellington's **Te Papa** (p338)

2 Scaling the lighthouse steps on wild and remote **Cape Palliser** (p358)

3 Meeting real live kiwi on a **Kapiti Island** (p354) night-time walk

4 Exploring the capital's creative side around **Cuba Street**

5 Rambling the dunes of **Queen Elizabeth Park** (p354) near beachy **Paekakariki**

6 Riding the ratchety **cable car** (p336) from Lambton Quay to the

leafy **Wellington Botanic Gardens** (p333)

7 Maintaining a straight line on your bicycle as you tour the picturesque **Martinborough wineries** (p357)

8 Discovering hidden shortcuts to surprising lookout points around **hilly Wellington** (p333) city

ⓘ Getting There & Around

Wellington is a major transport hub, being the North Island port for the interisland ferries. Long-distance **KiwiRail Scenic Journeys** (☎ 04-495 0775, 0800 872 467; www.kiwirails-cenic.co.nz) trains run from Wellington to Auckland via Palmerston North. Wellington Airport is serviced by international and domestic airlines.

InterCity (☎ 04-385 0520; www.intercity.co.nz) is the main North Island bus company, travelling just about everywhere. Approaching Wellington city from the north, you'll pass through either the Kapiti Coast to the west via State Hwy1 (SH1), or the Wairarapa and Hutt Valley to the east via State Hwy2 (SH2).

Getting into and out of Wellington on regional trains and buses is a breeze. **Metlink** (☎ 0800

801 700; www.metlink.org.nz) is the one-stop shop for regional transport services, from Wellington to the Kapiti Coast and the Wairarapa.

WELLINGTON

POP 190,950 (CITY), 488,160 (REGION)

A small city with a big reputation, Wellington is most famous for being NZ's constitutional and cultural capital. It is *infamous* for its weather, particularly the gale-force winds wont to barrel through, wrecking umbrellas and obliterating hairdos. It also lies on a major fault line. And negotiating the inner-city one-way system is like the Krypton Factor on acid.

But don't be deterred, for these are mere trifles on Welly's multilayered, jam-packed stand of sweet treats. For starters it's lovely to look at, draped around bushy hillsides encircling a freshly whipped harbour. There are super lookouts on hilltops, golden sand on the promenade, and spectacular craggy shores along the south coast. Downtown, the city is compact and vibrant, buoyed by

WELLINGTON REGION WELLINGTON

ESSENTIAL WELLINGTON

Eat Yourself silly: Wellington has a gut-busting number of great cafes and restaurants; bring trousers with an elasticated waistband

Drink Coffee – espresso, AeroPress, Chemex, siphon, Swissgold, V60...you name it

Read Rousing words along Wellington's waterfront Writers Walk

Listen to Radio New Zealand National (101.3FM, www.radionz.co.nz) – programming for the people

Watch 'Wellington Airport Landings' on YouTube

Festival Summer City (p340) – free fun in the sun, *in theory*

Go green Wairarapa's Pukaha Mt Bruce National Wildlife Centre is home to many species of native bird, as well as eels and tuatara

Online www.wellingtonnz.com, www. naturecoast.co.nz, www.wairarapanz. com; www.lonelyplanet.com/new-zealand/wellington

Area code 04

a decent smattering of museums, theatres, galleries and boutiques. A cocktail-, caffeine- and craft-beer-fuelled hospitality scene fizzes and pops among the throng.

History

Maori legend has it that the explorer Kupe was first to discover Wellington harbour. Wellington's original Maori name was Te Whanganui-a-Tara (great harbour of Tara), named after the son of a chief named Whatonga who had settled on the Hawke's Bay coast. Whatonga sent Tara and his half-brother to explore the southern part of the North Island. When they returned over a year later, their reports were so favourable that Whatonga's followers moved there, founding the Ngati Tara tribe.

The first European settlers arrived in the New Zealand Company's ship *Aurora* on 22 January 1840, not long after Colonel William Wakefield arrived to buy land from the Maori. However, Maori denied they had sold the land at Port Nicholson, or Poneke as they called it, as it was founded on hasty and illegal purchasing by the New Zealand Company. As in many parts of NZ, land rights struggles ensued, and would plague the country for years to come.

By 1850 Wellington was a thriving settlement of around 5500 people, despite a shortage of flat land. Originally the waterfront was along Lambton Quay, but reclamation of parts of the harbour began in 1852. In 1855 a significant earthquake raised many parts of Wellington, including the lower Hutt Valley and the land on which the modern Hutt Rd now runs.

In 1865 the seat of government was moved from Auckland to Wellington, although it took until the turn of the century for the city to really flourish. In the early 1900s the port prospered, while producer boards and banks sprung up in its surrounds. Other industries developed, pushing urban sprawl further afield into the Hutt Valley, Porirua, and the Kapiti Coast.

In modern times, the capital remains a stronghold of the public service, despite ongoing trims. It also boasts a good quotient of technology and creative industries.

◉ Sights

Museum of Wellington City & Sea MUSEUM
(Map p334; www.museumswellington.org.nz; Queens Wharf; ⊙10am-5pm) FREE For an imaginative, interactive experience of Welling-

MAORI NZ: WELLINGTON

In legend the mouth of Maui's Fish, and traditionally known as Te Whanganui-a-Tara, the Wellington area became known to Maori in the mid-19th century as 'Poneke' (a transliteration of Port Nicholas, its European name at the time).

The major *iwi* (tribes) of the region were Te Ati Awa and Ngati Toa. Ngati Toa was the *iwi* of Te Rauparaha, who composed the now famous 'Ka Mate' *haka*. Like most urban areas the city is now home to Maori from many *iwi*, sometimes collectively known as Ngati Poneke.

NZ's national museum, Te Papa (p338), presents excellent displays on Maori culture, traditional and modern, as well as a colourful *marae* (meeting house). In its gift store you can see excellent carving and other crafts, as you can in both Kura (p350) and Ora (p350) galleries nearby.

Kapiti Island Nature Tours (p354) offers an intimate insight into the Maori culture of the Wellington area, as does Kiwi Coastal Tours (p338).

ton's social and salty maritime history, swing into the Museum of Wellington. Highlights include a moving documentary about the tragedy of the *Wahine*, the interisland ferry that sank in the harbour entrance on a terrible, blustery day back in 1968, with a loss of 51 lives. Maori legends are also dramatically told using tiny hologram actors and special effects. The building itself is an old Bond Store dating from 1892.

★ **City Gallery**   GALLERY
(Map p342; www.citygallery.org.nz; Civic Sq, Wakefield St; charges may apply for major exhibits; ⊙10am-5pm) FREE Housed in the monumental old library in Civic Sq, Wellington's much-loved City Gallery does a cracking job of securing acclaimed contemporary international exhibitions, as well as unearthing and supporting those at the forefront of the NZ scene. A packed events calendar and excellent Nikau Cafe (p346) enhance the experience.

Academy Galleries   GALLERY
(Map p334; www.nzafa.com; 1 Queens Wharf; ⊙10am-5pm) FREE The showcase of the New Zealand Academy of Fine Arts, Academy Galleries presents frequently changing exhibitions by NZ artists.

New Zealand Portrait Gallery   GALLERY
(Map p334; www.nzportraitgallery.org.nz; Shed 11, Queens Wharf; ⊙10.30am-4.30pm) FREE Housed in the historic waterfront Shed 11, this gallery presents a diverse range of NZ portraiture from its own collection and frequently changing guest exhibitions.

Parliament House   CULTURAL BUILDING
(Map p334; www.parliament.nz; Bowen St; ⊙tours on the hour 10am-4pm) FREE The austere grey-

and-cream Parliament House was completed in 1922. Free one-hour tours depart from the ground-floor foyer (arrive 15 minutes prior). Next door is the 1899 neo-Gothic Parliamentary Library building, as well as the modernist **Beehive** (Map p334), designed by British architect Sir Basil Spence and built between 1969 and 1980. Controversy surrounded its construction and – love it or loathe it – it's the architectural symbol of the country. Across the road are the **Government Buildings** (Map p334), the largest wooden building in the southern hemisphere, doing a pretty good impersonation of stone.

★ **Mt Victoria Lookout**   LOOKOUT
(Map p334) The city's most accessible viewpoint is on the top of 196m-high Mt Victoria, east of the city centre. You can take the Roseneath bus some of the way up, but the rite of passage is to sweat it out on the walk (ask a local for directions or just follow your nose). If you've got your own wheels, take Oriental Pde along the waterfront and then scoot up Carlton Gore Rd. If this whets your appetite, ask a local how to get to the wind turbine or Mt Kaukau – both higher, better, blinkin' marvellous.

★ **Wellington Botanic Gardens**   GARDENS
(Map p334) FREE The hilly, 25-hectare botanic gardens can be *almost* effortlessly visited via a cable-car ride (nice bit of planning, eh?), although there are several other entrances hidden in the hillsides. They boast a tract of original native forest along with varied collections including a beaut rose garden and international plant collections. Add in fountains, a cheerful playground, sculptures, duck pond, cafe, magical city views and much more, and you've got a grand outing indeed.

Greater Wellington

Wellington Harbour

Wellington-Picton Ferry (Interislander Services)

Interislander

Cruise Ship
Passenger Terminal

Aotea Quay

Westpac
Stadium

Waterloo Quay

Port of Wellington
Container
Terminal

Hutt Rd

Wellington Urban Mwy

Thorndon Quay

Hobson St

Long Distance Bus
Departure Point

Wellington
Railway Station

Bluebridge
Ferries

WADESTOWN

Murphy St

Pipitea St

Local Bus
Terminal

Aitken St

Bunny St

21

Park St

Molesworth St

Kate

Sheppard Pl

Thorndon Quay

10

Wadestown Rd

Tinakori Rd

Hawkestone St

15

THORNDON

14

5

9

Lambton Quay

Grant Rd

Hill St

Bowen St

18

Te Ahumairangi
Hill

Sydney St W

Bolton St

Town
Belt

Northern
Walkway

Lady Norwood
Rose Garden

WILTON

Wilton Rd

13

500 m
0.25 miles

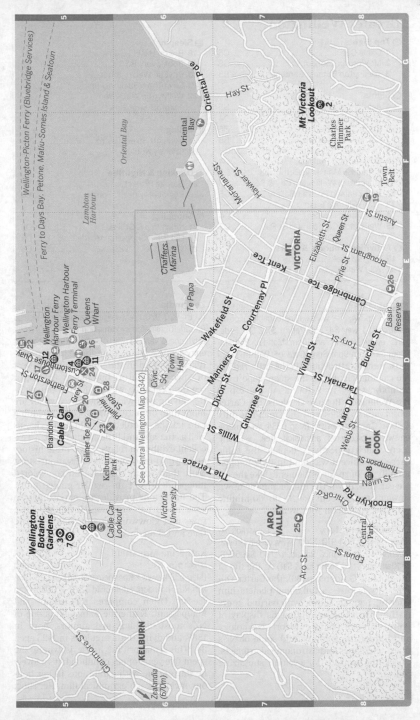

Greater Wellington

◎ Top Sights
1 Cable Car C5
2 Mt Victoria Lookout.............................. G8
3 Wellington Botanic Gardens................ B5

◎ Sights
4 Academy Galleries................................ D5
5 Beehive.. D4
6 Cable Car Museum................................ B5
7 Carter Observatory B5
8 Colonial Cottage Museum.................... C8
9 Government Buildings D4
10 Katherine Mansfield Birthplace D2
11 Museum of Wellington City & Sea....... D5
12 New Zealand Portrait Gallery.............. D5
13 Otari-Wilton's Bush A1
14 Parliament House.................................. D4
15 Wellington Cathedral of St Paul.......... D3

◎ Activities, Courses & Tours
16 Ferg's Kayaks.. D5
17 Wild Winds.. D5

◎ Sleeping
18 Bolton Hotel... C4
19 Booklovers B&B F8
20 CityLife Wellington............................... D5
21 Downtown Backpackers........................ D4
22 Wellington Waterfront
    Motorhome Park D5

◎ Eating
23 Boulcott Street Bistro........................... C5
24 Charley Noble D5

◎ Drinking & Nightlife
25 Garage Project....................................... B7
26 Regional Wines & Spirits...................... E8

◎ Shopping
27 Kirkcaldie & Stains............................... D5
28 Old Bank Shopping Arcade................... D5
29 Vault... C5

★ **Cable Car** CABLE CAR
(Map p334; www.wellingtoncablecar.co.nz; adult/child 1 way $4/1.50, return $7/2.50; ⊙ departs every 10min, 7am-10pm Mon-Fri, 8.30am-10pm Sat, 9am-9pm Sun) One of Wellington's most famous attractions is the little red cable car that clanks up the steep slope from Lambton Quay to Kelburn. At the top is the Wellington Botanic Gardens, the Carter Observatory (p336) and the small-but-nifty **Cable Car Museum** (Map p334; www.museumswellington.org.nz; admission free; ⊙ 10am-5pm), which evocatively depicts the cable car's story since it was built in 1902 to open up hilly Kelburn for settlement. Take the cable car back down the hill, or ramble down through the gardens (a 20- to 60-minute walk, depending on your wend).

Carter Observatory ASTRONOMY
(Map p334; ☎ 04-910 3140; www.carterobservatory.org; 40 Salamanca Rd; adult/child $18.50/8; ⊙ 10am-5pm, to 9.30pm Tue & Sat) At the top of the Botanic Gardens (p333), the Carter Observatory features a full-dome planetarium offering regular shows with virtual tours of the local skies; a multimedia display of Polynesian navigation, Maori cosmology and European explorers; and some of NZ's finest telescopes and astronomical artefacts. Check the website for evening stargazing times.

Zealandia WILDLIFE RESERVE
(☎ 04-920 9200; www.visitzealandia.com; Waiapu Rd; adult/child/family exhibition only $7.50/5/20, exhibition & valley $17.50/9/44; ⊙ 10am-5pm, last entry 4pm) 🍃 This groundbreaking ecosanctuary is tucked in the hills about 2km west of town (the Karori bus passes nearby, or see the Zealandia website for the free shuttle). Living wild within the fenced valley are more than 30 native bird species, including rare takahe, saddleback, hihi and kaka, as well as tuatara and little spotted kiwi. An excellent exhibition relays NZ's natural history and world-renowned conservation story. More than 30km of tracks can be explored independently, or on regular guided tours. The night tour provides an opportunity to spot nocturnal creatures including kiwi, frogs and glowworms (adult/child $75/36). Cafe and shop on site.

Katherine Mansfield Birthplace HISTORIC BUILDING
(Map p334; www.katherinemansfield.com; 25 Tinakori Rd, Thorndon; adult/child $8/2; ⊙ 10am-4pm Tue-Sun) Often compared to Chekhov and Maupassant, Katherine Mansfield is one of NZ's most distinguished authors, born in 1888, and dying of tuberculosis in 1923 aged 34. This Tinakori Rd house is where she spent five years of her childhood; it's a lovely heritage home with exhibitions in her honour, including a biographical film. Her short

stories can be found in one volume, *The Collected Stories of Katherine Mansfield*.

Otari-Wilton's Bush
PARK

(Map p334; 160 Wilton Rd; ⊙ dawn–dusk) FREE About 3km west of the city is Otari-Wilton's Bush, the only botanic gardens in NZ specialising in native flora. There are more than 1200 plant species here, including some of the city's oldest trees, as well as 11km of walking trails and delightful picnic areas. The Wilton bus from the city passes the gates.

Colonial Cottage Museum
MUSEUM

(Map p334; www.museumswellington.org.nz; 66 Nairn St, Mt Cook; adult/child $8/4; ⊙ noon–4pm Sat & Sun) Open daily during high summer, and weekends only the rest of the year, and just a five-minute amble from the top of Cuba St, Wellington's oldest cottage has been carefully restored (complete with an organic garden and chooks) to retell the stories of early settlers and life in their era. Check the website for current tour times, usually hourly.

Wellington Zoo
ZOO

(www.wellingtonzoo.com; 200 Daniell St; adult/child $20/10; ⊙ 9.30am-5pm, last entry 4.15pm) Committed to conservation and research, with an active captive-breeding program, Wellington Zoo is home to a menagerie of native and exotic wildlife, including lions and tamarins. The nocturnal house has kiwi and tuatara. 'Close encounters' allow you to meet the big cats, red pandas, giraffes and those cute little meerkats (for a fee). The zoo is 4km south of the city; catch the Newtown bus.

Weta Cave
MUSEUM

(www.wetanz.com; cnr Camperdown Rd & Weka St, Miramar; ⊙ 9am-5.30pm) FREE Film buffs will enjoy the Weta Cave, a fun, mind-boggling minimuseum of the Academy Award–winning company that brought *The Lord of the Rings, King Kong, The Adventures of Tintin* and *The Hobbit* to life. Learn how the company does it on the 45-minute 'Window into Workshop' guided tour (starting every half-hour, $20). The Weta Cave is 9km east of the city centre, a pleasant waterside bike ride or 20 minutes on the Miramar bus.

New Zealand Film Archive
CINEMA

(Map p342; ✍ film info line 04-499 3456; www.filmarchive.org.nz; cnr Taranaki & Ghuznee Sts; movies $8; ⊙ 9am-5pm Mon-Fri, evening screenings 7pm Wed-Sat) FREE The Film Archive is a veritable vortex of NZ moving images, into which you could well get sucked for days on end. Its library holds more than 30,000 titles spanning feature films, documentaries, short films, home movies, newsreels, TV programs and advertisements. There are regular screenings in the cinema ($8), as well as a viewing library (free) where you can ferret out and watch films until you're square-eyed. Groovy on-site cafe.

Dowse Art Museum
GALLERY

(www.dowse.org.nz; 45 Laings Rd, Lower Hutt; ⊙ 10am-5pm; ☎) FREE Fifteen minutes' drive or via regular buses from downtown Wellington, the Dowse is worth visiting for its architecture alone. It's also a friendly, accessible art museum showcasing NZ art, craft and design, with a nice cafe to boot.

WELLINGTON IN...

Two Days

To get a feel for the lie of the land, walk (or drive) up to the **Mt Victoria Lookout**, or ride the **cable car** up to the **Wellington Botanic Gardens**. After lunch on groovy **Cuba Street**, catch some Kiwi culture at **Te Papa** or the **Museum of Wellington City & Sea**. Top off the day by doing the rounds of the city's numerous craft-beer bars.

The next day, reconstitute with coffee and a plate of sage eggs at **Nikau** in the City Gallery, then head to **Zealandia** to meet the birds and learn about NZ conservation, or encounter some other bird-brains in a tour of **Parliament House**. Raid **Moore Wilson** for cheese and wine for a picnic supper in Waitangi Park, before heading back into the night lights for some live music, or a movie at the gloriously restored **Embassy Theatre**.

Four Days

Shake and bake the two-day itinerary, then decorate with the following: a seal-spotting safari along wild Cape Palliser, followed by a wine tasting or two around **Martinborough**. The next day, head to **Paekakariki** for an ocean swim and ice cream before wandering through the dunes of **Queen Elizabeth Park** next door.

TREASU...   ...E PAPA

★ **Te Pa...** ...; www.tepapa.govt.nz; 55 Cable St; ⊙10am-6pm Fri-Wed, to 9pm Thu) **FREE** i... ...ust-see' attraction, and for reasons well beyond the fact that it's NZ's natio... ... . It's highly interactive, fun and full of surprises.

Aptly, '... ...arewa' loosely translates as 'treasure box'. The riches inside include an ... ...ction of Maori artefacts and the museum's own colourful *marae* (meeting ... ...ral history and environment exhibitions; Pacific and NZ history galleries; ... ...Te Papa (the national art collection, see www.arts.tepapa.govt. nz), and ... ...covery centres' for children. Expect impressive gallery spaces and plent... ...n twists. Big-name, temporary exhibitions incur an admission fee, although ... ...ssion is free.

You cou... ...day exploring Te Papa's six floors but still not see it all. To cut to the chase, head to the information desk on level two and collect a map. For exhibition highlights and to get your bearings, the one-hour 'Introducing Te Papa' tour ($14) is a good idea; tours leave from the info desk at 10.15am, noon and 2pm daily in winter, more frequently in summer. Two cafes and two gift shops complete the Te Papa experience, one which could well take a couple of visits.

Petone Settlers Museum MUSEUM
(www.petonesettlers.org.nz; The Esplanade, Petone; ⊙10am-4pm Wed-Sun) **FREE** On the shell-strewn Petone foreshore, 10 minutes' drive from downtown Wellington or reachable by regular bus services, the art-deco Petone Settlers Museum recalls local migration and settlement in its charming *Tatou Tatou* exhibition.

🏃 Activities

Ferg's Kayaks KAYAKING
(Map p334; www.fergskayaks.co.nz; Shed 6, Queens Wharf; ⊙9am-8pm Mon-Fri, to 6pm Sat & Sun) Stretch your tendons with indoor rock climbing (adult/child $15/10), cruise the waterfront wearing in-line skates ($15 for two hours) or go for a paddle in a kayak or on a stand-up paddleboard (from $15 for one hour). There's also bike hire (one hour from $15) and guided kayaking trips.

Wild Winds WINDSURFING, PADDLEBOARDING
(Map p334; ☑04-473 3458; www.wildwinds.co.nz; 36 Customhouse Quay) With all this wind and water, Wellington was made for windsurfing, kiteboarding, and stand-up paddleboarding. Take on one or all three with Wild Winds; lessons start from $110 for two hours.

**Makara Peak
Mountain Bike Park** MOUNTAIN BIKING
(www.makarapeak.org; South Karori Rd, Karori; admission by donation) In the hills of Karori, 8km west of the city centre (on the Karori bus), this excellent 200-hectare park is laced with 60km of single-track ranging from be-

ginner to expert. The nearby **Mud Cycles** (☑04-476 4961; www.mudcycles.co.nz; 421 Karori Rd, Karori; half-day/full day/weekend bike hire from $30/45/75) has mountain bikes for hire, and runs guided tours for riders of all abilities. Wellington is a true MTB mecca – visit tracks.org.nz for the evidence.

👉 Tours

Walk Wellington WALKING TOUR
(www.walkwellington.org.nz; adult/child $20/10; ⊙tours 10am daily, plus 5.30pm Mon, Wed & Fri Nov-Mar) Informative and great-value two-hour walking tours focusing on the city and waterfront, departing the i-SITE. Book online, phone or just turn up.

Zest Food Tours GUIDED TOUR
(☑04-801 9198; www.zestfoodtours.co.nz; tours from $169) Runs three- to 5½-hour small-group foody tours; longer tours include lunch with matched wines at the legendary Logan Brown (p347).

Kiwi Coastal Tours 4WD TOURS
(☑0272 520 099; www.kiwicoastaltours.co.nz; 3/5hr tour $150/225) Excellent 4WD exploration of the rugged south coast in the company of a local Maori guide with plenty of stories to tell.

John's Hop On Hop Off BUS TOUR
(☑0274 535 880, 0800 246 877; www.hoponhopoff.co.nz; per person $45) Flexible two-hour scenic loop of the city with 18 stops en route, starting at the i-SITE. Tickets are valid for 24 hours.

🏃 City Walk
City Sculpture

START POST OFFICE SQ
END KARO DR
LENGTH 3.5KM; TWO TO THREE HOURS

Begin at Post Office Sq, where Bill Culbert's ❶ **SkyBlues** noodles into the air, then cross Jervois Quay to pass between the New Zealand Academy of Fine Arts and Museum of Wellington City & Sea. At the Queens Wharf waterfront, turn south, past the big shed to the ❷ **Water Whirler**, the largely lifeless needle of experimental kineticist Len Lye that whirrs crazily into life on the hour several times a day.

Continue along the promenade or deviate through Frank Kitts Park, passing the graceful ❸ **Albatross Fountain**. A short detour over the flotsam City to Sea Bridge, Civic Sq is surrounded by the i-SITE, library and City Gallery. Neil Dawson's ❹ **Ferns** hangs in the air, attendant by a stand of nikau palms.

Back on the waterfront, continue past Te Raukura *whare waka* (canoe house) and ❺ **Hikitia**, the world's oldest working crane

ship. Strip to your undies and jump off the diving platform, or perhaps just keep on trucking along wharf, past the bronze form of ❻ **Solace in the Wind** leaning over the edge, alongside Katherine Mansfield's breezy contribution to the Wellington Writers Walk.

Cross the footbridge to Waitangi Park to eyeball some roller action, before heading south to Courtenay Pl via Chaffers St, and Blair St with its century-old warehouses.

On Courtenay Pl, check out the leggy form of the industrial ❼ **Tripod**, before heading west. Cross Taranaki St to ❽ **Te Aro Park** with its canoe prow and trip hazards.

Turn south when you hit Cuba St, heading up the pedestrian mall. Watch out for the sly, sloshy ❾ **Bucket Fountain**.

Change down to granny gear and wander through doorways, all the way to the top of Cuba, into the remnant heritage precinct cut through by the controversial inner-city bypass. Bookend your sculpture walk with Regan Gentry's brilliant but ghostly ❿ **Subject to Change**, and the Tonks' Well alongside.

WORTH A TRIP

DAYS BAY & MATIU/SOMES ISLAND

The small **Wellington Harbour Ferry** (Map p334; ✆04-499 1282; www.eastbywest.co.nz; Queens Wharf) plies the harbour between Queens Wharf and Days Bay in Eastbourne, via Matiu/Somes Island, and on fine weekends Petone and Seatoun as well.

Locals have been jumping on a boat to Days Bay for decades, where there's a beach, a park and a cafe, and a boatshed with kayaks, row boats and bikes for hire. A 10-minute walk from Days Bay leads to Eastbourne, a beachy township with more cafes, a cute pub and numerous other diversions.

The ferry also stops at at Matiu/Somes Island in the middle of the harbour. It's a reserved managed by the Department of Conservation (DOC), where you might see weta, tuatara, kakariki and little blue penguins, among other critters. The island is rich in history, having once been a prisoner-of-war camp and quarantine station. Take a picnic lunch, or even stay overnight in the campsite (adult/child $10/5) or in the DOC house; book online at www.doc.govt.nz or at Wellington's DOC visitor centre (p351).

It's a 20- to 30-minute chug across the harbour. There are 16 sailings on weekdays, eight on Saturday and Sunday (return fare adult/child $22/12).

Flat Earth   CULTURAL TOUR
(✆04-472 9635, 0800 775 805; www.flatearth. co.nz; half- & full-day tours $175-385) An array of themed small-group tours (city highlights, Maori treasures, arts and Middle-earth filming locations).

Movie Tours   GUIDED TOUR
(✆0274 193 077; www.adventuresafari.co.nz; tours from adult/child $45/30) Half- and full-day tours with more props, clips, and Middle-earth film locations than you can shake a staff at.

South Coast Shuttles   GUIDED TOUR
(✆04-389 2161; www.southcoastshuttles.co.nz; 2½-hour tours $55; ⊗tours 10am & 1pm) Offers tailored tours as well as a scheduled daily two-hour city highlights tour including the south coast and Otari Wilton's Bush. Photographer's early-bird trip at 7am (two hours, $45).

Wellington Rover   GUIDED TOUR
(✆04-471 0044, 0800 426 211; www.wellington-rover.co.nz; tours from adult/child $95/50) Half-to full-day tours of the city, seal colony and Hobbit habitat.

✰✰ Festivals & Events

Check at the Wellington i-SITE or visit www. wellingtonnz.com/events for listings; ticketed events can be found and booked via **Ticketek** (www.ticketek.co.nz) and **TicketDirect** (✆0800 224 224; www.ticketdirect.co.nz).

Summer City   CULTURE
(www.wellington.govt.nz) A summertime event bonanza – many free and outdoors including the lovely 'Gardens Magic' concerts – from January to March.

New Zealand International Sevens   SPORTS
(www.sevens.co.nz) The world's top seven-a-side rugby teams compete, but it's the crowd that plays up. Held in February; book with lightning speed.

New Zealand International Arts Festival   CULTURE
(www.festival.co.nz) A month-long biennial (even years; around mid-February to mid-March) spectacular of theatre, dance, music, visual arts and literature. International acts aplenty.

Fringe NZ   CULTURE
(www.fringe.org.nz) Three weeks across February and March of way-out-there experimental visual arts, music, dance and theatre.

New Zealand Comedy Festival   COMEDY
(www.comedyfestival.co.nz) Three weeks of hysterics across April/May. World-famous-in-NZ comedians, and some truly world-famous ones, too.

Matariki   CULTURE
(www.tepapa.govt.nz) Celebrating the Maori New Year (in June) with a free festival of dance, music and other events at Te Papa.

International Film Festival   FILM
(www.nzff.co.nz) Two-week indie film fest screening the best of NZ and international cinema. Held over July/August.

Beervana   BEER
(www.beervana.co.nz) A barrel-load of craft-beer aficionados roll into town for a weekend of supping and beard-stroking. In August.

Wellington on a Plate
FOOD

(www.wellingtononaplate.com) Lip-smacking program of gastronomic events, and bargains aplenty at restaurants around the city. Held in August.

World of WearableArt
FASHION

(www.worldofwearableart.com) A two-week run in September of the spectacular nightly extravaganza of amazing garments. Tickets are hot property.

Toast Martinborough
FOOD & DRINK

(www.toastmartinborough.co.nz) A day of hedonism around the Martinborough vineyards. Tickets = hot cakes. Held in November.

🛏 Sleeping

Wellington accommodation is generally more expensive than in regional areas. Standards are reasonably high, and there are plenty of options right in or within easy walking distance of the city centre. One hassle is the lack of parking, so it will pay to ask in advance about options if you have your own wheels.

Wellington's budget accommodation largely takes the form of multistorey hostel megaliths. There's no 'motel alley' in Wellington, but motels are scattered around the city fringe. Being the hub of government and business, self-contained apartments are popular, with bargains often available at weekends.

During the peak season (December to February), or during major events, book your bed well in advance.

Campsites are as rare as bad coffee in Wellington. Tenters should head to Wellington Top 10 Holiday Park (p343) in Seaview, or Paekakariki Holiday Park (p354). Motorhomers, however, can enjoy the superconvenient Wellington Waterfront Motorhome Park.

★ YHA Wellington City
HOSTEL $

(Map p342; 📞 04-801 7280; www.yha.co.nz; cnr Cambridge Tce & Wakefield St; dm $29-36, d with/without bathroom $120/88; @ 🛜) 🏄 Wellington's best hostel wins points for fantastic communal areas including two big kitchens and dining areas, and separate rooms for games, reading and watching movies. Sustainable initiatives (recycling, composting and energy-efficient hot water) impress, and there's a comprehensive booking service at reception, along with espresso.

Nomads Capital
HOSTEL $

(Map p342; 📞 0508 666 237, 04-978 7800; www.nomadscapital.com; 118 Wakefield St; dm $28-36, d $95-105; @ 🛜) Smack-bang in the middle of town, Nomads has good security, spick-and-span rooms, an on-site cafe-bar (free modest nightly meals and happy hour) and discounts for longer stays. Kitchen and lounge spaces are short on elbow room, but slick service, heritage features and location stop you dwelling on the negatives.

Trek Global
HOSTEL $

(Map p342; 📞 0800 868 735, 04-471 3480; www.trekglobal.net; 9 O'Reilly Ave; dm $22-26, s $59, tw with/without bathroom $89/69; 🅿 @ 🛜) A highlight of this back-lane hostel is the funky and welcoming foyer hang-out and cosy TV lounge. The sleeping quarters and kitchens are squeezed into rabbit-warren corridors, but it's relatively quiet with clean rooms and laudable extras such as bike hire, parking ($20 per day), a women-only dorm with a suntrap terrace, and travel booking service.

WELLINGTON FOR CHILDREN

Let's cut to the chase: Welly's biggest hit for kids is Te Papa (p338), with the whole caboodle looking like it's curated by a team of five-year-old geniuses. It has interactive activities galore, more creepy, weird and wonderful things than you can shake a squid at, and heaps of special events for all ages. See the dedicated Kids page on the website for proof of Te Papa's prowess in this department.

Conveniently located either side of Te Papa are **Frank Kitts Park** and **Waitangi Park**, both with playgrounds and in close proximity to roller skates, ice cream and life-saving espresso for the grown-ups.

A ride up the cable car (p336) and a lap around the Wellington Botanic Gardens (p333) will get the wee ones pumped up, and when darkness descends head to the Carter Observatory (p336) to gaze at galaxies far, far away. On a more terrestrial bent, check out some crazy animals at the Wellington Zoo (p337) or Zealandia (p336).

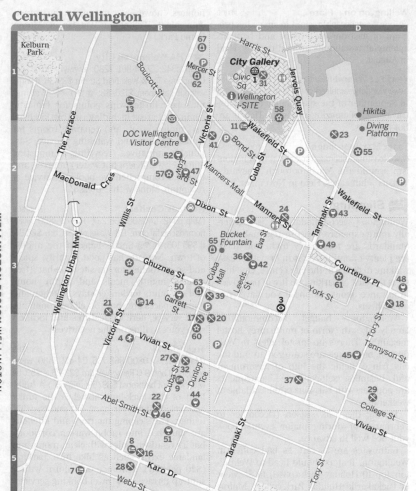

Downtown Backpackers

HOSTEL $

(Map p334; ✆04-473 8482, 0800 225 725; www.downtownbackpackers.co.nz; 1 Bunny St; dm $28-31, s $68, d $85-95; @ 🛜) Housed in a historic art-deco hotel at the railway end of town, Downtown has tidy, bright rooms and plenty of capacious, character-filled communal areas (be sure to check out the carved fireplace in the bar). Budget meals in the cafe morning and night.

Cambridge Hotel

HOSTEL $

(Map p342; ✆04-385 8829; www.cambridgehotel.co.nz; 28 Cambridge Tce; dm $25-30, with/without bathroom s $90/65, d $105/85; @ 🛜) Comfort-able accommodation in a heritage hotel with a ground-floor pub. En suite rooms have Sky TV, phone and fridge (try for a room at the back if you're a light sleeper). The backpacker wing has a snug kitchen-lounge, flash bathrooms and dorms with lit-tle natural light but sky-high ceilings. Bonus $3 breakfast.

Wellington Waterfront Motorhome Park

MOTORHOME PARK $

(Map p334; www.wwmp.co.nz; 12 Waterloo Quay; powered sites $50; 🛜) In reality it's simply a waterfront car park, but it's nonetheless unbelievably convenient, offering overnight stays, and modest hourly rates for dayparking. Facilities comprise a sharp ablution block and power supply. Book online.

Moana Lodge HOSTEL $
(☑ 04-233 2010; www.moanalodge.co.nz; 49 Moana Rd, Plimmerton; dm $34, d with shared bathroom $86-96; @ 🛜) Just off SH1 and only a 30-minute train ride or drive from Wellington (25km), this exceptional waterfront backpackers offers sea views and relaxation within easy reach of the city. The lovely old

house is immaculate and inviting, and your friendly host will happily direct you to local sights.

Wellington Top 10 Holiday Park HOLIDAY PARK $
(☑ 0800 948 686, 04-568 5913; www.wellington-top10.co.nz; 95 Hutt Park Rd, Seaview; sites $45, cabins $60-100, motels $115-170; @ 🛜) This park, 13km northeast of Wellington, is convenient for the ferry. Family-friendly facilities include communal kitchens, games room, jumping pillow and a playground, but its industrial location detracts. Follow the signs off SH2 for Petone and Seaview, or take regular public transport.

Comfort & Quality Hotels HOTEL $$
(Map p342; ☑ 0800 873 553, 04-385 2156; www. hotelwellington.co.nz; 223 Cuba St; d $104-200; P @ 🛜 🏊) In the heart of Cuba St, the CQ has two wings: the sympathetically renovated historic 'Trekkers' building with smaller, cheaper rooms (Comfort); and the snazzier high-rise 'Quality' which adjoins five fully self-contained apartments. Shared facilities include an in-house bar and restaurant (mains $14 to $35), and parking ($25 per day).

Booklovers B&B B&B $$
(Map p334; ☑ 04-384 2714; www.booklovers.co.nz; 123 Pirie St; s/d from $150/180; P @ 🛜) Author Jane Tolerton's gracious, book-filled B&B has three queen en suite guest rooms (one with an extra single bed). A bus service runs past the front gate to Courtenay Pl and the train station, and the city's 'green belt' begins right next door. Free wi-fi and parking.

Capital View Motor Inn MOTEL $$
(Map p342; ☑ 04-385 0515, 0800 438 505; www. capitalview.co.nz; 12 Thompson St; d $125-240; P 🛜) Many of the rooms in this well-maintained, multistorey building close to Cuba St do indeed enjoy capital views – especially the large, good-value penthouse (sleeps five). All are self-contained and spruce, and there's free parking.

Victoria Court MOTEL $$
(Map p342; ☑ 04-385 710, 0800 282 8502; www.victoriacourt.co.nz; 201 Victoria St; d $149-205; P 🛜) This central city option continues to deliver satisfaction in the inner city through its spacious studios and apartments with kitchenettes, quality joinery and soft furnishings, and recently refreshed bathrooms. There are two disabled-access units; larger units sleep up to six. Free on-site guest parking.

Central Wellington

◎ **Top Sights**
1 City Gallery C1
2 Te Papa E2

◎ **Sights**
3 New Zealand Film Archive C3

◎ **Activities, Courses & Tours**
4 On Yer Bike B4

◎ **Sleeping**
5 Apollo Lodge F4
6 Cambridge Hotel E4
7 Capital View Motor Inn A5
8 City Cottages B5
9 Comfort & Quality Hotels B4
10 Museum Art Hotel E2
11 Nomads Capital C2
12 Ohtel F3
13 Trek Global B1
14 Victoria Court B3
15 YHA Wellington City E3

◎ **Eating**
16 Arthur's B5
17 Aunty Mena's B4
Capitol .... (see 56)
18 Chow D3
19 City Market F2
20 Duke Carvell's C4
21 Farmers Market A3
22 Fidel's B4
23 Gelissimo Gelato D2
24 Great India C2
25 Harbourside Market E2
26 Little Penang C3
27 Logan Brown B4
28 Martha's Pantry B5
29 Moore Wilson Fresh D4
30 Mt Vic Chippery E3
31 Nikau Cafe C1
32 Ombra B4
33 Ortega Fish Shack F4

34 Pandoro Panetteria E3
35 Phoenician Falafel E4
36 Pizza Pomodoro C3
37 Prefab C4
38 Regal E4
39 Scopa C3
40 Sweet Mother's Kitchen E4
41 Tatsushi C2

◎ **Drinking & Nightlife**
42 Goldings Free Dive C3
43 Hashigo Zake D2
44 Havana B4
45 Hawthorn Lounge D4
46 Laundry B5
Library .... (see 18)
47 Little Beer Quarter B2
48 Malthouse D3
Matterhorn .... (see 65)
49 Molly Malone's D3
50 Rogue & Vagabond B3
51 Southern Cross B5
52 Vivo B2

◎ **Entertainment**
53 BATS E3
54 Bodega B3
55 Circa D2
56 Embassy Theatre E4
57 Meow B2
58 Michael Fowler Centre C1
59 Paramount E3
60 San Fran B4
61 St James Theatre D3

◎ **Shopping**
62 Bivouac Outdoor B1
63 Hunters & Collectors B3
64 Kura E3
65 Mandatory C3
66 Ora Design Gallery E3
67 Unity Books B1

Apollo Lodge   MOTEL **$$**
(Map p342; ☑ 04-385 1849, 0800 361 645; www.
apollolodge.co.nz; 49 Majoribanks St; d $140-160,
q $190-240; P 🐾) Within staggering distance
of Courtenay Pl, Apollo Lodge is a loose
collation of 35 varied units (one and two
bedrooms), ranging from studios to family-
friendly units with full kitchen. Nearby
apartments available for longer-term stays.

City Cottages   RENTAL HOUSE **$$**
(Map p342; ☑ 021 073 9232; www.citybedand-
breakfast.co.nz; Tonks Gr; d/q $170/200) These
two tiny 1880 cottages sit among a precious
precinct of historic Cuba St buildings. Clever

conversion has transformed them into all-
mod-con, self-contained one-bedroom pads,
comfortable for two but sleeping up to four
thanks to a sofa bed. Stylish, convenient and
veerrrry Cuba. Road noise may be an issue.

CityLife Wellington   APARTMENT **$$$**
(Map p334; ☑ 04-922 2800, 0800 368 888; www.
heritagehotels.co.nz; 300 Lambton Quay; d from
$189; P @🐾) Luxurious serviced apart-
ments in the city centre, ranging from stu-
dios to three-bedroom arrangements, some
with full kitchen and in-room laundry fa-
cilities, and some with a harbour glimpse.
Weekend rates are great bang for your buck.

The vehicle entrance is from Gilmer Tce, off Boulcott St (parking $15.50 per day).

Ohtel
BOUTIQUE HOTEL $$$
(Map p342; ✆04-803 0600; www.ohtel.com; 66 Oriental Parade; d $295-425; ❂) Enjoy a slice of beautiful life at this bijou hotel on Oriental Pde. Individually decorated rooms and suites feature stylish furniture and contemporary artwork and ceramics, avidly collected by the architect-owner. Mix yourself a cocktail, then take a soak in the luxurious bathtubs.

Museum Art Hotel
HOTEL $$$
(Map p342; ✆04-802 8900, 0800 994 335; www.museumhotel.co.nz; 90 Cable St; r & apt Mon-Thu $209-399, Fri-Sun $189-349; @❂❂) Formerly known as 'Museum Hotel de Wheels' (to make way for Te Papa, it was rolled here from its original location 120m away), this art-filled hotel keeps the quirk-factor high. Bright-eyed staff, a very good restaurant with flamboyant decor, and groovy tunes piped into the lobby make a refreshing change from homogenised business hotels. Tasty weekend and weekly rates.

Bolton Hotel
HOTEL $$$
(Map p334; ✆04-472 9966, 0800 996 622; www.boltonhotel.co.nz; cnr Bolton & Mowbray Sts; d $189-359; @❂❂) ✐ Slick and well serviced, the lofty Bolton deserves its five stars. Room options are varied but share a common theme of muted tones, fine linens and colourful artwork. Most are spacious with full kitchen facilities and some enjoy park or city views. Warm your cockles in the heated pool, spa and sauna.

✗ Eating

Wellington offers exciting dining, with a bewildering array of options packed into the city centre (and plenty of fabulous options in the suburbs). Varied, contemporary cafes and upmarket restaurants are complemented by a broad range of budget options including oodles of noodle houses, with stiff competition keeping standards high and prices keen across the board.

Three excellent inner-city food markets run from dawn till around 2pm on Sundays – the seriously fruit-and-veg **Farmers Market** (Map p342; cnr Victoria & Vivian Sts), and the more varied **Harbourside Market** (Map p342; Wakefield St) next to Te Papa, where you'll also find artisan producers se-ducing foodies with their wares in the **City Market** (Map p342; Chaffers Dock Bldg, 1 Herd St; ❂8.30am-12.30pm Sun).

Moore Wilson Fresh
SUPERMARKET $
(Map p342; www.moorewilson.co.nz; cnr College & Tory Sts; ❂7.30am-6pm) A call-out to self-caterers: this positively swoon-inducing grocer is one of NZ's most committed supporters of independently produced and artisanal produce. If you want to sample the best of Wellington and NZ, here's your chance.

Gelissimo Gelato
ICE CREAM $
(Map p342; www.gelissimo.co.nz; 11 Cable St, Taranaki Wharf; gelato $4-8; ❂8am-5.30pm) The hottest thing in coldness is the gelato and sorbet made by Graham, who grew up in a fruiterer's shop and sure knows his apples (and raspberries, and chocolate...). Outpost along Oriental Bay.

Pandoro Panetteria
BAKERY $
(Map p342; www.pandoro.co.nz; 2 Allen St; items $3-8; ❂7am-5pm; ✐) This excellent Italian bakery serves inexpensive deliciousness (cakes, pastries and various savoury, bready, scrolly, rolly things) along with smooth coffee in sit-down surrounds. Another outlet at 14 Woodward St.

Little Penang
MALAYSIAN $
(Map p342; Oaks Complex, Dixon St; mains $8-13; ❂10.30am-8.30pm Mon-Sat) Among a troupe of great Malaysian places, teeny tiny Little Penang steals the show with its fresh-flavoured, often-fiery street food. Pick a yummy curry for your *nasi lemak,* traditionally accompanied with the eggy, nutty, saucy stuff, or go for the bargain eight-buck *nasi goreng.* Then go back for yummy curry puffs. Aim to avoid the lunchtime rush.

Aunty Mena's
VEGETARIAN $
(Map p342; 167 Cuba St; meals $10-19; ❂11.30am-9.30pm; ✐) The lightest and healthiest of Welly's noodle houses is Aunty Mena's, a cheery cafe cranking out tasty vegie/vegan Malaysian and Chinese dishes to a diverse clientele. Easy-clean, over-lit interior.

Phoenician Falafel
LEBANESE $
(Map p342; 10 Kent Tce; meals $8-16; ❂11.30am-9.30pm; ✐) Authentic falafel, shish and *shawarma* (kebab) served up by cheery Lebanese owners. The best kebabs in town, although its sister ship, Phoenician Cuisine at 245 Cuba St, comes a very close second.

★ **Mt Vic Chippery** FISH & CHIPS $

(Map p342; www.mtvicchippery.co.nz; 5 Majoribanks St; meals $8-16; ⊘ noon-9pm Wed-Sun, 4-9pm Mon & Tue) Flash fish and chips by numbers. 1. Choose your fish (at least three varieties). 2. Choose your coating (beer batter, panko crumb, tempura...). 3. Choose your chips (five varieties!). 4. Add aioli, coleslaw, salad or sauce, and a quality soft drink. 5. Chow down inside or take away. Burgers and battered sausages will placate the piscophobes.

Havana Coffee Works CAFE $

(www.havana.co.nz; 163 Tory St; snacks $4-7; ⊘ 8.30am-5pm Mon-Fri) Hitched on to the Havana headquarters and roastery, this fantastical 'First Class' coffee lounge offers a step back and forwards in time with its invented history and modern attitude towards quality service with speed. Nibbles are limited to the likes of scones and pies from the warmer.

Fidel's CAFE $

(Map p342; www.fidelscafe.com; 234 Cuba St; snacks $4-7, mains $10-24; ⊘ 7.30am-10pm; ⫽) A Cuba St institution for caffeine-craving, alternative types. Eggs any-which-way, pizza and splendid salads are cranked out of the itsy kitchen, along with Welly's best milkshakes. Revolutionary memorabilia adorns the walls of the funky interior; decent outdoor areas too. A superbusy crew copes with the chaos admirably.

Martha's Pantry CAFE $

(Map p342; 276 Cuba St; snacks $4-9; ⊘ 9am-5pm Tue-Fri, 10am-5pm Sat & Sun) Run by the Ladies McLeod, whose roots lie in this neighbourhood, this tearoom commemorates their heritage in delicious style. Martha proffers finger sandwiches, delicate tarts, and tea in fine bone china, while across the road, **Arthur's** (Map p342; 272 Cuba St; mains $17-24; ⊘ 10am-late Wed-Sat) wears plaid and dishes up a manly fry-up, roasts and pork crackling snacks.

Sweet Mother's Kitchen AMERICAN $

(Map p342; www.sweetmotherskitchen.co.nz; 5 Courtenay Pl; mains $10-27; ⊘ 8am-10pm Sun-Thu, to late Fri & Sat; ⫽) Perpetually brimming with cool cats, Sweet Mother's serves dubious but darn tasty takes on the Deep South, such as burritos, nachos, po' boys, jambalaya and key lime pie. It's cheap, cute, has craft beer and good sun.

Pizza Pomodoro PIZZA $$

(Map p342; ⫽ 04-381 2929; www.pizzapomodoro. co.nz; 13 Leeds St; pizzas $13-24; ⊘ noon-2pm Wed-Fri, 5-9pm Mon-Sat; ⫽) Pomodoro's Mas-

simo is so serious about his wood-fired pizza he's a member of the Associazione Verace Pizza Napoletana, founded to protect and promote real pizza. Take away or dine in the microspace, or eat Welly's best pizza at Goldings Free Dive (p348) with a cold beer in hand. Yes, please.

Prefab CAFE $$

(Map p342; www.pre-fab.co.nz; 14 Jessie St; breakfast $5-18, lunch $14-20; ⊘ 7am-4pm Mon-Fri, 8am-4pm Sat) A big, industrial-minimalist space houses the city's slickest espresso bar and roastery, owned by folks who started the capital's coffee ball rolling. Beautiful house-baked bread features on a menu of flavourful and well-executed offerings such as smoked fish, asparagus and poached egg for brekkie, or pork belly with rocket, apple and fennel salad for lunch. Sunny terrace.

★ **Nikau Cafe** CAFE $$

(Map p342; www.nikaucafe.co.nz; City Gallery, Civic Sq; lunch $14-25; ⊘ 7am-4pm Mon-Fri, 8am-4pm Sat; ⫽) An airy affair at the sophisticated end of the cafe scene, Nikau consistently dishes up some of the simplest but most delightful fare in town. Refreshing aperitifs, legendary kedgeree and sage eggs, divine sweets and sunny courtyard.

Tatsushi JAPANESE $$

(Map p342; 99 Victoria St; dishes $4-27; ⊘ 11.30am-2.30pm Tue-Sat, 6-10pm Wed-Sat) A compact, Zen-like space reassuringly dominated by an open kitchen from which authentic Japanese dishes emerge, such as superfresh sashimi, homemade *agedashi* tofu, *chazuke* soup, *sunomono* (dressed salad) and moreish Karaage chicken. Tatsushi is the real deal. Sushi and bento boxes to takeaway.

Chow FUSION $$

(Map p342; www.chow.co.nz; 45 Tory St; dishes $7-24; ⊘ noon-midnight; ⩩⫽) Well-oiled Chow is a stylish pan-Asian restaurant-cum-bar, popular with folk with a penchant for zingy food in sociable surroundings, and creative cocktails. Daily deals, free wi-fi, and the fun Library bar (p349) through the back door.

Scopa ITALIAN $$

(Map p342; www.scopa.co.nz; cnr Cuba & Ghuznee Sts; mains $16-26; ⊘ 8am-late Mon-Fri, 9am-late Sat & Sun; ⫽) Authentic pizza, pasta and gnocchi make dining at this modern *cucina* a pleasure. The *bianche* (white) pizzas make a refreshing change as do the *pizzaiolo* (pizzas of the week). Watch the groovy 'Cubans' from a seat in the window. Lunchtime specials; sexy evenings complete with cocktails.

★ **Ombra** ITALIAN $$

(Map p342; www.ombra.co.nz; 199 Cuba St; snacks & small plates $4-18; ⊙10am-late; ✏) This Venetian-style *bacaro* (taverna) dishes up mouth-watering Italian fare in a lively, warm atmosphere. Admire the on-trend distressed interior while sipping an aperitif then share tasty morsels like *arancino* (fried risotto ball), *pizzette* (minipizza) and meatballs. Round things off with a classic dessert such as tiramisu or saffron and honey pannacotta. *Delizioso!*

Capitol MODERN NZ $$

(Map p342; www.capitolrestaurant.co.nz; cnr Kent Tce & Majoribanks St; mains $22-36; ⊙noon-2.30pm & 5.30-9.30pm) This consistent culinary star serves simple, seasonal fare using premium local ingredients, carefully prepared with a nod to the classic Italian style. Try the parmesan-crusted lamb's liver. The dining room is a bit cramped and noisy, but elegant nonetheless, and who's going to gripe when presented with such fine cuisine? It's well worth a wait at the wee bar (no dinner bookings).

Great India INDIAN $$

(Map p342; www.greatindia.co.nz; 141 Manners St; mains $15-32; ⊙lunch & dinner; ✏) This is not your average curry house. While a tad more expensive than its competitors, this place consistently earns its moniker with distinctly flavoured curry and other high-quality specialities. Opt for the rice and bread selection if asked.

Regal CHINESE $$

(Map p342; ✆04-384 6656; 7 Courtenay Pl; yum cha around $20) Yum cha is popular in Wellington, with many Chinese restaurants clustered around Courtenay Pl packing in the punters for their weekend ritual. The Regal pleases with speed, volume and quality, and excellence in the departments of prawn steamed dumplings, barbecue pork buns, Peking duck and coconut buns. Booking advised.

★ **Duke Carvell's** MEDITERRANEAN $$$

(Map p342; ✆04-385 2240; www.dukecarvell.co.nz; 6 Swan Lane; small plates $9-19, large plates $38-80; ⊙noon-late Mon-Fri, 9am-late Sat & Sun) Join the handsome Duke for an indulgent culinary romp of the Mediterranean, swinging through shared plates such as house-made charcuterie, paella, chocolate mousse and

noble cheeses. Heirloom artwork adorns the walls while low-cut chandeliers cast a sultry light on proceedings. Spectacular-value three-course lunch ($35 including a glass of wine).

★ **Ortega Fish Shack** SEAFOOD $$$

(Map p342; ✆04-382 9559; www.ortega.co.nz; 16 Marjoribanks St; mains $32-39; ⊙5.30-10pm Tue-Sat) Fishing floats, salty portraits and Egyptian floor tiles set a colourful Mediterranean scene, a good hook on which to hang a seafood dinner. Fish comes many ways (roasted with Malaysian gravy, sashimi with lime dressing) while the afters head straight for France courtesy of orange crêpes and one of Welly's best cheeseboards. Excellent food in a relaxed yet upbeat environment.

Boulcott Street Bistro BISTRO $$$

(Map p334; ✆04-499 4199; www.boulcottstreetbistro.co.nz; 99 Boulcott St; lunch mains $25-39, dinner mains $33-39; ⊙noon-3pm & 6pm-late Mon-Fri, 5.30pm-late Sat & Sun) Savour classic bistro fare ministered by the inimitable Rex Morgan, within a precious heritage cottage secreted in high-rise surrounds. With no evening bookings, you may be forced to wait with a flute of fizz or glass of craft beer in the convivial bar. It'll be tough. Top-value two-course Sunday roasts ($45) and lunchtime specials ($20).

Charley Noble MODERN NZ $$$

(Map p334; www.charleynoble.co.nz; Post Office Sq; starters & small plates $5-18, mains $22-40) Paul Hoather, chef-owner of the lauded and longstanding White House fine-dining restaurant, loosens up at this grand establishment in a newly renovated heritage building. Raw oysters and wood-fired meats follow fashion in ravishing style, but it's creative dishes such as pig's tail and pomegranate salad, and grilled octopus with crispy capers that really set this hot ticket alight.

★ **Logan Brown** MODERN NZ $$$

(Map p342; ✆04-801 5114; www.loganbrown.co.nz; 192 Cuba St; mains $45-51; ⊙noon-2pm Mon-Sat, 5.30pm-late Mon-Sun; 🍷) Routinely and deservedly touted as Wellington's best restaurant, Logan Brown oozes class without being pretentious or overly formal. Its 1920s banking chamber dining room is a stunner, as is the menu, which features such treats as Waikanae crab cakes and venison loin with goat's curd and cherry. The three-course bistro menu ($45) is an excellent and affordable way into Wellington's finest dining experience, although the epic wine list might force a blow-out. Bookings recommended.

🍷 Drinking & Nightlife

Wellingtonians love a late night, and it's common to see the masses heading into town at a time when normal folk would be boiling the kettle for cocoa. A lively music scene keeps things humming, along with respectable bar food, competitive cocktail concoctions, great NZ wines and tasty beer.

In fact the beer scene is where the action is, with Welly now a veritable whirlpool of crafty bars circled by a batch of local breweries. Put yourself in the pitcher at boho Aro's **Garage Project** (Map p334; www.garageproject.co.nz; 68 Aro Street; ⊙noon-8pm Tue-Sat) microbrewery or fill a flagon at the bamboozling **Regional Wines & Spirits** (Map p334; www.regionalwines.co.nz; 15 Ellice St; ⊙9am-10pm Mon-Sat, 11am-7.30pm Sun). See www.craftbeercapital.com for more propaganda.

The inner city is riddled with bars, with high concentrations around Courtenay Pl (short skirts, sexy shoes, and hair-raising hijinks); and Cuba/Victoria Sts (colourful and groovy with personality in spades). A short pub crawl can also be had along the waterfront.

Wellington's music scene predominates in pint-sized venues, most often in the corner of a bar. Big-gig listings can be found at www.undertheradar.co.nz and www.eventfinder.co.nz; look out for others as you walk the streets, or investigate venue websites and Facebook pages.

★**Goldings Free Dive**   CRAFT BEER
(Map p342; www.goldingsfreedive.co.nz; 14 Leeds St; ⊙noon-11pm; 🛜) Hidden down an upswinging back alley near Cuba St, gloriously garish Goldings is a bijoux craft-beer bar with far too many merits to mention, although we'll single out ex-casino swivel chairs, a nice wine list, a ravishing Reuben sandwich plus pizza from Pomodoro, next door. Plastic fantastic gewgaws add colourful buckets of battiness.

Hashigo Zake   CRAFT BEER
(Map p342; www.hashigozake.co.nz; 25 Taranaki St; ⊙noon-midnight; 🛜) This brick-walled bunker bar serves as the headquarters of a zealous importation business splicing a stimulating mix of big-flavoured international brewstars into a smartly selected NZ range. Ogling the oft-changing taps and brimming fridges is a wide range of hopheads, happy to stand elbow to elbow around the bar or squeeze into the acoustically sweet side-lounge on nano-gig nights (every Saturday at 10pm).

Malthouse   CRAFT BEER
(Map p342; www.themalthouse.co.nz; 48 Courtenay Pl; ⊙3pm-late Mon & Tue, noon-1am Wed-Sun) At last count there were nearly 200 reasons to drink at this, the capital's original craft-beer bar – still boasting a high beer-geek quotient, and now housed in a low-key concrete box with leaners, comfy corner lounge, and popular alfresco area where you can watch the world go by. Check the blackboard for new brews, or ask savvy staff to serve something to suit your mood.

★**Little Beer Quarter**   CRAFT BEER
(Map p342; www.littlebeerquarter.co.nz; 6 Edward St; 4pm-late Mon, noon-late Tue-Sat) Tucked away in a back lane, lovely LBQ is a lively bar handled with a lady's touch. It's warm, inviting, and soft in all the right places, but still packs a hop-headed punch with its well-curated taps and bottled selection. Good cocktails, wines and whiskies, too, plus tasty bar food along the lines of pizza and pork scratchings. Bargain specials Monday to Thursday.

Rogue & Vagabond   CRAFT BEER
(Map p342; www.rogueandvagabond.co.nz; 18 Garrett St) Right in the heart of Cuba fronting on to a precious pocket park, the Rogue is a lovably scruffy, colourful, kaleidoscopic craft-beer bar with heaps going on: 18 taps; voluminous, chewy-crust pizza ($15 to $22); regular, rockin' gigs; and sifting about on the patio or slouching around on the lawn.

Southern Cross   PUB
(Map p342; www.thecross.co.nz; 39 Abel Smith St; ⊙8am-late) Welcoming to all – from frenetic five-year-olds to Nana with her knitting – the fun, easygoing Cross rambles around a series of colourful rooms, combining a respectable restaurant, lively bar, dance floor, pool table and the best garden bar in town. There's interesting beer on tap, food to suit all budgets, and regular events including bingo, gigs and quiz night.

Laundry   BAR
(Map p342; www.laundry.net.nz; 240 Cuba St; ⊙10am-late Wed-Sun, 4pm-late Tue) Tumble into this junk-shop juke joint any time of the day or night for a tipple and a taco, and hang out with the hipsters in a wrinkle-free zone. Carousal is encouraged with regular gigs and deejays, lip-smacking libations and colourful, carnivalesque decor pasted up with a very rough brush. Trailer-trash backyard complete with a caravan.

Molly Malone's   IRISH PUB

(Map p342; www.mollymalones.co.nz; cnr Courtenay Pl & Taranaki St; ⏰11am-1am Sun-Thu, to 3am Fri & Sat) This highly polished Irish bar hosts live music nearly every night, and dishes up well-priced pub grub and a balcony overlooking the bustle. If the *craic* downstairs is too much for you, head up to the piano bar for a quiet dram.

Havana   BAR

(Map p342; www.havanabar.co.nz; 32 Wigan St; ⏰11.30am-late Mon-Fri, 3pm-late Sat) Go out of your way to find Havana, a mighty fine needle in Welly's hospitality haystack, hidden down a sidestreet and squeezed into two adjacent heritage cottages sharing a groovy backyard. Fortify yourself with tapas and top shelf, then chinwag, smoke or flirt, or all three, then break out your sexy legs in the microdisco.

Vivo   WINE BAR

(Map p342; www.vivowinebar.com; 19 Edward St; ⏰3pm-late Mon-Fri, 5pm-late Sat) If your idea of a good time is fine wine, tapas and conversation, head to Vivo. Match wines off an epic list with any of 30 delectable small plates, and relax in the brick-lined and timbered, cellarlike dining room. This is one of the city's real hidden gems – dark and twinkly, sensual and delicious.

Hawthorn Lounge   COCKTAIL BAR

(Map p342; www.hawthornlounge.co.nz; 82 Tory St; ⏰6pm-late Tue-Sat) This classy cocktail bar has a 1920s speakeasy feel, suited up in waistcoats and wide-brimmed fedoras. Sip a drink and play poker, or simply enjoy the behind-the-bar theatrics from the Hawthorn's serious mixologists twisting and turning classics into modern-day masterpieces. Kiss me, tease me, spoil me wines.

Library   BAR

(Map p342; www.thelibrary.co.nz; 53 Courtenay Pl; ⏰5pm-late) You'll find yourself in the right kind of bind at the book-filled Library, with its velveteen booths, board games and bestselling cocktails. An excellent all-round drink selection is complemented by a highly sharable menu of sweet and savoury treats including chocolate fondant and cheese. Live music on occasion.

Matterhorn   BAR

(Map p342; www.matterhorn.co.nz; 106 Cuba St; ⏰3pm-late) An early riser in Welly's 21st-century bar scene, the 'Horn still hovers around the top with its reputable food (tapas from mid-arvo, dinner daily, brunch weekends), snappy service and regular live music. The sultry, designerly style for which it is famous is now slightly faded and dated, but this matters little in the dimmed light of its bewitching hours.

☆ Entertainment

Wellington is home to a long-standing professional theatre, Circa, whose busy program is augmented by plenty of amateur companies and fringe performers, student shows and regular visiting tours. Peruse listings at www.eventfinder.co.nz. Many events are ticketed via **Ticketek** (www.ticketek.co.nz) box offices, located at **St James Theatre** (Map p342; 77 Courtenay Pl) and the **Michael Fowler Centre** (Map p342; 111 Wakefield St), as well as **TicketDirect** (www.ticketdirect.co.nz). Discount same-day tickets for some productions are often available at the i-SITE.

Wellywood has simply too many good indy cinemas to list, so here are a few innercity picks. Movie times are listed in the daily *Dominion Post* and at www.flicks.co.nz.

Circa   THEATRE

(Map p342; ☎04-801 7992; www.circa.co.nz; 1 Taranaki St; ⏰Tue-Sun) Waterfront Circa

WELCOME TO WELLYWOOD

In recent years Wellington has stamped its place firmly on the world map as the home of NZ's dynamic film industry, earning itself the nickname 'Wellywood'. Acclaimed director Peter Jackson still calls Wellington home; the success of his *The Lord of the Rings* films and subsequent productions such as *King Kong, The Adventures of Tintin* and *The Hobbit* have made him a powerful Hollywood player, and have bolstered Wellington's reputation.

Canadian director James Cameron is now in on the action, with three *Avatar* sequels set to be shot in New Zealand. Cameron and his family are New Zealand residents, with landholding in rural Wairarapa.

Movie buffs can experience some local movie magic by visiting minimuseum the Weta Cave (p337), or one of many film locations around the region – a speciality of local guided-tour companies.

houses two auditoriums in which it shows everything from edgy new works to Christmas panto. Standby tickets available an hour before the show.

BATS
THEATRE

($ 04-802 4175; www.bats.co.nz; 1 Kent Tce) Wildly alternative but accessible BATS presents cutting-edge and experimental NZ theatre – varied, cheap and intimate – in its freshly revamped theatre.

Light House Cinema
CINEMA

($ 04-385-3337; www.lighthousecuba.co.nz; 29 Wigan St; adult/child $17.50/12.50) Tucked away near the top end of Cuba St, this small, stylish and modern cinema screens a wide range of mainstream, art-house and foreign films in three small theatres. High-quality snacks.

Embassy Theatre
CINEMA

(Map p342; $ 04-384 7657; www.eventcinemas.co.nz; 10 Kent Tce; adult/child from $18.50/13.50) Wellywood's cinema mothership is an art-deco darling, built in the 1920s. Today she screens mainly mainstream films with state-of-the-art sound and vision. Bars and cafe on site.

Paramount
CINEMA

(Map p342; $ 04-384 4080; www.paramount.co.nz; 25 Courtenay Pl; adult/child $15.90/10.50; ☺ noon-midnight) A lovely old complex screening largely art-house, documentary and foreign flicks.

Meow
LIVE MUSIC, BAR

(Map p342; www.welovemeow.co.nz; 9 Edward St; ☺ 4.30pm-late Mon, 10am-late Tue-Sun) Truly the cat's pyjamas, Meow goes out on a limb to host a diverse range of gigs and other performances, at the same time offering good-quality, inexpensive food at almost any time of day. There are treats for the sweet tooth, and a good selection of keenly priced craft beers. Mishmashed retro decor gives the place a speakeasy feel.

San Fran
LIVE MUSIC

(Map p342; www.sanfran.co.nz; 171 Cuba St; ☺ noon-late) This much-loved, midsized music venue is moving to a new beat, having boarded the craft-beer bandwagon and rockin' out smoky, meaty food along the way. Gigs still rule, dancing is de rigueur and the balcony still gets good afternoon sun.

Bodega
LIVE MUSIC

(Map p342; www.bodega.co.nz; 101 Ghuznee St; ☺ 4pm-late) A trailblazer of the city's modern live-music scene, the good-old Bodge' has demonstrated admirable endurance, hosting a regular and varied program of gigs – including frequent international acts – in a pleasant space with solid acoustics and a respectable dance floor.

 ## Shopping

Wellington supports a high number of independent shops including scores of design stores and clothing boutiques. There's still plenty that's Kiwi-made – despite cheap imports and online shopping – with retailers flying their home-grown flags with pride.

Unity Books
BOOKS

(Map p342; www.unitybooks.co.nz; 57 Willis St; ☺ 9am-6pm Mon-Fri, 10am-6pm Sat, 11am-5pm Sun) Setting the standard for every bookshop in the land. Dedicated NZ table piled high.

Vault
ARTS & CRAFTS

(Map p334; www.thevaultnz.com; 2 Plimmer Steps; ☺ 9.30am-5.30pm Mon-Thu, 9.30am-7pm Fri, 10am-5pm Sat, 11am-4.30pm Sun) Jewellery, clothing, bags, ceramics, cosmetics – a bonny store with lots of NZ-made, beautiful things.

Kura
ARTS & CRAFTS

(Map p342; www.kuragallery.co.nz; 19 Allen St; ☺ 10am-6pm Mon-Fri, 11am-4pm Sat & Sun) Contemporary indigenous art: painting, ceramics, jewellery and sculpture.

Ora Design Gallery
ARTS & CRAFTS

(Map p342; 23 Allen St; ☺ 9am-6pm Mon-Fri, 9am-5pm Sat, 10am-4pm Sun) Fresh, bold, bright contempoary art including sculpture, weaving and jewellery.

Mandatory
CLOTHING

(Map p342; www.mandatory.co.nz; 108 Cuba Mall; ☺ 10am-6pm Mon-Thu, 10am-7pm Fri, 10am-4.30pm Sat, noon-4pm Sun) Great service and sharp men's tailoring for the capital's cool cats.

Hunters & Collectors
VINTAGE

(Map p342; 134 Cuba St; ☺ 10am-6pm Mon-Sat, 11am-5pm Sun) Off-the-rack and vintage clothing (punk, skate and mod), plus shoes and accessories. Best-dressed window in NZ.

Bivouac Outdoor
OUTDOOR EQUIPMENT

(Map p342; www.bivouac.co.nz; 39 Mercer St; ☺ 9am-5.30pm Mon-Fri, 10am-5pm Sat & Sun) The best of several outdoor shops, staffed by people who know because they go.

Old Bank Shopping Arcade SHOPPING CENTRE
(Map p334; www.oldbank.co.nz; cnr Lambton Quay
& Willis St; ⊙9am-6pm Mon-Fri, 10am-4pm Sat,
11am-3pm Sun) This dear old building is home
to indulgent boutiques, predominantly
clothing.

Kirkcaldie & Stains DEPARTMENT STORE
(Map p334; 165-177 Lambton Quay; ⊙9am-5.30pm
Mon-Fri, 10am-5pm Sat & Sun) NZ's answer to
Bloomingdale's or Harrods, established in
1863. Bring your travel documents with you
for tax-free bargains.

ℹ️ Information

INTERNET ACCESS
Free wi-fi is available in most of the CBD (see
www.cbdfree.co.nz); the i-SITE also has internet
access.

MEDICAL SERVICES
**Wellington Accident & Urgent Medical
Centre** (☑04-384 4944; www.wamc.co.nz;
17 Adelaide Rd, Newtown; ⊙8am-11pm) No
appointment necessary; also home to the
after-hours pharmacy. It's close to the Basin
Reserve around the northern end of Adelaide Rd.
Wellington Hospital (☑04-385 5999; www.
ccdhb.org.nz; Riddiford St, Newtown; ⊙24hr)
One kilometre south of the city centre.

POST
Post Office (Map p342; 2 Manners St;
⊙8.30am-5.30pm Mon-Fri, 9am-3pm Sat) This
branch has the longest opening hours of all city
branches.

TOURIST INFORMATION
DOC Wellington Visitor Centre (Map p342;
☑04-384 7770; www.doc.govt.nz; 18 Manners
St; ⊙9.30am-5pm Mon-Fri, 10am-3.30pm Sat)
Bookings, passes and information for local and
national walks (including Great Walks), parks,
huts and camping.
Wellington i-SITE (Map p342; ☑04-802 4860;
www.wellingtonnz.com; Civic Sq, cnr Wakefield
& Victoria Sts; ⊙8.30am-5pm) Staff book
almost everything, and cheerfully distribute
Wellington's *Official Visitor Guide*, along with
other maps and helpful pamphlets. Internet
access and cafe.

USEFUL WEBSITES
Best of Wellington (www.bestofwellington.
co.nz) Entertaining, long-standing independent guidebook aimed at longer-staying
visitors.
Stuff (www.stuff.co.nz) Online news service
incorporating Wellington's newspaper, the
Dominion Post.

ℹ️ Getting There & Away

AIR
Wellington is an international gateway to NZ.
Wellington Airport (WLG; ☑04-385 5100;
www.wellingtonairport.co.nz; Stewart Duff Dr,
Rongotai; ⊙4am-1.30am) has touch-screen
information kiosks in the luggage hall. There's
also currency exchange, ATMs, car-rental desks,
shops and, of course, spectacular espresso. If
you're in transit or have an early flight, you can't
linger overnight inside the terminal.
Air New Zealand (☑0800 737 000; www.
airnewzealand.co.nz) Offers flights between
Wellington and most domestic centres, including Auckland, Nelson, Christchurch, Dunedin
and Queenstown. It also flies direct to Sydney,
Melbourne and Brisbane.
Jetstar (☑0800 800 995; www.jetstar.com)
Offers economical flights from Wellington
to Auckland and Christchurch, but takes no
prisoners when it comes to late check-in. It also
flies direct to Sydney and Melbourne.
Qantas (☑0800 808 767; www.qantas.com.
au) Flies direct between Wellington and Sydney
and Melbourne.
Soundsair (☑03-520 3080, 0800 505 005;
www.soundsair.com) Flies between Wellington
and Picton up to eight times daily (from $95),
Nelson (from $113) and Blenheim (from $95).

For human assistance, try the helpful folks at
Flight Centre (www.flightcentre.co.nz; cnr Willis
& Manners Sts; ⊙9am-5.30pm Mon-Fri, 10am-
4pm Sat).

BOAT
On a clear day, sailing into Wellington Harbour
or through the Marlborough Sounds is magical.
Cook Strait can cut up rough, but the big ferries
handle it well, and sport lounges, cafes, bars, information desks and cinemas but no pool tables.
There are two options for crossing the strait
between Wellington and Picton: Bluebridge and
the Interislander.

Booking online is the cheapest option, but folks
at the i-SITE and hotels will happily book for you.
Bluebridge is based at Waterloo Quay, opposite
the Wellington train station. The Interislander
terminal is about 2km northeast of the city centre; a shuttle bus ($2) runs to the Interislander
from platform 9 at Wellington train station (where
long-distance buses also depart). It also meets
arriving ferries, returning passengers to platform
9. There's also a taxi stand at the terminal.

Car-hire companies allow you to pick up/drop
off vehicles at ferry terminals. If you arrive outside business hours, arrangements can be made
to collect your vehicle from the terminal car park.
Bluebridge Ferries (Map p334; ☑04-471
6188, 0800 844 844; www.bluebridge.co.nz;

50 Waterloo Quay) Crossing takes 3½ hours; up to four sailings in each direction daily. Cars and campervans from $118; motorbikes $51; bicycles $10. Passenger fares from adult/child $51/26.

Interislander (Map p334; ☎0800 802 802, 04-498 3302; www.interislander.co.nz; Aotea Quay) Crossing takes three hours 10 minutes; up to five sailings in each direction daily. Cars are priced from $118; campervans (up to 5.5m) from $133; motorbikes from $56; bicycles $15. Passenger fares start from adult/child $55/28.

BUS

Wellington is a major bus-travel hub, with **Inter-City** (☎04-385 0520; www.intercity.co.nz) boasting the most extensive network. Services depart from platform 9 at the train station north to Auckland (11 hours) and all major towns in between and beyond such as Palmerston North (2¼ hours), Rotorua (7½ hours), and Napier (5½ hours). Buy tickets from the Intercity ticket window in the train station, or online for discounted fares.

Naked Bus (☎0900 625 33; www.nakedbus. com) runs north from Wellington to all major North Island destinations, including Palmerston North (2½ hours), Napier (five hours), Taupo (6½ hours) and Auckland (11½ hours), with myriad stops en route. Buses depart from opposite the Amora Hotel in Wakefield St, and collect more passengers at Bunny St opposite the railway station. Book online or at Wellington i-SITE; get in early for the cheapest fares.

TRAIN

Wellington train station has six **ticket windows** (☎0800 801 700; ◷6.30am-8pm Mon-Thu, to 1am Fri & Sat, to 7pm Sun), two selling tickets for **KiwiRail Scenic Journeys** (☎04-495 0775, 0800 872 467; www.kiwirailscenic.co.nz) trains, Interislander ferries and InterCity coaches; the other four ticketing local/regional **Tranz Metro** (☎0800 801 700; www.tranzmetro.co.nz) trains (Johnsonville, Melling, Hutt Valley, Kapiti and Wairarapa lines).

KiwiRail Scenic runs the just-hanging-in-there *Northern Explorer* service from Wellington to Auckland on Tuesday, Friday and Sunday, returning from Auckland on Monday, Thursday, and Saturday (from $99, 12 hours). KiwiRail also runs the *Capital Connection* commuter service from Palmerston North, leaving at 6.15am for Wellington, and returning to Palmerston North at 5.15pm.

❶ Getting Around

Metlink (☎0800 801 700; www.metlink.org. nz) is the one-stop shop for Wellington's regional bus, train and harbour ferry networks.

TO/FROM THE AIRPORT

Co-op Shuttles (☎04-387 8787; www.co-opshuttles.co.nz; 1/2 passengers $20/26) provides a door-to-door minibus service between the city and airport, 8km southeast of the city. It's cheaper if two or more passengers are travelling to the same destination. Shuttles meet all arriving flights.

The **Airport Flyer** (☎0800 801 700; www. airportflyer.co.nz) bus runs between the airport, Wellington and the Hutt Valley, with a fare to downtown Wellington costing around $9. Buses run from around 6am to 8pm.

A taxi between the city centre and airport costs around $30.

BICYCLE

If you're fit or keep to the flat, cycling is a viable option. City hirers include **On Yer Bike** (Map p342; ☎04-384 8480; www.onyerbikeavantiplus.co.nz; 181 Vivian St; half-day $20-30, full day $30-40, week $150) near Cuba St, and Ferg's Kayaks (p338) on the waterfront. Wellington's Regional Council shows great encouragement via the maps and suggestions on its **Journey Planner** (www.journeyplanner.org.nz).

BUS

Frequent and efficient bus services cover the whole Wellington region and run between approximately 6am and 11.30pm. Major bus terminals are at the Wellington train station, and on Courtenay Pl near the Cambridge Tce intersection. Pick up route maps and timetables from the i-SITE and convenience stores, or online from Metlink. Fares are determined by zones: a trip across the city centre (Zone 1) costs $2, and all the way north to Masterton (Zone 14) costs $18.

Metlink also runs the After Midnight bus service, departing from two convenient city stops (Courtenay Pl and Cuba St) between midnight and 4.30am Saturday and Sunday, following a number of routes to the outer suburbs. Fares range from $6.50 to $13.50, depending on how far away your bed is.

CAR

There are a lot of one-way streets in Wellington, and parking gets tight (and pricey) during the day. If you've got a car or a caravan, park on the outskirts and walk or take public transport into the city centre. Campervans can also park during the day at the Wellington Waterfront Motorhome Park and the open-air car park outside Te Papa.

Aside from the major international rental companies, Wellington has several operators that will negotiate cheap deals, especially for longer-term rentals of two weeks or more, but rates generally aren't as competitive as in Auckland. Rack rates range from around $40 to $80 per day; cars are usually a few years old and in pretty good condition. Operators include the following:

Jucy Rentals (☎0800 399 736, 04-380 6211; www.jucy.co.nz; 5 Ropa Lane, Miramar)

Apex Car Rental (☎0800 300 110, 04-385 2163; www.apexrentals.co.nz; 186 Victoria St)

Omega Rental Cars (☑ 0800 667 722, 04-472 8465; www.omegarentalcars.com; 77 Hutt Rd)

If you plan on exploring both North and South Islands, most companies suggest you leave your car in Wellington and pick up another one in Picton after crossing Cook Strait. This is a common (and more affordable) practice, and car-hire companies make it a painless exercise.

There are often cheap deals on car relocation from Wellington to Auckland, as most renters travel in the opposite direction. The catch is that you may only have 24 or 48 hours to make the journey.

TAXI

Packed ranks can be found on Courtenay Pl, at the corner of Dixon and Victoria Sts, on Featherston St and outside the railway station. Two of many operators:

Green Cabs (☑ 0508 447 336; www.greencabs.co.nz)

Wellington Combined Taxis (☑ 04-384 4444; www.taxis.co.nz)

TRAIN

Tranz Metro (☑ 0800 801 700; www.tranzmetro.co.nz) operates four train routes running through Wellington's suburbs to regional destinations. Trains run frequently from around 6am to 11pm, departing Wellington train station. The routes: Johnsonville, via Ngaio and Khandallah; Kapiti, via Porirua, Plimmerton, Paekakariki and Paraparaumu; Melling, via Petone; the Hutt Valley via Waterloo to Upper Hut; and a Wairarapa service calling at Featherston, Carterton and Masterton. Timetables are available from convenience stores, the train station, Wellington i-SITE and online. Standard fares from Wellington to the ends of the five lines range from $5 to $18. A Day Rover ticket ($14) allows unlimited off-peak and weekend travel on all lines except Wairarapa.

KAPITI COAST

With wide, crowd-free beaches, the Kapiti Coast acts as a summer playground and suburban extension for Wellingtonians. The region takes its name from Kapiti Island, a wildlife sanctuary 5km offshore from Paraparaumu.

The mountainous Tararua Forest Park forms a dramatic backdrop along the length of the coastline and has some accessible day walks and longer tramps.

The Kapiti Coast makes an easy day trip from Wellington, but if you're after a few restful days there's enough of interest to keep you entertained.

ℹ Information

The Coast's official visitor centre is **Paraparaumu i-SITE** (☑ 04-298 8195; Coastlands Mall, Rimu Rd; ⏲ 9am-5pm Mon-Fri, 10am-2pm Sat & Sun), located within the Coastlands shopping centre, where you'll find all manner of other useful services such as banks, ATMs, post office and supermarkets.

ℹ Getting There & Around

AIR

The recently expanded **Kapiti Coast Airport** (PPQ; www.kapitiairport.co.nz; Toru Rd, Paraparaumu Beach) in Paraparumu is a regular destination for **Air2there** (☑ 0800 777 000; www.air2there.com), with daily flights to Blenheim and Nelson, and **Air New Zealand** (☑ 0800 737 000; www.airnewzealand.co.nz), which flies direct to Auckland.

BUS

InterCity (☑ 04-385 0520; www.intercity.co.nz) stops at major Kapiti Coast towns on its services between Wellington (45 minutes) and northern destinations including Taupo (5½ hours) and Auckland (10 hours). Book online for best fares.

Naked Bus (☑ 0900 625 33; www.nakedbus.com) also stops at major Kapiti Coast towns on its daily services.

Metlink (☑ 0800 801 700; www.metlink.org.nz) runs local bus services around Paraparumu, and up to Waikanae and Otaki, calling at highway and beach settlements.

CAR & MOTORCYCLE

Getting here from Wellington is a breeze by car: just follow SH1 for 30 minutes to Paekakariki, and around 45 to Paraparaumui. It's motorway most of the way.

TRAIN

Tranz Metro (p352) commuter trains between Wellington and the coast are easier and more frequent than buses. Services run from Wellington to Paraparaumu ($12, generally half-hourly off-peak between 6am and 11pm, with more services at peak times), stopping en route in Paekakariki ($10.50). Weekday off-peak fares (9am to 3pm) are up to $2 cheaper.

KiwiRail Scenic Journeys (☑ 04-495 0775, 0800 872 467; www.kiwirailscenic.co.nz) has long-distance *Northern Explorer* trains connecting Wellington and Auckland stopping at Paraparaumu, while the weekday-only, peak-hour *Capital Connection*, travelling to Wellington in the morning and back to Palmerston North in the evening, stops at Paraparaumu, Waikanae and Otaki.

Paekakariki

POP 1665

Paekakariki is an arty little seaside village stretched along a black-sand beach, serviced by a train station and passed by the highway to Wellington, 41km to the south.

◉ Sights & Activities

★ Queen Elizabeth Park   PARK

(SH1; ⊙ gates 8am-8pm) FREE One of the last relatively unchanged areas of dune and wetland along this coast, this undulating 650-hectare beachside park offers swimming, walking, cycling and picnicking opportunities, as well as the Tramway Museum and Stables on the Park. There are three entrances: off Wellington Rd in Paekakariki, at MacKay's Crossing on SH1, and off the Esplanade in Raumati to the north.

Tramway Museum   MUSEUM

(www.wellingtontrams.org.nz; MacKay's Crossing entrance, Queen Elizabeth Park; admission by donation, all-day tram rides adult/child/family $10/5/24; ⊙ museum 10am-4.30pm daily, trams 11am-4.30pm Sat & Sun, daily 26 Dec-late Jan) A glimpse into historic Wellington by way of restored wooden trams and museum displays housed in a large garage, and on a 2km tram ride through Queen Elizabeth Park down to the beach. On-site ice-cream kiosk.

Stables on the Park   HORSE RIDING

(☑ 027 448 6764, 06-364 3336; www.stablesonthepark.co.nz; MacKay's Crossing entrance, Queen Elizabeth Park; 30-90min ride $50-100; ⊙ open most days in summer) Mandy and friends run guided rides on well-mannered horses. The 1½-hour trek will see you trot along the beach with views of Kapiti Island before heading inland on park tracks. Beginners are welcome.

⌷ Sleeping & Eating

Paekakariki Holiday Park   HOLIDAY PARK $

(☑ 04-292 8292; www.paekakarikiholidaypark.co.nz; 180 Wellington Rd; sites per adult from $16, cabins & flats from $65; @ ☏) This large, leafy park has rather tired and dated facilities, but is well located, 1.5km north of the township at the southern entrance to Queen Elizabeth Park.

Finn's   HOTEL, PUB $$

(☑ 04-292 8081; www.finnshotel.co.nz; 2 Beach Rd; d $135-150; ☏) Finn's is the flashy beige suit of the low-key railway village, but redeems itself with spacious rooms, good-value meals (mains $17 to $29), craft beer on tap and an in-house 26-seat cinema. The hush glass keeps the highway at bay.

WORTH A TRIP

KAPITI ISLAND

Kapiti Island is the coastline's dominant feature, a 10km by 2km slice that since 1897 has been a protected reserve. Largely predator-free since 1998, it is home to a remarkable range and number of birds including many species that are now rare or extinct on the mainland.

The island is open to visitors, limited each day to 100 at **Rangatira**, where you can hike up to the 521m high point, Tuteremoana; and 60 visitors at the **northern end**, which has short, gentle walks to viewpoints and around a lagoon.

To visit the island, you must make your arrangements in advance with one of three licensed operators. Remember to reconfirm your arrangements on the morning of departure, as sailings are weather-dependent. All boats depart from Paraparaumu Beach, which can be reached by train. Services are provided by **Kapiti Marine Charter** (☑ 027 442 4850, 04-297 2585; www.kapitimarinecharter.co.nz; adult/child $95/55); **Kapiti Tours** (☑ 0800 527 484, 04-237 7965; www.ngatitoakapititours.co.nz; adult/child $105/65); and **Kapiti Island Nature Tours** (☑ 021 126 7525, 06-362 6606; www.kapitiislandnatureturetours.co.nz; boat transport adult/child $95/55), run by the Barrett and Clark *whanau* (family), who have a long-standing connection to the island. The latter offers day tours as well as a very special overnight stay (adult/child from $369/215), which includes an introduction to wildlife, history and Maori traditions, but also an after-dark walk in the bush to spot the cutest-ever bird, the rare little spotted kiwi. The price includes lodge accommodation in sole-occupancy rooms or bunk houses, with meals included.

More information can be found in the Department of Conservation (DOC) *Kapiti Island Nature Reserve* brochure or in person at the DOC Wellington Visitor Centre (p351).

Beach Road Deli
CAFE $

(5 Beach Rd; snacks $3-8, pizzas $13-22; ⊘7am-8pm Wed-Sat, to 4.30pm Sun) Bijou deli and wood-fired pizzeria, stocked with home-baked bread and pastries, cheese, charcuterie and assorted imported goodies. Heaven-sent for the highway traveller, picnicker, or those looking for a sausage to fry and a bun to put it in. Ace coffee.

Waikanae & Around

Heading north beyond Paekakariki, it's not long before it's time to slow down for another Kapiti Coast town. The first is **Para-paraumu** (population 17,190), the region's major commercial and residential hot spot. The town has two hubs: the main town on the highway, with shopping galore, and Paraparaumu Beach with its waterside park and walkway, decent swimming and other beachy attractions, including the stunning view out to Kapiti Island. The correct pronunciation is 'Pah-ra-pah-ra-oo-moo', meaning 'scraps from an oven', which is said to have originated when a Maori war party attacked the settlement and found only scraps of food remaining. It's a bit of a mouthful to pronounce; locals usually just corrupt it into 'Para-par-am'.

Around 15 minutes' drive (20km) north of Paraparamu is **Waikanae** (population 10,640), traditionally a retirees' favourite but in contemporary times a growing, go-ahead town encouraged by first-time-home-buyer flight from Wellington city. It's a pleasant and sunny seaside town, and a rewarding stop for some salt-tinged R&R.

◉ Sights & Activities

Nga Manu Nature Reserve   WILDLIFE RESERVE

(www.ngamanu.co.nz; 281 Ngarara Rd; adult/child/family $15/6/35; ⊘10am-5pm) Waikanae's main visitor attraction, Nga Manu Nature Reserve is a 15-hectare bird sanctuary dotted with picnic areas, bushwalks, aviaries and a nocturnal house with kiwi, owls and tuatara. The eels are fed at 2pm daily, and guided tours run on weekends at 2pm (Sunday only in winter). To get here, turn seawards from SH1 onto Te Moana Rd and then right down Ngarara Rd and follow the signs.

Tuatara Brewery   BREWERY

(www.tuatarabrewing.co.nz; 7 Sheffield St, Paraparaumu; ⊘11am-7pm Wed-Sun) Visit the oldest and most famous of Wellington's craft breweries at its industrial-estate premises where you can enjoy a tasting along with simple bar snacks (biersticks, pizza...) or preferably go on an enlightening tour of the brewery with Mr McInness, raconteur ($30, including tasting tray).

Southward Car Museum   MUSEUM

(www.southwardcarmuseum.co.nz; Otaihanga Rd; adult/child $13/3; ⊘9am-4.30pm) This museum has one of Australasia's largest collections of antique and unusual cars. Check out the DeLorean and the 1950 gangster Cadillac.

Waikanae Estuary Bird Tours   ECOTOUR

(☎04-905 1001; www.kapitibirdtours.co.nz; 2hr tours $35) The Waikanae Estuary is a hot spot for birds, with around 60 species visiting during the year. You can expect to see around 20 on these personalised outings with a passionate guide, which end with a cup of tea and a freshly baked scone ($25 without refreshments).

Hemi Matenga Memorial Park   WALKING

This 330-hectare native reserve overlooking Waikanae contains a large remnant of kohekohe forest. The reserve rises steeply from 150m to its highest point, Te Au (514m), a hike of around four hours. There are a couple of other tracks including the Kohekohe Walk, an easy 30-minute amble on a well-formed path. Access is off Reikorangi Rd, Waikanae.

🛏 Sleeping & Eating

Kapiti Gateway Motel   MOTEL $$

(☎0800 429 360, 04-902 5876; www.kapitigateway.co.nz; 114 Main Rd, Waikanae; d $115-155; 🛜 ❄) Tidy, airy motel on the highway with solar-heated pool, great hospitality and excellent local advice. Holiday hermits can make the most of the free wi-fi, kitchen facilities and Sky TV.

Long Beach   CAFE $$

(www.longbeach.net.nz; 40 Tutere St, Waikanae; meals $16-30; ⊘8.30am-10pm) Neighbourly, family-friendly Long Beach offers an extensive menu ranging from house-cured salmon and risotto through to pizza and fish and chips. With a large conservatory, it's bright and beachy, making it most suitable for socialising over a drink from an impeccable list. The Front Room cafe next door is also very good.

Ambience Café   CAFE $$

(10 Seaview Rd, Paraparaumu; lunch $13-22; ⊘8am-4pm Sun-Thu; ✍) A very 'Wellington' cafe, with both light and substantial meals made with relish, such as fish cakes, the BLT and colourful vegie options. Cake cabinet at full capacity, and great coffee (of course).

THE WAIRARAPA

The Wairarapa is the large tract of land east and northeast of Wellington, beyond the Tararua and Rimutaka Ranges. It is named after Wairarapa Moana – otherwise known as Lake Wairarapa and translating as 'sea of glistening waters'. This shallow 80-sq-km lake and the surrounding wetland is the focus of much-needed ecological restoration, redressing generations of sheep farming in its ambit. Fields of fluffy sheep still abound, as do vineyards and the associated hospitality which have turned the region into a decadent weekend retreat.

See www.wairarapanz.com for regional info, but also check out the **Classic New Zealand Wine Trail** (www.classicwinetrail. co.nz) – a useful tool for joining the dots throughout the Wairarapa and its neighbouring wine regions of Hawke's Bay and Marlborough.

Note that the telephone area code over here is 06, not 04 like most of the rest of the Wellington region.

Getting There & Around

From Wellington, **Tranz Metro** (0800 801 700; www.tranzmetro.co.nz) commuter trains run to Masterton ($17.50, five or six times daily on weekdays, two daily on weekends), calling at seven Wairarapa stations including Featherston and Carterton. For towns off the railway line, catch a Tranzit Coachlines bus (details available from **Metlink** (0800 801 700; www.metlink. org.nz) Its services run to all major Wairarapa towns as well as north to Palmerston North.

WAIRARAPA WINE COUNTRY

Wairarapa's world-renowned wine industry was nearly crushed in infancy. The region's first vines were planted in 1883, but the prohibition movement in 1908 soon put a cap on that corker idea. It wasn't until the 1980s that winemaking was revived, after Martinborough's *terroir* (natural environment) was discovered to be similar to Burgundy in France. A few vineyards soon sprang up, but the number has now ballooned to around 40 regionwide. Martinborough is the undisputed hub of the action, but vineyards around Gladstone and Masterton are also on the up. Keep an eye out for the occasional olive groves with tasting rooms, nestled among the vines.

Martinborough plays host to **Toast Martinborough** (www.toastmartinborough.co.nz; tickets $70), held annually on the third Sunday in November. Enjoyable on many levels (standing up and quite possibly lying on the grass), this is a hugely popular wine, food and music event, and you'll have to be quick on the draw to get a ticket.

The **Wairarapa Wines Harvest Festival** (www.wairarapawines.co.nz; tickets $45) celebrates the beginning of the harvest with an extravaganza of wine, food and family fun. It's held at a remote riverbank setting 10 minutes from Carterton on a Saturday in mid-March.

Wairarapa's wineries thrive on visitors; around half of Martinborough's 25-odd wineries welcome visitors every day, with most of the rest open at the weekends. Well-oiled cellar doors swing wide open for tastings; some places feature a cafe or restaurant, while some will rustle up a picnic platter to be enjoyed in their gardens. The *Wairarapa Wine Trail Map* (available from the Martinborough i-SITE and many other locations) will aid your navigations. Read all about it at www.winesfrommartinborough.com.

A handy place to sample and purchase many wines, and get advice on local cellar doors is the **Martinborough Wine Centre** (www.martinboroughwinecentre.co.nz; 6 Kitchener St; 10am-5pm), which also sells local olive oils, books, clothing and art.

The best and most ecofriendly way to explore the Wairarapa's wines is by bicycle, as the flat landscape makes for puff-free cruising. You can also knock off quite a few on foot. Should you require transport, however, hop on the daily tasting tour run by **Tranzit Tours** (06-370 6600, 0800 471 227; www.tranzittours.co.nz; tours from $150), which features four vineyard tastings, lunch and late-afternoon cheese and coffee.

Recommended Wineries

Ata Rangi (www.atarangi.co.nz; 14 Puruatanga Rd; 1-3pm Mon-Fri, noon-4pm Sat & Sun) One of the region's pioneering winemakers. Great drops across the board and cute cellar door.

Coney (03-306 8345; www.coneywines.co.nz; Dry River Rd; 11am-4pm Fri-Sun) Fingers crossed that your tasting host will be the inimitable Tim Coney, an affable character who

Martinborough

POP 1470

The sweetest visitor spot in the Wairarapa, Martinborough is a pretty town with a leafy town square and some charming old buildings, surrounded by a patchwork of pasture and a pinstripe of grapevines. It is famed for its wineries, which draw in visitors to nose the pinot and polish it off with good food, and snooze it off at boutique accommodation. Beyond the wineries, you'll need your own vehicle, with most of this area's notable sights out on the coast and along its rural roads. As is often the case, getting there is half the fun: the Martinborough area is splendid for a scenic drive.

🛏 Sleeping

★ Martinborough Top 10 Holiday Park
HOLIDAY PARK $

(☎06-306 8946, 0800 780 909; www.martinboroughholidaypark.com; cnr Princess & Dublin Sts; sites per person from $18, cabins $65-139; @🛜) An appealing camping ground with grapevine views, just five minutes' walk to town. It has shady trees and the town pool over the back fence, making it a cooling oasis on sticky days. Cabins are basic but great value, freeing up your dollars for the cellar door. Bike hire available from $25 per day.

Claremont
MOTEL $$

(☎0800 809 162, 06-306 9162; www.theclaremont.co.nz; 38 Regent St; d $130-158, 4-person apt $280; 🛜) A classy accommodation enclave 15

makes a mighty syrah and may sing at random. Home to the excellent **Trio Cafe** (mains $23-26) too; bookings recommended.

Haythornthwaite (www.ht3wines.co.nz; 45 Omarere Rd; ⊗1-5pm) Sustainable, hands-on winemaking producing complex drops including cherrylike pinot noir and gorgeous gewürztraminer.

Margrain (www.margrainvineyard.co.nz; cnr Ponatahi & Huangarua Rds; ⊗11am-5pm Fri-Sun) High-quailty wines across a wide range can be tasted at this character-filled cellar door, with a casual on-site cafe overlooking the vines.

Palliser (www.palliser.co.nz; Kitchener St; ⊗10.30am-4pm) Wines so good, even the Queen has some stashed away in her cellar. Slick outfit.

Poppies (www.poppiesmartinborough.co.nz; 91 Puruatanga Rd; ⊗11am-4pm) Delectable handcrafted wines served by the label's passionate winemaking and viticulturalist duo. Savour their wines alongside a well-matched platter at the stylishly simple cellar door.

Schubert (www.schubert.co.nz; 57 Cambridge Rd; ⊗11am-3pm) German imports who searched for and found the best spot in the world to produce their favourite wine: pinot noir. Compact cellar door large on personality with a fine range of wines including the unusual Tribianco, a blend of three white wine varieties.

Bicycle Rental

Bicycles are comfortable cruisers with saddle bags for your booty. Suffice to say, you ought to pay greater attention to your technique as the day wears on.

Christina Estate Vineyard (☎06-306 8920; christinaestate@xtra.co.nz; 28 Puruatanga Rd; full day bicycle/tandem $25/50; ⊗8.30am-6pm)

Green Jersey Cycle Tour Company (☎021 074 6640; www.greenjersey.co.nz; 3hr guided tour incl lunch $110)

March Hare (☎03-306 5010; www.march-hare.co.nz; 18 Kitchener St; full-day bike hire incl picnic lunch $65)

Martinborough Top 10 Holiday Park (☎06-306 8946, 0800 780 909; www.martinboroughholidaypark.com; cnr Princess & Dublin Sts; full day $35)

Martinborough Wine Centre (☎06-306 9040; www.martinboroughwinecentre.co.nz; 6 Kitchener St; half-/full day $25/35) minutes' walk to the town centre, the Claremont has two-storey, self-contained units in great nick, modern studios with spa baths, and sparkling two-bedroom apartments, all at reasonable rates (even cheaper in winter and/or midweek). Private outlooks, attractive gardens, barbecue areas and bike hire.

Aylstone Retreat BOUTIQUE HOTEL $$$
(✉06-306 9505; www.aylstone.co.nz; 19 Huangarua Rd; d incl breakfast $230-260; 🛜) Set among the vines on the edge of the village, this elegant retreat is a winning spot for the romantically inclined. Six en suite rooms exude a lightly floral, French-provincial charm, and share a pretty posh reading room, while the whole shebang is surrounded by micromansion garden sporting lawns, boxed hedges and chichi furniture.

✕ Eating & Drinking

Café Medici CAFE $$
(www.cafemedici.co.nz; 9 Kitchener St; breakfast & lunch $13-23, dinner $24-32; ⊘8.30am-4pm, dinner from 6.30pm Thu-Sat) A perennial favourite among townsfolk and regular visitors, this airy cafe has Florentine flourishes and a sunny courtyard. Tasty, home-cooked food includes muffins and pies, lovely brunch dishes such as Spanish eggs, and Med-flavoured dinner options such as Moroccan lamb tagine. Great coffee, too.

★ Tirohana Estate MODERN NZ $$
(✉06-306 9933; www.tirohanaestate.com; 42 Puruatanga Rd; lunch mains $16-33, 3-course prix fixe dinner $59; ⊘lunch noon-3pm, dinner 6pm-late Tue-Sun) A casual lunch over a glass or two will be much enjoyed on the terrace at this pretty vineyard, while evening dining in the elegant dining room is quite the occasion. The food, while 'comfort' in style (crumbed prawns, beef fillet and mash, bread-and-butter pudding), is amply proportioned, fresh and proficiently prepared. Impeccable service; dinner booking essential.

★ Micro Wine Bar WINE BAR
(www.microbar.co.nz; 14c Ohio St; ⊘3pm-late Thu-Mon) Moreish little Micro packs a punch with its excellent wine list (mostly local with some far-flung stars), notable craft-beer selection and yummy nibbles ranging from Asian dim sum to Mediterranean tapas. Catch the sun streetside, hole up in the romantic bar, or head to the sociable courtyard where an evening might slip very easily by.

Martinborough Hotel PUB
(www.themartinboroughhotel.com; Memorial Sq; ⊘8am-late) The historic Martinborough Hotel is home to the Settlers Bar, a friendly, well-run pub with a decent drinks list and both a bistro and bar menu (mains $18 to $32). Set yourself up in the sunshine on pavement tables or mingle inside with a mix of locals and out-of-towners.

☆ Entertainment

Circus CINEMA
(✉movieline 06-306 9434; www.circus.net.nz; 34 Jellicoe St; adult/child $16/11; ⊘3pm-late Wed-Mon) Lucky old Martinborough sports its own art-house cinema, and a stylish one it is too. This modern, microsize complex has two comfy studio theatres and a cafe opening out on to a sunny, somewhat Zen garden. Reasonably priced food (mains $22 to $32) includes bar snacks, pizza, mains with plenty of seasonal veg, and gelato.

❶ Information

Martinborough i-SITE (✉06-306 5010; www.wairarapanz.com; 18 Kitchener St; ⊘9am-5pm Mon-Fri, 10am-4pm Sat & Sun) This small office stocks wine-region maps, including one produced by the folks behind the useful site www.martinboroughnz.com.

Cape Palliser

The Wairarapa coast south of Martinborough around Palliser Bay and Cape Palliser is remote and sparsely populated, and a trip to its landmark lighthouse is a must-do if you can spare the time and have your own wheels. The drive to the Cape is just over an hour, but depending on stops you could take half- to a full day.

From Martinborough, the road wends through picturesque farmland before hitting the coast along Cape Palliser Road. This section of the drive is intensely scenic as it hugs the coast between the vast, wild ocean and black-sand beaches on the shoreside, and sheer cliffs on the other. Look for shadows of the South Island, visible on a clear day.

In these environs lies a significant wilderness area, Aorangi (Haurangi) Forest Park, which offers backcountry tramping, camping and a DOC cottage for rent. Detailed information is available from Martinborough i-SITE. Within the park are the Putangirua Pinnacles, accessed through the Putangirua Scenic Reserve where there is a DOC campsite and car park. Standing like giant organ pipes, these 'hoodoos' were formed by rain washing silt and sand away and exposing the underlying bedrock. It's an easy 1½-hour walk to the lookout, or take the 3½-hour loop track past hills and coastal viewpoints.

Heading south further along the coast is the wind-worn fishing village of **Ngawi**. The first things you'll notice here are the rusty bulldozers on the beach, used to drag fishing boats ashore. Note the grassy picnic spot next door. You won't find coffee here, but you will get a taste of salt.

Next stop is the malodorous **seal colony**, the North Island's largest breeding area for these fellers. Whatever you do in your quest for a photo, don't get between the seals and the sea. If you block their escape route they're likely to have a go at you!

Just beyond stands the **Cape Palliser Lighthouse**, where you can get a few puffs into the lungs on the 250-step climb to its foot. It's a beaut view from here, and a great place to linger if the wind isn't blowing your eyeballs into the back of your head.

On the way there or back, take the short detour to the crusty waterside settlement of **Lake Ferry**, overlooking Lake Onoke. The tastiest attraction here is the **Lake Ferry Hotel** (www.lakeferryhotel.co.nz; 1 Lake Ferry Rd; mains $12-28; ⊙from 11am), happily trapped in a time warp with its formica tables and resident old-timers. Pull up a pew in the window and enjoy a good feed of fish and chips.

However, don't leave Lake Ferry without venturing beyond the pub to the grey, shingled dunes at the rivermouth where the water rushes and swirls while big black-backed gulls circle overhead. This is a classic coastal corner of NZ where nothing ever happens but there's plenty to see.

Martinborough i-SITE can help with accommodation options in the Lake Ferry and Cape Palliser area, which include campsites and holiday homes for rent.

Greytown

POP 2200

The most seductive of several small towns along SH2, Greytown has tarted itself up over recent years and is now home to a permanent population at critical mass, and waves of Wellington weekenders. It has plenty of accommodation, some decent food, three high-street pubs and some swanky shopping. Check out www.greytown.co.nz for more information.

⊙ Sights

Cobblestones Village Museum   MUSEUM
(www.cobblestonesmuseum.org.nz; 169 Main St; adult/child/family $5/2/10; ⊙10am-4.30pm) Greytown was the country's first planned inland town: intact Victorian architectural specimens line the main street. Sporting a spruce new information centre, this darling museum is an enclave of period buildings and various historic objects, dotted around pretty grounds inviting a lie-down on a picnic blanket.

Schoc Chocolates   CHOCOLATIERIE
(www.chocolatetherapy.com; 177 Main St) No picnic? No worries. Visit Schoc in its 1920s cottage beside Cobblestones Village Museum. Sublime flavours, worth every single penny of 12 bucks a tablet. Truffles, rocky road and peanut brittle, too. Free tastings.

Stonehenge Aotearoa   MONUMENT
(☑06-377 1600; www.stonehenge-aotearoa.co.nz; tours adult/child $16/13; ⊙10am-4pm Wed-Sun, tours 11am Sat & Sun & by appointment) About 10km from Greytown, this full-scale adaptation of the UK's Stonehenge is oriented for its southern-hemisphere location on a grassy knoll overlooking the Wairarapa Plain. Its mission: to bring the night sky to life, even in daylight. The pretour talk and audiovisual presentation are excellent, and the henge itself a pretty surreal sight. Self-guided 'Stone Trek' tours are also available for adult/child $8/4.

🛌 Sleeping & Eating

Greytown Campground   CAMPSITE $
(☑027 449 4980, 06-304 9387; www.greytowncampground.co.nz; Kuratawhiti St; sites per person $14, cabins $40) A basic camping option with equally basic facilities inluding two handkerchief-sized cabins, scenically spread through Soldiers Memorial Park, 500m from town.

Greytown Hotel   HOTEL $
(☑06-304 9138; www.greytownhotel.co.nz; 33 Main St; s/d with shared bathroom $50/80; ☎) A serious contender for 'oldest hotel in New Zealand', the Top Pub (as it's known) is looking tidy for her age. Upstairs rooms are small and basic but comfortable, with no-frills furnishings and shared bathrooms. Downstairs is a modern dining room, alongside an ol' faithful lounge-bar (meals $14 to $34) and popular garden-courtyard.

Oak Estate Motor Lodge
MOTEL $$

(☑0800 843 625, 06-304 8188; www.oakestate.co.nz; cnr Main St & Hospital Rd; r $125-190; ☎) A stand of gracious roadside oaks and pretty gardens shield a smart complex of self-contained units: studios, one- and two-bedroom options.

French Baker
BAKERY $

(81 Main St; light meals $7-13; ☒8am-3pm Mon-Fri, to 4pm Sat & Sun) Buttery croissants, tempting tarts and authentic breads – this artisan baking is le real McCoy. Grab and go from the cabinet, or tuck into a breakfast of muesli, toast or a bacon buttie washed down with espresso.

Saluté
TAPAS $$

(www.salute.net.nz; 83 Main St; tapas $8-17, pizzas $20; ☒noon-late Wed-Sat, 10.30-3.30pm Sun; ✐) Moroccan-flavoured Saluté will suit you down to the ground if you like saucy, succulent, crisp, charred and fried, along with lashings of olive oil and wedges of lemon. Food so colourful you'll forget you're in grey-town.

Masterton & Around

Masterton (population 20,100) is the Wairarapa's utilitarian hub, an unselfconscious town getting on with its business. Its main claim to immortality is the 50-year-old sheep-shearing competition, the international **Golden Shears** (www.goldenshears.co.nz), held annually in the first week of March.

Masterton spins the wool out a bit longer at the **Wool Shed** (www.thewoolshednz.com; Dixon St; adult/child/family $8/2/15; ☒10am-4pm), a baaaa-loody marvellous little museum dedicated to NZ's sheep-shearing and wool-production industries. It's also a good place to get yourself a home-knit hat.

Next door is the region's foremost cultural institution, the small but rather splendid **Aratoi Wairarapa Museum of Art & History** (www.aratoi.co.nz; cnr Bruce & Dixon Sts; admission by donation; ☒10am-4.30pm), which hosts an impressive program of exhibitions and events (and has a very nice shop!).

Opposite the Wool Shed and Aratoi is **Queen Elizabeth Park** (Dixon St), perfect for stretching your legs. Feed the ducks, dump someone on the see-saw, have a round of minigolf or practise your high catches on the cricket oval. Refuel with a magnificent meat pie, purchased from Masterton's notable bakery, the **Ten O'Clock Cookie** (180 Queen St; ☒7am-4.30pm Mon-Fri, 8am-2.30pm Sat).

If none of this is sounding particularly rock and roll, we've got news for you. Masterton has an absolutely ace music venue. **King Street Live** (www.kingstreetlive.co.nz; ☒4pm late Thu-Sat, plus other event nights) lures a diverse range of performers to play in its properly outfitted and professionally run, acoustically excellent, groovalicious, complete-with-garden-bar music venue, co-owned by gentleman-player Warren Maxwell (of legendary Trinity Roots – play catch-up where you can).

There are a few interesting sights further afield, one of which is **Castlepoint**, on the coast 68km east of Masterton. It's a truly awesome, end-of-the-world place, with a reef, the lofty 162m-high Castle Rock, largely safe swimming and walking tracks. There's an easy (but sometimes ludicrously windy) 30-minute return walk across the reef to the lighthouse, where 70-plus shell species are fossilised in the cliffs. Another one-hour return walk runs to a huge limestone cave (take a torch), or take the 1½-hour return track from Deliverance Cove to Castle Rock. Keep well away from the lower reef when there are heavy seas. Ask the staff at Masterton i-SITE about accommodation here.

Thirty kilometres north of Masterton on SH2, **Pukaha Mt Bruce National Wildlife Centre** (www.pukaha.org.nz; aduld/child/family $20/6/50; ☒9am-4.30pm) is not only one of NZ's most successful wildlife and captive breeding centres, it's also the most readily accessible bush experience off the highway. Get a good overview of the 1000-hectare wilderness on the scenic 1½-hour loop walk which affords good vantage points. The visitor centre has various exhibits including an interactive gallery, while alongside is a kiwi house with roaming adult birds, an incubation area and nursery. A series of aviaries allows viewing of other special native birds. The daily visitor program allows you to see tuatara being fed (11.30am), attend the eel-feeding (1.30pm) and watch the kaka circus (3pm). There are also guided walks, day time and at night (adult/child from $20/6). There's a cafe and shop on site.

The turn-off to the main eastern entrance of the **Tararua Forest Park** (www.doc.govt.nz) is just south of Masterton on SH2; follow Norfolk Rd about 15km to the gates. Mountain streams dart through virgin forest in this reserve, known as **Holdsworth**. A recreation area has swimming holes, picnic spots, campsites and a lodge. Heading into the hills, walks include short, easy family tramps, excellent one- or two-day tramps, and longer, challenging tramps for experienced bush-bods (west through to Otaki Forks). The resident caretaker has maps and hut accommodation info. Check weather and track updates before setting off, and be prepared to be baked, battered and buffeted by fickle conditions.

Further south is **Carterton**, another of the small rural towns that punctuates SH2. It boasts by far the best hanging flower baskets of the lot, and adds a raft of good secondhand shopping and some good cafes to boot – don't pass through without stopping for a wander.

As you've had the stamina to read this far, it's only fair that we share with you one final tip. If you've got your own wheels, and you like a good garden bar, head to the **Gladstone Inn** (51 Gladstone Rd, Gladstone). Cheers!

ⓘ Information

Masterton i-SITE (☏ 370 0900; www.wairarapanz.com; cnr Dixon & Bruce Sts; ⊙ 9am-5pm Mon-Fri, 10am-4pm Sat & Sun) Can sort you out with oodles of information including a copy of the *Wairarapa Visitor Guide*, advice on accommodation, and directions to the Gladstone Inn.

Understand the North Island

THE NORTH ISLAND TODAY...................364

Auckland emerging as a cosmopolitan international city, sporting successes and musical mastery – time to take a Kiwi temperature check.

HISTORY 366

Tread a New Zealand timeline from Maori origins to Pakeha arrivals and recent ructions.

ENVIRONMENT..............................376

Get the low-down on the land, flora and fauna, national parks and environmental issues.

MAORI CULTURE 383

Read up on NZ's first people: history, religion, legends, traditions and the arts (and, of course, the *haka*).

THE KIWI PSYCHE 391

Global psychiatry: lie down on this couch NZ, and tell us all about yourself.

ARTS & MUSIC 396

The best Kiwi books, movies, TV, music and visual arts – this little nation punches well above its artistic weight.

The North Island Today

New Zealand has had a bad run on the disaster front in recent years, between devastating earthquakes and a mining tragedy, not to mention the usual storms, droughts, drownings, sinkings and suchlike that make headline news. The global financial crisis hasn't helped either, with money troubles well and truly trickling down to ground level. Despite this, a typically plucky New Zealand public has turned to the sporting arena – and increasingly the arts – to put a smile on its dial.

Top Films

The Hobbit trilogy (Sir Peter Jackson; 2012–14)
Lord of the Rings trilogy (Sir Peter Jackson; 2001–03)
The Piano (Jane Campion; 1993)
Whale Rider (Niki Caro; 2002)
Once Were Warriors (Lee Tamahori; 1994)

Etiquette

Rugby Try to feign some enthusiasm. If in doubt, mumble 'forward pass' or 'offside'.
Possums Don't express any affection for the tree-munching possum.
Australanders Be sure never to mistake a New Zealander for an Australian.
Dinnertime In Maori culture, sitting on a table is bad manners.

Top Books

The Luminaries (Eleanor Catton; 2013)
Mister Pip (Lloyd Jones; 2007)
Live Bodies (Maurice Gee; 1998)
The 10pm Question (Kate De Goldi; 2009)
The Collected Stories of Katherine Mansfield (2007)

Emerging International City

New Zealand may be a long way away from everywhere, but it is not immune to the vagaries of the global economy. In September 2010, just as the country was edging out of its worst recession in 30 years, a magnitude 7.1 earthquake struck near Christchurch, the nation's second-largest city, in the South Island. The damage was extensive but miraculously no lives were lost.

Then, on 22 February 2011, a magnitude 6.3 earthquake struck Christchurch. This time, 185 people lost their lives. Numerous buildings, already weakened by the September 2010 quake were damaged beyond repair and had to be demolished completely.

The nation's nerves were jangled yet again in July and August 2013 as moderate earthquakes struck the top of the South Island. Widely felt in NZ's capital Wellington on the North Island, they served as a seismic and shaky reminder to New Zealanders.

Through the admirable resilience and innovation of the city's residents, Christchurch is now re-emerging as one of the country's most exciting cities, and was named by Lonely Planet as one of the world's top 10 cities in *Best in Travel 2013*. On the North Island, the country's economic hub of Auckland was named one of the world's must-visit cities in *Best in Travel 2014,* and is rapidly emerging as the country's only truly international city.

Around one in three New Zealanders now lives in Auckland, and through immigration and better employment opportunities the city is growing faster than the provinces. Housing prices continue to outstrip the rest of the country, and important decisions need to be taken regarding public transport, housing density and urban sprawl. Significant investment in the hospitality industry has boosted new restaurant precincts, and finally the city is showcasing its stunning waterfront location on the Hauraki Gulf.

At the opposite end of the North Island, Wellington maintains its reputation as one of the world's coolest and more interesting capital cities, channelling Portland and San Francisco in its laid-back combination of coffee, craft beer and heritage wooden housing in hilly central suburbs.

Reasons to be Cheerful

Christchurch's recovery and rebuild is still a major preoccupation across NZ, producing good news and bad stories in equal measure. On one hand it is testing relationships between the citizens and government agencies, as tough decisions are made about fix-ups and pay-outs. On the other, the city's recovery reinforces Kiwis' perceptions of themselves as 'battlers' with strong communities and civic pride.

New Zealanders have little difficulty in finding something to feel proud about. While the All Blacks remain a foundation – not only for their sporting achievements but as figureheads for 'brand NZ' – the depth of Kiwi talent ranges far beyond the rugby pitch. Following the All Blacks' success at the 2011 Rugby World Cup, this featherweight country punched well above its weight at the 2012 London Olympics. Claiming six gold medals, Team NZ gave traditional rival and sporting giant Australia a run for its money as it only managed to win one more. Other Kiwi sporting stars making their mark around the globe include young golfing sensation Lydia Ko, NBA rookie Steve Adams, IndyCar speedster Scott Dixon, and Valerie Adams, the greatest female shot putter the world has ever seen.

While Sir Peter Jackson holds his position as a heavyweight in cinema with his blockbusting adaptations of *The Hobbit,* another major player has thrown his hat into the ring. Canadian director James Cameron has set up a rural home base near Wellington and will create the *Avatar* sequels in the capital, bringing substantial investment and cementing NZ's reputation as a world-class filmmaking destination.

Pop pundits are also taking note of new Kiwi stars, with Grammy Award–winning Lorde (she of *Pure Heroine,* one of *Rolling Stone*'s albums of 2013) and Kimbra (of Goyte's 2012 smash-hit *Somebody That I Used to Know*) making huge impressions. Pages are also being turned on the international literary scene, as evidenced by Cantabrian Eleanor Catton. She claimed one of the world's most coveted publishing accolades in 2013, the Man Booker Prize, with her voluminous historical novel *The Luminaries* – only the second New Zealander to do so.

POPULATION: **3.4 MILLION**

AREA: **113,729 SQ KM**

GDP GROWTH: **1.4% (2013)**

INFLATION: **1.4% (2013)**

UNEMPLOYMENT: **6.2% (2013)**

if the North Island were 100 people

66 would be European
15 would be Maori
10 would be Asian
8 would be Pacific Islanders
1 would be other

Where they live

(% of New Zealanders)

64 North Island
20 South Island
10 Australia
5 Rest of the World
1 Travelling

population per sq km

NORTH ISLAND   SOUTH ISLAND   AUSTRALIA

≈ 3 people

History

by James Belich

New Zealand's history is not long, but it is fast. In less than a thousand years these islands have produced two new peoples: the Polynesian Maori and European New Zealanders. The latter are often known by their Maori name, 'Pakeha' (though not all like the term). NZ shares some of its history with the rest of Polynesia, and with other European settler societies, but has unique features as well. It is the similarities that make the differences so interesting, and vice versa.

One of New Zealand's foremost modern historians, James Belich has written a number of books on NZ history and hosted the TV documentary series *The New Zealand Wars*.

Making Maori

Despite persistent myths, there is no doubt that the first settlers of NZ were the Polynesian forebears of today's Maori. Beyond that, there are a lot of question marks. Exactly where in east Polynesia did they come from – the Cook Islands, Tahiti, the Marquesas? When did they arrive? Did the first settlers come in one group or several? Some evidence, such as the diverse DNA of the Polynesian rats that accompanied the first settlers, suggests multiple founding voyages. On the other hand, only rats and dogs brought by the founders have survived, not the more valuable pigs and chickens. The survival of these cherished animals would have had high priority, and their failure to be successfully introduced suggests fewer voyages.

NZ seems small compared with Australia, but it is bigger than Britain, and very much bigger than other Polynesian islands. Its regions vary wildly in environment and climate. Prime sites for first settlement were warm coastal gardens for the food plants brought from Polynesia (kumara or sweet potato, gourd, yam and taro); sources of workable stone for knives and adzes; and areas with abundant big game. NZ has no native land mammals apart from a few species of bat, but 'big game' is no exaggeration: the islands were home to a dozen species of moa (a large flightless bird), the largest of which weighed

TIMELINE	AD 1000–1200	1642	1769
	Possible date of the arrival of Maori in NZ. Solid archaeological evidence points to about AD 1200, but much earlier dates have been suggested for the first human impact on the environment.	First European contact: Abel Tasman arrives on an expedition from the Dutch East Indies (Indonesia) to find the 'Great South Land'. His party leaves without landing, after a sea skirmish with Maori.	European contact recommences with visits by James Cook and Jean de Surville. Despite some violence, both manage to communicate with Maori. This time NZ's link with the outside world proves permanent.

up to 240kg, about twice the size of an ostrich. There were also other species of flightless birds and large sea mammals such as fur seals, all unaccustomed to being hunted. For people from small Pacific islands, this was like hitting the jackpot. The first settlers spread far and fast, from the top of the North Island to the bottom of the South Island within the first 100 years. High-protein diets are likely to have boosted population growth.

By about 1400, however, with big-game supply dwindling, Maori economics turned from big game to small game – forest birds and rats – and from hunting to gardening and fishing. A good living could still be made, but it required detailed local knowledge, steady effort and complex communal organisation, hence the rise of the Maori tribes. Competition for resources increased, conflict did likewise, and this led to the building of increasingly sophisticated fortifications, known as *pa*. Vestiges of *pa* earthworks can still be seen around the country (on the hilltops of Auckland, for example).

The Maori had no metals and no written language (and no alcoholic drinks or drugs). But their culture and spiritual life was rich and distinctive. Below Ranginui (sky father) and Papatuanuku (earth mother) were various gods of land, forest and sea, joined by deified ancestors over time. The mischievous demigod Maui was particularly important. In legend, he vanquished the sun and fished up the North Island before meeting his death between the thighs of the goddess Hine-nui-te-po in an attempt to conquer the human mortality embodied in her. Maori traditional performance art, the group singing and dancing known as *kapa haka*, has real power, even for modern audiences. Visual art, notably woodcarving, is something special – 'like nothing but itself', in the words of 18th-century explorer-scientist Joseph Banks.

Similarities in language between Maori and Tahitian indicate close contact in historical times. Maori is about as similar to Tahitian as Spanish is to French, despite the 4294km separating these island groups.

THE MORIORI & THEIR MYTH

One of NZ's most persistent legends is that Maori found mainland NZ already occupied by a more peaceful and racially distinct Melanesian people, known as the Moriori, whom they exterminated. This myth has been regularly debunked by scholars since the 1920s, but somehow hangs on.

To complicate matters, there were real 'Moriori', and Maori did treat them badly. The real Moriori were the people of the Chatham Islands, a windswept group about 900km east of the mainland. They were, however, fully Polynesian, and descended from Maori – 'Moriori' was their version of the same word. Mainland Maori arrived in the Chathams in 1835, as a spin-off of the Musket Wars, killing some Moriori and enslaving the rest. But they did not exterminate them. The mainland Moriori remain a myth.

1772	1790s	1818–36	1837
Marion du Fresne's French expedition arrives; it stays for some weeks at the Bay of Islands. Relations with Maori start well, but a breach of Maori *tapu* (sacred law) leads to violence.	Whaling ships and sealing gangs arrive in the country. Relations are established with Maori, with Europeans depending on the contact for essentials such as food, water and protection.	Intertribal Maori 'Musket Wars' take place: tribes acquire muskets and win bloody victories against tribes without them. The war tapers off in 1836, probably due to the equal distribution of weapons.	Possums are introduced to New Zealand from Australia. Brilliant.

Enter Europe

NZ became an official British colony in 1840, but the first authenticated contact between Maori and the outside world took place almost two centuries earlier in 1642, in Golden Bay at the top of the South Island. Two Dutch ships sailed from Indonesia, to search for southern land and anything valuable it might contain. The commander, Abel Tasman, was instructed to pretend to any natives he might meet 'that you are by no means eager for precious metals, so as to leave them ignorant of the value of the same'.

When Tasman's ships anchored in the bay, local Maori came out in their canoes to make the traditional challenge: friends or foes? Misunderstanding this, the Dutch challenged back, by blowing trumpets. When a boat was lowered to take a party between the two ships, it was attacked. Four crewmen were killed. Tasman sailed away and did not come back; nor did any other European for 127 years. But the Dutch did leave a name: 'Nieuw Zeeland' or 'New Sealand'.

Contact between Maori and Europeans was renewed in 1769, when English and French explorers arrived, under James Cook and Jean de Surville. Relations were more sympathetic, and exploration continued, motivated by science, profit and great power rivalry. Cook made two more visits between 1773 and 1777, and there were further French expeditions.

Unofficial visits, by whaling ships in the north and sealing gangs in the south, began in the 1790s. The first mission station was founded in 1814, in the Bay of Islands, and was followed by dozens of others: Anglican, Methodist and Catholic. Trade in flax and timber generated small European–Maori settlements by the 1820s. Surprisingly, the most numerous category of Western visitor was probably American. New England whaling ships favoured the Bay of Islands for rest and recreation; 271 called there between 1833 and 1839 alone. To whalers, 'rest and recreation' meant sex and drink. Their favourite haunt, the little town of Kororareka (now Russell) was known to the missionaries as 'the hellhole of the Pacific'. New England visitors today might well have distant relatives among the local Maori.

One or two dozen bloody clashes dot the history of Maori–European contact before 1840 but, given the number of visits, interracial conflict was modest. Europeans needed Maori protection, food and labour, and Maori came to need European articles, especially muskets. Whaling stations and mission stations were linked to local Maori groups by intermarriage, which helped keep the peace. Most warfare was between Maori and Maori: the terrible intertribal 'Musket Wars' of 1818–36. Because Northland had the majority of early contact with Europe, its

Abel Tasman named NZ Statenland, assuming it was connected to Staten Island near Argentina. It was subsequently named after the province of Zeeland in Tasman's Holland.

The Ministry for Culture & Heritage's history website (www. nzhistory.net.nz) is an excellent source of info on NZ history.

1840	1844	1858	1860–69
Starting at Waitangi in the Bay of Islands on 6 February, around 500 chiefs countrywide sign the Treaty of Waitangi to 'settle' sovereignty once and for all. NZ becomes a nominal British colony.	Young Ngapuhi chief Hone Heke challenges British sovereignty, first by cutting down the British flag at Kororareka (now Russell), then by sacking the town itself. The ensuing Northland war continues until 1846.	The Waikato chief Te Wherowhero is installed as the first Maori King.	First and Second Taranaki wars, starting with the controversial swindling of Maori land by the government at Waitara, and continuing with outrage over the confiscation of more land as a result.

CAPTAIN JAMES COOK

If aliens ever visit earth, they may wonder what to make of the countless obelisks, faded plaques and graffiti-covered statues of a stiff, wigged figure gazing out to sea from Alaska to Australia, from NZ to North Yorkshire, from Siberia to the South Pacific. James Cook (1728–79) explored more of the earth's surface than anyone in history, and it's impossible to travel the Pacific without encountering the captain's image and his controversial legacy in the lands he opened to the West.

For a man who travelled so widely, and rose to such fame, Cook came from an extremely pinched and provincial background. The son of a day labourer in rural Yorkshire, he was born in a mud cottage, had little schooling, and seemed destined for farm work – and for his family's grave plot in a village churchyard. Instead, Cook went to sea as a teenager, worked his way up from coal-ship servant to naval officer, and attracted notice for his exceptional charts of Canada. But Cook remained a little-known second lieutenant until, in 1768, the Royal Navy chose him to command a daring voyage to the South Seas.

In a converted coal ship called *Endeavour*, Cook sailed to Tahiti, and then became the first European to land at NZ and the east coast of Australia. Though the ship almost sank after striking the Great Barrier Reef, and 40% of the crew died from disease and accidents, the *Endeavour* limped home in 1771. On a return voyage (1772–75), Cook became the first navigator to pierce the Antarctic Circle and circle the globe near its southernmost latitude, demolishing the myth that a vast, populous and fertile continent surrounded the South Pole. Cook criss-crossed the Pacific from Easter Island to Melanesia, charting dozens of islands between. Though Maori killed and cooked 10 sailors, the captain remained sympathetic to islanders. 'Notwithstanding they are cannibals,' he wrote, 'they are naturally of a good disposition.'

On Cook's final voyage (1776–79), in search of a northwest passage between the Atlantic and Pacific, he became the first European to visit Hawaii, and coasted America from Oregon to Alaska. Forced back by Arctic pack ice, Cook returned to Hawaii, where he was killed during a skirmish with islanders who had initially greeted him as a Polynesian god. In a single decade of discovery, Cook had filled in the map of the Pacific and, as one French navigator put it, 'left his successors with little to do but admire his exploits'.

But Cook's travels also spurred colonisation of the Pacific, and within a few decades of his death, missionaries, whalers, traders and settlers began transforming (and often devastating) island cultures. As a result, many indigenous people now revile Cook as an imperialist villain who introduced disease, dispossession and other ills to the Pacific (hence the frequent vandalising of Cook monuments). However, as islanders revive traditional crafts and practices, from tattooing to *tapa* (traditional barkcloth), they have turned to the art and writing of Cook and his men as a resource for cultural renewal. For good and ill, a Yorkshire farm boy remains the single most significant figure in the shaping of the modern Pacific.

Tony Horwitz is a Pulitzer Prize–winning reporter and nonfiction author. In researching Blue Latitudes (or Into the Blue), *Tony travelled the Pacific – 'boldly going where Captain Cook has gone before'.*

1861	1863–64	1868–72	1886–87
Gold discovered in Otago by Gabriel Read, an Australian prospector. As a result, the population of Otago climbs from less than 13,000 to over 30,000 in six months.	Waikato Land War. Up to 5000 Maori resist an invasion mounted by 20,000 imperial, colonial and 'friendly' Maori troops. Despite surprising successes, Maori are defeated and much land is confiscated.	East Coast war. Te Kooti, having led an escape from his prison on the Chatham Islands, leads a holy guerrilla war in the Urewera region. He finally retreats to establish the Ringatu Church.	Tuwharetoa tribe gifts the mountains of Ruapehu, Ngauruhoe and Tongariro to the government to establish the world's fourth national park.

Ngapuhi tribe acquired muskets first. Under their great general Hongi Hika, Ngapuhi then raided south, winning bloody victories against tribes without muskets. Once they acquired muskets, these tribes saw off Ngapuhi, but also raided further south in their turn. The domino effect continued to the far south of the South Island in 1836. The missionaries claimed that the Musket Wars then tapered off through their influence, but the restoration of the balance of power through the equal distribution of muskets was probably more important.

Europe brought such things as pigs (at last) and potatoes, which benefited Maori, while muskets and diseases had the opposite effect. The negative effects have been exaggerated, however. Europeans expected peoples like the Maori to simply fade away at contact, and some early estimates of Maori population were overly high – up to one million. Current estimates are between 85,000 and 110,000 for 1769. The Musket Wars killed perhaps 20,000, and new diseases did considerable damage too (although NZ had the natural quarantine of distance: infected Europeans usually recovered or died during the long voyage, and smallpox, for example, which devastated native Americans, did not make it here). By 1840, the Maori had been reduced to about 70,000, a decline of at least 20%. Maori bent under the weight of European contact, but they certainly did not break.

Making Pakeha

By 1840, Maori tribes described local Europeans as 'their Pakeha', and valued the profit and prestige they brought. Maori wanted more of both, and concluded that accepting nominal British authority was the way to get them. At the same time, the British government was overcoming its reluctance to undertake potentially expensive intervention in NZ. It too was influenced by profit and prestige, but also by humanitarian considerations. It believed, wrongly but sincerely, that Maori could not handle the increasing scale of unofficial European contact. In 1840, the two peoples struck a deal, symbolised by the treaty first signed at Waitangi on 6 February that year. The Treaty of Waitangi now has a standing not dissimilar to that of the Constitution in the US, but is even more contested. The original problem was a discrepancy between British and Maori understandings of it. The English version promised Maori full equality as British subjects in return for complete rights of government. The Maori version also promised that Maori would retain their chieftainship, which implied local rights of government. The problem was not great at first, because the Maori version applied outside the small European settlements. But as those settlements grew, conflict brewed.

In 1840, there were only about 2000 Europeans in NZ, with the shanty town of Kororareka (now Russell) as the capital and biggest settlement.

Scottish influence can still be felt in NZ, particularly in the south of the South Island. NZ has more Scottish pipe bands per capita than Scotland itself.

The Waitangi Treaty Grounds, where the Treaty of Waitangi was first signed in 1840, is now a tourist attraction for Kiwis and non-Kiwis alike. Each year on 6 February, Waitangi hosts treaty commemorations and protests.

1893	1901	1908	1914–18
NZ becomes the first country in the world to grant the vote to women, following a campaign led by Kate Sheppard, who petitioned the government for years.	NZ politely declines the invitation to join the new Commonwealth of Australia.	NZ physicist Ernest Rutherford is awarded the Nobel Prize in chemistry for 'splitting the atom', investigating the disintegration of elements and the chemistry of radioactive substances.	NZ's contribution to WWI is staggering for a country of just over one million people: about 100,000 NZ men serve overseas. Some 60,000 become casualties, mostly on the Western Front in France.

By 1850, six new settlements had been formed with 22,000 settlers between them. About half of these had arrived under the auspices of the New Zealand Company and its associates. The company was the brainchild of Edward Gibbon Wakefield, who also influenced the settlement of South Australia. Wakefield hoped to short-circuit the barbarous frontier phase of settlement with 'instant civilisation', but his success was limited. From the 1850s, his settlers, who included a high proportion of upper-middle-class gentlefolk, were swamped by succeeding waves of immigrants that continued to wash in until the 1880s. These people were part of the great British and Irish diaspora that also populated Australia and much of North America, but the NZ mix was distinctive. Lowland Scots settlers were more prominent in NZ than elsewhere, for example, with the possible exception of parts of Canada. NZ's Irish, even the Catholics, tended to come more from the north of Ireland. NZ's English tended to come from the counties close to London. Small groups of Germans, Scandinavians and Chinese made their way in, though the last faced increasing racial prejudice from the 1880s, when the Pakeha population reached half a million.

Much of the mass immigration from the 1850s to the 1870s was assisted by the provincial and central governments, which also mounted large-scale public works schemes, especially in the 1870s under Julius Vogel. In 1876, Vogel abolished the provinces on the grounds that they were hampering his development efforts. The last imperial governor with substantial power was the talented but Machiavellian George Grey, who ended his second governorship in 1868. Thereafter, the governors (governors-general from 1917) were largely just nominal heads of state; the head of government, the premier or prime minister, had more power. The central government, originally weaker than the provincial governments, the imperial governor and the Maori tribes, eventually exceeded the power of all three.

The Maori tribes did not go down without a fight, however. Indeed, their resistance was one of the most formidable ever mounted against European expansion, comparable to that of the Sioux and Seminole in the US. The first clash took place in 1843 in the Wairau Valley, now a wine-growing district. A posse of settlers set out to enforce the myth of British control, but encountered the reality of Maori control. Twenty-two settlers were killed, including Wakefield's brother, Arthur, along with about six Maori. In 1845, more serious fighting broke out in the Bay of Islands, when Hone Heke sacked a British settlement. Heke and his ally Kawiti baffled three British punitive expeditions, using a modern variant of the traditional *pa* fortification. Vestiges of these innovative earthworks can still be seen at Ruapekapeka (south of Kawakawa). Governor Grey claimed victory in the north, but few were convinced at the time. Grey

Rumours of late survivals of the giant moa bird abound, but none have been authenticated. So if you see a moa in your travels, photograph it – you'll have just made the greatest zoological discovery of the last 100 years.

'I believe we were all glad to leave New Zealand. It is not a pleasant place. Amongst the natives there is absent that charming simplicity...and the greater part of the English are the very refuse of society.' Charles Darwin, referring to Kororareka (Russell), in 1860.

1931	1935–49	1936	1939–45
Napier earthquake kills 131 people.	First Labour government in power, under Michael Savage. This government creates NZ's pioneering version of the welfare state, and also takes some independent initiatives in foreign policy.	NZ aviatrix Jean Batten becomes the first aviator to fly solo from Britain to NZ.	NZ troops back Britain and the Allied war effort during WWII; from 1942 around 100,000 Americans arrive to protect NZ from the Japanese.

To find out more about the New Zealand Wars, visit www.newzealandwars.co.nz.

had more success in the south, where he arrested the formidable Ngati Toa chief Te Rauparaha, who until then wielded great influence on both sides of Cook Strait. Pakeha were able to swamp the few Maori living in the South Island, but the fighting of the 1840s confirmed that the North Island at that time comprised a European fringe around an independent Maori heartland.

In the 1850s, settler populations and aspirations grew, and fighting broke out again in 1860. The wars burned on sporadically until 1872 over much of the North Island. In the early years, a Maori nationalist organisation, the King Movement, was the backbone of resistance. In

LAND WARS

Five separate major conflicts made up what are now collectively known as the New Zealand Wars (also referred to as the Land Wars or Maori Wars). Starting in Northland and moving throughout the North Island, the wars had many complex causes, but *whenua* (land) was the one common factor. In all five wars, Maori fought both for and against the government, on whose side stood the Imperial British Army, Australians and NZ's own Armed Constabulary. Land confiscations imposed on the Maori as punishment for involvement in these wars are still the source of conflict today, with the government struggling to finance compensation for what are now acknowledged to have been illegal seizures.

Northland war (1844–46) 'Hone Heke's War' began with the famous chopping of the flagpole at Kororareka (now Russell) and 'ended' at Ruapekapeka (south of Kawakawa). In many ways, this was almost a civil war between rival Ngapuhi factions, with the government taking one side against the other.

First Taranaki war (1860–61) Starting in Waitara, the first Taranaki war inflamed the passions of Maori across the North Island.

Waikato war (1863–64) The largest of the five wars. Predominantly involving Kingitanga, the Waikato war was caused in part by what the government saw as a challenge to sovereignty. However, it was land, again, that was the real reason for friction. Following defeats such as Rangiriri, the Waikato people were pushed entirely from their own lands, south into what became known as the King Country.

Second Taranaki war (1865–69) Caused by Maori resistance to land confiscations stemming from the first Taranaki war, this was perhaps the war in which the Maori came closest to victory, under the brilliant, one-eyed prophet-general Titokowaru. However, once he lost the respect of his warriors (probably through an indiscretion with the wife of one of his warriors), the war was lost.

East Coast war (1868–72) Te Kooti's holy guerrilla war.

Errol Hunt

1948	1953	1973	1974
Maurice Scheslinger invents the Buzzy Bee, NZ's most famous children's toy.	New Zealander Edmund Hillary, with Tenzing Norgay, 'knocks the bastard off'; the pair become the first men to reach the summit of Mt Everest.	Fledgling Kiwi prog-rockers Split Enz enter a TV talent quest…finishing second to last.	Pacific Island migrants who have outstayed visas ('overstayers') are subjected to Dawn Raids by immigration police under Robert Muldoon and the National government. These raids continue until the early 1980s.

later years, some remarkable prophet-generals, notably Titokowaru and Te Kooti, took over. Most wars were small-scale, but the Waikato war of 1863–64 was not. This conflict, fought at the same time as the American Civil War, involved armoured steamships, ultramodern heavy artillery, telegraph and 10 proud British regular regiments. Despite the odds, the Maori won several battles, such as that at Gate Pa, near Tauranga, in 1864. But in the end they were ground down by European numbers and resources. Maori political, though not cultural, independence ebbed away in the last decades of the 19th century. It finally expired when police invaded its last sanctuary, the Urewera Mountains, in 1916.

Welfare & Warfare

From the 1850s to the 1880s, despite conflict with Maori, the Pakeha economy boomed on the back of wool exports, gold rushes and massive overseas borrowing for development. The crash came in the 1880s, when NZ experienced its Long Depression. In 1890, the Liberals came to power, and stayed there until 1912, helped by a recovering economy. The Liberals were NZ's first organised political party, and the first of several governments to give NZ a reputation as 'the world's social laboratory'. NZ became the first country in the world to give women the vote in 1893, and introduced old-age pensions in 1898. The Liberals also introduced a long-lasting system of industrial arbitration, but this was not enough to prevent bitter industrial unrest in 1912–13. This happened under the conservative 'Reform' government, which had replaced the Liberals in 1912. Reform remained in power until 1928, and later transformed itself into the National Party. Renewed depression struck in 1929, and the NZ experience of it was as grim as any. The derelict little farmhouses still seen in rural areas often date from this era.

In 1935, a second reforming government took office: the First Labour government, led by Michael Joseph Savage, easily NZ's favourite Australian. For a time, the Labour government was considered the most socialist government outside Soviet Russia. But, when the chips were down in Europe in 1939, Labour had little hesitation in backing Britain.

NZ had also backed Britain in the Boer War (1899–1902) and WWI (1914–18), with dramatic losses in WWI in particular. You can count the cost in almost any little NZ town. A central square or park will contain a memorial lined with names – more for WWI than WWII. Even in WWII, however, NZ did its share of fighting: around 100,000 New Zealanders fought in Europe and the Middle East. NZ, a peaceful-seeming country, has spent much of its history at war. In the 19th century it fought at home; in the 20th, overseas.

HISTORY WELFARE & WARFARE

'Kaore e mau te rongo – ake, ake!' (Peace never shall be made – never, never!) War chief Rewi Maniapoto in response to government troops at the battle of Orakau, 1864.

'God's own country, but the devil's own mess.' Prime Minister Richard (King Dick) Seddon, speaking on the source of NZ's self-proclaimed nickname 'Godzone'.

1981	1985	1992	1995
Springbok rugby tour divides the nation. Many New Zealanders show a strong anti-apartheid stance by protesting the games. Others feel sport and politics shouldn't mix, and support the tour going ahead.	*Rainbow Warrior* is sunk in Auckland Harbour by French government agents to prevent the Greenpeace protest ship from making its intended voyage to Moruroa, where the French are conducting nuclear tests.	Government begins reparations for the Land Wars, and confirms Maori fishing rights in the 'Sealord deal'. Major settlements follow, including, in 1995, reparations for the Waikato land confiscations.	Peter Blake and Russel Coutts win the America's Cup for NZ, sailing *Black Magic*; red socks become a matter of national pride.

Better Britons?

British visitors have long found NZ hauntingly familiar. This is not simply a matter of the British and Irish origin of most Pakeha. It also stems from the tightening of NZ links with Britain from 1882, when refrigerated cargoes of food were first shipped to London. By the 1930s, giant ships carried frozen meat, cheese and butter, as well as wool, on regular voyages taking about five weeks one way. The NZ economy adapted to the feeding of London, and cultural links were also enhanced. NZ children studied British history and literature, not their own. NZ's leading scientists and writers, such as Ernest Rutherford and Katherine Mansfield, gravitated to Britain. This tight relationship has been described as 'recolonial', but it is a mistake to see NZ as an exploited colony. Average living standards in NZ were normally better than in Britain, as were the welfare and lower-level education systems. New Zealanders had access to British markets and culture, and they contributed their share to the latter as equals. The list of 'British' writers, academics, scientists, military leaders, publishers and the like who were actually New Zealanders is long. Indeed, New Zealanders, especially in war and sport, sometimes saw themselves as a superior version of the British – Better Britons.

'Recolonial' NZ prided itself, with some justice, on its affluence, equality and social harmony. But it was also conformist, even puritanical. Until the 1950s, it was technically illegal for farmers to allow their cattle to mate in fields fronting public roads, for moral reasons. The 1953 American movie, *The Wild One,* was banned until 1977. Sunday newspapers were illegal until 1969, and full Sunday trading was not allowed until 1989. Licensed restaurants hardly existed in 1960, nor did supermarkets or TV. Notoriously, from 1917 to 1967, pubs were obliged to shut at 6pm. Opposition to Sunday trading stemmed, not so much from belief in the sanctity of the Sabbath, but from the belief that workers should have weekends too. Six o'clock closing was a standing joke in rural areas, notably the marvellously idiosyncratic region of the South Island's West Coast. There was always something of a Kiwi counterculture, even before imported countercultures took root from the 1960s.

There were also developments in cultural nationalism, beginning in the 1930s but really flowering from the 1970s. Writers, artists and filmmakers were by no means the only people who 'came out' in that era.

Coming In, Coming Out

The 'recolonial' system was shaken several times after 1935, but managed to survive until 1973, when Mother England ran off and joined the Franco-German commune now known as the EU. NZ was beginning

The Six o'clock Swill referred to the frantic after-work drinking at pubs when men tried to drink as much as possible from 5.05pm until strict closing time at 6pm.

Wellington-born Nancy Wake (codenamed 'The White Mouse') led a guerrilla attack against the Nazis with a 7000-strong army. She had the multiple honours of being the Gestapo's most-wanted person and being the most decorated Allied servicewoman of WWII.

2004	2005	2008	2010
Maori TV begins broadcasting – for the first time, a channel committed to NZ content and the revitalisation of Maori language and culture hits the small screen.	New Zealand is the first country in the world where women hold all the highest offices: the head of state, governor-general, prime minister, attorney general and the chief justice.	Sir Edmund Hillary dies. Among the mourners at the funeral is Norbu Tenzing Norgay – the son of Tenzing Norgay.	A cave-in at Pike River coalmine on the South Island's West Coast kills 29 miners.

to develop alternative markets to Britain, and alternative exports to wool, meat and dairy products. Wide-bodied jet aircraft were allowing the world and NZ to visit each other on an increasing scale. NZ had only 36,000 tourists in 1960, compared with more than two million a year now. Women were beginning to penetrate first the upper reaches of the workforce and then the political sphere. Gay people came out of the closet, despite vigorous efforts by moral conservatives to push them back in. University-educated youths were becoming more numerous and more assertive.

From 1945, Maori experienced both a population explosion and massive urbanisation. In 1936, Maori were 17% urban and 83% rural. Fifty years later, these proportions had reversed. The immigration gates, which until 1960 were pretty much labelled 'whites only', widened, first to allow in Pacific Islanders for their labour, and then to allow in (East) Asians for their money. These transitions would have generated major socioeconomic change whatever happened in politics. But most New Zealanders associate the country's recent 'Big Shift' with the politics of 1984.

In 1984, NZ's third great reforming government was elected – the Fourth Labour government, led nominally by David Lange and in fact by Roger Douglas, the Minister of Finance. This government adopted an antinuclear foreign policy, delighting the left, and a more-market economic policy, delighting the right. NZ's numerous economic controls were dismantled with breakneck speed. Middle NZ was uneasy about the antinuclear policy, which threatened NZ's ANZUS alliance with Australia and the US. But in 1985, French spies sank the antinuclear protest ship *Rainbow Warrior* in Auckland Harbour, killing one crewman. The lukewarm American condemnation of the French act brought middle NZ in behind the antinuclear policy, which became associated with national independence. Other New Zealanders were uneasy about the more-market economic policy, but failed to come up with a convincing alternative. Revelling in their new freedom, NZ investors engaged in a frenzy of speculation, and suffered even more than the rest of the world from the economic crash of 1987.

The early 21st century is an interesting time for NZ. Food, wine, film and literature are flowering as never before, and the new ethnic mix is creating something very special in popular music. There are continuities, however – the pub, the sportsground, the quarter-acre section, the bush, the beach and the bach – and they too are part of the reason people like to come here. Realising that NZ has a great culture and an intriguing history, as well as a great natural environment, will double the bang for your buck.

TE KOOTI

Maurice Shadbolt's *Season of the Jew* (1987) is a semifictionalised story of bloody campaigns led by warrior Te Kooti against the British in Poverty Bay in the 1860s. Te Kooti and his followers compared themselves to the Israelites who were cast out of Egypt.

2011	2011	2013	2013
A severe earthquake strikes Christchurch, killing 185 people and badly damaging the central business district.	NZ hosts (and wins!) the Rugby World Cup.	New Zealand becomes one of just 15 countries in the world to legally recognise same-sex marriage.	Eleanor Catton wins the Man Booker prize for her novel *The Luminaries*, only the second New Zealander (and the youngest author ever) to win.

Environment

by Vaughan Yarwood

New Zealand is a young country – its present shape is less than 10,000 years old. Having broken away from the supercontinent of Gondwanaland (which included Africa, Australia, Antarctica and South America) in a stately geological dance some 85 million years ago, it endured continual uplift and erosion, buckling and tearing, and the slow fall and rise of the sea, as ice ages came and went.

Vaughan Yarwood is a historian and travel writer who is widely published in New Zealand and internationally. He is the author of *The History Makers: Adventures in New Zealand Biography*

The Land

Straddling the boundary of two great colliding slabs of the earth's crust – the Pacific plate and the Indian/Australian plate – to this day NZ remains the plaything of nature's strongest forces.

The result is one of the most varied and spectacular series of landscapes in the world, ranging from snow-dusted mountains and drowned glacial valleys to rainforests, dunelands and an otherworldly volcanic plateau. It is a diversity of landforms you would expect to find across an entire continent rather than a small archipelago in the South Pacific.

Evidence of NZ's tumultuous past is everywhere. The South Island's mountainous spine – the 650km-long ranges of the Southern Alps – is a product of the clash of the two plates; the result of a process of rapid lifting that, if anything, is accelerating. Despite NZ's highest peak, Aoraki/Mt Cook, losing 10m from its summit overnight in a 1991 landslide, the Alps are on an express elevator that, without erosion and landslides, would see them 10 times their present height within a few million years.

On the North Island, the most impressive changes have been wrought by volcanoes. Auckland is built on an isthmus peppered by scoria cones, on many of which you can still see the earthworks of *pa* (fortified villages) built by early Maori. The city's biggest and most recent volcano, 600-year-old Rangitoto Island, is just a short ferry ride from the downtown wharves. Some 300km further south, the classically shaped cone of snowcapped Mt Taranaki/Egmont overlooks tranquil dairy pastures.

But the real volcanic heartland runs through the centre of the North Island, from the restless bulk of Mt Ruapehu in Tongariro National Park northeast through the Rotorua lake district out to NZ's most active volcano, White Island, in the Bay of Plenty. Called the Taupo Volcanic Zone, this great 250km-long rift valley – part of a volcano chain known as the 'Pacific Ring of Fire' – has been the seat of massive eruptions that have left their mark on the country physically and culturally.

Most spectacular were the eruptions that created Lake Taupo. Considered the world's most productive volcano in terms of the amount of material ejected, Taupo last erupted 1800 years ago in a display that was the most violent anywhere on the planet within the past 5000 years.

ENVIRONMENTAL ISSUES IN NEW ZEALAND

Employing images of untouched landscapes, Tourism New Zealand's 100% Pure marketing campaign has been critically acclaimed, and is the envy of tourism organisations worldwide. Such portrayals of a pristine environment have, however, been repeatedly rumbled in recent years as environmentalists – and the media – place NZ's 'clean green' credentials under the microscope. Mining, offshore oil and gas exploration, pollution, biodiversity loss, conservation funding cuts and questionable urban planning – there have been endless hooks for bad-news stories, and numerous reasons to protest.

A 2013 university study found that New Zealanders rate water quality as the country's most serious environmental issue. Their concern is well founded, with one-third of NZ's 425 lakes, rivers and beaches deemed unsafe for swimming; research from diverse quarters confirms that the health of NZ's waterways is in serious decline. The primary culprit is 'dirty dairying' – cow effluent leaching into freshwater ecosystems, carrying with it high levels of nitrates, as well as bacteria and parasites such as E. coli and giardia.

The dairy industry is NZ's biggest export earner, and it continues to boom with more land being converted, despite clear evidence of its detrimental effects, which include the generation of half of NZ's greenhouse gas emissions. Parliamentary Commissioner for the Environment, Jan Wright, has referred to the matter as a 'classic economy versus environment dilemma'. NZ's dominant dairy cooperative – Fonterra – has expressed a commitment to upping its game to ensure farm management practices 'preserve New Zealand's clean green image'; some farmers are indeed cleaning up their act.

There are many other threats to water and land ecosystems, including proliferation of invasive weeds and pests, with biodiversity loss continuing in parallel. The worst offenders are possums, stoats and rats, which chomp through swathes of forest and kill wildlife, particularly birds. Controversy rages at the Department of Conservation's use of 1080 poison (sodium fluoroacetate) to control these pests, despite it being sanctioned by prominent environmental groups such as Forest & Bird and the Parliamentary Commissioner for the Environment. Vehement opposition to 1080 is expressed by such diverse camps as hunters and animal-rights activists, who cite detriments such as by-kill and the poison's transmittal into waterways.

This is just one of the DOC's increasing range of duties, which includes processing applications for mining within the conservation estate. Public feeling runs high on this issue, too, as demonstrated by recent ructions over opencast coalmining on the West Coast's Denniston Plateau. DOC has increasingly found itself in the thick of it; at the same time as budget cuts and major internal restructuring have left it appearing thinner on the ground.

Meanwhile, NZ's principle legislation governing the NZ environment – the 1991 Resource Management Act – is undergoing controversial reforms suspected of opening the door to further exploitation of the environment. NGOs and community groups – ever-vigilant and already making major contributions to the welfare of NZ's environment – will find plenty to keep them occupied in the years to come.

Sarah Bennett & Lee Slater

You can experience the aftermath of volcanic destruction on a smaller scale at Te Wairoa (the Buried Village), near Rotorua on the shores of Lake Tarawera. Here, partly excavated and open to the public, lie the remains of a 19th-century Maori village overwhelmed when nearby Mt Tarawera erupted without warning. The famous Pink and White Terraces (one of several claimants to the popular title 'eighth wonder of the world') were destroyed overnight by the same upheaval.

But when nature sweeps the land clean with one hand she often rebuilds with the other: Waimangu Valley, born of all that geothermal violence, is the place to go to experience the hot earth up close and personal amid geysers, silica pans, bubbling mud pools and the world's biggest hot spring. Or you can wander around Rotorua's Whakarewarewa Thermal

GEYSERS

Village, where descendants of Maori displaced by the eruption live in the middle of steaming vents and prepare food for visitors in boiling pools.

A second by-product of movement along the tectonic plate boundary is seismic activity – earthquakes. Not for nothing has NZ been called 'the Shaky Isles'. Most quakes only rattle the glassware, but one was indirectly responsible for creating an internationally celebrated tourist attraction…

In 1931, an earthquake measuring 7.9 on the Richter scale levelled the Hawke's Bay city of Napier, causing huge damage and loss of life. Napier was rebuilt almost entirely in the then-fashionable art-deco architectural style, and walking its streets today you can relive its brash exuberance in what has become a mecca for lovers of art deco.

However, the North Island doesn't have a monopoly on earthquakes. In September 2010 Christchurch was rocked by a magnitude 7.1 earthquake. Less than six months later, in February 2011, a magnitude 6.3 quake destroyed much of the city's historic heart and claimed 185 lives, making it the country's second-deadliest natural disaster. NZ's second city continues to be jostled by aftershocks as it begins to build anew.

The South Island can also see some evidence of volcanism – if the remains of the old volcanoes of Banks Peninsula weren't there to repel the sea, the vast Canterbury Plains, built from alpine sediment washed down the rivers from the Alps, would have eroded away long ago.

But in the south it is the Southern Alps themselves that dominate, dictating settlement patterns, throwing down engineering challenges and offering outstanding recreational opportunities. The island's mountainous backbone also helps shape the weather, as it stands in the path of the prevailing westerly winds which roll in, moisture-laden, from the Tasman Sea. As a result bush-clad lower slopes of the western Southern Alps are among the wettest places on earth, with an annual precipitation of some 15,000mm. Having lost its moisture, the wind then blows dry across the eastern plains towards the Pacific coast.

The North Island has a more even rainfall and is spared the temperature extremes of the South – which can plunge when a wind blows in from Antarctica. The important thing to remember, especially if you are tramping at high altitude, is that NZ has a maritime climate. This means weather can change with lightning speed, catching out the unprepared.

NZ is one of the most spectacular places in the world to see geysers. Rotorua's short-lived Waimangu geyser, formed after the Mt Tarawera eruption, was once the world's largest, often gushing to a dizzying height of 400m.

Wildlife

NZ may be relatively young, geologically speaking, but its plants and animals go back a long way. The tuatara, for instance, an ancient reptile unique to these islands, is a Gondwanaland survivor closely related to the dinosaurs, while many of the distinctive flightless birds (ratites) have distant African and South American cousins.

Due to its long isolation, the country is a veritable warehouse of unique and varied plants, most of which are found nowhere else. And with separation of the landmass occurring before mammals appeared on the scene, birds and insects have evolved in spectacular ways to fill the gaps.

The now extinct flightless moa, the largest of which grew to 3.5m tall and weighed over 200kg, browsed open grasslands much as cattle do today (skeletons can be seen at Auckland Museum), while the smaller kiwi still ekes out a nocturnal living rummaging among forest leaf litter for insects and worms much as small mammals do elsewhere. One of the country's most ferocious-looking insects, the mouse-sized giant weta, meanwhile, has taken on a scavenging role elsewhere filled by rodents.

As one of the last places on earth to be colonised by humans, NZ was for millennia a safe laboratory for such risky evolutionary strategies, but with the arrival first of Maori and soon after of Europeans, things went downhill fast.

Many endemic creatures, including moa and the huia, an exquisite songbird, were driven to extinction, and the vast forests were cleared for their timber and to make way for agriculture. Destruction of habitat and the introduction of exotic animals and plants have taken a terrible environmental toll and New Zealanders are now fighting a rearguard battle to save what remains.

Birds & Animals

The first Polynesian settlers found little in the way of land mammals – just two species of bat – but forests, plains and coasts alive with birds. Largely lacking the bright plumage found elsewhere, NZ's birds – like its endemic plants – have an understated beauty that does not shout for attention.

Among the most musical is the bellbird, common in both native and exotic forests everywhere except Northland, though like many birds it is more likely to be heard than seen. Its call is a series of liquid bell notes, most often sounded at dawn or dusk.

The tui, another nectar eater and the country's most beautiful songbird, is a great mimic, with an inventive repertoire that includes clicks, grunts and chuckles. Notable for the white throat feathers that stand out against its dark plumage, the tui often feeds on flax flowers in suburban gardens but is most at home in densely tangled forest ('bush' to New Zealanders).

Fantails are commonly encountered on forest trails, swooping and jinking to catch insects stirred up by passing hikers, while pukeko, elegant swamp-hens with blue plumage and bright-red beaks, are readily seen along wetland margins and even on the sides of roads nearby – be warned, they have little road sense.

If you spend any time in the South Island high country, you are likely to come up against the fearless and inquisitive kea – an uncharacteristically drab green parrot with bright-red underwings. Kea are common in the car parks of the Fox and Franz Josef Glaciers, where they hang out for food scraps or tear rubber from car windscreens.

Then there is the takahe, a rare flightless bird thought extinct until a small colony was discovered in 1948, and the equally flightless kiwi, NZ's national emblem and the nickname for New Zealanders themselves.

The kiwi has a round body covered in coarse feathers, strong legs and a long, distinctive bill with nostrils at the tip for sniffing out food. It

The icon in reviews marks places that demonstrate a commitment to sustainability. Travellers seeking other sustainable tourism operators should look for operators accredited with Qualmark Green (www.qualmark.co.nz) or listed at Organic Explorer (www.organicexplorer.co.nz).

KIWI SPOTTING

A threatened species, the kiwi is also nocturnal and difficult to see in the wild, although you can do this in **Trounson Kauri Park** (p144) in Northland, Okarito on the West Coast and on Stewart Island. They can, however, be observed in many artificially dark 'kiwi houses':

➡ **Auckland Zoo** (p55)
➡ **Kiwi North**, Whangarei (p111)
➡ **Rainbow Springs**, Rotorua (p272)
➡ **Otorohanga Kiwi House & Native Bird Park** (p168)
➡ **National Aquarium of New Zealand**, Napier (p317)
➡ **Nga Manu Nature Reserve**, Waikanae (p355)
➡ **Pukaha Mt Bruce National Wildlife Centre**, near Masterton (p360)
➡ **Wellington Zoo** (p337)

is not easy to find them in the wild, but they can be seen in simulated environments at excellent nocturnal houses. One of the best is the Otorohanga Kiwi House, which also has other birds, including native falcons, moreporks (owls) and weka.

To get a feel for what the bush used to be like, take a trip to Tiritiri Matangi island. This regenerating island is an open sanctuary and one of the country's most successful exercises in community-assisted conservation.

Bird-Watching

B Heather and H Robertson's *Field Guide to the Birds of New Zealand* is a comprehensive guide for bird-watchers and a model of helpfulness for anyone even casually interested in the country's remarkable bird life.

The flightless kiwi is the species most sought after by bird-watchers. Sightings of the Stewart Island subspecies are common at all times of the year. Elsewhere, wild sightings of this increasingly rare nocturnal species are difficult, apart from in enclosures. Other birds that twitchers like to sight are the royal albatross, white heron, Fiordland crested penguin, yellow-eyed penguin, Australasian gannet and wrybill.

On the Coromandel Peninsula, the Firth of Thames (particularly Miranda) is a haven for migrating birds, while the Wharekawa Wildlife Refuge at Opoutere Beach is a breeding ground of the endangered NZ dotterel. There's also a very accessible Australasian gannet colony at Muriwai, west of Auckland, and one in Hawke's Bay. On the South Island, there are popular trips to observe pelagic birds out of Kaikoura, and royal albatross viewing on the Otago Peninsula.

Two good guides are the revised *Field Guide to the Birds of New Zealand,* by Barrie Heather and Hugh Robertson, and *Birds of New Zealand: Locality Guide* by Stuart Chambers.

Marine Mammal-Watching

Kaikoura, on the northeast coast of the South Island, is NZ's nexus of marine mammal-watching. The main attraction here is whale-watching, but this is dependent on weather conditions, so don't expect to just be able to rock up and head straight out on a boat for a dream encounter. The sperm whale, the largest toothed whale, is pretty much a year-round resident, and depending on the season you may also see migrating humpback whales, pilot whales, blue whales and southern right whales. Other mammals – including fur seals and dusky dolphins – are seen year-round.

Kaikoura is also an outstanding place to swim with dolphins. Pods of up to 500 playful dusky dolphins can be seen on any given day. Dolphin swimming is common elsewhere in NZ, with the animals gathering off the North Island near Whakatane, Paihia, Tauranga, and in the Hauraki Gulf, and off Akaroa on the South Island's Banks Peninsula. Seal swimming is possible in Kaikoura and in the Abel Tasman National Park.

Trees

No visitor to NZ (particularly Australians!) will go for long without hearing about the damage done to the bush by that bad-mannered Australian import, the brush-tailed possum. The long list of mammal pests introduced to NZ accidentally or for a variety of misguided reasons includes deer, rabbits, stoats, pigs and goats. But the most destructive by far is the possum, 70 million of which now chew through millions of tonnes of foliage a year despite the best efforts of the Department of Conservation (DOC) to control them.

Among favoured possum food are NZ's most colourful trees: the kowhai, a small-leaved tree growing to 11m that in spring has drooping clusters of bright-yellow flowers (NZ's national flower); the pohutukawa, a beautiful coastal tree of the northern North Island which bursts into vivid red flower in December, earning the nickname 'Christmas tree'; and

National Parks & Forest Parks

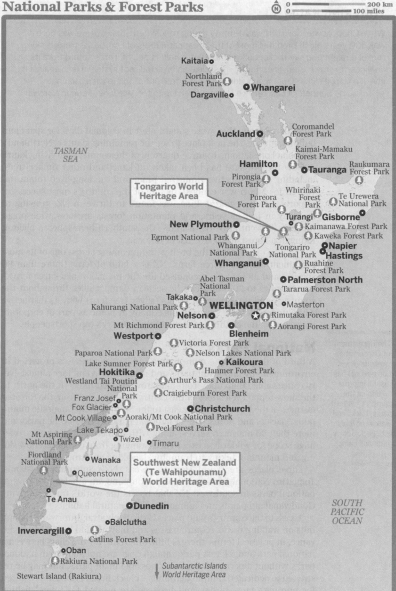

a similar crimson-flowered tree, the rata. Rata species are found on both islands; the northern rata starts life as a climber on a host tree (that it eventually chokes).

The few remaining pockets of mature centuries-old kauri are stately emblems of former days. Their vast hammered trunks and towering, epiphyte-festooned limbs, which dwarf every other tree in the forest, are

TOWERING KAURI

When Chaucer was born this was a sturdy young tree. When Shakespeare was born it was 300 years old. It predates most of the great cathedrals of Europe. Its trunk is sky-rocket straight and sky-rocket bulky, limbless for half its height. Ferns sprout from its crevices. Its crown is an asymmetric mess, like an inverted root system. I lean against it, give it a slap. It's like slapping a building. This is a tree out of Tolkien. It's a kauri.

Joe Bennett (A Land of Two Halves) referring to the McKinney kauri in Northland.

reminders of why they were sought after in colonial days for spars and building timber. The best place to see the remaining giants is Northland's Waipoua Forest, home to three-quarters of the country's surviving kauri.

Now the pressure has been taken off kauri and other timber trees, including the distinctive rimu (red pine) and the long-lived totara (favoured for Maori war canoes), by one of the country's most successful imports – *Pinus radiata*. Pine was found to thrive in NZ, growing to maturity in just 35 years, and plantation forests are now widespread through the central North Island – the southern hemisphere's biggest, Kaingaroa Forest, lies southeast of Rotorua.

You won't get far into the bush without coming across one of its most prominent features – tree ferns. NZ is a land of ferns (more than 80 species) and most easily recognised are the mamaku (black tree fern) – which grows to 20m and can be seen in damp gullies throughout the country – and the 10m-high ponga (silver tree fern) with its distinctive white underside. The silver fern is equally at home as part of corporate logos and on the clothing of many of the country's top sportspeople.

National Parks

The Department of Conservation website (www.doc.govt.nz) has useful information on the country's national parks, tracks and walkways. It also lists backcountry huts and campsites.

A third of the country – more than 5 million hectares – is protected in environmentally important parks and reserves that embrace almost every conceivable landscape: from mangrove-fringed inlets in the north to the snow-topped volcanoes of the Central Plateau, and from the forested fastness of the Ureweras in the east to the Southern Alps' majestic mountains, glaciers and fiords. The 14 national parks, three marine parks and more than 30 marine reserves, along with numerous forest parks, offer huge scope for wilderness experiences, ranging from climbing, snow skiing and mountain biking to tramping, kayaking and trout fishing.

Three places are World Heritage Areas: NZ's Subantarctic Islands, Tongariro National Park and Te Wahipounamu, an amalgam of several national parks in southwest NZ that boasts the world's finest surviving Gondwanaland plants and animals in their natural habitats.

Access to the country's wild places is relatively straightforward, though huts on walking tracks require passes and may need to be booked in advance. In practical terms, there is little difference for travellers between a national park and a forest park, though dogs are not allowed in national parks without a permit. Camping is possible in all parks, but may be restricted to dedicated camping grounds – check first. Permits are required for hunting (game birds), and licences are needed for inland fishing (trout, salmon); both can be bought online at www.fishandgame.org.nz.

Maori Culture

by John Huria

'Maori' once just meant 'common' or 'everyday', but now it means...let's just begin by saying that there is a lot of 'then' and a lot of 'now' in the Maori world. Sometimes the cultural present follows on from the past quite seamlessly; sometimes things have changed hugely; sometimes we just want to look to the future.

Maori today are a diverse people. Some are engaged with traditional cultural networks and pursuits; others are occupied with adapting tradition and placing it into a dialogue with globalising culture. The Maori concept of *whanaungatanga* – family relationships – is important to the culture. And families spread out from the *whanau* (extended family) to the *hapu* (subtribe) and *iwi* (tribe) and even, in a sense, beyond the human world and into the natural and spiritual worlds.

Maori are New Zealand's *tangata whenua* (people of the land), and the Maori relationship with the land has developed over hundreds of years of occupation. Once a predominantly rural people, many Maori now live in urban centres, away from their traditional home base. But it's still common practice in formal settings to introduce oneself by referring to home: an ancestral mountain, river, sea or lake, or an ancestor. There's no place like home, but it's good to be away as well.

If you're looking for a Maori experience in NZ you'll find it – in performance, in conversation, in an art gallery, on a tour...

> John Huria (Ngai Tahu, Muaupoko) has an editorial, research and writing background with a focus on Maori writing and culture. He was senior editor for Maori publishing company Huia (NZ) and now runs an editorial and publishing services company, Ahi Text Solutions Ltd (www.ahitextsolutions.co.nz).

Maori Then

Some three millennia ago people began moving eastward into the Pacific, sailing against the prevailing winds and currents (hard to go out, easier to return safely). Some stopped at Tonga and Samoa, and others settled the small central East Polynesian tropical islands.

The Maori colonisation of Aotearoa began from an original homeland known to Maori as Hawaiki. Skilled navigators and sailors travelled across the Pacific, using many navigational tools – currents, winds, stars, birds and wave patterns – to guide their large, double-hulled ocean-going craft to a new land. The first of many was the great navigator Kupe, who arrived, the story goes, chasing an octopus named Muturangi. But the distinction of giving NZ its well-known Maori name – Aotearoa – goes to his wife, Kuramarotini, who cried out, '*He ao, he ao tea, he ao tea roa!*' (A cloud, a white cloud, a long white cloud!).

Kupe and his crew journeyed around the land, and many places around Cook Strait (between the North and South Islands), and the Hokianga in Northland still bear the names that they gave them and the marks of his passage. Kupe returned to Hawaiki, leaving from (and naming) Northland's Hokianga. He gave other seafarers valuable

> The best way to learn about the relationship between the land and the *tangata whenua* is to get out there and start talking with Maori.

HOW THE WORLD BEGAN

In the Maori story of creation, first there was the void, then the night, then Rangi-nui (sky father) and Papa-tu-a-nuku (earth mother) came into being, embracing with their children nurtured between them. But nurturing became something else. Their children were stifled in the darkness of their embrace. Unable to stretch out to their full dimensions and struggling to see clearly in the darkness, their children tried to separate them. Tawhiri-matea, the god of winds, raged against them; Tu-mata-uenga, the god of war, assaulted them. Each god child in turn tried to separate them, but still Rangi and Papa pressed against each other. And then Tane-mahuta, god of the great forests and of humanity, placed his feet against his father and his back against his mother and slowly, inexorably, began to move them apart. Then came the world of light, of demigods and humanity.

In this world of light Maui, the demigod ancestor, was cast out to sea at birth and was found floating in his mother's topknot. He was a shape-shifter, becoming a pigeon or a dog or an eel if it suited his purposes. He stole fire from the gods. Using his grandmother's jawbone, he bashed the sun so that it could only limp slowly across the sky, so that people would have enough time during the day to get things done (if only he would do it again!). Using the South Island as a canoe, he used the jawbone as a hook to fish up Te Ika a Maui (the fish of Maui) – the North Island. And, finally, he met his end trying to defeat death itself. The goddess of death, Hine Nui Te Po, had obsidian teeth in her vagina (obsidian is a volcanic glass that takes a razor edge when chipped). Maui attempted to reverse birth (and hence defeat death) by crawling into her birth canal to reach her heart as she slept. A small bird – a fantail – laughed at the absurd sight. Hine Nui Te Po awoke, and crushed Maui between her thighs. Death one, humanity nil.

navigational information. And then the great *waka* (ocean-going craft) began to arrive.

The *waka* that the first setters arrived on, and their landing places, are immortalised in tribal histories. Well-known *waka* include *Takitimu, Kurahaupo, Te Arawa, Mataatua, Tainui, Aotea* and *Tokomaru*. There are many others. Maori trace their genealogies back to those who arrived on the *waka* (and further back as well).

What would it have been like making the transition from small tropical islands to a much larger, cooler land mass? Goodbye breadfruit, coconuts, paper mulberry; hello moa, fernroot, flax – and immense space (relatively speaking). NZ has over 15,000km of coastline. Rarotonga, by way of contrast, has a little over 30km. There was land, lots of it, and a flora and fauna that had developed more or less separately from the rest of the world for 80 million years. There was an untouched, massive fishery, a great seaside mammalian convenience stores – seals and sea lions – as well as a fabulous array of birds.

The early settlers went on the move, pulled by love, by trade opportunities and greater resources; pushed by disputes and threats to security. When they settled, Maori established *mana whenua* (regional authority), whether by military campaigns, or by the peaceful methods of intermarriage and diplomacy. Looking over tribal history it's possible to see the many alliances, absorptions and extinctions that went on.

Histories were carried by the voice, in stories, songs and chants. Great stress was placed on accurate learning – after all, in an oral culture where people are the libraries, the past is always a generation or two away from oblivion.

Maori lived in *kainga,* small villages, which often had associated gardens. Housing was quite cosy by modern standards – often it was hard to stand upright while inside. From time to time people would leave their home base and go to harvest seasonal foods. When peaceful

Kupe's passage is marked around NZ: he left his sails (Nga Ra o Kupe) near Cape Palliser as triangular landforms; he named the two islands in Wellington Harbour Matiu and Makoro after his daughters; his blood stains the red rocks of Wellington's south coast.

life was interrupted by conflict, the people would withdraw to *pa*, fortified dwelling places.

And then Europeans began to arrive.

Maori Today

Today's culture is marked by new developments in the arts, business, sport and politics. Many historical grievances still stand, but some *iwi* (Ngai Tahu and Tainui, for example) have settled historical grievances and are major forces in the NZ economy. Maori have also addressed the decline in Maori language use by establishing *kohanga reo, kura kaupapa Maori* and *wananga* (Maori-medium preschools, schools and universities). There is now a generation of people who speak Maori as a first language. There is a network of Maori radio stations, and Maori TV is attracting a committed viewership. A recently revived Maori event is becoming more and more prominent – Matariki, or Maori New Year. The constellation Matariki is also known as Pleiades. It begins to rise above the horizon in late May or early June and its appearance traditionally signals a time for learning, planning and preparing as well as singing, dancing and celebrating. Watch out for talks and lectures, concerts, dinners, and even formal balls.

Religion

Christian churches and denominations are important in the Maori world: televangelists, mainstream churches for regular and occasional worship, and two major Maori churches (Ringatu and Ratana) – we've got it all.

But in the (non–Judaeo Christian) beginning there were the *atua Maori*, the Maori gods, and for many Maori the gods are a vital and relevant force still. It is common to greet the earth mother and sky father when speaking formally at a *marae*. The gods are represented in art and carving, sung of in *waiata* (songs), invoked through *karakia* (prayer and incantation) when a meeting house is opened, when a *waka* is launched, even (more simply) when a meal is served. They are spoken of on the *marae* and in wider Maori contexts. The traditional Maori creation story is well known and widely celebrated.

The Arts

There are many collections of Maori *taonga* (treasures) around the country. Some of the largest and most comprehensive are at Wellington's Te Papa Museum and the Auckland Museum. Canterbury Museum in Christchurch also has a good collection, and Hokitika Museum has an exhibition showing the story of *pounamu* (nephrite jade, or greenstone).

You can stay up to date with what is happening in the Maori arts by reading *Mana* magazine (available from most newsagents), listening to *iwi* stations (www.irirangi.net) or weekly podcasts from Radio New Zealand (www.radionz.co.nz). Maori TV also has regular features on the Maori arts – check out www.maoritelevision.com.

Maori TV went to air in 2004, an emotional time for many Maori who could at last see their culture, their concerns and their language in a mass medium. Over 90% of content is NZ-made, and programs are in both Maori and English: they're subtitled and accessible to everyone. If you want to really get a feel for the rhythm and meter of spoken Maori from the comfort of your own chair, switch to Te Reo, a Maori-language-only channel.

MAORI CULTURE MAORI TODAY

Arriving for the first time in NZ, two crew members of *Tainui* saw the red flowers of the pohutakawa tree, and they cast away their prized red feather ornaments, thinking that there were plenty to be had on shore.

Maori legends are all around you as you tour NZ: Maui's *waka* became today's Southern Alps; a *taniwha* (supernatural creature) formed Lake Waikaremoana in its death throes; and a rejected Mt Taranaki walked into exile from the central North Island mountain group, carving the Whanganui River.

See Ngahuia Te Awekotuku's *Mau Moko: The World of Maori Tattoo* (2007) for the big picture, with powerful, beautiful images and an incisive commentary.

Ta Moko

Ta moko is the Maori art of tattoo, traditionally worn by men on their faces, thighs and buttocks, and by women on their chins and lips. *Moko* were permanent grooves tapped into the skin using pigment (made from burnt caterpillar or kauri gum soot), and bone chisels: fine, sharp combs for broad work, and straight blades for detailed work. Museums in the major centres – Auckland, Wellington and Christchurch – all display traditional implements for *ta moko*.

The modern tattooist's gun is common now, but bone chisels are coming back into use for Maori who want to reconnect with tradition. Since the general renaissance in Maori culture in the 1960s, many artists have taken up *ta moko* and now many Maori wear *moko* with quiet pride and humility.

Can visitors get involved, or even get some work done? The term *kirituhi* (skin inscriptions) has arisen to describe Maori motif–inspired modern tattoos that non-Maori can wear.

Carving

Traditional Maori carving, with its intricate detailing and curved lines, can transport the viewer. It's quite amazing to consider that it was done with stone tools, themselves painstakingly made, until the advent of iron (nails suddenly became very popular).

Some major traditional forms are *waka* (canoes), *pataka* (storage buildings), and *wharenui* (meeting houses). You can see sublime examples of traditional carving at Te Papa in Wellington, and at the following:

Auckland Museum (p52) Maori Court

Hell's Gate (p273) Carver in action every day; near Rotorua

Putiki Church (p215) Interior covered in carvings and *tukutuku* (wall panels), Whanganui

Taupo Museum (p233) Carved meeting house

Te Manawa (p224) Museum with a Maori focus, Palmerston North

Waikato Museum (p153) Beautifully carved *waka taua* (war canoe), Hamilton

Wairakei Terraces (p235) Carved meeting house, Taupo

Waitangi Treaty Grounds (p126) *Whare runanga* and *waka taua*

Whakarewarewa Thermal Village (p260) The 'living village' – carving, other arts, meeting house and performance, Rotorua

Whanganui Regional Museum (p214) Wonderful carved *waka*, Whanganui

The apex of carving today is the *whare whakairo* (carved meeting house). A commissioning group relates its history and ancestral stories to a carver, who then draws (sometimes quite loosely) on traditional motifs to interpret or embody the stories and ancestors in wood or composite fibreboard.

See Hirini Moko Mead's *Tikanga Maori*, Pat and Hiwi Tauroa's *Visiting a Marae*, and Anne Salmond's *Hui* for detailed information on Maori customs.

Rongomaraeroa Marae, by artist Cliff Whiting, at Te Papa in Wellington is a colourful example of a contemporary re-imagining of a traditional art form. The biggest change in carving (as with most traditional arts) has been in the use of new mediums and tools. Rangi Kipa uses a synthetic polymer called Corian to make his *hei tiki* (figure motif worn around the neck), the same stuff that is used to make kitchen benchtops. You can check out his gallery at www.rangikipa.com.

Weaving

Weaving was an essential art that provided clothing, nets and cordage, footwear for rough country travel, mats to cover earthen floors, and *kete* (bags). Many woven items are beautiful as well as practical. Some were major works – *korowai* (cloaks) could take years to finish.

VISITING MARAE

As you travel around the North Island, you will see many *marae* complexes. Often *marae* are owned by a descent group. They are also owned by urban Maori groups, schools, universities and church groups, and they should only be visited by arrangement with the owners. Some *marae* that may be visited include **Huria Marae** (p278) in Tauranga; **Koriniti Marae** (p219) on the Whanganui River Rd; **Te Manuka Tutahi Marae** (p289) in Whakatane; and **Te Papa** (p338) in Wellington.

Marae complexes include a *wharenui* (meeting house), which often embodies an ancestor. Its ridge is the backbone, the rafters are ribs, and it shelters the descendants. There is a clear space in front of the *wharenui* (ie the *marae atea*). Sometimes there are other buildings: a *wharekai* (dining hall); a toilet and shower block; perhaps even classrooms, play equipment and the like.

Hui (gatherings) are held at *marae*. Issues are discussed, classes conducted, milestones celebrated and the dead farewelled. *Te reo Maori* (the Maori language) is prominent, sometimes exclusively so.

Visitors sleep in the meeting house if a *hui* goes on for longer than a day. Mattresses are placed on the floor, someone may bring a guitar, and stories and jokes always go down well as the evening stretches out...

The Powhiri

If you visit a *marae* as part of an organised group, you'll be welcomed in a *powhiri* (formal welcome). The more common ones are outlined here.

There may be a *wero* (challenge). Using *taiaha* (quarter-staff) moves, a warrior will approach the visitors and place a baton on the ground for a visitor to pick up.

There is a *karanga* (ceremonial call). A woman from the host group calls to the visitors and a woman from the visitors responds. Their long, high, falling calls begin to overlap and interweave and the visiting group walks on to the *marae atea*.

It is then time for *whaikorero* (speechmaking). The hosts welcome the visitors, the visitors respond. Speeches are capped off by a *waiata* (song), and the visitors' speaker places *koha* (gift, usually an envelope of cash) on the *marae*. The hosts then invite the visitors to *hariru* (shake hands) and *hongi* (press foreheads together). Visitors and hosts are now united and will share light refreshments or a meal.

The Hongi

Press forehead and nose together firmly, shake hands, and perhaps offer a greeting such as '*Kia ora*' or '*Tena koe*'. Some prefer one press (for two or three seconds, or longer), others prefer two shorter (press, release, press). Men and women sometimes kiss on one cheek. Some people mistakenly think the *hongi* is a pressing of noses only (awkward to aim!) or the rubbing of noses (even more awkward).

Tapu

Tapu (spiritual restrictions) and *mana* (power and prestige) are taken seriously in the Maori world. Sit on chairs or seating provided (never on tables), and walk around people, not over them. The *powhiri* is *tapu*, and mixing food and *tapu* is right up there on the offence-o-meter. Do eat and drink when invited to do so by your hosts. You needn't worry about starvation: an important Maori value is *manaakitanga* (kindness).

Depending on the area, the *powhiri* has gender roles: women *karanga* (call), men *whaikorero* (orate); women lead the way on to the *marae*, men sit on the *paepae* (the speakers' bench at the front). In a modern context, the debate around these roles continues.

Woven predominantly with flax and bird feathers, they are worn now on ceremonial occasions, a stunning sight.

Working with natural materials for the greater good of the people involved getting things right by maintaining the supply of raw material and ensuring that it worked as it was meant to. Protocols were necessary, and women were dedicated to weaving under the aegis of the gods. Today, tradition is greatly respected, but not all traditions are necessarily followed.

Flax was (and still is) the preferred medium for weaving. To get a strong fibre from flax leaves, weavers scraped away the leaves' flesh with a mussel shell, then pounded until it was soft, dyed it, then dried it. But contemporary weavers are using everything in their work: raffia, copper wire, rubber – even polar fleece and garden hoses!

The best way to experience weaving is to contact one of the many weavers running workshops. By learning the art, you'll appreciate the examples of weaving in museums even more. And if you want your own? Woven *kete* and backpacks have become fashion accessories and are on sale in most cities. Weaving is also found in dealer art galleries around the country.

Music plays an important role in traditional and contemporary Maori culture.

Haka

Experiencing *haka* can get the adrenaline flowing, as it did for one Pakeha observer in 1929 who thought of dark Satanic mills: 'They looked like fiends from hell wound up by machinery'. *Haka* can be awe-inspiring; they can also be uplifting. The *haka* is not only a war dance – it is used to welcome visitors, honour achievement, express identity or to put forth very strong opinions.

Haka involve chanted words, vigorous body movements, and *pukana* (when performers distort their faces, eyes bulging with the whites showing, perhaps with tongue extended).

The well-known *haka* 'Ka Mate', performed by the All Blacks before rugby test matches, is credited to the cunning fighting chief Te Rauparaha. It celebrates his escape from death. Chased by enemies, he hid himself in a food pit. After they had left, a friendly chief named Te Whareangi (the 'hairy man' referred to in the *haka*), let him out; he climbed out into the sunshine and performed 'Ka Mate'.

On the North Island, you can experience *haka* at various cultural performances in Rotorua, including at Mitai Maori Village (p271), Tamaki Maori Village (p271), Te Puia (p259) and Whakarewarewa Thermal Village (p260). In the Bay of Islands, *haka* is performed at the Waitangi Treaty Grounds (p126), and in Auckland at the Auckland Museum (p52).

But the best displays of *haka* are at the Te Matatini National Kapa Haka Festival when NZ's top groups compete. It is held every two years, with the next festival in March 2015 to take place in Christchurch.

Contemporary Visual Art

You can check out a map that shows *iwi* distribution and a good list of *iwi* (tribe) websites on Wikipedia (www.wikipedia. org).

A distinctive feature of Maori visual art is the tension between traditional Maori ideas and modern artistic mediums and trends. Shane Cotton produced a series of works that conversed with 19th-century painted meeting houses, which themselves departed from Maori carved houses. Kelcy Taratoa uses toys, superheroes and pop urban imagery alongside weaving and carving design.

Of course not all Maori artists use Maori motifs. Ralph Hotere is a major NZ artist who 'happens to be Maori' (his words), and his career-long exploration of black speaks more to modernism than the traditional *marae* context.

Contemporary Maori art is by no means only about painting. Many other artists use installations as the preferred medium – look out for work by Jacqueline Fraser and Peter Robinson.

There are some great permanent exhibitions of Maori visual arts in the major centres. Both the Auckland and Christchurch Art Galleries hold strong collections, as does Wellington's Te Papa.

Contemporary Theatre

The 1970s saw the emergence of many Maori playwrights and plays, and theatre is a strong area of the Maori arts today. Maori theatre drew heavily on the traditions of the *marae*. Instead of dimming the lights and immediately beginning the performance, many Maori theatre groups began with a stylised *powhiri*, had space for audience members to respond to the play, and ended with a *karakia* or a farewell.

Taki Rua is an independent producer of Maori work for both children and adults and has been in existence for over 25 years. As well as staging its shows in the major centres, it tours most of its work – check out its website (www.takirua.co.nz) for the current offerings. Maori drama is also often showcased at the professional theatres in the main centres as well as the biennial New Zealand International Festival. Hone Kouka and Briar Grace-Smith (both have published play scripts available) have toured their works around NZ and to festivals in the UK.

Contemporary Dance

Contemporary Maori dance often takes its inspiration from *kapa haka* and traditional Maori imagery. The exploration of pre-European life also provides inspiration. For example, a Maori choreographer, Moss Patterson, used *kokowai* (a body-adorning paste made from reddish clay and shark oil) as the basis of his most recent piece of the same name.

NZ's leading specifically Maori dance company is the Atamira Dance Collective (www.atamiradance.co.nz), which has been producing critically acclaimed, beautiful and challenging work since 2000. If that sounds too earnest, another choreographer to watch out for is Mika Torotoro, who happily blends *kapa haka* (cultural dance), drag, opera, ballet and disco into his work. You can check out clips of his work at www.mika.co.nz.

Maori Film-Making

Although there had already been successful Maori documentaries (*Patu!* and the *Tangata Whenua* series are brilliant, and available from some urban video stores), it wasn't until 1987 that NZ had its first fiction feature-length movie by a Maori director with Barry Barclay's *Ngati*. Mereta Mita was the first Maori woman to direct a fiction feature, with *Mauri* (1988). Both Mita and Barclay had highly political aims and ways of working, which involved a lengthy pre-production phase, during which they would consult with and seek direction from their *kaumatua* (elders). Films with significant Maori participation or control include the harrowing *Once Were Warriors* and the uplifting *Whale Rider*. Oscar-shortlisted Taika Waititi, of Te Whanau-a-Apanui descent, wrote and directed *Eagle vs Shark* and *Boy*.

The New Zealand Film Archive (www.filmarchive.org.nz) is a great place to experience Maori film, with most showings being either free or relatively inexpensive. It has offices in Auckland and Wellington.

The first NZ hip-hop song to become a hit was Dalvanius Prime's 'Poi E', which was sung entirely in Maori by the Patea Maori Club. It was the highest-selling single of 1984 in NZ, outselling all international artists.

Maori Writing

There are many novels and collections of short stories by Maori writers, and personal taste will govern your choices. How about approaching Maori writing regionally? Read Patricia Grace (*Potiki, Cousins, Dogside Story, Tu*) around Wellington, and maybe Witi Ihimaera (*Pounamu, Pounamu, The Matriarch, Bulibasha, The Whale Rider*) on the North Island's East Coast. Keri Hulme (*The Bone People, Stonefish*) and the South Island go together like a mass of whitebait bound in a frying pan by a single egg (ie very well). Read Alan Duff (*Once Were Warriors*) anywhere, but only if you want to be saddened, even shocked. Definitely take James George (*Hummingbird, Ocean Roads*) with you to Auckland's West Coast beaches and Northland's Ninety Mile Beach. Paula Morris (*Queen of Beauty, Hibiscus Coast, Trendy but Casual*) and Kelly Ana Morey (*Bloom, Grace Is Gone*) – hmm, Auckland and beyond? If poetry appeals you can't go past the giant of Maori poetry in English, the late, lamented Hone Tuwhare (*Deep River Talk: Collected Poems*). Famously sounding like he's at church and in the pub at the same time, you *can* take him anywhere.

For information on Maori arts today, check out Toi Maori www.maoriart.org.nz.

The Kiwi Psyche

New Zealand is like that little guy at school when they're picking rugby teams – quietly waiting to be noticed, desperately wanting to be liked. Then, when he does get the nod, his sheer determination to prove himself propels him to score a completely unexpected try. When his teammates come to congratulate him he stares at the ground and mumbles, 'It was nothing, ay'.

What Makes Kiwis Tick?

While NZ is a proud little nation, Kiwis traditionally don't have time for show-offs. Jingoistic flag-waving is generally frowned upon. People who make an impression on the international stage are respected and admired, but flashy tall poppies have traditionally had their heads lopped off. This is perhaps a legacy of NZ's early egalitarian ideals – the ones that sought to avoid the worst injustices of the 'mother country' (Britain) by breaking up large land holdings and enthusiastically adopting a 'cradle to grave' welfare state. 'Just because someone's got a bigger car than me, or bigger guns, doesn't make them better' is the general Kiwi attitude.

NZ has rarely let its size get in the way of making a point on the international stage. A founding member of the League of Nations (the precursor to the UN), it ruffled feathers between the world wars by failing to blindly follow Britain's position. It was in the 1980s, however, when things got really interesting.

For many, Sir Edmund Hillary, the first person to climb Mt Everest, was the consummate New Zealander: humble, practical and concerned for social justice. A public outpouring of grief followed his death in 2008.

A Turbulent Decade

Modern Kiwi culture pivots on the decade of the 1980s. Firstly, the unquestioned primacy of rugby union as a source of social cohesion (which rivalled the country's commitment to the two world wars as a foundation of nation-building) was stripped away when tens of thousands of New Zealanders took to the streets to protest a tour by the South African rugby side in 1981. The protestors held that the politics of apartheid not only had a place in sport, they trumped it. The country was starkly divided; there were riots in paradise. The scar is still strong enough that most New Zealanders over the age of 40 will recognise the simple phrase 'The Tour' as referring to those events.

The tour protests both harnessed and nourished a political and cultural renaissance among Maori that had already been rolling for a decade. Three years later, that renaissance found its mark when a reforming Labour government gave statutory teeth to the Waitangi Tribunal, an agency that has since guided a process of land return, compensation for past wrongs and interpretation of the Treaty of Waitangi – the 1840 pact between Maori and the Crown – as a living document.

At the same time antinuclear protests that had been rumbling for years gained momentum, with mass blockades of visiting US naval ships. In 1984 Prime Minister David Lange barred nuclear-powered or armed ships from entering NZ waters. The mouse had roared. As a result the US threw NZ out of ANZUS, the country's main strategic

People born in other countries make up 23% of NZ residents. Of these, the main regions of origin are the UK and Ireland (29%), the Pacific Islands (15%), Northeast Asia (15%) and Australia (7%).

military alliance, which also included Australia, declaring NZ 'a friend but not an ally'.

However, it was an event in the following year that completely changed the way NZ related to the world, when French government agents launched an attack in Auckland Harbour, sinking Greenpeace's antinuclear flagship *Rainbow Warrior* and killing one of its crew. Being bombed by a country that NZ had fought two world wars with – and the muted or nonexistent condemnation by other allies – left an indelible mark. It strengthened NZ's resolve to follow its own conscience in foreign policy, and in 1987 the New Zealand Nuclear Free Zone, Disarmament, and Arms Control Act became law.

'...a sordid act of international state-backed terrorism...' – Prime Minister David Lange, describing the bombing of the *Rainbow Warrior* (1986)

From the Boer to Vietnam Wars, NZ had blithely trotted off at the behest of the UK or US. Not anymore, as is demonstrated by its lack of involvement in the invasion of Iraq. That's not to say that the country shirks its international obligations: NZ troops continue to be deployed in peacekeeping capacities throughout the world and are currently active in Afghanistan.

If that wasn't enough upheaval for one decade, 1986 saw another bitter battle split the community – this time over the decriminalisation of homosexuality. The debate was particularly rancorous, but the law that previously incarcerated consenting gay adults was repealed, paving the way for the generally accepting society that NZ is today. In 1999 Georgina Beyer, an openly transsexual former prostitute, would win a once-safe rural seat off a conservative incumbent – and in 2013 NZ legalised same-sex marriage.

'SO, WHAT DO YOU THINK OF NEW ZEALAND?'

That, by tradition, is the question that visitors are asked within an hour of disembarking in NZ. Sometimes they might be granted an entire day's research before being asked to pronounce, but asked they are. The question – composed equally of great pride and creeping doubt – is symbolic of the national consciousness.

When George Bernard Shaw visited for four weeks in 1934, he was deluged with what-do-you-think-of questions from newspaper reporters the length of the country. Although he never saw fit to write a word about NZ, his answers to those newspaper questions were collected and reprinted as *What I Saw in New Zealand: the Newspaper Utterances of George Bernard Shaw in New Zealand*. Yes, people really were that keen for vindication.

Other visitors were more willing to pronounce in print, including the British Liberal MP, David Goldblatt, who wrote an intriguing and prescient little book called *Democracy At Ease: a New Zealand Profile*. Goldblatt found New Zealanders a blithe people: kind, prosperous and fond of machines.

For the bon vivant Goldblatt, the attitude towards food and drink was all too telling. He found only 'the plain fare and even plainer fetch and carry of the normal feeding machine of this country' and shops catering 'in the same pedestrian fashion for a people never fastidious – the same again is the order of the day'.

Thus, a people with access to some of the best fresh ingredients on earth tended to boil everything to death. A nation strewn almost its entire length with excellent microclimates for viticulture produced only fortified plonk. Material comfort was valued, but was a plain thing indeed.

It took New Zealanders a quarter of a century more to shuck 'the same dull sandwiches', and embrace a national awareness – and, as Goldblatt correctly anticipated, it took 'hazards and misfortunes' to spur the 'divine discontent' for change.

But when it did happen, it really happened.

Russell Brown is a journalist and manager of the popular Public Address blog site (www. publicaddress.net).

Yet while the 1980s saw the country jump to the left on social issues, simultaneously economic reforms were carried out that were an extreme step to the right (to paraphrase one-time Hamiltonian Richard O'Brien's song 'The Time Warp'). The bloated public sector was slashed, any state assets that weren't bolted to the floor were sold off, regulation was removed from many sectors, trade barriers dismantled and the power of the unions greatly diminished.

If there is broad agreement that the economy had to be restructured, the reforms carried a heavy price. The old social guarantees are not as sure. New Zealanders work long hours for lower wages than their Australian cousins would ever tolerate. Compared with other Organisation for Economic Co-operation and Development (OECD) nations, NZ family incomes are low, child poverty rates are high and the gap between rich and poor is widening.

A New New Zealand

There is a dynamism about NZ today that was rare in the 'golden weather' years before the reforms. Today NZ farmers take on the world without the massive subsidies of yore, and Wellington's inner city – once virtually closed after dark by oppressive licensing laws – now thrives with great bars and restaurants.

As with the economic reforms, the 'Treaty process' of redress and reconciliation with Maori made some New Zealanders uneasy, more in their uncertainty about its extent than that it happened at all. The Maori population sat somewhere between 85,000 and 110,000 at the time of first European contact 200 years ago. Disease and warfare subsequently decimated the population, but a high birth rate sees about 15% of New Zealanders (599,000 people) identify as Maori, and that proportion is likely to grow.

The implication of the Treaty is one of partnership between Maori and the British Crown, together forging a bicultural nation. After decades of attempted cultural assimilation it's now accepted in most quarters that the indigenous culture has a special and separate status within the country's ethnic mix. For example, Maori is an official language and there is a separate electoral roll granting Maori guaranteed parliamentary seats.

Yet room has had to be found for the many New Zealanders of neither British nor Maori heritage. In each new wave of immigration there has been a tendency to demonise before gradually accepting and celebrating what the new cultures have to offer. This happened with the Chinese in the mid-19th century, Pacific Islanders in the 1970s, the Chinese again in the 1990s and, most recently, Croatians at the beginning of the 20th. That said, NZ society is more integrated and accepting than most. People of all races are represented in all levels of society and race isn't an obstacle to achievement.

For the younger generation, for whom the reformist 1980s are prehistory, political apathy is the norm today. In the 2011 general election only 75% of the population turned out to vote; for the under 30s this figure dropped to less than 64%. Perhaps it's because a decade of progressive government has given them little to kick against – unlike those politicised by the anti–Iraq War movements elsewhere. Ironically, as NZ has finally achieved its own interesting, independent cultural sensibility, the country's youth seem more obsessed with US culture than ever. This is particularly true within the hip-hop scene, where a farcical identification with American gangsta culture has developed into a worrying youth gang problem.

GLOBAL PEACE

In 2009 and 2010 NZ topped the Global Peace Index, earning the distinction of being rated the world's most peaceful country. In 2011 it dropped to second place behind Iceland – something to do with all those *haka* performed during the Rugby World Cup, perhaps?

NZ is defined as a state in the Australian constitution. At the time of Australia's federation into one country it was hoped that NZ would join. On this side of the Tasman that idea proved as unpopular then as it does now.

A SPORTING CHANCE

The arena where Kiwis have most sated their desperation for recognition on the world stage is sport. In 2012, NZ was ranked the most successful sporting nation per capita in the world (in 2013 it slipped to third behind Slovenia and Norway). NZ's teams are the current world champions in rugby union, holding both the men's and women's world cup in each code.

For most of the 20th century, NZ's All Blacks dominated international rugby union, with one squad even dubbed 'The Invincibles'. Taking over this pastime of the British upper class did wonders for national identity and the game is now interwoven with NZ's history and culture. The 2011 Rugby World Cup victory did much to raise spirits after a year of tragedy and economic gloom.

For all rugby's influence on the culture, don't go to a game expecting to be caught up in an orgy of noise and cheering. Rugby crowds at Auckland's Eden Park are as restrained as their teams are cavalier, but they get noisier as you head south. In contrast, a home game for the NZ Warriors rugby league team at Auckland's Mt Smart Stadium is a thrilling spectacle, especially when the Polynesian drummers kick in.

Despite the everyman appeal of rugby union in NZ (unlike in the UK), rugby league retains the status of the working-class sport and support is strongest from Auckland's Maori, Polynesian and other immigrant communities.

Netball is the leading sport for women and the one in which the national team, the Silver Ferns, perpetually vies for world supremacy with the Australians – one or other of the countries has taken the world championship at every contest (except for a three-way tie in 1979).

In 2010 the All Whites, NZ's national soccer (football) squad, competed in the FIFA World Cup for the second time ever, emerging with the totally unanticipated distinction of being the only unbeaten team in the competition. They didn't win any games either, but most Kiwis were overjoyed to have seen their first ever World Cup goals and three draws. Sadly, they failed to qualify for the 2014 tournament.

Other sports in which NZ punches above its weight include sailing, rowing, canoeing, equestrian, cycling and triathlon. The most Olympic medals NZ has won have been in athletics, particularly in track and field events. Cricket is the established summer team sport, and a series of good results in early 2014 promised a more consistent and successful future for the Black Caps, NZ's national cricket team.

If you truly want to discover the good, the bad and the ugly of the national psyche, the sporting field isn't a bad place to start.

A Long Way from Britain

Most Kiwis (except perhaps the farmers) would probably wish it rained a little less and they got paid a little more, but it sometimes takes a few months travelling on their 'Big OE' (Overseas Experience – a traditional rite of passage) beforfe they realise how good they've got it.

No matter where you are in NZ, you're never more than 128km from the sea.

In a 2012 study of the quality of life in the world's major cities, Auckland was rated third and Wellington 13th. In 2014, US-based Social Progress Index (SPI) ranked NZ as the most socially progressive country (followed by Switzerland, Iceland, the Netherlands and Norway) for personal rights and freedom, internet access and school enrollment.

Despite all the change, key elements of the NZ identity are an unbroken thread, and fortune is still a matter of economics rather than class. If you are well served in a restaurant or shop, it will be out of politeness or pride in the job, rather than servility.

In country areas and on bushwalks don't be surprised if you're given a cheery greeting from passers-by. In a legacy of the British past, politeness is generally regarded as one of the highest virtues. A 'please' and 'thank

IT'S A WOMAN'S WORLD

New Zealand is justifiably proud of being the first country in the world to give women the vote (in 1893). Kate Sheppard, the hero of the women's suffrage movement, features on the country's $10 bill. Despite that early achievement, the real role for women in public life was modest for many years. That can hardly be said now. Since 1997 the country has had two female prime ministers and for a time in the 2000s every key constitutional position was held by a woman, including the prime minister, attorney general, chief justice, governor general and head of state – although New Zealanders can't take credit for choosing Betty Windsor for that last role. At the same time a Maori queen headed the Kingitanga (King Movement) and a woman led NZ's biggest listed corporation. Things have slipped a little since and only two of those roles are held by women – and, yes, one of those is filled by Queen Elizabeth II.

you' will get you a long way. The three great exceptions to this rule are: a) on the road, where genteel Dr Jekylls become raging Mr Hydes, especially if you have the misfortune of needing to change lanes in Auckland; b) if you don't speak English very well; and c) if you are Australian.

The latter two traits are the product of insularity and a smallness of world view that tends to disappear among Kiwis who have travelled (and luckily many do). The NZ/Australian rivalry is taken much more seriously on this side of the Tasman. Although it's very unlikely that Kiwis will be rude outright, visiting Aussies must get pretty sick of the constant ribbing, much of it surprisingly ill-humoured. It's a sad truth that while most Australians would cheer on a NZ sports team if they were playing anyone other than their own, the opposite is true in NZ.

Number-Eight Wire

You might, on your travels, hear the phrase 'number-eight wire' and wonder what on earth it means. It's a catchphrase New Zealanders still repeat to themselves to encapsulate a national myth: that NZ's isolation and its pioneer stock created a culture in which ingenuity allowed problems to be solved and tools to be built from scratch. A NZ farmer, it was said, could solve pretty much any problem with a piece of number-eight wire (the gauge used for fencing on farms).

It's actually largely true – NZ farms are full of NZ inventions. One reason big offshore film and TV producers bring their projects here – apart from the low wages and huge variety of locations – is that they like the can-do attitude and ability to work to a goal of NZ technical crews. Many more New Zealanders have worked as managers, roadies or chefs for famous recording artists (everyone from Led Zeppelin and U2 to Madonna) than have enjoyed the spotlight themselves. Which just goes to show that New Zealanders operate best at the intersection of practicality and creativity, with an endearing (and sometimes infuriating) humility to boot.

ERNEST RUTHERFORD

Ironically, the person responsible for the nuclear age was a New Zealander. In 1917 Ernest Rutherford was the first to split the nucleus of an atom. His face appears on the $100 note.

Arts & Music

It took a hundred years for post-colonial New Zealand to develop its own distinctive artistic identity. In the first half of the 20th century it was writers and visual artists who led the charge. By the 1970s NZ pub rockers had conquered Australia, while in the 1980s, indie music obsessives the world over hooked into Dunedin's weird and wonderful alternative scene. However, it took the success of the film industry in the 1990s to catapult the nation's creativity into the global consciousness.

Literature

In 2013 New Zealanders rejoiced when 28-year-old Eleanor Catton became only the second NZ writer to win the Man Booker Prize, one of the world's most prestigious awards for literature. Lloyd Jones had come close in 2007 when his novel *Mister Pip* was shortlisted, but it had been a long wait between drinks since Keri Hulme took the prize in 1985. Interestingly, both Catton's epic historical novel *The Luminaries* and Hulme's haunting *The Bone People* were set on the numinous West Coast of the South Island – both books capturing something of the raw and mysterious essence of the landscape.

A wide range of cultural events are listed on www.eventfinder. co.nz. This is a good place to find out about concerts, classical music recitals and *kapa haka* (traditional Maori song and dance performances) performances. For more specific information on the NZ classical music scene, see www.sounz. org.nz.

Catton and Hulme continue in a proud line of NZ women writers, starting in the early 20th century with Katherine Mansfield. Mansfield's work began a Kiwi tradition in short fiction, and for years the standard was carried by novelist Janet Frame, whose dramatic life was depicted in Jane Campion's film of her autobiography, *An Angel at My Table*. Frame's novel *The Carpathians* won the Commonwealth Writers' Prize in 1989.

Less recognised internationally, Maurice Gee has gained the nation's annual top fiction gong six times, most recently with *Blindsight* (2005). His much-loved children's novel *Under the Mountain* (1979) was made into a seminal NZ TV series in 1981 and then a major motion picture in 2009. In 2004 the adaptation of another of his novels, *In My Father's Den* (1972), won major awards at international film festivals and is one of the country's highest-grossing films.

Maurice is an auspicious name for NZ writers, with the late Maurice Shadbolt also achieving much acclaim for his many novels, particularly those set during the New Zealand Wars. Try *Season of the Jew* (1987) or *The House of Strife* (1993).

MAORI VOICES IN PRINT

Some of the most interesting and enjoyable NZ fiction voices belong to Maori writers, with Booker winner Keri Hulme leading the way. Witi Ihimaera's novels give a wonderful insight into small-town Maori life on the East Coast – especially *Bulibasha* (1994) and *The Whale Rider* (1987), which was made into an acclaimed film. Patricia Grace's work is similarly filled with exquisitely told stories of rural *marae*-centred life: try *Mutuwhenua* (1978), *Potiki* (1986), *Dogside Story* (2001) or *Tu* (2004).

MIDDLE-EARTH TOURISM

If you are one of those travellers inspired to come down under by the scenery of the *Lord of the Rings (LOTR)* movies, you won't be disappointed. Jackson's decision to film in NZ wasn't mere patriotism. Nowhere else on earth will you find such wildly varied, unspoiled landscapes – not to mention poorly paid actors.

You will doubtless recognise some places from the films. For example, Hobbiton (near Matamata), Mt Doom (instantly recognisable as towering Ngauruhoe) and the Misty Mountains (the South Island's Southern Alps). The visitor information centres in Wellington, Twizel or Queenstown should be able to direct you to local *LOTR* sites of interest. If you're serious about finding the exact spots where scenes were filmed, buy a copy of Ian Brodie's nerdtastic *The Lord of the Rings: Location Guidebook,* which includes instructions, and even GPS coordinates, for finding all the important places.

Cinema & TV

If you first got interested in NZ by watching it on the silver screen, you're in good company. Sir Peter Jackson's NZ-made *The Hobbit* and *Lord of the Rings* (*LOTR*) trilogies were the best thing to happen to NZ tourism since Captain Cook. Yet NZ cinema is hardly ever easygoing. In his BBC-funded documentary, *Cinema of Unease,* NZ actor Sam Neill described the country's film industry as 'uniquely strange and dark', producing bleak, haunted work. One need only watch Lee Tamahori's harrowing *Once Were Warriors* (1994) to see what he means.

Film critic Philip Matthews makes a slightly more upbeat observation: 'Between (Niki Caro's) *Whale Rider,* (Christine Jeffs') *Rain* and *Lord of the Rings,* you can extract the qualities that our best films possess. Beyond slick technical accomplishment, all share a kind of land-mysticism, an innately supernatural sensibility'.

You could add to this list Jane Campion's *The Piano* (1993), Brad McGann's *In My Father's Den* (2004) and Jackson's *Heavenly Creatures* (1994) – all of which use magically lush scenery to couch disturbing violence. It's a land-mysticism constantly bordering on the creepy.

Even when Kiwis do humour it's as resolutely black as their rugby jerseys; check out Jackson's early splatter-fests and Taika Waititi's *Boy* (2010). Exporting NZ comedy hasn't been easy, yet the HBO-produced TV musical parody *Flight of the Conchords* – featuring a mumbling, bumbling Kiwi folk-singing duo trying to get a break in New York – has found surprising international success.

It's the Polynesian giggle-factor that seems likeliest to break down the bleak house of NZ cinema, with feel-good-through-and-through *Sione's Wedding* (2006) netting the second-biggest local takings of any NZ film.

New Zealanders have gone from never seeing themselves in international cinema to having whole cloned armies of Temuera Morrisons invading the universe in *Star Wars.* Familiar faces such as Cliff Curtis and Karl Urban seem to constantly pop up playing Mexican or Russian gangsters in action movies. Many of them got their start in long-running soap opera *Shortland St.*

Visual Arts

The NZ 'can do' attitude extends to the visual arts. If you're visiting a local's home don't be surprised to find one of the owner's paintings on the wall or one of their mate's sculptures in the back garden, pieced together out of bits of shell, driftwood and a length of the magical 'number-eight wire'.

This is symptomatic of a flourishing local art and crafts scene cultivated by lively tertiary courses churning out traditional carvers and

Other than 2003's winner *Return of the King, The Piano* is the only NZ movie to be nominated for a Best Picture Oscar. Jane Campion was the first Kiwi nominated for the Best Director Oscar, and Peter Jackson the first to win it.

The only Kiwi actors to have won an Oscar are Anna Paquin (for *The Piano*) and Russell Crowe (for *Gladiator*). Paquin was born in Canada but moved to NZ when she was four, while Crowe moved from NZ to Australia at the same age.

weavers, jewellery-makers, multimedia boffins, and moulders of metal and glass.

The larger cities have excellent dealer galleries representing interesting local artists working across all media. Not all the best galleries are in Auckland or Wellington. The energetic Govett-Brewster Art Gallery (p200) – home to the legacy of sculptor and film-maker Len Lye – is worth a visit to New Plymouth in itself.

Traditional Maori art has a distinctive visual style with well-developed motifs that have been embraced by NZ artists of every race. In the painting medium, these include the cool modernism of Gordon Walters and the more controversial pop-art approach of Dick Frizzell's *Tiki* series. Likewise, Pacific Island themes are common, particularly in Auckland. An example is the work of Niuean-born Auckland-raised John Pule.

It should not be surprising that in a nation so defined by its natural environment, landscape painting constituted the first post-European body of art. John Gully and Petrus van der Velden were among those to arrive and paint memorable (if sometimes overdramatised) depictions of the land.

A little later, Charles Frederick Goldie painted a series of compelling, realist portraits of Maori, who were feared to be a dying race. Debate over the political propriety of Goldie's work raged for years, but its value is widely accepted now: not least because Maori themselves generally acknowledge and value them as ancestral representations.

From the 1930s NZ art took a more modern direction and produced some of the country's most celebrated artists including Rita Angus, Toss Woollaston and Colin McCahon. McCahon is widely regarded to have been the country's most important artist. His paintings might seem inscrutable, even forbidding, but even where McCahon lurched into Catholic mysticism or quoted screeds from the Bible, his spirituality was rooted in geography. His bleak, brooding landscapes evoke the sheer power of NZ's terrain.

Music
by Gareth Shute

Gareth Shute wrote this music section. He is the author of four books, including *Hip Hop Music in Aotearoa* and *NZ Rock 1987–2007.* He is also a musician and has toured the UK, Europe and Australia as a member of The Ruby Suns and The Brunettes. He now plays in indie soul group The Cosbys.

NZ music began with the *waiata* (songs) developed by Maori following their arrival in the country. The main musical instruments were wind instruments made of bone or wood, the most well known of which is the *nguru* (also known as the 'nose flute'), while percussion was provided by chest- and thigh-slapping. These days, the liveliest place to see Maori music being performed is at *kapa haka* competitions in which groups compete with their own routines of traditional song and dance: track down the **Te Matatini National Kapa Haka Festival** (www.tematatini. co.nz) which happens in March in odd-numbered years at different venues (Christchurch in 2015). In a similar vein, Auckland's Pasifika Festival (p61) represents each of the Pacific Islands. It's a great place to see both traditional and modern forms of Polynesian music: modern hip-hop, throbbing Cook Island drums, or island-style guitar, ukulele and slide guitar.

Classical & Opera

Early European immigrants brought their own styles of music and gave birth to local variants during the early 1900s. In the 1950s Douglas Lilburn became one of the first internationally recognised NZ classical composers. More recently the country has produced a number of world-renowned musicians in this field, including opera singer Dame Kiri Te Kanawa, million-selling pop diva Hayley Westenra, composer John Psathas (who created music for the 2004 Olympic Games) and composer/percussionist Gareth Farr (who also performs in drag under the name Lilith).

Rock

New Zealand also has a strong rock scene, its most acclaimed exports being the revered indie label Flying Nun and the Finn Brothers.

In 1981 Flying Nun was started by Christchurch record store owner Roger Shepherd. Many of the early groups came from Dunedin, where local musicians took the DIY attitude of punk but used it to produce a lo-fi indie-pop that received rave reviews from the likes of *NME* in the UK and *Rolling Stone* in the US. *Billboard* even claimed in 1989: 'There doesn't seem to be anything on Flying Nun Records that is less than excellent.'

Many of the musicians from the Flying Nun scene still perform live to this day, including David Kilgour (from The Clean) and Shayne Carter (from the Straitjacket Fits, and subsequently Dimmer and The Adults). The Bats are still releasing albums, and Martin Phillipps' band The Chills released a live album in 2013.

Reggae, Hip-Hop & Dance

The genres of music that have been adopted most enthusiastically by Maori and Polynesian New Zealanders are reggae (in the 1970s) and hip-hop (in the 1980s), which has led to distinct local forms. In Wellington a thriving jazz scene took on a reggae influence to create a host of groups that blended dub, roots, and funky jazz – most notably Fat Freddy's Drop. The national public holiday, Waitangi Day, on 6 February, also happens to fall on the birthday of Bob Marley and annual reggae concerts are held on this day in Auckland and Wellington.

The local hip-hop scene has its heart in the suburbs of South Auckland, which have a high concentration of Maori and Pacific Island residents. This area is home to one of New Zealand's foremost hip-hop labels, Dawn

For indie rock fans, a great source of local info is www.cheeseontoast.co.nz, which lists gigs and has band interviews and photos. For more on local hip-hop, pop and rock, check out www.thecorner.co.nz and the long-running www.muzic.net.nz.

ARTS & MUSIC MUSIC

THE BROTHERS FINN

There are certain tunes that all Kiwis can sing along to, given a beer and the opportunity. A surprising proportion of these were written by Tim and Neil Finn, and have been international hits.

Tim Finn first came to prominence in the 1970s group Split Enz. When the original guitarist quit, Neil flew over to join the band in the UK, despite being only 15 at the time. Split Enz amassed a solid following in Australia, NZ and Canada before disbanding in 1985.

Neil then formed Crowded House with two Australian musicians (Paul Hester and Nick Seymour) and one of their early singles, 'Don't Dream It's Over', hit number two on the US charts. Tim later did a brief spell in the band, during which the brothers wrote 'Weather With You' – a song that reached number seven on the UK charts, pushing their album *Woodface* to gold sales. The original line-up of Crowded House played their final show in 1996 in front of 100,000 people on the steps of the Sydney Opera House (though Finn and Seymour reformed the group in 2007 and continue to tour and record occasionally). Tim and Neil have both released a number of solo albums, as well as releasing material together as the Finn Brothers.

More recently, Neil has also remained busy organising a set of shows/releases under the name Seven Worlds Collide – a collaboration with well-known overseas musicians including Jeff Tweedy (Wilco), Johnny Marr (The Smiths) and members of Radiohead. His latest band is the Pajama Club, a collaboration with wife Sharon and Auckland musicians Sean Donnelly and Alana Skyring.

Neil's son Liam also has a burgeoning solo career, touring the US with Eddie Vedder and The Black Keys and appearing on *The Late Show with David Letterman*. Both Tim and Neil were born in the small town of Te Awamutu: the local museum has a collection documenting their work.

GOOD LORDE!

Of course, the big news in Kiwi music recently has been the success of Lorde, a singer-songwriter from Devonport on Auckland's North Shore. Known less regally to her friends as Ella Yelich-O'Connor, 16-year-old Lorde cracked the number-one spot on the US Billboard charts in 2013 with her magical, schoolyard-chant-evoking hit 'Royals' – the first NZ solo artist to top the American charts. 'Royals' then went on to win the Song of the Year Grammy in 2014. Her debut album *Pure Heroine* has spawned a string of hits and is selling millions of copies worldwide. Not bad for 16!

Raid, which takes its name from the infamous early-morning house raids of the 1970s that police performed on Pacific Islanders suspected of outstaying their visas. Dawn Raid's most successful artist is Savage, who sold a million copies of his single 'Swing' after it was featured in the movie *Knocked Up*. Within New Zealand, the most well-known hip-hop acts are Scribe, Che Fu, and Smashproof (whose song 'Brother' held number one on the NZ singles charts longer than any other local act).

Dance music gained a foothold in Christchurch in the 1990s, spawning dub/electronica outfit Salmonella Dub and its offshoot act, Tiki Taane. Drum 'n' bass remains popular locally and has spawned internationally renowned acts such as Concord Dawn and Shapeshifter.

The TV show *Popstars* originated in New Zealand, though the resulting group, True Bliss, was short-lived. The series concept was then picked up in Australia, the UK and the US, inspiring the *Idol* series.

New Music

Since 2000 the NZ music scene has developed new vitality after the government convinced commercial radio stations to adopt a voluntary quota of 20% local music. This enabled commercially oriented musicians to develop solid careers. Rock groups such as Shihad, The Feelers and Op-shop have thrived in this environment, as have a set of soulful female solo artists (who all happen to have Maori heritage): Bic Runga, Anika Moa and Brooke Fraser. NZ also produced two internationally acclaimed garage rock acts over this time: the Datsuns and the D4.

Current Kiwis garnering international recognition include the gifted songstress Kimbra (who sang on Gotye's global smash 'Somebody That I Used To Know'); indie anthem alt-rockers The Naked & Famous; singer-songwriter Ladyhawke; the arty Lawrence Arabia; and the semi-psychedelic Unknown Mortal Orchestra. Aaradhna is a much-touted R&B singer currently making a splash with her album *Trebel & Reverb*, which won Album of the Year at the 2013 New Zealand Music Awards.

Venues

In Auckland the main rock venues are the Kings Arms Tavern (p75) and Cassette Nine (p74), though two joint venues in St Kevins Arcade (off Karangahape Rd) are also popular – the Wine Cellar & Whammy Bar (p75). Ding Dong Lounge (p74) and Portland Public House (p76) are also worth a look. Wellington is rife with live-music venues – mostly around Cuba St – from Meow (p350) to Bodega (p350).

An up-to-date list of gigs in the main centres is listed at www.ripitup.co.nz. Tickets for most events can be bought at www.ticketek.co.nz, www.ticketmaster.co.nz, or, for smaller gigs, www.undertheradar.co.nz.

Festivals

A number of festivals happen over summer, including new year's celebration **Rhythm & Vines** (www.rhythmandvines.co.nz) in Gisborne. The touring international alt-rock fest **Big Day Out** (www.bigdayout.com) seemed destined for the scrapheap but was relaunched in Auckland in 2014. Also recommended is the underground festival held early each year by A Low Hum (www.alowhum.com). World music fans flock to the local version of **WOMAD** (World of Music Arts & Dance; www.womad.co.nz) in New Plymouth, which features both local and overseas acts.

Survival Guide

DIRECTORY A–Z . . . 402

Accommodation 402

Children 404

Climate 405

Customs Regulations . . . 405

Discount Cards 405

Electricity 406

Embassies &
Consulates 406

Food & Drink 406

Gay & Lesbian
Travellers 406

Health 407

Insurance 408

Internet Access 408

Legal Matters 408

Maps 409

Money 409

Opening Hours 409

Post 410

Public Holidays 410

Safe Travel 410

Telephone 410

Time 411

Toilets 411

Tourist Information 411

Travellers with
Disabilities 412

Visas 412

Volunteering 413

Women Travellers 413

Work 413

TRANSPORT 415

GETTING THERE
& AWAY 415

Entering the Country 415

Air .415

Sea 416

GETTING AROUND 416

Air .416

Bicycle 417

Boat 417

Bus 417

Car & Motorcycle 418

Hitching &
Ride-Sharing 421

Local Transport 421

Train 422

LANGUAGE 423

GLOSSARY 425

Directory A–Z

Accommodation

Across the North Island, you can bed down in historic guesthouses, facility-laden hotels, uniform motel units, beautifully situated campsites, and hostels that range in character from clean-living to tirelessly party-prone.

If you're travelling during peak tourist seasons, book your bed well in advance. Accommodation is most in demand (and at its priciest) during the summer holidays from Christmas to late January, and at Easter.

Visitor information centres provide reams of local accommodation information, often in the form of folders detailing facilities and up-to-date prices; many can also make bookings on your behalf.

For online listings, check out the websites of the **Automobile Association** (AA; www.aa.co.nz) and **Jasons** (www.jasons.com).

B&Bs

Bed and breakfast (B&B) accommodation in NZ's North Island pops up in the middle of cities, in rural hamlets and on stretches of isolated coastline, with rooms on offer in everything from suburban bungalows to stately manors.

Breakfast may be 'continental' (cereal, toast and tea or coffee), 'hearty continental' (add yoghurt, fruit, home-baked bread or muffins), or a stomach-loading cooked meal (eggs, bacon, sausages...). Some B&B hosts may also cook dinner for guests and advertise dinner, bed and breakfast (DB&B) packages.

B&B tariffs are typically in the $120 to $180 bracket (per double), though some places charge upwards of $300 per double. Some hosts cheekily charge hefty prices for what is, in essence, a bedroom in their home. Off-street parking is often a bonus in Auckland and Wellington.

Online resources:

Bed & Breakfast Book (www.bnb.co.nz)

Bed and Breakfast Directory (www.bed-and-breakfast. co.nz)

Camping & Holiday Parks

Campers and campervan drivers alike converge upon NZ's hugely popular 'holiday parks', slumbering peacefully in powered and unpowered sites, cheap bunk rooms (dorm rooms), cabins and self-contained units (often called motels or tourist flats). Well-equipped communal kitchens, dining areas, and games and TV rooms often feature. In cities, holiday parks are usually a fair way from the action, but in smaller towns they can be impressively central or near lakes, beaches, rivers and forests.

The nightly cost of camping at a holiday park is usually between $15 and $20 per adult, with children charged half price; powered sites are a couple of dollars more. Cabins or units normally ranges from $70 to $120 per double. Unless noted otherwise, the prices we've listed for campsites, campervan sites, huts and cabins are for two people.

DOC CAMPSITES & FREEDOM CAMPING

A fantastic option for those in campervans is the 250-plus vehicle-accessible Conservation Campsites run by the **Department of Conservation** (DOC; www.doc.govt. nz), with fees ranging from free (basic toilets and fresh water) to $15 per adult (flush

---

BOOK YOUR STAY ONLINE

For more accommodation reviews by Lonely Planet authors, check out http://lonelyplanet.com/hotels/. You'll find independent reviews, as well as recommendations on the best places to stay. Best of all, you can book online.

toilets and showers). DOC publishes free brochures with detailed descriptions and instructions to find every campsite (even GPS coordinates). Pick up copies from DOC offices before you hit the road, or visit the website.

DOC also looks after hundreds of backcountry huts and backcountry campsites which can only be reached on foot. See the website for details. Great Walk huts and campsites are also managed by DOC: see the Active North Island section (p29) for info.

New Zealand is so photogenic, it's tempting to just pull off the road at a gorgeous viewpoint and camp the night. But never just assume it's OK to camp somewhere: always ask a local or check with the local i-SITE, DOC office or commercial campground. If you are freedom camping, treat the area with respect. Note that if your chosen campsite doesn't have toilet facilities and neither does your campervan, it's illegal for you to sleep there (your campervan must also have an on-board grey-water storage stytem). Legislation allows for $200 on-the-spot fines for camping in prohibited areas, or for improper disposal of waste (in cases where dumping waste could damage the environment, fines are up to $10,000). See www.camping.org.nz for more freedom-camping tips.

Farmstays

Farmstays open the door to the agricultural side of NZ life, with visitors encouraged to get some dirt beneath their fingernails at orchards and dairy, sheep and cattle farms. Costs can vary widely, with B&Bs generally ranging from $80 to $120. Some farms have separate cottages where you can fix your own food, while others offer low-cost, shared, backpacker-style accommodation.

Farm Helpers in NZ (FHINZ; www.fhinz.co.nz) Produces a booklet ($25) that lists around 350 NZ farms providing lodging in exchange for four to six hours' work per day.

Rural Holidays NZ (www.ruralholidays.co.nz) Lists farmstays and homestays throughout the country.

Hostels

NZ is packed to the rafters with backpacker hostels, both independent and part of large chains, ranging from small, homestay-style affairs with a handful of beds, to refurbished hotels and towering modern structures in the big cities. Hostel bed prices listed throughout this book are nonmember rates, usually between $25 and $35 per night.

Hostel organisations include:

Budget Backpacker Hostels (BBH; www.bbh.co.nz) NZ's biggest hostel group with around 275 hostels. Membership costs $45 for 12 months and entitles you to stay at member hostels at rates listed in the annual (free) *BBH Backpacker Accommodation* booklet. Nonmembers pay an extra $3 per night. Pick up a membership card from any member hostel or order one online for $50; see the website for details.

YHA New Zealand (Youth Hostels Association; www.yha.co.nz) More than 50 hostels in prime NZ locations. The YHA is part of the **Hostelling International** (HI; www.hihostels.com) network, so if you're an HI member in your own country, membership entitles you to use NZ hostels. If you don't already have a home membership, you can join at major NZ YHA hostels or online for $42, valid for 12 months. Nonmembers pay an extra $3 per night.

Base Backpackers (www.stayatbase.com) Nationwide chain with seven hostels around NZ, including North Island locations in the Bay of Islands, Auckland, Rotorua and Taupo. Expect clean dorms, women-only areas and party opportunities aplenty. Offers a 10-night 'Base Jumping' accommodation card for $239, bookable online.

VIP Backpackers (www.vipbackpackers.com) International organisation affiliated with around 20 NZ hostels (not BBH or YHA), mainly in the cities and tourist hot-spots. For around $61 (including postage) you'll receive a 12-month membership entitling you to a $1 discount off nightly accommodation. Join online or at VIP hostels.

Nomads Backpackers (www.nomadsworld.com) Seven franchises in NZ with North Island properties in Auckland, Rotorua, Taupo, Waitomo and Wellington. Membership costs $49 for 12 months and, like VIP, offers NZ$1 off the cost of nightly accommodation. Join at participating hostels or online.

Pubs, Hotels & Motels

➡ The least expensive form of North Island hotel accommodation is the humble pub. NZ's old pubs are often full of character (and characters), while others are grotty, ramshackle places that are best avoided, especially by women travelling solo. Check whether there's a band playing the night you're staying – you could be in for a sleepless night. In the cheapest pubs, singles/doubles might cost as little as $30/60 (with a shared bathroom down the hall), though $50/80 is more common.

➡ At the top end of the hotel scale are five-star international chains, resort complexes and splendid boutique hotels, all of which charge a hefty premium for their mod cons, snappy service and/or historic opulence. We quote 'rack rates' (official advertised rates) for such places, but discounts and special deals often apply.

➡ NZ's towns have a glut of nondescript, low-rise motels and motor lodges, charging between $80 and $180 for double rooms. These tend to be squat structures skulking by highways on the edges of towns. Most are modernish (though decor is often mired in the early 2000s) and have similar facilities, namely tea- and coffee-making equipment, fridge, and TV – prices vary with standard.

Rental Accommodation

The basic Kiwi holiday home is called a 'bach' (short for 'bachelor', as they were historically used by single men as hunting and fishing hideouts). These are simple self-contained cottages that can be rented in rural and coastal areas, often in isolated locations. Prices are typically $80 to $150 per night, which isn't bad for a whole house or self-contained bungalow. For more upmarket holiday houses, expect to pay anything from $150 to $400.

Online resources include:

Baches and Holiday Homes To Rent (www.holidayhomes.co.nz)

Bookabach (www.bookabach.co.nz)

Holiday Houses (www.holidayhouses.co.nz)

New Zealand Apartments (www.nzapartments.co.nz)

Children

NZ is a terrific place to travel with kids as it is safe and affordable, with loads of playgrounds, kid-centric activities, a moderate climate and chilli-free cuisine. For helpful general tips, see Lonely Planet's *Travel with Children*. Handy online resources for kids' activities and travel info include:

Kidz Go New Zealand (www.kidzgo.co.nz)

Kidspot (www.kidspot.co.nz)

KidsNewzealand (www.kidsnewzealand.com)

Tips

➡ Many motels and holiday parks have playgrounds, games and DVDs, and, occasionally, fenced swimming pools and trampolines. Cots and highchairs aren't always available at budget and midrange accommodation, but top-end hotels supply them and often provide child-minding services. Many B&Bs promote themselves as kid-free, and hostels tend to focus on the backpacker demographic, but there are plenty of hostels (including YHA) that do allow kids.

➡ For specialised childcare, try www.rockmybaby.co.nz, or look under 'babysitters' and 'child care centres' in the *Yellow Pages* directory.

➡ Check that your car-hire company can supply the right-sized seat for your child, and that the seat will be properly fitted. Some companies legally require you to fit car seats yourself.

PRACTICALITIES

➡ **News** Leaf through Auckland's *New Zealand Herald* or Wellington's *Dominion Post* newspapers. Online see www.nzherald.co.nz or www.stuff.co.nz.

➡ **TV** Watch one of the national government-owned TV stations (TV One, TV2, TVNZ 6, Maori TV and the 100% Maori language Te Reo) or the subscriber-only Sky TV (www.skytv.co.nz).

➡ **Radio** Tune in to Radio National for current affairs and Concert FM for classical and jazz (see www.radionz.co.nz for frequencies). Radio Hauraki (www.hauraki.co.nz) cranks out the rock, while Newstalk ZB (www.newstalkzb.co.nz) has the most lively of talkback discussions on New Zealand issues.

➡ **DVDs** Kiwi DVDs are encoded for Region 4, which includes Mexico, South America, Central America, Australia, the Pacific and the Caribbean.

➡ **Electrical** To plug yourself into the electricity supply (240V AC, 50Hz), use a three-pin adaptor (the same as in Australia; different to British three-pin adaptors).

➡ **Weights & measures** NZ uses the metric system.

Climate

Auckland

Rotorua

Wellington

→ Most Kiwis are relaxed about public breastfeeding. Alternatively, cities and major towns have public rooms where parents can go to feed a baby or change a nappy (diaper); check with the local visitor information centre, or ask a local.

→ Kids' and family rates are often available for accommodation, tours, attraction entry fees, and air, bus and train transport, with discounts of as much as 50% off the adult rate. Note that the definition of 'child' can vary from under 12 to under 18 years; toddlers (under four years old) usually get free admission and transport.

→ There are plenty of family-friendly restaurants in NZ with highchairs and kids' menus. Pubs often serve kids' meals and most cafes and restaurants (with the exception of upmarket eateries) can handle the idea of child-sized portions.

→ NZ's medical services and facilities are world-class. Goods like formula and disposable nappies are widely available.

Customs Regulations

For the low-down on what you can and can't bring into NZ, see the **New Zealand Customs Service** (www. customs.govt.nz). Per-person duty-free allowances:

→ 1125mL of spirits or liqueur

→ 4.5L of wine or beer

→ 200 cigarettes (or 50 cigars or 250g of tobacco)

→ dutiable goods up to the value of $700

It's a good idea to declare any unusual medicines. Tramping gear (boots, tents etc) will be checked and may need to be cleaned before being allowed in. You must declare any plant or animal products (including anything made of wood), and food of any kind. Weapons and fire-arms are either prohibited or require a permit and safety testing.

Discount Cards

→ The internationally recognised **International Student Identity Card** is produced by the **International Student Travel Confederation** (ISTC; www.istc.org), and issued to full-time students aged 12 and over. It provides discounts on accommodation, transport and admission to attractions. The ISTC also produces the **International Youth Travel Card**, available to folks under 30 who are not full-time students, with equivalent benefits to the ISIC. Also similar is the **International Teacher Identity Card**, available to teaching professionals. All three cards (NZ$30 each) are available online at www. isiccard.co.nz, or from student travel companies such as STA Travel.

→ The **New Zealand Card** (www.newzealandcard.com) is a $35 discount pass that'll score you between 5% and 50% off a range of accommodation, tours, sights and activities.

→ Travellers over 60 with some form of identification (eg an official seniors card from your home country) are often eligible for concession prices.

Electricity

240V/50Hz

Embassies & Consulates

Most principal diplomatic representations to NZ are in Wellington, with a few in Auckland.

Australian High Commission (☎04-473 6411; www.australia.org.nz; 72-76 Hobson St, Thorndon, Wellington)

Canadian High Commission (☎04-473 9577; Lvl 11, 125 The Terrace, Wellington)

Chinese Embassy (☎04-474 9631; www.chinaembassy.org.nz; 2-6 Glenmore St, Kelburn, Wellington)

Fiji High Commission (☎04-473 5401; www.fiji.org.nz; 31 Pipitea St, Thorndon, Wellington)

French Embassy (☎04-384 2555; www.ambafrance-nz.org; 34-42 Manners St, Wellington)

German Embassy (☎04-473 6063; www.wellington.diplo.de; 90-92 Hobson St, Thorndon, Wellington)

Irish Consulate (☎09-977 2252; www.ireland.co.nz; Lvl 3, Tower 1, 205 Queen St, Auckland)

Israeli Embassy (☎04-439 9500; http://embassies.gov.il/wellington; Lvl 13, Bayleys Building, 36 Brandon St, Wellington)

Japanese Embassy (☎04-473 1540; www.nz.emb-japan.go.jp; Lvl 18, The Majestic Centre, 100 Willis St, Wellington)

Netherlands Embassy (☎04-471 6390; http://newzealand.nlembassy.org; Lvl 10, Cooperative Bank Building, cnr Featherston & Ballance Sts, Wellington)

UK High Commission (☎04-924 2888; www.gov.uk; 44 Hill St, Thorndon, Wellington)

US Embassy (☎04-462 6000; http://newzealand.usembassy.gov; 29 Fitzherbert Tce, Thorndon, Wellington)

Food & Drink

New Zealand's restaurants and cafes are adept at throwing together traditional staples (lamb, beef, venison, green-lipped mussels) with Asian, European and pan-Pacific flair. Eateries themselves range from fish-and-chip shops and pub bistros to retro-styled cafes, restaurant-bars with full à la carte service and crisp-linen fine dining. Tipping is not mandatory, but feel free to if you've had a happy culinary experience (about 10% of the bill). For online listings check out:

Dine Out (www.dineout.co.nz)

Menus NZ (www.menus.co.nz)

On the liquid front, NZ wine is world class (especially sauvignon blanc and pinot noir), and you'll be hard-pressed to find a NZ town of any size without decent espresso. Auckland, Wellington and other smaller North Island cities have specialist beer bars showcasing NZ's excellent craft-beer scene.

Vegetarians & Vegans

Most large urban centres have at least one dedicated vegetarian cafe or restaurant: see the **Vegetarians New Zealand** (www.vegetarians.co.nz) website for listings. Beyond this, almost all restaurants and cafes offer some vegetarian menu choices (although sometimes only one or two). Many eateries also provide gluten-free and vegan options. Always check that stocks and sauces are vegetarian, too.

In this book, the vegetarian icon (🌱) in Eating listings indicates a good vegetarian selection.

Gay & Lesbian Travellers

The gay and lesbian tourism industry in NZ isn't as high-profile as it is in neighbouring Australia, but homosexual communities are prominent in Auckland and Wellington and there are myriad support organisations across both islands. NZ has progressive laws protecting the rights of gays and lesbians, and same-sex marriage was

---

EATING PRICE RANGES

Listings within this book are in order of author preference within their respective budget ranges. The following price indicators used throughout refer to the average price of a main course:

$ less than $15

$$ $15–32

$$$ more than $32

legalised here in 2013. Generally speaking, Kiwis are fairly relaxed and accepting about homosexuality, but that's not to say that homophobia doesn't exist.

Resources

There are loads of websites dedicated to gay and lesbian travel in NZ. **Gay Tourism New Zealand** (www.gaytourismnewzealand.com) is a good starting point, with links to various sites. Other worthwhile queer websites include the following:

Gay NZ (www.gaynz.com)

Lesbian NZ (www.lesbian.net.nz)

Gay Stay (www.gaystay.co.nz)

Check out the nationwide magazine *express* (www.gayexpress.co.nz) every second Wednesday for the latest happenings, reviews and listings on the NZ gay scene.

Festivals & Events

Big Gay Out (www.biggayout.co.nz) Free festival (food, drink, entertainment) held every February in Auckland.

Out Takes (www.outtakes.org.nz) G&L film festival staged in Auckland and Wellington in May/June.

Health

New Zealand is one of the healthiest countries in the world in which to travel. Diseases such as malaria and typhoid are unheard of, and the absence of poisonous snakes or other dangerous animals makes outdoor adventures here less risky than in neighbouring Australia.

Before You Go
MEDICATIONS

Bring medications in their original, clearly labelled containers. A signed and dated letter from your physician describing your medical conditions and medications (including generic names) and any requisite syringes or needles, is also wise.

VACCINATIONS

NZ has no vaccination requirements for any traveller, but the World Health Organization recommends that all travellers should be covered for diphtheria, tetanus, measles, mumps, rubella, chickenpox and polio, as well as hepatitis B, regardless of their destination. Ask your doctor for an *International Certificate of Vaccination* (or 'the yellow booklet'), which will list all the vaccinations you've received.

HEALTH INSURANCE

Health insurance is essential for all travellers. While health care in NZ is of a high standard and not overly expensive by international standards, considerable costs can be built up and repatriation can be pricey.

If your current health insurance doesn't cover you for medical expenses incurred overseas, consider extra insurance – see www.lonelyplanet.com/travel-insurance for more information. Find out in advance if your insurance plan will make payments directly to providers or reimburse you later for overseas health expenditures.

In New Zealand
AVAILABILITY & COST OF HEALTH CARE

➡ NZ's public hospitals offer a high standard of care (free for residents). All travellers are covered for medical care resulting from accidents that occur while in NZ (eg motor-vehicle accidents, adventure-activity accidents) by the **Accident Compensation Corporation** (ACC; www.acc.co.nz). Costs incurred due to treatment of a medical illness that occurs while in NZ will only be covered by travel insurance. For more details, see www.moh.govt.nz and www.acc.co.nz.

➡ The 24-hour, free-call **Healthline** (📞 0800 611 116; www.health.govt.nz) offers health advice throughout NZ.

PHARMACEUTICALS

Over-the-counter medications are widely available in NZ through private chemists. These include painkillers, antihistamines and skin-care products. Some medications, such as antibiotics and the contraceptive pill, are only available via a prescription obtained from a general practitioner. If you take regular medications, bring an adequate supply and details of the generic name, as brand names differ country-to-country.

INFECTIOUS DISEASES

The giardia parasite is widespread in NZ waterways: drinking untreated water from streams and lakes is not recommended. Using water filters and boiling or treating water with iodine are effective ways of preventing the disease. Symptoms consist of intermittent diarrhoea, abdominal bloating and wind. Effective treatment is available (tinidazole or metronidazole).

ENVIRONMENTAL HAZARDS

➔ Hypothermia is a significant risk, especially during winter and year-round at altitude. Mountain ranges and/or strong winds produce a high chill factor, which can cause hypothermia even in moderate temperatures. Early signs include the inability to perform fine movements (such as doing up buttons), shivering and a bad case of the 'umbles' (fumbles, mumbles, grumbles, stumbles). To treat, minimise heat loss: remove wet clothing, add dry clothes with wind- and waterproof layers, and consume water and carbohydrates to allow shivering to build the internal temperature. In severe hypothermia, shivering actually stops; this is a medical emergency requiring rapid evacuation in addition to the above measures.

➔ NZ has exceptional surf beaches. The power of the surf can fluctuate as a result of the varying slope of the seabed at many beaches. Check with local surf-lifesaving organisations before entering the surf and be aware of your own limitations and expertise.

Insurance

➔ A watertight travel insurance policy covering theft, loss and medical problems is essential. Some policies specifically exclude designated 'dangerous activities' such as scuba diving, bungy jumping, whitewater rafting, skiing and even tramping. If you plan on doing any of these things (a distinct possibility in NZ!), make sure your policy covers you fully.

➔ It's worth mentioning that under NZ law, you cannot sue for personal injury (other than exemplary damages). Instead, the country's **Accident Compensation Corporation** (ACC; www. acc.co.nz) administers an accident compensation scheme that provides accident insurance for NZ residents and visitors to the country, regardless of fault. This scheme, however, does not negate the necessity for your own comprehensive travel-insurance policy, as it doesn't cover you for such things as income loss, treatment at home or ongoing illness.

➔ Consider a policy that pays doctors or hospitals directly, rather than you paying on the spot and claiming later. If you have to claim later, keep all documentation. Some policies ask you to call (reverse charges) to a centre in your home country where an immediate assessment of your problem is made. Check that the policy covers ambulances and emergency medical evacuations by air.

➔ Worldwide travel insurance is available at www.lonelyplanet.com/travel-insurance. You can buy, extend and claim online anytime – even if you're already on the road.

Internet Access

Wi-fi & Internet Service Providers

➔ You'll be able to find wi-fi access around the country, from hotel rooms to pub beer gardens to hostel dorms. Usually you have to be a guest or customer to log-on; you'll be issued with an access code. Sometimes it's free, sometimes there's a charge.

➔ The country's main telecommunications company is **Telecom New Zealand** (www.telecom.co.nz), which has wireless hotspots around the country where you can purchase prepaid access cards. Alternatively, purchase a prepaid number from the login page at any wireless hotspot using your credit card. See Telecom's website for hotspot listings.

➔ If you've brought your palmtop or laptop, consider buying a prepay USB modem (aka a 'dongle') with a local SIM card: both Telecom and **Vodafone** (www.vodafone. co.nz) sell these from around $100. If you want to get connected via a local internet service provider (ISP), options include the following:

Clearnet (☎0508 888 800; www.clearnet.co.nz)

Earthlight (☎03-479 0303; www.earthlight.co.nz)

Slingshot (☎0800 892 000; www.slingshot.co.nz)

INTERNET CAFES

There are fewer internet cafes around these days than there were five years ago (thanks to the advent of smartphones and wi-fi) but you'll still find them in most sizable towns. Access at cafes ranges anywhere from $4 to $6 per hour.

Most youth hostels have both computers for internet access and wi-fi, as do many hotels and caravan parks. Many public libraries have internet access, including wi-fi, but generally it's provided for research, not for travellers to check Facebook.

Legal Matters

➔ Marijuana is widely indulged in but illegal: anyone caught carrying this or other illicit drugs will have the book thrown at them.

➔ Drink-driving is a serious offence and remains a significant problem in NZ. The legal blood alcohol limit is 0.08% for drivers over 20, and zero for those under 20.

➔ If you are arrested, it's your right to consult a lawyer before any formal questioning begins.

Maps

→ New Zealand's **Automobile Association** (AA; ☎0800 500 444; www.aa.co.nz/travel) produces excellent city, town, regional, island and highway maps, available from its local offices. The AA also produces a detailed *New Zealand Road Atlas*. Other reliable countrywide atlases, available from visitor information centres and bookshops, are published by Hema, KiwiMaps and Wises.

→ **Land Information New Zealand** (LINZ; www.linz.govt.nz) publishes several exhaustive map series, including street, country and holiday maps, national park and forest park maps, and topographical trampers' maps. Scan the larger bookshops, or try the nearest DOC office or visitor information centre for topo maps.

→ Online, log onto **AA Maps** (www.aamaps.co.nz) or **Yellow Maps** (www.maps.yellowpages.co.nz) to pinpoint exact NZ addresses.

Money
ATMs & Eftpos

→ Branches of the country's major banks across both islands have ATMs, but you won't find them everywhere (eg not in small towns).

→ Many NZ businesses use electronic funds transfer at point of sale (Eftpos), allowing you to use your bank card (credit or debit) to make direct purchases and often withdraw cash as well. Eftpos is available practically everywhere: just like an ATM, you'll need a personal identification number (PIN).

Bank Accounts

We've heard mixed reports on the subject of travellers opening bank accounts in NZ, and bank websites are vague. Some sources say opening an account is as simple as flashing a few pieces of ID; other sources say banks won't allow visitors to open an account unless the application is accompanied by proof of employment. Either way, do your homework before you arrive and be prepared to shop around to get the best deal.

Credit & Debit Cards
CREDIT CARDS

Credit cards such as Visa and MasterCard are widely accepted for everything from a hostel bed to a bungy jump, and are pretty much essential for car hire. They can also be used for over-the-counter cash advances at banks and from ATMs, but be aware that such transactions will incur charges. Diners Club and American Express cards are not as widely accepted.

DEBIT CARDS

Debit cards enable you to draw money directly from your home bank account using ATMs, banks or Eftpos facilities. Any card connected to the international banking network (Cirrus, Maestro, Visa Plus and Eurocard) should work with your PIN. Fees will vary depending on your home bank; ask before you leave. Alternatively, companies such as Travelex offer debit cards with set withdrawal fees and a balance you can top-up from your personal bank account while on the road.

Currency

NZ's currency is the NZ dollar, comprising 100 cents. There are 10c, 20c, 50c, $1 and $2 coins, and $5, $10, $20, $50 and $100 notes. Prices are often still marked in single cents and then rounded to the nearest 10c when you hand over your money.

Moneychangers

Changing foreign currency or travellers cheques is usually no problem at NZ banks or at licensed moneychangers (eg Travelex) in the major cities. Moneychangers can be found in all major tourist areas, cities and airports.

Taxes & Refunds

The Goods and Services Tax (GST) is a flat 15% tax on all domestic goods and services. Prices in this book include GST. There's no GST refund available when you leave NZ.

Travellers Cheques

Amex, Travelex and other international brands of travellers cheques are a bit old-fashioned these days, but they're easily exchanged at banks and moneychangers. Present your passport for identification when cashing them; shop around for the best rates.

Opening Hours

Note that most attractions close on Christmas Day and Good Friday.

Banks 9.30am to 4.30pm Monday to Friday; some city branches also open Saturday mornings.

Cafes 7am to 4pm or 5pm.

Post offices 8.30am to 5pm Monday to Friday; larger branches also 9.30am to 1pm Saturday. Postal desks in news-agencies open later.

Pubs Noon until late; food from noon to 2pm and from 6pm to 8pm.

Restaurants Noon to 2.30pm and 6.30 to 9pm, often until 11pm Fridays and Saturdays.

Shops & businesses 9am to 5.30pm Monday to Friday, and 9am to 12.30pm or 5pm Saturday. Late-night shopping (until 9pm) in larger cities on Thursday and/or Friday nights. Sunday trading in most big towns and cities.

Supermarkets 8am to 7pm, often 9pm or later in cities.

Post

The services offered by **New Zealand Post** (☎0800 501 501; www.nzpost.co.nz) are reliable and reasonably inexpensive. See the website for current info on national and international zones and rates, plus post office locations.

Public Holidays

NZ's main public holidays:

New Year 1 and 2 January

Waitangi Day 6 February

Easter Good Friday and Easter Monday; March/April

Anzac Day 25 April

Queen's Birthday First Monday in June

Labour Day Fourth Monday in October

Christmas Day 25 December

Boxing Day 26 December

In addition, each NZ province has its own anniversary-day holiday. The dates of these provincial holidays vary: when they fall on Friday to Sunday, they're usually observed the following Monday; if they fall on Tuesday to Thursday, they're held on the preceding Monday.

Provincial North Island anniversary holidays:

Wellington 22 January

Auckland 29 January

Northland 29 January

Taranaki 31 March

Hawke's Bay 1 November

School Holidays

The Christmas holiday season, from mid-December to late January, is part of the summer school vacation: expect transport and accommodation to book-out in advance, and queues at tourist attractions. There are three shorter school-holiday periods during the year: from mid- to late April, early to mid-July, and mid-September to early October.

For exact dates see the **Ministry of Education** (www.minedu.govt.nz) website.

Safe Travel

Although it's no more dangerous than other developed countries, violent crime does happen in NZ, so take sensible precautions on the streets at night or if staying in remote areas. Gang culture permeates some parts of the country; give any black-jacketed, insignia-wearing groups a wide berth.

Theft from cars is a problem around NZ – travellers are viewed as easy marks. Avoid leaving valuables in vehicles, no matter where they're parked; you're tempting fate at tourist parking areas and trailhead car parks.

Don't underestimate the dangers posed by NZ's unpredictable, ever-changing climate, especially in high-altitude areas. Hypothermia is a real risk.

NZ has been spared the proliferation of venomous creatures found in neighbouring Australia (spiders, snakes, jellyfish...). Sharks patrol NZ waters, but rarely nibble on humans. Much greater ocean hazards are rips and undertows, which can quickly drag swimmers out to sea: heed local warnings.

Kiwi roads are often made hazardous by speeding locals, wide-cornering campervans and traffic-ignorant sheep. Set yourself a reasonable itinerary and keep your eyes on the road. Cyclists take care: motorists can't always overtake easily on skinny roads.

In the annoyances category, NZ's sandflies are a royal pain (the intense itching can last for months). Lather yourself with insect repellent in coastal areas, even if you're only sitting on the edge of a beach for a minute or two.

Telephone

Telecom New Zealand (www.telecom.co.nz) The country's key domestic player, with a stake in the local mobile (cell) market.

Vodafone (www.vodafone.co.nz) Mobile network option.

2 Degrees (www.2degreesmobile.co.nz) Mobile network option.

Mobile Phones

➡ Local mobile phone numbers are preceded by the prefix ☎021, ☎022, ☎025 or ☎027. Mobile phone coverage is good in cities and towns of the North Island, but can be patchy away from urban centres.

➡ If you want to bring your own phone and use a prepaid service with a local SIM card, **Vodafone** (www.vodafone.co.nz) is a practical option. Any Vodafone shop (found in most major towns) will set

---

GOVERNMENT TRAVEL ADVICE

The following government websites offer travel advisories and information on current hot spots:

Australian Department of Foreign Affairs (www.smarttraveller.gov.au)

British Foreign & Commonwealth Office (www.gov.uk/fco)

Foreign Affairs, Trade & Development Canada (www.international.gc.ca)

US Department of State (www.travel.state.gov)

you up with a SIM card and phone number (about $40); top-ups can be purchased at newsagencies, post offices and petrol stations in most places.

➡ Alternatively, if you don't bring your own phone from home, you can rent one from **Vodafone Rental** (www.vodarent.co.nz) priced from $5 per day (for which you'll also need a local SIM card), with pick-up and drop-off outlets at NZ's major airports. We've also had some positive feedback on **Phone Hire New Zealand** (www.phonehirenz.com), which hires out mobile phones, SIM cards, modems and GPS systems.

Local Calls

Local calls from private phones are free. Local calls from payphones cost $1 for the first 15 minutes, and $0.20 per minute thereafter, though coin-operated payphones are scarce (and if you do find one, chances are the coin slot will be gummed up); you'll generally need a phonecard. Calls to mobile phones attract higher rates.

International Calls

Payphones allow international calls, but the cost and international dialling code for calls will vary depending on which provider you're using. International calls from NZ are relatively inexpensive and subject to specials that reduce the rates even more, so it's worth shopping around – consult the *Yellow Pages* for providers.

To make international calls from NZ, you need to dial the international access code ✆00, then the country code and the area code (without the initial 0). So for a London number, you'd dial ✆00-44-20, then the number.

If dialling NZ from overseas, the country code is ✆64, followed by the appropriate area code minus the initial zero.

Long Distance Calls & Area Codes

NZ uses regional two-digit area codes for long-distance calls, which can be made from any payphone. If you're making a local call (ie to someone else in the same town), you don't need to dial the area code. But if you're dialling within a region (even if it's to a nearby town with the same area code), you do have to dial the area code.

Information & Toll-Free Calls

Numbers starting with ✆0900 are usually recorded information services, charging upwards of $1 per minute (more from mobiles); these numbers cannot be dialled from payphones.

Toll-free numbers in NZ have the prefix ✆0800 or ✆0508 and can be called free of charge from anywhere in the country, though they may not be accessible from certain areas or from mobile phones. Telephone numbers beginning with ✆0508, ✆0800 or ✆0900 cannot be dialled from outside NZ.

Phonecards

NZ has a wide range of phonecards available, which can be bought at hostels, newsagencies and post offices for a fixed-dollar value (usually $5, $10, $20 and $50). These can be used with any public or private phone by dialling a toll-free access number and then the PIN number on the card. Shop around – rates vary from company to company.

Time

NZ is 12 hours ahead of GMT/UTC and two hours ahead of Australian Eastern Standard Time. The Chathams are 45 minutes ahead of NZ's main islands.

In summer, NZ observes daylight-saving time, where clocks are wound forward by one hour on the last Sunday in September; clocks are wound back on the first Sunday of the following April.

Toilets

Toilets in NZ are sit-down Western style. Public toilets are plentiful, and (to make a sweeping generalisation) are usually reasonably clean with working locks and toilet paper.

See www.toiletmap.co.nz for public toilet locations around the country.

Tourist Information

Tourism New Zealand

The website for the official national tourism body, **Tourism New Zealand** (www.newzealand.com), is the best place for pre-trip research. Emblazoned with the hugely successful 100% Pure New Zealand branding, the site has information in several languages, including German and Japanese, and also lists Tourism New Zealand contact offices overseas (Australia, UK, USA etc).

Local Tourist Offices

➡ Almost every North Island city or town seems to have a visitor information centre. The bigger centres stand united within the outstanding **i-SITE** (www.newzealand.com/travel/i-sites) network – around 80 info centres affiliated with Tourism New Zealand. i-SITEs have trained staff, information on local activities and attractions, and free brochures and maps. Staff can also book activities, transport and accommodation.

➡ Bear in mind that some information centres only promote accommodation and tour operators who are paying members of the local tourist association, and that sometimes staff aren't supposed to recommend one activity or accommodation provider over another.

➡ There's also a network of **Department of Conservation** (Department of Conservation; www.doc.govt.nz) visitor centres to help you plan activities and make bookings. DOC visitor centres – in national parks, regional centres and major cities – usually also have displays on local lore, flora, fauna and biodiversity.

Travellers with Disabilities

Kiwi accommodation generally caters fairly well for travellers with disabilities, with a significant number of hostels, hotels, motels and B&Bs equipped with wheelchair-accessible rooms. Many tourist attractions similarly provide wheelchair access, with wheelchairs often available.

Tour operators with accessible vehicles operate from most major centres. Key cities are also serviced by 'kneeling' buses (buses that hydraulically stoop down to kerb level to allow easy access), and taxi companies offer wheelchair-accessible vans. Large car-hire firms (Avis, Hertz etc) provide cars with hand controls at no extra charge (advance notice required).

Activities

➡ Want to tackle a wilderness pathway? Pick up a copy of *Accessible Walks* by Anna and Andrew Jameson ($30 including postage), with first-hand descriptions of 100-plus South Island walks. It's available online at www.accessiblewalks.co.nz.

➡ If cold-weather activity is more your thing, see the **Disabled Snowsports NZ** (www.disabledsnowsports.org.nz) website.

Resources

Weka (www.weka.net.nz) Good general information, with categories including Transport and Travel.

Royal New Zealand Foundation of the Blind (www.rnzfb.org.nz)

National Foundation for the Deaf (www.nfd.org.nz)

Mobility Parking (www.mobilityparking.org.nz) Info on mobility parking permits and online applications.

Visas

Visa application forms are available from NZ diplomatic missions overseas, travel agents and **Immigration New Zealand** (☑09-914 4100, 0508 558 855; www.immigration.govt.nz). Immigration New Zealand has over a dozen offices overseas; consult the website.

Visitor Visa

➡ Citizens of Australia don't need a visa to visit NZ and can stay indefinitely (provided they have no criminal convictions). UK citizens don't need a visa either and can stay in the country for up to six months.

➡ Citizens of another 56 countries that have visa-waiver agreements with NZ don't need a visa for stays of up to three months, provided they have an onward ticket and sufficient funds to support their stay: see the Immigration New Zealand website for details. Nations in this group include Canada, France, Germany, Ireland, Japan, the Netherlands, South Africa and the USA.

➡ Citizens of other countries must obtain a visa before entering NZ. Visas come with three months' standard validity and cost NZ$130 if processed in Australia or certain South Pacific countries (including Samoa and Fiji), or around NZ$165 if processed elsewhere in the world.

➡ A visitor's visa can be extended for stays of up to nine months within one 18-month period, or to a maximum of 12 months in the country. Applications are assessed on a case-by-case basis; you may need to provide proof of adequate finds to sustain you during your visit (NZ$1000 per month) plus an onward ticket establishing your intent to leave. Apply for extensions at any Immigration New Zealand office – see the website for locations.

Work Visa & Working Holiday Scheme
WORK VISA

It's illegal for foreign nationals to work in NZ on a visitor's visa, except for Australians who can legally gain work without a visa or permit. If you're visiting NZ to find work, or you already have an employment offer, you'll need to apply for a work visa, which translates into a work permit once you arrive and is valid for up to three years. You can apply for a work permit after you're in NZ, but its validity will be backdated to when you entered the country. The fee for a work visa fluctuates between NZ$230 and $360, depending on where and how it's processed (paper or online) and the type of application.

WORKING HOLIDAY SCHEME

➡ Eligible travellers who are only interested in short-term employment to supplement their travels can take part in one of NZ's working holiday schemes (WHS). Under these schemes citizens aged 18 to 30 years from 40 countries – including Canada, France, Germany, Ireland, Japan, Malaysia, the Netherlands, Scandinavian countries, the UK and the USA – can apply for a visa. For most nationalities the visa is valid for 12 months. It's only issued to those seeking a genuine working holiday, not permanent work, so you're not supposed to work for one employer for more than three months.

➜ Most WHS-eligible nationals must apply for this visa from within their own country; residents of some countries can apply online. Applicants must have an onward ticket, a passport valid for at least three months from the date they will leave NZ and evidence of at least NZ$4200 in accessible funds. The application fee is NZ$165 regardless of where you apply, and isn't refunded if your application is declined.

➜ The rules vary for different nationalities, so make sure you read up on the specifics of your country's agreement with NZ at www.immigration.govt.nz/migrant/stream/work/workingholiday.

Volunteering

NZ presents a swathe of active, outdoorsy volunteer opportunities for travellers to get some dirt under their fingernails and participate in conservation programs. Programs can include anything from tree-planting and weed removal to track construc-tion, habitat conservation and fencing. Ask about local opportunities at any regional i-SITE visitor information centre, or check out www.conservationvolunteers.org.nz and www.doc.govt.nz/getting-involved, both of which allow you to browse for opportunities by region. Another resource is www.helpx.net, which lists volunteering opportunities on farms where you can work in exchange for accommodation.

Women Travellers

NZ is generally a very safe place for women travellers, although the usual sensible precautions apply: avoid walking alone late at night and never hitchhike alone. If you're out on the town, always keep enough money aside for a taxi back to your accommodation. Lone women should also be wary of staying in basic pub accommodation unless it looks safe and well managed. Sexual harassment is not a widely reported problem in NZ.

See www.womentravel.co.nz for more information.

WWOOFING

If you don't mind getting your hands dirty, an economical way of travelling around NZ involves doing some voluntary work as a member of the international **Willing Workers on Organic Farms** (WWOOF; ☑03-544 9890; www.wwoof.co.nz) scheme. Down on the farm, in exchange for a hard day's work, owners provide food, accommodation and some hands-on organic farming experience. Contact farm owners a week or two beforehand to arrange your stay, as you would for a hotel or hostel – don't turn up unannounced!

A one-year online membership costs $40; an online membership and a farm-listing book, which is mailed to you, costs an extra $10 plus postage. You should have a working holiday visa when you visit NZ, as the immigration department considers WWOOFers to be working.

Work

➜ If you arrive in NZ on a visitor visa, you're not allowed to work for pay. If you're caught breaching this (or any other) visa condition, you could be booted back to where you came from.

➜ If you have been approved for a WHS visa, look into the possibilities for temporary employment. There's plenty of casual work around, mainly in agriculture (fruit picking, farming, wineries), hospitality (bar work, waiting tables) or at ski resorts. Office-based work can be found in IT, banking, finance and telemarketing. Register with a local office-work agency to get started.

➜ Seasonal fruit picking, pruning and harvesting is prime short-term work for visitors. More than 30,000 hectares of apples, kiwifruit and other fruit and veg are harvested from December to May. Rates are around $12 to $17 an hour (not much) for physically taxing toil, working in the dirt under the hot sun – turnover of workers is high. You're usually paid by how much you pick (per bin, bucket or kilogram): if you stick with it for a while, you'll get faster and fitter and can actually make some reasonable cash. Prime North Island picking locations include the Bay of Islands (Kerikeri and Paihia), rural Auckland, Tauranga and the Bay of Plenty, Gisborne and Hawke's Bay (Napier and Hastings).

➜ Winter work at ski resorts and their service towns includes bartending, waiting, cleaning, ski-tow operation and, if you're properly qualified, ski or snowboard instructing.

Resources

Backpacker publications, hostel managers and other travellers are the best sources of info on local work possibilities. **Base Backpackers** (www.stayatbase.com/work) runs an employment service via its website, while the Notice Boards page on **Budget Backpacker Hostels** (BBH; www.bbh.co.nz) lists job vacancies in BBH hostels and a few other possibilities.

Kiwi Careers (www.careers.govt.nz) lists professional opportunities in various fields (agriculture, creative, health, teaching, volunteer work and recruitment), while **Seek** (www.seek.co.nz) is one of the biggest NZ job-search networks, with thousands of jobs listed.

Check ski-resort websites for work opportunities in the snow; in the fruit-picking/horticultural realm, try the following websites:

Seasonal Work (www.seasonalwork.co.nz)

Seasonal Jobs in New Zealand (www.seasonal-jobs.co.nz)

Picking Jobs (www.picking-jobs.com)

Income Tax

Death and taxes – no escape! For most travellers, Kiwi dollars earned in NZ will be subject to income tax, deducted from payments by employers – a process called Pay As You Earn (PAYE). Standard NZ income tax rates are 12.2% for annual salaries up to $14,000, then 19.2% up to $48,000, 31.7% up to $70,000, then 34.7% for higher incomes. A NZ Accident Compensation Corporation (ACC) scheme levy (around 2%) will also be deducted from your pay packet. Note that these rates tend to change slightly year-to-year.

If you visit NZ and work for a short time (eg on a working-holiday scheme), you may qualify for a tax refund when you leave. Complete a *Refund Application – People Leaving New Zealand IR50* form and submit it with your tax return, along with proof of departure (eg air-ticket copies) to the **Inland Revenue Department** (www.ird.govt.nz). For more info, see the IRD website, or contact the **Inland Revenue Non-Resident Centre** (☑03-951 2020; nonres@ird.govt.nz; Private Bag 1932, Dunedin 9054).

IRD Number

Travellers undertaking paid work in NZ must obtain an IRD (Inland Revenue Department) number. Download the *IRD Number Application – Individual IR595* form from the **Inland Revenue Department** website. IRD numbers normally take eight to 10 working days to be issued.

Transport

GETTING THERE & AWAY

New Zealand is a long way from almost everywhere – most travellers jet in from afar. Flights, tours and rail tickets can be booked online at lonelyplanet.com/bookings.

Entering the Country

Disembarkation in New Zealand is generally a straightforward affair, with only the usual customs declarations and the luggage-carousel scramble to endure. Under the the Orwellian title of 'Advance Passenger Screening', documents that used to be checked after you touched down in NZ (passport, visa etc) are now checked before you board your flight – make sure all your documentation is in order so that your check-in is stress-free.

Passport

There are no restrictions when it comes to foreign citizens entering NZ. If you have a current passport and visa (or don't require one), you should be fine.

Air

There are a number of competing airlines that service NZ if you're flying in from Asia, Europe or North America, though ultimately you'll still pay a lot for a flight unless you jet in from Australia. NZ's abundance of year-round activities means that airports are busy most of the time: if you want to fly at a particularly popular time of year (eg over the Christmas period), book well in advance.

The high season for flights into NZ is during summer (December to February), with slightly less of a premium on fares over the shoulder months (October to November and March to April). The low season generally tallies with the winter months (June to August), though this is still a busy time for airlines ferrying ski bunnies and powder hounds.

International Airports

A number of North Island airports handle international flights, with Auckland receiving most traffic:

Auckland International Airport (AKL; ☎09-275 0789; www.aucklandairport.co.nz; Ray Emery Dr, Mangere)

Hamilton International Airport (HIA; ☎07-848 9027; www.hamiltonairport.co.nz; Airport Rd)

Rotorua International Airport (ROT; ☎07-345 8800; www.rotorua-airport.co.nz; SH30)

Wellington Airport (WLG; ☎04-385 5100; www.wellingtonairport.co.nz; Stewart Duff Dr, Rongotai)

CLIMATE CHANGE & TRAVEL

Every form of transport that relies on carbon-based fuel generates CO_2, the main cause of human-induced climate change. Modern travel is dependent on aeroplanes, which might use less fuel per kilometre per person than most cars but travel much greater distances. The altitude at which aircraft emit gases (including CO_2) and particles also contributes to their climate change impact. Many websites offer 'carbon calculators' that allow people to estimate the carbon emissions generated by their journey and, for those who wish to do so, to offset the impact of the greenhouse gases emitted with contributions to portfolios of climate-friendly initiatives throughout the world. Lonely Planet offsets the carbon footprint of all staff and author travel.

DEPARTURE TAX

An international departure tax of NZ$25 applies when leaving three of NZ's smaller international airports: Hamilton, Rotorua and the sporadically international Palmerston North. At all other airports the tax has been replaced with a NZ$12.50 Passenger Service Charge (PSC), which is included in your ticket price. At Hamilton, Rotorua and Palmerston North, departure tax must be paid separately at the airport before you board your flight (via credit card or cash). For kids under 12 it's NZ$10, and free for kids under two.

International Airlines

New Zealand's own international carrier is **Air New Zealand** (www.airnewzealand.co.nz), which flies to runways across Europe, North America, eastern Asia and the Pacific, and has an extensive network across NZ.

Winging-in from Australia, **Virgin Australia** (www.virginaustralia.com), **Qantas** (www.qantas.com.au), **Jetstar** (☑0800 800 995; www.jetstar.com) and Air New Zealand are the key players. Air New Zealand also flies in from North America, but you can head south with **Air Canada** (www.aircanada.com) and **American Airlines** (www.aa.com), too.

From Europe, the options are a little broader, with **British Airways** (www.britishairways.com), **Lufthansa** (www.lufthansa.com) and **Virgin Atlantic** (www.virginatlantic.com) entering the fray, and plenty of others stopping in NZ on broader round-the-world routes.

From Asia and the Pacific there are myriad options, with direct flights from China, Japan, Singapore, Malaysia, Thailand and many Pacific Island nations.

Sea

It's possible (though by no means easy or safe) to make your way between NZ and Australia, and some smaller Pacific islands, by hitching rides or crewing on yachts. Try asking around at harbours, marinas, and yacht and sailing clubs. Popular yachting harbours in NZ include the Bay of Islands and Whangarei (both in Northland), Auckland and Wellington. March and April are the best months to look for boats heading to Australia. From Fiji, October to November is a peak departure season to beat the cyclones that soon follow in that neck of the woods.

If you're looking for something with a slower pace, plenty of passenger cruise liners stop in NZ on the South Pacific legs of their respective schedules: try **P&O Cruises** (www.pocruises.com.au) for starters.

Alternatively, a berth on a cargo ship or freighter to/from New Zealand is a quirky way to go: check out websites such as www.freightercruises.com and www.freighterexpeditions.com.au for more info.

GETTING AROUND

Air

Those who have limited time to get between NZ's attractions can make the most of a widespread (and very reliable and safe) network of intra- and inter-island flights.

Domestic Airlines

The country's major domestic carrier, Air New Zealand, has an aerial network covering most of the country, often operating under the Air New Zealand Link moniker on less popular routes. Australia-based Jetstar also flies between main urban areas. Between them, these two airlines carry the vast majority of domestic passengers in NZ. Beyond this, several small-scale regional operators provide essential transport services to outlying islands such as Great Barrier Island in the Hauraki Gulf. Operators include the following:

Air Chathams (www.airchathams.co.nz) Services to the remote Chatham Islands from Wellington, Christchurch and Auckland.

Air New Zealand (www.airnewzealand.co.nz) Offers flights between 30-plus domestic destinations, plus myriad overseas destinations.

Air2there.com (www.air2there.com) Connects destinations across Cook Strait, including Paraparaumu, Wellington, Nelson and Blenheim.

FlyMySky (www.flymysky.co.nz) At least three flights daily from Auckland to Great Barrier Island.

Great Barrier Airlines (www.greatbarrierairlines.co.nz) Plies the skies over Great Barrier Island, Auckland, Tauranga and Whangarei.

Jetstar (www.jetstar.com) Joins the dots between key tourism centres: Auckland, Wellington, Christchurch, Dunedin and Queenstown (and flies Queenstown to Melbourne and Sydney; Christchurch to Melbourne, Sydney and the Gold Coast; and Auckland to Melbourne, Adelaide, the Gold Coast and Cairns).

Salt Air (www.saltair.co.nz) Charter flights from Auckland to the Bay of Islands.

Soundsair (www.soundsair.co.nz) Numerous flights each day between Picton and

Wellington, plus flights from Wellington to Blenheim, Nelson and Wanganui.

Sunair (www.sunair.co.nz) Flies to Whitianga from Auckland, Great Barrier Island and Tauranga, plus numerous other North Island connections between Hamilton, Napier, Rotorua and Gisborne and New Plymouth.

Air Passes

With discounting being the norm these days, and a number of budget airlines now serving the trans-Tasman route as well as the Pacific islands, the value of air passes isn't as red-hot as in the past.

Available exclusively to travellers from the USA or Canada who have bought an Air New Zealand fare to NZ from the USA or Canada, Australia or the Pacific islands, Air New Zealand offers the good-value **New Zealand Explorer Pass**. The pass lets you fly between up to 27 destinations in New Zealand, Australia and the South Pacific islands (including Norfolk Island, Tonga, Vanuatu, Tahiti, Fiji, Niue and the Cook Islands). Fares are broken down into four discounted, distance-based zones: zone one flights start at US$79 (eg Auckland to Christchurch); zone two from US$109 (eg Auckland to Queenstown); zone three from US$214 (eg Wellington to Sydney); and zone four from US$295 (eg Tahiti to Auckland). You can buy the pass before you travel, or after you arrive in NZ.

Star Alliance (www.staralliance.com) offers the sector-based **South Pacific Airpass**, valid for selected journeys within NZ, and between NZ, Australia and several Pacific islands, including Fiji, New Caledonia, Tonga, the Cook Islands and Samoa. Passes are available to nonresidents of these countries, must be issued outside NZ in conjunction with Star Alliance international tickets, and are valid for three months. A typical Sydney–Christchurch–Wellington–Auckland–Nadi pass cost NZ$1050 at the time of research.

Bicycle

Touring cyclists proliferate in NZ, particularly over summer. The country is clean, green and relatively uncrowded, and has lots of cheap accommodation (including camping) and abundant fresh water. The roads are generally in good nick, and the climate is usually not too hot or cold. Road traffic is the biggest danger: trucks overtaking too close to cyclists are a particular threat. Bikes and cycling gear are readily available to rent or buy in the main centres, as are bicycle repair shops.

By law all cyclists must wear an approved safety helmet (or risk a fine); it's also vital to have good reflective safety clothing. Cyclists who use public transport will find that major bus lines and trains only take bicycles on a 'space available' basis and charge up to $10. Some of the smaller shuttle bus companies, on the other hand, make sure they have storage space for bikes, which they carry for a surcharge.

If importing your own bike or transporting it by plane within NZ, check with the relevant airline for costs and the degree of dismantling and packing required.

See www.nzta.govt.nz/traffic/ways/bike for more bike safety and legal tips, and www.nzcycletrail.com/ for info on Nga Haerenga, New Zealand Cycle Trail – a network of 22 'Great Rides' across NZ.

Hire

Rates offered by most outfits for renting road or mountain bikes range from $10 to $20 per hour and $30 to $50 per day. Longer-term rentals may be available by negotiation. You can often hire bikes from your accommodation (hostels, campgrounds, etc), or rent more reputable machines from bike shops in the larger towns.

Buying a Bike

Bicycles can be readily bought in NZ's larger cities, but prices for newer models are high. For a decent hybrid bike or rigid mountain bike you'll pay anywhere from $800 to $1800, though you can get a cheap one for around $500 (but you still then need to buy panniers, helmet, lock etc, and the cost quickly climbs). Other options include the post-Christmas sales and midyear stocktakes, when newish cycles can be heavily discounted.

Boat

NZ may be an island nation but there's virtually no long-distance water transport around the country. Obvious exceptions include the boat services between Auckland and various islands in the Hauraki Gulf and the inter-island ferries that chug across Cook Strait between Wellington and Picton.

If you're cashed-up, consider the cruise liners that chug around the NZ coastline as part of broader South Pacific itineraries: **P&O Cruises** (www.pocruises.com.au) is a major player.

Bus

Bus travel in NZ is relatively easy and well organised, with services transporting you to the far reaches of both islands (including the start/end of various walking tracks), but it can be expensive, tedious and time-consuming.

NZ's dominant bus company is **InterCity** (www.intercity.co.nz), which can drive you to just about anywhere on the North Island. **Naked Bus** (www.nakedbus.com) has similar routes and remains the main competition. Both bus lines offer fares as low as $1.

Seat Classes & Smoking

There are no allocated economy or luxury classes on NZ buses (very democratic), and smoking on the bus is a definite no-no.

Reservations

Over summer, school holidays and public holidays, book well in advance on popular routes (a week or two if possible). At other times a day or two ahead is usually fine. The best prices are generally available online, booked a few weeks in advance.

Bus Passes

If you're covering a lot of ground, both **InterCity** (www. intercity.co.nz) and **Naked Bus** (www.nakedbus.com) offer bus passes that can be cheaper than paying as you go, but they do of course lock you into using their respective networks. InterCity also offers a 10% discount for YHA, ISIC, Nomads, BBH or VIP card holders, and passes are generally valid for 12 months.

NATIONWIDE PASSES

➡ **Flexipass** A hop-on/hop-off InterCity pass, allowing travel to pretty much anywhere in NZ, in any direction, including the Interislander ferry across Cook Strait. The pass is purchased in blocks of travel time: minimum 15 hours ($119), maximum 60 hours ($449). The average cost of each block becomes cheaper the more hours you buy. You can top up the pass if you need more time.

➡ **Flexitrips** (5/15/30 trips including the ferry cost $210/383/550, $54 less if you don't need the ferry) An InterCity bus-pass system whereby you purchase a specific number of bus trips

(eg Auckland to Tauranga would count as one trip) in blocks of five, with or without the Cook Strait ferry trip included.

➡ **Aotearoa Adventurer**, **Kiwi Explorer**, **Kia Ora New Zealand** and **Tiki Tour New Zealand** Hop-on/hop-off, fixed-itinerary nationwide passes offered by InterCity. These passes link up tourist hot spots and range in price from $645 to $1219. See www.travelpass.co.nz for details.

➡ **Naked Passport** (www. nakedpassport.com; 5/15/30 trips cost $151/318/491.) A Naked Bus pass that allows you to buy trips in blocks of five, which you can add to at any time and book each trip as needed. An unlimited pass costs $597 – great value if you're travelling NZ for many moons.

NORTH ISLAND PASSES

➡ InterCity also offers 13 hop-on/hop-off, fixed-itinerary North Island bus passes, ranging from short $43 runs between Rotorua and Taupo, to $249 trips from Auckland to Wellington via the big sights in between. See www.travelpass.co.nz for details.

Shuttle Buses

As well as InterCity and Naked Bus, regional shuttle buses fill in the gaps between the smaller towns. North Island operators include the following:

Alpine Scenic Tours (www. alpinescenictours.co.nz) Runs tours around Taupo and into Tongariro National Park, plus the ski fields around Mt Ruapehu and Mt Tongariro.

Go Kiwi Shuttles (www.go-kiwi.co.nz) Links Auckland with Whitianga on the Coromandel Peninsula daily, with extensions to Rotorua in summer.

Waitomo Wanderer (www. travelheadfirst.com) Does a loop from Rotorua or Taupo to Waitomo.

Backpacker Buses

If you feel like clocking up some kilometres with like-minded fellow travellers, the following operators run fixed-itinerary bus tours, nationwide or on the North or South Island. Accommodation and hop-on/hop-off flexibility are often included.

Adventure Tours New Zealand (www.adventure-tours.com.au)

Flying Kiwi (www.flyingkiwi. com)

Kiwi Experience (www. kiwiexperience.com)

Haka Tours (www.hakatours. com)

Stray Travel (www. straytravel.com)

Car & Motorcycle

The best way to explore NZ in depth is to have your own wheels. It's easy to hire cars and campervans at good rates. Alternatively, if you're in NZ for a few months, you might consider buying your own vehicle.

Automobile Association (AA)

NZ's **Automobile Association** (AA; ☎0800 500 444; www.aa.co.nz/travel) provides emergency breakdown services, maps and accommodation guides (from holiday parks to motels and B&Bs).

Members of overseas automobile associations should bring their membership cards – many of these bodies have reciprocal agreements with the AA.

Drivers Licences

International visitors to NZ can use their home country drivers licence – if your licence isn't in English, it's a good idea to carry a certified translation with you. Alternatively, use an International Driving Permit (IDP), which will usually be issued on the spot (valid for 12 months) by your home country's automobile association.

ROAD DISTANCES (KM)

	Auckland	Cape Reinga	Dargaville	Gisborne	Hamilton	Hicks Bay	Kaitaia	Napier	New Plymouth	Paihia	Palmerston North	Rotorua	Taupo	Tauranga	Thames	Waitomo Caves	Whanganui	Wellington	Whakatane
Cape Reinga	430																		
Dargaville	175	280																	
Gisborne	490	920	675																
Hamilton	125	555	300	390															
Hicks Bay	510	945	690	180	400														
Kaitaia	325	115	170	820	440	800													
Napier	420	860	590	215	300	395	735												
New Plymouth	360	790	530	570	240	580	680	410											
Paihia	225	220	130	720	340	720	120	645	590										
Palmerston North	520	950	690	395	400	570	840	180	230	750									
Rotorua	235	670	405	295	110	285	550	220	300	460	325								
Taupo	280	720	450	330	155	365	600	140	300	505	250	80							
Tauranga	210	635	385	290	110	290	525	300	330	435	400	85	155						
Thames	115	540	280	410	110	400	430	360	340	345	470	170	210	115					
Waitomo Caves	200	620	360	440	75	440	515	300	180	420	340	165	170	150	175				
Whanganui	455	880	615	465	330	645	770	250	160	670	75	310	225	375	430	270			
Wellington	640	1080	805	530	520	730	960	320	350	860	140	450	375	530	590	460	190		
Whakatane	300	740	470	200	190	204	620	300	380	525	410	85	160	95	210	240	380	540	
Whangarei	160	280	55	640	280	650	165	580	515	70	680	390	430	350	265	345	600	790	450

Fuel

Fuel (petrol, aka gasoline) is available from service stations across NZ: unless you're cruising around in something from the '70s, you'll be filling up with 'unleaded' or LPG (gas). LPG is not always stocked by rural suppliers; if you're on gas, it's safer to have dual-fuel capability. Aside from remote locations, petrol prices don't vary much from place to place: per-litre costs at the time of research were around $2.40.

Campervan Hire

Check your rear-view mirror on any far-flung NZ road and you'll probably see a shiny white campervan (aka mobile home, motor home, RV) packed with liberated travellers, mountain bikes and portable barbecues cruising along behind you.

Most towns of any size have a campground or holiday park with powered sites (where you can plug your vehicle in) for around $35 per night. There are also 250-plus vehicle-accessible **Department of Conservation** (DoC; www.doc.govt.nz) campsites around NZ, ranging in price from free to $15 per adult: check the website for info.

You can hire campervans from dozens of companies. Prices vary with season, vehicle size and length of rental.

A small van for two people typically has a minikitchen and foldout dining table, the latter transforming into a double bed when dinner is done and dusted. Larger 'superior' two-berth vans include shower and toilet. Four- to six-berth campervans are the size of trucks (and similarly sluggish) and, besides the extra space, usually contain a toilet and shower.

Over summer, rates offered by the main rental firms for two-/four-/six-berth vans start at around $160/200/290 per day for a month-long rental, dropping to as low as $45/60/90 per day during winter.

Major operators include the following:

Apollo (✆0800 113 131, 09-889 2976; www.apollocamper.co.nz)

Britz (✆0800 831 900, 09-255 3910; www.britz.co.nz)

Also does 'Britz Bikes' (add a mountain or city bike from $13 per day).

Kea (☎0800 520 052, 09-448 8800)

Maui (☎0800 651 080, 09-255 3910; www.maui.co.nz)

United Campervans (☎0800 759 919, 09-275 9919; www.unitedcampervans.co.nz)

Wilderness Motorhomes (☎09-255 5300; www.wilderness.co.nz)

BACKPACKER VAN RENTALS

Budget players in the campervan industry offer slick deals and funky (often gregariously spray-painted with Jimi Hendrix, *Where The Wild Things Are*, Sly Stone etc), well-kitted-out vehicles for backpackers. Rates are competitive (from $35/50 per day for a two-/four-berth van May to September; from $100/150 per day December to February). Operators include the following:

Backpacker Sleeper Vans (☎0800 321 939, 03-359 4731; www.sleepervans.co.nz)

Escape Campervans (☎0800 216 171; www.escape-rentals.co.nz)

Hippie Camper (☎0800 113 131; www.hippiecamper.co.nz)

Jucy (☎0800 399 736, 09-374 4360; www.jucy.co.nz)

Mighty Cars & Campers (☎0800 422 267; www.mightycampers.co.nz)

Spaceships (☎0800 772 237, 09-526 2130; www.spaceshipsrentals.co.nz)

Wicked Campers (☎0800 246 870, 09-634 2994; www.wickedcampers.co.nz)

Car Hire

Competition between car-rental companies in NZ is torrid, particularly in the big cities. Remember that if you want to travel far, you need unlimited kilometres. Some (but not all) companies require drivers to be at least 21 years old – ask around.

Most car-hire firms suggest (or insist) that you don't take their vehicles between islands on the Cook Strait ferries. Instead, you leave your car at either Wellington or Picton terminal and pick up another car once you've crossed the strait. This saves you paying to transport a vehicle on the ferries, and is a pain-free exercise.

INTERNATIONAL RENTAL COMPANIES

The big multinational companies have offices in most major cities, towns and airports. Firms sometimes offer one-way rentals (eg collect a car in Auckland, leave it in Wellington), but there are often restrictions and fees. On the other hand, an operator in Christchurch may need to get a vehicle back to Auckland and will offer an amazing one-way car relocation deal (sometimes free!).

The major companies offer a choice of either unlimited kilometres, or 100km (or so) per day free, plus so many cents per subsequent kilometre. Daily rates in main cities typically start at around $40 per day for a compact, late-model, Japanese car, and around $75 for medium-sized cars (including GST, unlimited kilometres and insurance).

Avis (☎0800 655 111, 09-526 2847; www.avis.co.nz)

Budget (☎0800 283 438, 09-529 7784; www.budget.co.nz)

Europcar (☎0800 800 115; www.europcar.co.nz)

Hertz (☎0800 654 321, 03-358 6789; www.hertz.co.nz)

Thrifty (☎0800 737 070, 03-359 2721; www.thrifty.co.nz)

LOCAL RENTAL COMPANIES

Local rental firms dapple the *Yellow Pages*. These are almost always cheaper than the big boys – sometimes half the price – but the cheap rates may come with serious restrictions: vehicles are

often older, and with less formality sometimes comes a less protective legal structure for renters.

Rentals from local firms start at around $30 per day for the smallest option. It's obviously cheaper if you rent for a week or more, and there are often low-season and weekend discounts.

Affordable, independent operators with national networks include the following:

a2b Car Rentals (☎0800 545 000; www.a2b-carrentals.co.nz)

Ace Rental Cars (☎0800 502 277, 09-303 3112; www.acerentalcars.co.nz)

Apex Rentals (☎0800 939 597, 03-379 6897; www.apex-rentals.co.nz)

Go Rentals (☎0800 467 368, 09-525 7321; www.go-rentals.co.nz)

Omega Rental Cars (☎0800 525 210, 09-377 5573; www.omegarentalcars.com)

Pegasus Rental Cars (☎0800 803 580, 03-548 2852; www.rentalcars.co.nz)

Transfercar (☎09-630 7533; www.transfercar.co.nz) One-way relocation specialists.

Motorcycle Hire

Born to be wild? NZ has great terrain for motorcycle touring, despite the fickle weather in some regions. Most of the North Island's motorcycle-hire shops are in Auckland, where you can hire anything from a little 50cc moped (aka nifty-fifty) to a throbbing 750cc touring motorcycle and beyond. Recommended operators (who also run guided tours) with rates from $80 to $345 per day include:

New Zealand Motorcycle Rentals & Tours (☎09-486 2472; www.nzbike.com)

Te Waipounamu Motorcycle Tours (☎03-377 3211; www.motorcycle-hire.co.nz)

Insurance

Rather than risk paying out wads of cash if you have an

accident, you can take out your own comprehensive insurance policy, or (the usual option) pay an additional fee per day to the rental company to reduce your excess. This brings the amount you must pay in the event of an accident down from around $1500 or $2000 to around $200 or $300. Smaller operators offering cheap rates often have a compulsory insurance excess, taken as a credit-card bond, of around $900.

Most insurance agreements won't cover the cost of damage to glass (including the windscreen) or tyres, and insurance coverage is often invalidated on beaches and certain rough (4WD) unsealed roads – read the fine print.

See p 407 for info on NZ's **Accident Compensation Corporation** (ACC; www. acc.co.nz) insurance scheme (fault-free personal injury insurance).

Purchase

Buying a car then selling it at the end of your travels can be one of the cheapest and best ways to see NZ. Auckland is the easiest place to buy a car. **Turners Auctions** (www. turners.co.nz) is NZ's biggest car-auction operator, with 11 locations.

LEGALITIES

Make sure your prospective vehicle has a Warrant of Fitness (WoF) and registration valid for a reasonable period: see the **Land Transport New Zealand** (www. landtransport.govt.nz) website for details.

Buyers should also take out third-party insurance, covering the cost of repairs to another vehicle in an accident that is your fault: try the **Automobile Association** (AA; ✆0800 500 444; www. aa.co.nz/travel). NZ's no-fault Accident Compensation Corporation scheme covers personal injury, but make sure you have travel insurance, too.

If you're considering buying a car and want someone to check it out for you, various car-inspection companies inspect cars for around $150; find them at car auctions, or they will come to you. Try **Vehicle Inspection New Zealand** (VINZ; ✆0800 468 469, 09-573 3230; www. vinz.co.nz) or the AA.

Before you buy it's wise to confirm ownership of the vehicle, and find out if there's anything dodgy about the car (eg stolen, or outstanding debts). The AA's **Lemon-Check** (✆0800 536 662, 09-420 3090; www.lemoncheck. co.nz) offers this service ('Pry before you buy'...).

BUY-BACK DEALS

You can avoid the hassle of buying/selling a vehicle privately by entering into a buy-back arrangement with a dealer. Predictably, dealers often find sneaky ways of knocking down the return-sale price, which may be 50% less than what you paid, so hiring or buying and selling a vehicle yourself (if you have the time) is usually a better bet.

Road Hazards

Kiwi traffic is usually pretty light, but it's easy to get stuck behind a slow-moving truck or campervan – pack plenty of patience. There are also lots of slow wiggly roads, one-way bridges and plenty of gravel roads, all of which require a more cautious driving approach. And watch out for sheep!

To check road conditions call ✆0800 444 449 or see www.nzta.govt.nz/traffic/ current-conditions.

Road Rules

➡ Kiwis drive on the left-hand side of the road; cars are right-hand drive. Give way to the right at intersections.

➡ At single-lane bridges (of which there are a surprisingly large number), a smaller red arrow pointing in your direction of travel means that *you* give way.

➡ Speed limits on the open road are generally 100km/h; in built-up areas the limit is usually 50km/h. Speed cameras and radars are used extensively.

➡ All vehicle occupants must wear a seatbelt or risk a fine. Small children must be belted into approved safety seats.

➡ Always carry your licence when driving. Drink-driving is a serious offence and remains a significant problem in NZ, despite widespread campaigns and severe penalties. The legal blood alcohol limit is 0.08% for drivers over 20, and 0% (zero!) for those under 20.

Hitching & Ride-Sharing

NZ is no longer immune from the perils of solo hitching. Those who decide to hitch are taking a small but potentially serious risk. That said, it's not unusual to see hitchhikers along country roads.

Alternatively, check hostel noticeboards for ride-share opportunities, or have a look online at www.carpoolnz.org or www.nationalcarshare. co.nz.

Local Transport
Bus, Train & Tram

The North Island's larger cities have extensive bus services but, with a few honourable exceptions, they are mainly daytime, weekday operations; weekend services can be infrequent or nonexistent. Negotiating inner-city Auckland is made easier by the Link and free City Circuit buses, and Hamilton also has a free city-centre loop bus. Most smaller North Island cities have late-night buses for boozy Friday and Saturday nights.

The only cities with decent train services are Auckland and Wellington, with four and five suburban routes respectively.

Taxi

The main cities have plenty of taxis and even small towns may have a local service.

Train

NZ train travel is about the journey, not about getting anywhere in a hurry. **KiwiRail Scenic Journeys** (☎0800 872 467, 04-495 0775; www.tranzscenic.co.nz) operates two North Island

routes, listed below; reservations can be made through KiwiRail Scenic Journeys directly, or at most train stations (notably not at Palmerston North or Hamilton), travel agents and visitor information centres:

➡ **Capital Connection**
Weekday commuter service between Palmerston North and Wellington.

➡ **Northern Explorer**
Between Auckland and Wellington.

Train Passes

A KiwiRail Scenic Journeys **Scenic Journey Rail Pass** (www.kiwirailscenic.co.nz/

scenic-rail-pass) allows unlimited travel on all of its rail services, including passage on the Wellington–Picton Interislander ferry. There are two types of pass, both requiring you to book your seats a minimum of 24 hours before you want to travel:

➡ **Fixed Pass** (1/2/3 weeks, per adult $599/699/799) Limited duration fares. It's a little bit less for kids.

➡ **Freedom Pass** (3/7/9-day pass $417/903/1161) Affords you travel on a certain number of days over a 12-month period.

Language

New Zealand has three official languages: English, Maori and NZ sign language. Although English is what you'll usually hear, Maori has been making a comeback. You can use English to speak to anyone in New Zealand, but there are some occasions when knowing a small amount of Maori is useful, such as when visiting a *marae*, where often only Maori is spoken. Some knowledge of Maori will also help you interpret the many Maori place names you'll come across.

KIWI ENGLISH

Like the people of other English-speaking countries in the world, New Zealanders have their own, unique way of speaking the language. The flattening of vowels is the most distinctive feature of Kiwi pronunciation. For example, in Kiwi English, 'fish and chips' sounds more like 'fush and chups'. On the North Island sentences often have 'eh!' attached to the end. In the far south a rolled 'r' is common, which is a holdover from that region's Scottish heritage – it's especially noticeable in Southland.

MAORI

The Maori have a vividly chronicled history, recorded in songs and chants that dramatically recall the migration to New Zealand from Polynesia as well as other important events. Early missionaries were the first to record the

language in a written form using only 15 letters of the English alphabet.

Maori is closely related to other Polynesian languages such as Hawaiian, Tahitian and Cook Islands Maori. In fact, New Zealand Maori and Hawaiian are quite similar, even though more than 7000km separates Honolulu and Auckland.

The Maori language was never dead – it was always used in Maori ceremonies – but over time familiarity with it was definitely on the decline. Fortunately, recent years have seen a revival of interest in it, and this forms an integral part of the renaissance of *Maoritanga* (Maori culture). Many Maori people who had heard the language spoken on the *marae* for years but had not used it in their day-to-day lives, are now studying it and speaking it fluently. Maori is taught in schools throughout New Zealand, some TV programs and news reports are broadcast in it, and many English place names are being renamed in Maori. Even government departments have been given Maori names: for example, the Inland Revenue Department is also known as Te Tari Taake (the last word is actually *take*, which means 'levy', but the department has chosen to stress the long 'a' by spelling it 'aa').

In many places, Maori have come together to provide instruction in their language and culture to young children; the idea is for them to grow up speaking both Maori and English, and to develop a familiarity with Maori tradition. It's a matter of some pride to have fluency in the language. On some *marae* only Maori can be spoken.

WANT MORE?

For in-depth language information and handy phrases, check out Lonely Planet's *South Pacific Phrasebook*. You'll find it at **shop.lonelyplanet.com**, or you can buy Lonely Planet's iPhone phrasebooks at the Apple App Store.

Pronunciation

Maori is a fluid, poetic language and surprisingly easy to pronounce once you remember to split each word (some can be amazingly long) into separate syllables. Each syllable ends in a vowel. There are no 'silent' letters.

Most consonants in Maori – *h, k, m, n, p, t* and *w* – are pronounced much the same as in English. The Maori *r* is a flapped sound (not rolled) with the tongue near the front of the mouth. It's closer to the English 'l' in pronunciation.

The *ng* is pronounced as in the English words 'singing' or 'running', and can be used at the beginning of words as well as at the end. To practise, just say 'ing' over and over, then isolate the 'ng' part of it.

The letters *wh,* when occuring together, are generally pronounced as a soft English 'f'. This pronunciation is used in many place names in New Zealand, such as Whakatane, Whangaroa and Whakapapa (all pronounced as if they begin with a soft 'f'). There is some local variation: in the region around the Whanganui River, for example, *wh* is pronounced as in the English word 'when'.

The correct pronunciation of the vowels is very important. The examples below are a rough guideline – it helps to listen carefully to someone who speaks the language well. Each vowel has both a long and a short sound, with long vowels often denoted by a line over the letter or a double vowel. We have not indicated long and short vowel forms in this book.

Vowels

a	as in 'large', with no 'r' sound
e	as in 'get'
i	as in 'marine'
o	as in 'pork'
u	as the 'oo' in 'moon'

Vowel Combinations

ae, ai	as the 'y' in 'sky'
ao, au	as the 'ow' in 'how'
ea	as in 'bear'
ei	as in 'vein'
eo	as 'eh-oh'
eu	as 'eh-oo'
ia	as in the name 'Ian'
ie	as the 'ye' in 'yet'
io	as the 'ye o' in 'ye old'
iu	as the 'ue' in 'cue'
oa	as in 'roar'
oe	as in 'toe'
oi	as in 'toil'
ou	as the 'ow' in 'how'
ua	as the 'ewe' in 'fewer'

Greetings & Small Talk

Maori greetings are becoming increasingly popular – don't be surprised if you're greeted with *Kia ora*.

Welcome!	*Haere mai!*
Hello./Good luck./ Good health.	*Kia ora.*
Hello. (to one person)	*Tena koe.*
Hello. (to two people)	*Tena korua.*
Hello. (to three or more people)	*Tena koutou.*
Goodbye. (to person staying)	*E noho ra.*
Goodbye. (to person leaving)	*Haere ra.*
How are you? (to one person)	*Kei te pehea koe?*
How are you? (to two people)	*Kei te pehea korua?*
How are you? (to three or more people)	*Kei te pehea koutou?*
Very well, thanks./ That's fine.	*Kei te pai.*

Maori Geographical Terms

The following words form part of many Maori place names in New Zealand, and help you understand the meaning of these place names. For example: Waikaremoana is the Sea *(moana)* of Rippling *(kare)* Waters *(wai)*, and Rotorua means the Second *(rua)* Lake *(roto)*.

a – of
ana – cave
ara – way, path or road
awa – river or valley
heke – descend
hiku – end; tail
hine – girl; daughter
ika – fish
iti – small
kahurangi – treasured possession; special greenstone
kai – food
kainga – village
kaka – parrot
kare – rippling
kati – shut or close
koura – crayfish
makariri – cold
manga – stream or tributary
manu – bird
maunga – mountain
moana – sea or lake
moko – tattoo
motu – island
mutu – finished; ended; over
nga – the (plural)

noa – ordinary; not *tapu*
nui – big or great
nuku – distance
o – of, place of...
one – beach, sand or mud
pa – fortified village
papa – large blue-grey mudstone
pipi – common edible bivalve
pohatu – stone
poto – short
pouri – sad; dark; gloomy
puke – hill
puna – spring; hole; fountain
rangi – sky; heavens
raro – north
rei – cherished possession
roa – long
roto – lake
rua – hole in the ground; two
runga – above
tahuna – beach; sandbank
tane – man
tangata – people
tapu – sacred, forbidden or taboo
tata – close to; dash against; twin islands
tawaha – entrance or opening
tawahi – the other side (of a river or lake)
te – the (singular)
tonga – south
ure – male genitals
uru – west

waha – broken
wahine – woman
wai – water
waingaro – lost; waters that disappear in certain seasons
waka – canoe
wera – burnt or warm; floating
wero – challenge
whaka... – to act as ...
whanau – family
whanga – harbour, bay or inlet
where – house
whenua – land or country
whiti – east

Here are some more place names composed of words in the list:

Aramoana – Sea *(moana)* Path *(ara)*
Awaroa – Long *(roa)* River *(awa)*
Kaitangata – Eat *(kai)* People *(tangata)*
Maunganui – Great *(nui)* Mountain *(maunga)*
Opouri – Place of *(o)* Sadness *(pouri)*
Te Araroa – The *(te)* Long *(roa)* Path *(ara)*
Te Puke – The *(te)* Hill *(puke)*
Urewera – Burnt *(wera)* Penis *(ure)*
Waimakariri – Cold *(makariri)* Water *(wai)*
Wainui – Great *(nui)* Waters *(wai)*
Whakatane – To Act *(whaka)* as a Man *(tane)*
Whangarei – Cherished *(rei)* Harbour *(whanga)*

GLOSSARY

Following is a list of abbreviations, 'Kiwi English', Maori and slang terms used in this book and which you may hear in New Zealand.

All Blacks – NZ's revered national rugby union team
Anzac – Australia and New Zealand Army Corps
Aoraki – Maori name for Mt Cook, meaning 'Cloud Piercer'
Aotearoa – Maori name for NZ, most often translated as 'Land of the Long White Cloud'
aroha – love

B&B – bed and breakfast accommodation
bach – holiday home (pronounced 'batch'); see also crib
black-water rafting – rafting or tubing underground in a cave

boozer – public bar
bro – literally 'brother'; usually meaning mate
BYO – 'bring your own' (usually applies to alcohol at a restaurant or cafe)

choice/chur – fantastic; great
crib – the name for a bach in Otago and Southland

DB&B – bed and breakfast accommodation including dinner
DOC – Department of Conservation (or Te Papa Atawhai); government department that administers national parks, tracks and huts

eh? – roughly translates as 'don't you agree?'

farmstay – accommodation on a Kiwi farm
football – rugby, either union or league; occasionally soccer

Great Walks – set of nine popular tramping tracks within NZ
greenstone – jade; *pounamu*
gumboots – rubber boots or Wellingtons; originated from diggers on the gum-fields

haka – any dance, but usually a war dance
hangi – oven whereby food is steamed in baskets over embers in a hole; a Maori feast
hapu – subtribe or smaller tribal grouping
Hawaiki – original homeland of the Maori

hei tiki – carved, stylised human figure worn around the neck; also called a *tiki*

homestay – accommodation in a family house

hongi – Maori greeting; the pressing of foreheads and noses, and sharing of life breath

hui – gathering; meeting

i-SITE – information centre

iwi – large tribal grouping with common lineage back to the original migration from *Hawaiki*; people; tribe

jandals – contraction of 'Japanese sandals'; flip-flops; thongs; usually rubber footwear

jersey – jumper, usually woollen; the shirt worn by rugby players

kauri – native pine

kia ora – hello

Kiwi – New Zealander; an adjective to mean anything relating to NZ

kiwi – flightless, nocturnal brown bird with a long beak

Kiwiana – things uniquely connected to NZ life and culture, especially from bygone years

kiwifruit – small, succulent fruit with fuzzy brown skin and juicy green flesh; aka Chinese gooseberry or zespri

kumara – Polynesian sweet potato, a Maori staple food

Kupe – early Polynesian navigator from *Hawaiki*, credited with the discovery of the islands that are now NZ

mana – spiritual quality of a person or object; authority or prestige

Maori – indigenous people of NZ

Maoritanga – things Maori, ie Maori culture

marae – sacred ground in front of the Maori meeting house; more commonly used to refer to the entire complex of buildings

Maui – figure in Maori (Polynesian) mythology

mauri – life force/principle

moa – large, extinct flightless bird

moko – tattoo; usually refers to facial tattoos

nga – the (plural); see also *te*

ngai/ngati – literally, 'the people of' or 'the descendants of'; tribe (pronounced 'kai' on the South Island)

NZ – universal term for New Zealand; pronounced 'en zed'

pa – fortified Maori village, usually on a hilltop

Pacific Rim – modern NZ cuisine; local produce cooked with imported styles

Pakeha – Maori for a white or European person

Pasifika – Pacific Island culture

paua – abalone; iridescent paua shell is often used in jewellery

pavlova – meringue cake topped with cream and kiwifruit

PI – Pacific Islander

poi – ball of woven flax

pounamu – Maori name for *greenstone*

powhiri – traditional Maori welcome onto a *marae*

rip – dangerously strong current running away from the shore at a beach

Roaring Forties – the ocean between 40° and 50° south, known for very strong winds

silver fern – symbol worn by the *All Blacks* and other national sportsfolk on their jerseys; the national netball team is called the Silver Ferns

sweet, sweet as – all-purpose term like *choice*; fantastic, great

tapu – strong force in Maori life, with numerous meanings; in its simplest form it means sacred, forbidden, taboo

te – the (singular); see also *nga*

te reo – literally 'the language'; the Maori language

tiki – short for *hei tiki*

tiki tour – scenic tour

tramp – bushwalk; trek; hike

tuatara – prehistoric reptile dating back to the age of dinosaurs

tui – native parson bird

wahine – woman

wai – water

wairua – spirit

Waitangi – short way of referring to the Treaty of Waitangi

waka – canoe

Warriors – NZ's popular rugby league club, affiliated with Australia's NRL

Wellywood – Wellington, because of its thriving film industry

zorbing – rolling down a hill inside an inflatable plastic ball

Behind the Scenes

SEND US YOUR FEEDBACK

We love to hear from travellers – your comments keep us on our toes and help make our books better. Our well-travelled team reads every word on what you loved or loathed about this book. Although we cannot reply individually to postal submissions, we always guarantee that your feedback goes straight to the appropriate authors, in time for the next edition. Each person who sends us information is thanked in the next edition – the most useful submissions are rewarded with a selection of digital PDF chapters.

Visit **lonelyplanet.com/contact** to submit your updates and suggestions or to ask for help. Our award-winning website also features inspirational travel stories, news and discussions.

Note: We may edit, reproduce and incorporate your comments in Lonely Planet products such as guidebooks, websites and digital products, so let us know if you don't want your comments reproduced or your name acknowledged. For a copy of our privacy policy visit lonelyplanet.com/privacy.

OUR READERS

Many thanks to the travellers who used the last edition and wrote to us with helpful hints, useful advice and interesting anecdotes: Daniel Trocme-Latter, Florian Poppe, Helen McGuire, Michael Monson, Phil Smith.

AUTHOR THANKS

Brett Atkinson

Thanks to all of the i-SITE, DOC and information centre staff who patiently answered all my questions. Cheers to the clever craft brewers of New Zealand for sustenance on the road, and to Carol for support on occasional forays to offshore islands. Thanks to my fellow authors, the most professional and wittiest bunch one could aspire to work with, and huge thanks and friendship to the mighty Errol Hunt.

Sarah Bennett & Lee Slater

Thanks to everyone who helped us on the road, including RTO and visitor information centre staff, tourism operators and travellers. Special thanks to DOC staff, especially Penny McIntosh and Katrina Henderson. Big ups to everyone in-house at Lonely Planet, and to our fellow authors – Brett and Charles. Thanks also to Sarah Ewing. To all who provided a park for our camper, a fridge for the flagon, and even a feed of *kaimoana* on occasion: *arohanui, e hoa ma*.

Charles Rawlings-Way

Thanks to the many generous, knowledgeable and quietly self-assured Kiwis I met on the road, especially the staff at the Palmerston North, Hastings and New Plymouth i-SITEs who flew through my questions with the greatest of ease. Huge thanks to Errol Hunt for signing me up (again), and the in-house Lonely Planet staff who schmoozed this book through production. Humongous gratitude to my tireless, witty and professional co-authors – Sarah, Brett and Lee – who infused this book with humour and local low-down. Most of all, thank you Meg, Ione and Remy for holding the fort while I was away.

ACKNOWLEDGMENTS

Climate Map Data (CRMS and Discover titles) Climate map data adapted from Peel MC, Finlayson BL & McMahon TA (2007) 'Updated World Map of the Köppen-Geiger Climate Classification', *Hydrology and Earth System Sciences*, 11, 1633–44.

Cover photograph: Mt Taranaki, Radius Images/Corbis

THIS BOOK

This 3rd edition of Lonely Planet's *New Zealand's North Island* guidebook was researched and written by Brett Atkinson, Sarah Bennett, Charles Rawlings-Way and Lee Slater. They also wrote the previous edition along with Peter Dragicevich. This guidebook was commissioned in Lonely Planet's Melbourne office, and produced by the following:

Commissioning Editors Errol Hunt, Glenn van der Knijff

Destination Editor Tasmin Waby

Product Editor Tracy Whitmey

Senior Cartographer Diana Von Holdt

Book Designer Wendy Wright

Assisting Editors Nigel Chin, Samantha Forge, Paul Harding, Kate Mathews

Cover Researcher Naomi Parker

Thanks to Sasha Baskett, Ryan Evans, Larissa Frost, Genesys India, Jouve India, Catherine Naghten, Claire Naylor, Karyn Noble, Martine Power

Index

A

accommodation 402-4, see also individual locations
activities 29-39, see also individual activities, locations
adventure sports, see extreme sports
Ahipara 138-40
air travel 415-17
All Blacks 12, 77, 394
Anaura Bay 304
Anchor Bay 102
animals 378-80, see also birds, zoos & wildlife reserves, individual species
Anzac Bay 193
aquariums
Kelly Tarlton's Sealife Aquarium 53
National Aquarium of New Zealand 317
Tongariro National Trout Centre 243
Arahaki Lagoon 273
Aramoana Hill 219
area codes 19
Aroha Island 129-30
art galleries, see also museums
Academy Galleries 333
ArtsPost 153
Auckland Art Gallery 46-7
Chronicle Glass Studio 215
City Gallery 333
Dowse Art Museum 337
Govett-Brewster Art Gallery 200-1
Hastings City Art Gallery 323
Lopdell House Gallery 94

New Zealand Portrait Gallery 333
Old Library Arts Centre 111
Old School Arts Centre 157
Percy Thomson Gallery 210
Real Tart Gallery 201
Sarjeant Gallery 215
Tauranga Art Gallery 277
Wallace Arts Centre 56
Whangarei Art Museum 111
Zealandia Sculpture Garden 101
arts 396-400
arts festivals, see also festivals & events
Auckland Art Fair 61
Auckland Arts Festival 61
Erupt Festival 240
Hamilton Gardens Arts Festival 153
New Zealand International Arts Festival 340
Sculpture on the Gulf 86
Taranaki International Arts Festival 204
Tauranga Arts Festival 279
Wanganui Festival of Glass 215
Atene 219
ATMs 409
Auckland 8, 40, 44-81, **45**, **48**, **50-1**, **54**, **62**, **65**, **68**, **70**, **9**
accommodation 63-6
activities 56-8
children, travel with 60
drinking & nightlife 74-6
entertainment 76-7
festivals & events 60-1, 63
food 66-73
highlights 45
history 46
information 78
internet resources 46

itineraries 47
music 75
shopping 77-8
sights 46-9, 52-6
tours 58, 60
travel to/from 78-80
travel within 80-1
walking tour 59, **59**
Auckland region 40, 44-104, **45**
accommodation 44
climate 44
food 44
highlights 45
Maori culture 61
travel seasons 44
Auckland Zoo 55
Awakino 174

B

ballooning
Auckland 58
Hamilton 153
bathrooms 121, 411
Bay of Islands 10, 40, 105, 118-32, **106-7**, **119**, **11**
accommodation 105
climate 105
food 105
highlights 106-7
travel seasons 105
travel to/from 108
Bay of Plenty 41, 257, 276-97, **258**
accommodation 257
activities 257
climate 257
highlights 258
travel seasons 257
travel to/from 259
Baylys Beach 145
beaches 20
Aramoana 328
Auckland 58
Back Beach 203

Baylys Beach 145
Blackhead 328
Buffalo Beach 186
Cathedral Cove 189
East End Beach 203
Foxton Beach 228
Great Exhibition Bay 137
Hahei Beach 189
Hot Water Beach 190-1
Kai Iwi Beach 215
Kairakau 328
Mangakuri 328
Mangawhai 108
Matauri Bay 132
Midway Beach 308
New Chum's Beach 185
Ngarunui Beach 160
Ocean Beach (Kawhia) 167
Ocean Beach (Raglan) 160
Ocean Beach (Whangarei Heads) 115
Omaha 103
Orewa 99
Otama Beach 186
Pakiri Beach 104
Porangahau 328
Pourerere 328
Puheke Beach 136
Russell 123
Shipwreck Bay 139
Tauranga Bay 132
Tawharanui Regional Park 102
Te Werahi Beach 136
Tokerau Beach 135
Waiheke Island 82
Waihi Beach 193
Waikanae Beach 308
Waipu 109
Beehive 333
beer 22, see also breweries
bicycle travel, see cycling, mountain biking
birds 378-80, see also zoos & wildlife reserves, individual species

bird-watching 380
  Miranda 178
  Thames 179
black-water rafting 171, see also white-water rafting
boat travel 416, see also sailing
books 364, 375, 380, 386, 396, see also literature
Bream Bay 109-10
Bream Head 115
breweries
  Gisborne 307
  Leigh 104
  New Plymouth 203
  Palmerston North 225
  Paraparaumu 355
  Whenuakite 189
Bridge to Nowhere 220, **17**
budget 19
bungy jumping 35
  Auckland 57
  Rotorua 263
  Taupo 238
bus travel 417-18
bushwalking, see tramping
business hours 409

C
Cable Bay 134
Cambridge 163-4
campervan hire 419-20
Campion, Jane 396, 397
canoeing & kayaking 38-9
  Ahipara 139
  Auckland 57
  Bay of Islands 118
  Cambridge 163
  Coromandel Town 182
  Goat Island Marine Reserve 104
  Hahei 190
  Horeke 141
  Kawhia 167
  Mt Maunganui 284
  Napier 319
  National Park Village 252
  New Plymouth 204
  Ohakune 254
  Ohope 294
  Puhoi 100
  Raglan 158
  Rotorua 264-5
  Taupo 237

Map Pages **000**
Photo Pages **000**

Tauranga 278
Tauranga Bay 133
Urupukapuka Island 129
Waiheke Island 85
Wellington 338
Whangamata 192-3
Whanganui National Park 220-1
Whangarei 112
canyoning
  Thames 180
  Waitakere Ranges 95
Cape Kidnappers 327-8
Cape Maria van Diemen 136
Cape Palliser 358-9
Cape Reinga 136-8
car travel 418-22
  driving licences 418
  hire 420
  insurance 420-1
  road distance chart 419
  road rules 421
Carterton 361
Cathedral Cove 189, **15**, **21**
cathedrals, see churches & cathedrals
caves & caving
  Abbey Caves 111
  Aranui Cave 170
  Glowworm Cave 170
  Kawiti Glowworm Caves 121
  Muriwai's Cave 290-1
  Raglan 158
  Ruakuri Cave 170
  Ruatapu Cave 237
  Waitomo Caves 10, 169-73, **10**
cell phones 18, 410-11
Central Plateau region 41, 246-56, **231**
  accommodation 230
  climate 230
  food 230
  highlights 231
  travel seasons 230
  travel to/from 232
children, travel with 404-5
  Auckland 60
  Wellington 341
churches & cathedrals
  Christ Church 122-3
  Church of Sts Peter & Paul 100
  Hiona St Stephen's Church 295
  Holy Trinity Cathedral 53
  Matakohe Pioneer Church 146

Matawhero Church 307
Putiki Church 215
St Mary's Church (Mitimiti) 140
St Mary's Church (Tikitiki) 303
St Patrick's Cathedral 47
St Paul's Church (Paihia) 127
St Paul's Church (Rangiaowhia) 162-3
Taranaki Cathedral 201
cinema 349, 364, 365, 397, see also film festivals, Hobbit, Lord of the Rings
climate 18, 405, see also individual regions
climbing, see rock climbing
Colville 184
consulates 406
Cook, Captain James 369
Coopers Beach 134
Coroglen 189
Coromandel Peninsula 14, 41, 176-96, **148, 177, 5, 15, 21**
  accommodation 147
  activities 147
  climate 147
  highlights 148
  travel seasons 147
  travel to/from 149
Coromandel Town 181-4
costs 19, 403, 406
credit cards 409
Croatian immigrants 139
culture 364-5, 391-5
currency 18, 409
customs regulations 405
cycling 36, 417, see also mountain biking
  Cambridge 163
  Gisborne 309
  Hauraki Rail Trail 178
  Hawke's Bay 315
  New Plymouth 204
  Nga Haerenga, New Zealand Cycle Trail 36
  Pou Herenga Tai Twin Coast Cycle Trail 118
  Taupo 235
  Thames 180
  Timber Trail (Taumarunui) 175
  Tongariro River Trail 243
  Waiheke Island 85
  Wairarapa 357

D
dangers, see safety
Dargaville 145-6
Darwin, Charles 122, 371
Days Bay 340
debit cards 409
Department of Conservation (DOC) 403
departure tax 416
Dickey's Flat 195
disabilities, travellers with 412
distance chart 419
diving 36-8, see also snorkelling
  Auckland 57
  Bay of Islands 118
  Gisborne 308
  Great Barrier Island 90
  Hahei 190
  Karikari Peninsula 136
  Leigh 103-4
  Poor Knights Islands 116
  Tairua 191
  Tauranga 279
  Te Tapuwae o Rongokako Marine Reserve 305
  Whakatane 291
  Whitianga 186
dolphins
  Bay of Islands 120
  Tauranga 278
  Whakatane 291
Dome Forest 101
Doubtless Bay 134-5
drinking, see breweries, wine regions, individual locations
driving, see car travel
driving licences 418
DVDs 404

E
earthquakes 364, 378
East Cape 12, 299-314, **12**
East Coast 42, 298-329, **300-1**
  accommodation 298
  activities 298
  climate 298
  highlights 300-1
  travel seasons 298
  travel to/from 299
economy 364-5
Egmont National Park 207-9
electricity 406
embassies 406
emergencies 19

entertainment, see individual locations
environment 376-82
etiquette 364
events, see festivals & events, sporting events
exchange rates 19
extreme sports 22, 35-9, 57, see also individual sports

F

festivals & events 22, 23-6, see also arts festivals, film festivals, food & wine festivals, music festivals, sporting events
Art Deco Weekend 320
Auckland International Cultural Festival 61
Auckland Pride Festival 60-1
Christmas in the Park 61
Diwali Festival of Lights 61
Festival of Cultures 226
Festival of Lights 204
Fringe NZ 340
Great New Zealand Muster 173
Grey Lynn Park Festival 61
Hastings Blossom Festival 324
Heritage Festival 61
Lantern Festival 60
Matariki 340
New Zealand Comedy Festival 340
NZ Fashion Week 61
NZ International Comedy Festival 61
Pasifika Festival 61
Polyfest 61
Royal Easter Show 61
Russell Birdman 121
Santa Parade 61
Summer City 340
Taranaki Garden Spectacular 204
Vintage Weekend 215
Waitangi Day 121
Whanganui Literary Festival 216
Winterfest 240
World of WearableArt 341
film 349, 364, 365, 397, see also Hobbit, Lord of the Rings, film festivals, film locations

film festivals
International Film Festival 340
Movies In Parks 60
NZ International Film Festival 61
Out Takes 61
Silo Park Markets 63
film locations 165, 174
Finn, Neil 399
Finn, Tim 399
fishing
Gisborne 308
Great Barrier Island 90
Napier 319
Rotorua 266
Taupo 238-9
Tauranga 279
Turangi 243
Fletcher Bay 185
food 22, 406, see also individual locations
food & wine festivals
Bay of Islands Food & Wine Festival 121
Beervana 340
Carrot Carnival 253
Devonport Food & Wine Festival 61
Feast Gisborne 309
Manawatu Harvest Festival 226
Manawatu Wine & Food Festival 226
Rhythm & Vines 309
Scallop Festival 188
Toast Martinborough 341, 356
Waiheke Island of Wine Vintage Festival 86
Wairarapa Wines Harvest Festival 356
Wellington on a Plate 341
forest parks, see national parks, regional parks & reserves
Forgotten World Hwy 210
fortified villages (pa) 101
Foxton 228
Frying Pan Lake 276

G

galleries, see art galleries
gannets 98
gardens, see parks & gardens
gay travellers 74, 406-7
Gemstone Bay 189
geography 376-8
geology 376-8

geysers 166, 235, 237, 259, 260-1, 276, 378
giardia 407-8
Gisborne 305-11
Gladstone 361
glowworms 170
Goat Island Marine Reserve 104
Godzone 373
Goldmine Experience 179
golf
Rotorua 266
Taupo 239
Great Barrier Island 90-4, **92**
Great Walks 31-3, **32**
Lake Waikaremoana Track 313, **312-13**
Tongariro Northern Circuit 247, **248**
Whanganui Journey 220-1
Greytown 359-60
guided walks 33-4
gumdigging 137

H

Hackfalls Arboretum 311
Hahei 189-90
haka 388
Hamilton 151-6, **152**
Hamilton Zoo 153
Hastings 323-7, **324**
Hauraki Gulf 8, 81-94
Havelock North 323-7
Hawai 299
Hawera 213
Hawke's Bay 17, 314-29, **316**
health 407-8
Helena Bay 117
Hells Gate 273
Hicks Bay 303
hiking, see tramping
Hillary, Sir Edmund 391
Hinemoa 263
Hiruharama 219
history 20, 366-75
hitching 421
Hobbit 174
Hokianga 140-3
Holdsworth 360-1
holidays 410
Hone Heke 123
Horeke 141
horse riding 35
Ahipara 139
Bay of Islands 119

Baylys Beach 145
Manawatu Gorge 229
Napier 319
Ohakune 254
Paekakariki 354
Paengaroa 289
Pakiri 104
Rangitukia 303
River Valley 256
Rotorua 266
Taupo 238
Waireinga (Bridal Veil Falls) 161
Whakatane 291
Whitianga 187
hot springs
Athenree Hot Springs 194
Awakeri Hot Springs 292
Great Barrier Island 90
Hot Water Beach 190-1
Lost Spring 186
Mangatutu Hot Pools 329
Miranda Hot Springs 178
Morere Hot Springs 311
Opal Hot Springs 165
Parakai Springs 98
Polynesian Spa 265
Taranaki Thermal Spa 203
Te Aroha Mineral Spa 166
Te Puia Hot Springs 167
Tokaanu Thermal Pools 244-5
Wairakei Terraces & Thermal Health Spa 235
Waiwere Thermal Resort 100
Hot Water Beach 190-1
hot-air ballooning
Auckland 58
Hamilton 153
Huka Prawn Park 239
Hukutaia Domain 295
hypothermia 408

I

immigration 415
Inferno Crater Lake 276
Inglewood 209-10
insurance 408
car & motorcycle 420-1
health 407
travel 408
internet access 408
internet resources 19, 368, 372, 390, 398, 399
i-SITE 411

itineraries 27-8, **27**, **28**
  Auckland 47
  Rotorua 264
  Wellington 337
iwi 388

J
Jackson, Sir Peter 365
jetboating 35
  Auckland 58
  Bay of Islands 120
  Cambridge 163
  Opotiki 296
  Palmerston North 225
  Rotorua 263-4
  Taumarunui 176
  Taupo 238
  Whanganui National
    Park 221
jetskiing
  Bay of Islands 118
  Tauranga 279

K
Kai Iwi Lakes 144-5
Kaitaia 138
Kapiti Coast 353-5
Kapiti Island 354
Karangahake Gorge 195-6
Karekare 95-6
Karikari Peninsula 135-6
Katikati 287-8
Katikati Bird Gardens 288
kauri 111, 143-4, 146, 382
Kawakawa 121
Kawau Island 89-90
Kaweka J 329
Kaweka ranges 329
Kawhia 167-8
kayaking, *see* canoeing &
  kayaking
Kelly Tarlton's Sealife
  Aquarium 53
Kennedy Bay 185
Kerikeri 129-32, **130**
King Country 166-76, **150**
Kingdom of Zion 111-12
Kingitanga 167
Kiritehere 173
kitesurfing
  Karikari Peninsula 136
  Ocean Beach (Raglan)
    160
  Wellington 338

Map Pages **000**
Photo Pages **000**

kiwifruit 288
kiwis 379
Kohukohu 140-1
Koriniti 219
Kuaotunu 185
Kumara Box 145
Kumeu 97-8

L
Lake Ferry 359
Lake Karapiro 163
Lake Rotorua 262
Lake Tarawera 275-6
Lake Taupo region 230,
  232-46, **231**
  accommodation 230
  climate 230
  food 230
  highlights 231
  travel to/from 232
  travel seasons 230
Lake Tutira 314-15
Lake Waikareiti 314
Land Wars 372
language 18, 423-6
legal matters 408
Leigh 103-4
lesbian travellers 74, 406-7
Levin 228
literature 216, 396, *see also*
  books
Long Bay Regional Park 99
Lord of the Rings 164,
  246, 397
Lorde 400

M
Mahia Peninsula 311
Mahurangi Regional
  Park 101
Maitai Bay 135
Maketu 289
Makorori 308
Manawatu Gorge 228-9
Mangapurua Trig 222
Mangawhai 108-9
Mangonui 134
Maniapoto, Rewi 373
Maniaroa Marae 174
Mansfield, Katherine 336-7
Manu Bay 160
Maori language 367, 423-6
Maori people
  arts 385-90
  carvings 233
  concerts 271
  culture 13, 20, 383-90
  hangi 271

history 291, 294, 308,
  366-73
  language 367, 423-6
  legends 384, 385
  literature 390, 396
  religion 137, 385
  tattoos 386
Maori regional highlights
  Auckland 61
  Central Plateau 233
  East Coast 302
  Northland 110
  Rotorua & Bay of Plenty
    262
  Taranaki & Whanganui
    201
  Waikato &
    Coromandel 151
  Wellington 333
maps 409
marae 387
  Hokianga 140
  Koriniti 219
  Maketu 167
  Maniaroa 174
  Nuhaka 312
  Papatea Bay 302
  Tauranga 278
  Turangawaewae 151
  Whakatane 289
marine reserves 750
  Goat Island Marine
    Reserve 104
  Hauraki Gulf Maritime
    Park 81-94
  Sugar Loaf Islands
    Marine Park 201
  Te Angiangi Marine
    Reserve 328
  Te Tapuwae o Rongokako
    Marine Reserve 305
markets 22, 407
  Auckland Fish
    Market 49
  Gisborne Farmers
    Market 307
  Hastings Farmers Market
    323
  Napier Urban Food
    Market 317
  Silo Park Markets 63
Marokopa 173
Martinborough 357-8
Masterton 360
Matakana 102-3
Matakana Island 287
Matakohe 146
Matamata 164-5
Matapouri 116
Matariki 46

Matauri Bay 132-3
Matheson Bay 103
Matiu/Somes Island 340
Mauao 284
Maungakiekie (One Tree
  Hill) 55-6
measures 404
medical services 407
Mill Bay 134
Miranda 178
Mitimiti 140
moa 371
mobile phones 18, 410-11
Moeatoa 173
Mohaka River 329
Mokai Gravity Canyon 256
Mokau 174, 203
money 18, 19, 405, 409
Morto people 367
motorcycle travel 418-21
Motu River 299
Motuhora (Whale Island)
  294
Motuihe Island 82
Motuora Island 89
Moturiki Island 284
Motutapu Island 81-2
Motuti 140
mountain biking 36, *see
  also* cycling
  Great Barrier Island 90
  Hawke's Bay 315
  Helensville 98
  Mt Te Aroha 166
  National Park Village 252
  Ohakune 253, 254
  Opotiki 295-6
  Owhango 176
  Redwoods Whaka-
    rewarewa Forest 273
  Rotorua 264
  Taupo 235
  Tauranga 278
  Wellington 338
  Whangamata 192-3
  Whanganui National
    Park 222
  Whirinaki Forest Park 273
movie locations 165, 174
Mt Eden 49
Mt Hikurangi 304
Mt Humphries 222
Mt Karioi 161
Mt Manaia 115
Mt Maunganui 282-6, **283**
Mt Pirongia 161
Mt Pureora 175
Mt Taranaki (Egmont
  National Park) 207-9

Mt Titiraupenga 175
Muriwai Beach 98
museums 20-1, *see also* art galleries
Aratoi Wairarapa Museum of Art & History 360
Auckland Museum 52-3
Bohemian Museum 100
Buried Village 275
Butler Point Whaling Museum 134
Cambridge Museum 163
Central Hawke's Bay Settlers Museum 328
Clapham's Clocks 111
Classic Flyers NZ 277
Classics Museum 153
Cobblestones Village Museum 359
Colonial Cottage Museum 337
Coromandel Mining & Historic Museum 182
Dargaville Museum 145
East Coast Museum of Technology 307
Fun Ho! National Toy Museum 210
Gumdiggers Park 137
Historical Museum (Thames) 179
Katikati Heritage Museum 287
Kauri Museum 146
Kawhia Regional Museum & Gallery 167
KD's Elvis Presley Museum 213
Kiwi North 111
Mangawhai Museum 108
McCahon House 94
Mercury Bay Museum 186
MOTAT (Museum of Transport & Technology) 55
MTG Hawke's Bay 317
Museum of Wellington City & Sea 332-3
National Army Museum 256
Navy Museum 55
New Zealand Rugby Museum 224
Opotiki Museum 295
Petone Settlers Museum 338
Puke Ariki 200
Rewa's Village 129
Rotorua Museum 261
Russell Museum 123

School of Mines & Mineralogical Museum 179
Shalfoon & Francis Museum 295
Southward Car Museum 355
Tainui Historical Society Museum 174
Tairawhiti Museum 305, 307
Taranaki Aviation, Transport & Technology Museum 203
Taranaki Pioneer Village 210
Taupo Museum 233
Tawhiti Museum 213
Te Aroha Museum 166
Te Awamutu Museum 161
Te Manawa 224
Te Papa 338
Tramway Museum 354
Victoria Battery Tramway & Museum 195
Volcanic Activity Centre 234
Voyager - New Zealand Maritime Museum 49
Waiheke Museum & Historic Village 83
Waihi Arts Centre & Museum 194
Waikato Museum 153
Waipu Museum 109
Wairoa Museum 314
Waitomo Caves Discovery Centre 170
Warkworth & District Museum 102
Weta Cave 337
Whakatane District Museum 289
Whanganui Regional Museum 214-15
Whanganui Riverboat Centre 215
music 75, 388, 398-400
music festivals
Coromandel Gold Festival 188
Country Rock Festival 121
International Jazz & Blues Festival 226
Jazz & Blues Festival 121
Laneway Festival 60
Music In Parks 60
National Jazz Festival 279
Rhythm & Vines 309

Splore 61
Waiheke Island International Jazz Festival 86
Waiheke Island of Wine Vintage Festival 86
WOMAD 204
MV *Rena* 284

N

Napier 14, 315-23, **318**, **15**
National Aquarium of New Zealand 317
National Jazz Festival 24
National Park Village 251-3
national parks, regional parks & reserves 382, **381**, *see also* marine reserves
Aorangi (Haurangi) Forest Park 358-9
AH Reed Memorial Kauri Park 111
Bellbird Bush Scenic Reserve 315
Boundary Stream Scenic Reserve 315
Coromandel Forest Park 182
Doneraille Park 311
Hemi Matenga Memorial Park 355
Long Bay Regional Park 99
Mahurangi Regional Park 101
Mangapohue Natural Bridge Scenic Reserve 173
Mimiwhangata Coastal Park 117
Morere Springs Scenic Reserve 311
Mt Taranaki (Egmont National Park) 207-9
Nga Manu Nature Reserve 355
Ngaiotonga Scenic Reserve 117
Opouahi Scenic Reserve 315
Piripiri Caves Scenic Reserve 173
Pirongia Forest Park 161
Puerora Forest Park 175
Rangikapiti Pa Historic Reserve 134
Redwoods Whaka-rewarewa Forest 273, 275
Rotokura Ecological Reserve 255

Ruakuri Scenic Reserve 172
Ruapekapeka Pa Historic Reserve 123
Scandrett Regional Park 101
Shakespear Regional Park 99
Tangoio Falls Scenic Reserve 315
Tararua Forest Park 360-1
Tawharanui Regional Park 102
Te Mata Peak 323
Te Paki Recreation Reserve 136-7
Te Urewera National Park 312-14
Tongariro National Park 246-50, **248**
Trounson Kauri Park 144
Waipatiki Scenic Reserve 315
Wairere Boulders Nature Park 141
Wenderholm Regional Park 100
Whanganui National Park 219, **220**
Whangaruru North Head Scenic Reserve 117
Whirinaki Forest Park 273
White Pine Bush Scenic Reserve 315
Native Bird Recovery Centre 111
New Plymouth 200-7, **202**
New Zealand International Sevens 23
newspapers 404
Nga Haerenga, New Zealand Cycle Trail 36
Ngaruawahia 151
Ngarunui Beach 160
Ngarupupu Point 173
Nga-Tapuwae-o-te-Mangai 137
Ngawi 359
Ngunguru 116
Ninety Mile Beach 136-8
Northland region 40, 105-46, **106-7**
accommodation 105
climate 105
food 105
highlights 106
travel seasons 105
travel to/from 108
Northland War 123
number-eight wire 395

O

Oakura 211-12
Ocean Beach 160
Ohakune 253-6
Ohinemutu 262
Omahuta Forest 132
Omaio 299
Omapere 142-3
One Tree Hill 55-6
Ongaonga 328
Opapake Pa 172
opening hours 409
Opito 186
Opononi 142-3
Opotiki 295-7
Opoutere 192
Opua Forest 127
Opunake 212-13
Orakau 163
Orakei Korako 237
Orewa 99-100
Oriuwaka Ecological Area 273
Orokawa Bay 193
Oscars 397
Otorohanga 168-9
Otorohanga Kiwi House & Native Bird Park 168
Owhango 176

P

pa 101
Paaku 191
Pacific Coast Hwy 299-305
Pacific Islanders 24, 77, **10**, **25**
paddle boarding
   Bay of Islands 119
   Wellington 338
   Whangamata 193
Paekakariki 354-5
Paeroa 196
Paihia 125-9, **126**
Pakiri 104
Palmerston North 224-8, **225**
Papamoa 287
Papatea Bay 302
Paradise Valley Springs 273
paragliding 323
Paraparaumu 355
parasailing 35-6
   Bay of Islands 118
   Taupo 238

Parihaka 211
Paritutu 201
parks & gardens, *see also* national parks, regional parks & reserves
   Albert Park 47
   Auckland Botanic Gardens 56
   Auckland Domain 53
   Bastion Point 53
   Botanica & Cafler Park 111
   Brooklands Park 201
   Butterfly & Orchid Garden 179
   Connells Bay 83
   Dead Dog Bay 83
   Eastwoodhill Arboretum 307
   Eden Garden 49
   Gisborne Botanic Gardens 307
   Government Gardens 262
   Hamilton Gardens 151-2
   Jubilee Gardens 163
   Kuirau Park 262
   Monmouth Redoubt 277-8
   One Tree Hill 55-6
   Otari-Wilton's Bush 337
   Parnell Rose Gardens 53
   Parry Kauri Park 102
   Pukeiti 201-2
   Pukekura Park 200
   Quarry Gardens 111
   Queen Elizabeth Park (Masterton) 360
   Queen Elizabeth Park (Paekakariki) 354
   Rapaura Water Gardens 181
   Robbins Park 277-8
   Rose Garden 161
   Titirangi Park 307
   Wellington Botanic Gardens 333
   Western Springs 55
   Zealandia Sculpture Garden 101
Parua Bay 115
Pasifika Festival 24, **10**, **25**
passports 415
Pataua 115
Peach Cove 115
penguins 53, 55, 89, 96, 119, 187, 340
phonecards 411
Piha 96-7
Pipiriki 219-20

Pirongia Forest Park 161
place names 424-5
planning, *see also* individual regions
   activities 29-39
   budgeting 19
   calendar of events 23-6
   children, travel with 60, 341, 404-5
   internet resources 19
   itineraries 27-8, **27**, **28**
   North Island basics 18-19
   North Island's regions 40-2
   travel seasons 18
plants 380-2
politics 391-5
Poor Knights Islands 115-17
population 365, 391
Port Charles 185
postal services 410
Pouto Point 146
public holidays 410
pubs 22
Puhoi 100-1
Pukaha Mt Bruce National Wildlife Centre 360
Pukearuhe 203
Puketapu 291
Puketi Forest 132
Puketui Valley 192
Pungarehu 212
Putangirua Pinnacles 358-9

Q

quad biking
   Ahipara 139
   Horeke 141

R

radio 404
rafting, *see* black-water rafting, white-water rafting
Raglan 157-60, **157**, **37**
railways
   Driving Creek Railway & Potteries 182
   Gabriel the Steam Engine 121
   Goldfields Railway 194
   Rain Forest Express 95
   Raurimu Spiral 175
   Thames Small Gauge Railway 180
   Waitakere Tramline Society 95
Rainbow Springs 272

Rainbow Warrior 133, 392
Rainbow's End 56
Ranana 219
Rangatira 354
Rangiaowhia 162-3
Rangipo Desert 256
Rangiputa 135-6
Rangiriri 150-1
Rangitoto Island 81-2
Rangitukia 303
Rawene 141-2
Rawhiti 117
regional parks, *see* national parks, regional parks & reserves
road distance chart 419
rock climbing 36, **37**
   Hamilton 153
   Mt Maunganui 284
   Raglan 158
   Rotorua 263
   Wharepapa South 163
ropes courses
   Helensville 98
   Taupo 238
   Whitianga 187
Rotoroa Island 89
Rotorua 10, 41, 259-72, **260**, **11**
   accommodation 267-9
   activities 262-6
   drinking & nightlife 270-1
   entertainment 270-1
   food 269-70
   history 259
   information 271-2
   itineraries 264
   shopping 271
   tours 266-7
   travel to/from 272
   travel within 272
Rotorua region 257-97, **258**
   accommodation 257
   activities 257
   climate 257
   highlights 258
   travel seasons 257
   travel to/from 259
Ruahina ranges 329
Ruatoria 304
rugby 12, 23, 224, 340
Russell 122-5, **122**
Russell Rd 117
Rutherford, Ernest 394

S

safety 410
   hitching 421

road 421
tramping 30, 247
sailing
  Auckland 56-7
  Bay of Islands 118, 119-20
  Coromandel 182
  Napier 319
  Taupo 237
  Tauranga 279
  Whitianga 187
Sanctuary Mountain Maungatautari 162
sandboarding 142
Sandy Bay (Cape Reinga) 136
Sandy Bay (Matapouri) 116
Scandrett Regional Park 101
scenic reserves, see national parks, regional parks & reserves
scuba diving, see diving
sea kayaking, see canoeing & kayaking
seals 359
Shakespear Regional Park 99
Shannon 228
Sheepworld 102
shopping, see markets, individual locations
skiing & snowboarding 34-5
  Manganui Ski Area 208
  Orewa 99
  Taupo 238
  Tongariro National Park 249-50
skydiving 38
  Auckland 57
  Rotorua 263
  Taupo 238
  Tauranga 279
  Whangarei 112
Smugglers Bay 115
snorkelling, see also diving
  Gisborne 308
  Goat Island Marine Reserve 104
  Hahei 190
  Leigh 103-4
  Tairua 191
  Te Angiangi Marine Reserve 328
  Whangamata 192-3
snowboarding, see skiing & snowboarding
Spirits Bay 136
Sponge Bay 308

sporting events
  Auckland Anniversary Day Regatta 60
  Auckland Cup Week 61
  Auckland International Boat Show 61
  Balloons Over Waikato 153
  Cemetery Circuit Motorcycle Race 216
  Golden Shears 360
  Ironman New Zealand 240
  Lake Taupo Cycle Challenge 240
  New Zealand International Sevens 340
  Opotiki Rodeo 296
  Tall Ship Race 121
  Weekend Coastal Classic 121
sports 394, see also individual sports
Stardome Observatory 56
Stingray Bay 189
Stony Bay 185
Stratford 210
Sugar Loaf Islands Marine Park 201
Surf Highway 45 211-13
surfing 38
  Ahipara 139
  Auckland 58
  Gisborne 308
  Great Barrier Island 90
  Kumara Patch 212
  Manu Bay 160
  Mt Maunganui 282, 284
  Napier 319
  New Plymouth 203
  Ngarunui Beach 160
  Oakura 211
  Ohope 294
  Opunake 212
  Poor Knights Islands 116
  Raglan 158
  Stent Rd 212
  Taupo Bay 134
  Whale Bay 160
  Whangamata 192-3
Surville Cliffs 136
sustainable travel 379

T
ta moko 386
Taihape 256
Taipa 134
Tairua 191-2
Tapotupotu Bay 136

Tapu 181
Taranaki 41, 197-229, **198-9**
  accommodation 197
  activities 197
  climate 197
  highlights 198
  travel seasons 197
  travel to/from 200
Tararua Wind Farm 229
tattoos 386
Taumarunui 175-6
Taumata Trig 222
Taumatawhakatangihanga-koauauotamateaturipu-kakapikimaungahoro-nukupokaiwhenuaki-tanatahu 328
Taupiri 155
Taupo 41, 232-42, **234, 236**
  accommodation 240-1
  activities 235-9
  drinking & nightlife 242
  entertainment 242
  festivals & events 240
  food 241-2
  history 232-3
  information 242
  sights 233-5
  tours 239
  travel to/from 242
  travel within 242
Taupo region 230, 232-46, **231**
  accommodation 230
  climate 230
  food 230
  highlights 231
  travel seasons 230
  travel to/from 232
Tauranga 276-82, **277**
Tauranga Bay 132-3
Tawarau Forest 173
Tawharanui Regional Park 102
taxes 414
Te Angiangi Marine Reserve 328
Te Apiti Wind Farm 229
Te Araroa 34, 303
Te Aroha 165-6
Te Awamutu 161-2
Te Hana Te Ao Marama 101
Te Haruhi Bay 99
Te Henga (Bethells Beach) 97
Te Kaha 302
Te Kooti 308, 375
Te Kuiti 173-4

Te Papa 338, **21**
Te Papaka 291
Te Puia 259-60
Te Puia Springs 304
Te Puke 288-9
Te Puru 181
Te Tapuwae o Rongokako Marine Reserve 305
Te Urewera National Park 312-14
telephone services 18, 410-11
Te-Waha-O-Rerekohu 303
Thames 178-81, **179**
thermal springs, see hot springs
Tikitiki 303
time 411
Tiritiri Matangi Island 89
Titirangi 94-5
toilets 121, 411
Tokomaru Bay 304
Tolaga Bay 304
Tongariro Alpine Crossing 17, 248-9, **16**
Tongariro National Park 246-50, **248**
Tongariro National Trout Centre 243
Torere 299
Toto Gorge 161
tourist information 411-12
tours, see individual locations
train travel 422, see also railways
tramping 21, 29-34, **32**, see also Great Walks
  Anaura Bay Walkway 304
  Arai te Uru Heritage Walk 142
  Around-the-Mountain Circuit 208
  Atene Skyline Track 222
  Atene Viewpoint Walk 222
  Auckland 58
  Bridge to Nowhere Track 221-2
  Cape Reinga Coastal Walkway 136
  Coastal Walkway 203
  Cooks Cove Walkway 304
  Coromandel Coastal Walkway 182, 185
  Crater Lake 249
  Doubtless Bay 134
  Duke's Nose Track 134
  Dundle Hill Walk 172
  Eastern Okataina Walkway 265

tramping *continued*
Gentle Annie Road 329
Great Barrier Island 90-1
Great Lake Trail 235
Great Lake Walkway 235
Hatea River Walk 112
Hemi Matenga Memorial Park 355
Heritage & Tree Trail 163
Hillary Trail 95
Hinemihi's Track 243
Huatok Walkway 203
Huka Falls Walkway 236
Kaimai Mamaku Forest Park 278
Karangahake Gorge Historic Walkway 195
Kauri Grove Nature Walk 117
Kerikeri River Track 130
Lake Surprise Track 253
Lake Waikaremoana Track 313, **312-13**
Mangapurua/ Kaiwhakauka Track 222
Mangawhai Cliff Top Walkway 108
Mangawhero Forest Walk 253
Manginangina Kauri Walk 132
Matemateaonga Track 222
Mauao Base Track 284
Maunganamu Track 243
Miranda 178
Mt Taranaki 208
Mt Te Aroha 166
New Plymouth Heritage Trail 203
Northern Tarawera Track 265
Omahuta Forest 132
Owhango 176
Pinnacles 182
Pit Rim Walkway 194
Pouakai Circuit 208
Puerora Forest Park 175
Puketi Forest 132
Puketui Valley 182
Rainbow Mountain Track 265
Riverbank Walk 175
Ruapani Circuit Track 314

Silica Rapids Track 250
Six Foot Track 142
Tama Lakes Track 250
Tangoio Walkway 315
Taranaki Falls Track 250
Tauranga-Taupo River Walk 243
Tawarau Forest 173
Te Hoe Track 273
Te Kuri Walkway 308
Te Puia Track 329
Tongariro Alpine Crossing 248-9
Tongariro River Trail 243
Trounson Kauri Park 144
Tutukaka 116
Twin Bole Kauri Walk 117
Waiheke Island 85
Waikato River Trails 163
Waipapa River Track 132
Waipu Caves Walking Track 109
Wairakau Stream Track 133-4
Wairake Track 161
Waitakere Ranges 95
Waitomo Caves 172
Waitonga Falls Track 253
Wentworth Falls walk 193
Western Okataina Walkway 265
Whakapapa Nature Walk 250
Whangamata 192-3
Whangamumu Scenic Reserve 117
Whanganui National Park 221-2
Whangarei 112
Whangarei Heads 115
Wharekirauponga walk 193
Whirinaki Track 273
White Cliffs Walkway 203
travel to/from New Zealand 415-16
travel within New Zealand 416-22
Treaty of Waitangi 125, 126-7, 370
trees 380-2
trekking, *see* tramping
Trounson Kauri Park 144
trout 243, 244
Tryphena 90
Tuamotu Island 308
Tuhua (Mayor Island) 287
Turangi 243-6, **243**
Tutukaka 116
TV 397, 404

U
Under the Mountain 46
Urenui 203
Urquharts Bay 115
Urupukapuka Island 129

V
vacations 410
visas 18, 412-13
visual arts 397-8
volcanoes
Auckland 57
Maunganui Bluff 144
Motuhora (Whale Island) 294
Mt Eden 49
Mt Ngauruhoe 246
Mt Ruapehu 246
Mt Taranaki (Egmont National Park) 207-9
Mt Tongariro 246
Mt Victoria 54-5
One Tree Hill 55-6
Rangitoto 57, 81-2
Whakaari (White Island) 293-4
volunteering 413

W
Waihau Bay 303
Waiheke Island 82-8, **84**, **8**
Waihi 193-5
Waikanae 355
Waikato 41, 149-66, **148**
accommodation 147
activities 147
climate 147
highlights **148**
travel seasons 147
travel to/from 149
Waikato River 153
Waikawau 173
Waikawau Bay 185
Waimamaku 143
Waimangu Volcanic Valley 276
Wainui 308
Waioeka Gorge 299
Wai-O-Tapu Thermal Wonderland 276
Waiotemarama 143
Waiouru 256
Waipawa 328
Waipiro Bay 304
Waipoua Forest 143-4
Waipu 109-10
Waipukurau 328
Wairakei **234**

Wairarapa, the 356-61
Wairoa 314
Waitakere Ranges 95
Waitangi 125-9
Waitangi Treaty Grounds 126-7
Waitomo Caves 10, 169-73, **169**, **10**
Waiwera 100
Wake, Nancy 374
walking, *see* tramping
walking tours
Auckland 59, **59**
Wellington 339, **339**
Wanganui, *see* Whanganui
Warkworth 101-2
waterfalls
Aratiatia Rapids 233-4
Haruru Falls 127
Huka Falls 233
Marokopa Falls 173
Okere Falls 265
Owharoa Falls 195
Tarawera Falls 265
Te Reinga Falls 311
Te Wairoa Falls 275
Waiau Falls 186
Waireinga (Bridal Veil Falls) 161
Wairere Falls (Matamata) 165
Wairere Falls (Whakatane) 289
Whangarei Falls 111
weather 18, 405, *see also individual regions*
websites 19, 368, 372, 390, 398, 399
weights 404
Wellington 12, 42, 332-53, **334-5**, **342-3**, **13**
accommodation 341-5
activities 338
children, travel with 341
drinking & nightlife 348-9
entertainment 349-50
festivals & events 340-1
food 345-7
history 332
information 351
itineraries 337
shopping 350-1
sights 332-3, 336-8
tours 338, 340
travel to/from 351-2
travel within 352-3
walking tour 339, **339**
Wellington region 42, 330-62, **331**

climate 330
drinking & nightlife 330
food 330
highlights 331
travel seasons 330
travel to/from 331
Wellington Zoo 337
Wellywood 349
Wenderholm Regional
Park 100
Whakaari (White Island)
293-4
Whakapapa Village 250-1
Whakatane 289-93, **290**
Whale Bay 116, 160
whale-watching 380
Whananaki 116
Whanarua Bay 302
Whangamata 192-3
Whangamomona 210
Whangamumu Harbour 117
Whanganui 41, 213-19, **214**
Whanganui National Park
17, 219, **220**, **17**
Whanganui region 41, 197,
198-9
accommodation 197
activities 197
climate 197
highlights 198-9
travel seasons 197

travel to/from 200
Whanganui River Road 219
Whangaparapara 90
Whangapoua 185
Whangarei 110-15, **112-13**
Whangarei Heads 115
Whangaroa Harbour 133-4
Wharekawa Wildlife Refuge
192
Whareorino Forest 173
Wharepapa South 163
Wharerata State
Forest 311
Whatuwhiwhi 135
Whenuakite 189
White Cliffs 203
white-water rafting 39, see
also black-water rafting
Motu River 299, 302
Napier 319
Ohakune 254
Opotiki 296
River Valley 256
Rotorua 264-5
Taupo 237
Turangi 243-4
Whitianga 186-9, **187**
wi-fi 408
wildlife 378-80, see also
birds, zoos & wildlife
reserves, individual
species

Wilsons Bay 181
windsurfing
Napier 319
Ocean Beach 160
Tauranga 279
Wellington 338
wine festivals, see food &
wine festivals
wine regions 22
Auckland 79
Gisborne 305
Hawke's Bay 326
Kaitaia 138
Karangahake Gorge
195-6
Karikari Peninsula 136
Katikati 288
Kumeu 97-8
Napier 319
Tauranga 278
Waiheke Island 82-3
Wairarapa 356-7
Wingspan National Bird of
Prey Centre 273
WOMAD 24
women in New Zealand 395
women travellers 413
work 413-14
World of WearableArt
Award Show 26
WWOOF 413

Z
Zealandia 336
ziplining
Rotorua 262-3
Waiheke Island 85
zoos & wildlife reserves
Aroha Island 129
Auckland Zoo 55
Hamilton Zoo 153
Katikati Bird Gardens
288
Native Bird Recovery
Centre 111
Nga Manu Nature
Reserve 355
Otorohanga Kiwi House
& Native Bird Park 168
Paradise Valley Springs
273
Pukaha Mt Bruce
National Wildlife
Centre 360
Rainbow Springs 272
Tiritiri Matangi Island 89
Wharekawa Wildlife
Refuge 192
Wellington Zoo 337
Wingspan National Bird
of Prey Centre 273
Zealandia 336
zorbing 263

Map Legend

Sights

- Beach
- Bird Sanctuary
- Buddhist
- Castle/Palace
- Christian
- Confucian
- Hindu
- Islamic
- Jain
- Jewish
- Monument
- Museum/Gallery/Historic Building
- Ruin
- Sento Hot Baths/Onsen
- Shinto
- Sikh
- Taoist
- Winery/Vineyard
- Zoo/Wildlife Sanctuary
- Other Sight

Activities, Courses & Tours

- Bodysurfing
- Diving
- Canoeing/Kayaking
- Course/Tour
- Skiing
- Snorkelling
- Surfing
- Swimming/Pool
- Walking
- Windsurfing
- Other Activity

Sleeping

- Sleeping
- Camping

Eating

- Eating

Drinking & Nightlife

- Drinking & Nightlife
- Cafe

Entertainment

- Entertainment

Shopping

- Shopping

Information

- Bank
- Embassy/Consulate
- Hospital/Medical
- Internet
- Police
- Post Office
- Telephone
- Toilet
- Tourist Information
- Other Information

Geographic

- Beach
- Hut/Shelter
- Lighthouse
- Lookout
- Mountain/Volcano
- Oasis
- Park
- Pass
- Picnic Area
- Waterfall

Population

- Capital (National)
- Capital (State/Province)
- City/Large Town
- Town/Village

Transport

- Airport
- Border crossing
- Bus
- Cable car/Funicular
- Cycling
- Ferry
- Metro station
- Monorail
- Parking
- Petrol station
- Subway station
- Taxi
- Train station/Railway
- Tram
- Underground station
- Other Transport

Routes

- Tollway
- Freeway
- Primary
- Secondary
- Tertiary
- Lane
- Unsealed road
- Road under construction
- Plaza/Mall
- Steps
- Tunnel
- Pedestrian overpass
- Walking Tour
- Walking Tour detour
- Path/Walking Trail

Boundaries

- International
- State/Province
- Disputed
- Regional/Suburb
- Marine Park
- Cliff
- Wall

Hydrography

- River, Creek
- Intermittent River
- Canal
- Water
- Dry/Salt/Intermittent Lake
- Reef

Areas

- Airport/Runway
- Beach/Desert
- Cemetery (Christian)
- Cemetery (Other)
- Glacier
- Mudflat
- Park/Forest
- Sight (Building)
- Sportsground
- Swamp/Mangrove

Note: Not all symbols displayed above appear on the maps in this book

Tony Horwitz wrote the Captain James Cook boxed text in the History chapter. Tony is a Pulitzer-winning reporter and nonfiction author. His fascination with James Cook, and with travel, took him around NZ, Australia and the Pacific while researching *Blue Latitudes* (alternatively titled *Into the Blue*), part biography of Cook and part travelogue.

John Huria (Ngai Tahu, Muaupoko) wrote the Maori Culture chapter. John has an editorial, research and writing background with a focus on Maori writing and culture. He was senior editor for Maori publishing company Huia and now runs an editorial and publishing services company, Ahi Text Solutions Ltd (www.ahitextsolutions.co.nz).

Josh Kronfeld wrote the Surfing in New Zealand boxed text in the Active North Island chapter. Josh is an ex–All Black flanker, whose passion for surfing NZ's beaches is legendary and who found travelling for rugby a way to surf other great breaks around the world.

Gareth Shute wrote the Music section in the Arts & Music chapter. Gareth is the author of four books, including *Hip Hop Music in Aotearoa* and *NZ Rock 1987–2007*. He is also a musician and has toured the UK, Europe and Australia as a member of the Ruby Suns and the Brunettes. He now plays in indie soul group The Cosbys.

Vaughan Yarwood wrote the Environment chapter. Vaughan is an Auckland-based writer whose books include *The History Makers: Adventures in New Zealand Biography, The Best of New Zealand: A Collection of Essays on NZ Life and Culture by Prominent Kiwis,* which he edited, and the regional history *Between Coasts: From Kaipara to Kawau.* He has written widely for NZ and international publications and is the former associate editor of *New Zealand Geographic,* for which he has also written for many years.

OUR STORY

A beat-up old car, a few dollars in the pocket and a sense of adventure. In 1972 that's all Tony and Maureen Wheeler needed for the trip of a lifetime – across Europe and Asia overland to Australia. It took several months, and at the end – broke but inspired – they sat at their kitchen table writing and stapling together their first travel guide, *Across Asia on the Cheap*. Within a week they'd sold 1500 copies. Lonely Planet was born.

Today, Lonely Planet has offices in Franklin, London, Melbourne, Oakland, Beijing and Delhi, with more than 600 staff and writers. We share Tony's belief that 'a great guidebook should do three things: inform, educate and amuse'.

OUR WRITERS

Brett Atkinson

Coordinating Author, Auckland, Bay of Islands & Northland, Waikato & Coromandel Peninsula Resident in Auckland, Brett leapt at the chance to research his home town for this edition. Highlights include exploring the city's emerging restaurant scene around Wynyard Quarter, and journeying to the diverse islands of the Hauraki Gulf. Excursions further afield to Northland and Coromandel echoed family holidays in an earlier century. Brett's contributed to Lonely Planet guidebooks spanning Europe, Asia and the Pacific, and covered almost 50 countries as a food and travel writer. See www.brett-atkinson.net for his latest travels.

Sarah Bennett & Lee Slater

Taupo & the Central Plateau, Wellington Region Lee and Sarah live in Wellington, but spend many months on the road each year in their small campervan, boots on board, mountain bikes on the back. Specialists in 'soft-core adventure' (tramping without crampons), they re-imagine their journeys into magazine features, and guidebooks including Lonely Planet's *Hiking & Tramping in New Zealand*, four editions of *New Zealand*, as well as *The New Zealand Tramper's Handbook* and *Let's Go Camping*. Read more at www.bennettandslater.co.nz and follow on Twitter @BennettnSlater.

Charles Rawlings-Way

Taranaki & Whanganui, Rotorua & the Bay of Plenty, The East Coast English by birth, Australian by chance, All Blacks fan by choice: Charles' early understanding of Aotearoa was less than comprehensive (sheep, mountains, sheep on mountains...). He realised there was more to it when a wandering uncle returned with a faux-jade tiki in 1981. He wore it with pride until he saw the NZ cricket team's beige uniforms in 1982... Mt Taranaki's snowy summit, Napier's art-deco deliverance and Whanganui's raffish charm have helped him forgive: he's once again smitten with the country's phantasmal landscapes, disarming locals, and determination to sculpt its own political and indigenous destiny.

Contributing Writers

Professor James Belich wrote the History chapter. James is one of NZ's pre-eminent historians and the award-winning author of *The New Zealand Wars*, *Making Peoples* and *Paradise Reforged*. He has also worked in TV – *New Zealand Wars* was screened in NZ in 1998.

OVER PAGE | MORE WRITERS

Published by Lonely Planet Publications Pty Ltd
ABN 36 005 607 983
3rd edition – October 2014
ISBN 978 1 74220 790 2
© Lonely Planet 2014   Photographs © as indicated 2014
10 9 8 7 6 5 4 3 2 1
Printed in China

32953012555795